Lecture Notes in Artificial Intelligence 10233

Subseries of Lecture Notes in Computer Science

More information about this series at http://www.springer.com/series/1244

Malek Mouhoub · Philippe Langlais (Eds.)

Advances in Artificial Intelligence

30th Canadian Conference on Artificial Intelligence, Canadian AI 2017 Edmonton, AB, Canada, May 16–19, 2017 Proceedings

Editors
Malek Mouhoub
University of Regina
Regina, SK
Canada

Philippe Langlais
University of Montreal
Montreal, QC
Canada

ISSN 0302-9743 ISSN 1611-3349 (electronic)
Lecture Notes in Artificial Intelligence
ISBN 978-3-319-57350-2 ISBN 978-3-319-57351-9 (eBook)
DOI 10.1007/978-3-319-57351-9

Library of Congress Control Number: 2017937581

LNCS Sublibrary: SL7 – Artificial Intelligence

Printed on acid-free paper

This Springer imprint is published by Springer Nature
The registered company is Springer International Publishing AG
The registered company address is: Gewerbestrasse 11, 6330 Cham, Switzerland

Preface

It is with great pleasure and excitement that we present the proceedings of the 30th Canadian Conference on Artificial Intelligence (AI 2017). The conference took place for the first time in Edmonton, Alberta, during May 16–19, 2017. As done in the past, this forum was collocated with the 43rd Graphics Interface (GI 2017) and the 14th Computer and Robot Vision (CRV 2017) conferences.

AI 2017 received 62 submissions from Canada and the following countries: Brazil, China, France, India, Iran, Mexico, Moldova, New Zealand, Nigeria, South Africa, Taiwan, Turkey, USA, and UK. Each submission was carefully reviewed by three members of the Program Committee. For the final conference program and for inclusion in these proceedings, 19 regular papers, with allocation of 12 pages each, were selected. Additionally, 24 short papers, with allocation of six pages each, were accepted. Finally, six papers accepted and presented at the Graduate Student Symposium, are also included in these proceedings. These six papers were selected from nine submissions through a reviewing process conducted by a separate Program Committee.

The conference program was enriched by three keynote presentations, several tutorials, and an industry session. The keynote speakers were Hugo Larochelle, Université de Sherbrooke, Adnan Darwiche, University of California Los Angeles, and Robert Holte, University of Alberta. We would like to thank the Program Committee members and the external reviewers of the conference and the Graduate Student Symposium, for their time and effort in providing valuable reviews in a timely manner. We thank all the authors for submitting their contributions and the authors of accepted papers for preparing the final version of their papers and presenting their work at the conference. We thank Daniel Silver, Colin Berlinger, and Shiven Sharma for organizing the Graduate Student Symposium, and chairing the related Program Committee.

The Canadian Conference on Artificial Intelligence is sponsored by the Canadian Artificial Intelligence Association (CAIAC). In this regard, we would like to thank the CAIAC Executive Committee members for their advice and guidance based on their past experience with the conference organization. We would like to express our sincere gratitude to Pierre Boulanger and Nilanjan Ray, the AI/GI/CRV general chairs, to Grzegorz Kondrak, the AI local arrangements chair, and to Fatiha Sadat, the publicity chair, for their help with the organization of the conference. Finally, we are in debt to Andrei Voronkov and the rest of the development team of the EasyChair Conference System. This system made the process of paper submission and evaluation, as well as the preparation of the proceedings, easy and saved us a significant amount of time.

March 2017

Malek Mouhoub
Philippe Langlais

Organization

Executive Committee

AI General Chairs

Pierre Boulanger	University of Alberta, Canada
Nilanjan Ray	University of Alberta, Canada

AI Program Co-chairs

Malek Mouhoub	University of Regina, Canada
Philippe Langlais	Université de Montréal, Canada

AI Publicity Chair

Fatiha Sadat	Université du Québec à Montréal (UQAM), Canada

AI Local Arrangement Chair

Grzegorz Kondrak	University of Alberta, Canada

AI Graduate Student Symposium Program Co-chairs

Daniel Silver	Acadia University, Canada
Colin Bellinger	University of Alberta, Canada
Shiven Sharma	University of Ottawa, Canada

AI Graduate Student Symposium Program Committee

Karim Abou-Moustafa	University of Alberta, Canada
Ebrahim Bagheri	Ryerson University, Canada
Scott Buffett	National Research Council Canada IIT e-Business, Canada
Cory Butz	University of Regina, Canada
Scott Goodwin	University of Windsor, Canada
Diana Inkpen	University of Ottawa, Canada
Nathalie Japkowicz	American University, USA
Anna Kazantseva	National Research Council Canada, Canada
Alistair Kennedy	SoundHound Inc., USA
Ziad Kobti	University of Windsor, Canada

Adam Krzyzak	Concordia University, Canada
Philippe Langlais	Université de Montréal, Canada
Xiao Luo	Indiana University–Purdue University Indianapolis, USA
Brad Malin	Vanderbilt University, USA
Stan Matwin	Dalhousie University, Canada
Malek Mouhoub	University of Regina, Canada
Gerald Penn	University of Toronto, Canada
Marina Sokolova	University of Ottawa, Canada
Alex Thomo	University of Victoria, Canada

Program Committee

Esma Aimeur	University of Montréal, Canada
Otmane Ait Mohamed	Concordia University, Canada
Reda Alhajj	University of Calgary, Canada
Xiangdong An	York University, Canada
Periklis Andritsos	University of Toronto, Canada
Dirk Arnold	Dalhousie University, Canada
Ebrahim Bagheri	Ryerson University, Canada
Caroline Barriere	Computer Research Institute of Montréal, Canada
Sotiris Batsakis	University of Huddersfield, UK
Colin Bellinger	University of Alberta, Canada
Salem Benferhat	Cril, CNRS UMR8188, Université d'Artois, France
Virendra Bhavsar	University of New Brunswick, Canada
Ismaïl Biskri	Université du Québec àTrois-Rivières, Canada
Narjes Boufaden	KeaText Inc., Canada
Maroua Bouzid	GREYC-CNRS, France
Scott Buffett	National Research Council Canada, IIT - e-Business, Canada
Cory Butz	University of Regina, Canada
Eric Charton	Yellow Pages, Canada
David Chiu	University of Guelph, Canada
Lyne Dasylva	Université de Montréal, Canada
Ali Dewan	Athabasca University, Canada
Angelo Di Iorio	University of Bologna
Chrysanne Dimarco	University of Waterloo, Canada
Larbi Esmahi	Athabasca University, Canada
Ahmed Esmin	Universidade Federal de Lavras, Brazil
Jocelyne Faddoul	Saint Mary's University, UK
Behrouz Far	University of Calgary, Canada
Atefeh Farzindar	NLP Technologies Inc., Canada
Stefano Ferilli	Università di Bari, Italy
Enrico Francesconi	ITTIG-CNR, Italy
Fred Freitas	Universidade Federal de Pernambuco (UFPE), Brazil
Michel Gagnon	Polytechnique Montréal, Canada

Yong Gao	UBC Okanagan, Canada
Zahia Guessoum	LIP6, Université de Paris 6, France
Orland Hoeber	University of Regina, Canada
Jimmy Huang	York University, Canada
Diana Inkpen	University of Ottawa, Canada
Ilya Ioshikhes	University of Ottawa, Canada
Aminul Islam	Dalhousie University, Canada
Nathalie Japkowicz	SITE, University of Ottawa, Canada
Igor Jurisica	Ontario Cancer Institute, Canada
Vangelis Karkaletsis	NCSR Demokritos, Greece
Vlado Keselj	Dalhousie University, Canada
Fazel Keshtkar	St. John's University, USA
Svetlana Kiritchenko	NRC, Canada
Ziad Kobti	University of Windsor, Canada
Grzegorz Kondrak	University of Alberta, Canada
Leila Kosseim	Concordia University, Canada
Lars Kotthoff	University of British Columbia, Canada
Anastasia Krithara	NCSR Demokritos, Greece
Adam Krzyzak	Concordia University, Canada
Philippe Langlais	Université de Montréal, Canada
Guy Lapalme	Université de Montréal, Canada
Kate Larson	University of Waterloo, Canada
Fuhua Lin	Athabasca University, Canada
Pawan Lingras	Saint Mary's University, UK
Simone Ludwig	North Dakota State University, USA
Yannick Marchand	Dalhousie University, Canada
Stan Matwin	Dalhousie University, Canada
Gordon McCalla	University of Saskatchewan, Canada
Wagner Meira Jr.	UFMG, Brazil
Mohamed El Bachir Menai	King Saud University, KSA
Robert Mercer	The University of Western Ontario, Canada
Marie-Jean Meurs	Université du Québec à Montréal, Canada
Shamima Mithun	Concordia University, Canada
Abidalrahman Moh'D	Dalhousie University, Canada
Malek Mouhoub	University of Regina, Canada
Gabriel Murray	University of the Fraser Valley, Canada
Eric Neufeld	University of Saskatchewan, Canada
Jian-Yun Nie	Université de Montréal, Canada
Roger Nkambou	Université du Québec à Montréal, Canada
Seyednaser Nourashrafeddin	Dalhousie University, Canada
Gerald Penn	University of Toronto, Canada
Fred Popowich	Simon Fraser University, Canada
Sheela Ramanna	University of Winnipeg, Canada
Robert Reynolds	Wayne State University, USA
Samira Sadaoui	University of Regina, Canada

Fatiha Sadat	Université du Quebec à Montréal, Canada
Eugene Santos	Dartmouth College, USA
Shiven Sharma	University of Ottawa, Canada
Weiming Shen	National Research Council Canada
Daniel L. Silver	Acadia University, Canada
Michel Simard	National Research Council Canada
Marina Sokolova	University of Ottawa, Canada
Axel Soto	University of Manchester, UK
Bruce Spencer	University of New Brunswick, Canada
Stan Szpakowicz	EECS, University of Ottawa, Canada
Andrea Tagarelli	University of Calabria, Italy
Thomas Tran	University of Ottawa, Canada
Peter van Beek	University of Waterloo, Canada
Julien Velcin	Université de Lyon 2, France
Xin Wang	University of Calgary, Canada
Leo Wanner	Pompeu Fabra University, Spain
Dan Wu	University of Windsor
Yang Xiang	University of Guelph, Canada
Jingtao Yao	University of Regina, Canada
Yiyu Yao	University of Regina, Canada
Jia-Huai You	University of Alberta, Canada
Harry Zhang	University of New Brunswick, Canada
Xinghui Zhao	Washington State University, USA
Bing Zhou	Sam Houston State University, USA
Xiaodan Zhu	National Research Council Canada
Sandra Zilles	University of Regina, Canada
Nur Zincir-Heywood	Dalhousie University, Canada

Additional Reviewers

Alharthi, Haifa
Chen, Qian
Chowdhury, Md. Solimul
Karimi, Arash
Makonin, Stephen
Nyamen Tato, Ange Adrienne
Ochoa, Erick
Odilinye, Lydia
Ouchani, Samir
Pereira Junior, Romualdo
Shil, Shubhashis
Solinas, Christopher
Tsiakas, Konstantinos
Zhang, Congsong

Contents

AI Applications

Natural Language Processing

Uncertainty and Preference Reasoning

Agent Systems

Graduate Student Symposium

Data Mining and Machine Learning

On Generalized Bellman Equations and Temporal-Difference Learning

Huizhen Yu(✉), Ashique Rupam Mahmood, and Richard S. Sutton

RLAI Lab, Department of Computing Science,
University of Alberta, Edmonton, Canada
janey.hzyu@gmail.com

Abstract. We consider off-policy temporal-difference (TD) learning in discounted Markov decision processes, where the goal is to evaluate a policy in a model-free way by using observations of a state process generated without executing the policy. To curb the high variance issue in off-policy TD learning, we propose a new scheme of setting the λ parameters of TD, based on generalized Bellman equations. Our scheme is to set λ according to the eligibility trace iterates calculated in TD, thereby easily keeping these traces in a desired bounded range. Compared to prior works, this scheme is more direct and flexible, and allows much larger λ values for off-policy TD learning with bounded traces. Using Markov chain theory, we prove the ergodicity of the joint state-trace process under nonrestrictive conditions, and we show that associated with our scheme is a generalized Bellman equation (for the policy to be evaluated) that depends on both λ and the unique invariant probability measure of the state-trace process. These results not only lead immediately to a characterization of the convergence behavior of least-squares based implementation of our scheme, but also prepare the ground for further analysis of gradient-based implementations.

Keywords: Markov decision process · Policy evaluation · Generalized bellman equation · Temporal differences · Markov chain · Randomized stopping time

1 Introduction

We consider off-policy temporal-difference (TD) learning in discounted Markov decision processes (MDPs), where the goal is to evaluate a policy in a model-free way by using observations of a state process generated without executing the policy. Off-policy learning is an important part of the reinforcement learning methodology [25] and has been studied in the areas of operations research and machine learning (see e.g., [3,5,6,8–11,17,18,20,29]). Available algorithms, however, tend to have very high variances due to the use of importance sampling, an issue that limits their applicability in practice. The purpose of this paper is to introduce a new TD learning scheme that can help address this problem.

This work was supported by a grant from Alberta Innovates—Technology Futures.

M. Mouhoub and P. Langlais (Eds.): Canadian AI 2017, LNAI 10233, pp. 3–14, 2017.
DOI: 10.1007/978-3-319-57351-9_1

Our work is motivated by the recently proposed Retrace [15] and ABQ [12] algorithms, and by the Tree-Backup algorithm [18] that existed earlier. These algorithms, as explained in [12], all try to use the λ-parameters of TD to curb the high variance issue in off-policy learning. In this paper we propose a new scheme of setting the λ-parameters of TD, based on generalized Bellman equations. Our scheme is to set λ according to the eligibility trace iterates calculated in TD, thereby easily keeping those traces in a desired range. Compared to the previous works, this is a direct way to bound the traces in TD, and it is also more flexible, allowing much larger λ values for off-policy learning.

Regarding generalized Bellman equations, they are a powerful tool. In classic MDP theory they have been used in some intricate optimality analyses. Their computational use, however, seems to emerge primarily in the field of reinforcement learning (see [24], [1, Chap. 5.3] and [28] for related early and recent research). Like the earlier works [12,15,18,28,33], our work aims to employ this tool to make off-policy learning more efficient.

Our analyses of the new TD learning scheme will focus on its theoretical side. Using Markov chain theory, we prove the ergodicity of the joint state and trace process under nonrestrictive conditions (see Theorem 2.1), and we show that associated with our scheme is a generalized Bellman equation (for the policy to be evaluated) that depends on both λ and the unique invariant probability measure of the state-trace process (see Theorem 3.1). These results not only lead immediately to a characterization of the convergence behavior of least-squares based implementation of our scheme (see Corrolary 2.1 and Remark 3.1), but also prepare the ground for further analysis of gradient-based implementations.

We note that due to space limit, in this paper we can only give the ideas or outlines of our proofs. The full details will be given in the longer version of this paper, which will also include numerical examples that we will not cover here.

The rest of the paper is organized as follows. In Sect. 2, after a brief background introduction, we present our scheme of TD learning with bounded traces, and we establish the ergodicity of the joint state-trace process. In Sect. 3 we derive the generalized Bellman equation associated with our scheme.

2 Off-Policy TD Learning with Bounded Traces

2.1 Preliminaries

The off-policy learning problem we consider in this paper concerns two Markov chains on a finite state space $\mathcal{S} = \{1, \ldots, N\}$. The first chain has transition matrix P, and the second P^o. Whatever physical mechanisms that induce the two chains shall be denoted by π and π^o, and referred to as the target policy and behavior policy, respectively. The second Markov chain we can observe; however, it is the system performance for the first Markov chain that we want to evaluate. Specifically, we consider a one-stage reward function $r_\pi : \mathcal{S} \to \Re$ and an associated discounted total reward criterion with state-dependent discount factors $\gamma(s) \in [0, 1]$, $s \in \mathcal{S}$. Let Γ denote the $N \times N$ diagonal matrix with diagonal entries $\gamma(s)$. We assume that P and P^o satisfy the following conditions:

Condition 2.1 (Conditions on the target and behavior policies). (i) P *is such that the inverse* $(I - P\Gamma)^{-1}$ *exists, and* (ii) P^o *is such that for all* $s, s' \in \mathcal{S}$, $P^o_{ss'} = 0 \Rightarrow P_{ss'} = 0$, *and moreover,* P^o *is irreducible.*

The performance of π is defined as the expected discounted total rewards for each initial state $s \in \mathcal{S}$:

$$v_\pi(s) := \mathbb{E}^\pi_s \left[r_\pi(S_0) + \textstyle\sum_{t=1}^{\infty} \gamma(S_1)\, \gamma(S_2) \cdots \gamma(S_t) \cdot r_\pi(S_t) \right], \qquad (2.1)$$

where the notation $\mathbb{E}^\pi_s$ means that the expectation is taken with respect to (w.r.t.) the Markov chain $\{S_t\}$ starting from $S_0 = s$ and induced by π (i.e., with transition matrix P). The function v_π is well-defined under Condition 2.1(i). It is called the *value function* of π, and by standard MDP theory (see e.g., [19]), we can write it in matrix/vector notation as

$$v_\pi = r_\pi + P\Gamma\, v_\pi, \qquad \text{i.e.,} \quad v_\pi = (I - P\Gamma)^{-1} r_\pi.$$

The first equation above is known as the Bellman equation (or dynamic programming equation) for a stationary policy.

We compute an approximation of v_π of the form $v(s) = \phi(s)^\top \theta$, $s \in \mathcal{S}$, where $\theta \in \Re^n$ is a parameter vector and $\phi(s)$ is an n-dimensional feature representation for each state s ($\phi(s), \theta$ are column vectors and $^\top$ stands for transpose). Data available for this computation are:

(i) the Markov chain $\{S_t\}$ with transition matrix P^o generated by π^o, and
(ii) rewards $R_t = r(S_t, S_{t+1})$ associated with state transitions, where the function r relates to $r_\pi(s)$ as $r_\pi(s) = \mathbb{E}^\pi_s[r(s, S_1)]$ for all $s \in \mathcal{S}$.

To find a suitable parameter θ for the approximation $\phi(s)^\top \theta$, we use the off-policy TD learning scheme. Define $\rho(s, s') = P_{ss'}/P^o_{ss'}$ (the importance sampling ratio);[1] denote $\rho_t = \rho(S_t, S_{t+1}), \gamma_t = \gamma(S_t)$. Given an initial $e_0 \in \Re^n$, for each $t \geq 1$, the eligibility trace vector $e_t \in \Re^n$ and the scalar temporal-difference term $\delta_t(v)$ for any approximate value function $v : \mathcal{S} \to \Re$ are calculated according to

$$e_t = \lambda_t\, \gamma_t\, \rho_{t-1}\, e_{t-1} + \phi(S_t), \qquad (2.2)$$

$$\delta_t(v) = \rho_t \left(R_t + \gamma_{t+1} v(S_{t+1}) - v(S_t) \right). \qquad (2.3)$$

Here $\lambda_t \in [0, 1], t \geq 1$, are important parameters in TD learning, the choice of which we shall elaborate on shortly.

[1] Our problem formulation entails both value function and state-action value function estimation for a stationary policy in the standard MDP context. In these applications, it is the state-action space of the MDP that corresponds to the state space $\mathcal{S}$ here; see [29, Examples 2.1, 2.2] for details. The third application is in a simulation context where P^o corresponds to a simulated system and both P^o, P are known so that the ratio $\rho(s, s')$ is available. Such simulations are useful, for example, in studying system performance under perturbations, and in speeding up the computation when assessing the impacts of events that are rare under the dynamics P.

Using e_t and δ_t, a number of algorithms can be formed to generate a sequence of parameters θ_t for approximate value functions. One such algorithm is LSTD [2,29], which obtains θ_t by solving the linear equation for $\theta \in \Re^n$,

$$\tfrac{1}{t} \sum_{k=0}^{t-1} e_k \, \delta_k(v) = 0, \quad v = \Phi\theta \tag{2.4}$$

(if it admits a solution), where Φ is a matrix with row vectors $\phi(s)^\top, s \in \mathcal{S}$. LSTD updates the equation (2.4) iteratively by incorporating one by one the observation of (S_t, S_{t+1}, R_t) at each state transition. We will discuss primarily this algorithm in the paper, as its behavior can be characterized directly using our subsequent analyses of the joint state-trace process. As mentioned earlier, our analyses will also provide bases for analyzing other gradient-based TD algorithms [9,10] using stochastic approximation theory. However, due to its complexity, this subject is better to be treated separately, not in the present paper.

2.2 Our Choice of λ

We now come to the choices of λ_t in the trace iterates (2.2). For TD with function approximation, one often lets λ_t be a constant or a function of S_t [23,25,27]. If neither the behavior policy nor the λ_t's are further constrained, $\{e_t\}$ can have unbounded variances and is also unbounded in many natural situations (see e.g., [29, Sect. 3.1]), and this makes off-policy TD learning challenging.[2] If we let the behavior policy to be close enough to the target policy so that $P^o \approx P$, then variance can be reduced, but it is not a satisfactory solution, for the applicability of off-policy learning would be seriously limited.

Without restricting the behavior policy, the two recent works [12,15] (as well as the closely related early work [18]) exploit state-dependent λ's to control variance. Their choices of λ_t are such that $\lambda_t \rho_{t-1} < 1$ for all t, so that the trace iterates e_t are made bounded, which can help reduce the variance of the iterates.

Our proposal, motivated by these prior works, is to set λ_t according to e_{t-1} directly, so that we can keep e_t in a desired range straightforwardly and at the same time, allow a much larger range of values for the λ-parameters. As a simple example, if we use λ_t to scale the vector $\gamma_t \rho_{t-1} e_{t-1}$ to be within a ball with some given radius, then we keep e_t bounded always.

In the rest of this paper, we shall focus on analyzing the iteration (2.2) with a particular choice of λ_t of the kind just mentioned. We want to be more general than the preceding simple example. However, we also want to retain certain Markovian properties that are very useful for convergence analysis. This leads us to consider λ_t *being a certain function of the previous trace and past states.* More specifically, we will let λ_t be a function of the previous trace and a certain memory state that is a summary of the states observed so far, and the formulation is as follows.

Denote the memory state at time t by y_t. For simplicity, we assume that y_t can only take values from a finite set $\mathcal{M}$, and its evolution is Markovian:

[2] Asymptotic convergence is still ensured, however, for several algorithms [29–31], thanks partly to a powerful law of large numbers for stationary processes.

$y_t = g(y_{t-1}, S_t)$ for some given function g. The joint process $\{(S_t, y_t)\}$ is then a simple finite-state Markov chain. Each y_t is a function of $(S_0, \ldots, S_t)$ and y_0. We further require, besides the irreducibility of $\{S_t\}$ (cf. Condition 2.1(ii)), that[3]

Condition 2.2 (Evolution of memory states). *Under the behavior policy π^o, the Markov chain $\{(S_t, y_t)\}$ on $\mathcal{S} \times \mathcal{M}$ has a single recurrent class.*

Thus we let y_t and λ_t evolve as

$$y_t = g(y_{t-1}, S_t), \qquad \lambda_t = \lambda(y_t, e_{t-1}) \tag{2.5}$$

where $\lambda : \mathcal{M} \times \Re^n \to [0, 1]$. We require the function λ to satisfy two conditions.

Condition 2.3 (Conditions for λ). *For some norm $\|\cdot\|$ on $\Re^n$, the following hold for each memory state $y \in \mathcal{M}$:*

(i) *For any $e, e' \in \Re^n$, $\|\lambda(y, e)\, e - \lambda(y, e')\, e'\| \leq \|e - e'\|$.*

(ii) *For some constant C_y, $\|\gamma(s')\rho(s, s') \cdot \lambda(y, e)\, e\| \leq C_y$ for all possible state transitions (s, s') that can lead to the memory state y.*

In the above, the second condition is to restrict $\{e_t\}$ in a desired range (as it makes $\|e_t\| \leq \max_{y \in \mathcal{M}} C_y + \max_{s \in \mathcal{S}} \|\phi(s)\|$). The first condition is to ensure that the traces e_t jointly with (S_t, y_t) form a Markov chain with nice properties (as will be seen in the next subsection).

Consider the simple scaling example mentioned earlier. In this case we can let $y_t = (S_{t-1}, S_t)$, and for each $y = (s, s')$, define $\lambda(y, \cdot)$ to scale back the vector $\gamma(s')\rho(s, s')\, e$ when it is outside the Euclidean ball with radius $C_{ss'}$: $\lambda(y, e) = 1$ if $\gamma(s')\rho(s, s')\|e\|_2 \leq C_{ss'}$; and $\lambda(y, e) = \frac{C_{ss'}}{\gamma(s')\rho(s,s')\|e\|_2}$ otherwise.

2.3 Ergodicity Result

The properties of the joint state-trace process $\{(S_t, y_t, e_t)\}$ are important for understanding and characterizing the behavior of the proposed TD learning scheme. We study them in this subsection; most importantly, we shall establish the ergodicity of the state-trace process. The result will be useful in convergence analysis of several associated TD algorithms, although in this paper we discuss only the LSTD algorithm. In the next section we will also use the ergodicity result when we relate the LSTD equation (2.4) to a generalized Bellman equation for the target policy, which will then make the meaning of the LSTD solutions clear.

As a side note, one can introduce nonnegative coefficients $i(y)$ for memory states y to weight the state features (similarly to the use of "interest" weights in the ETD algorithm [26]) and update e_t according to

$$e_t = \lambda_t\, \gamma_t\, \rho_{t-1}\, e_{t-1} + i(y_t)\, \phi(S_t). \tag{2.6}$$

The results given below apply to this update rule as well.

Let us start with two basic properties of $\{(S_t, y_t, e_t)\}$ that follow directly from our choice of the λ function:

[3] These conditions are nonrestrictive. If the Markov chains have multiple recurrent classes, each recurrent class can be treated separately using the same arguments.

(i) By Condition 2.3(i), for each y, $\lambda(y,e)e$ is a continuous function of e, and thus e_t depends continuously on e_{t-1}. This, together with the finiteness of $\mathcal{S} \times \mathcal{M}$, ensures that $\{(S_t, y_t, e_t)\}$ is a weak Feller Markov chain.[4]
(ii) Then, by a property of weak Feller Markov chains [14, Theorem 12.1.2(ii)], the boundedness of $\{e_t\}$ ensured by Condition 2.3(ii) implies that $\{(S_t, y_t, e_t)\}$ has at least one invariant probability measure.

The third property, given in the lemma below, concerns the behavior of $\{e_t\}$ for different initial e_0. It is an important implication of Condition 2.3(i) (actually it is our purpose of introducing the condition 2.3(i) in the first place). Due to space limit, we omit the proof, which is similar to the proof of [29, Lemma 3.2].

Lemma 2.1. *Let $\{e_t\}$ and $\{\hat{e}_t\}$ be generated by the iteration (2.2) and (2.5), using the same trajectory of states $\{S_t\}$ and initial y_0, but with different initial e_0 and $\hat{e}_0$, respectively. Then under Conditions 2.1(i) and 2.3(i), $e_t - \hat{e}_t \overset{a.s.}{\to} 0$.*

We use the preceding lemma and ergodicity properties of weak Feller Markov chains [13] to prove the ergodicity theorem given below (for lack of space, we again omit the proof). Before stating this result, we note that for $\{(S_t, y_t, e_t)\}$ starting from the initial condition $x = (s, y, e)$, the occupation probability measures $\{\mu_{x,t}\}$ are random probability measures on $\mathcal{S} \times \mathcal{M} \times \Re^n$ given by

$$\mu_{x,t}(D) := \tfrac{1}{t} \textstyle\sum_{k=0}^{t-1} \mathbb{1}\big((S_k, y_k, e_k) \in D\big)$$

for all Borel sets $D \subset \mathcal{S} \times \mathcal{M} \times \Re^n$, where $\mathbb{1}(\cdot)$ is the indicator function. We write $\mathbf{P}_x$ for the probability distribution of $\{(S_t, y_t, e_t)\}$ with initial condition x.

Theorem 2.1. *Under Conditions 2.1–2.3, $\{(S_t, y_t, e_t)\}$ is a weak Feller Markov chain and has a unique invariant probability measure ζ. For each initial condition $(S_0, y_0, e_0) = (s, y, e) =: x$, the occupation probability measures $\{\mu_{x,t}\}$ converge weakly[5] to ζ, $\mathbf{P}_x$-almost surely.*

Let $\mathbb{E}_\zeta$ denote expectation w.r.t. the stationary state-trace process $\{(S_t, y_t, e_t)\}$ with initial distribution ζ. Since the traces and hence the entire process lie in a bounded set under Condition 2.3(ii), the weak convergence of $\{\mu_{x,t}\}$ to ζ implies that the sequence of equations, $\frac{1}{t} \sum_{k=0}^{t-1} e_k \, \delta_k(v) = 0$, as given in (2.4) for LSTD, has an asymptotic limit that can be expressed in terms of the stationary state-trace process as follows.

Corollary 2.1. *Let Conditions 2.1–2.3 hold. Then for each initial condition of (S_0, y_0, e_0), almost surely, the first equation in (2.4), viewed as a linear equation in v, tends to[6] the equation $\mathbb{E}_\zeta[e_0 \delta_0(v)] = 0$ in the limit as $t \to \infty$.*

---

[4] This means that for any bounded continuous function f on $\mathcal{S} \times \mathcal{M} \times \Re^n$ (endowed with the usual topology), with $X_t = (S_t, y_t, e_t)$, $\mathbb{E}\big[f(X_1) \mid X_0 = x\big]$ is a continuous function of x [14, Prop. 6.1.1].

[5] This means $\int f d\mu_{x,t} \to \int f d\zeta$ as $t \to \infty$, for every bounded continuous function f.

[6] By this we mean that as linear equations in v, the random coefficients in this sequence of equations converge to the corresponding coefficients in the limiting equation.

3 Generalized Bellman Equations

In this section we continue the analysis started in Sect. 2.3. Our goal is to relate the linear equation $\mathbb{E}_\zeta[e_0\delta_0(v)] = 0$, the asymptotic limit of the linear equation (2.4) for LSTD as just shown by Corrolary 2.1, to a generalized Bellman equation for the target policy π. Then, we can interpret solutions of (2.4) as solutions of approximate versions of that generalized Bellman equation.

To simplify notation in subsequent derivations, we shall use the following shorthand notation: For $k \leq m$, denote $S_k^m = (S_k, S_{k+1}, \ldots S_m)$, and denote

$$\rho_k^m = \prod_{i=k}^m \rho_i, \qquad \lambda_k^m = \prod_{i=k}^m \lambda_i, \qquad \gamma_k^m = \prod_{i=k}^m \gamma_i, \tag{3.1}$$

whereas by convention we treat $\rho_k^m = \lambda_k^m = \gamma_k^m = 1$ if $k > m$.

3.1 Randomized Stopping Times

Consider the Markov chain $\{S_t\}$ induced by the target policy π. Let Condition 2.1(i) hold. Recall that for the value function v_π, we have

$$v_\pi(s) = \mathbb{E}_s^\pi\big[\textstyle\sum_{t=0}^\infty \gamma_1^t\, r_\pi(S_t)\big] \text{ (by definition), and } v_\pi(s) = r_\pi(s) + \mathbb{E}_s^\pi[\gamma_1 v_\pi(S_1)]$$

for each state s. The second equation is the standard one-step Bellman equation.

To write generalized Bellman equations for π, we need the notion of *randomized stopping times* for $\{S_t\}$. They generalize stopping times for $\{S_t\}$ in that whether to stop at time t depends not only on S_0^t but also on certain random outcomes. A simple example is to toss a coin at each time and stop as soon as the coin lands on heads, regardless of the history S_0^t. (The corresponding Bellman equation is the one associated with TD(λ) for a constant λ.) Of interest here is the general case where the stopping decision does depend on the entire history.

To define a randomized stopping time formally, first, the probability space of $\{S_t\}$ is enlarged to take into account whatever randomization scheme that is used to make the stopping decision. (The enlargement will be problem-dependent, as the next subsection will demonstrate.) Then, on the enlarged space, a randomized stopping time τ for $\{S_t\}$ is by definition a stopping time relative to some increasing sequence of sigma-algebras $\mathcal{F}_0 \subset \mathcal{F}_1 \subset \cdots$, where the sequence $\{\mathcal{F}_t\}$ is such that (i) for all $t \geq 0$, $\mathcal{F}_t \supset \sigma(S_0^t)$ (the sigma-algebra generated by S_0^t), and (ii) w.r.t. $\{\mathcal{F}_t\}$, $\{S_t\}$ remains to be a Markov chain with transition probability P, i.e., $\text{Prob}(S_{t+1} = s \mid \mathcal{F}_t) = P_{S_t s}$. (See [16, Chap. 3.3].)

The advantage of this abstract definition is that it allows us to write Bellman equations in general forms without worrying about the details of the enlarged space which are not important at this point. For notational simplicity, we shall still use $\mathbb{E}^\pi$ to denote expectation for the enlarged probability space and write $\mathbf{P}^\pi$ for the probability measure on that space, when there is no confusion.

If τ is a randomized stopping time for $\{S_t\}$, the strong Markov property [16, Theorem 3.3] allows us to express v_π in terms of $v_\pi(S_\tau)$ and the total discounted rewards R^τ prior to stopping:

$$\begin{aligned} v_\pi(s) &= \mathbb{E}^\pi_s \left[\sum_{t=0}^{\tau-1} \gamma_1^t \, r_\pi(S_t) + \sum_{t=\tau}^{\infty} \gamma_1^\tau \cdot \gamma_{\tau+1}^t \, r_\pi(S_t) \right] \\ &= \mathbb{E}^\pi_s \left[R^\tau + \gamma_1^\tau \, v_\pi(S_\tau) \right], \end{aligned} \tag{3.2}$$

where $R^\tau = \sum_{t=0}^{\tau-1} \gamma_1^t \, r_\pi(S_t)$ for $\tau \in \{0, 1, 2, \ldots\} \cup \{+\infty\}$.[7] We can also write the Bellman equation (3.2) in terms of $\{S_t\}$ only, by taking expectation over τ:

$$v_\pi(s) = \mathbb{E}^\pi_s \left[\sum_{t=0}^{\infty} \left(q_t^+(S_0^t) \cdot \gamma_1^t \, r_\pi(S_t) + q_t(S_0^t) \cdot \gamma_1^t \, v_\pi(S_t) \right) \right], \tag{3.3}$$

$$\text{where} \quad q_t^+(S_0^t) = \mathbf{P}^\pi(\tau > t \mid S_0^t), \qquad q_t(S_0^t) = \mathbf{P}^\pi(\tau = t \mid S_0^t). \tag{3.4}$$

The r.h.s. of (3.2) or (3.3) defines an associated generalized Bellman operator $T : \Re^N \to \Re^N$ that has several equivalent expressions; e.g., for all $s \in \mathcal{S}$,

$$(Tv)(s) = \mathbb{E}^\pi_s \left[R^\tau + \gamma_1^\tau \, v(S_\tau) \right] = \mathbb{E}^\pi_s \left[\sum_{t=0}^{\infty} \left(q_t^+(S_0^t) \cdot \gamma_1^t \, r_\pi(S_t) + q_t(S_0^t) \cdot \gamma_1^t \, v(S_t) \right) \right].$$

If $\tau \geq 1$ a.s., then as in the case of the one-step Bellman operator, the value function v_π is the unique fixed point of T, i.e., the unique solution of $v = Tv$.[8]

3.2 Bellman Equation for the Proposed TD Learning Scheme

With the terminology of randomized stopping times, we are now ready to write down the generalized Bellman equation associated with the TD-learning scheme proposed in Sect. 2.2. It corresponds to a particular randomized stopping time. We shall first describe this random time, from which a generalized Bellman equation follows as seen in the preceding subsection. That this is indeed the Bellman equation for our TD learning scheme will then be proved.

Consider the Markov chain $\{S_t\}$ *under the target policy* π. We define a randomized stopping time τ for $\{S_t\}$:

- Let $y_t, \lambda_t, e_t, t \geq 1$, evolve according to (2.5) and (2.2).
- Let the initial (S_0, y_0, e_0) be distributed according to ζ, the unique invariant probability measure in Theorem 2.1.
- At time $t \geq 1$, we stop the system with probability $1 - \lambda_t$ if it has not yet been stopped. Let τ be the time when the system stops ($\tau = \infty$ if the system never stops).

To make the dependence on the initial distribution ζ explicit, we write $\mathbf{P}^\pi_\zeta$ for the probability measure of this process.

---

[7] In the case $\tau = 0$, $R^0 = 0$. In the case $\tau = \infty$, $R^\infty = \sum_{t=0}^{\infty} \gamma_1^t \, r_\pi(S_t)$, and the second term $\gamma_1^\tau \, v_\pi(S_\tau)$ in (3.2) is 0 because $\gamma_1^\infty := \prod_{k=1}^{\infty} \gamma_k = 0$ a.s. under Condition 2.1(i).

[8] It can be shown in this case that the substochastic matrix involved in the affine operator T is a linear contraction w.r.t. a weighted sup-norm on $\Re^N$, by using Condition 2.1(i) and nonnegative matrix theory (see also [1, Prop. 2.2]).

Note that by definition λ_t and λ_1^t are functions of the initial (y_0, e_0) and states S_0^t. From how the random time τ is defined, we have for all $t \geq 1$,

$$\mathbf{P}_\zeta^\pi(\tau > t \mid S_0^t, y_0, e_0) = \lambda_1^t =: h_t^+(y_0, e_0, S_0^t), \tag{3.5}$$

$$\mathbf{P}_\zeta^\pi(\tau = t \mid S_0^t, y_0, e_0) = \lambda_1^{t-1}(1 - \lambda_t) =: h_t(y_0, e_0, S_0^t), \tag{3.6}$$

and hence

$$q_t^+(S_0^t) := \mathbf{P}_\zeta^\pi(\tau > t \mid S_0^t) = \int h_t^+(y, e, S_0^t)\, \zeta(d(y, e) \mid S_0), \tag{3.7}$$

$$q_t(S_0^t) := \mathbf{P}_\zeta^\pi(\tau = t \mid S_0^t) = \int h_t(y, e, S_0^t)\, \zeta(d(y, e) \mid S_0), \tag{3.8}$$

where $\zeta(d(y, e) \mid s)$ is the conditional distribution of (y_0, e_0) given $S_0 = s$, w.r.t. the initial distribution ζ. As before, we can write the generalized Bellman operator T associated with τ in several equivalent forms. Let $\mathbb{E}_\zeta^\pi$ denote expectation under $\mathbf{P}_\zeta^\pi$. Based on (3.2) and (3.5)–(3.6), it is easy to derive that[9] for all $v : \mathcal{S} \to \Re, s \in \mathcal{S}$,

$$(Tv)(s) = \mathbb{E}_\zeta^\pi \left[\sum_{t=0}^\infty \lambda_1^t \gamma_1^t\, r_\pi(S_t) + \sum_{t=1}^\infty \lambda_1^{t-1}(1 - \lambda_t)\gamma_1^t\, v(S_t) \mid S_0 = s\right]. \tag{3.9}$$

Alternatively, by integrating over (y_0, e_0) and using (3.7)–(3.8), we can write

$$(Tv)(s) = \mathbb{E}_\zeta^\pi \left[\sum_{t=0}^\infty \left(q_t^+(S_0^t) \cdot \gamma_1^t\, r_\pi(S_t) + q_t(S_0^t) \cdot \gamma_1^t\, v(S_t)\right) \mid S_0 = s\right], \tag{3.10}$$

for all $v : \mathcal{S} \to \Re, s \in \mathcal{S}$, where in the case $t = 0$, $q_0^+(\cdot) \equiv 1 = \mathbf{P}_\zeta^\pi(\tau > 0 \mid S_0)$ and $q_0(\cdot) \equiv 0 = \mathbf{P}_\zeta^\pi(\tau = 0 \mid S_0)$ (since $\tau > 0$ by construction).

Comparing the two expressions of T, we remark that the expression (3.9) reflects the role of the λ_t's in determining the stopping time, whereas the expression (3.10), which has eliminated the auxiliary memory states y_t, shows more clearly the dependence of the stopping time on the entire history S_0^t. It can also be seen from the initial distribution ζ that the behavior policy asserts a significant role in determining the Bellman operator T for the target policy. This is in contrast with off-policy TD learning that uses a constant λ, where the behavior policy affects only how one approximates the Bellman equation underlying TD, not the Bellman equation itself.

We now proceed to show how the Bellman equation $v = Tv$ given above relates to the off-policy TD learning scheme in Sect. 2.2. Some notation is needed. Denote by $\zeta_\mathcal{S}$ the marginal of ζ on $\mathcal{S}$. Note that $\zeta_\mathcal{S}$ coincides with the invariant probability measure of the Markov chain $\{S_t\}$ *induced by the behavior policy.* For two functions v_1, v_2 on $\mathcal{S}$, we write $v_1 \perp_{\zeta_\mathcal{S}} v_2$ if $\sum_{s \in \mathcal{S}} \zeta_\mathcal{S}(s)\, v_1(s)\, v_2(s) = 0$. If $\mathcal{L}$ is a linear subspace of functions on $\mathcal{S}$ and $v \perp_{\zeta_\mathcal{S}} v'$ for all $v' \in \mathcal{L}$, we write $v \perp_{\zeta_\mathcal{S}} \mathcal{L}$. Recall that ϕ is a function that maps each state s to an n-dimensional feature vector. Denote by $\mathcal{L}_\phi$ the subspace spanned by the n component functions of ϕ,

[9] Rewrite (3.2) as $v_\pi(s) = \mathbb{E}_s^\pi \left[\sum_{t=0}^\infty \mathbb{1}(\tau > t)\, \gamma_1^t\, r_\pi(S_t) + \sum_{t=0}^\infty \mathbb{1}(\tau = t)\, \gamma_1^t\, v_\pi(S_t)\right]$ and for the tth terms in the r.h.s., take expectation over τ conditioned on (S_0^t, y_0, e_0).

which is the space of approximate value functions for our TD learning scheme. Recall also that $\mathbb{E}_\zeta$ denotes expectation w.r.t. the *stationary* state-trace process $\{(S_t, y_t, e_t)\}$ under the behavior policy (cf. Theorem 2.1).

Theorem 3.1. *Let Conditions 2.1–2.3 hold. Then as a linear equation in v, $\mathbb{E}_\zeta\big[e_0\, \delta_0(v)\big] = 0$ is equivalently $Tv - v \perp_{\zeta_S} \mathcal{L}_\phi$, where T is the generalized Bellman operator for π given in (3.9) or (3.10).*

Remark 3.1 (On LSTD). Note that $Tv - v \perp_{\zeta_S} \mathcal{L}_\phi, v \in \mathcal{L}_\phi$ is a projected version of the generalized Bellman equation $Tv - v = 0$ (projecting the l.h.s. onto the approximation subspace $\mathcal{L}_\phi$ w.r.t. the ζ_S-weighted Euclidean norm). Theorem 3.1 and Corrolary 2.1 together show that this is what LSTD solves in the limit. If this projected Bellman equation admits a unique solution $\bar{v}$, then the approximation error $\bar{v} - v_\pi$ can be characterized as in [22,32].

Proof (outline). We divide the proof into three parts. The first part is more subtle than the other two, which are mostly calculations. Due to space limit, we can only outline the proof here, leaving out the details of some arguments.

(i) We extend the stationary state-trace process to $t = -1, -2, \ldots$ and work with a double-ended stationary process $\{(S_t, y_t, e_t)\}_{-\infty<t<\infty}$ (such a process exists by Kolmogorov's theorem [4, Theorem 12.1.2]). We keep using the notation P_ζ and $\mathbb{E}_\zeta$ for this double-ended stationary Markov chain. Then, by unfolding the iteration (2.2) for e_t backwards in time, we show that[10]

$$e_0 = \phi(S_0) + \textstyle\sum_{t=1}^{\infty} \lambda_{1-t}^{0} \gamma_{1-t}^{0} \rho_{-t}^{-1}\, \phi(S_{-t}) \quad P_\zeta\text{–a.s.}, \tag{3.11}$$

or with $\lambda_1^0 = \rho_0^{-1} = 1$ by convention, we can write $e_0 = \sum_{t=0}^{\infty} \lambda_{1-t}^{0} \gamma_{1-t}^{0} \rho_{-t}^{-1}\, \phi(S_{-t})$ P_ζ-a.s. The proof of (3.11) uses the stationarity of the process, Condition 2.1(i) and a theorem on integration [21, Theorem 1.38] among others.

(ii) Using the expression (3.11) of e_0, we calculate $\mathbb{E}_\zeta\big[e_0 \cdot \rho_0 f(S_0^1)\big]$ for any bounded measurable function f on $\mathcal{S} \times \mathcal{S}$. In particular, we first obtain

$$\mathbb{E}_\zeta\big[e_0 \cdot \rho_0 f(S_0^1)\big] = \textstyle\sum_{t=0}^{\infty} \mathbb{E}_\zeta\Big[\phi(S_0) \cdot \mathbb{E}_\zeta\big[\lambda_1^t \gamma_1^t \rho_0^t\, f(S_t^{t+1}) \mid S_0\big]\Big] \tag{3.12}$$

by using (3.11) and the stationarity of the state-trace process. Next we relate the expectations in the summation in (3.12) to expectations w.r.t. the process with probability measure $\mathbf{P}_\zeta^\pi$, which we recall is induced by the target policy π and introduced at the beginning of this subsection. Let $\tilde{\mathbb{E}}_\zeta^\pi$ denote expectation w.r.t. the marginal of $\mathbf{P}_\zeta^\pi$ on the space of $\{(S_t, y_t, e_t)\}_{t\geq 0}$. From the change of measure performed through ρ_0^t, we have

$$\mathbb{E}_\zeta\big[\lambda_1^t \gamma_1^t \rho_0^t\, f(S_t^{t+1}) \mid S_0, y_0, e_0\big] = \tilde{\mathbb{E}}_\zeta^\pi\big[\lambda_1^t \gamma_1^t\, f(S_t^{t+1}) \mid S_0, y_0, e_0\big], \quad t \geq 0. \tag{3.13}$$

Combining this with (3.12) and using the fact that ζ is the marginal distribution of (S_0, y_0, e_0) in both processes, we obtain

$$\mathbb{E}_\zeta\big[e_0 \cdot \rho_0 f(S_0^1)\big] = \textstyle\sum_{t=0}^{\infty} \tilde{\mathbb{E}}_\zeta^\pi\Big[\phi(S_0) \cdot \tilde{\mathbb{E}}_\zeta^\pi\big[\lambda_1^t \gamma_1^t\, f(S_t^{t+1}) \mid S_0\big]\Big]. \tag{3.14}$$

---
[10] Recall the shorthand notation (3.1) introduced at the beginning of Sect. 3.

(iii) We now use (3.14) to calculate $\mathbb{E}_\zeta\big[e_0\,\delta_0(v)\big]$ for a given function v. Recall from (2.3) $\delta_0(v) = \rho_0 \cdot \big(r(S_0^1) + \gamma_1 v(S_1) - v(S_0)\big)$, so we let $f(S_t^{t+1}) = r(S_t^{t+1}) + \gamma_{t+1} v(S_{t+1}) - v(S_t)$ in (3.14). Then a direct calculation shows that[11]

$$\mathbb{E}_\zeta\big[e_0\,\delta_0(v) \mid S_0\big] = \phi(S_0) \cdot \big\{ - v(S_0) + (Tv)(S_0)\big\}. \tag{3.15}$$

Therefore $\mathbb{E}_\zeta\big[e_0\,\delta_0(v)\big] = \sum_{s\in\mathcal{S}} \zeta_{\mathcal{S}}(s)\,\phi(s) \cdot (Tv - v)(s)$, and this shows that $\mathbb{E}_\zeta\big[e_0\,\delta_0(v)\big] = 0$ is equivalent to $Tv - v \perp_{\zeta_{\mathcal{S}}} \mathcal{L}_\phi$. □

Concluding Remark. This completes our analysis of the LSTD algorithm for the proposed TD-learning scheme. To conclude the paper, we note that the preceding results also prepare the ground for analyzing gradient-based algorithms similar to [9, 10] in a future work. Specifically, like LSTD, these algorithms would aim to solve the same projected generalized Bellman equation as characterized by Theorem 3.1 (cf. Remark 3.1). Their average dynamics, which is important for analyzing their convergence using the mean ODE approach from stochastic approximation theory [7], can be studied based on the ergodicity result of Theorem 2.1, in essentially the same way as we did in Sect. 2.3 for the LSTD algorithm.

References

1. Bertsekas, D.P., Tsitsiklis, J.N.: Neuro-Dynamic Programming. Athena Scientific, Belmont (1996)
2. Boyan, J.A.: Least-squares temporal difference learning. In: Proceedings of the 16th International Conference Machine Learning (ICML) (1999)
3. Dann, C., Neumann, G., Peters, J.: Policy evaluation with temporal differences: a survey and comparison. J. Mach. Learn. Res. **15**, 809–883 (2014)
4. Dudley, R.M.: Real Analysis and Probability. Cambridge University Press, Cambridge (2002)
5. Geist, M., Scherrer, B.: Off-policy learning with eligibility traces: a survey. J. Mach. Learn. Res. **15**, 289–333 (2014)
6. Glynn, P.W., Iglehart, D.L.: Importance sampling for stochastic simulations. Manag. Sci. **35**, 1367–1392 (1989)
7. Kushner, H.J., Yin, G.G.: Stochastic Approximation and Recursive Algorithms and Applications, 2nd edn. Springer, New York (2003)
8. Liu, B., Liu, J., Ghavamzadeh, M., Mahadevan, S., Petrik, M.: Finite-sample analysis of proximal gradient TD algorithms. In: The 31st Conference on Uncertainty in Artificial Intelligence (UAI) (2015)
9. Maei, H.R.: Gradient temporal-difference learning algorithms. Ph.D. thesis, University of Alberta (2011)
10. Mahadevan, S., Liu, B., Thomas, P., Dabney, W., Giguere, S., Jacek, N., Gemp, I., Liu, J.: Proximal reinforcement learning (2014). arXiv:1405.6757

[11] Note $\sum_{t=0}^\infty \tilde{\mathbb{E}}_\zeta^\pi\left[\lambda_1^t \gamma_1^t r(S_t^{t+1}) \mid S_0\right] = \sum_{t=0}^\infty \tilde{\mathbb{E}}_\zeta^\pi\left[\lambda_1^t \gamma_1^t\, r_\pi(S_t) \mid S_0\right]$ (since $\tilde{\mathbb{E}}_\zeta^\pi[r(S_t^{t+1}) \mid S_0^t] = r_\pi(S_t)$). By rearranging terms, $\sum_{t=0}^\infty \tilde{\mathbb{E}}_\zeta^\pi\left[\lambda_1^t \gamma_1^t \cdot \big(\gamma_{t+1} v(S_{t+1}) - v(S_t)\big) \mid S_0\right]$ equals $-v(S_0) + \sum_{t=1}^\infty \tilde{\mathbb{E}}_\zeta^\pi\left[\lambda_1^{t-1}(1-\lambda_t) \cdot \gamma_1^t v(S_t) \mid S_0\right]$. Putting these together and using the expression of T in (3.9), we obtain (3.15).

11. Mahmood, A.R., van Hasselt, H., Sutton, R.S.: Weighted importance sampling for off-policy learning with linear function approximation. In: Advances in Neural Information Processing Systems (NIPS), vol. 27 (2014)
12. Mahmood, A.R., Yu, H., Sutton, R.S.: Multi-step off-policy learning without importance-sampling ratios (2017). arXiv:1702.03006
13. Meyn, S.: Ergodic theorems for discrete time stochastic systems using a stochastic Lyapunov function. SIAM J. Control Optim. **27**, 1409–1439 (1989)
14. Meyn, S., Tweedie, R.L.: Markov Chains and Stochastic Stability, 2nd edn. Cambridge University Press, Cambridge (2009)
15. Munos, R., Stepleton, T., Harutyunyan, A., Bellemare, M.G.: Safe and efficient off-policy reinforcement learning. In: Advances in Neural Information Processing Systems (NIPS), vol. 29 (2016)
16. Nummelin, E.: General Irreducible Markov Chains and Non-Negative Operators. Cambridge University Press, Cambridge (1984)
17. Precup, D., Sutton, R.S., Dasgupta, S.: Off-policy temporal-difference learning with function approximation. In: The 18th International Conference on Machine Learning (ICML) (2001)
18. Precup, D., Sutton, R.S., Singh, S.: Eligibility traces for off-policy policy evaluation. In: The 17th International Conference on Machine Learning (ICML) (2000)
19. Puterman, M.L.: Markov Decision Processes: Discrete Stochastic Dynamic Programming. Wiley, New York (1994)
20. Randhawa, R.S., Juneja, S.: Combining importance sampling and temporal difference control variates to simulate Markov chains. ACM Trans. Model. Comput. Simul. **14**(1), 1–30 (2004)
21. Rudin, W.: Real and Complex Analysis. McGraw-Hill, New York (1966)
22. Scherrer, B.: Should one compute the temporal difference fix point or minimize the Bellman residual? In: The 27th International Conference on Machine Learning (ICML) (2010)
23. Sutton, R.S.: Learning to predict by the methods of temporal differences. Mach. Learn. **3**, 9–44 (1988)
24. Sutton, R.S.: TD models: modeling the world at a mixture of time scales. In: The 12th International Conference on Machine Learning (ICML) (1995)
25. Sutton, R.S., Barto, A.G.: Reinforcement Learning. MIT Press, Cambridge (1998)
26. Sutton, R.S., Mahmood, A.R., White, M.: An emphatic approach to the problem of off-policy temporal-difference learning. J. Mach. Learn. Res. **17**(73), 1–29 (2016)
27. Tsitsiklis, J.N., Van Roy, B.: An analysis of temporal-difference learning with function approximation. IEEE Trans. Autom. Control **42**(5), 674–690 (1997)
28. Ueno, T., Maeda, S., Kawanabe, M., Ishii, S.: Generalized TD learning. J. Mach. Learn. Res. **12**, 1977–2020 (2011)
29. Yu, H.: Least squares temporal difference methods: an analysis under general conditions. SIAM J. Control Optim. **50**, 3310–3343 (2012)
30. Yu, H.: On convergence of emphatic temporal-difference learning. In: The 28th Annual Conference on Learning Theory (COLT) (2015). arXiv:1506.02582
31. Yu, H.: Weak convergence properties of constrained emphatic temporal-difference learning with constant and slowly diminishing stepsize. J. Mach. Learn. Res. **17**(220), 1–58 (2016)
32. Yu, H., Bertsekas, D.P.: Error bounds for approximations from projected linear equations. Math. Oper. Res. **35**(2), 306–329 (2010)
33. Yu, H., Bertsekas, D.P.: Weighted Bellman equations and their applications in approximate dynamic programming. LIDS Technical report 2876, MIT (2012)

Person Identification Using Discriminative Visual Aesthetic

Samiul Azam(✉) and Marina Gavrilova

University of Calgary, 2500 University Dr NW, Calgary, AB, Canada
{samiul.azam,mgavrilo}@ucalgary.ca

Abstract. A person's image aesthetic is defined as a set of principles that influences the person to choose favorite images over a list of options. Different persons have different visual preferences which can be used to discriminate a person from another. Recently, some research has been carried in the area of behavioral biometric and image aesthetic. Researchers prove that it is possible to identify a person from discriminative visual cues. In this paper, we develop a new and improved method for person recognition using aesthetic features. The proposed approach uses 14 perceptual and 3 content features collected from the state-of-the-art researches. To achieve significant improvement in rank 1 recognition rate, we utilize local perceptual features and Histogram Oriented Gradient (HOG) feature for the first time. However, the new feature space is 975 dimensional which increases the elapsed time of enrollment and recognition phases. To minimize it, we apply Principle Component Analysis (PCA) that reduces the dimension of the feature vector by 50% without affecting the actual recognition performance. The proposed method has been evaluated on 200 user's 40,000 images from the benchmark Flickr database. Experiment shows that the proposed method achieves 84% and 97% recognition rates in rank 1 and 5, whereas most well-performed state-of-the-art method shows 73% and 92%, respectively.

1 Introduction

Behavioral biometric is the field of study that allows identification and verification of an individual based on discriminative activity and behavioral attributes [10,15]. Person's styles, preferences, interactions, expressions and attitudes, such as typing pattern, gait, social interaction, mouse dynamic and browsing history are the sources of behavioral traits. In contrast to physiological biometric, it has few advantages [24]. It is easily collectible through the low cost devices without the physical contact. However, as it is a highly intrinsic aspect of a person, analyzing and extracting discriminative features of behavioral traits are much more difficult. Also, it changes over time, so periodic data collection is needed depending on the type of the behavioral trait. Recently, researchers introduced visual aesthetic as a new behavioral biometric trait [14]. It is a person's set of cognitive rules that guides the person to prefer one object over others. Simply, what a person prefer can be utilized to identify that person. However, it is not a

M. Mouhoub and P. Langlais (Eds.): Canadian AI 2017, LNAI 10233, pp. 15–26, 2017.
DOI: 10.1007/978-3-319-57351-9_2

unique trait like fingerprint. It changes over time, and can be overlapped among peoples from same social environment, family, age, group and ethnicity [11]. However, researchers experimentally prove that collection of aesthetic data from a person contains sufficient discriminative features to identify the person from others [13]. Also, researchers utilize this biometric trait to predict gender information [3,4]. With the rapid advancement of Online Social Media (OSN), aesthetic data is becoming available to the researchers for analysis. People share their likeness, choices and preferences in the form of texts, images, videos and musics. For example, the OSN Flickr contains user's favorite set of images with few soft biometric informations, such as age and gender [9]. In 2014, a group of researchers conducted experiment on 200 Flickr user's 40,000 favorite images, and reconstructed individual's visual preference model for biometric identification and verification [14]. However, it is not feasible or practical as a biometric authentication and recognition system where high security is needed.

According to literature, forensic security is the potential application area of aesthetic biometric [13]. Forensic experts investigate a crime scene to collect physiological and behavioral traits of the suspects and victims. In many cases, absence of physiological traits pushes them to rely only on the behavioral biometric traits. Collected hand held devices can be analyzed to estimate demographic information of the suspect using aesthetic features of the images inside media directory. Moreover, various OSNs are carrying aesthetic data that can be investigated to identify list of suspects. To perform this, automated system is needed to process large image data from OSNs. As biometric identification, visual aesthetic has been rarely studied. It was first introduced by P. Lovato, in 2014, who defined it as "personal aesthetic" trait of people (that distinguishes people from each other) [14]. So far, a few state-of-the-art researches exist in this area, as well as no commercially deployed aesthetic biometric system has been found. The maximum reported recognition rates are 73% and 92% in rank 1 and 5 by the authors of [18], which is not significant enough compare to other behavioral biometric systems [24]. Motivated by this fact, we propose an improved person identification method using discriminative visual aesthetic. It shows 84% and 97% recognition rates in rank 1 and 5, respectively. The main contributions of the paper are as follows:

- Proposed an improved methodology for aesthetic based person identification that outperforms other state-of-the-art methods. It is validated based on the benchmark Flickr database [13].
- Achieved significant improvement by utilizing Histogram Oriented Gradient (HOG) and local perceptual visual features.
- Enhanced feature vector (length of 975) allowed to increase the one-vs-all learning time (as enrollment time in Biometric domain) which is mitigated using Principle Component Analysis (PCA).

2 Literature Review

The preliminary concept of aesthetic biometric was first introduced by the authors of [13]. They created the benchmark image database consists of 40,000 favorite images from 200 Flickr users. They extracted a pool of low and high level image features, and exploited linear regression to learn the most discriminative features. Experiment showed that, if 100 images are used in the enrollment and recognition phase (from each person), then the system can recognize people with only 55% accuracy in rank 5. Although the method didn't able to show good accuracy, the literature introduced various primary aspects of aesthetic biometric and the Flickr image database. Later, the same authors improved the method by incorporating new features [14]. The previous work used 62 dimensional feature vector, whereas the new technique considered 111 feature. They kept the same linear regression method to build person specific preference models, and evaluated it on the benchmark database (shows 79% accuracy in rank 5). At the same time, another group of researchers introduced a different solution of the problem [17]. They used K-means clustering to divide the whole training space into 6 clusters. Similar thematic images were considered under same cluster. Then bagging strategy was designed to improve the stability and accuracy of the machine learning algorithm. In general, they combined the idea of clustering and bagging to create surrogate images (a different representation of the input). Then LASSO (least absolute shrinkage and selection operator) regression [21] was applied to build discriminative models. During experiment, authors considered the method [13] for comparison and normalized area under the curve (nAUC) as performance metric. The new technique was able to outperforms method [13] by 7% in nAUC. So far, the best approach is proposed by the authors of [18]. Powerful concept of counting grid [16] is applied with support vector machine (SVM) to improve the performance. It shows 92% recognition rate in rank 5 which is the highest accuracy reported in the literature. In this paper, we introduce a new approach for person identification method which is able to reach the recognition rate of 84% in rank 1 and 97% in rank 5. This significant improvement is achieved by incorporating histogram oriented gradient (HOG) feature and local feature extraction process. We apply LASSO regression with the enhanced feature vector to learn a person's preference model in one-vs-all training. The next two sections describe the proposed method and the experimental evaluation steps.

3 Proposed Methodology

3.1 Global Image Feature

The existing state-of-the-art methods [13,14,17,18] use 14 perceptual and 3 content features for modeling a person's visual aesthetic. These features are heterogeneous, contain various aesthetic cues of a person [2,7]. In our proposed method, we have considered these state-of-the-art features, as they showed promising result in person identification. Each type of feature has its own dimension. Figure 1 shows the list of features and their dimensions. Total length of the perceptual feature vector is 57, and content feature vector is 54. All these features are extracted globally from an image. So the total length of the global feature vector is 111.

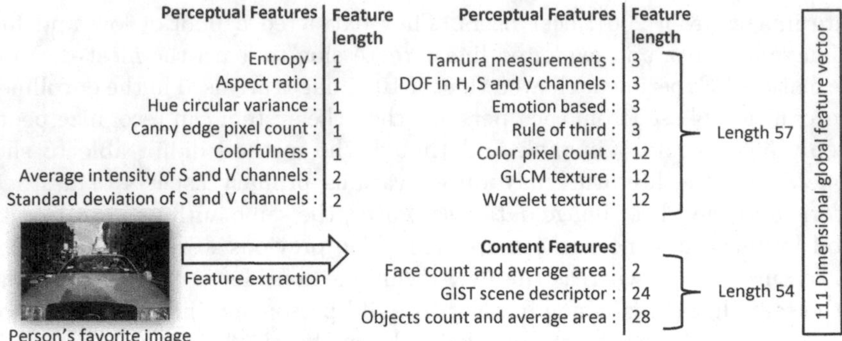

Fig. 1. List of perceptual and content features collected from [13,14,17,18].

3.2 Local Image Feature

The existing methods extract all features globally which lacks the local information of an image. On the other hand, we can extract features locally where an image is divided into number of image patches. Many researchers have argued that local image features are more robust and informative than global, which improves the recognition performance of machine learning algorithms [1,5]. Moreover, same image feature in different segments of images may create discrimination of aesthetics among persons. Hence, to improve the performance, we apply local feature extraction process. We divide an image into 9 equal size subregions, and apply feature extraction for each sub-region. During local processing, only the perceptual features are considered, as they are not affected by the image partition process. However, content features (such as faces, objects, image scene category, and shapes) are excluded from the local process as they are vulnerable to unaware segmentation. We also exclude the aspect ratio (a perceptual feature), as because it is same in local regions. Figure 2 shows the construction of local feature vector from an image.

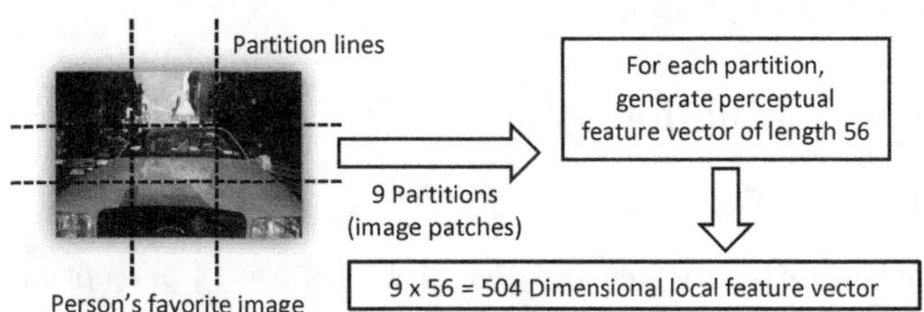

Fig. 2. Construction of local feature vector from an image.

3.3 Histogram Oriented Gradient (HOG) Feature

As content feature, state-of-art-methods use face [22], objects (14 specific items) [8] and scene descriptor [23]. In addition to these, we use HOG feature which is a powerful shape and appearance descriptor of image contents. HOG feature was first introduced by Navneet and Bill in 2005 for the purpose of pedestrian detection [6]. Later, it was widely used by other researchers for various computer vision tasks, such as object detection [25], text extraction [20] and face recognition [19]. Motivated by this fact, we use HOG image descriptor to add more discriminative visual cues among persons. For simplicity, we use HOG descriptor with cell size of 1. Figure 3 shows the steps of generating HOG descriptor from an image. It contains 360 bins where each bin is filled up based on pixel's gradient information. We can easily generate the gradient images (angle and magnitude) using 1st order derivative filter in both x and y directions (G_x and G_y). For each pixel location, a bin is selected based on calculated angle value on that location, and add the magnitude value with the selected bin. The HOG bins describe the local orientation information of an image and magnitude of intensity change, which is sufficient to get rough idea of an object shape and appearance. Lastly the global, local and HOG feature vectors are concatenated together to make a high dimensional vector of length 975.

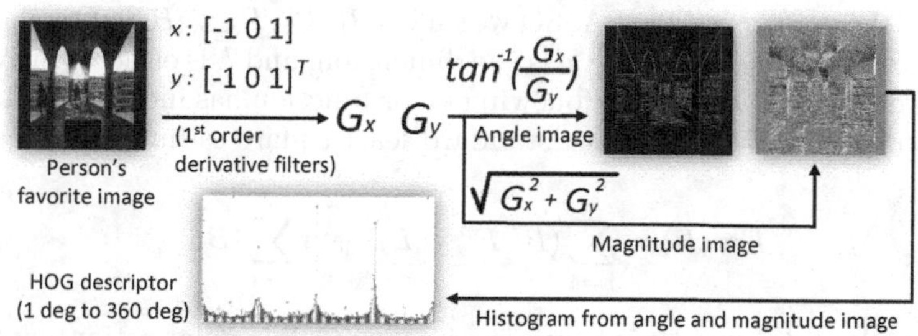

Fig. 3. Steps of generating HOG descriptor from an image.

3.4 Principle Component Analysis for Dimension Reduction

The feature vector used in the proposed model has dimension of 975 per image which increases the training time of a person's preference model. In the proposed method, we apply LASSO regression [21] to learn preference model of a person in one-vs-all manner. To enroll and recognize 50 persons, the proposed method takes 5,334 s which is significantly high. To speed up the training process, we apply Principle Component Analysis (PCA) for dimensionality reduction without having significant deviation from the actual model performance. PCA is a well known and widely used approach for data dimension reduction [12]. It is a statistical procedure that transform a set of d-dimensional observations into linearly uncorrelated variables (or principle components) using orthogonal projection. As output it gives d principle components where the first component has highest variance, and the last component has lowest variance. Top k ($k < d$) components contain most of the variances of the data. Systemically selecting top k components, and applying reverse transformation will give the k-dimensional data having most of variances in it. In our case d is 975, and k has been assigned experimentally training time of a person is minimized without having much performance degradation.

3.5 LASSO Regression for Aesthetic Template Generation

To generate aesthetic template of a person, existing methods use LASSO regression [21] as binary classifier where positive class is the person, and negative class is all others. It performs automatic variable selection (through weight assignment) and regularization to improve prediction accuracy. This model has simple interpretation which can be used to find impact of heterogeneous features toward positive and negative classes [14]. Due simplicity and easy feature analysis, we also use LASSO regression for learning preference model and generating matching score for recognition. To apply LASSO regression, an image is represented as linear combination of features:

$$L = B_1F_1 + B_2F_2 + B_3F_3 + \dots\dots\dots + B_dF_d \tag{1}$$

where B is the person specific LASSO weights $\{B_1, B_2, B_3 \dots B_d\}$, F is the image feature vector $\{F_1, F_2, F_3 \dots F_d\}$, d is the dimension, and L is either positive (+1) or negative (-1) class label. The following error function has incorporated to find the person specific B vector using standard least square estimates.

$$Err(B) = \sum_{n=1}^{N} (B^T F^n - L)^2 + \alpha \sum_{i=1}^{d} |B_i|. \tag{2}$$

Here, N is the total number of training images, α is regularization parameter, and T is matrix transpose operator. In the error function the only parameter is α. From a range of α values, we select optimum α where minimum number of LASSO weights are zero. Finally, the solution B is the template (or preference model) for the person. In the recognition phase, matching score of a person is calculated by averaging all regression scores generated from test images and person specific weight vector B. The person with highest matching score will be the identified person.

4 Experiment and Analysis

4.1 Experimental Setup

The only publicly available database exists in this domain is the Flickr database created by Lovato [13]. It contains 40,000 color images in JPEG file format belonging to 200 randomly selected Flickr users. Each user's first 200 images under the "Favorite" tab have been considered. The process of adding favorite images is a continuous process over 23 to 441 weeks. This ensures time variance acquisition of favorite images. The database has 0.05% overlapping of images among 200 users. Samples from the database are provided in Fig. 4. For reducing

Fig. 4. Example of favorite images from one anonymous Flickr user [9].

the experimentation time, we randomly select 50 user's 10,000 images (one fourth of the database [13]) for PCA component selection, initial evaluation of the proposed method, as well as comparing 3 existing state-of-the-art methods. At the end of Sect. 4.4, we report the rank 1 and 5 recognition rates for the full database. The workstation used in the experiment has Windows 8.1 as operating system, AMD A8-7410 APU 2.2 GHz processor and 8 GB RAM. Since all the features have heterogeneous range of values, we apply z-score normalization.

4.2 PCA Component Selection

Due to large feature vector (length of 975), the training phase of the proposed method takes significant amount of time. From the point of view of biometric system, training of a person's preference model is the enrollment phase. In the proposed method, the elapsed time for enrollment and recognition of 50 persons takes 5,334 s. To reduce the training time, we apply PCA for dimensionality reduction. However, finding appropriate number of principle components is an important issue. In this experiment, we use iterative approach to select top k components (higher to lower variance of data). Starts from $k = 100$ and step size 100, we plot the recognition rate of 50 persons in rank 1 (black bars). Figure 5 shows that for $k = 500$, the recognition rate is equal to the rate of actual feature vector (without applying PCA). The elapsed time showing in the plot is the average enrollment and recognition time per person (gray bars). The time for

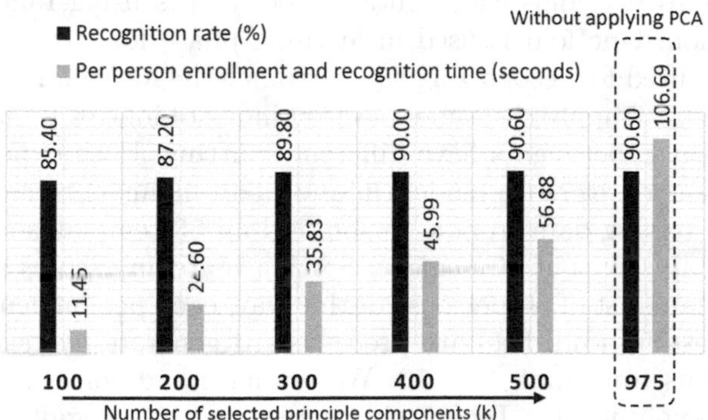

Fig. 5. Effect of number of PCA components in recognition rate and elapsed time.

feature extraction is not counted here, as it is significantly higher than the training and testing time. Experiment shows that at $k = 500$, the dimension of the feature vector and elapsed time are reduced by 48.71% and 44.82%, respectively, without affecting the recognition rate.

4.3 Implementation of Existing Methods

In the area of visual aesthetic biometric, four different state-of-the-art methods were evaluated on the benchmark Flickr database. According to the articles [13,14,17,18], the authors use 5 to 20 random splitting of training and testing dataset, and report average experimental results in the literature. However, they didn't report the splitting information, used various evaluation metrics, as well as didn't compare other approaches using CMC curve. For fare comparison, we implemented existing methods, and applied same random splitting information, metrics, and CMC curve in all experiments. Method [18] is not implemented, as it is very complex and challenging, as well as lacks enough details in the original article. However, at the end of the experiment, we compare the recognition rate (in rank 1 and 5) as per the reported results [18].

In all experiments, the number of training and testing images are set to 100. For 200 users, the accuracies in rank 5 reported (using CMC curve) in the articles for the methods [13,14] are 55% and 79%, whereas our implementations show 53.4% and 78.1%. According to article [17], use of surrogate image has shown 7% improvement in recognition rate. Our implementation of method [17] with the extended feature vector from the method [14] shows 5.45% improvement of recognition rate (83.55%) over [14]. In summary, our implementations show similar results close to the source implementations.

4.4 Performance Comparison

Instead of using all 200 users from the benchmark database, we evaluate the proposed method on randomly selected 50 users (justification is provided in Sect. 4.1). Each user contributed 200 of his (or her) favorite images. We split this image set into two folds each contains 100 images using random selection without repetition. One fold is used in learning phase for enrollment purpose, and other fold is used for recognizing the person at the identification phase. In a single experiment, we apply the same selection index of images for all 50 persons. However, different experiments have different splitting. Each experiment needs to learn 50 person's preference model (in one-vs-all manner) to create aesthetic template. Then testing data from a person and all 50 templates are utilized to generate matching scores of 50 persons. Sorting matching scores in descending order gives the rank list of 50 persons. In this way, each person generates a rank list. Finally, these 50 rank lists are processed to generate average recognition rate of 50 persons from rank 1 to 10. We evaluate and compare the methods in 10 different experiments. Table 1 shows the rank 1 recognition rate for 10 experiments. It is clear that model performances are sensitive to training and testing splitting as standard deviation for methods [14,17] are 4.43 and 4.50.

Table 1. Recognition rate **(in rank 1)** over 10 different experiments (consider 50 users from the benchmark Flickr database).

Exp. no.	Proposed method: Rank 1 recognition rate (%)	Method [14]: Rank 1 recognition rate (%)	Method [17]: Rank 1 recognition rate (%)
1	94	74	84
2	94	78	76
3	92	70	80
4	90	70	76
5	90	64	68
6	88	68	80
7	88	72	72
8	90	68	76
9	88	78	74
10	92	72	78
Avg	90.6	71.4	76.4
Std dev	2.32	4.43	4.50

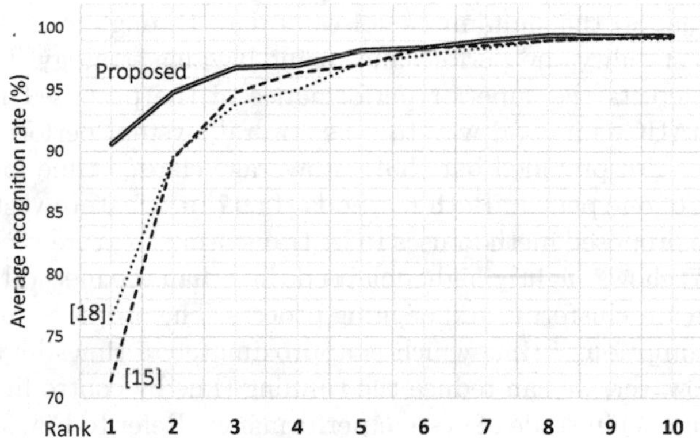

Fig. 6. Cumulative matching characteristic (CMC) curves for the proposed method, as well as existing methods [14,17] upto rank 10. The curves have been obtained by averaging 10 different experiments with different training and testing splitting.

However, the proposed method shows significantly higher average recognition rate (90.60%), and lower standard deviation (2.32%) than other twos. Figure 6 shows the CMC curve up to rank 10 for different methods. We see that the curve for the proposed method is always above the other two curves. However, all of them show similar performances after rank 5. We exclude the method [13] from the comparison as it shows significantly poor performance (41.20%) in rank 1.

In Fig. 7, we use bar charts to compare the methods. The bar chart of average recognition rate shows that the proposed method can recognize persons

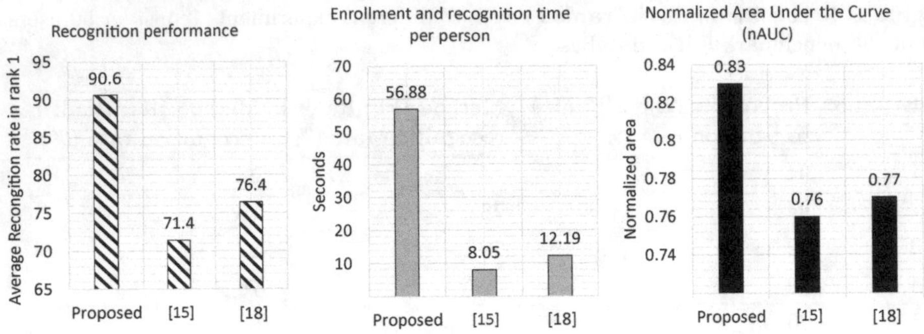

Fig. 7. Bar charts showing recognition rate, nAUC and elapsed time for the methods [14, 17] and the proposed one.

14.2% more accurately. The reason is that, use of local feature extraction and shape information add more discrimination of visual aesthetic which helps the LASSO regression to recognize people more efficiently. On the other hand, none of the existing methods use local and HOG features. Method [17] shows 5% improved performance than [14] due to imposing k-means clustering (to generate surrogate images) that minimizes noises of data through averaging. Also, it increases model stability and performance using bagging strategy. The bar chart of nAUC also depicts the superior performance of the proposed method over existing ones. nAUC is a good way to sense overall system performance in different ranks. We also provided bar chart of average elapsed time for enrollment and recognition of one person. Both methods [14, 17] use feature vector of length 111 whereas the proposed method uses PCA transformed feature vector of length 500. Method [17] shows slightly higher elapsed time than the method [14] because of applying k-means clustering and bagging process. The proposed method shows significant consumption of time which is approximately 5 times higher than the method [17]. However, we can reduce the running time by controlling number of PCA components (k) in trade of system performance. Refer to Fig. 5, we see that when $k = 100$, the elapsed time is only 11.46 s, but system performance become 85.4% (reduced by 5.2%). However, the accuracy is still 9% and 14% higher than the methods [14, 17].

We also compare the proposed method with the most well performed state-of-the-art approach [18] for all 200 user's 40,000 images. According to the literature, method [18] shows 73% and 92% of recognition rate in rank 1 and 5, whereas our proposed method gives 84% and 97%. In summary, the proposed method outperforms all existing state-of-the-art methods.

5 Conclusions

In biometric community, human aesthetic is a new concept. It is defined as a behavioral biometric trait which is sufficiently unique to differentiate a person from. However, reconstructing a person's discriminative aesthetic preferences from favorite images is not a trivial task. Due to variability over time and similarity within same group, the area become more challenging to the researcher. However, most recently, researchers show that it possible to identify people in rank 5 with 92% accuracy using only the visual aesthetic as cue. The reported accuracy is not significant enough compare to other behavioral biometric trait. In this paper, we develop an improved method for person identification using personal aesthetic information. It achieves 84% and 97% recognition rates in rank 1 and 5 on 200 Flickr user's 40,000 favorite images. Experiment shows that the proposed method outperforms all existing state-of-the-art methods in terms of rank 1 recognition rate. As future work, we will apply more sophisticated machine learning algorithms, such as Convolutional Neural Network (CNN), Convolutional Deep Belief Network (CDBN) to improve the performance.

Acknowledgment. The authors would like to thank NSERC Discovery program grant RT731064, URGC, NSERC ENGAGE, NSERC Vanier CGS, and Alberta Ingenuity for partial support of this project.

References

1. Ahmed, F., Paul, P.P., Gavrilova, M.: Music genre classification using a gradient-based local texture descriptor. In: Czarnowski, I., Caballero, A.M., Howlett, R.J., Jain, L.C. (eds.) Intelligent Decision Technologies 2016. SIST, vol. 57, pp. 455–464. Springer, Cham (2016). doi:10.1007/978-3-319-39627-9_40
2. Aydn, T.O., Smolic, A., Gross, M.: Automated aesthetic analysis of photographic images. IEEE Trans. Vis. Comput. Graph. **21**(1), 31–42 (2015)
3. Azam, S., Gavrilova, M.: Gender prediction using individual perceptual image aesthetics. J. Winter Sch. Comput. Graph. **24**(02), 53–62 (2016)
4. Azam, S., Gavrilova, M.: Soft biometric: give me your favorite images and I will tell your gender. In: Proceedings of 15th International Conference on Cognitive informatics and Cognitive computing (ICCICC), pp. 535–541, August 2016
5. Costa, Y.M., Oliveira, L.S., Koerich, A.L., Gouyon, F., Martins, J.G.: Music genre classification using LBP textural features. Sig. Process. **92**(11), 2723–2737 (2012)
6. Dalal, N., Triggs, B.: Histograms of oriented gradients for human detection. In: Proceedings of IEEE Computer Society Conference on Computer Vision and Pattern Recognition, vol. 01, pp. 886–893 (2005)
7. Datta, R., Joshi, D., Li, J., Wang, J.Z.: Studying aesthetics in photographic images using a computational approach. In: Leonardis, A., Bischof, H., Pinz, A. (eds.) ECCV 2006. LNCS, vol. 3953, pp. 288–301. Springer, Heidelberg (2006). doi:10.1007/11744078_23
8. Felzenszwalb, P., McAllester, D., Ramanan, D.: A discriminatively trained, multiscale, deformable part model. In: Proceedings of IEEE Conference on Computer Vision and Pattern Recognition, pp. 1–8, June 2008
9. Flickr (2004). https://www.flickr.com/. Accessed 19 Jan 2016
10. Gavrilova, M., Monwar, M.: Multimodal Biometrics and Intelligent Image Processing for Security Systems. IGI Global, Hershey (2013)

11. Gavrilova, M.L., Ahmed, F., Azam, S., Paul, P.P., Rahman, W., Sultana, M., Zohra, F.T.: Emerging trends in security system design using the concept of social behavioural biometrics. In: Alsmadi, I.M., Karabatis, G., AlEroud, A. (eds.) Information Fusion for Cyber-Security Analytics. SCI, vol. 691, pp. 229–251. Springer, Cham (2017). doi:10.1007/978-3-319-44257-0_10
12. Kambhatla, N., Leen, T.K.: Dimension reduction by local principal component analysis. Neural Comput. **9**(7), 1493–1516 (1997)
13. Lovato, P., Perina, A., Sebe, N., Zandonà, O., Montagnini, A., Bicego, M., Cristani, M.: Tell me what you like and I'll tell you what you are: discriminating visual preferences on flickr data. In: Lee, K.M., Matsushita, Y., Rehg, J.M., Hu, Z. (eds.) ACCV 2012. LNCS, vol. 7724, pp. 45–56. Springer, Heidelberg (2013). doi:10.1007/978-3-642-37331-2_4
14. Lovato, P., Bicego, M., Segalin, C., Perina, A., Sebe, N., Cristani, M.: Faved! biometrics: tell me which image you like and I'll tell you who you are. IEEE Trans. Inf. Forensics Secur. **9**(3), 364–374 (2014)
15. Monwar, M.M., Gavrilova, M., Wang, Y.: A novel fuzzy multimodal information fusion technology for human biometric traits identification. In: Proceedings of IEEE International Conference on Cognitive Informatics and Cognitive Computing, pp. 112–119, August 2011
16. Perina, A., Jojic, N.: Image analysis by counting on a grid. In: Proceedings of IEEE Conference on Computer Vision and Pattern Recognition, pp. 1985–1992, June 2011
17. Segalin, C., Perina, A., Cristani, M.: Biometrics on visual preferences: a pump and distill regression approach. In: Proceedings of 2014 IEEE International Conference on Image Processing, pp. 4982–4986 (2014)
18. Segalin, C., Perina, A., Cristani, M.: Personal aesthetics for soft biometrics: a generative multi-resolution approach. In: Proceedings of 16th International Conference on Multimodal Interaction, pp. 180–187, November 2015
19. Tan, H., Yang, B., Ma, Z.: Face recognition based on the fusion of global and local HOG features of face images. IET Comput. Vis. **08**(03), 224–234 (2014)
20. Terasawa, K., Tanaka, Y.: Slit style HOG feature for document image word spotting. In: Proceedings of 10th International Conference on Document Analysis and Recognition (ICDAR), pp. 116–120, July 2009
21. Tibshirani, R.: Regression shrinkage and selection via the lasso. J. Roy. Stat. Soc. Ser. B (Methodol.) **58**, 267–288 (1996)
22. Viola, P., Jones, M.: Rapid object detection using a boosted cascade of simple features. In: 2001 IEEE Computer Society Conference on Computer Vision and Pattern Recognition (CVPR), vol. 1, p. I-511 (2001)
23. Wu, J., Rehg, J.M.: CENTRIST: a visual descriptor for scene categorization. IEEE Trans. Pattern Anal. Mach. Intell. **33**(8), 1489–1501 (2011)
24. Yampolskiy, R.V., Gavrilova, M.: Artimetrics: biometrics for artificial entities. IEEE Robot. Autom. Mag. **19**(4), 48–58 (2012)
25. Yamauchi, Y., Matsushima, C., Yamashita, T., Fujiyoshi, H.: Relational HOG feature with wild-card for object detection. In: Proceedings of IEEE International Conference on Computer Vision Workshops (ICCV Workshops), pp. 1785–1792, November 2011

A Global Search Approach for Inducing Oblique Decision Trees Using Differential Evolution

Rafael Rivera-Lopez[1] and Juana Canul-Reich[2(✉)]

[1] Departamento de Sistemas y Computación, Instituto Tecnológico de Veracruz, Veracruz, Mexico
rrivera@itver.edu.mx

[2] División Académica de Informática y Sistemas, Universidad Juárez Autónoma de Tabasco, Cunduacán, Mexico
juana.canul@ujat.mx

Abstract. This paper describes the application of a Differential Evolution based approach for inducing oblique decision trees in a global search strategy. By using both the number of attributes and the number of class labels in a dataset, this approach determines the size of the real-valued vector utilized for encoding the set of hyperplanes used as test conditions in the internal nodes of an oblique decision tree. Also a scheme of three steps to map the linear representation of candidate solutions into feasible oblique decision trees is described. Experimental results obtained show that this approach induces more accurate classifiers than those produced by other proposed induction methods.

Keywords: Machine learning · Classification · Evolutionary algorithms

1 Introduction

Evolutionary algorithms (EAs) are population-based search methods that have been successfully applied for providing near-optimal solutions for many computationally complex problems in almost all areas of science and technology. The effectiveness of EAs is due to two factors: (1) they combine a clever exploration of the search space to identify promising areas, and (2) they perform an efficient exploitation of these areas aiming to improve the known solution or solutions. EAs are inspired by evolutionary theories that synthesize the Darwinian evolution through natural selection with the Mendelian genetic inheritance. In particular, Differential Evolution (DE) algorithm is an EA designed for solving optimization problems with variables in continuous domains that, instead of implementing traditional crossover and mutation operators, it applies a linear combination of several randomly selected candidate solutions to produce a new solution [28]. DE has been applied for solving optimization problems arising in several domains of science and engineering including economics, medicine, biotechnology, manufacturing and production, big data and data mining, etc., [25]. In data mining, DE has been utilized for constructing models of classification [19], clustering [7], and rule generation [8] with the aim of identifying

M. Mouhoub and P. Langlais (Eds.): Canadian AI 2017, LNAI 10233, pp. 27–38, 2017.
DOI: 10.1007/978-3-319-57351-9_3

hidden relationships among known instances. DE has been used in conjunction with neural networks [19], support vector machines [20], bayesian classifiers [13], instance based classifiers [12] and decision trees [30] for the induction of classifiers.

In this paper, a differential evolution-based approach named DE-ODT for inducing oblique decision trees in a global search strategy is described. The representation scheme of candidate solutions used by DE-ODT allows to apply DE operators without any modification, and the procedure for mapping a real-valued chromosome into a feasible decision tree ensures to carry out an efficient search in the solution space. DE-ODT is compared with three approaches for inducing oblique decision trees: the Oblique Classifier 1 (OC1) [24], the Perceptron Decision Tree (PDT) method [23], and the EFTI algorithm [32], and with the J48 method [34]. Experimental results obtained in this work show that DE-ODT induces more accurate classifiers than those found by the other methods. In order to describe the implementation of DE-ODT method, this paper is organized as follows: Sect. 2 describes the elements of differential evolution algorithm. The use of evolutionary algorithms for inducing oblique decision trees is presented in Sect. 3, and in Sect. 4 details of DE-ODT method with emphasis in both the determination of the size of candidate solutions and the induction of feasible oblique decision trees are given. Section 5 describes experimental results, and finally, Sect. 6 gives conclusions and future work.

2 Differential Evolution Algorithm

DE is a population-based metaheuristic that evolves a set of candidate solutions by applying evolutionary operators in order to find near-optimal solutions to optimization problems. Each candidate solution is encoded using a real-valued vector $\mathbf{x}_i = (x_{i,1}, x_{i,2}, \cdots, x_{i,m})^T$ of m variables.

In this paper, the standard DE algorithm [28], named DE/rand/1/bin in accordance to the nomenclature adopted for referencing DE variants, is used as a procedure for oblique decision tree induction that implements a global search strategy. DE/rand/1/bin uses the following evolutionary operators:

1. **Mutation:** Three randomly selected candidate solutions ($\mathbf{x}_a$, $\mathbf{x}_b$ and $\mathbf{x}_c$) are linearly combined, using Eq. (1), to yield a mutated solution $\mathbf{x}_{mut}$.
$$\mathbf{x}_{mut} = \mathbf{x}_a + F(\mathbf{x}_b - \mathbf{x}_c) \tag{1}$$
where F is a scale factor for controlling the differential variation.
2. **Crossover:** The mutated solution is utilized to perturb another candidate solution $\mathbf{x}_{cur}$ using the binomial crossover operator defined as follows:
$$x_{new,j} = \begin{cases} x_{mut,j} & \text{if } r \leq Cr \vee j = k \\ x_{cur,j} & \text{otherwise} \end{cases} ; j \in \{1, \ldots, m\} \tag{2}$$
where $x_{new,j}$, $x_{mut,j}$ and $x_{cur,j}$ are the values in the j-th position of $\mathbf{x}_{new}$, $\mathbf{x}_{mut}$ and $\mathbf{x}_{cur}$, respectively, $r \in [0, 1)$ and $k \in \{1, \ldots, m\}$ are uniformly distributed random numbers, and Cr is the crossover rate.

3. **Selection:** $\mathbf{x}_{new}$ is selected as member of the new population if it has a better fitness value than that of $\mathbf{x}_{cur}$.

DE/rand/1/bin, described in Algorithm 1, starts with a population of randomly generated candidate solutions whose values are uniformly distributed in the range $[x_{min}, x_{max}]$ as follows:

$$x_{i,j} = x_{min} + r\,(x_{max} - x_{min})\,; i \in \{1,\ldots,NP\} \wedge j \in \{1,\ldots,m\} \qquad (3)$$

where NP is the population size. New populations of candidate solutions are iteratively created until a stop condition is reached and then the best solution of the last population is returned. It can be observed that DE requires few control parameters (Cr, F, and NP) in comparison to other EAs.

Algorithm 1. Standard DE algorithm introduced in [28].

$k \leftarrow 0$
$\mathbf{X}_k \leftarrow \emptyset$
for i in $\{1,\ldots,NP\}$ **do**
  $\mathbf{x}_i \leftarrow$ Randomly generated candidate solution using (3)
  $\mathbf{X}_k \leftarrow \mathbf{X}_k \cup \{\mathbf{x}_i\}$
end for
while stop condition is not reached **do**
  $k \leftarrow k+1$
  $\mathbf{X}_k \leftarrow \emptyset$
  for cur in $\{1,\ldots,NP\}$ **do**
    $\{\mathbf{x}_a, \mathbf{x}_b, \mathbf{x}_c\} \leftarrow$ Randomly selected candidate solutions of $\mathbf{X}_{k-1}$
    $\mathbf{x}_{mut} \leftarrow$ Mutated candidate solution using (1)
    $\mathbf{x}_{new} \leftarrow$ Perturbed candidate solution of $\mathbf{x}_{cur}$ using (2)
    $\mathbf{x}_{sel} \leftarrow \begin{cases} \mathbf{x}_{new} & \text{if } fitness(\mathbf{x}_{new}) \text{ is better than } fitness(\mathbf{x}_{cur}) \\ \mathbf{x}_{cur} & \text{otherwise} \end{cases}$
    $\mathbf{X}_k \leftarrow \mathbf{X}_k \cup \{\mathbf{x}_{sel}\}$
  end for
end while
return The best candidate solution in $\mathbf{X}_k$

3 EAs for Inducing Oblique Decision Trees

A decision tree (DT) is a hierarchical structure composed of a set of nodes containing both test conditions (internal nodes) and class labels (leaf nodes) that are joined by arcs representing the possible result values of each test condition. A DT is a classification model induced through a set of training instances which is used for predicting the class membership of new unclassified instances. Each training instance is encoded as a vector $\mathbf{v} = (v_1, v_2, \ldots, v_d, c)^T$ of d variables (attributes or features) and a label c that determines the class membership of the instance. The simplicity and the high level of interpretability of a DT along with its predictive power has made it one of the most widely used classifiers.

The number of attributes used in the test conditions of a DT determines its type (univariate or multivariate). Since efficient induction methods such as CART [5] and C4.5 [27] generate univariate DTs (also called axis-parallel DTs) it is the most known type of DTs. On the other hand, oblique DTs and nonlinear DTs are multivariate DTs in which a linear combination and a nonlinear composition of attributes in test conditions is utilized, respectively. In particular, oblique DTs use a set of not axis-parallel hyperplanes for splitting the instance space in order to predict the class membership of unclassified instances. A hyperplane is defined as follows:

$$\sum_{i=1}^{d} x_i v_i + x_{d+1} > 0 \tag{4}$$

where v_i is the value of attribute i, x_i is a real-valued coefficient used in the hyperplane and x_{d+1} represents the independent term. Oblique DTs are generally smaller and more accurate than univariate DTs but they are generally more difficult to interpret [6].

EAs have been previously applied for DT induction (DTI) and there exist several surveys that describe their implementation [2,11]. Some approaches implement a recursive partitioning strategy in which an EA is used for finding a near-optimal test condition for each tree internal node [6], however, the approach most commonly used is to perform a global search in the solution space with the aim of finding near-optimal DTs [3,17,18,23,31–33]. A genetic algorithm (GA) is an EA that generally employs a linear representation of candidate solutions and its implementation for DTI is associated to the problem of mapping an oblique DT from a linear structure [17]. However, with the application of special genetic operators, GA can use a tree representation for DTI [3,18]. An special GA that evolves a unique candidate solution is used in EFTI method [32] for inducing a complete oblique DT. Furthermore, DE has been utilized for finding the parameter settings of a DTI method [30] and for constructing both univariate DTs [31] and oblique DTs [23]. Finally, since genetic programming (GP) represents its candidate solutions as trees, standard GP [22] and GP variants such as strongly-typed GP [4] and grammar-based GP [1] have been applied for oblique DTI.

4 DE-ODT Method for Inducing Oblique DTs

DE-ODT is proposed in this paper as a method for oblique DTI in a global search strategy that evolves a population of candidate solutions encoded as fixed-length real-valued vectors. A similar approach known as PDT method is described in [23] but, although DE-ODT and PDT share the same objective and both implement a global search strategy for DTI with DE, substantial differences in the representation scheme used in DE-ODT allows for induction of more accurate and compact oblique DTs than PDT and other similar approaches. In the next paragraphs the main elements of DE-ODT method are described.

4.1 Global Search Strategy to Generate Near-Optimal Oblique DTs

The great majority of algorithms for DTI apply a recursive partitioning strategy that implements some splitting criterion in order to separate the training instances. Several studies point out that this strategy has three fundamental problems: overfitting [14], selection bias towards multi-valued attributes [15] and instability to small changes in the training set [29]. On the other hand, algorithms that implement a global search strategy can ensure a more efficient exploration of the solution space although it is known that building optimal DTs is NP-Hard [16].

DE-ODT implements a global search strategy with the aim of constructing more accurate oblique DTs, and also for overcoming the inherent problems of the recursive partitioning strategy. Since oblique DTs use hyperplanes with real-valued coefficients as test conditions, the search for near-optimal oblique DTs can be considered a continuous optimization problem, and DE has proven to be a very competitive approach for solving this type of problems. Although other metaheuristic-based approaches have been previously used for classifications tasks, DE-ODT is introduced in this work as a simple and straightforward method in which DE is applied for finding near-optimal solutions, and where each real-valued chromosome encodes only a feasible oblique DT.

4.2 Linear Representation of Oblique DTs

Two schemes for encoding candidate solutions in EAs can be used: tree or linear representation. When tree representation is adopted, special crossover and mutation operators must be implemented in order to ensure the construction of only feasible candidate solutions [3,18]. An advantage of this representation is that EAs can evolve DTs with different sizes but it is known that crossover has a destructive effect on the offsprings [18]. On the other hand, if a linear representation is utilized then a scheme for mapping the sequence of values into a DT must be applied [17]. The main advantage of linear representation is that it is applied for encoding candidate solutions in several EAs such as GA, DE and evolutionary strategies and they can be implemented for DTI without any modification. Nevertheless, since these EAs use a fixed-length representation, it is necessary to define a priori this length and this can limit the performance of the induced DTs.

In DE-ODT method each candidate solution encodes only the internal nodes of a complete binary oblique DT stored in breadth-first order in a fixed-length real-valued vector (Fig. 1). This vector encodes the set of hyperplanes used as test conditions of the oblique DT. Vector size is determined using both the number of attributes and the number of class labels.

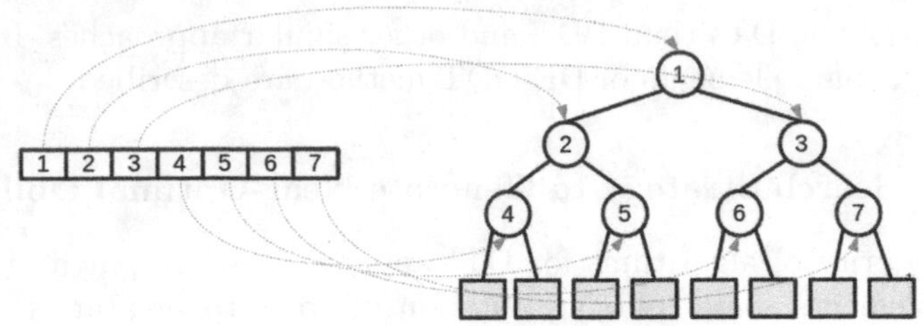

Fig. 1. Linear encoding scheme for the internal nodes of a complete binary tree.

4.3 Estimated Number of Tree Internal Nodes

Since each internal node of an oblique DT has a hyperplane as test condition, the size of real-valued vector used for encoding each candidate solution is fixed as $n_e(d+1)$, where n_e is the estimated number of internal nodes of a complete binary DT and d is the number of attributes of the training set. Considering that: (1) an oblique DTs is more compact than an univariate DTs when they are induced with the same training set, and (2) the DT size is related to the structure of the training set, DE-ODT determines the value of n_e using both the number of attributes (d) and the number of class labels (k) in the training set. If, for one complete binary DT, h is the depth, n_i is the number of internal nodes and n_l is the number of leaf nodes, respectively, then d and k can be used as lower bounds for n_i and n_l ($n_i = 2^{h-1} - 1 \geq d$ and $n_l = 2^{h-1} \geq k$), respectively. Using these relations, two estimated depths ($h_i = \lceil \log_2(d+1) + 1 \rceil$ and $h_l = \lceil \log_2(k) + 1 \rceil$) are calculated and n_e is obtained as follows:

$$n_e = 2^{\max(h_i, h_l)-1} - 1 \tag{5}$$

4.4 Induction of Feasible Oblique DTs

Since the training set must be utilized for inducing one DT, DE-ODT uses it for mapping each candidate solution into a feasible oblique DT, including its leaf nodes. DE applies the training accuracy of a DT as fitness value within the evolutionary process. The induction of a feasible oblique DT (Fig. 2) in DE-ODT has three steps:

1. **Construction:** First, an empty complete binary DT with n_e nodes (7 nodes in example of Fig. 2) is created. Then, the coefficient values of a hyperplane are assigned to each node in this DT by applying the next criterion: Values on positions $\{1, \ldots, d+1\}$ of this vector are used in the hyperplane of the first node, values on positions $\{d+2, \ldots, 2d+2\}$ are used in the hyperplane of the second node, and so on.
2. **Assignment:** One instance set is assigned to a node (the complete training set for the root node of the tree) and it is labeled as an internal node. For evaluating each instance in this set using the hyperplane associated to the

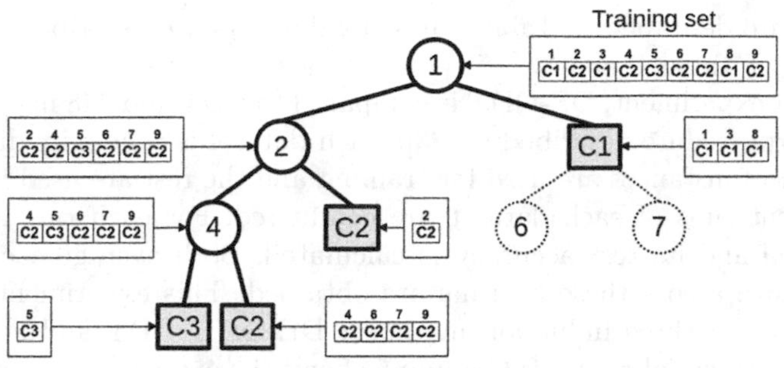

Fig. 2. Construction and assignment of a feasible oblique DT.

internal node, two instance subsets are created and they are assigned to the successor nodes of this node. This assignment is repeated for each node of the DT. If the internal node is located at the end of a branch of the DT (node 4 in Fig. 2, for example), then two leaf nodes are created and are designated children of the ending node of the branch. The subsets created are assigned to these leaf nodes. On the other hand, if all instances in the set assigned to the internal node have the same class label, it is labeled as a leaf node (nodes 3 and 5 in Fig. 2) and its successor nodes are removed, if they exist (nodes 6 and 7 in Fig. 2).

3. **Pruning:** Finally, when the assignment of training instances is completed, a pruning procedure is applied for removing tree branches in order to improve the accuracy of the DT induced.

These steps allow to induce feasible oblique DTs with different number of nodes, although the candidate solutions are encoded using fixed-length real-valued vectors.

5 Experiments

In order to evaluate the performance of DE-ODT method and for comparison to other approaches, two experiments were conducted using several datasets with numerical attributes chosen from UCI repository [21]. DE-ODT is implemented in Java language using the JMetal library [10]. The parameters used in the

Table 1. Parameters used in experiments with DE-ODT.

Parameter	Value	Parameter	Value
Scale factor	1	Num. of generations	50
Crossover rate	0.9	Population size	$20\sqrt{d}$ (proposed in [6])
Fitness function	DT accuracy	Pruning method	Reduced error pruning [26]

experiments are described in Table 1 and the datasets are described in the first four columns of Tables 2 and 3.

In the first experiment, DE-ODT is compared to PDT and J48 methods using the sampling procedure described in [23]: Each dataset is randomly divided into two sets, 85% of instances are used for training and the rest are used for testing. 30 independent runs of each dataset are conducted. For each run, an oblique DT is induced and its test accuracy is calculated. Both average accuracy and average DT size across these 30 runs are obtained. This experimental scheme is replicated using three induction methods: DE-ODT, PDT and J48. Table 2 shows the experimental results[1]: Column 5 shows the average accuracy reported by [23]. Columns 6 and 7 show the average accuracy and the average DT size produced by DE-ODT method and the results obtained by J48 are shown in columns 8 and 9. In this table can be observed that accuracies obtained by DE-ODT method are better than: (1) the accuracies produced by J48 for all datasets, and (2) the accuracies reported by PDT for 7 of 8 datasets. DE-ODT produces more compact oblique-DTs than those produced for J48. In the case of DT size for PDT method, these results were not reported in [23]. Figure 3(a) shows a comparative plot of the average accuracies obtained.

Table 2. Results obtained for PDT, DE-ODT and J48.

(1)	(2)	(3)	(4)	(5)	(6)	(7)	(8)	(9)
				PDT	DE-ODT		J48	
Dataset	Inst.	Attr.	Classes	Acc.	Acc.	Size	Acc.	Size
Breast tissue	106	9	6	39.92	**64.44**	**5.97**	33.70	7.6
Vertebral column	310	6	2	84.11	**93.04**	**2.90**	79.29	5.0
Ecoli	336	7	8	76.73	**87.33**	**5.83**	80.47	9.1
Glass	214	9	7	58.08	**71.04**	**7.03**	64.42	11.5
Hill valley	1212	100	2	**99.45**	81.35	3.83	50.49	**1.0**
Iris	150	4	3	94.35	**99.97**	**3.37**	93.77	3.5
Libras movement	360	90	15	31.85	**56.34**	**26.1**	55.80	26.2
Sonar	208	60	2	77.29	**94.73**	**4.03**	71.13	5.4

In the second experiment, DE-ODT is compared to OC1 and EFTI methods using 5 independents runs of 10-fold stratified cross-validation. EFTI is a novel approach that reports better results with several datasets than other EA-based algorithms. Results are shown in Table 3: Columns 5–8 show the average accuracy and the average DT size reported in [32] for both OC1 and EFTI methods. Columns 9 and 10 show the average accuracy and the average DT size produced by DE-ODT method. In Table 3 can be observed that the accuracies obtained for DE-ODT are better than those obtained by both EFTI and OC1 methods

[1] Highest values for each dataset are in bold.

in 10 of 13 datasets, although the DT size are slightly larger than the DT size reported for EFTI method. Figure 3(b) shows a comparative plot of the average accuracies obtained in this experiment.

Table 3. Results obtained by OC1, EFTI and DE-ODT.

(1)	(2)	(3)	(4)	(5)	(6)	(7)	(8)	(9)	(10)
				OC1		EFTI		DE-ODT	
Dataset	Inst.	Attr.	Classes	Acc.	Size	Acc.	Size	Acc.	Size
Breast-w	683	9	2	95.53	3.68	96.59	**2.02**	**99.56**	3.48
Diabetes	768	8	2	73.03	6.54	74.94	**2.35**	**81.25**	3.70
Glass	214	9	7	62.04	13.12	70.82	7.31	**75.05**	**7.22**
Iris	150	4	3	95.60	3.54	94.13	**3.00**	**100.00**	3.20
Vehicle	846	18	4	68.16	33.54	**68.75**	**5.44**	55.51	6.70
Vowel	990	10	11	**74.55**	51.68	54.90	17.86	55.11	**9.96**
Heart-statlog	270	13	2	76.30	4.70	81.28	**2.12**	**83.70**	3.38
Australian	690	14	2	83.63	6.10	**84.51**	**2.28**	77.10	4.08
Balance-scale	625	4	3	71.58	3.08	87.85	**2.40**	**92.70**	3.06
Ionosphere	351	34	2	88.26	6.18	86.39	**2.49**	**97.61**	6.26
Sonar	208	60	2	70.39	6.76	74.64	**2.38**	**96.54**	5.38
Liver-disorders	345	6	2	67.23	5.38	70.36	**2.33**	**81.97**	2.92
Page-blocks	5473	10	5	97.05	23.78	93.16	**2.04**	**97.17**	5.12

In order to evaluate the performance of DE-ODT a statistical test of the results obtained was realized. Friedman test is applied for detecting the existence of significant differences between the performance of two or more methods and the Nemenyi post-hoc test is utilized for checking these differences. Nemenyi test uses the average ranks of each classifier and checks for each pair of classifiers

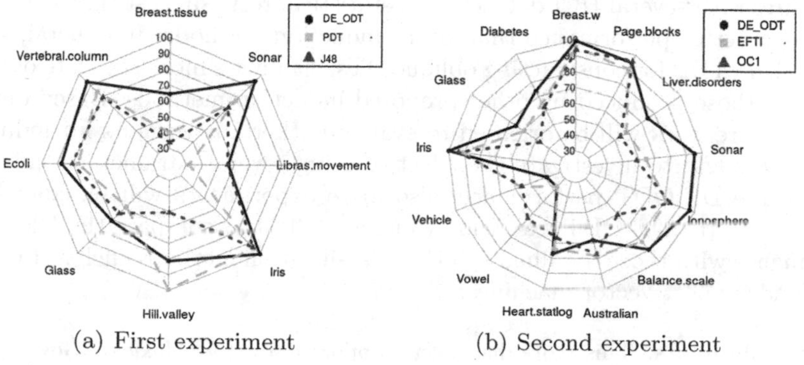

(a) First experiment (b) Second experiment

Fig. 3. Average accuracies obtained in experiments.

whether the difference between their ranks is greater than the critical difference $\left(CD = q_\alpha\sqrt{k(k+1)/(6N)}\right)$ defined in [9], where k is the number of methods, N is the number of datasets, and q_α is a critical value associated of the significance level α. For the first experiment, Friedman statistic for 3 methods using 8 datasets is 9.75 and the p-value obtained is 0.007635 for 2° of freedom (dof) of chi-square distribution. This p-value indicates the existence of statistical differences between these methods and then Nemenyi test post-hoc is conducted. Figure 4(a) shows the CDs obtained for Nemenyi test and it shown as well that DE-ODT has better performance than PDT and J48. For the second experiment, Friedman statistic for 3 methods using 13 datasets is 8.0, the p-value is 0.01832 with 2 dof and it also indicates statistical differences between these methods. Figure 4(b) shows the CDs obtained for Nemenyi test and in it can be observed that DE-ODT has better performance than EFTI and OC1 methods.

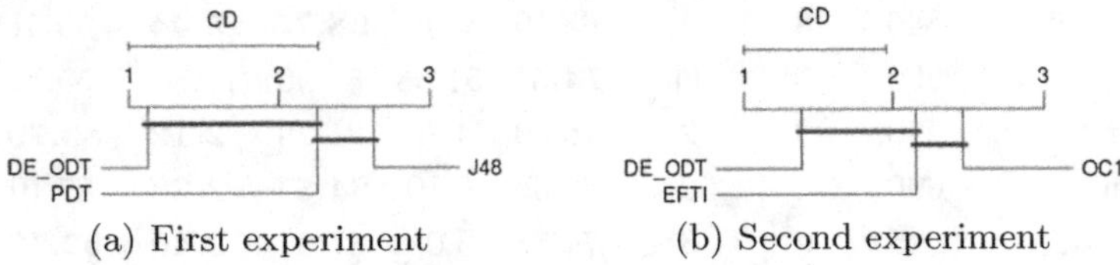

(a) First experiment (b) Second experiment

Fig. 4. Comparison of classifiers using Nemenyi post-hoc test.

6 Conclusions

In this paper, a DE-based method implementing a global search strategy for finding a near-optimal oblique DTs is introduced. This search strategy ensures a more efficient exploration of solution space in order to reach more compact and accurate DTs. DE-ODT uses a fixed-length linear representation of oblique DTs that permits to apply DE operators without any modification. By using the training set in the mapping scheme implemented in this work, the induction of feasible oblique DTs is guaranteed. DE-ODT was evaluated using two sampling procedures with several UCI datasets and statistical tests suggest that DE-ODT achieves a better performance than other induction methods. In general, since DE-ODT uses DE for constructing oblique DTs, it induces more accurate oblique DTs than those produced by other proposed induction methods. Based on our results, future work will be oriented to evaluate other DE variants for inducing oblique DTs and to investigate the effect of using several parameter configurations on the DE-ODT performance, also more experiments will be conducted for analyzing the DE-ODT execution time, as well as to compare the DE-ODT performance with those obtained by other classification methods such as random forest and support vector machines.

Acknowledgments. This work has been supported by the Mexican Government (CONACyT FOMIX-DICC project No. TAB-2014-C01-245876 and the PROMEP-SEP project No. DSA/103.5/15/6409).

References

1. Agapitos, A., O'Neill, M., Brabazon, A., Theodoridis, T.: Maximum margin decision surfaces for increased generalisation in evolutionary decision tree learning. In: Silva, S., Foster, J.A., Nicolau, M., Machado, P., Giacobini, M. (eds.) EuroGP 2011. LNCS, vol. 6621, pp. 61–72. Springer, Heidelberg (2011). doi:10.1007/978-3-642-20407-4_6
2. Barros, R.C., Basgalupp, M.P., Carvalho, A., Freitas, A.A.: A survey of evolutionary algorithms for decision-tree induction. IEEE Trans. Syst. Man Cybern.-Part C: Appl. Rev. **42**(3), 291–312 (2012). doi:10.1109/TSMCC.2011.2157494
3. Basgalupp, M.P., Barros, R.C., de Carvalho, A.C., Freitas, A.A.: Evolving decision trees with beam search-based initialization and lexicographic multi-objective evaluation. Inf. Sci. **258**, 160–181 (2014). doi:10.1016/j.ins.2013.07.025
4. Bot, M.C.J., Langdon, W.B.: Improving induction of linear classification trees with genetic programming. In: Whitley, L.D., Goldberg, D.E., Cantú-Paz, E., Spector, L., Parmee, I.C., Beyer, H.G. (eds.) GECCO-2000, pp. 403–410. Morgan Kaufmann, Burlington (2000)
5. Breiman, L., Friedman, J., Olshen, R., Stone, C.: Classification and Regression Trees. Taylor & Francis, Abingdon (1984)
6. Cantú-Paz, E., Kamath, C.: Inducing oblique decision trees with evolutionary algorithms. IEEE Trans. Evol. Comput. **7**(1), 54–68 (2003). doi:10.1109/TEVC.2002.806857
7. Das, S., Abraham, A., Konar, A.: Automatic clustering using an improved differential evolution algorithm. IEEE Trans. Syst. Man Cybern.-Part A: Syst. Hum. **38**(1), 218–237 (2008). doi:10.1109/tsmca.2007.909595
8. De Falco, I.: Differential evolution for automatic rule extraction from medical databases. Appl. Soft Comput. **13**(2), 1265–1283 (2013). doi:10.1016/j.asoc.2012.10.022
9. Demšar, J.: Statistical comparisons of classifiers over multiple data sets. J. Mach. Learn. Res. **7**(Dec), 1–30 (2006)
10. Durillo, J.J., Nebro, A.J.: jMetal: a Java framework for multiobjective optimization. Adv. Eng. Softw. **42**(10), 760–771 (2011). doi:10.1016/j.advengsoft.2011.05.014
11. Espejo, P.G., Ventura, S., Herrera, F.: A survey on the application of genetic programming to classification. IEEE Trans. Syst. Man Cybern.-Part C: Appl. Rev. **40**(2), 121–144 (2010). doi:10.1109/TSMCC.2009.2033566
12. García, S., Derrac, J., Triguero, I., Carmona, C.J., Herrera, F.: Evolutionary-based selection of generalized instances for imbalanced classification. Knowl.-Based Syst. **25**(1), 3–12 (2012). doi:10.1016/j.knosys.2011.01.012
13. Geetha, K., Baboo, S.S.: An empirical model for thyroid disease classification using evolutionary multivariate Bayesian prediction method. Glob. J. Comput. Sci. Technol. **16**(1), 1–9 (2016)
14. Hawkins, D.M.: The problem of overfitting. ChemInform **35**(19) (2004). doi:10.1002/chin.200419274
15. Hothorn, T., Hornik, K., Zeileis, A.: Unbiased recursive partitioning: a conditional inference framework. J. Comput. Graph. Stat. **15**(3), 651–674 (2006). doi:10.1198/106186006x133933
16. Hyafil, L., Rivest, R.L.: Constructing optimal binary decision trees is NP-complete. Inf. Process. Lett. **5**(1), 15–17 (1976). doi:10.1016/0020-0190(76)90095-8
17. Kennedy, H.C., Chinniah, C., Bradbeer, P., Morss, L.: The contruction and evaluation of decision trees: a comparison of evolutionary and concept learning methods. In: Corne, D., Shapiro, J.L. (eds.) AISB EC 1997. LNCS, vol. 1305, pp. 147–161. Springer, Heidelberg (1997). doi:10.1007/BFb0027172

18. Krętowski, M., Grześ, M.: Evolutionary learning of linear trees with embedded feature selection. In: Rutkowski, L., Tadeusiewicz, R., Zadeh, L.A., Żurada, J.M. (eds.) ICAISC 2006. LNCS (LNAI), vol. 4029, pp. 400–409. Springer, Heidelberg (2006). doi:10.1007/11785231_43
19. Leema, N., Nehemiah, H.K., Kannan, A.: Neural network classifier optimization using differential evolution with global information and back propagation algorithm for clinical datasets. Appl. Soft Comput. **49**, 834–844 (2016). doi:10.1016/j.asoc.2016.08.001
20. Li, J., Ding, L., Li, B.: Differential evolution-based parameters optimisation and feature selection for support vector machine. Int. J. Comput. Sci. Eng. **13**(4), 355–363 (2016)
21. Lichman, M.: UCI Machine Learning Repository (2013). University of California, Irvine. http://archive.ics.uci.edu/ml
22. Liu, K.H., Xu, C.G.: A genetic programming-based approach to the classification of multiclass microarray datasets. Bioinformatics **25**(3), 331–337 (2009). doi:10.1093/bioinformatics/btn644
23. Lopes, R.A., Freitas, A.R.R., Silva, R.C.P., Guimarães, F.G.: Differential evolution and perceptron decision trees for classification tasks. In: Yin, H., Costa, J.A.F., Barreto, G. (eds.) IDEAL 2012. LNCS, vol. 7435, pp. 550–557. Springer, Heidelberg (2012). doi:10.1007/978-3-642-32639-4_67
24. Murthy, S.K., Kasif, S., Salzberg, S., Beigel, R.: OC1: a randomized algorithm for building oblique decision trees. In: Proceedings of AAAI 1993, vol. 93, pp. 322–327 (1993)
25. Plagianakos, V.P., Tasoulis, D.K., Vrahatis, M.N.: A review of major application areas of differential evolution. In: Chakraborty, U.K. (ed.) Advances in Differential Evolution. SCI, vol. 143, pp. 197–238. Springer, Heidelberg (2008). doi:10.1007/978-3-540-68830-38
26. Quinlan, J.R.: Simplifying decision trees. Int. J. Hum.-Comput. Stud. **27**(3), 221–234 (1987). doi:10.1006/ijhc.1987.0321
27. Quinlan, J.R.: C4.5: Programs for Machine Learning. Morgan Kaufmann, Burlington (1993)
28. Storn, R., Price, K.: Differential evolution-a simple and efficient heuristic for global optimization over continuous spaces. J. Glob. Optim. **11**(4), 341–359 (1997). doi:10.1023/A:1008202821328
29. Strobl, C., Malley, J., Tutz, G.: An introduction to recursive partitioning: rationale, application, and characteristics of classification and regression trees, bagging, and random forests. Psychol. Methods **14**(4), 323–348 (2009). doi:10.1037/a0016973
30. Tušar, T.: Optimizing accuracy and size of decision trees. In: ERK-2007, pp. 81–84 (2007)
31. Veenhuis, C.B.: Tree based differential evolution. In: Vanneschi, L., Gustafson, S., Moraglio, A., Falco, I., Ebner, M. (eds.) EuroGP 2009. LNCS, vol. 5481, pp. 208–219. Springer, Heidelberg (2009). doi:10.1007/978-3-642-01181-8_18
32. Vukobratović, B., Struharik, R.: Evolving full oblique decision trees. In: CINTI 2015, pp. 95–100. IEEE (2015). doi:10.1109/CINTI.2015.7382901
33. Wang, P., Tang, K., Weise, T., Tsang, E.P.K., Yao, X.: Multiobjective genetic programming for maximizing ROC performance. Neurocomputing **125**, 102–118 (2014). doi:10.1016/j.neucom.2012.06.054
34. Witten, I., Frank, E.: Data Mining: Practical Machine Learning Tools and Techniques. Morgan Kaufmann, Burlington (2005)

Improving Active Learning for One-Class Classification Using Dimensionality Reduction

Mohsen Ghazel[1(✉)] and Nathalie Japkowicz[1,2]

[1] School of Electrical Engineering and Computer Science, University of Ottawa, Ottawa, ON, Canada
mghaz007@uottawa.ca

[2] Department of Computer Science, American University, Washington, DC, USA
japkowic@american.edu

Abstract. This work aims to improve the performance of active learning techniques for one-class classification (OCC) via dimensionality reduction (DR) and pre-filtering of the unlabelled input data. In practice, the input data of OCC problems is high-dimensional and often contains significant redundancy of negative examples. Thus, DR is typically an important pre-processing step to address the high-dimensionality challenge. However, the redundancy has not been previously addressed. In this work, we propose a framework to exploit the detected DR basis functions of the instance space in order to filter-out most of the redundant data. Instances are removed or maintained using an adaptive thresholding operator depending on their distance to the identified DR basis functions. This reduction in the dimensionality, redundancy and size of the instance space results in significant reduction of the computational complexity of active learning for OCC process. For the preserved instances, their distance to the identified DR basis functions is also used in order to select more efficiently the initial training batch as well as additional instances at each iteration of the active training algorithm. This was done by ensuring that the labelled data always contains nearly uniform representation along the different DR basis functions of the instance space. Experimental results show that applying the DR and pre-filtering steps results in better performance of the active learning for OCC.

Keywords: Active learning · One-class learning · Dimensionality reduction · PCA · ICA · Supervised learning · Anomaly detection

1 Introduction

Active learning aims to minimize the costs associated with human experts data labelling efforts while prioritizing the order in which instances are labelled in order to achieve well trained supervised classification models. In some binary classification applications, such as medical diagnosis and gamma-ray anomaly detection, we are often faced with extreme levels of class imbalance between the majority (negative) class and the minority (positive) class, in the sense that negative examples are abundant, or even redundant, while very few or in extreme

M. Mouhoub and P. Langlais (Eds.): Canadian AI 2017, LNAI 10233, pp. 39–44, 2017.
DOI: 10.1007/978-3-319-57351-9_4

cases no positive examples are available. In such extreme imbalance level, it was shown that the most effective way to deal with the problem is to first reduce the highly imbalanced binary classification task into a OCC problem, and then apply suitable active learning methods designed to deal with such extreme class imbalance [1,2]. Several general active learning strategies as well as those specifically designed for OCC have been proposed in the literature and nicely reviewed in [3]. Most of these approaches differ in one significant aspect, which is how instances are selected for labelling by a human expert.

In most OCC applications, the input data is high dimensional and often contains significant redundancy of negative examples. These two distinct features of the input data may be the key sources of the inherent computational complexity of active learning for OCC applications. Several works have explored applying DR techniques for addressing the high-dimensionality challenge [5–7]. These DR-based techniques attempt to reduce the dimensionality of the feature space but they do not address the redundancy in the negative examples data. As such, an applied active learning technique may needlessly end up selecting many similar or equally informative examples for labelling when selecting the best representative of these examples may be sufficient. In this work, we propose an additional pre-processing step after applying a DR operation in order to pre-filter available unlabelled data and reduce the redundancy in the negative examples data. This results in data thinning and reduction of the number of the instances available for labelling, hence resulting in reduction of the computational complexity.

This paper is organized as follows: Sect. 2 outlines the proposed approach while Sect. 3 provides the experimental setup and results. Finally, Sect. 4 contains concluding remarks and proposed future work.

2 The Proposed Approach

The proposed approach basically consists of applying a DR technique, such as PCA or ICA, in order to detect the significant basis vectors of the instance space. A data thinning process is then applied on the unlabelled instances in order to determine whether they should be preserved or removed, depending on their closeness to the significant basis vectors identified by the DR algorithm.

2.1 Dimensionality Reduction

Various DR methods have been proposed to reduce the dimensionality of measured data into a smaller set of components [4]. In this work we consider the widely used PCA and ICA DR techniques [4]. PCA is based on the second-order statistics and it is adequate if the data is Gaussian, linear, and stationary. In cases where when the data is not Gaussian, ICA, which exploits inherently non-Gaussian features of the data and minimizes higher-order statistics such as kurtosis, can be a more appropriate DR technique. For our data, we cannot make validated assumptions about the nature of the distribution of the feature vectors. Thus, we have implemented both PCA and ICA DR algorithms in order to assess and compare their performances.

2.2 Data Pre-filtering

Once the significant basis vectors have been identified by the applied DR method, instances are then maintained or removed depending on their closeness to these basis functions, as described next.

Data Projection: Suppose that we have n unlabelled input instances I_k with associated feature vectors $\mathbf{x}_k$, $k = 1, 2, \ldots, n$. Assume that the applied DR technique has reduced the dimensionality from n to m with $m \leq n$ and let us denote these DR basis functions by $\mathbf{p}_j$, $j = 1, 2, \ldots, m$. The closeness between a feature vector $\mathbf{x}_k$ and each of the $\mathbf{p}_j$ basis vectors is given by: $\gamma_{kj} = \frac{||\hat{\mathbf{x}}_{kj}||}{||\mathbf{x}_k||}$, for $k = 1, 2, \ldots, n$ and $j = 1, 2, \ldots, m$, where $\hat{\mathbf{x}}_{kj}$ is the orthogonal projection of $\mathbf{x}_k$ onto $\mathbf{p}_j$. We can then assign instance I_k with feature vector $\mathbf{x}_k$, to its closest DR basis function, depending on the values of its corresponding weights γ_{kj}, $j = 1, 2, \ldots, m$, as follows: $\mathbf{x}_k \mapsto \mathbf{p}_l$ if $\gamma_{kl} \geq \gamma_{kj}$ for $j \neq l$. Next, we outline how to pre-filter instances based on their weights.

Adaptive Thresholding: We have explored various ways of thinning the unlabelled instances by thresholding their associated weights, γ_{kl} and we have found that it is best to apply a staircase adaptive thresholding operator on the range $[0, 1]$, as follows: First, the interval $[0, 1]$ is uniformly partitioned into $N \geq 2$ equal sub-intervals with endpoints: $t_i = \frac{i}{N}$, for $i = 0, 1, \ldots, N$. The proposed adaptive threshold is defined by: $T(t) = \frac{f_T(t_{i-1}) + f_T(t_i)}{2}$ if $t_{i-1} \leq t < t_i$ and $i = 1, 2, \ldots, N$, where: $f_T(t) = \frac{1-e^{-\alpha t}}{1-e^{-\alpha}}$, for $0 \leq t \leq 1$, and $\alpha > 0$. The decision regarding the fate of instance I_k is then to keep it if $f_T(\gamma_{kl}) \geq T(\gamma_{kl})$ and remove otherwise.

The above adaptive thresholding strategy results in filtering-out many of the instances that are closely aligned with one of DR basis vector. This is desirable because typically we expect to have many such typical instances with similar feature vectors along each DR basis vector, so it is important to thin-out these instances and reduce the redundancy in the data. On the other, the above adaptive thresholding strategy is more conservative in dealing with instances that are further away from the DR basis vectors. Again, this is desirable because these instances are quite distinct from the identified DR basis functions and may be interpreted as data outliers. Thus, it is important to preserve them and confirm, through domain expert labelling, that these instances do belong to the majority (negative) class and include them into the training set in order to reduce the false positive rate of the classification model.

The above adaptive thresholding mechanism allows us to pre-filter the unlabelled input data and reduce its dimensionality and size by reducing any duplication and redundancy. Note that, this is done only once and any active learning scheme with associated selection criterion and classification model can then be applied on the remaining pre-filtered data.

3 Experimental Results

In this section, we describe the experimental setup including the input dataset, the experimental setup and results.

3.1 Dataset

The input dataset was obtained from the Radiation Protection Bureau of Health Canada. It consists of 19113 samples from a Sodium iodide detector in the city of Saanich, British Columbia, collected over a period of 7 months. The sampling period was of 15 min. Each sample consists of photon counts over 512 energy bins, but only the first 250 were used following advice from domain experts. The photon counts are non-negative integers. Of the 19113 instances, 95 are anomalies and 19018 are normal, which supports treating this as an OCC problem.

3.2 Experiment

For comparative purposes, we implemented the activate learning technique proposed in [3] and followed the same experimental setup described in that work. In particular, we considered the OCC-SVM as the classification model of choice. Also, in order to obtain a more reliable estimate of the classification performance and reduce the impact of the assignment of instances to the test set, initial training set, and unlabelled pool, we used a 10-fold cross-validation. This process was repeated at each iteration, without data pre-filtering and then with data pre-filtering using PCA and then ICA DR algorithms for comparison purposes.

We also made some modifications to the experimental setup outlined in [3] by exploiting the weight γ_{kl} associated with each remaining instance I_k. For the active learning technique proposed in [3], a randomly selected initial batch of instances were labelled and used for training the initial model. In our implementation, we selected the initial batch of instances to contain an almost equal number of instances associated with each of the DR basis functions. This was done by selecting a sufficient number of instances with highest weights γ_{kl} along each basis DR basis function. Similarly, the weight γ_{kl} of each remaining instance was also used within the selection criterion of the active learning process to ensure that the labelled data is always almost evenly balanced along the different identified DR basis functions. Furthermore, these weights are also used during the 10-fold cross validation to ensure that each group contains an almost equal number of representative instances along each of DR basis function of the instance space.

3.3 Results

Figure 1 illustrates the performance of the initial classification model, as estimated from the initial batch of instances, and the final classification model obtained at the end of the active learning process. For each case, the figure illustrates the results without applying the proposed pre-filtering step, as well as after applying the DR filtering step using PCA and ICA algorithms. The performance of the classification model is assessed in terms of the area under the ROC curve (AUROC) obtained by varying the threshold at which instances are determined to belong to one class or the other. Clearly, applying the pre-filtering step using either DR technique results, on average, in an increase in the AUROC performance measure of the classification model before and after applying the active learning process. It should also be noted that higher gains are achieved when applying the ICA instead of PCA DR algorithm. This may indicate that the instance data and its features do not fit a Gaussian distribution. As mentioned earlier, in such cases, the ICA is a more suitable option for DR than PCA on this particular dataset.

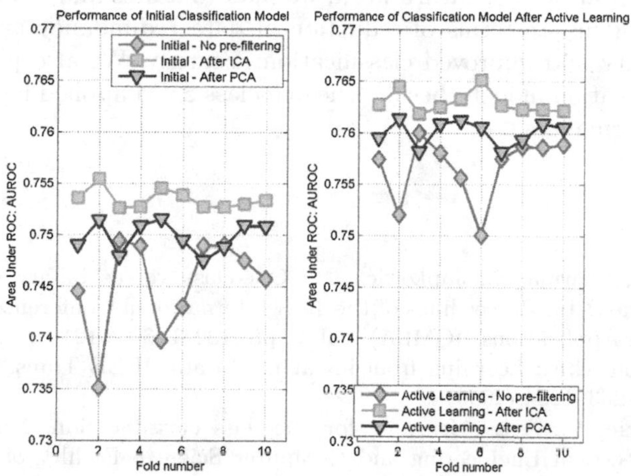

Fig. 1. Performance evaluation, as measured by AUROC of the classification model before and after applying active learning, with and without the DR pre-filtering step.

4 Conclusions

In this work, we implemented an PCA/ICA-based Dimensionality Reduction (DR) pre-processing step to reduce the dimensionality and filter-out the redundancy in the input unlabelled data and hence reduce the number of instances available for labelling. The aim was to accomplish this without removing the most informative instances, which are most valuable in training the classification model. The proposed approach allows us to select the initial batch of instances that is typically required by standard active learning techniques. The initial batch set is selected more systematically in a way that ensures nearly uniform representations from the different DR basis functions of the instance space. This ensures that the initial batch training set captures much of the variability in the instance space and hence the resulting original model should be more accurate.

The pre-filtering step was also shown to enhance the selection criterion used during the active learning process. Since each instance of the remaining data is known to be associated with one of the basis vectors of the instance space, we can easily keep track of the number of instances already labelled, which belong to each of the identified DR basis functions. We can then add a mechanism to the selection process that ensures that the labelled data is evenly balanced along the different identified DR basis functions. Experimental results show that applying the proposed pre-filtering step first results in improved overall performance of the implemented active learning for OCC process, as measured by the area under the ROC curve. The proposed data pre-filtering approach is classifier independent and reduces the amount of input data since many of the instances can be discarded before active learning is applied. This results in significant reduction of the computational complexity of the applied active learning process, regardless of it selection criterion. For future work, we plan to assess and more accurately quantify these gains, in terms of reduction of data redundancy and computational complexity and improved classification accuracy. We also plan to apply different classification models, besides the one-class SVM applied here, and compare their performances.

References

1. Bellinger, C., Sharma, S., Japkowicz, N.: One-class versus binary classification: which and when? In: Proceedings of the 11th International Conference on Machine Learning and Applications (ICMLA), vol. 2, pp. 102–106 (2012)
2. He, H., Garcia, E.A.: Learning from imbalanced data. IEEE Trans. Knowl. Data Eng. **21**(9), 1263–1284 (2009)
3. Barnabe-Lortie, V.: Active learning for one-class classiffication. Master's thesis, School of Electrical Engineering and Computer Science, Faculty of Engineering, University of Ottawa (2015)
4. Fodor, I.K.: A survey of dimension reduction techniques. Technical report UCRLID-148494. Lawrence Livermore National Laboratory, US Department of Energy (2002)
5. Villalba, S., Cunningham, P.: An evaluation of dimension reduction techniques for one-class classification. J. Artif. Intell. Rev. **27**(4), 273–294 (2007)
6. Bilgic, M.: Combining active learning and dynamic dimensionality reduction. In: SIAM International Conference on Data Mining, pp. 696–707 (2012)
7. Davy, M., Luz, S.: Dimensionality reduction for active learning with nearest neighbour classifier in text categorisation problems. In: International Conference on Machine Learning and Applications, pp. 1–8 (2007)

Local and Global Influence on Twitter

Shan Zong[1], Richard Khoury[2(✉)], and Rachid Benlamri[1]

[1] Department of Software Engineering, Lakehead University, Thunder Bay, Canada
{szong, rbenlamr}@lakeheadu.ca

[2] Department of Computer Science and Software Engineering, Université Laval, Québec City, Canada
richard.khoury@ift.ulaval.ca

Abstract. In this paper, we present a new metric to measure the influence a user has on an online social network. We define this influence as a 2D coordinate, comprising the user's local influence on their immediate followers, and their global influence on the entire network. We present the general idea underlying our metrics, and demonstrate their usefulness by applying them over 300 Twitter users. Our results show how the metrics can model and predict different classes of users in 2D space.

Keywords: Social network analysis · Twitter · Microblog · Influence scoring

1 Introduction

Social network analysis (SNA) is the process of investigating social activity through the use of networks made up of nodes (individuals) and edges (relationships or interactions) [1]. In this research, we will focus specifically on measuring a user's social influence; a concept we can define informally as the degree to which a user's activity will propagate through the network and be seen by other users. A user with a greater social influence is one whose opinions will reach and affect more other users, and thus is a target for political and marketing campaigns. A key contribution of our metric is its simplicity. While we have chosen to study Twitter, our measures have general definitions and can be ported to other social networks with minimal changes.

2 Background

Twitter is a social networking site that allows users to publish 140-character-long microblog messages, called tweets, to their followers, and to read the tweets of other users they are following (their followees). A user may mark a followee's tweet as a "favorite" or re-publish (retweet) it to their own followers. Limited information about each user and their recent tweets can be obtained through the Twitter API. We will focus here on research related to identifying and quantifying influential users.

The authors of [2] focused on identifying influential users in Canadian federal political party communities. They studied six different metrics: indegree (the number of

M. Mouhoub and P. Langlais (Eds.): Canadian AI 2017, LNAI 10233, pp. 45–50, 2017.
DOI: 10.1007/978-3-319-57351-9_5

incoming connections), eigenvector centrality (how connected a node's connections are), clustering coefficient (how embedded within the network a node is), knowledge (the number of tweets featuring context-specific terms), and interaction (the number of mentions of that node). They show that indegree and eigenvector centrality are both useful metrics of the influence of a node in the network. In [3], the authors proposed that there are two categories of actions that signal influence: conversation actions (replies and mentions), and content actions (retweets and attributions). The ratio of these actions to the total number of tweets a user makes is a measure of that user's influence in their social group, but fails to account for the size of that group. The influence metric proposed in [4] is a product of two components: the ratio of original tweets to retweets posted by the user, and the count of retweets and mentions of the user by others. The most influential user will thus be one that creates a lot of original posts and whose posts are repeated a lot, thus penalizing users with an important impact on a smaller community. In [5], researchers proposed the IARank ranking system, a weighted sum of buzz and structural advantage. Buzz is a measure of attention the user receives on a specific issue. It is the ratio of mentions the user receives to the total number of tweets the user has made related to an event. Structural advantage is a measure of the user's general influence, defined as the ratio of the number of followers he has to the sum of his followers and followees. They thus measures a user's influence as a combination of the attention of a specific subset of his tweets and of his connections in the network.

3 Methodology

In this paper, we follow the lead of [4, 5] and propose an influence metric that is a combination of two factors. Our factors aim to model the local and global influence of the user. Our underlying philosophy is that a user can have a strong influence on his or her immediate surroundings and thus be an important local actor, independently of whether or not their influence spreads globally throughout the entire network.

The local influence of a user is the impact the user has on his or her immediate network. We measure this in two parts. First, we consider the attention that the user's messages receive from their contacts through retweeting and marking as favourite. Since these are strongly correlated [6], we have opted to use only retweets, which we can count through the Twitter API. However, such a measure would be strongly biased in favour of users who have more followers. To account for this, we normalize by the number of followers the user has. This is the left-hand side of the multiplication in Eq. (1). The second part of the local score, the right-hand side of the multiplication in Eq. (1), considers the rate at which the user writes posts, as a function of the number of days it took for the user to write their 100 most recent tweets. The local score is the product of these two values, as shown in Eq. (1). Note that, in the rare cases where the value of the local score goes above 1, we cap it at 1 for simplicity.

$$Local = \min\left(1, \frac{\log(\#retweets)}{\log(\#followers \times 100)} \times \log\left(\frac{100}{\#days} + 1\right)\right) \tag{1}$$

The global influence is the impact the user has globally on the entire social network. This metric is also composed of two parts. The first is the proportion of the network reached by the user, or the ratio of the user's number of followers to the total number of users (310 million on Twitter), as shown in the left-hand side of the multiplication in Eq. (2). The second part is the user's activity compared to their number of followers. Our intuition is that a user that posts scarcely but is followed by a large crowd must attract more attention than one who spams the same number of followers. We compute this as 1 minus the ratio of the user's number of tweets to their number of followers, fixing a minimum score of zero, as shown in the right-hand side of the multiplication of Eq. (2). The global score is the product of these values.

$$Global = \frac{\log(\#followers)}{\log(310{,}000{,}000)} \times \max\left(0, 1 - \frac{\#tweets}{\#followers}\right) \tag{2}$$

Of important note is the simplicity of our metric. Attributes like tweets, retweets, and followers are specific to Twitter, but they could become posts, share, and friends on Facebook, or pictures, mentions, and followers on Instagram. The metrics are only computed using information from the user's profile, and do not require information from elsewhere in the social network, average user information over time, or private information. This means our metric only requires one API call to the social network to get a snapshot of the user's profile, which makes it very efficient computationally.

4 Experimental Results

In order to study our two metrics, we built a varied corpus of 234 Twitter users, with 54 US politicians (federal, state, and municipal levels; red squares in Fig. 1), 33 Canadian politicians (federal, provincial, and municipal levels; yellow squares with X), 20 international politicians (national and municipal levels; brown squares with + signs), 34 celebrities (pop stars, actors, entertainers, and athletes; green triangles), 56 CEOs of various software and traditional companies (blue diamonds), and 37 ordinary users

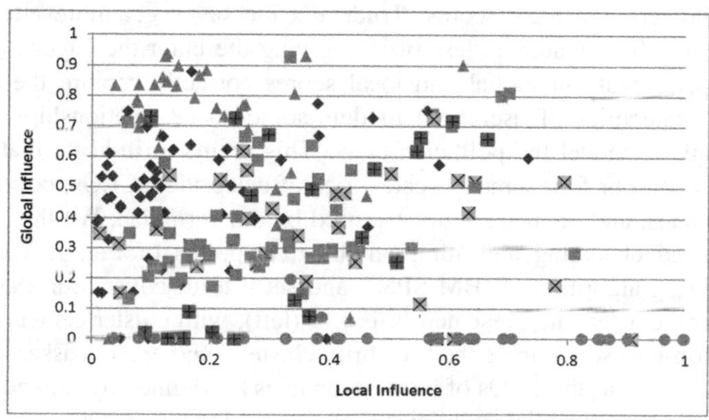

Fig. 1. Local and global influence of different categories of users. (Color figure online)

(purple circles). Figure 1 shows some clear regions by category of users. Ordinary users are at the bottom of the global influence axis (average 0.02), but their local influence varies the most of any category, going from almost 0 for a user with almost no followers to 1 for users who are very popular. Celebrities with very high number of followers have the highest global influence score (average 0.72), but are mainly clustered in a low local influence region (average 0.20) since many of them do not tweet much. The CEO category is a variation of celebrities, with fewer followers and fewer tweets, leading to lower scores (average 0.45 and 0.17 respectively).

There are outliers to each of these categories. One ordinary user gets a global score of 0.20 thanks to a low number of tweets to a high number of followers. The celebrity who tops both scores (global: 0.90, local: 0.62) is Kim Kardashian, a user who is both a very active author and who has a large number of followers retweeting her messages, while comedian Donovan Goliath has a high local influence but an unusually low global influence (global: 0.07, local: 0.43) thanks to a very low number of tweets but high recent activity. We can observe some CEOs reaching celebrity-like high global scores, such as Bill Gates (0.88) and Elon Musk (0.77), while others are very active authors and score high local influence, like Marc Benioff (0.73). However, there are no "Kim Kardashian" CEOs with high global and local influence scores.

Users in the political category are much more irregularly distributed and show no dominant cluster. There is important overlap between the scatter of US, Canadian, and international politicians. The cluster of national politicians shows a higher average global score than that of regional politicians, which is slightly higher than that of municipal politicians. There are nonetheless interesting relationships to observe between individual politicians. This dataset being from summer 2016, then-US President Barack Obama (global: 0.93, local: 0.33) shows a higher global importance but lower local importance than either candidates Hillary Clinton (global: 0.80, local: 0.69) or Donald Trump (global: 0.81, local: 0.70). This is due to him having more than 10 times the number of followers but writing tweets at a lower rate, as would be expected of a sitting world leader vs. campaigning candidates. On the Canadian side, the sitting Prime Minister, Justin Trudeau (global: 0.73, local: 0.57) also has a higher global score than either opposition leader Rona Ambrose (global: 0.42, local: 0.63) or third-party leader Thomas Mulcair (global: 0.62, local: 0.26), again thanks to a much higher number of followers. On local scores, Trudeau's messages get more attention than those of Ambrose, but he authors less tweets, giving the latter the edge.

It thus appears that our global and local scores correctly capture the distinction between some categories of users and models some social relationships, but allow outliers and fails to model the politician class. This seems to indicate that there is a distinction between our four semantic categories of celebrities, CEOs, politicians, and random individuals, and the behaviours captured by our formulae. We thus decided to run an automated clustering algorithm on the data points of Fig. 1. We used the k-means clustering algorithm of IBM SPSS, and set it to discover four clusters.

The resulting clusters are presented in Fig. 2 (left), with cluster centers marked as $\times$. Cluster 1 (top-left) seems to be the "celebrity cluster", and encompasses most of our 34 celebrities, as well as the CEOs of large companies (as defined by LinkedIn) and the most internationally-influential politicians (such as President Obama). Cluster 2 (lower-left) covers mainly ordinary politicians and CEOs of small and medium

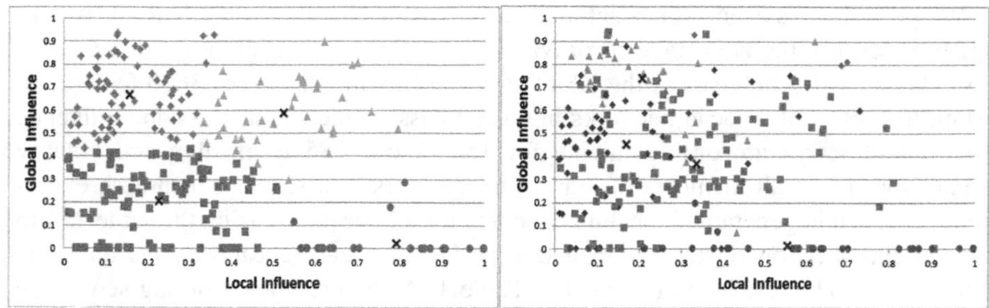

Fig. 2. k-means generation of 4 clusters (left), and category clusters for politicians, celebrities, CEOs, and ordinary users (right).

companies. Cluster 3 (top-right) covers politicians that are temporarily famous (including then-campaigning Donald Trump and Hilary Clinton). Finally, cluster 4 (bottom-right) shows the lowest global influence score, and is composed mostly of ordinary users.

To compare, we generated in Fig. 2 (right) the four clusters corresponding to the four semantic categories of politicians, celebrities, CEOs, and ordinary users. The results show that the celebrity cluster centre (top-left side) and the ordinary user cluster centre (bottom-right side) in the right-hand graph line up well with the cluster 1 and cluster 4 centres in the left-hand graph. However, the business and politician cluster centres are not near the centres of clusters 2 and 3; these two categories are likewise the ones divided over multiple clusters by k-means.

A final question is: is it possible to predict a user's class based on their statistics? To check, we collected a test set of 50 additional Twitter users: 13 politicians, 11 celebrities, 14 CEOs, and 12 ordinary users; or 20 users from cluster 1, 6 from cluster 2, 10 from cluster 3, and 14 from cluster 4. We ran two tests: a "classification" test to sort the test users into the semantic category clusters of Fig. 2 right, and a "clustering" test to sort the test users into the four k-means clusters of Fig. 2 left.

We computed the local and global influence of each test user with Eqs. (1) and (2). We then computed the Euclidean distance to each cluster center, and assigned each user to the nearest one. We computed precision and recall for each cluster, averaged it over all classes, and compute the F-measure of the classification. The results are presented in Table 1. They show that the using the clusters gives almost 20% better results than using the categories. This was expected; the categories are useful human-level constructs but are noisy reflections of the influence quantified by our formulae.

Table 1. Experimental results and benchmarks.

Experiment	Precision	Recall	F-Measure
Our system – categorization test	0.62	0.65	0.64
Our system – clustering test	0.80	0.84	0.82
IARank – categorization test	0.32	0.43	0.37
IARank – clustering test	0.59	0.57	0.58
Klout – categorization test	0.28	0.28	0.28
Klout – clustering test	0.54	0.52	0.53

We picked two systems for benchmark comparison. The first is the IARank system of [5], which has the advantage of providing two-dimensional influence metrics like ours. The second benchmark is the Klout system [7], which analyses 3600 features of 750 million users of 9 social networks in order to assign them a single-value influence score. Klout scores are only available for 150 of our 285 users; they are notably missing for almost all members of our "ordinary users" class. Our benchmark experiment consisted in generating benchmark scores for all our users, using the same 234 to discover classification cluster centres and to perform k-means clustering, and the same 50 for testing. The results are included in Table 1. As before, the clustering scores are about 20% higher than the categorization scores. However, our metric performs significantly better than the benchmarks in all measures.

5 Conclusion

In this paper, we have presented a new approach to modelling a user's influence on social networks. Our model consists of two metrics, namely the local influence the user has on his or her immediate set of contacts, and the global influence the user has on the entire social network. We presented both general definitions of these two metrics and showed how to implement them for a real social network, namely the Twitter network. Our case study using Twitter showed that our model can create clusters of users in 2D space corresponding to their social standing, and can further be used to classify previously-unseen users into the correct classes with an f-measure of 0.82, which is significantly higher than benchmark algorithms.

References

1. Otte, E., Rousseau, R.: Social network analysis: a powerful strategy, also for the information sciences. J. Inf. Sci. **28**(6), 441–453 (2002)
2. Dubois, E., Gaffney, D.: Identifying political influentials and opinion leaders on Twitter. Am. Behav. Sci. **58**(10), 1260–1277 (2014)
3. Leavitt, A., Burchard, E., Fisher, D., Gilbert, S.: New approaches for analyzing influence on twitter. Web Ecol. Project **4**(2), 1–18 (2009)
4. Noro, T., Fei, R., Xiao, F., Tokuda, T.: Twitter user rank using keyword search. Inf. Model. Knowl. Bases XXIV **251**(8), 31–48 (2013)
5. Cappelletti, R., Sastry, N.: IARank: ranking users on Twitter in near real-time, based on their information amplification potential. In: IEEE International Conference on Social Informatics, pp. 70–77, 14 December 2012
6. Mei, Y., Zhong, Y., Yang, J.: Finding and analyzing principal features for measuring user influence on Twitter. In: IEEE First International Conference on Big Data Computing Service and Applications, San Francisco Bay, USA, pp. 478–486, 30 March–2 April 2015
7. Rao, A., Spasojevic, N., Li, Z., DSouza, T.: Klout score: measuring influence across multiple social networks. In: Proceedings of the IEEE International Conference on Big Data, Santa Clara, USA, pp. 2282–2289, 29 October–1 November 2015

The Impact of Toxic Language on the Health of Reddit Communities

Shruthi Mohan[1(✉)], Apala Guha[1], Michael Harris[2], Fred Popowich[1], Ashley Schuster[2], and Chris Priebe[2]

[1] School of Computing Science, Simon Fraser University, Burnaby, BC, Canada
shruthim@sfu.ca

[2] Two Hat Security Ltd, Kelowna, BC, Canada

Abstract. There are numerous on-line communities in which people converse about various topics and issues. It is usually necessary to monitor on-line forums to ensure that conversations and content are appropriate. Disturbing trends are starting to emerge, including cyberbullying, cyber threats, on-line harassment, hate speech, and abuse — referred to collectively as 'toxicity'. Researchers have already started investigating automatic and semi-automatic monitoring of social networking sites for aspects of toxicity. We are investigating the relationship between on-line toxicity and forum health. Specifically, we provide results of the evaluation of the impact of toxicity on community health as a function of its size, while correcting for community topic.

1 Introduction

With the rising use of the internet and other digital technologies, we are seeing some disturbing trends starting to emerge, including cyberbullying, cyber threats, online harassment, hate speech, and abuse – referred to collectively as "toxicity". For instance, McAfee released findings from the company's 2014 Teens and The Screen study: Exploring Online Privacy, Social Networking and Cyberbullying. According to this study, 87% of youth in the US have witnessed cyberbullying. When users experience toxicity, there are psychological costs to both individuals and society. Additionally, there are revenue costs to businesses due to lower user engagement. The goal of this paper is to study the relationship between online toxicity and forum health.

We use Reddit as an example online forum for this study. We define online toxicity as language involving bullying, racism, hate speech, vulgarity, fraud, and, threats. In this paper, health is defined as a measure of user engagement in Reddit communities or subreddits. Engagement can be used to predict both revenue and user attitude, therefore it is a good metric for this study. Our hypothesis is that engagement is negatively correlated with toxicity. We also aim to study how the relationship between toxicity and health is impacted by the nature of the subreddit. For example, the subreddit topic may determine the baseline level of toxicity i.e. users in certain subreddits expect some toxicity while others do not. The nature of a subreddit can also be captured by subreddit size, and we hypothesize that subreddits of different sizes react differently to toxicity.

M. Mouhoub and P. Langlais (Eds.): Canadian AI 2017, LNAI 10233, pp. 51–56, 2017.
DOI: 10.1007/978-3-319-57351-9_6

2 Background

The primary dataset for this research was Reddit 2009. Reddit is an online community forum, which is organized into *subreddits* by topic. Subreddits can cover topics like science, gaming, music, books, news, movies, fitness, food, and more. Registered community members can submit content, such as text posts or direct links. Users can then vote submissions up or down and the submissions with the most positive votes appear on the front page or at the top of a category. Also, users may reply to comments. A sequence of comments and replies forms a *thread*. As of 2016, Reddit had 542 million monthly visitors (234 million unique users). The dataset is essentially a json corpus containing information like subreddit name, text of the comments, timestamp, number of ups the thread has received, number of downs the thread has received, and so on.

To label the data, we partnered with Community Sift, a leading company in text filtering which has spent over four years building a comprehensive list of toxic words, phrases, and n-grams using supervised learning. Community Sift sells this list commercially to many of the largest social media and video games sites to keep kids safe. They rate words and phrases (called rules) on a sliding scale of risk level from 1–7, with linguistic and cultural annotation guidelines for each level. Level 1 and 2 are words that are safe to ignore (like "table", "sky"). Level 3 and 4 are words that are spelling mistakes, keyboard smashing (like "asldkjksjkl") and words that are questionable but require context (eg. "ugly"). Level 5 involves controversial words that might be allowed in some context but not others. Level 6 are words that are typically considered inappropriate and offensive whereas level 7 are very high-risk content like rape threats and abuse.

3 Forming the Feature Vectors

The goal is to study the relationship between toxicity levels and health of several subreddits. The toxicity level of each subreddit for the year 2009 is represented as a 52-dimensional feature vector i.e. each dimension represents the perceived toxicity in a particular week of 2009. Similarly, the health of each subreddit is represented as a 52-dimensional vector. We only considered subreddits that had activity for at least half the number of weeks (i.e. 26) of the whole year. Approximately 180 subreddits were studied for the whole year.

3.1 Forming the Toxicity Feature Vectors

We considered posts with labels of 6 or 7 as toxic posts, and all other posts as non-toxic posts. After such classification, we considered the number of toxic posts in a subreddit per week as well the total number of posts in that subreddit in that week. We normalized the toxicity level by taking the ratio of these two quantities to represent the perceived toxicity for that subreddit for that week.

We then computed the moving average of the toxicity score for each week. The last week's toxicity score is the average of the toxicity scores of all the weeks in that year. The final feature vector for a subreddit contains the moving average toxicity score for each week of the year 2009. Moving averages were computed to focus on the long-term toxicity trends.

3.2 Forming the Subreddit Health Feature Vectors

Health, in this paper, is a measure of engagement. For each week and for each subreddit, we considered the number of posts and the number of unique authors of these posts. The number of posts definitely signify health but in some cases a high number of posts may not represent high user engagement. For example, when a small number of users are engaged in toxic fights, although the number of posts shoots up, the community may be actually diminishing.

Both these features were standardized using range scaling. Thus, each week produces two engagement scores for each subreddit. We needed to compute an overall score for each week which accounts for both these values, since these are both important indicators. In order to combine these two scores into a single score, we simply added them and then mapped them to the $[0, 1]$ range by applying the sigmoid function to the sum. Similar to the toxicity score, a moving average is computed over the health score throughout the year. Thus the health score vector represents the moving average for each week for each subreddit.

4 Studying the Health Impact of Subreddit Toxicity

4.1 Relationship Between Subreddit Toxicity and Health

Figure 1 shows the scatter plot of subreddit toxicity and health. Each subreddit is represented by a different color. There are 52 points representing each subreddit, one for each week. At lower levels of toxicity, the points are distributed all over the y-axis i.e. subreddits exhibit the whole range of health. However, as

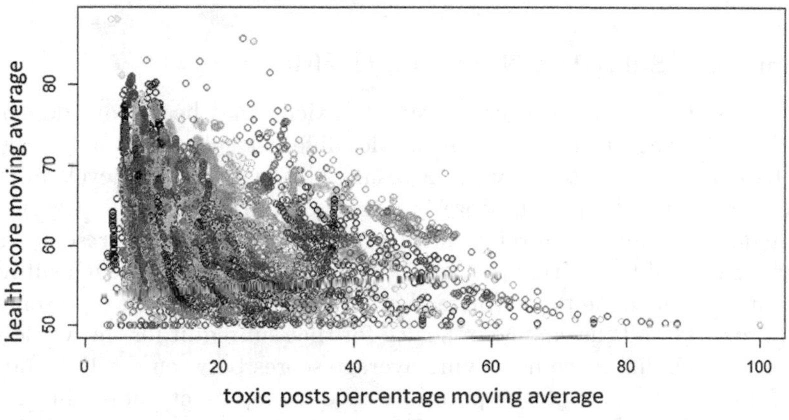

Fig. 1. Health score versus toxic posts percentage (Color figure online)

toxicity increases, the points are more concentrated at lower health values. This phenomenon seems to suggest that when toxicity is low, other factors determine the health of a subreddit. As toxicity increases, it becomes a major factor in the health of a subreddit.

Two categories of subreddits are visible in this chart. The first category is one in which toxicity level remains fairly constant throughout the year. The other category is in which toxicity levels change significantly throughout the year. In the first case, where toxicity levels remain constant, the health score varies in many cases, again indicating that health is determined by other factors when toxicity is low and stable. However, when toxicity varies, the negative correlation is evident i.e. lower health scores correspond to higher values of toxicity.

Figure 2 shows the histogram of correlation coefficients for all the subreddits. About 50% of the subreddits exhibit a highly negative correlation of -0.8 and -0.9. This confirms our hypothesis that there is a strong relationship between subreddit toxicity and health. The bins representing high positive correlation coefficients have the lowest frequencies in the histogram i.e. it is rare to have high toxicity and good health and vice-versa.

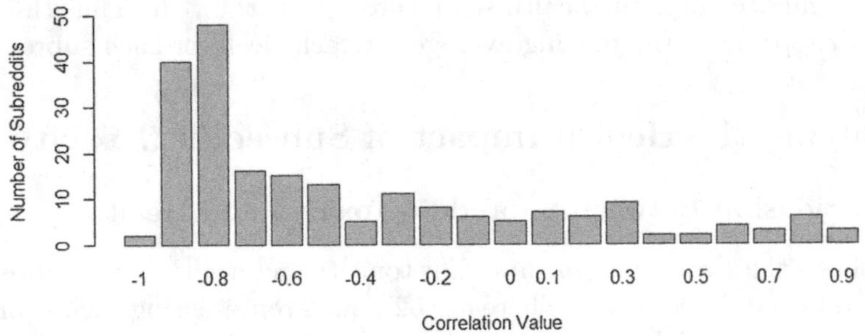

Fig. 2. Overall correlation between toxicity and health score for each subreddit

4.2 Impact of Subreddit Nature on Health

In this section we study whether subreddit toxicity and health are dependent upon subreddit characteristics. For example, different subreddits may generate certain baseline levels of toxicity. As a result, although toxicity levels are high in these subreddits, the health score is not much impacted. Similarly the size of a subreddit may affect the relationship. In order to do so, we present a more summarized view of the scatter plot in Fig. 3. In this scatter plot, each subreddit is represented by a single point (instead of 52 points). The point represents the change in toxicity and the change in health for that subreddit for the whole year. The change is the difference in moving average scores between the last and first weeks of 2009. The color of the points is used to represent subreddit size i.e. the average number of posts per week. The change in scores over the whole year allows correcting for the baseline toxicity of a particular subreddit topic.

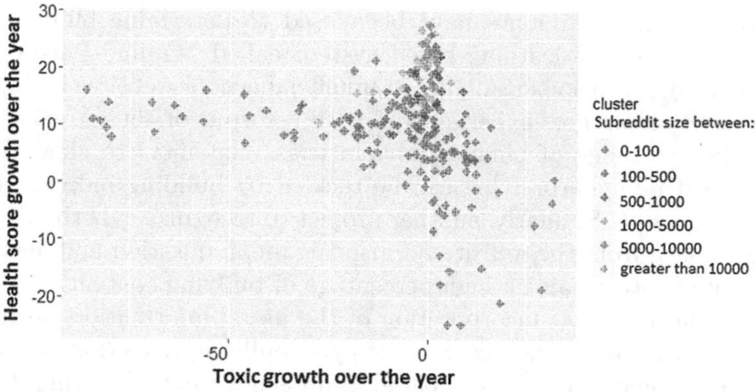

Fig. 3. Growth in health score versus growth in toxic posts percentage (Color figure online)

The scatter plot shows that most subreddits did not experience a significant change in toxicity over the whole year i.e. most points are distributed around the $x = 0$ line. However, among these subreddits, there was varying change in health score. Some subreddits exhibited growing health while others exhibited declining health. Interestingly, most of the subreddits with growing health were the larger subreddits (100 or more posts per week) and while the ones with declining health were the smaller subreddits (less than 100 posts per week). Also there were more subreddits with growing health than with declining health. In fact, a majority of the subreddits had their health grow by 10% or more. This observation indicates that stable toxicity levels are more often rewarded with community growth.

When toxicity declines, health almost always grows. However, most of the communities exhibiting toxicity decline are the smaller subreddits. It is probably unlikely that toxicity will decline in large subreddits. Also this fact may indicate a diminishing interest in the subreddit which ultimately leads to less toxicity.

When toxicity grows by a small amount (around 10%), health grows in many cases. However, this holds true only for small subreddits and the growth is small (less than 10%). Health declines for several subreddits when toxicity increases by a small amount. Here too, the subreddits are small. Higher levels of toxicity increase are always exhibited by small subreddits with declining health. It looks like any increase in toxicity level limits the size of a subreddit and also its growth. Thus there is more incentive to prevent toxicity levels from shooting up.

5 Related Work

Efforts to study the desirability of automatic monitoring of cyberbullying on social networking sites concluded that automatic monitoring was favoured, but specified clear conditions under which such systems should be implemented, including effective follow-up strategies, protecting the users' privacy and safeguarding their self-reliance [5].

Machine learning techniques have been used to determine bullying words and phrases. A machine learning-based system called "Online Patrol Agent" was developed to detect cyberbullying in unofficial school websites in Japan [3]. In another case, researchers experimented with a corpus of 4500 YouTube comments, applying a range of binary and multiclass classifiers to show that the detection of textual cyberbullying can be tackled by building individual topic-sensitive classifiers [2]. Similarly, another project to recognize cyberbullying content collected data from the website Formspring.me, a question-and-answer formatted website that contains a high percentage of bullying content [4]. Another research hypothesized that incorporation of the users' information, such as age and gender, will improve the accuracy of cyberbullying detection [1]. In their study, they investigated the gender-based approach for cyberbullying detection in MySpace corpus and showed that author information can be leveraged to improve the detection in online social networks.

6 Conclusions

We studied toxicity and health for 180 subreddits in the year 2009. We found that community health and toxicity exhibit high negative correlation. In fact, more than 50% of the subreddits we studied exhibited a negative correlation of −0.8 or more. Although subreddits exhibited fluctuations in toxicity and health throughout 2009, most of them had stable levels of toxicity on average. Subreddits with stable toxicity levels more often witness growth in health, with the growth percentage being higher for larger communities, regardless of the subreddit topic. Small increases in toxicity may also sometimes lead to growth in health. But large increases in toxicity always leads to health decline. These facts combined indicate that it is worthwhile to maintain stable toxicity levels subreddits to ensure that they grow in size. However, the actual level that is desirable in a subreddit may be dependent on the topic.

References

1. Dadvar, M., De Jong, F.: Cyberbullying detection: a step toward a safer internet yard. In: Proceedings of the 21st International Conference on World Wide Web. pp. 121–126. ACM (2012)
2. Dinakar, K., Reichart, R., Lieberman, H.: Modeling the detection of textual cyberbullying. Soc. Mob. Web **11**(02) (2011)
3. Kovacevic, A., Nikolic, D.: Automatic detection of cyberbullying to make internet a safer environment. In: Handbook of Research on Digital Crime, Cyberspace Security, and Information Assurance, p. 277 (2014)
4. Reynolds, K., Kontostathis, A., Edwards, L.: Using machine learning to detect cyberbullying. In: 2011 10th International Conference on Machine Learning and Applications and Workshops (ICMLA), vol. 2, pp. 241–244. IEEE (2011)
5. Van Royen, K., Poels, K., Daelemans, W., Vandebosch, H.: Automatic monitoring of cyberbullying on social networking sites: from technological feasibility to desirability. Telemat. Inform. **32**(1), 89–97 (2015)

Somatic Copy Number Alteration-Based Prediction of Molecular Subtypes of Breast Cancer Using Deep Learning Model

Md. Mohaiminul Islam[1,2,3], Rasif Ajwad[1,2,3], Chen Chi[1,3], Michael Domaratzki[2], Yang Wang[2], and Pingzhao Hu[1,3,4](✉)

[1] Department of Biochemistry and Medical Genetics, University of Manitoba, Winnipeg, Canada
{islammm5,ajwadr,chic3}@myumanitoba.ca, pingzhao.hu@umanitoba.ca

[2] Department of Computer Science, University of Manitoba, Winnipeg, Canada
{mdomarat,yang.wang}@umanitoba.ca

[3] George and Fay Yee Centre for Healthcare Innovation, University of Manitoba, Winnipeg, Canada

[4] Department of Electrical and Computer Engineering, University of Manitoba, Winnipeg, Canada

Abstract. Statistical analysis of high throughput genomic data, such as gene expressions, copy number alterations (CNAs) and single nucleotide polymorphisms (SNPs), has become very popular in cancer studies in recent decades because such analysis can be very helpful to predict whether a patient has a certain cancer or its subtypes. However, due to the high-dimensional nature of the data sets with hundreds of thousands of variables and very small numbers of samples, traditional machine learning approaches, such as Support Vector Machines (SVMs) and Random Forests (RFs), cannot analyze these data efficiently. To overcome this issue, we propose a deep neural network model to predict molecular subtypes of breast cancer using somatic CNAs. Experiments show that our deep model works much better than traditional SVM and RF.

Keywords: Bioinformatics · Classification · Genomic data · Deep learning

1 Introduction

Rather than being a single disease, breast cancer is a collection of diseases with multiple subtypes. Breast cancer can be classified into estrogen-receptor-positive (ER+) and estrogen-receptor-negative (ER−). A patient has ER+ breast cancer if her cancer cells have receptors for the hormone estrogen. Classifying patients into hormone receptor positive or negative is important for physicians because they need to determine whether the patients need hormonal treatments or chemotherapy. With the advent of technologies researchers were able to use gene expression profiles to identify four intrinsic molecular subtypes of breast cancer (i.e., PAM50 subtypes): Luminal A, Luminal B, HER-2 enriched and Basal-like [1].

M. Mouhoub and P. Langlais (Eds.): Canadian AI 2017, LNAI 10233, pp. 57–63, 2017.
DOI: 10.1007/978-3-319-57351-9_7

CNAs represent the somatic changes of copy numbers in a DNA sequence. According to Beroukhim et al. [2], CNAs are predominant in different type of cancers. It is expected that this data type can also be used to predict different molecular subtypes (such as ER status and PAM50 subtypes) of breast cancer using patient-specific CNA profiles. Previously, machine learning models were built to predict these subtypes [3]. CNA profile data is a high-throughput data and traditional machine learning methods, such as SVMs and RFs, can be easily overfitted if such high-throughput data is used directly as an input into these learners.

Deep convolutional neural network (DCNN) based models do not use any hand crafted features, rather they use the raw information about training samples and produce a complex form of generic features to represent the input data. Unlike SVMs and RFs, these deep models are able to take an input vector of any length. To avoid the over-fitting problem, deep learning provides a useful technique known as dropout [4]. Deep learning has achieved many state-of-the-art results in different computer vision fields such as image classification [5]. Currently, deep learning methods are used to solve different problems in bioinformatics. For example, Denas et al. proposed a DCNN model for binding site prediction [6].

In this paper, we propose to build a DCNN based model using CNA profile-based data to predict molecular subtypes of breast cancer: the status of estrogen-receptor (ER+ and ER−) and the PAM50 subtypes (Luminal A, Luminal B, HER-2 enriched and Basal-like). The former is a standard supervised binary classification problem while the latter is a supervised multi-class classification problem.

2 Deep Learning Model for the Prediction of Molecular Subtypes of Breast Cancer

Specifically, we propose to use a deep convolutional neural network (DCNN) for the prediction of molecular subtypes of breast cancer (Fig. 1). Our network receives a single vector (X) as an input to the input layer of the DCNN, which is followed by convolutional layers. Each neuron of a convolutional layer receives some input and performs a dot product operation. These convolutional layers are considered a strong pattern detector of local features.

The two convolutional layers (Fig. 1) are followed by a one-dimensional pooling layer. The outputs of the convolution layers are considered low-level features. Pooling over these features creates higher-level features that can help smooth the noisiness in training data. This pooling layer partitions the outputs from the convolutional layers into a set of sub-regions and for each of those regions the maximum value is taken as an output. The pooling layer reduces the size of its input vector to decrease the large number of parameters to be estimated, which is also useful to avoid potential overfitting and to make model invariant to input features.

In our experiment, there is a complex non-linear relationship between the response variable (such as the prediction score assigned to a patient for a specific molecular subtype of breast cancer) and the predictors (such as the gene-specific CNA profiles).

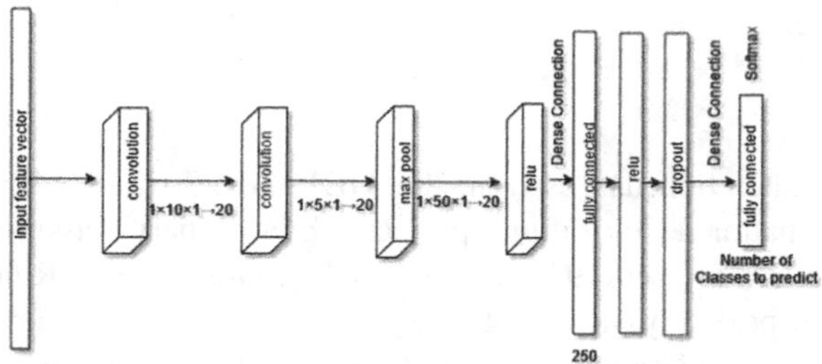

Fig. 1. Proposed architecture of DCNN. The number and size of different filters that must be learned is shown in the figure. Here, $1 \times 10 \times 1 \to 20$ means the kernel size is 1×10 and this is a one-dimensional feature while the total number of convolutional feature maps is 20. The stride size for the convolutional layer is 1×1 and for the pooling layer is 1×2. The number of outputs of the first fully connected layer is 250. The size of the output of the last fully connected layer will be two for binary classification (ER status prediction) and four for multiclass classification (PAM50 subtype prediction).

Therefore, we use the Relu (Rectified Linear Units) layer after the pooling layer to model this non-linear relationship. Relu performs a threshold operation as:

$$f(t) = \begin{cases} t, t \geq 0 \\ 0, t < 0 \end{cases} \quad (1)$$

Here, t represents the input to a neuron.

To complete the higher-level reasoning of our network we use the fully connected layer ($F1$), as used in a traditional neural network, and the output of this layer can be calculated as a matrix multiplication tailed via a bias offset. Then, we pass the output of $F1$ to another fully connected layer ($F2$) using a Relu layer and a dropout layer as medium. This helps our model overcome the potential overfitting problem and provides generalizability.

The output of $F2$ is a K-dimensional vector (a) that provides the prediction scores of test samples assigned to each of the classes. We use a softmax classification layer to transform the prediction scores into probability scores. This layer implements the softmax function using the prediction scores (a) and estimated parameters (e.g., w) from $F2$ to produce k-th probability scores for test samples assigned to each of the classes. Therefore, the probabilities that the test samples are assigned to the i-th class can be calculated as follows:

$$P(h = i|a) = \frac{e^{a^T w_i}}{\sum_{k=1}^{K} e^{a^T w_k}} \quad (2)$$

Here, $a^T w$ represents the inner product of a and w and K represents the number of classes. We train our network using the backpropagation approach and we use softmax loss to allow us explain the prediction results as probabilities.

3 Experiments

3.1 Dataset

Our copy number alteration data is from the METABRIC (Molecular Taxonomy of Breast Cancer International Consortium) project [7]. For binary classification, we have 991 samples in the training set (794 samples and 197 samples for ER positive and ER negative classes respectively) and 984 samples in the test set. For the multiclass classification we have 935 samples for the training set (for Luminal A, Luminal B, HER-2 enriched and Basal-like classes we have 464, 268, 87 and 116 samples, respectively) and 842 samples for the test set. We have three discrete copy number calls: −1 = copy number loss, 0 = diploid, 1 = copy number gain in our CNA mutation matrix (patients-by-genes).

3.2 Informative Feature Section for DCNN

In total, we retrieved 18,305 genes. Since different genes have different numbers of CNAs across all patients, the genes are more informative if they have more somatic CNAs. We calculated the CNA frequency for each of the 18,305 genes as follows:

$$f_{CNA} = \frac{N_{CNA}}{M} \tag{3}$$

Here, f_{CNA} means CNA frequency of a gene, N_{CNA} means the number of copy number gains and losses of a gene and M represents the total number of samples (i.e., patients). We selected few cutoffs (0.0101, 0.0492, 0.0685, 0.1102 and 0.1283) based on the five-number summary statistics (minimum, first quartile, median, third quartile and maximum) and mean of the CNA frequency.

3.3 Construction of DCNN Model

To implement the DCNN model (Fig. 1) for both the binary and multiclass classification tasks, we used publicly available C++ based deep learning library called CAFFE [8]. For each of the tasks, we trained several DCNN models using different CNA frequency cutoffs: 0.0101, 0.0492, 0.0685, 0.1102 and 0.1283. The number of genes or features selected by the unsupervised approach at these cutoffs is 18305, 13476, 8857, 5192 and 4377, respectively. We used learning rate 0.001, batch size 64 and dropout ratio 0.5 to train our network.

3.4 Performance Evaluation Metrics and Baseline Models

We use overall accuracy and Receiver Operating Characteristics (ROC) curve to evaluate the performance of our DCNN classifiers. We use area under the ROC curve (AUC) as the quantitative measure of the ROC curve. To compare the performance of our DCNN models, we use two state-of-the-art supervised classification models: SVM and RF, as our baseline models. We use two R packages known as e1071 and randomForest to build SVM and RF models, respectively. For each sample we have more than 18,000 genes while we have only ~1000 samples. SVM and RF are not able to use such high-throughput data as input vectors. Using such input will result in these models being overfitted. So, we performed nonparametric supervised Chi-square (χ^2) test to calculate the significance of each of the genes. Then we selected the top (most significant) hundreds of genes to build our baseline models.

4 Results

Prediction accuracies and AUCs based on our DCNN models using different numbers of features selected at different CNA frequencies are shown in Figs. 2 and 3.

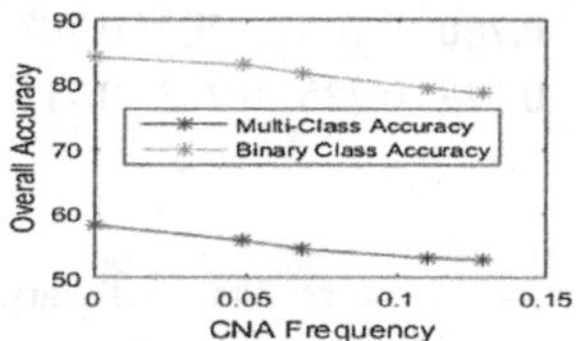

Fig. 2. Overall accuracy (%) of the proposed DCNN model at different CNA frequencies

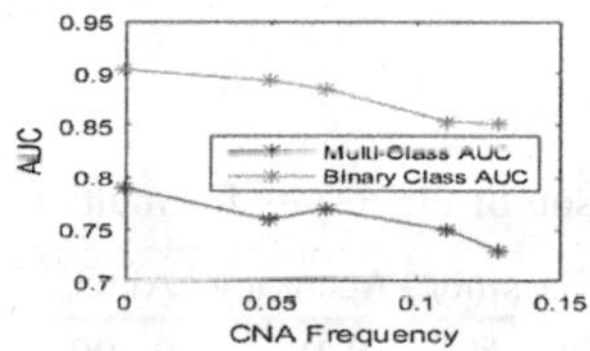

Fig. 3. AUC of the proposed DCNN model at different CNA frequencies

In general, the somatic CNA-based profiles have much larger power to predict ER status (binary classification) than PAM50 subtypes (multiclass classification). The models have highest prediction performance when all the features are used. Their performance decreases when the number of features used in the models decreases.

The prediction results of our baseline models are shown in Table 1 (accuracies) and Table 2 (AUCs) for binary classification (B_SVM, B_RF) and multiclass classification (M_SVM, M_RF). The numbers in bold color mean that it is the best result among different numbers of the selected top genes. We use an R function called multiclass.roc to generate multiple ROC curves to compute the multiclass AUC.

Comparisons of the results (Tables 3 and 4) of our proposed DCNN models with our baseline models clearly confirms that our DCNN models outperform the results of SVM and RF. Tables 3 and 4 show the best result among the binary and multiclass classifiers from Figs. 2, 3, Tables 1 and 2.

Table 1. Overall accuracy (%)

Classifiers	Top selected genes				
	100	250	350	400	500
B_SVM	**76.5**	76.4	**76.5**	75.8	76.0
B_RF	81.5	**82.7**	**82.7**	82.3	81.7
M_SVM	42.7	43.7	43.8	**45.0**	43.7
M_RF	44.8	47.0	48.6	**49.5**	48.6

Table 2. Area under the curve (AUC)

Classifiers	Top selected genes				
	100	250	350	400	500
B_SVM	0.693	0.686	**0.702**	**0.702**	0.693
B_RF	0.764	0.798	0.804	0.815	**0.817**
M_SVM	**0.780**	0.703	0.702	0.708	0.707
M_RF	**0.729**	0.725	0.723	0.715	0.725

Table 3. Comparison of the results for binary classification.

Classifier	Accuracy	AUC
DCNN	84.1	0.904
SVM	76.5	0.702
RF	82.7	0.817

Table 4. Comparison of the results for multiclass classification.

Classifier	Accuracy	AUC
DCNN	58.19	0.790
SVM	45.0	0.780
RF	49.5	0.729

5 Conclusion and Discussions

In this paper, we showed that the proposed DCNN models achieve much better results than SVMs and RFs for both binary and multiclass classification tasks. We also demonstrated that the DCNN models can work well for data sets with larger numbers of features than samples, which often results in overfitting in SVM- or RF-based models. Although there are great advances using traditional machine learning models in different bioinformatics applications, recent research including this paper shows that deep convolutional neural networks have significant advantages over them.

We use DCNN model rather than deep belief network (DBN) because DCNN models are more invariant to the translation of the data. DCNN can also provide a model which is more robust to the unwanted noisiness in the data than DBN. In our future work, we will incorporate DBN network into our experiments for both binary and multiclass classification.

Acknowledgement. This work was supported in part by Canadian Breast Cancer Foundation – Prairies/NWTRegion, Natural Sciences and Engineering Research Council of Canada, Manitoba Research Health Council and University of Manitoba.

References

1. Perou, C.M., et al.: Molecular portraits of human breast tumours. Nature **406**, 747–752 (2000)
2. Beroukhim, R., et al.: Assessing the significance of chromosomal aberrations in cancer: methodology and application to glioma. Proc. Natl. Acad. Sci. **104**, 20007–20012 (2007)
3. Han, L., et al.: The Pan-Cancer analysis of pseudogene expression reveals biologically and clinically relevant tumour subtypes. Nat. Commun. **5**, 3963 (2014)
4. Srivastava, N., et al.: Dropout: a simple way to prevent neural networks from overfitting. J. Mach. Learn. Res. **15**, 1929–1958 (2014)
5. Russakovsky, O., et al.: Imagenet large scale visual recognition challenge. Int. J. Comput. Vis. **115**, 211–252 (2015)
6. Denas, O., Taylor, J.: Deep modeling of gene expression regulation in an erythropoiesis model. In: Representation Learning, ICML Workshop (2013)
7. Curtis, C., et al.: The genomic and transcriptomic architecture of 2,000 breast tumours reveals novel subgroups. Nature **486**, 346–352 (2012)
8. Jia, Y., et al.: An open source convolutional architecture for fast feature embedding (2013). http://caffe.berkeleyvision.org

An Improved Data Sanitization Algorithm for Privacy Preserving Medical Data Publishing

A.N.K. Zaman(✉), Charlie Obimbo, and Rozita A. Dara

School of Computer Science, University of Guelph,
50 Stone Road East, Guelph, ON N1G 2W1, Canada
{azaman,cobimbo,drozita}@uoguelph.ca

Abstract. Data sharing is critical due to the possibility of privacy breaches. In contrast, it is very important to design and implement public-spirited policies to expedite effective services and development (e.g., public health care). This research proposes a randomization algorithm for data sanitization that satisfies ϵ-differential privacy to publish privacy preserving data. The proposed algorithm has been implemented, and tested with two different data sets. The obtained results show that the proposed algorithm has promising performance compared to other existing works.

Keywords: Differential privacy · Data anonymization · Privacy preserving medical data publishing · Re-identification risk

1 Introduction

Removing personal identifiable information from a data set is not enough to secure privacy of a person. As a result, anonymization algorithms are needed to overcome these shortcomings. Ideas of interactive, and non-interactive anonymization techniques are mentioned in [1]. In the literature, differential privacy (DP) method is widely used in interactive framework [2–4]. In the case of a non-interactive framework, sanitized data set is published by a data custodian for public use. In this research, the non-interactive framework is adopted as this approach has a number of advantages [1,5] over its counterpart (interactive approach).

2 Contributions

The key contributions are enlisted below:

- The proposed algorithm adopted the non-interactive model for data sanitization and release, thus data miners have full access of the published data set for further processing, to promote data sharing in a safe way.
- The published data set will be independent of adversary's background knowledge.
- Also the proposed algorithm can handle real life data sets contain categorical, numerical, and set-valued attributes and keeps data usable in case of classification.
- Reduced and/or neutralized the re-identification risk.

M. Mouhoub and P. Langlais (Eds.): Canadian AI 2017, LNAI 10233, pp. 64–70, 2017.
DOI: 10.1007/978-3-319-57351-9_8

3 Related Works

There are various algorithms for privacy preserving data mining (PPDM) and privacy preserving data publishing (PPDP), however, not much is found in literature that addresses the privacy preservation to achieve the goal of classification [5,6]. Some of the recent works on privacy preserving data publishing are reported below:

In [7], Qin et al., proposed a local differential privacy algorithm called LDP-Miner to anoymize set-valued data. They claimed that the algorithmic analysis of their method is practical in terms of efficiency. In [8], Fan and Jin implemented two methods: Hand-picked algorithm (HPA), and Simple random algorithm (SRA) which are variations of l-diversity [9] technique, and use Laplace mechanism [10] for adding noise to make data secure. Wu et al., [11] proposed a privacy preserving algorithm by changing quasi-identifiers, and anonymization, and evaluated the published data using classification accuracy, and F-measure. In [1], Mohammad et al., proposed a DP based algorithm, and measured classification accuracy of the sanitized data set. In literature, it is also found that, several authors modified existing machine learning techniques to adopt privacy to publish privacy preserving results e.g., classification results [12], histogram [13] of data sets. Those methods are only useful for publishing result, but not for publishing secure data set for sharing.

4 Problem Statement

The aim of this research is to develop a framework that satisfies differential privacy standards [10], and ensures maximum data usability. This proposed work has followed two phases:

- To find a feasible way to apply generalization, and suppression to sanitize micro-data to its anonymous form that satisfies ϵ-differential privacy.
- To keep the sanitized data usable, and accurate for the data miners for further processing for various application e.g., data classification, and to reduce the possibility of re-identification.

5 Proposed System and Experimental Design

The following sections will discuss implementation of the propose system, and the experimental setup:

5.1 Privacy Constraint

In literature, it is found that many privacy preserving models suffer with different attacks to breach privacy. In the proposed system, ϵ-differential privacy will be used which is capable to protect published data set from different attacks. From literature [5,10,14], it is found that ϵ-differential privacy is able to protect most attacks.

Definition (ϵ-differential privacy): $DB1$ and $DB2$ are two data sets, and they differ only in one element. For both data sets, $DB1$ and $DB2$, a certain query response Rs should be the same as well as satisfy the following probability distribution Pr:

$$\frac{Pr(An(DB1) = Rs)}{Pr(An(DB2) = Rs)} \leq e^{\epsilon} \tag{1}$$

where, An presents an anonymization algorithm. The parameter $\epsilon > 0$ is chosen by the data publisher. Stronger privacy guarantee could be achieved by choosing a lower value of ϵ. The values could be 0.01, 0.1, or may be $\ln 2$ or $\ln 3$ [15]. If it is a very small ϵ then, $e^{\epsilon} \approx 1 + \epsilon$. To process numeric and non-numeric data with differential privacy model, following techniques will be needed.

5.2 Laplace Mechanism

Dwork et al.,[2] proposed the Laplace mechanism to add noise for numerical values, and ensure DP. The Laplace mechanism takes a database DB as input and consists of a function f and the privacy parameter λ. The privacy parameter λ specifies how much noise should be added to produce the privacy preserved output. The mechanism first computes the true output $f(DB)$, and then perturbs the noisy output. A Laplace distribution having a probability density function

$$pdf(\frac{x}{\lambda}) = \frac{1}{2\lambda} e^{-}|x|/\lambda \tag{2}$$

generates noise, where, x is a random variable; its variance is $2\lambda^2$ and mean is 0. The sensitivity of the noise is defined by this formula: $\hat{f}(DB) = f(DB) + lap(\lambda)$, where, $lap(\lambda)$ is sampled from Laplace distribution. The mechanism, $\hat{f}(DB) = f(DB) + lap(\frac{1}{\epsilon})$ ensures ϵ-differential privacy. A recent publish work [16] also proves that adding Laplace noise secures data from the adversary.

5.3 Anonymization

Data anonymization is a procedure that converts data in a new form to produce secure data, and prevents information leakage from that data set. Data suppression, and generalization are common methods to implement data anonymization.

Generalization. To anonymize a data set DB, the process of generalization takes place by substituting an original value of an attribute with a more general form of a value. The general value is chosen according to the characteristics of an attribute. For examples, profession: **filmmaker**, and **singer** are generalized with the **artist**, and the **age 34** is generalized with a range [**30–35**). Let $DB = r_1, r_2, ..., r_n$ be a set of records, where every record r_i represent the information of an individual with attributes $A = A_1, A_2, ..., A_d$. It is assumed that each attribute A_i has a finite domain, denoted by $\Omega(A_i)$. The domain of DB is defined as $\Omega(DB) = \Omega(A_1) \times \Omega(A_2) \times ... \times \Omega(A_d)$.

Suppression. Suppression replaces an attribute value fully or partially by a special symbol (e.g., "*" or "Any"), which indicates that the value has been suppressed. Suppression is used to prevent disclosure of any value from a data set. Figure 2 shows the taxonomy tree (TT) of the zip code suppression of two German cities. First two digits of a code represents a city, for example the number 42 presents the City of Velbert. At the root of the TT, there is 'any/*****', and a full zip code is placed at the leaf of that TT. Taxonomy tree depth (TTD), plays a role in the usability of the published data.

5.4 Proposed Algorithm

Figure 1 represents the ADiffP algorithm. In the line-1, the algorithm generalizes the raw data set to its generalize form to add a layer of privacy to prevent data breaches. Taxonomy tree helps find the hierarchical relations between the actual attribute to its general form. The proposed algorithm then (line-2) groups the generalized data set based on the similarities of the predictor attributes, and taxonomy tree. In this stage in line-3, the algorithm recalculates the initial privacy budget based on the size of the group to add Laplace noise to that certain group. This process repeats until noise added to all groups of the generalized data set (line-4 to 8). As the proposed algorithm recalculate the privacy budget depending on the size of the group, we consider this procedure as an adaptive noise addition. As soon as the algorithm end up the noise addition process it merges all the sub-groups to form the anonymize differential private sanitize data set (line-9).

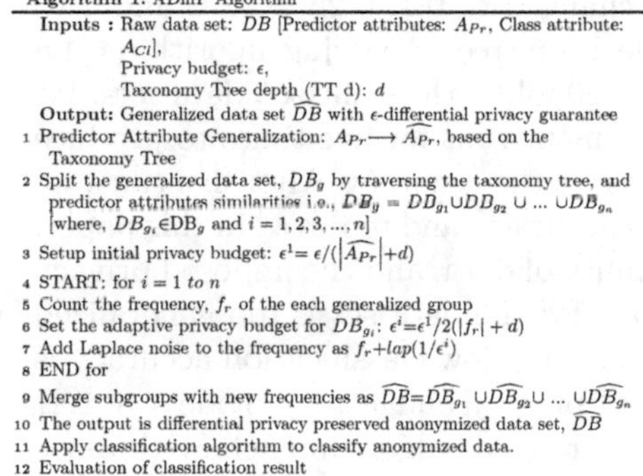

Algorithm 1: ADiffP Algorithm

Inputs : Raw data set: DB [Predictor attributes: A_{Pr}, Class attribute: A_{Cl}],
Privacy budget: ϵ,
Taxonomy Tree depth (TT d): d

Output: Generalized data set $\widehat{DB}$ with ϵ-differential privacy guarantee

1 Predictor Attribute Generalization: $A_{Pr} \longrightarrow \widehat{A_{Pr}}$, based on the Taxonomy Tree
2 Split the generalized data set, DB_g by traversing the taxonomy tree, and predictor attributes similarities i.e., $DB_g = DD_{g_1} \cup DD_{g_2} \cup \ldots \cup DB_{g_n}$ [where, $DB_{g_i} \in \mathrm{DB}_g$ and $i = 1, 2, 3, \ldots, n$]
3 Setup initial privacy budget: $\epsilon^1 = \epsilon / (\left|\widehat{A_{Pr}}\right| + d)$
4 START: for $i = 1$ *to* n
5 Count the frequency, f_r of the each generalized group
6 Set the adaptive privacy budget for DB_{g_i}: $\epsilon^i = \epsilon^1 / 2(|f_r| + d)$
7 Add Laplace noise to the frequency as $f_r + lap(1/\epsilon^i)$
8 END for
9 Merge subgroups with new frequencies as $\widehat{DB} = \widehat{DB}_{g_1} \cup \widehat{DB}_{g_2} \cup \ldots \cup \widehat{DB}_{g_n}$
10 The output is differential privacy preserved anonymized data set, $\widehat{DB}$
11 Apply classification algorithm to classify anonymized data.
12 Evaluation of classification result

Fig. 1. Proposed algorithm

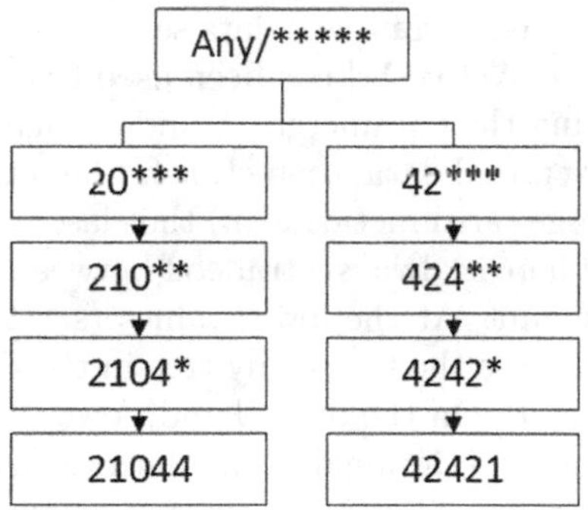

Fig. 2. Taxonomy tree of the zip code of two German Cities (Hamburg mid, and Velbert)

6 Data Sets

There are two different data sets, the Adult[1], and the Doctor's Bills data sets (DBDS)[2] are used to test the proposed algorithm for sanitizing and publishing secure data. Table 1 represents the details of the data sets.

[1] https://archive.ics.uci.edu/ml/datasets/Adult.
[2] http://madm.dfki.de/downloads-ds-doctor-bills.

Table 1. Data set descriptions

Data sets	Numerical attributes	Categorical attributes	Set-valued attributes	Class information
Adult	6	8	Not applicable	>50 K, ≤50 K
Doctor's Bills	3	3	1	>60, ≤60

Table 2. Classification accuracy of the Doctor's Bill data set (Left), and the Adult data set (right)

TTD	ϵ =0.1	ϵ =0.25	ϵ =0.5	ϵ =1	ϵ =2	ϵ =4
16	82.76	82.25	77.53	62.93	70.1	51.66
12	81.98	83.58	77.11	64.38	55.13	52.44
8	82.38	80.7	77.98	63.28	58.81	55.1
4	82.66	80.95	76.16	66.82	64.8	53.94
2	76.04	79.57	78.62	70.1	63.17	58.07

TTD	ϵ =0.1	ϵ =0.25	ϵ =0.5	ϵ =1	ϵ =2	ϵ =4
16	83.56	81.69	79.34	75.79	75.51	75.25
12	82.14	81.22	79.86	76.93	75.3	79.21
8	77.91	80.93	80.4	77.37	78.76	78.25
4	77.28	76.6	79.24	75.93	75.92	75.44
2	76.09	75.63	76.32	75.5	75.37	75.88

7 Results and Discussion

The sanitized, and published data set is evaluated to measure the usability in case of data classification, and associated re-identification risk. Table 2 (left and right), are representing the classification accuracy numerically, and the corresponding graphs are presented at Figs. 3, and 4. There are five sets of experiments completed at different values of taxonomy tree (TT) depths, $d = 2$, 4, 8, 12, and 16. For every TT depth d, values of ϵ are changed to 0.1, 0.25, 0.5, 1, and 2 to generate the sanitized data set. Then, the decision tree classifying algorithm C4.5 (J48 in Weka) [17] has been used to classify (10 folds) the sanitized data sets. By varying the parameters d, and ϵ, each experiment runs for five times to produce anonymized data, then classify them to measure the accuracy. After five runs, we average (arithmetic mean) the classification accuracy, and reported in this paper.

There is always a tradeoff between, usability of data, and the imposed privacy constraint. At the lower values (say 2 or 4) of d the data set is too generalized (please see the taxonomy tree in the Fig. 2), so, the low classification accuracy is expected. On the other hand, lower values of privacy budget, ϵ provide stronger privacy [18] in making the data secure. The proposed algorithm achieved above 83% of classification accuracy at the lowest value of ϵ = 0.1 with the higher values of d, for example 16, 12, and 8.

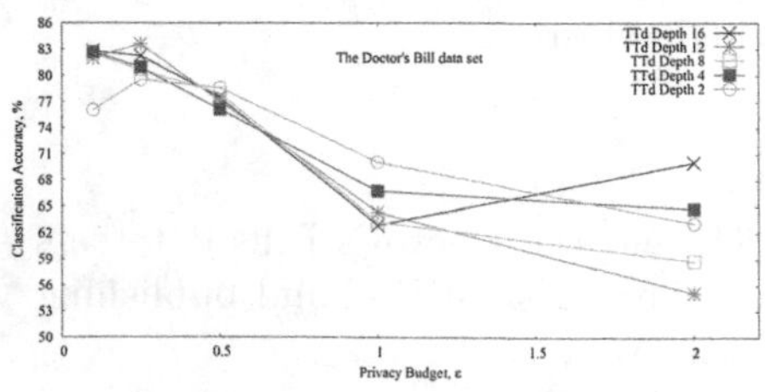

Fig. 3. Doctor's Bill data set

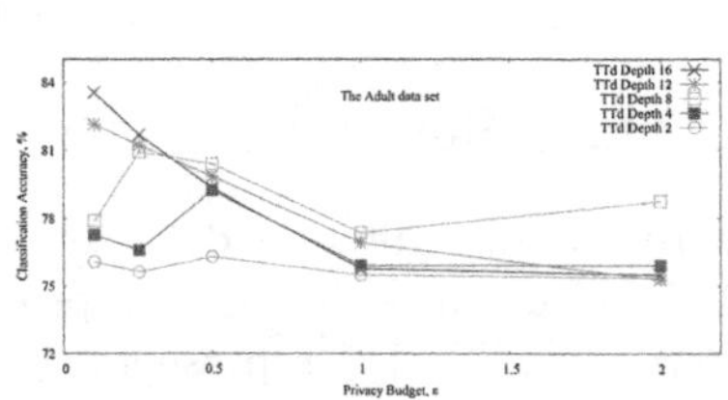

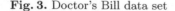

Fig. 4. The Adult data set

The performance of the proposed algorithm, ADiffP, has compared with five other anonymization algorithms: DiffGen [1], k-anonymity ($k = 5$), k-Map ($k = 5$), δ-Presence ($0.5 \leq \delta \leq 1.0$), and (e, d)-Differential Privacy ($e = 2, d = 1e - 6$) algorithms [19,20]. The implementations of those mentioned algorithms are adopted from the [1], and the ARX-Powerful Data Anonymization Tool [20]. In case of Decision Tree classifier, ADiffP algorithm showed better performance compared to five other algorithms. Figure 5 is presenting the comparison of the accuracy among ADiffP and five others algorithms for the Adult, and the Doctor's Bill data sets.

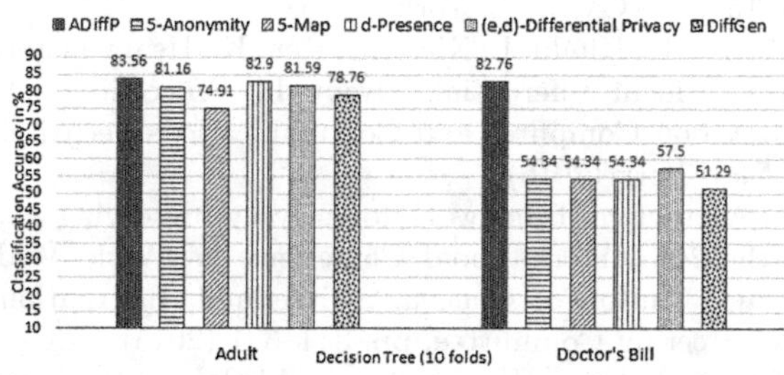

Fig. 5. Comparisons among proposed algorithm and five other algorithms

The published data sets are also tested with three different attack models [19,20] called Prosecutor, Journalist, and Marketer attacker models showing that the Adult data set has only 0.0001%, and the Doctor's Bill data set has only 0.002% risk of re-identification. The risk of the re-identification is very low, thus the published data is safe, and sanitized.

8 Conclusion

This research proposes a new algorithm called ADiffP that utilizes generalization, suppression techniques, and Laplace noise in an adaptive way for generating and publishing anonymized data set from a micro data set. Also, AdiffP ensures ϵ-Differential Privacy guarantee. While working with this algorithm, the Adult (benchmark) data set, and a new data set called Doctor's Bills data set, are used to perform experiments for testing, and evaluating the performance of the proposed algorithm. Experiments indicate that the proposed ADiffP algorithm is capable of publishing useful anonymized data set.

References

1. Mohammed, N., Chen, R., Fung, B.C., Yu, P.S.: Differentially private data release for data mining. In: Proceedings of the 17th ACM SIGKDD International Conference on Knowledge Discovery and Data Mining, KDD 2011, pp. 493–501. ACM, New York (2011)
2. Dwork, C., McSherry, F., Nissim, K., Smith, A.: Calibrating noise to sensitivity in private data analysis. In: Halevi, S., Rabin, T. (eds.) TCC 2006. LNCS, vol. 3876, pp. 265–284. Springer, Heidelberg (2006). doi:10.1007/11681878_14

3. Roth, A., Roughgarden, T.: Interactive privacy via the median mechanism. In: Proceedings of the Forty-Second ACM Symposium on Theory of Computing, STOC 2010, pp. 765–774. ACM, New York (2010)
4. Friedman, A., Schuster, A.: Data mining with differential privacy. In: Proceedings of the 16th ACM SIGKDD International Conference on Knowledge Discovery and Data Mining, KDD 2010, pp. 493–502. ACM, New York (2010)
5. Fung, B.C.M., Wang, K., Chen, R., Yu, P.S.: Privacy-preserving data publishing: a survey of recent developments. ACM Comput. Surv. **42**(4), 14:1–14:53 (2010)
6. Boyd, K., Lantz, E., Page, D.: Differential privacy for classifier evaluation. In: Proceedings of the 8th ACM Workshop on Artificial Intelligence and Security. AISec 2015, pp. 15–23. ACM, New York (2015)
7. Qin, Z., Yang, Y., Yu, T., Khalil, I., Xiao, X., Ren, K.: Heavy hitter estimation over set-valued data with local differential privacy. In: Proceedings of the 2016 ACM SIGSAC Conference on Computer and Communications Security. CCS 2016, pp. 192–203. ACM, New York (2016)
8. Fan, L., Jin, H.: A practical framework for privacy-preserving data analytics. In: Proceedings of the 24th International Conference on World Wide Web, WWW 2015, Republic and Canton of Geneva, Switzerland. International World Wide Web Conferences Steering Committee, pp. 311–321 (2015)
9. Chen, B.C., Kifer, D., LeFevre, K., Machanavajjhala, A.: Privacy-preserving data publishing. Found. Trends Databases **2**(1–2), 1–167 (2009)
10. Dwork, C., Roth, A.: The algorithmic foundations of differential privacy. Found. Trends Theor. Comput. Sci. **9**(3–4), 211–407 (2014)
11. Wu, L., He, H., Zaïane, O.R.: Utility enhancement for privacy preserving health data publishing. In: Motoda, H., Wu, Z., Cao, L., Zaiane, O., Yao, M., Wang, W. (eds.) ADMA 2013. LNCS (LNAI), vol. 8347, pp. 311–322. Springer, Heidelberg (2013). doi:10.1007/978-3-642-53917-6_28
12. Vaidya, J., Shafiq, B., Basu, A., Hong, Y.: Differentially private naive bayes classification. In: Proceedings of the 2013 IEEE/WIC/ACM International Joint Conferences on Web Intelligence (WI) and Intelligent Agent Technologies (IAT), vol. 01, WI-IAT 2013, pp. 571–576. IEEE Computer Society, Washington, DC (2013)
13. Chawla, S., Dwork, C., McSherry, F., Talwar, K.: On privacy-preserving histograms. CoRR abs/1207.1371 (2012)
14. Zaman, A., Obimbo, C.: Privacy preserving data publishing: a classification perspective. Int. J. Adv. Comput. Sci. Appl. (IJACSA) **5**(9), 129–134 (2014)
15. Dwork, C.: A firm foundation for private data analysis. Commun. ACM **54**(1), 86–95 (2011)
16. Lee, J., Clifton, C.: Differential identifiability. In: Proceedings of the 18th ACM SIGKDD International Conference on Knowledge Discovery and Data Mining. KDD 2012, pp. 1041–1049. ACM, New York (2012)
17. Smith, T.C., Frank, E.: In: Introducing Machine Learning Concepts with WEKA. Springer New York, New York (2016)
18. Hsu, J., Gaboardi, M., Haeberlen, A., Khanna, S., Narayan, A., Pierce, B.C., Roth, A.: Differential privacy: an economic method for choosing epsilon. CoRR abs/1402.3329 (2014)
19. Fabian, P., Florian, K., Ronald, L., Klaus, A.K.: Arx - a comprehensive tool for anonymizing biomedical data. In: Proceedings of the AMIA 2014 Annual Symposium, Washington D.C., USA, pp. 984–993, November 2014
20. Fabian, P., Florian, K., Contributors: ARX - powerful data anonymization tool, June 2016. http://arx.deidentifier.org/

Reflexive Regular Equivalence for Bipartite Data

Aaron Gerow[1(✉)], Mingyang Zhou[2], Stan Matwin[1], and Feng Shi[3]

[1] Faculty of Computer Science, Dalhousie University, Halifax, NS, Canada
gerow@dal.ca

[2] Department of Computer Science, University of Chicago, Chicago, USA

[3] University of North Carolina, Chapel Hill, NS, USA

Abstract. Bipartite data is common in data engineering and brings unique challenges, particularly when it comes to clustering tasks that impose strong structural assumptions. This work presents an unsupervised method for assessing similarity in bipartite data. The method is based on *regular equivalence* in graphs and uses spectral properties of a bipartite adjacency matrix to estimate similarity in both dimensions. The method is reflexive in that similarity in one dimension informs similarity in the other. The method also uses local graph transitivities, a contribution governed by its only free parameter. Reflexive regular equivalence can be used to validate assumptions of co-similarity, which are required but often untested in co-clustering analyses. The method is robust to noise and asymmetric data, making it particularly suited for cluster analysis and recommendation in data of unknown structure. (An extended preprint of this paper is available at arxiv.org/abs/1702.04956.)

In bipartite data, co-similarity is the notion that similarity in one dimension is matched by similarity in some other dimension. Such data occurs in a many areas: text mining, gene expression networks, consumer co-purchasing data and social affiliation. In bipartite analyses, co-clustering is an increasingly prominent technique in a range of applications [11], but has strong co-similarity assumptions. One example of co-similar structure is in text analysis where similar words appear in similar documents, where there is assumed to be a permutation of the word-document co-occurrence matrix that exposes co-similarity among words and documents [4]. The work here describes a way to *assess* co-similarity using regular equivalence [8] with a reflexive conception of similarity that accommodates nodes' (data-points) local structures. This assessment is a kind of precondition for co-clustering: if there is little co-similarity, co-clustering will yield a poor clustering solution. Assessing co-similarity will produce similarity in one dimension to expose potential clustering without requiring it across dimensions. This is particularly useful for asymmetric data when a non-clustered dimension informs, but does not reciprocate clustering in the other. Whereas as co-clustering finds clusters across dimensions, our method provides a decoupled solution in each mode. Reflexive regular equivalence is able to quantify how much one dimension informs similarity in the other. Additionally, our results show that by incorporating local structures, it can better overcome noise and accommodate asymmetry.

M. Mouhoub and P. Langlais (Eds.): Canadian AI 2017, LNAI 10233, pp. 71–77, 2017.
DOI: 10.1007/978-3-319-57351-9_9

Background. Measuring co-similarity amounts to calculating similarity in two dimensions. In a graph setting, this can be done with bipartite generalizations of regular equivalence [1,5], which measure similarity based on the similarity of neighboring nodes. Bipartite regular equivalence makes sense of *within-dimension regularity* and *between-dimension structure.* As we will see, allowing the inter-dimensional structure to be "reflexive", as defined below, greatly helps assess co-similarity. Specifically, we conceive of bipartite data as a two-mode network. In simple networks, vertex similarity can be measured using pairwise metrics like the Jaccard index, the cosine of a pair's connectivity patterns, their correlation or simply the overlap of neighbors. Recent efforts have sought to account for structure beyond nodes' immediate neighbors. *Regular equivalence* proposes that nodes are similar to the extent their neighbors are similar [8], a method common in social network analysis [7].

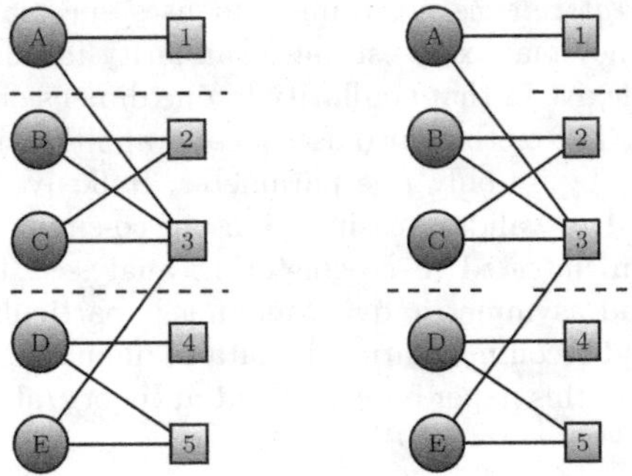

Fig. 1. With the same network (left; a) a biclustering solution yields partitions that group vertices in both modes. On the right (b) is a hypothetical grouping based on similarities produced by reflexive regular equivalence; there may not be a mapping between clusters in each mode and groupings are exposed by similarity, not by partitioning.

In a social setting, co-similarity was formalized by Ronald Breiger in 1974 where similar people were found to participate in similar groups [2]. With the adjacency structure, A, of *people* × *groups*, similarity can be measured as $S_{people} = AA^{\mathsf{T}}$ and $S_{groups} = A^{\mathsf{T}}A$. Such multi-modal conceptions of social structures are now common in models of social search and recommendation [6,10]. Our method extends regular equivalence and Breiger's notion of co-similarity. Crucially, it considers structural equivalence by adding contributions from local transitivity – two nodes are similar if their neighbors are similar within and across dimensions. Our goal is not to find partitions that optimally group nodes across dimensions, but to measure similarity in each mode of the data using information from the other. Only by extension, may any clustered structure be revealed in the data. Figure 1 depicts a bipartite network and hypothetical co-clustering solution (a) and a potential solution based on reflexive regular equivalence (b). Though different from our method, co-clustering algorithms have much in common with reflexive regular equivalence. Co-clustering algorithms yield partitions across modes that group self-similar rows with self-similar columns, and assume co-similarity just as clustering assumes similarity. Reflexive equivalence assess co-similarity, which *may* justify a co-clustering strategy. For examples of co-clustering algorithms that implement related notions of similarity see [3,9,12].

Method. Our reflexive equivalence method is an unsupervised approach to measuring vertex similarity in a bipartite network. This notion is equivalent to a pairwise similarity metric that operates on row- and column-vectors of the adjacency structure in bimodal data. Bipartite networks are equivalent to what are normally treated as rows and columns in a matrix. Our method iterates between each mode incorporating information from the other. There is no restriction to binary-valued data: edges may be weighted.

Let G be a bipartite graph with two sets of nodes, V and V' and A be the adjacency matrix in which $A_{ij} > 0$ represents how strongly $i \in V$ is connected to $j \in V'$. Let S be a square $|V|$ matrix where entry S_{ij} is the similarity between i and j in V, and S' be a square $|V'|$ matrix where S'_{ij} is the similarity between i and j in V'. Assuming the similarity of i and j in one mode is informed by similarity between neighbors of i and any neighbor of j in the other mode, then

$$S_{ij} = \sum_k \sum_l A_{ik} A_{jl} S'_{kl}, \tag{1}$$

$$S'_{ij} = \sum_k \sum_l A_{ki} A_{lj} S_{kl}, \tag{2}$$

This provides a procedure for inferring similar nodes in the adjacency matrix. Starting from randomly initialized S and S', Eqs. 1 and 2 can be applied iteratively until convergence of $\|S\|_{\mathsf{F}}$ and $\|S'\|_{\mathsf{F}}$. This formulation, however, treats all neighbors equally, regardless of their structural importance to the pair of nodes in question. Thus, we weight similarity between common neighbors more than non-common neighbors. Denoting neighbors of i and j by Γ_i and Γ_j respectively, we define this similarity as follows:

$$S_{ij} = (1-\alpha)\Big[\sum_{k\in(\Gamma_i-\Gamma_i\cap\Gamma_j)} \sum_{l\in\Gamma_j} S'_{kl} + \sum_{k\in\Gamma_i\cap\Gamma_j} \sum_{l\in(\Gamma_j-\Gamma_i\cap\Gamma_j)} S'_{kl}\Big] + \sum_{k\in\Gamma_i\cap\Gamma_j} \sum_{l\in\Gamma_i\cap\Gamma_j} S'_{kl},$$

$$S'_{ij} = (1-\alpha)\Big[\sum_{k\in(\Gamma_i-\Gamma_i\cap\Gamma_j)} \sum_{l\in\Gamma_j} S_{kl} + \sum_{k\in\Gamma_i\cap\Gamma_j} \sum_{l\in(\Gamma_j-\Gamma_i\cap\Gamma_j)} S_{kl}\Big] + \sum_{k\in\Gamma_i\cap\Gamma_j} \sum_{l\in\Gamma_i\cap\Gamma_j} S_{kl}.$$

This combines structural equivalence, regular equivalence and reflexivity into a single model. A parameter α balances the contribution of non-common and common neighbors. Rearranging the terms, the equations can be rewritten as

$$S_{ij} = (1-\alpha)\sum_k \sum_l A_{ik} A_{jl} S'_{kl} + \alpha \sum_k \sum_l A_{ik} A_{jk} A_{il} A_{jl} S'_{kl}, \tag{3}$$

$$S'_{ij} = (1-\alpha)\sum_k \sum_l A_{ki} A_{lj} S_{kl} + \alpha \sum_k \sum_l A_{ki} A_{kj} A_{li} A_{lj} S_{kl}, \tag{4}$$

or in matrix form:

$$S = (1-\alpha)AS'A^{\mathsf{T}} + \alpha(A \otimes A^{\mathsf{T}}) \cdot S' \cdot (A \otimes A^{\mathsf{T}})^{\mathsf{T}}, \tag{5}$$

$$S' = (1-\alpha)A^{\mathsf{T}}SA + \alpha(A^{\mathsf{T}} \otimes A) \cdot S \cdot (A^{\mathsf{T}} \otimes A)^{\mathsf{T}}, \tag{6}$$

where $(\cdot)$ is the conventional inner product defined in tensor algebra. Equations 5 and 6 compute reflexivity between the two dimensions and the effect of local structure is controlled by α. When $\alpha = 0$, the method is a bipartite form of regular equivalence. As α increases, similarity between common neighbors plays a larger role. A is normalized prior to applying the algorithm, and S and S' are normalized after every iteration by their L_1-, L_2- or L_∞-vector norm.

Results. We evaluated the method on data with known structure. A set of semi-random $n \times m$ versions of A were generated with diagonal blocks of random sizes: the resulting similarity matrices should have diagonal blocks proportional to the row- and column-wise block sizes in A. The test is to run the algorithm on randomly permuted data, $\hat{A}$, after which if we apply the original ordering of A to $\hat{S}$ and $\hat{S}'$. The solution is then assessed as

$$\mu = \frac{1}{2}\|S - \hat{S}\|_{\mathsf{F}}\frac{1}{|S|} + \frac{1}{2}\|S' - \hat{S}'\|_{\mathsf{F}}\frac{1}{|S'|}. \tag{7}$$

Here, μ is simply the mean difference between results on A and $\hat{A}$, and in the perfect case will be 0. We compare reflexive similarity to three pairwise metrics operating on the rows and columns of A. The results show that reflexive variants perform marginally better (Fig. 2b); α had no effect, which is expected given all node interactions are purely local.

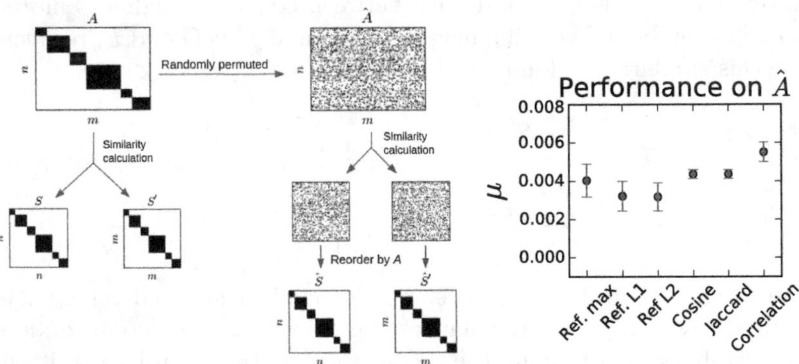

Fig. 2. (a; left) Similarity of $\hat{A}$ should produce results similar to those computed for A. (b; right) Performance (μ; lower is better) on $\hat{A}$ using variants of reflexive similarity method. Error-bars are ± 2 s.e. of the mean over ten versions of A.

Robustness to Noise. Because real-world data is often noisy, we evaluated the method with noise added to A of the form $\mathcal{N}(0, \sigma)$ to produce $\tilde{A}$. Note that adding noise breaks the element-wise symmetry of A but the underlying block-structure remains symmetric. Figure 3 shows results with respect to noise, normalization variant and α. With little noise, the L_∞-norm variant outperforms other methods when $\alpha > 0.5$. As noise is increased, pairwise metrics perform worse, as do the reflexive methods with $\alpha = 0$. This confirms that our method is well-suited to finding co-similarity structure in both dimensions of noisy data where the L_∞ variant with $\alpha = 1$ performs best.

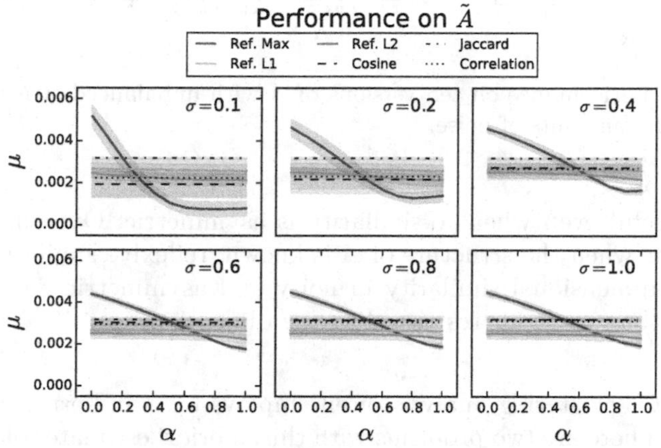

Fig. 3. Performance (μ; lower is better) with respect to noise, σ, in $\tilde{A}$ for different values of α. Error-bands are ± 2 s.e. of the mean over ten versions of A.

Unbalanced Co-similarity. Because clusters exposed by similarity in S and S' are not coupled as they are in co-clustering tasks, reflexive similarity is able to find unbalanced co-similarity structure. With this kind of data, the reflexive method should produce similarity matrices with different structure. For this task, another set of semi-random versions of A were generated with random unbalanced block structure, which were then randomly permuted to get $\hat{A}$. Results on $\hat{A}$ were compared to results from A. Figure 4a shows the results on variants of reflexive regular equivalence and the pairwise metrics. Results show that all variants of reflexive similarity outperform the pairwise metrics, but that neither normalization choice nor α make significant difference.

The parameter α is crucial to our method's ability to overcome noise in symmetric data. The same task was run on asymmetric data with added noise. Figure 4b shows performance with different noise levels. The results show that after adding a small amount of noise, the reflexive variants significantly outperform pairwise metrics. In particular, for low levels of noise, the L_∞-norm variant performs best, but for higher levels ($\sigma > 0.2$) the L_1- and L_2-norms are better. In all variants, higher values of α yield better performance. This suggests local

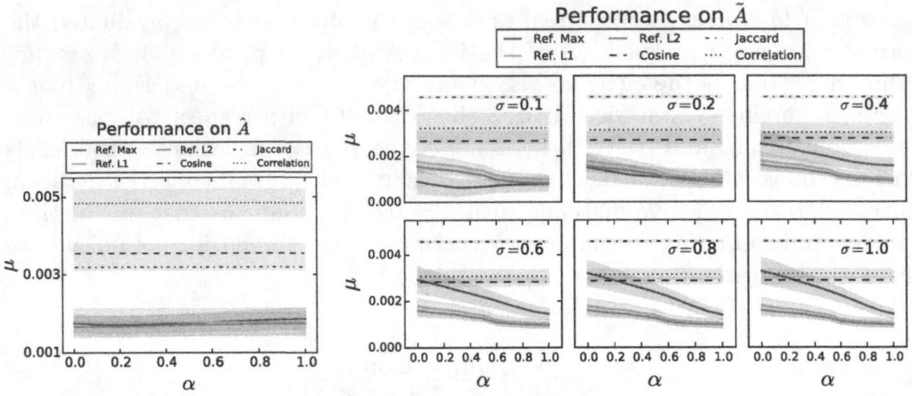

Fig. 4. (a; left) Performance on ten versions of $\hat{A}$ with unbalanced structure and, (b; left) with varying amounts of noise.

structure is useful even when co-similarity is asymmetric. Overall, the evaluations show that when the structure of A is known, reflexive similarity is able to leverage inter-dimensional similarity in noisy and asymmetric data to provide better results than methods restricted to one dimension.

Discussion. Co-clustering analysis often employs trial-and-error when assessing similarity. There are two problems with this: a priori estimates of the number of clusters can be hard to make, and clusters may not be coupled across dimension. Reflexive regular equivalence offers a way to attenuate inter-dimensional structure and local transitivities in similarity calculations. The results show this is particularly important in noisy data. The method also offers a way to validate co-similarity assumptions: if the same permutation for S and S' exposes block structure in each, then A is co-similar. By varying α, one can enhance or reduce the contribution of local equivalence, essentially backing off to spectral similarity. In this way, our method offers a way to measure co-similarity across dimensions, helping confirm assumptions of co-similarity.

References

1. Borgatti, S.P.: 2-mode concepts in social network analysis. In: Encyclopedia of Complexity and System Science, vol. 6 (2009)
2. Breiger, R.L.: The duality of persons and groups. Soc. Forces **53**, 181–190 (1974)
3. Codocedo, V., Napoli, A.: Lattice-based biclustering using partition pattern structures. In: ECAI 2014, pp. 213–218 (2014)
4. Dhillon, I.S.: Co-clustering documents and words using bipartite spectral graph partitioning. In: Proceedings of the SIGKDD 2001, pp. 269–274 (2001)
5. Doreian, P., Batagelj, V., Ferligoj, A.: Generalized blockmodeling of two-mode network data. Soc. Netw. **26**(1), 29–53 (2004)

6. Gerow, A., Lou, B., Duede, E., Evans, J.: Proposing ties in a dense hypergraph of academics. Social Informatics. LNCS, vol. 9471, pp. 209–226. Springer, Cham (2015). doi:10.1007/978-3-319-27433-1_15
7. Gnatyshak, D., Ignatov, D.I., Semenov, A., Poelmans, J.: Gaining insight in social networks with biclustering and triclustering. In: Aseeva, N., Babkin, E., Kozyrev, O. (eds.) BIR 2012. LNBIP, vol. 128, pp. 162–171. Springer, Heidelberg (2012). doi:10.1007/978-3-642-33281-4_13
8. Leicht, E.A., Holme, P., Newman, M.E.: Vertex similarity in networks. Phys. Rev. E **73**(2), 026120 (2006)
9. Pensa, R.G., Ienco, D., Meo, R.: Hierarchical co-clustering: off-line and incremental approaches. Data Min. Knowl. Disc. **28**(1), 31–64 (2014)
10. Shi, F., Foster, J.G., Evans, J.A.: Weaving the fabric of science: dynamic network models of science's unfolding structure. Soc. Netw. **43**, 73–85 (2015)
11. Tanay, A., Sharan, R., Shamir, R.: Biclustering algorithms: a survey. Handb. Comput. Mol. Biol. **9**(1–20), 122–124 (2005)
12. Teng, L., Tan, K.: Finding combinatorial histone code by semi-supervised biclustering. BMC Genom. **13**(1), 301 (2012)

Investigating Citation Linkage with Machine Learning

Hospice Houngbo(✉) and Robert E. Mercer

Department of Computer Science, The University of Western Ontario, London, ON, Canada
hhoungbo@uwo.ca, mercer@csd.uwo.ca

Abstract. Scientists face the challenge of having to navigate the deluge of information contained in the articles published in their domain of research. Tools such as citation indexes link papers but do not indicate the passage in the paper that is being cited. In this study, we report our early attempts to design a framework for finding sentences that are cited in a given article, a task we have called *citation linkage*. We first discuss our building of a corpus annotated by domain experts. Then, with datasets consisting of all possible citing sentence-candidate sentence pairs, some deemed not to be cited and others deemed to be by the annotators with confidence ratings 1 to 5 (lowest to highest), we have built regression models whose outputs are used to predict the degree of similarity for any pair of sentences in a target paper. Even though the Pearson correlation coefficient between the predicted values and the expected values is low (0.2759 with a linear regression model), we have shown that the citation linkage goal can be achieved. When we use the learning models to rank the predicted scores for sentences in a target article, 18 papers out of 22 have at least one sentence ranked in the top k positions (k being the number of relevant sentences per paper) and 10 papers (45%) have their Normalized Discounted Cumulative Gain (NDCG) scores greater than 71% and Precision greater than 44%. The mean average NDCG is 47% and the Mean Average Precision is 29% over all the papers.

1 Introduction

An academic research paper is distinguished by it being part of a research mosaic. In research literature, the writer is obliged to place the research contribution of the current article in its research context. The method to achieve this placement is to refer explicitly to other research works. References to other works are then manifested as *citations*. Citations are thus an important instrument for connecting the ideas in the research literature.

This importance has led to a variety of tools to assist researchers. For instance, citation indexes, an idea conceived in 1964 [6], contain a subset of all of the citations in research articles. More recently, methods have been proposed to classify the purpose of a citation [7,15]. Potential uses of citations include

M. Mouhoub and P. Langlais (Eds.): Canadian AI 2017, LNAI 10233, pp. 78–83, 2017.
DOI: 10.1007/978-3-319-57351-9_10

multiple article summarization [13] and the tracking of scientific argumentation [12] across multiple papers. Citations, when used in science research papers, cite papers, so some of the more sophisticated uses of citations are not immediately realizable because of the coarse granularity of the citation itself. Being able to extract this span of text in the referenced article which is significantly smaller than a complete paper, a paragraph or a sentence or a set of sentences, say, would be beneficial for some of the more complex applications mentioned above.

This work aims at investigating how to determine the target sentences that citation sentences in science research papers refer to in a given cited paper. We call this operation *citation linkage* and believe that this is a very practical problem that can be solved using machine learning and information retrieval techniques. The contribution of our work in this paper is twofold. We have provided the Computational Linguistics research community with an initial corpus of 22 biochemical research articles annotated with citation target sentences by two graduate students with biochemistry knowledge. We have also investigated machine learning techniques for text matching applied to the citation linkage context. We test with two regression models using a feature pool comprising many similarity measures to predict the degree of similarity between citation sentences and their candidate target sentences. The rest of this paper is organized as follows. The next section reviews some related works. In Sect. 3, a detailed methodology of the citation linkage task is presented. In Sect. 4, the results are described. We conclude the paper by a summary and directions for future work.

2 Related Work

Many state-of-the-art text similarity detection techniques use linear combinations of text similarity measures. For instance, two corpus-based and six knowledge-based measures were tested in [11]. A method for measuring the semantic similarity between sentences or very short texts, based on semantic and word order information was presented in [10]. [9] used string similarity and semantic word similarity, and common-word order similarity. The authors of [1] used a hybrid method that combines corpus-based semantic relatedness measures over the whole sentence along with the knowledge-based semantic similarity scores that were obtained for the words that belong to the same syntactic role labels in both sentences. Furthermore, a promising correlation between manual and automatic similarity results were achieved in [3] by combining similarity between sentences using N-gram based similarity, and the similarity between concepts in the two sentences using a concept similarity measure and WordNet. Also, the similarity detection system called UKP [2] used string similarity, semantic similarity, text expansion mechanisms and measures related to structure and style.

3 Methodology

We discuss the following contributions below: the construction of a corpus, the development of a machine learning model and the ranking of chosen candidate sentences by the model to see how they compare with the annotation.

3.1 Building of a Citation Linkage Corpus

The text in which a citation occurs can span one or more sentences in the paper. In this study, this span is limited to one sentence, and the linkage task is assumed to be a sentence-level matching operation. An expert reads a citation sentence taken in isolation and determines the candidate sentences that have been cited in a reference paper. After candidate sentences are selected, the expert gives a confidence rating for each candidate sentence, 1 (lowest) to 5 (strongest).

We have chosen the papers to annotate from the open-access BioMed Central's research articles corpus in such a way that they belong to a citation network that shows the links between cited and citing papers. Annotators' feedback has been collected. It indicates that candidate sentences were chosen based on surface level similarity as well as non-explicit factors such as background domain knowledge and inference from the surrounding text.

We have limited the current research to the biomedical domain (experimental biochemistry, in particular) and our final corpus is curated with papers from this domain. We also chose to work only with citing sentences that referred to experimental methodology since we hypothesized that the language in the cited sentences would be less linguistically varying. Starting with 26 papers, the final corpus is comprised of 22 papers. This resulted after an analysis and removal of four papers that have non-zero similarity scores ranging from 1 to 2. They seemed to be review papers rather than descriptions of experiments.

The final 22 papers have a total of 4258 sentences and 22 citations. These citation-sentence pairs were annotated with the following ratings (0 meaning the annotator indicated that the sentence is not being cited by the citation, and numbers 1–5 giving the annotators' confidence that the citation is citing the sentence). These statistics are given as triples: (rating, number of candidate sentences with that confidence rating, proportion of total sentences): (0, 4049, 95%), (1, 44, 1.33%), (2, 42, 0.98%), (3, 42, 0.98%), (4, 48, 1.13%), (5, 33, 0.77%).

3.2 Building Learning Models

We test our hypothesis with a multi-linear regression and SVM regression with the linear kernel by combining the scores of similarity measures between pairs of sentences. These pairs comprise the citation sentences and individual sentences from the target paper. The resulting feature vector is assigned the rating value given by the annotator. We used the implementation of both algorithms provided by the open-source Java-based machine-learning library Weka 3.7 [8].

3.3 Feature Pool

We use the following three types of similarity measures for features. The first type are distance and term-based features: the number of non-stop words in common between two sets, JaroWinkler, edit distance, longest common sequence of characters, cosine of angle between texts represented as vectors, ROUGEW, ROUGES, ROUGEN, Jaccard, and QGram. The second set are knowledge-based features using WordNet to measure word-to-word similarity: Lin's method, Resnik's method, and a path-based method. The third group is a corpus-based feature using the TASA corpus LSA-based word-to-word similarity model [14].

All the features are combined into three sets: distance and term-based features only (System 1), distance and term-based and knowledge-based features (System 2), all features (System 3).

4 Results and Discussion

We use five datasets, one with the six rating categories 0-1-2-3-4-5, and four others built by combining the ratings in the following patterns: 0-1-2-3-45, 0-12-3-45, 0-123-45, and 0-12345. Evaluation is performed by computing the Pearson correlation coefficient between the annotators' ratings and the scores produced by the machine learning algorithms, SVM Regression and Linear Regression.

Table 1. Evaluation of the five datasets

Data	System 1		System 2		System 3	
	SVMReg (r)	LinearReg (r)	SVMReg (r)	LinearReg (r)	SVMReg (r)	LinearReg (r)
0-1-2-3-4-5	0.2016	0.27	0.1862	0.2652	0.2183	0.2759
0-1-2-3-45	0.2136	0.2658	0.1852	0.2614	0.2018	0.2737
0-12-3-45	0.1926	0.2667	0.1816	0.2651	0.1613	**0.2762**
0-123-45	0.1521	0.2443	0.1968	0.2426	0.1837	0.2711
0-12345	0.1521	0.2443	0.1968	0.2426	0.1848	0.2442

Table 1 shows that the best results are obtained with Linear Regression when distance-based, knowledge- based, and corpus-based features are used (System 3). Also, in this column dataset combinations with the patterns 0-1-2-3-4-5, 0-1-2-3-45, 0-12-3-45, 0-123-45 show similar performances (maximum value of 0.2762 (low correlation)). The citing sentences chosen in this study are sentences discussing (experimental) Methods. When considering only the candidate sentences that can be categorized as Method sentences, we are able to improve the best Pearson correlation coefficient to 0.4217 (medium correlation) for System 3.

Because the linear regression model using System 3 features performed the best, we chose that model as the ranking algorithm for the linkage operation. In order to rank the sentences in a target paper, we performed a Leave-One-Out cross validation by building a learning model with 21 papers. The resulting model is then used to predict the scores for the citation-sentence pairs in the target paper. To determine the effectiveness of the result, we compare the ranked scores with the ratings given to the candidate sentences by the annotators. Two evaluation metrics are used: the Normalized Discounted Cumulative Gain (NDCG) score at top k, and the precision at top k score. The mean average NDCG is 0.46740 and the mean average precision is 0.2949 for the 22 papers.

Most of the features used to build the learning models rely on word overlap techniques or some of their variants in the computation of the similarity scores between citation sentences and their targets. We noticed in our results that fewer sentences rated 5 and 4 have been rated as a 0 compared to those rated 3, 2 and 1. However, only 51% and 46% of the 5 s and 4 s are found, suggesting that there is still room for improvement. Annotator's comments suggest that higher rated candidate sentences share common surface level information with citation sentences. We might expect citation linkage to be more straightforward in many of such cases. This may also suggest that the 1 s, 2 s, and 3 s may also require biochemical knowledge and more background information for the linkage to be effective.

The results that we have obtained compare favourably with previous works that match citation sentences and related cited papers. In [5], an attempt to match citation text and cited spans in biomedical literature proved to be a difficult task with limited performance. In that work, a matching candidate can be formed by more than one sentence and relevant spans can overlap. Their best performing system achieved only 0.224 precision. However, the authors reported promising results with query reduction to noun phrases and UMLS expansion. A comparison with our results suggests that citation sentence reformulation might be of great value in most cases. However, the current study can only partially be compared to [5] as they limit their work to only binary relevance. Also [4], uses similar techniques for citation-based summarization of biomedical literature and shows that such a task is difficult compared to regular text retrieval tasks.

5 Conclusions and Future Work

In this study we have shown that the matching operation between citation sentences and cited sentences can be reasonably performed. We have presented the citation linkage problem as a machine learning task and showed that a number of higher rated target sentences can be matched using linear regression models. This study has focused on sentence-to-sentence matching, because most text applications are primarily concerned with individual sentence units. However a citation context can span many sentences and consequently, the target text can comprise more than one sentence.

Acknowledgements. Support for this work was provided through a Natural Sciences and Engineering Research Council of Canada (NSERC) Discovery Grant to Robert E. Mercer.

References

1. Aggarwal, N., Asooja, K., Buitelaar, P.: DERI&UPM: pushing corpus based relatedness to similarity: shared task system description. In: Proceedings of the First Joint Conference on Lexical and Computational Semantics (Volume 2: Proceedings of the Sixth International Workshop on Semantic Evaluation), pp. 643–647. Association for Computational Linguistics (2012)

2. Bär, D., Biemann, C., Gurevych, I., Zesch, T.: UKP: computing semantic textual similarity by combining multiple content similarity measures. In: Proceedings of the First Joint Conference on Lexical and Computational Semantics (Volume 2: Proceedings of the Sixth International Workshop on Semantic Evaluation), pp. 435–440. Association for Computational Linguistics (2012)
3. Buscaldi, D., Tournier, R., Aussenac-Gilles, N., Mothe, J.: IRIT: textual similarity combining conceptual similarity with an n-gram comparison method. In: Proceedings of the First Joint Conference on Lexical and Computational Semantics (Volume 2: Proceedings of the Sixth International Workshop on Semantic Evaluation), pp. 552–556. Association for Computational Linguistics (2012)
4. Cohan, A., Soldaini, L.: Towards citation-based summarization of biomedical literature. In: Proceedings of the Text Analysis Conference (TAC 2014) (2014)
5. Cohan, A., Soldaini, L., Goharian, N.: Matching citation text and cited spans in biomedical literature: a search-oriented approach. In: Human Language Technologies: The 2015 Annual Conference of the North American Chapter of the ACL (NAACL HLT 2015) (2015)
6. Garfield, E.: Science citation index—a new dimension in indexing. Science **144**(3619), 649–654 (1964)
7. Garzone, M., Mercer, R.E.: Towards an automated citation classifier. In: Hamilton, H.J. (ed.) AI 2000. LNCS (LNAI), vol. 1822, pp. 337–346. Springer, Heidelberg (2000). doi:10.1007/3-540-45486-1_28
8. Hall, M., Frank, E., Holmes, G., Pfahringer, B., Reutemann, P., Witten, I.H.: The WEKA data mining software: an update. ACM SIGKDD Explor. Newslett. **11**(1), 10–18 (2009)
9. Islam, A., Inkpen, D.: Semantic text similarity using corpus-based word similarity and string similarity. ACM Trans. Knowl. Discov. Data **2**(2), Article No. 10 (2008)
10. Li, Y., McLean, D., Bandar, Z.A., O'Shea, J.D., Crockett, K.: Sentence similarity based on semantic nets and corpus statistics. IEEE Trans. Knowl. Data Eng. **18**(8), 1138–1150 (2006)
11. Mihalcea, R., Corley, C., Strapparava, C.: Corpus-based and knowledge-based measures of text semantic similarity. In: Proceedings of the 21st National Conference on Artificial Intelligence - Volume 1, AAAI 2006, pp. 775–780. AAAI Press (2006)
12. Palau, R.M., Moens, M.F.: Argumentation mining: the detection, classification and structure of arguments in text. In: Proceedings of the 12th International Conference on Artificial Intelligence and Law, pp. 98–107. ACM (2009)
13. Radev, D.R., Jing, H., Budzikowska, M.: Centroid-based summarization of multiple documents: sentence extraction, utility-based evaluation, and user studies. In: Proceedings of the 2000 NAACL-ANLP Workshop on Automatic Summarization, pp. 21–30. Association for Computational Linguistics (2000)
14. Stefuanescu, D., Banjade, R., Rus, V.: Latent semantic analysis models on Wikipedia and TASA. In: Language Resources Evaluation Conference (LREC) (2014)
15. Teufel, S., Siddharthan, A., Tidhar, D.: Automatic classification of citation function. In: Proceedings of the 2006 Conference on Empirical Methods in Natural Language Processing (EMNLP 2006), pp. 103–110. Association for Computational Linguistics (2006)

Classification of Imbalanced Auction Fraud Data

Swati Ganguly and Samira Sadaoui(✉)

University of Regina, Regina, Canada
sadaouis@uregina.ca

Abstract. Online auctioning has attracted serious fraud given the huge amount of money involved and anonymity of users. In the auction fraud detection domain, the class imbalance, which means less fraud instances are present in bidding transactions, negatively impacts the classification performance because the latter is biased towards the majority class i.e. normal bidding behavior. The best-designed approach to handle the imbalanced learning problem is data sampling that was found to improve the classification efficiency. In this study, we utilize a hybrid method of data over-sampling and under-sampling to be more effective in addressing the issue of highly imbalanced auction fraud datasets. We deploy a set of well-known binary classifiers to understand how the class imbalance affects the classification results. We choose the most relevant performance metrics to deal with both imbalanced data and fraud bidding data.

Keywords: In-Auction Fraud · Shill bidding · Imbalanced fraud data · Data sampling · Binary classification · Performance metrics

1 Introduction

The e-auction industry has greatly encouraged the buying and selling of goods and services. This sector, which involves million of dollars, makes it however very attractive to fraudsters. The scope of criminal activities ranges from selling illegitimate products to inflating the price of products to non-payment of delivered products. As per the Internet Crime Complaint Center, auction fraud is one of the most frequently reported cybercrimes. It is very difficult to detect fraud happening during the bidding process that is In-Auction Fraud (IAF), such as shill bidding, bid shielding and bidder collusion. Shill bidding, which leads to money loss for the winner of an auction, is the hardest IAF to detect due to its similarity to usual bidding behavior. According to numerous empirical studies being done over the years in detecting shill bidding in commercial auctions [Ford2012, Nikitkov2015, Sadaoui2016], this fraud is very common. Researchers examined shill activities along with the history of users to develop efficient fraud detection systems [Ford2012, Sadaoui2016]. A successful detection of IAF requires two important aspects: (1) dealing with the tremendous amount of information about bidders, sellers and auctions. In auction sites, hundreds of auctions operate simultaneously; (2) learning from existing fraudulent data characteristics to classify unseen data. These requirements can be addressed with Machine Learning Techniques (MLTs). Several supervised MLTs, such as Naive Bayes,

M. Mouhoub and P. Langlais (Eds.): Canadian AI 2017, LNAI 10233, pp. 84–89, 2017.
DOI: 10.1007/978-3-319-57351-9_11

Decision Trees, Random Forests, Neural Networks and Support Vector Machines, have been deployed to handle fraud in industries, like credit cards, telecommunication, banking insurance, e-auctions and power utility. One of the biggest challenges in fraud classification is the class distribution factor that denotes the ratio of training instances present in each of the class categories. Whenever the two numbers differ a lot, i.e. one class (negative) contains more instances than the other class (positive), the training dataset is said to be highly imbalanced. There are several common areas that suffer from the issue of class imbalance, including fraud detection, medical diagnosis, network intrusion detection and oil spill detection.

Learning from training data that are highly imbalanced is erroneous since MLTs often misclassify the minority events as majority ones [Koknar-Tezel2009]. This is a serious concern in the fraud detection domain because the minority instances i.e. fraudulent activities are misclassified as normal. In auctions, once actual shill bidders have been predicted as honest ones, they can never be tracked thereafter. Several studies have been devised to fight shill-bidding crimes using MLTs but did not address the class imbalance of their fraud datasets. Various techniques have been introduced to correctly classify highly imbalanced datasets such as data sampling methods that have been proven to increase the classification performance [He2009, Koknar-Tezel2009]. In this research, based on commercial auction data, we first apply a hybrid data sampling method (over-sampling and under-sampling) to handle our highly imbalanced auction fraud dataset and also to improve the classification efficiency. After labeling the IAF training data with a robust clustering technique, we deploy three well-known baseline classifiers, Naive Bayes, Decision Trees and Neural Networks. It is worth mentioning that labelled shill-bidding datasets are lacking and unavailable. To have a better idea about the learning performance of each classifier, we employ four metrics that are the most relevant for both fraud data and imbalanced data. Next, we examine how the classifier performance changes before and after the sampling process is applied to the auction fraud dataset. We will determine which classifier achieves the lowest misclassification rate of suspicious bidders. The consequence of misclassifying fraudsters as normal is serious.

2 Hybrid Sampling of Imbalanced IAF Data

Imbalanced training data can lead to several problems regarding the output of the classification model [Ganganwar2012] as explained below: (1) The classifier assumes that the samples are uniformly distributed, which is false in this case; (2) The classification model is biased towards the dominant class; (3) Since the classification evaluation is accuracy driven, it does not portray the correct picture from the minority class perspective; (4) The costs of misclassifying instances from all the classes are considered equal, which again is not acceptable since the misclassification cost should be more for the class of interest that is the set of fraudulent instances. As an example, if among 100 samples, 95 are negative and 5 are positive, the classifier predicts all data as negative. So, the accuracy is 95% since all the 95 negative samples are classified correctly but the accuracy for the positive class is 0% as none of the samples among those 5 is correctly classified [Chawla2002]. This is called 'Accuracy Paradox', which means the model rather than depicting its accuracy is actually reflecting its class distribution [Brownlee2015]. Two different approaches have been introduced to handle the imbalanced classification issue:

- Data sampling that is either over-sampling the minority class, or under-sampling the majority class, or both. This process is also called 're-sampling'.
- Cost-sensitive learning that is assigning weights or costs to the classes. For instance, we can allocate a higher cost to the positive class, which is the most important class in fraud detection problems.

In any real-world fraud detection scenario, the number of negative instances, which refers to legitimate records, far outnumbers the number of positive instances, which refers to illegitimate records. The ratio of negative to positive instances may vary as much as 100:1 [Provost2001] in the fraud domain. In our particular case of auction fraud, the number of "normal" instances (honest bidding behavior) exceeds the number of "suspicious" instances (shill bidding behavior). An instance here denotes the misbehavior of a bidder in a certain auction. So to deal with this imbalanced learning problem, we need to select the best strategy. For our auction fraud classification task, we choose data sampling over cost-sensitive learning due to the reasons below [Weiss2007]:

- Sampling methods perform with somewhat similar effectiveness, if not better, than that of cost-sensitive learning.
- Cost-sensitive learning algorithms are efficient when processing very large training datasets, and on comparatively moderate size of datasets, like that of ours, cost-sensitive learning does not work well.
- In cost-sensitive learning, determining the cost depends on the problem domain and it is considered a challenging task.

Over-sampling and under-sampling techniques have been widely adopted in the literature. Again, it was seen that neither of them is a clear winner, and which kind of sampling that yields to better results largely depends on the training dataset on which it is applied to [Weiss2007]. Additionally, the hybrid strategy of over-sampling and under-sampling arguably works better than either one [Chawla2002]. Thus instead of selecting any one method, we employ a hybrid of the most used over-sampling and under-sampling schemes to balance our IAF training dataset: Synthetic Minority Over-sampling Technique (SMOTE) and SpreadSubsample. SMOTE over-samples the original dataset by creating near-duplicates of the minority class and inversely SpreadSubsample under-samples the dominant class. SMOTE has been proven to enhance the learning rate of the rare events. When compared to other over-sampling techniques, it has been found that SMOTE is more useful in creating a generalized decision region [Akbani2004]. SMOTE relatively achieves better results than other re-sampling methods and probabilistic estimating techniques. After sampling, sometimes instances for a particular class may get dense at some places in the dataset. If cross validation is performed in this un-uniformly spread dataset, some of the folds may be classified wrongly because folds may contain only positive or only negative examples. So to avoid this, randomization of instances is performed to randomly shuffle the order of instances as per the seed interval set as parameter.

3 Shill-Bidding Classification

To obtain a maximum profit, the fraudulent seller and his accomplices inflate the price of the product by placing aggressive bids through phony accounts. Once the price is high enough, the colluding users stop competing, and thus making the honest bidder win the auction. This way the winner actually pays more than the product is worthy. The goal of this study is to classify shill-bidding data using three well-known baseline classifiers, Decision Trees, Naïve Bayes and Neural Networks, and check how they behave with and without pre-processing the imbalanced data. We employ four metrics given their efficiency with respect to handling imbalanced data without getting biased towards the majority class and also their suitability with respect to fraud detection domain: (1) Recall focuses on the significant class (fraud) and is not sensitive to data distribution, (2) F-measure is a good metric due to its non-linear nature and has been used for fraud detection, (3) MCC is the best singular assessment measure and is less influenced by imbalanced data, (4) AUC evaluates the overall classifier performance and is very appropriate for class imbalance. Below we describe the auction fraud classification procedure.

A. Collection of Raw Auction Data: Here we employ actual auction data that have been made public in the following site: www.modelingonlineauctions.com/datasets. We utilize transactional data of 149 auctions of the Pilot PDA product auctioned in eBay. All the PDA auctions have a long duration (7 days). The longer the auction duration, the more shill bidders have a chance to imitate normal behaviour. So, our auction dataset is appropriate for shill-bidding detection.

B. Construction of IAF Training Dataset: We select eight shill patterns as the classification features because they have been found to be dominant across infected auctions as seen in numerous studies [Ford2012, Nikitkov2015]. The metrics of these fraud patterns, which are calculated from the raw auction data, are provided in [Sadaoui2016]. We obtain an IAF training set of 1488 observations. Each instance comprises of 10 features: auction ID, bidder ID, values of eight shill patterns.

C. Labeling IAF Training Data: To label the 1488 training data as 'normal' or 'suspicious', we apply the robust Hierarchical Clustering technique with the centroid linkage function. The resulting clusters consist of around 95% of non-fraud data and only 5% of shill-bidding data. Thus we can see that our training dataset is highly imbalanced with a ratio of 19:1. Thus, it requires sampling before the classification task.

D. Hybrid Sampling of IAF Dataset: To be more effective in solving the issue of class imbalance, we combine both SMOTE and SpreadSubsample to re-balance our fraud training dataset. It has been found that a ratio of 2:1 is preferable to achieve an efficient distribution between negative and positive instances in a training set [Chang2011].

E. Classification of IAF Data: Now we launch Naïve Bayes, Decision Tree (J48) and Neural Network (Voted Perceptron) on the re-balanced IAF training data. To build any optimal fraud classifier, we need to tune efficiently its parameters. This is done through

K-fold cross-validation. The latter ensures that each instance is randomly predicted at least once, thus increasing the efficiency of the classifier. With cross validation, we obtain a non-biased estimation of the model performance, which in turn helps in increasing the performance of the shill-bidding classifier being built. Here we show how data sampling affects the classification results. In Table 1, it can be seen that before sampling is done, the classifiers did not perform well with a very low MCC value of 59.3% for Naive Bayes, 56.5% for Neural Network and 33.9% for Decision Tree. Furthermore, it is clear from the Recall values that the 'completeness' of the classifiers in predicting the minority class is not good at all and that is why there is a large number of False Positives. The Decision Tree appears to be the most affected by the data imbalance problem whereas Naïve Bayes with an AUC of 71% seems to be less sensible to this problem. The F-measure values also demonstrate that the classifiers do not work well when the data is not balanced as this quality measure represents the combined metrics of Precision and Recall, both of which concentrate on predicting the minority class properly.

Table 1. Classification results before hybrid data sampling

	Recall	F-measure	MCC	AUC
Naïve Bayes	0.44	0.582	0.593	0.711
Neural network	0.380	0.534	0.565	0.708
Decision tree	0.271	0.397	0.339	0.584

Table 2 reports the classification results once hybrid sampling is applied to our IAF training dataset. The after-sampling performance of the three classifiers has improved considerably. The highest improvement can be witnessed for Decision Tree with an MCC value of 98% whereas Naïve Bayes and Neural Network also show great improvement. The Recall and F-measure values show that now the classifiers are able to do justice to the positive class with acceptable fraud detection rates. So we can see that Decision Tree is performing significantly better than others when the data is re-sampled and its higher Recall rate ensures that the number of suspicious bidders incorrectly classified is very small. On the other hand, Neural Network is less performing for our IAF training dataset.

Table 2. Classification results after hybrid data sampling

	Recall	F-measure	MCC	AUC
Naïve Bayes	0.707	0.817	0.711	0.952
Neural network	0.695	0.804	0.687	0.935
Decision tree	0.996	0.991	0.981	0.989

4 Conclusion

The class imbalance issue is present in any fraud detection problem where the number of fraud data is much less than non-fraud data. This issue has a negative effect on the classification algorithms since they return low performance results, especially for the minority class because in most of the times classifiers are biased towards the majority class. In this study, it was witnessed that the pre-processing phase of sampling highly imbalanced data has a considerable impact on well-known classifiers. The concluding points are the following: (1) Naïve Bayes is less sensitive to data quality problem than Neural Network and Decision Tree, and performs better when the fraud data is not pre-processed; (2) After the fraud training dataset was re-balanced, Decision Tree works much better than others. In the future, we would like to apply SVM on our IAF dataset. [Zhang2015] has found that SVM outperforms Naïve Bayes and Decision Tree after a certain level of dual sampling was done on five imbalanced UCI datasets (with different sizes, dimensionalities and imbalance ratios).

References

[Akbani2004] Akbani, R., Kwek, S., Japkowicz, N.: Applying support vector machines to imbalanced datasets. In: Boulicaut, J.-F., Esposito, F., Giannotti, F., Pedreschi, D. (eds.) ECML 2004. LNCS (LNAI), vol. 3201, pp. 39–50. Springer, Heidelberg (2004). doi:10.1007/978-3-540-30115-8_7

[Brownlee2015] Brownlee, J.: 8 Tactics to Combat Imbalanced Classes in Your Machine Learning Dataset (2015). www.machinelearningmastery.com

[Chang2011] Chang, W.-H., Chang, J.-S.: A novel two-stage phased modeling framework for early fraud detection in online auctions. Expert Syst. Appl. **38**(9), 11244–11260 (2011)

[Chawla2002] Chawla, N.V., et al.: SMOTE: synthetic minority over-sampling technique. J. Artif. Intell. Res. **16**, 321–357 (2002)

[Ford2012] Ford, B.J., Xu, H., Valova, I.: A real-time self-adaptive classifier for identifying suspicious bidders in online auctions. Comput. J. **56**, 646–663 (2012)

[Ganganwar2012] Ganganwar, V.: An overview of classification algorithms for imbalanced datasets. Int. J. Emerg. Technol. Adv. Eng. **2**(4), 42–47 (2012)

[He2009] He, H., Garcia, E.A.: Learning from imbalanced data. IEEE Trans. Knowl. Data Eng. **21**(9), 1263–1284 (2009)

[Koknar-Tezel2009] Köknar-Tezel, S., Latecki, L.J.: Improving SVM classification on imbalanced data sets in distance spaces. In: 9th IEEE International Conference on Data Mining (2009)

[Nikitkov2015] Nikitkov, A., Bay, D.: Shill bidding: empirical evidence of its effectiveness and likelihood of detection in online auction systems. Int. J. Account. Inf. Syst. **16**, 42–54 (2015)

[Provost2001] Provost, F., Fawcett, T.: Robust classification for imprecise environments. Mach. Learn. **42**(3), 203–231 (2001)

[Sadaoui2016] Sadaoui, S., Wang, X.: A dynamic stage-based fraud monitoring framework of multiple live auctions. Appl. Intell. **46**, 1–17 (2016). doi:10.1007/s10489-016-0818-7

[Weiss2007] Weiss, G.M., McCarthy, K., Zabar, B.: Cost-sensitive learning vs. sampling: which is best for handling imbalanced classes with unequal error costs? DMIN **7**, 35–41 (2007)

[Zhang2015] Zhang, S., Sadaoui, S., Mouhoub, M.: An empirical analysis of imbalanced data classification. Comput. Inf. Sci. **8**(1), 151–162 (2015)

Multi-label Learning Through Minimum Spanning Tree-Based Subset Selection and Feature Extraction

Payel Sadhukhan(✉) and C.A. Murthy

Machine Intelligence Unit, Indian Statistical Institute, Kolkata, India
payel0410@gmail.com

Abstract. Extracting an effective feature set on the basis of dataset characteristics can be a useful proposition to address a classification task. For multi-label datasets, the positive and negative class memberships for the instance set vary from label to label. In such a scenario, a dedicated feature set for each label can serve better than a single feature set for all labels. In this article, we approach multi-label learning addressing the same concern and present our work Multi-label learning through Minimum Spanning Tree based subset selection and feature extraction (MuMST-FE). For each label, we estimate the positive and negative class shapes using respective Minimum Spanning Trees (MSTs), followed by subset selection based on the key lattices of the MSTs. We select a unique subset of instances for each label which participates in the feature extraction step. A distance based feature set is extracted for each label from the reduced instance set to facilitate final classification. The classifiers modelled from MuMST-FE is found to possess improved robustness and discerning capabilities which is established by the performance of the proposed schema against several state-of-the-art approaches on ten benchmark datasets.

Keywords: Multi-label classification · Multi-label ranking · Minimum Spanning Tree · Feature extraction

1 Introduction

Multi-label datasets differ from traditional datasets by virtue of the membership of instances to more than one overlapping labels. In traditional datasets, an instance possess exactly one label. Traditional classifiers dealing with single-label data expect the instances to originate from a single and prefixed distribution. Unlike single-label datasets, multi-label datasets have variedly skewed and differently oriented class distributions for different labels. Hence, when tried against multi-label datasets such (traditional) classifiers generally do not provide optimal performance.

Beginning with text categorization, data with multi-label characteristics have emerged from different genres [7] namely images, music, bioinformatics, tag recommendation systems, video, henceforth multi-label classification and learning

M. Mouhoub and P. Langlais (Eds.): Canadian AI 2017, LNAI 10233, pp. 90–96, 2017.
DOI: 10.1007/978-3-319-57351-9_12

have gained momentum. Diverse techniques have been applied in this regard, and consistent improvement in performance has been achieved, which we will discuss next.

Multi-label classification approaches can be broadly divided into – *Problem transformation (PT) approach* and *Algorithm adaptation (AA) approach* [7]. In *problem transformation approach*, a multi-label learning task is transformed into one or more classification tasks where output is obtained by considering the assimilated output from the group of classifiers. Binary relevance, B_R is the most primitive form of PT approach, where a series of binary classifiers is generated, one for each label. The other extreme in this direction was given by [1], who considered the powerset of labels for analysis. RAKEL [6] considered a more feasible approach by taking random subsets of labels. In another sub-category of PT methods called pair-wise ranking, a binary classifier was considered for each pair of labels and final output was given based on the results from the group of such classifiers. Calibrated Label ranking [2] scheme provides multi-label output on the basis of pair-wise classification, considering a synthetic label to distinguish the relevant and irrelevant group of labels. Classifier Chains approach [5] considers a single binary classifier for each label but tries to capture label correlations by packing the input space of each subsequent classifier with the output from the preceding labels. In *algorithm adaptation approach*, existing algorithms in literature are suitably applied to facilitate multi-label learning. A number of methods like K-NN [10], Bayesian learning, neural networks [7] and others are applied to classify and rank multi-label data. [4] used clustering to find the local patterns of the feature space and classified an instance in the context of its nearest cluster. In recent years, feature space transformation through multi-label data was done effectively by LIFT [9]. It uses clustering to construct a transformed feature-set for each label, which can be easily used in conjunction with other available techniques to classify multi-label data. We present our work in the context of generating an intrinsic input subspace for each label followed by generation of a distance-based transformed feature set as in LIFT. The transformed feature set is used to classify multi-label data.

2 Approach and Algorithm

A feature extraction scheme can be effective if it can competently capture the dissimilarities which separates the different classes of an instance set. A multi-label dataset has a single instance set with contra-distinct partitions for different labels. To be precise, it has dissimilar positive class and negative class structures for different labels (considering two-class multi-label datasets). Here, we present a feature extraction scheme which bank on this characteristic of such datasets to generate a discriminative feature set for each label by initially selecting a shape-related discriminative subset of instances per label. In this work, we follow *first-order approach* of multi-label learning where we learn a single classifier for each label. The discriminative feature sets obtained by our schema are used to learn the classifiers. The following three steps are sequentially performed for each label to obtain its corresponding distinctive feature set.

- *Shape of the classes:* The contra-distinct partitions of the same instance set for different labels is the motivation of our schema. We obtain the shapes of both positive as well as negative classes of a label following this step twice, once for each. Here, we assume that the set of all points in a class (i.e., not only the given points belonging to the class, but also all those points which belong to the class but are not given) is a connected set. Note that we are given finitely many points from a class, even though the original set is uncountable (considering real space). The minimal connected set that can be obtained from the given points in the class is the Minimal Spanning Tree of the given points [3], where the edge weight is taken as the distance between the points. We are considering Minimal Spanning Tree (MST) to represent the geometry or shape of the class.
- *Key Point Subset/lattice of a shape:* Once we have the positive and negative class geometries of a label, we would like to select the 'key points or lattice' of their respective geometries. In a graph, a node or point can be denoted important if its removal along with its connected neighbours results in substantial distortion to the original geometry. By this rationale, it is evident that the potential candidates for the Key Point Subset are the higher degree vertices of the MST [8]. We select the higher degree vertices of the both the positive class MST and negative class MST individually into the Key Point Subset for a label (till they cover a predefined fraction of edges). Selection of the points is done from the actual set of instances. Hence, from a single instance set for all labels we select a dedicated set of instances for each label.
- *Feature extraction:* An instance is likely to be closer to the members of the class it belongs than it is to the members of the other class. A natural extension of this is followed by extracting a distance-based feature vector for each instance. The transformed feature vector of an instance for a label is obtained by calculating its distance from the Key Point Subset members of that label. If there are k labels, an instances gets k transformations, one for each label.

The transformed feature set for the training instance set with respect to a label is employed to model its corresponding classifier and this process is repeated across all labels. While classifying a test instance over a label, its transformed mapping (extracted feature vector) is obtained by calculating its distance from the Key Point Subset of that label and it is fed to the respective label classifier to obtain the class prediction. The action is repeated across all labels to obtain classification over the entire label set.

MuMST-FE has two stages. First stage is the feature extraction and classifier modelling step, where we derive the transformed feature set for each label from a single instance set. In this stage, we employ the set of training instances to select the Key Point Subset for each label from both positive and negative Minimum Spanning Trees followed by extraction of a distance based feature set. Next, we model a set of classifiers, one for each label, modelled upon the distance-based feature set. In the second stage, classification of a test point is done according to its new set of mapping for each label and feeding it to the respective label classifier. Algorithm 1 gives a formal sketch of our approach.

Algorithm 1. *MuMST-FE*

Input: Training attribute set S, Training label set Y, $covG$
Output: Classifiers – $C_1, C_2, ..., C_k$, Key Point Sets – $KPS_1, KPS_2, .., KPS_k$

procedure TRAINING(S, Y, $covG$)
  for each label $j \rightarrow 1, k$ **do**
    Segregate P_j, N_j according to their membership to label j as in Eqn (1)
    Form $Tree_{P_j}, Tree_{N_j}$ by taking MST of P_j and N_j respectively as in Eqn (2)
    Sort elements of P_j, N_j into $P_{j\_sorted}, N_{j\_sorted}$ according to the *normalized degree* values of the nodes as in Eqn (3)
    Select KPS_{j_p}, KPS_{j_n} from $P_{j\_sorted}, N_{j\_sorted}$ respectively till the summation of *normalized degrees* just equals or exceeds $covG$ as in Eqn (4)
    Obtain KPS_j by taking union of KPS_{j_p} and KPS_{j_n} as in Eqn (5)
    Transformed training feature set with respect to label j, $\beta_j(S)$ is obtained from KPS_j by considering each instance's distance from the KPS_j members as in Eqn (6)
    Classifier C_j is modelled on $\beta_j(S)$ and Y
  end for
end procedure

——————————————— **Input**: Classifier – $C_1, ..., C_k$, Key Point Sets – $KPS_1, .., KPS_k$, test point p
Output: Predicted labels for p

procedure TEST($C_1, C_2, ..., C_k$, $KPS_1, KPS_2, .., KPS_k$, p)
  for each label $j \rightarrow 1, k$ **do**
    $\beta_j(p)$ is obtained
    C_j is fed with $\beta_j(p)$ to get the jth label prediction for p
  end for
end procedure

3 Empirical Evaluation and Comparisons

- **Multi-label Evaluation Indices.** To get a vivid picture of multi-label competence of the methods, in addition to accuracy based metric, more refined metrics which consider ranking of labels and cumulative label accuracies are employed. The first index, namely *Hamming Loss*, is used to estimate the classification performance of the learners, while the next four, *Average Precision*, *Coverage*, *One Error* and *Ranking Loss* assess the ranking results and *Macro-f1* and *Micro-f1* provide us with cumulative performance averaged over all labels.
- **Datasets.** Two principal categories of real-life, two-class, multi-label datasets are used: *five* datasets with numeric attributes and *five* datasets containing nominal attributes. Multi-label datasets are described in terms of standard parameters like domain, number of instances, attribute types, number of attributes, number of labels as well as two additional multi-label parameters, label cardinality and label density. The description of the *ten* benchmark datasets is given in Table 1.
- **Comparing Methods and Experimental Settings.** We have considered five popular diversified multi label schemes for empirical comparison with MuMST-FE, *Binary Relevance* B_R, *Calibrated Label Ranking*, *LIFT* with $r = 0.1$, *MLKNN* with $k = 10$, *11 or 12* and *RAKEL* following parameter settings $k = 3$ *and number of subsets equal to twice the number of labels*. MuMST-FE is implemented in the framework of B_R, that is one classifier for each label. Euclidean distance and Hamming distances are considered for numeric

Table 1. Description of datasets

Dataset	Domain	Att. type	(D)	(L)	(F)	$(L.Card)$	$(L.Uniq)$
Corel5k	Image	Nominal	5000	374	499	3.522	3175
Enron	Text	Nominal	1702	53	1001	3.378	753
Lang log	Text	Nominal	1460	75	1004	1.180	286
Medical	Biology	Nominal	978	45	1449	1.245	94
Slashdot	Text	Nominal	3782	22	1079	1.181	156
CAL500	Music	Numeric	502	174	68	26.044	502
Image	Image	Numeric	2000	5	294	1.236	20
Music	Music	Numeric	592	6	72	1.869	27
Scene	Image	Numeric	2407	6	294	1.047	15
Yeast	Biology	Numeric	2417	14	103	4.037	198

datasets and for nominal datasets respectively. The only user supplied parameter is *covG* and its value is set to 0.6 for all datasets.

- **Results and Discussions.** Comparisons in terms of *seven* evaluating metrics is done for the proposed method, and *five* other baseline approaches. For each dataset, *50%* of the samples are randomly selected and used as the training set while the remaining samples are used as the test set. Mean and standard deviation values on the metric outputs are computed over *ten* independent runs and reported in the tables. Table 2 present the performance of the methods on accuracy based, ranking based and label-based metrics in sequence. The estimated mean values for *ten* runs as well the corresponding standard deviations are given in the mentioned tables. The best performance on each dataset is indicated in bold face in the column for the corresponding method. From Table 2 number of best outcomes achieved by each method (comparing and proposed) is calculated. This summarization manifests competence of the proposed method which achieves *forty-two* out of *seventy-four* best results with next higher score attained by LIFT, (*13 out of 74*) and CLR (*10 out of 74*). RAKEL gives best results on *6* cases, B_R and MLKNN in *two* and *one* cases respectively. The above stated results require some more analysis with respect to individual performances on each of the *seven* evaluating metrics to provide a vivid picture.
  MuMST-FE achieves lowest Hamming Loss on *nine* out of *ten* datasets, best value on the remaining dataset is given by LIFT for dataset *Enron*. On *four* datasets, for LLOG, Medical, Slashdot and CAL500 the proposed method shares best value with LIFT, RAKEL, LIFT and CLR respectively.
  MuMST-FE achieves competitive performance on Ranking-based criteria. On Average Precision it achieves best result on *five* datasets and *six* best outcomes are attained on each of Coverage and One-Error. On Ranking Loss MuMST-FE accomplishes best result on *seven* cases. Rest of the best outcomes are principally shared by CLR and LIFT with B_R getting best Coverage value on

Table 2. Predictive performance of methods in terms of multi-label evaluation metrics—↑ indicates higher is better and ↓ indicates lower is better, best outcome is indicated in bold-face

	Corel5k		Enron		LLOG		Medical		Slash		CAL500		Image		Music		Scene		Yeast	
Hamming Loss ↓																				
	mean	std	mean	std	mean	std	mean	std	mean	std	mean	std	mean	std	mean	std	mean	std	mean	std
B_R	0.010	0.001	0.060	0.002	0.017	0.002	0.013	0.001	0.050	0.001	0.138	0.003	0.187	0.007	0.286	0.002	0.108	0.004	0.202	0.005
CLR	0.011	0.001	0.055	0.001	0.018	0.001	0.038	0.002	0.052	0.001	**0.137**	0.003	0.185	0.006	0.272	0.002	0.106	0.004	0.201	0.005
LIFT	0.010	0.001	**0.047**	0.001	**0.015**	0.002	0.014	0.001	**0.040**	0.001	0.138	0.003	0.166	0.004	0.194	0.001	0.083	0.002	0.198	0.003
MLKNN	0.010	0.001	0.054	0.003	0.016	0.002	0.017	0.002	0.046	0.001	0.140	0.003	0.181	0.004	0.209	0.002	0.093	0.002	0.197	0.004
MuMST-FE	**0.009**	0.001	0.048	0.002	**0.015**	0.001	**0.012**	0.001	**0.040**	0.001	**0.137**	0.003	**0.156**	0.002	**0.190**	0.001	**0.081**	0.002	**0.192**	0.003
RAKEL	0.013	0.001	0.075	0.003	0.018	0.003	**0.012**	0.001	0.047	0.001	0.198	0.004	0.172	0.008	0.299	0.001	0.141	0.003	0.201	0.006
Average Precision ↑																				
	mean	std	mean	std	mean	std	mean	std	mean	std	mean	std	mean	std	mean	std	mean	std	mean	std
B_R	0.115	0.002	0.427	0.009	0.184	0.009	0.785	0.007	0.564	0.004	0.493	0.003	0.713	0.005	0.741	0.002	0.782	0.004	0.568	0.002
CLR	0.275	0.003	0.673	0.008	0.368	0.007	0.502	0.004	**0.672**	0.003	**0.498**	0.004	0.786	0.004	0.736	0.001	0.844	0.003	0.652	0.001
LIFT	**0.287**	0.004	**0.683**	0.010	**0.382**	0.007	0.843	0.004	0.670	0.003	0.492	0.003	0.812	0.004	0.808	0.001	0.876	0.002	0.762	0.001
MLKNN	0.239	0.002	0.609	0.008	0.290	0.006	0.777	0.007	0.589	0.004	0.484	0.003	0.774	0.004	0.789	0.002	0.853	0.003	0.758	0.002
MuMST-FE	0.265	0.003	0.656	0.008	0.328	0.012	**0.863**	0.003	0.667	0.003	0.497	0.004	**0.824**	0.003	**0.816**	0.001	**0.882**	0.002	**0.769**	0.002
RAKEL	0.124	0.003	0.556	0.008	0.192	0.010	0.777	0.006	0.609	0.004	0.383	0.004	0.794	0.005	0.722	0.002	0.847	0.002	0.622	0.003
Coverage ↓																				
	mean	std	mean	std	mean	std	mean	std	mean	std	mean	std	mean	std	mean	std	mean	std	mean	std
B_R	0.894	0.004	0.582	0.007	0.425	0.005	**0.044**	0.005	0.117	0.005	0.952	0.008	0.296	0.002	0.362	0.001	0.111	0.001	0.626	0.002
CLR	0.316	0.008	**0.223**	0.009	**0.154**	0.008	0.088	0.006	**0.108**	0.003	0.763	0.005	0.185	0.004	0.348	0.002	0.128	0.002	0.472	0.004
LIFT	0.319	0.007	0.245	0.008	0.194	0.006	0.058	0.005	0.111	0.004	0.762	0.004	0.181	0.003	0.291	0.002	0.070	0.002	0.456	0.003
MLKNN	0.316	0.009	0.263	0.011	0.182	0.011	0.075	0.006	0.186	0.005	0.762	0.005	0.207	0.004	0.311	0.003	0.084	0.002	0.458	0.006
MuMST-FE	**0.289**	0.006	0.251	0.007	0.165	0.005	0.050	0.004	0.113	0.004	**0.756**	0.004	**0.168**	0.003	**0.288**	0.002	**0.067**	0.002	**0.449**	0.003
RAKEL	0.882	0.002	0.527	0.007	0.438	0.004	0.081	0.005	0.196	0.004	0.967	0.004	0.212	0.002	0.389	0.002	0.118	0.002	0.526	0.003
One Error ↓																				
	mean	std	mean	std	mean	std	mean	std	mean	std	mean	std	mean	std	mean	std	mean	std	mean	std
B_R	0.829	0.013	0.506	0.014	0.856	0.011	0.252	0.012	0.502	0.009	0.283	0.010	0.408	0.009	0.357	0.011	0.346	0.014	0.248	0.012
CLR	0.708	0.012	0.265	0.010	0.718	0.008	0.386	0.007	0.433	0.009	0.124	0.010	0.329	0.009	0.276	0.011	0.252	0.008	0.228	0.010
LIFT	**0.687**	0.011	0.253	0.010	**0.704**	0.013	0.191	0.012	**0.425**	0.013	0.123	0.011	0.286	0.008	0.254	0.010	0.208	0.009	0.235	0.011
MLKNN	0.744	0.014	0.330	0.012	0.816	0.012	0.312	0.008	0.642	0.010	0.125	0.011	0.345	0.009	0.283	0.013	0.247	0.014	0.229	0.009
MuMST-FE	0.706	0.010	**0.240**	0.008	0.765	0.011	**0.170**	0.010	0.441	0.012	**0.118**	0.009	**0.270**	0.011	**0.251**	0.010	**0.198**	0.009	**0.218**	0.009
RAKEL	0.823	0.012	0.406	0.014	0.845	0.014	0.254	0.009	0.462	0.010	0.312	0.012	0.303	0.015	0.388	0.008	0.247	0.009	0.253	0.013
Ranking Loss ↓																				
	mean	std	mean	std	mean	std	mean	std	mean	std	mean	std	mean	std	mean	std	mean	std	mean	std
B_R	0.624	0.004	0.248	0.005	0.244	0.006	0.040	0.005	0.158	0.010	0.412	0.005	0.293	0.004	0.232	0.003	0.168	0.006	0.309	0.005
CLR	0.129	0.003	**0.078**	0.004	**0.134**	0.007	0.052	0.004	**0.096**	0.005	**0.182**	0.003	0.173	0.003	0.229	0.004	0.076	0.004	0.171	0.002
LIFT	0.132	0.003	0.086	0.004	0.184	0.004	0.039	0.005	0.098	0.004	0.189	0.003	0.157	0.003	0.154	0.002	0.068	0.004	0.171	0.003
MLKNN	0.138	0.002	0.100	0.006	0.175	0.003	0.042	0.006	0.172	0.006	0.184	0.005	0.192	0.002	0.175	0.003	0.086	0.003	0.168	0.004
MuMST-FE	**0.124**	0.003	0.091	0.005	0.156	0.007	**0.036**	0.003	0.101	0.004	**0.182**	0.004	**0.143**	0.003	**0.148**	0.002	**0.065**	0.003	**0.163**	0.003
RAKEL	0.603	0.004	0.226	0.007	0.325	0.006	0.078	0.005	0.285	0.003	0.467	0.008	0.192	0.003	0.252	0.001	0.103	0.004	0.226	0.006
macro f_1 ↑																				
	mean	std	mean	std	mean	std	mean	std	mean	std	mean	std	mean	std	mean	std	mean	std	mean	std
B_R	0.216	0.001	0.167	0.001	**0.201**	0.005	0.303	0.004	0.366	0.006	0.143	0.002	0.561	0.002	0.571	0.001	0.623	0.002	0.415	0.002
CLR	0.242	0.001	0.225	0.002	0.123	0.005	0.267	0.003	0.416	0.003	0.183	0.001	0.586	0.002	0.634	0.001	0.687	0.002	0.43	0.001
LIFT	**0.243**	0.001	**0.267**	0.002	0.155	0.004	0.265	0.002	0.463	0.003	0.193	0.002	0.621	0.001	0.662	0.001	0.740	0.002	0.441	0.001
MLKNN	0.205	0.002	0.226	0.002	0.104	0.003	0.184	0.002	0.421	0.002	**0.195**	0.002	0.553	0.001	0.623	0.001	0.611	0.002	0.438	0.002
MuMST-FE	0.234	0.001	0.242	0.002	0.107	0.003	0.289	0.003	0.466	0.002	0.193	0.002	**0.627**	0.001	**0.666**	0.001	**0.742**	0.001	**0.445**	0.002
RAKEL	0.228	0.001	0.181	0.003	0.191	0.003	**0.327**	0.004	**0.481**	0.002	0.161	0.001	0.581	0.001	0.622	0.002	0.661	0.001	0.426	0.002
micro f_1 ↑																				
	mean	std	mean	std	mean	std	mean	std	mean	std	mean	std	mean	std	mean	std	mean	std	mean	std
B_R	0.036	0.002	0.533	0.005	0.051	0.002	0.757	0.002	0.221	0.002	0.362	0.003	0.555	0.002	0.591	0.001	0.611	0.002	0.594	0.002
CLR	0.062	0.003	**0.568**	0.005	0.018	0.002	0.703	0.002	0.240	0.003	0.318	0.002	0.586	0.001	0.642	0.001	0.672	0.002	0.640	0.001
LIFT	**0.076**	0.002	0.564	0.003	**0.062**	0.003	0.727	0.002	0.256	0.003	0.321	0.001	0.618	0.001	0.669	0.001	0.730	0.001	0.640	0.001
MLKNN	0.034	0.002	0.468	0.004	0.056	0.004	0.609	0.003	0.178	0.002	0.349	0.002	0.557	0.002	0.621	0.001	0.704	0.001	0.640	0.001
MuMST-FE	0.064	0.002	0.532	0.004	0.057	0.003	0.743	0.002	0.242	0.002	0.326	0.003	**0.624**	0.002	**0.672**	0.001	**0.737**	0.002	**0.642**	0.001
RAKEL	0.035	0.003	0.525	0.003	0.055	0.003	**0.777**	0.002	**0.268**	0.004	**0.378**	0.002	0.578	0.002	0.627	0.001	0.676	0.001	0.607	0.001

medical dataset. Ranking performance of MuMST-FE substantiates the presence of MuMST-FE's aptitude to predict the correct hierarchy of the labels. In terms of label-based metrics, *macro-f1* and *micro-f1*, MuMST-FE gets highest (best) value in *four* out of *ten* datasets. *Six* and *four* of the remaining best outcomes are delivered by RAKEL and LIFT respectively. CLR and B_R gives one each of the remaining *two* cases. In terms of label-based metrics, MuMST-FE exhibits moderate efficacy, RAKEL too manifests considerable competence by virtue of its ability to capture label correlations.

4 Concluding Remarks and Future Work

A novel multi-label learning method, MuMST-FE, has been presented in this work. The key contribution of MuMST-FE lies in improving the classification and ranking results on standard benchmark multi-label datasets. The improvement is corroborated through empirical evidences.

In MuMST-FE, subset selection for each label is performed on the basis of the structures given by the positive and negative classes of the concerned label. MuMST-FE presents a novel approach in this regard by selecting a shape-related discriminative subset of instances for each label, which in turn is used to extract a discriminative feature set for classification and learning. In the present work, MuMST-FE has been implemented in the framework of correlation-independent learning using B_R. Comparative studies indicate that the extracted features of MuMST-FE prove to be more effective in multi-label context than other label-correlated approaches like CLR and RAKEL. Extracted feature set of MuMST-FE also outperforms the label-specific feature set of LIFT in multi-label learning. MuMST-FE can also be implemented in the framework of higher order approaches like CLR, CC, RAKEL and others.

MST implementation poses a computational bottle-neck in MuMST-FE and it aggravates with increasing number of data points. In future, we would like to address this issue so that we can more accommodate higher dimensional datasets.

References

1. Boutell, M.R., Luo, J., Shen, X., Brown, C.M.: Learning multi-label scene classification. Pattern Recogn. **37**(9), 1757–1771 (2004)
2. Fürnkranz, J., Hüllermeier, E., Mencía, E.L., Brinker, K.: Multilabel classification via calibrated label ranking. Mach. Learn. **73**(2), 133–153 (2008)
3. Graham, R.L., Hell, P.: On the history of the minimum spanning tree problem. IEEE Ann. Hist. Comput. **7**(1), 43–57 (1985). http://dx.doi.org/10.1109/MAHC.1985.10011
4. Nasierding, G., Tsoumakas, G., Kouzani, A.Z.: Clustering based multi-label classification for image annotation and retrieval. In: IEEE International Conference on Systems, Man and Cybernetics, SMC 2009, pp. 4514–4519, October 2009
5. Read, J., Pfahringer, B., Holmes, G., Frank, E.: Classifier chains for multi-label classification. Mach. Learn. **85**(3), 333–359 (2011)
6. Tsoumakas, G., Katakis, I., Vlahavas, I.: Random k-labelsets for multilabel classification. IEEE Trans. Knowl. Data Eng. **23**(7), 1079–1089 (2011)
7. Tsoumakas, G., Katakis, I.: Multi-label classification: an overview. Int. J. Data Wareh. Min. **3**, 1–13 (2007)
8. Zachariasen, M., Winter, P.: Concatenation-based greedy heuristics for the Euclidean Steiner tree problem. Algorithmica **25**(4), 418–437 (1999)
9. Zhang, M.L., Wu, L.: LIFT: multi-label learning with label-specific features. IEEE Trans. Pattern Anal. Mach. Intell. **37**(1), 107–120 (2015)
10. Zhang, M.L., Zhou, Z.H.: ML-KNN: a lazy learning approach to multi-label learning. Pattern Recogn. **40**(7), 2038–2048 (2007)

Comparative Study of Dimensionality Reduction Methods Using Reliable Features for Multiple Datasets Obtained by rs-fMRI in ADHD Prediction

Rodolfo Garcia(✉), Emerson Cabrera Paraiso, and Julio Cesar Nievola

Pontifícia Universidade Católica do Paraná, Curitiba, Brazil
{rodolfobbgarcia,paraiso,nievola}@ppgia.pucpr.br

Abstract. ADHD is the most commonly diagnosed psychiatric disorder in children and, although its diagnosis is done in a subjective way, it can be characterized by abnormality work of specific brain regions. Datasets obtained by rs-fMRI cooperate to the large amount of brain information, but they lead to the curse-of-dimensionality problem. This paper aims to compare dimensionality reduction methods belonging to feature selection task using reliable features for multiple datasets obtained by rs-fMRI in ADHD prediction. Experiments showed that features evaluated in multiple datasets were able to improve the correct labeling rate, including the 87% obtained by MRMD that overcomes the higher accuracy in rs-fMRI ADHD prediction. They also eliminated the curse-of-dimensionality problem and identified relevant brain regions related to this disorder.

Keywords: ADHD prediction · Feature selection · rs-fMRI

1 Introduction

The Attention-Deficit/Hyperactivity Disorder (ADHD) affects 5.3% of the population under 12 years old, being the most commonly diagnosed psychiatric disorder in children [1]. Symptoms like inattention, impulsivity and hyperactivity affect the cognitive development and difficult the integration of an individual with others, causing social constraints. Its diagnosis is done in a subjective way by interviews with family or teachers about the patient behavior, resulting sometimes in inappropriate conducts in medicines or treatments. On the other hand, ADHD can be characterized by abnormality work of specific brain regions detected in neuroimages [2]. The main problem in neuroimages analysis is the high dimensional nature which leads to the problem called curse-of-dimensionality when the number of features is much higher than the number of observations.

Resting-state functional Magnetic Resonance Image (rs-fMRI) technique measures interactions between brain regions in low activation frequency and cooperates for this large amount of brain information usually stored in connectivity matrices. Since many brain regions do not provide useful information for ADHD diagnostic, dimensionality

M. Mouhoub and P. Langlais (Eds.): Canadian AI 2017, LNAI 10233, pp. 97–102, 2017.
DOI: 10.1007/978-3-319-57351-9_13

reduction using feature selection methods is essential to identify those regions responsible to the disorder characterization and to mitigate the curse-of-dimensionality problem [3]. In [4] is listed some regions obtained by structural MRI studies (e.g. frontal, parietal and occipital lobes, basal ganglia and cerebellum) and obtained by rs-fMRI studies (e.g. anterior cingulate cortex, frontal and temporal lobes, and again cerebellum). Lim and colleagues listed in [2] some regions with abnormalities related to ADHD (e.g. fronto-striatal, temporo-parietal and fronto-cerebellar).

As can be seen in [3, 5], it is unusual to find works involving ADHD and dimensionality reduction in neuroimages obtained by rs-fMRI technique. Beyond this, none of them compare methods and the generalization level is low because only a single dataset is used [6–8]. In [4] PCA and FDA (Fisher Discriminative Analysis) were combined to build classifiers that reached 85% of correct labeling, the higher accuracy related to rs-fMRI in ADHD prediction [5].

This paper presents a comparative study of feature selection methods in connectivity matrices obtained by rs-fMRI technique focused on ADHD. In order to select features with high quality level, an evaluation step guarantees that the subset of features is reliable for multiple datasets with the same ADHD focus, and to identify the relevant regions that are represented by these features. The rest of this paper is organized as follows: Sect. 2 describes the experimental details and the results are revealed in Sect. 3. Section 4 is dedicated to the conclusions.

2 Experiments

Compare feature selection methods using reliable features for multiple datasets involves two steps: the main step composed by a unique dataset, and the feature subset evaluation by the remaining datasets. Were used in this paper four groups of connectivity matrices, or four datasets, whose samples belong to individuals diagnosed with ADHD and with typically developing control (Typ), aged between 7 and 21 years old. These datasets are: KKI (58 Typ and 20 ADHD samples), NeuroIMAGE (22 Typ and 17 ADHD samples), NYU (91 Typ and 96 ADHD samples) and Peking (93 Typ and 57 ADHD samples). Each dataset was captured from different places and it dissimilarity samples make them independents, although the same 17955 features corresponding to the activity level between two brain regions measured by Pearson correlation. All datasets were published by ADHD-200 Consortium and are available in the USC Multimodal Connectivity Database website[1].

The experiments were organized as follows: first, each dataset was analyzed independently as a main dataset with n samples. To reduce the loss of information motivated by the small sample size and they high dimensionality, the main dataset was partitioned using leave-one-out cross validation (LOOCV). In each fold, the train dataset was submitted to a feature selection method. The ranking of features is used as input to the evaluation step, which will be detailed later and determines the optimal feature subset. After that, five classifiers (SVM, KNN, Perceptron, C4.5 and Naive

[1] http://umcd.humanconnectomeproject.org/.

Bayes) were trained by reduced train dataset to label the reduced test dataset. At the end of all LOOCV folds, a quality measure defined by *(sensitivity + specificity)/2* was calculated. This measure is in the range [0,1] and the highest value shows good distinction between typically developing and ADHD individuals samples.

With respect to the evaluation step, it guaranteed that the optimal feature subset for each classifier had high correct labeling rates in multiple datasets. This step uses the ranking of features as input data to the evaluation train and evaluation test datasets, which were generated by randomized half-split. The feature subset size varies from the most relevant feature alone to n most relevant, in order to eliminate curse-of-dimensionality. The same five classifiers labeled the evaluation test dataset and get the quality measure. This step was executed for the remaining datasets and returns for each classifier the feature subset with higher quality measure average.

This paper used five selection methods belonging to filter and embedded approaches, which are not expensive computationally and practicable in high dimensionality data. Most of the methods used here was cited in bioinformatics specialized reviews, including ones for other psychiatric disorders [3, 9], and was executed in Matlab. As PCC works with numerical classes, the score function adopted as label classes –1 for typically developing and 1 for ADHD. The SVM cost in RFE was 1.0 and each iteration removes 20% of the less relevant features until reaches the n features. The LASSO method used 10-fold cross validation to generate more accurate models, which the best was that with lower error rate. In MRMD, the distance function used was the Euclidean one because it got better results in [10]. The weights for Euclidean distance was 10^{-5} and for PCC was 1.

The classifiers belong to different approaches and are available in Weka: libSVM using linear kernel with 1.0 as cost; KNN considering 5 nearest neighbors; C4.5 considering at least 5 samples per leaf; Voted Perceptron and Naive Bayes. Multiple classifiers were used to provide better comparisons, once each dataset has the behavior observed under different classifications approaches.

Another objective of this work is to identify the relevant brain regions represented in the features selected. All the experiments were performed in an Intel i7 CPU, 1.73 GHz with 6 GB of RAM machine, using Java Eclipse IDE[2], Matlab[3] and Weka[4].

3 Results

This section shows the results of applying high quality features for multiple datasets to predict ADHD connectivity matrices from rs-fMRI. Tables 1, 2 and 3 present the quality measured and it average for the feature selection methods and for the dataset composed by the entire set of features.

For KKI dataset (Table 1), the feature selection methods worked well since they have increased or maintained the average of classification rates. PCC, RFE and

[2] https://eclipse.org/.

[3] www.mathworks.com/products/matlab/.

[4] www.cs.waikato.ac.nz/ml/weka.

Table 1. Results for KKI dataset

	PCC	Wilcoxon	LASSO	RFE	MRMD	Entire dataset
SVM	0.57	0.57	0.54	0.51	0.53	0.47
KNN	0.6	0.62	0.55	0.54	0.56	0.51
Perceptron	0.55	0.54	0.61	0.5	0.51	0.49
C4.5	0.65	0.68	0.47	0.65	0.47	0.63
Naive Bayes	0.56	0.56	0.57	0.51	0.52	0.47
Average	0.58	0.59	0.54	0.54	0.51	0.51

Table 2. Results for NeuroIMAGE dataset

	PCC	Wilcoxon	LASSO	RFE	MRMD	Entire dataset
SVM	0.55	0.54	0.59	0.8	0.6	0.6
KNN	0.61	0.56	0.56	0.63	0.55	0.45
Perceptron	0.66	0.54	0.53	0.65	0.62	0.47
C4.5	0.81	0.66	0.53	0.69	0.87	0.78
Naive Bayes	0.65	0.59	0.51	0.7	0.7	0.58
Average	0.65	0.57	0.54	0.69	0.66	0.57

Table 3. Results for NYU dataset

	PCC	Wilcoxon	LASSO	RFE	MRMD	Entire dataset
SVM	0.48	0.48	0.58	0.54	0.47	0.53
KNN	0.53	0.52	0.58	0.47	0.54	0.52
Perceptron	0.53	0.5	0.55	0.5	0.52	0.45
C4.5	0.58	0.52	0.57	0.52	0.57	0.39
Naive Bayes	0.52	0.6	0.6	0.58	0.52	0.49
Average	0.52	0.52	0.57	0.52	0.52	0.47

Wilcoxon improved the quality measures for all classifiers when comparing with the entire dataset. This last obtained the highest average and was considered the best.

In NeuroIMAGE dataset results (Table 2), only LASSO had worse average than the entire dataset. Although the remaining methods had better averages, MRMD was the unique to improve all classifiers and the one that obtained the highest value in this paper (0.87 for C4.5). RFE obtained the best average with 0.69. PCC obtained a high average despite it did not improve the rate for SVM. Despite the few samples to train, it was possible increase rates and eliminate the curse-of-dimensionality.

Equal to KKI dataset experiment, none of methods had worse average than the full NYU dataset, but only LASSO could improve the quality measures for all classifiers (Table 3). It was clearly the best feature selection method for this dataset since also returned the best average and the higher value in the current experiment.

Differently from what was observed until here, the feature selection methods did not work well for Peking dataset and the higher average was obtained by the entire dataset. In RFE and MRMD cases, no classifier had an increased rate. For PCC, Wilcoxon and LASSO, only for KNN classifier were increased the quality measure.

Another objective of this paper is to identify the most relevant brain regions represented in the features selected by the best methods for each dataset (Wilcoxon for KKI, MRMD for NeuroIMAGE, LASSO for NYU and PCC for Peking), considering the top five relevant regions ordered by the number of presences in the features subsets. Based on the lists presented in introduction, some regions were common for all methods like the Frontal, Occipital and Parietal lobes. The Cerebellum was another important relevant region for most of datasets. Some evidences of the importance of fronto-striatal region, temporo-parietal region and Anterior Cingulate Cortex had appeared. The unique region not presented in the list is the Insular lobe, relevant for NeuroIMAGE dataset.

4 Conclusions

This paper compared feature selection methods applying reliable features for multiple datasets obtained by rs-fMRI for prediction of ADHD samples in four datasets.

The results in Sect. 3 showed that evaluating features using multiple datasets was crucial to increase the correct labeling rate and was able to eliminate the curse-of-dimensionality. In three of four datasets, there is at least one feature selection method able to increase the quality measures for all classifiers when compared to the entire dataset. These are the cases of Wilcoxon in KKI dataset, MRMD in NeuroIMAGE dataset and LASSO for NYU dataset. Additionally, the MRMD resulted in 87% of correct labeling in NeuroIMAGE with C4.5 classifier, which is better than the result obtained by [4], considered the higher accuracy for rs-fMRI ADHD neuroimage. On the contrary, Peking dataset was the negative case since any method had increased the classification quality. The reason for it or to find a method that works well can be addressed as future work. The best feature selection method for the experiments here executed was PCC for the fact that it is always between the best methods for all datasets.

Other objective of this paper is to identify the relevant regions represented in the features that characterize the ADHD disorder. The regions listed in [4] and [2] were considerable relevant at least once. Some common regions in all methods were the Frontal, Occipital and Parietal lobes. The Cerebellum region was an important relevant one for most of datasets as well. The only region absent in these lists was the left Insular lobe obtained by MRMD in the NeuroIMAGE dataset.

Although the improvements of correct labeling rate using reliable feature for multiples dataset focused on ADHD, the ideal scene is still not reached to support specialists in the ADHD diagnosis. For future work, ensemble of feature selection methods can generate more reliable feature subset, identifying even more the relevance of brain regions to ADHD and increasing our knowledge about this disorder.

Acknowledgement. The authors of this paper would like to acknowledge CAPES (Coordenação de Aperfeiçoamento de Pessoal de Nível Superior) for the financial support of this research.

References

1. Banaschewski, T., Zuddas, A., Asherson, P., et al.: ADHD and Hyperkinetic Disorder, 2nd edn. Oxford University Press, USA (2015)
2. Lim, L., Marquand, A., Cubillo, A., et al.: Disorder-specific predictive classification of adolescents with attention deficit hyperactivity disorder (ADHD) relative to autism using structural magnetic resonance imaging. PLoS ONE **8**(5), e63660 (2013). doi:10.1371/journal.pone.0063660
3. Mwangi, B., Tian, T., Soares, T.: A review of feature reduction techniques in neuroimaging. Neuroinformatics **12**(2), 229–244 (2014). doi:10.1007/s12021-013-9204-3
4. Zhu, C., Zang, Y., Cao, Q., et al.: Fisher discriminative analysis of resting-state brain function for attention-deficit/hyperactivity disorder. Neuroimage **40**(1), 110–120 (2008). doi:10.1016/j.neuroimage.2007.11.029
5. Wolfers, T., Buitelaar, J., Beckmann, C., et al.: From estimating activation locality to predicting disorder: a review of pattern recognition for neuroimaging-based psychiatric diagnostics. Neurosci. Biobehav. Rev. **57**, 328–349 (2015). doi:10.1016/j.neubiorev.2015.08.001
6. Wang, X., Jiao, Y., Lu, Z.: Discriminative analysis of resting-state brain functional connectivity patterns of attention-deficit hyperactivity disorder using kernel principal component analysis. In: 2011 Eighth International Conference on Fuzzy Systems and Knowledge Discovery (FSKD), pp. 1938–1941 (2011). doi:10.1109/FSKD.2011.6019911
7. Liang, S., Hsieh, T., Chen, P., et al.: Differentiation between resting-state fMRI data from ADHD and normal subjects: based on functional connectivity and machine learning. In: IEEE International Conference on Fuzzy Theory and it's Applications (iFUZZY), pp. 294–298 (2012). doi:10.1109/iFUZZY.2012.6409719
8. Sato, J., Hoexter, M., Fujita, A., et al.: Evaluation of pattern recognition and feature extraction methods in ADHD prediction. Front. Syst. Neurosci. **6**, 68 (2012). doi:10.3389/fnsys.2012.00068
9. Lazar, C., Taminau, J., Meganck, S., et al.: A survey on filter techniques for feature selection in gene expression microarray analysis. IEEE/ACM Trans. Comput. Biol. Bioinform. (TCBB) **9**(4), 1106–1119 (2012). doi:10.1109/TCBB.2012.33
10. Zou, Q., Zeng, L., Ji, R.: A novel features ranking metric with application to scalable visual and bioinformatics data classification. Neurocomputing **173**, 346–354 (2016). doi:10.1016/j.neucom.2014.12.123

Time-Dependent Smart Data Pricing Based on Machine Learning

Yi-Chia Tsai[1(✉)], Yu-Da Cheng[1(✉)], Cheng-Wei Wu[1(✉)], Yueh-Ting Lai[2], Wan-Hsun Hu[2], Jeu-Yih Jeng[2], and Yu-Chee Tseng[1]

[1] Department of Computer Science, National Chiao Tung University, Hsinchu, Taiwan, ROC
{yctsai5865, yuda0556098, cww0403, yctseng}@cs.nctu.edu.tw

[2] Chunghwa Telecom Laboratories, Taoyuan, Taiwan, ROC

Abstract. The purpose of *time-dependent smart data pricing* (abbreviated as *TDP*) is to relieve network congestion by offering network users different prices over varied periods. However, traditional TDP has not considered applying *machine learning concepts* in determining prices. In this paper, we propose a new framework for TDP based on machine learning concepts. We propose two different pricing algorithms, named *TDP-TR* (*TDP based on Transition Rules*) and *TDP-KNN* (*TDP based on K-Nearest Neighbors*). TDP-TR determines prices based on users' past willingness to pay given different prices, while TDP-KNN determines prices based on the similarity of users' past network usages. The main merit of TDP-TR is low computational cost, while that of TDP-KNN is low maintenance cost. Experimental results on simulated datasets show that the proposed algorithms have good performance and profitability.

Keywords: K-nearest neighbor · Machine learning · Network congestion management · Smart data pricing

1 Introduction and Background

Smart data pricing (abbreviated as *SDP*) [1–3] is to apply variable prices to incentivize users to adjust their behaviors in Internet access. A good pricing mechanism can relieve network congestion, thus enhancing network utilization, providing users good quality of experience, reducing costs on operators, and increasing companies' revenue. SDP has attracted a lot of attention from both industrial and academic institutions. Several pricing mechanisms [4, 5, 8, 9] have been proposed, such as *flat-rate pricing*, *usage-based pricing*, *location-dependent pricing*, and *transaction-based pricing*. Although these pricing mechanisms may work well in some specific applications or domains, they do not take into account the variation of network traffics over time.

In view of the above observations, the concept of *time-dependent smart data pricing* (abbreviated as *TDP*) was proposed [6, 7]. Its main idea is to dynamically adjust prices based on the estimation of users' future network traffic over various periods. Hence, TDP can incentivize users to shift their network usages to other periods where the network traffic is less congested. However, traditional TDP solutions assume

M. Mouhoub and P. Langlais (Eds.): Canadian AI 2017, LNAI 10233, pp. 103–108, 2017.
DOI: 10.1007/978-3-319-57351-9_14

that the degree that users will be incentivized (i.e., willingness to pay) may follow a mathematical model without considering the users' actual behaviors in the past. In this work, we propose the concept of *machine learning* [10] to improve the effectiveness of TDP. The main idea of machine learning is to make good use of historical data to make accurate prediction or estimation on future status.

In this paper, we apply the concept of machine learning to TDP and propose a new framework for mobile data networks. It consists of four main modules. (1) *Network usage collection*: this module collects network usages from users' mobile phones and sends it to the server of ISPs. (2) *Transition rule extraction*: this module extracts transition rules from users' historical behavior and uses these extracted rules to estimate the impact of prices on users' incentive. (3) *Future network usage estimation*: this module integrates extracted rules and machine learning methods to estimate users' future network usages under a set of prices. (4) *Utility maximization*: this module calculates an optimal set of prices to maximize the utility for ISPs and its users as much as possible. Moreover, we propose two different pricing algorithms, named *TDP-TR* (*TDP based on Transition Rules*) and *TDP-KNN* (*TDP based on K-Nearest Neighbors*), respectively. TDP-TR determines the prices based on the users' past willingness to pay under the TDP architecture, while TDP-KNN determines that based on the similar users' past network usages. The main merit of TDP-TR is low computational cost, while that of TDP-KNN is low maintenance cost. Experiments on synthetic datasets show that the proposed algorithms have good performance and profitability.

The rest of this paper is organized as follows. Section 2 introduces the proposed solutions and algorithms. Section 3 evaluates the performance of experimental results. The conclusion is described in Sect. 4.

2 Proposed Solutions

2.1 TDP-TR Pricing Algorithm

The TDP-TR algorithm adopts the *day-ahead dynamic pricing scheme* [7], which is often used in electricity pricing. In this scheme, a day will be partitioned into N time slots $\langle T_1, T_2, \ldots, T_N \rangle$. For example, if $N = 24$, a day will be partitioned into 24 time slots. Besides, each time slot is associated with a discount ratio. For the i-th time slot $T_i (1 \leq i \leq N)$, its discount is denoted by d_i. The system will determine a set of discounts $\theta = \langle d_1, d_2, \ldots d_N \rangle$ for the next day with the objective of maximizing the total utility of ISP and its users. Users will be informed of θ one day in advance. Therefore, users can plan when to access Internet over the next day. TDP-TR determines θ based on the following four main modules: (1) *network usage collection*, (2) *transition rule extraction*, (3) *Future network usage estimation*, and (4) *utility maximization*.

2.1.1 Network Usage Collection

To collect related information of users' network usages, each user's mobile phone is installed an App called *Collector*. This App will collect the following information and sends it to an ISP-side database called *TDP usage database*: (1) the user's Id, (2) the date, (3) the time slot number, (4) the user's network usage in the time slot and the corresponding discount over various time slots. If the user switches to *time-independent pricing* (abbreviated as *TIP*) mode (e.g., *flat-rate pricing* [7]), the App will still continuously collect the above information, but the information of discounts will be ignored and the collected information will be sent to another database called *TIP usage database*.

2.1.2 Transition Rule Extraction

The purpose of this module is to calculate users' willingness for transiting their Internet access behaviors from a time slot T_i of discount α to another time slot T_j of discount β. To get such information, whenever a user opens an App S at T_i, Collector will pop out a window to inquire the user whether he/she wants to use S right away. If the user answers "*Yes*", then such behavior will be treated as that the user is unwilling to transit his/her Internet access behavior. In this case, the system will generate a *transition rule* "$(T_i, d_i) \Rightarrow (T_i, d_i)$" and send it to a *transition rule database*. If the user answers "*No*" and re-opens the App S again at T_j and $(T - T_i) \leq \xi$, where ξ is a time threshold defined by ISP, then the user's behavior will be treated as willing to transit his/her network usages from T_i to T_j. In this case, the system will send a transition rule $(T_i, d_i) \Rightarrow (T_j, d_j)$ to the transition rule database. From the transition rule database, we can calculate users' transition probabilities to model the impact of prices on users' willingness for transition. Let r be any transition rule "$(T_i, \alpha) \Rightarrow (T_j, \beta)$" collected from a user, the transition probability for r is defined as $Pr(r) = Z/M$, where M is the number of rules whose antecedents are (T_i, α) and Z is the number of rules whose antecedents and consequents are (T_i, α) and (T_i, β), respectively.

2.1.3 Future Network Usage Estimation

Given a set of non-negative discounts $\pi = \langle d_1, d_2, \ldots, d_N \rangle$, this module will estimate each user's network usages over various time slots $\langle T_1, T_2, \ldots, T_N \rangle$ for the next day. Let $\sigma(u, J, D)$ denote user u's network usage of the J-th time slot on the D-th day and Q denote the total number of days on which u ever accessed Internet in the TIP model. We define the *TIP usage pattern* for user u as $\langle p_{u1}, p_{u2}, \ldots, p_{uN} \rangle$, where p_{uJ} $(1 \leq J \leq N)$ is defined as $P_{uJ} = \sum_{D=1}^{Q} \frac{\sigma(u,J,D)}{Q}$. In other words, p_{uJ} is user u's average network usage at the J-th time slot in the TIP model. Then, we estimate user u's expected network usages in the TDP model. While adopting TDP, user u's expected network usage transiting from time slot T_J to time slot T_k ($J \neq k$ and $1 \leq J \leq k \leq N$) is defined as $outflow(u, J, \pi) = \sum_{i=1}^{N} P_{uJ} \times Pr((T_i, d_i) \Rightarrow (T_j, d_j))$. By subtracting the outflow from p_{uJ}, the remaining usage for T_J is defined as $rm(u, J, \pi) = p_{uJ} - outflow(u, J, \pi)$. The expected network usage transiting from T_i to T_J ($i \neq J$ and $1 \leq i \leq J \leq N$) is defined as $inflow(u, J, \pi) = \sum_{i=1}^{N} P_{ui} \times Pr((T_i, d_i) \Rightarrow (T_j, d_j))$. User u's expected network usage for T_J in the TDP model is defined as $E_{uJ} = rm(u, J, \pi) + inflow(u, J, \pi)$. Therefore, user u's estimated network usages for the next day is $E_u = \langle E_{u1}, E_{u2}, \ldots, E_{uN} \rangle$.

2.1.4 Utility Maximization

Let U denotes the total number of users. Then, in the TDP model, the sum of the expected network usage of all users for T_J $(1 \leq J \leq N)$ is defined as $E_J = \sum_{u=1}^{U} E_{uJ}$. In the TIP model, the sum of the average network usage of all users for T_J $(1 \leq J \leq N)$ is defined as $P_J = \sum_{u=1}^{U} P_{uJ}$. By comparing E_J and P_J $(1 \leq J \leq N)$, the expected gain or loss of the ISP's revenue is $expGL(\pi) = \sum_{J=1}^{N} (E_J - (d_J \times E_J) - P_J) \times \gamma$, where γ is the unit profit per megabyte usage (i.e., \$/MB). If *expGL*(π) is higher than a capacity threshold *C* defined by the ISP, then the network congestion problem may occur, which may cause additional costs on the ISP and reduce some users' willingness to pay. We use a penalty function *penalty*(*J*, π) to represent such loss. On the contrary, if *expGL*(*J*, π)/γ is not higher than *C*, then with a higher discount d_J, T_J may attract more users to use the network services, which may increase the additional revenues for the ISP. We use a bonus function denoted by *bonus*(*J*, π) to represent such gain. The penalty and bonus functions can be defined by based on the ISP's requirements. Let π* be the set of all combinations of *N* discounts. This module will apply some optimization algorithms (e.g., *genetic algorithm*) to find an optimal set of discounts θ to maximize the objective utility function.

$$\theta = \max\left\{ expGL(\pi) + \sum_{J=1}^{N} [penalty(J, \pi) + bonus(J, \pi)] | \forall \pi \in \pi^* \right\}$$

2.2 TDP-KNN Pricing Algorithm

In this subsection, we propose another pricing algorithm called *TDP-KNN* (*TDP based on K-Nearest Neighbors*). It is similar to TDP-TR, but applies a classical machine learning algorithm, *k-nearest neighbor*, to estimate user *u*'s network usages for the next day (i.e., $E_u = \langle E_{u1}, E_{u2}, \ldots, E_{uN} \rangle$). So we will only focus on how the TDP-KNN calculate E_u.

Given a non-negative discounts $\pi = \langle d_1, d_2, \ldots, d_N \rangle$, the algorithm will estimate each user *u*'s network usages $E_u = \langle E_{u1}, E_{u2}, \ldots, E_{uN} \rangle$ over various time slots $\langle T_1, T_2, \ldots, T_N \rangle$ for the next day. In the off-line stage of the algorithm, it can adopt the *Euclidean distance* [10] or other similarity metrics to calculate the similarity between each pair of users in terms of their TDP network usages. The result is stored in a similarity matrix. The on-line stage of the algorithm works as follows. Let *K* and *L* be the input parameters for the algorithm. Each E_{ui} ($1 \leq i \leq N$) in E_u is first initialized to zero. To estimate the value of E_{ui} the algorithm proceeds as follows. It first initializes a variable *varN* to 0 and stores *u*'s *K* most similar users in *NB*(*u*), called *u*'s *neighbors*. By retrieving the similarity matrix, *u*'s neighbors can be easily obtained.

For each $y \in NB(u)$, the algorithm sets *VarL* as 0 and visits *y*'s historical TDP data. Suppose that *y* has *X* records and these records are sorted by their generation time. Let *y*[*j*] be the *j*-th record in *Y*. A smaller *j* represents that the generation time of the record is closer to the present. For each visited data *y*[*j*] ($1 \leq j \leq X$), the algorithm checks whether its time slot and discount are equal to *i* and d_i, respectively. If the condition is true, E_{ui} will be accumulated by the usage of *y*[*j*]. Besides, *varL* will be increased by 1. After the accumulation, the algorithm checks whether *varL* is equal to *L*. If *varL* is equal to *L*, the algorithm stops visiting the rest of the historical TDP data of *y* and processes the next neighbor of u. If all the neighbors in *NB*(u) have been processed, e_i will be divided by *K*. After that, we can obtain user *u*'s future estimated usage for the time slot T_i w.r.t. π. If $i = N + 1$, the algorithm outputs the estimation result $\langle E_{u1}, E_{u2}, \ldots, E_{uN} \rangle$ and completes the process. Otherwise, *i* is increased by 1 and the algorithm repeats the above process until $i = N + 1$.

3 Experimental Results

Experiments were performed on a computer with an Intel Core i5-3210 M CPU@2.50 GHz, 8 GB of memory, running on Windows 10 OS. All the compared algorithms are implemented in Java. We implemented a data generator to simulate TIP, TDP and transition rule databases. The parameters for generating data are described as follows. The unit profit of network usage per megabyte is 10. The total numbers of users in TIP (or TDP) database is 20. The total numbers of days and time slots in a day are 5 and 30, respectively. The maximum and minimum network usages are 100 and 0, respectively. Parameters C, K, and L are set to 80, 5, 5, respectively. As shown in Fig. 1(a) and (c), TDP-TR generally runs much faster than TDP-KNN. This is because TDP-KNN estimates future network usages of users by searching historical TDP data of users' neighbors, which may cause TDP-KNN to suffer from higher computational costs, while TDP-TR estimates that mainly relying on transition probabilities of rules, which only involves simple operations on additions and multiplications without time-consuming search operations. In Fig. 1(b) and (d), the profits gained by the two algorithms are different. This is reasonable because TDP-TR and TDP-KNN use different approaches to estimate future network usages of users. In Fig. 1, the execution time of TDP-TR are generally better than that of TDP-KNN. However, TDP-KNN does not need to maintain a transition rule database for the system, which can significantly decrease the costs on updating the transfer rule database and calculation of transition probabilities. Therefore, TDP-KNN is much easier to be maintained.

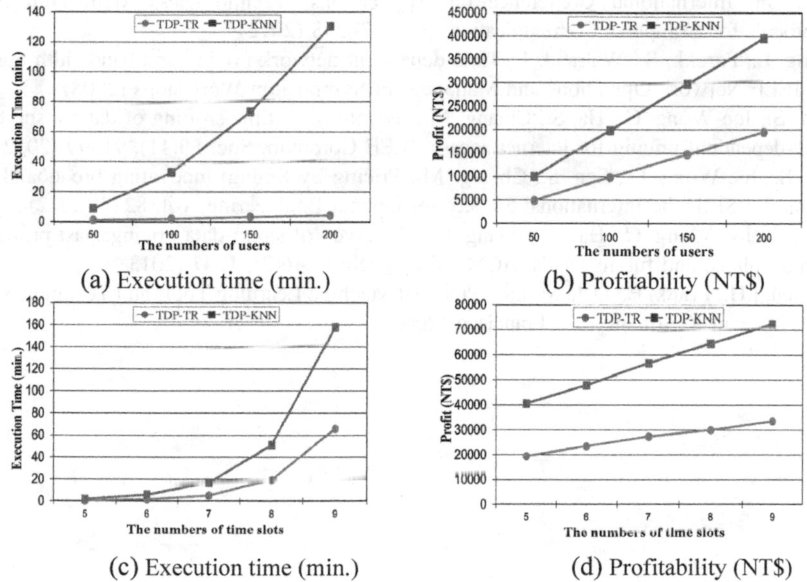

(a) Execution time (min.)

(b) Profitability (NT$)

(c) Execution time (min.)

(d) Profitability (NT$)

Fig. 1. The performance of TDP-TR and TDP-KNN under varied parameter settings.

4 Conclusion

This paper proposes a new framework for time-dependent smart data pricing based on machine learning concepts. It consists of four core modules: (1) *network usage collection*, (2) *transition rule extraction*, (3) *future network usage estimation*, and (4) *utility maximization*. Moreover, we propose two efficient algorithms, *TDP-TR* and *TDP-KNN*. Experimental results on simulated data show that the proposed algorithms have good performance under different parameter settings.

References

1. Chawla, C., Chana, I.: Optimal time dependent pricing model for smart cloud with cost based scheduling. In: International Symposium on Women in Computing and Informatics, pp. 522–526 (2015)
2. Chang, C.-H., Lin, P., Zhang, J., Jeng, J.-Y.: Time dependent adaptive pricing for mobile internet access. In: IEEE Conference on Computer Communication Workshops, pp. 540–545 (2015)
3. Chang, C.-H., Lin, P., Zhang, J., Jeng, J.-Y.: Time dependent pricing in wireless data networks: flat-rate vs. usage-based schemes. In: IEEE International Conference on Computer and Communications, pp. 700–708 (2014)
4. Falkner, M., Devetsikiotis, M.: An overview of pricing concepts for broadband IP networks. IEEE Commun. Surv. Tutorials **3**(2), 2–13 (2000)
5. Ha, S., Sen, S., Wong, C.J., Im, Y., Chiang, M.: TUBE: time-dependent pricing for mobile data. In: International Conference on Applications, Technologies, Architectures, and Protocols for Computer Communication, pp. 247–258 (2012)
6. Jiang, L., Parekh, S., Walrand, J.: Time-dependent network pricing and bandwidth trading. In: IEEE Network Operations and Management Symposium Workshops (2008)
7. Sen, S., Joe-Wong, C., Ha, S., Chiang, M.: Incentivizing time-shifting of data: a survey of time-dependent pricing for internet access. IEEE Commun. Soc. **50**(11), 91–99 (2012)
8. Ha, S., Joe-Wong, C., Sen, S., Chiang, M.: Pricing by timing: innovating broadband data plans. In: SPIE the International Society for Optical Engineering, vol. 8282 (2012)
9. Sen, S., Joe-Wong, C., Ha, S., Chiang, M.: A survey of smart data pricing: past proposals, current plans, and future trends. ACM Comput. Surv. **46**(2), 1–37 (2013)
10. Witten, I.H., Frank, E.: Data Mining: Practical Machine Learning Tools and Techniques, 2nd edn. Morgan Kaufmann, San Francisco (2005)

Time Prediction of the Next Refueling Event: A Case Study

S. Mohammad Mirbagheri(✉) and Howard J. Hamilton

University of Regina, Regina, SK, Canada
{mirbaghs,Howard.Hamilton}@uregina.ca

Abstract. A case study of finding the best algorithm for predicting the time of the next refueling event from an incomplete, crowd-sourced data set is presented. We considered ten algorithms including nine experts plus one ensemble (learner) method that performs machine learning using the other nine experts. An experiment on one dimensional crowd-sourced data showed that prediction with the ensemble method is more accurate than prediction with any of the individual experts.

1 Introduction

The goal of this research is to determine the effectiveness of existing and novel methods for the task of predicting the next time when users will refuel their cars, based on their self-recorded refueling information. The information given by users is not necessarily correct or complete, which complicates the prediction task. Therefore, a method is required to extract and filter the relevant information first and then perform a prediction with high accuracy. To achieve this, a sample data set is selected and then nine prediction methods (experts) are applied to it. The learner receives the results of their predictions and produces the tenth prediction based on Weighted Majority Algorithm (WMA). The ten predictions are evaluated on the sample data to assess the effectiveness of the methods.

The main contribution of this work is a model for predicting temporal events from crowd-sourced data. Previous work on temporal event prediction has used complete data sets. Yang et al. [1] showed how to use an extension of the association rule classification method to predict the time when a web page access will occur. Huang et al. [2] applied continuous time Markov chains and Kolmogorov's backward equations to predict when an online user will leave a current page and which page the user will request next. Both of these approaches were applied to web log data from a NASA server. Other work on predicting air cargo demand applied the Potluck problem approach along with WMA to non-temporal events [3]. All of the mentioned approaches were applied to complete data sets.

2 Input Data and Preprocessing

Data Set: The data set for the case study contains user-supplied records of fuel purchases for a period of more than six years from January 2010 to August 2016.

M. Mouhoub and P. Langlais (Eds.): Canadian AI 2017, LNAI 10233, pp. 109–114, 2017.
DOI: 10.1007/978-3-319-57351-9_15

car_id	purch_dt	prev_purch_dt	D_purch	add_dt	prev_add_dt	D_add_dt	D_hours	curr_km	prev_km	D_km
22222	2013-09-19	2013-09-09	10	2013-09-19 15:37:16	2013-09-09 22:47:55	10	233	122,849	122,580	269
22222	2013-09-28	2013-09-19	9	2013-09-28 12:52:21	2013-09-19 15:37:16	9	213	122,962	122,849	113
22222	2013-09-29	2013-09-28	1	2013-09-29 19:21:54	2013-09-28 12:52:21	1	31	123,238	122,962	276
22222	2013-10-04	2013-09-29	5	2013-10-04 17:25:36	2013-09-29 19:21:54	5	118	123,457	123,238	219
22222	2013-10-11	2013-10-04	7	2013-10-11 18:51:21	2013-10-04 17:25:36	7	169	123,686	123,457	229

Fig. 1. The first five rows of the data set with the synthetic delta variables

We define several synthetic variables to represent relevant differences (deltas) of the times and odometers values reported by users. The difference between the dates of successive purchases is calculated and recorded as *D_purch*. The difference between the dates of successive reports of purchases (in days, ignoring partial days) is *D_add_dt*, the difference between the times of successive reports (in hours) is *D_hours*, and the difference in odometer readings is *D_km*. Figure 1 shows the first five rows of data after the deltas for each car were calculated.

Filtering Records: The smallest unit in purch_dt (date of purchase) is *day*. Because *hour* as a unit of prediction could possibly give us better results than *day*, we wanted to have *hour* instead of *day*. However, in this data set, *hour* exists only in the add_dt (time of report) attribute. Therefore, we matched the *date* values of these two attributes and removed entries with inconsistent dates. For the remaining entries, we used *add_dt* to determine values for *D_hours* as an independent variable in predictions.

Since the data consists of self-reported values, filtering is applied to improve data quality. Any prediction method should be provided with a minimum number of data points (entries) with which to work. The minimum required number of entries for each car is set to $m+1$ (to give m deltas). As well, cars with unlikely deltas for times and odometer readings are filtered out. The average delta time is restricted to between 0 and 100 days and the average delta distance is restricted to between 100 km and 500 km.

Removing Outliers from Records: The median absolute deviation from the median (MAD) is used to find and remove outliers [4]. Given a data set $x = \{x_1, \ldots, x_n\}$, MAD is calculated:

$$MAD = median(|x_i - median(x)|) \quad (1)$$

For this purpose, the median and standard deviation of delta times are calculated for each car. An entry is identified as an outlier if the absolute deviation of its delta time from the median is more than two times greater than MAD. The outliers are then removed from the record for the car.

3 Methods of Prediction

We consider ten methods to predict the time of the next refueling event. The methods can be categorized in four major classes: statistical, empirical, data mining, and machine learning. Nine of these methods, which are called experts, predict the next value separately and the tenth method, which is an ensemble learning algorithm, makes a final prediction based on a weighted average of the predictions from the nine methods.

We require a minimum of m delta values as input to the nine experts. To avoid any Cold-Start anomalies, we only start performing predictions after the first $m+1$ values have accumulated and thus the first m deltas can be calculated. For example, suppose m is 20. The nine experts wait to get the first 20 delta times. They then each predict the next value (21st delta time). The learning algorithm (tenth method) puts the nine predicted values together and estimates one prediction for the 21st delta time. In the next step, the experts receive the actual 21st data point and the 22nd data point is predicted based on all entries so far. This process is iterated until the last data point is reached.

The first four experts use statistical calculations and the fifth one uses a simple empirical rule to make a prediction from all entries so far.

M1 - Mean: This method predicts the mean value of all entries so far.

M2 - Median: This method predicts the median value of all entries so far.

M3 - Linear Regression: Linear regression analysis requires at least two variables to estimate a regression line. However, since our data set has only one variable (delta time), we use the previous delta time as the independent variable (x) and the immediate next delta time as the dependent variable (y) [5].

M4 - Autoregressive Integrated Moving Average (ARIMA): In time series analysis, the ARIMA method can provide different models to predict future points in a series, depending on the data characteristics. It represents Autoregressive (AR), Moving Average (MA), or combination of both models with or without differencing (the operations to produce stationary time series) [6].

M5 - Repeat the Last Value: Since the training set is constructed and updated chronologically, the last value of the training set is the most recent one. This empirical method returns the last value of the training set as the predicted value.

Partitional clustering with the k-means algorithm [7] is employed in this research to divide the delta times into clusters. The following four approaches first cluster the data using the k-means algorithm and then apply a specialized method to predict the next value based on the resulting clusters.

M6 - Most Frequent Cluster: After running the k-means algorithm on data, this method counts the number of members in each cluster. The cluster with the most members, which is called the *most frequent cluster*, is identified and its center is picked for the prediction. If two or more clusters are tied for the most members, the average of their cluster centers is used for prediction. Figure 2 depicts an example of a prediction with the most frequent cluster method.

M7 - Last Entry Cluster: After constructing clusters with the k-means algorithm, the Last Entry method considers only the last entry. It maps this entry to its cluster and then selects the center of this cluster as the next predicted value. Figure 3 illustrates this method with an example.

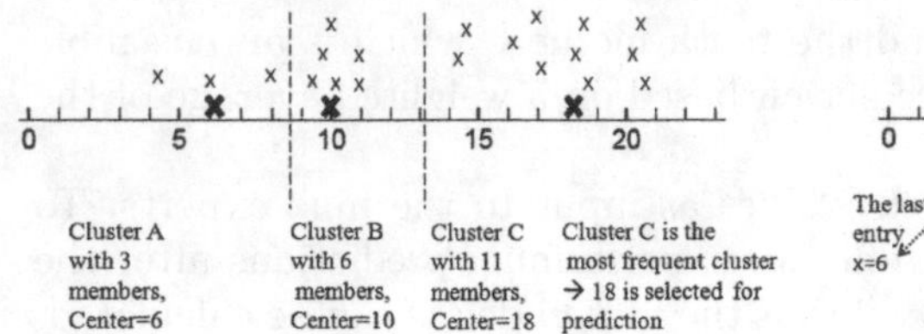

Fig. 2. Example of the most frequent cluster method

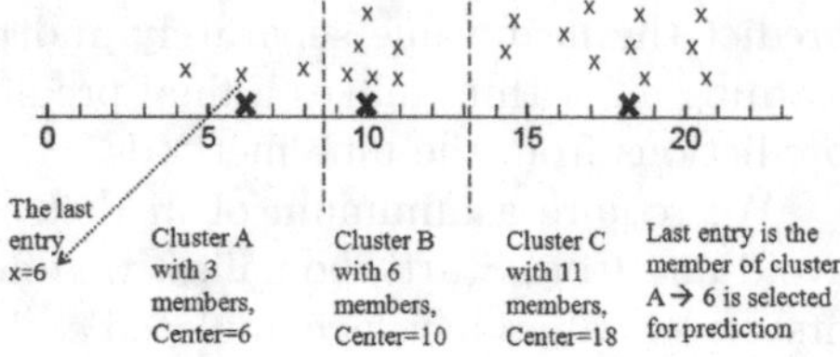

Fig. 3. Example of the last entry cluster method

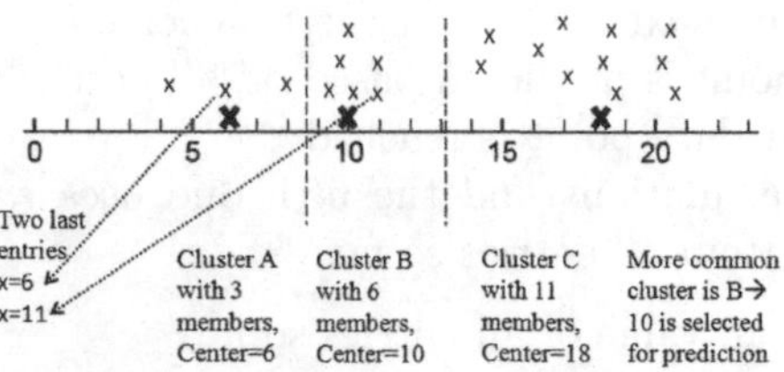

Fig. 4. Example of the two last entries-more common cluster method

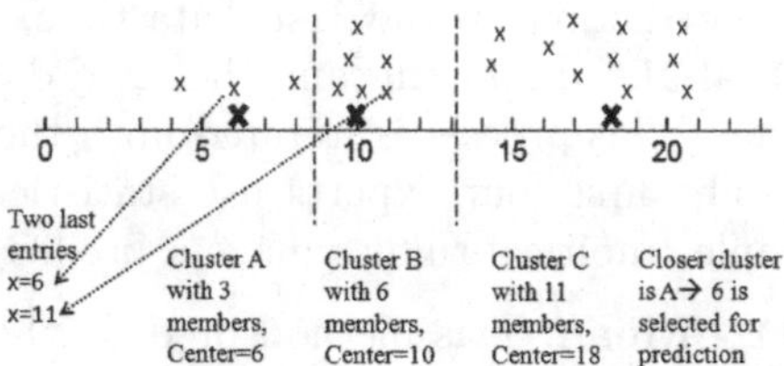

Fig. 5. Example of the two last entries-closer cluster method

M8 - Two Last Entries-More Common Cluster: This method uses a combination of the Most Frequent Cluster method and the Last Entry method. It maps the two last entries to their corresponding clusters and then selects the cluster with more members, which is called the *more common cluster*. The center of the more common cluster is selected for prediction. Figure 4 demonstrates an example of a prediction with the Two Last Entries-More Common Cluster method.

M9 - Two Last Entries-Closer Cluster: This method, like the previous method, maps the two last entries to their corresponding clusters. Then, it calculates the distances of the last two entries to their corresponding cluster centers. The cluster that has the smaller distance, which is called the *closer cluster*, is selected. Finally, the method selects the center of the closer cluster for prediction. Figure 5 depicts the Two Last Entries-Closer Cluster method.

The learning algorithm (tenth method) combines the predicted values from the nine methods and estimates one prediction for the next value.

M10 - Weighted Majority Algorithm–Continuous Version [8]**:** The continuous version of Weighted Majority Algorithm [8,9] for combining the result of N componenet algorithms (experts) is applied. In the beginning, all N experts (in this research, $N = 9$) are initialized with equal weights (1). Then, every time any expert makes a mistake in the prediction, it loses some weight. A new weight for every expert $i \in [1 \ldots N]$ can be obtained based on the following formula:

$$w_i^{t+1} = w_i^t.exp^{-\eta \cdot |\xi_i^t - y^t|} \tag{2}$$

where $|\xi_i^t - y^t|$ is the error of the prediction for expert i. An optimal upper bound η is calculated as $\eta = \sqrt{8lnN/T}$, where T is the number of predictions [10].

4 Empirical Evaluation

We applied the ten methods to crowd-sourced data to predict the next refueling times. We describe the experimental methodology and the results.

Experiment Environment and Implementation: We used the R statistical package, version 3.3.0 to implement the ten methods mentioned in Sect. 3. For the experiment, we randomly selected 1000 out of 6,057 cars in the cleaned data set. Data normalization between 0 and 1 is required, since the weighted majority algorithm (method M10), requires data in the range [0,1]. After prediction, the result is re-scaled to the original data range. The following steps are *repeated* by our software for every car to make predictions:

1. The data for a car are obtained and sorted chronologically.
2. The weights of all $N = 9$ component methods (experts) are set to 1.
3. The training set is constructed for the current car by taking the first m delta times. In the experiment, m is 10.
4. The ten methods are applied to predict the next delta time.
5. The predicted delta time is compared with the actual delta time to calculate the error of the prediction, and the new weights for the experts.
6. If the last data of the car has not been reached, the actual delta time is added to the training set and the next prediction round starts.

Experiment Results: The predictions from all methods for one sample car are presented in Table 1. All experts and the learning algorithm use normalized values between 0 and 1. The actual value and its normalized value are labeled "Act_val" and "Nrm_val," respectively. The prediction from the learning algorithm M10 is shown as "Act_M10." The actual value "Act_val," the prediction "Act_M10," and the error of the prediction "Error_M10" are in hours.

Table 1 can be explained by an example. The second column describes information for the car with id 3550. The actual value of the delta time is 160 h. The predicted value is 301.35 h after inverting the result of the learning algorithm (0.521823) and the error is 141.35 h. The user with car_id "3550" was predicted to purchase gas 301.35 h after the last purchase but the user actually purchased gas after 160 h. In the other words, the learning algorithm predicted 141.35 h (almost 6 days) earlier than the actual time.

Table 2 summarizes the results of an experiment based on 21,383 predictions, which is all the predictions made for the 1000 users. As seen in Table 2 for Weighted Majority Algorithm (M10), the number of the predictions with an error of at most 24 h is 7,905 (37% of 21,383 predictions). Similarly, for an error of at most 72 h, the number of predictions is 16,087 (75.2%) and for ±148 h (one week), it is 92.8%. By further analysis of the data (not shown), we determined that the mean absolute error for the 21,383 predictions is 55.5 h (less than 3 days).

5 Conclusion

This paper presented a case study attempting to predict the next refueling time from crowd-sourced data. We applied preprocessing to obtain the time differences (deltas) between refueling events and we also cleaned the data using the

Table 1. The results of the predictions for a sample car

car_id	3550
Act_val	160
Nrm_val	0.26151
M1	0.488766
M2	0.522099
M3	0.479282
M4	0.488766
M5	0.762431
M6	0.488766
M7	0.488766
M8	0.488766
M9	0.488766
M10	0.521823
Act_M10	301.35
Error_M10	141.35

Table 2. Accuracy of the methods for the experiment based on 21,383 predictions

Method	Delta time		
	$\pm 24h$	$\pm 72h$	$\pm 148h$
M1	7716 (0.361)	15953 (0.746)	19806 (0.926)
M2	7772 (0.363)	15847 (0.741)	19703 (0.921)
M3	7812 (0.365)	16045 (0.750)	**19881 (0.930)**
M4	7852 (0.367)	15939 (0.745)	19769 (0.925)
M5	7100 (0.332)	14691 (0.687)	18969 (0.887)
M6	7411 (0.345)	15412 (0.721)	19496 (0.912)
M7	7497 (0.351)	15485 (0.724)	19565 (0.915)
M8	7530 (0.352)	15523 (0.726)	19565 (0.915)
M9	7525 (0.352)	15485 (0.724)	19531 (0.913)
M10	**7905 (0.370)**	**16087 (0.752)**	19840 (0.928)

MAD method. Nine experts and a learning algorithm (the Weighted Majority Algorithm) were used to predict the next refueling time. The results of the experiment showed that the learning method outperformed any of the individual experts except for on the least important period of at most 148 h.

References

1. Yang, Q., Wang, H., Zhang, W.: Web-log mining for quantitative temporal-event prediction. IEEE Comput. Intell. Bull. **1**, 10–18 (2002)
2. Huang, Q., Yang, Q., Huang, J.Z., Ng, M.K.: Mining of Web-page visiting patterns with continuous-time Markov models. In: Dai, H., Srikant, R., Zhang, C. (eds.) PAKDD 2004. LNCS (LNAI), vol. 3056, pp. 549–558. Springer, Heidelberg (2004). doi:10.1007/978-3-540-24775-3_65
3. Totamane, R., Dasgupta, A., Rao, S.: Air cargo demand modeling and prediction. IEEE Syst. J. **8**(1), 52–62 (2014)
4. Weiner, I., Freedheim, D., Schinka, J., Velicer, W.: Handbook of Psychology, Research Methods in Psychology. Wiley, Hoboken (2003)
5. Chai, D.J., Kim, E.H., Jin, L., Hwang, B., Ryu, K.H.: Prediction of frequent items to one dimensional stream data. In: ICCSA 2007, pp. 353–361 (2007)
6. Zhang, G.: Time series forecasting using a hybrid ARIMA and neural network model. Neurocomputing **50**, 159–175 (2003)
7. Tan, P.: Introduction to Data Mining. Pearson Education, London (2006)
8. Agarwal, S.: Online Learning from Experts: Weighted Majority and Hedge, Course notes: E0 370. University of Pennsylvania, Philadelphia (2011)
9. Littlestone, N., Warmuth, M.: The weighted majority algorithm. Inf. Comput. **108**(2), 212–261 (1994)
10. Cesa-Bianchi, N., Lugosi, G.: Prediction, Learning, and Games. Cambridge University Press, Cambridge (2006)

Planning and Combinatorial Optimization

A Worst-Case Analysis of Constraint-Based Algorithms for Exact Multi-objective Combinatorial Optimization

Jianmei Guo[1(✉)], Eric Blais[2], Krzysztof Czarnecki[2], and Peter van Beek[2(✉)]

[1] East China University of Science and Technology, Shanghai, China
gjm@ecust.edu.cn
[2] University of Waterloo, Waterloo, Canada
{eric.blais,k2czarnecki,peter.vanbeek}@uwaterloo.ca

Abstract. In a multi-objective combinatorial optimization (MOCO) problem, multiple objectives must be optimized simultaneously. In past years, several constraint-based algorithms have been proposed for finding Pareto-optimal solutions to MOCO problems that rely on repeated calls to a constraint solver. Understanding the properties of these algorithms and analyzing their performance is an important problem. Previous work has focused on empirical evaluations on benchmark instances. Such evaluations, while important, have their limitations. Our paper adopts a different, purely theoretical approach, which is based on characterizing the search space into subspaces and analyzing the worst-case performance of a MOCO algorithm in terms of the expected number of calls to the underlying constraint solver. We apply the approach to two important constraint-based MOCO algorithms. Our analysis reveals a deep connection between the search mechanism of a constraint solver and the exploration of the search space of a MOCO problem.

1 Introduction

In a *multi-objective combinatorial optimization (MOCO)* problem, multiple objectives must be optimized simultaneously. MOCO problems arise in many areas where there are tradeoffs, such as engineering, finance, and logistics. For example, in the design of systems, one often has to choose between different candidate designs that balance multiple objectives, such as low cost, high performance, and high reliability. Since these objectives are often conflicting, there is usually no single optimal solution that excels in all objectives. Therefore, decision makers would like to know various, ideally all, Pareto-optimal solutions that trade off the multiple objectives, such that they can choose a posteriori the solution that best meets their needs.

Over the last four decades, *constraint programming* has emerged as a fundamental technology for solving hard combinatorial problems, as it provides rich languages to express combinatorial structures and to specify search procedures at a high level of abstraction [16]. Building on the strengths of this work,

M. Mouhoub and P. Langlais (Eds.): Canadian AI 2017, LNAI 10233, pp. 117–128, 2017.
DOI: 10.1007/978-3-319-57351-9_16

constraint-based algorithms and improvements to those algorithms have been proposed for finding Pareto-optimal solutions to MOCO problems [8, 11–13, 15]. These MOCO algorithms rely on modeling using constraint programming and on solving by repeated calls to a constraint solver to find feasible solutions.[1]

Understanding the properties of these constraint-based MOCO algorithms and analyzing their performance is an important problem. This is true both to understand their strengths and weaknesses, and also for the design of improved algorithms. Previous work has focused on empirical evaluations on benchmark instances. Such evaluations, while important, have their limitations, as any conclusions may not necessarily generalize to all instances. Our paper adopts a different, purely theoretical approach, which is based on characterizing the search space into subspaces and analyzing the worst-case performance of a MOCO algorithm in terms of an upper bound on the expected number of calls to the underlying solver to find each Pareto-optimal solution to a given MOCO instance. Our worst-case analysis holds for every MOCO instance and, in contrast to an average-case analysis, our bounds do not rely on any assumptions about the distribution of the input instances.

To determine the expected number of calls to a constraint solver, we build a general probability model that takes into account two uncertain factors: (a) how are all solutions distributed in the search space of a given MOCO instance, and (b) how likely is an arbitrary solution to be returned by the constraint solver. To address the first factor, we introduce a *good ordering property* that labels all solutions in the search space and identifies an important total-order relation on all solutions. To address the second factor, we introduce a *bounded bias assumption* where it is (weakly) assumed that for every solution s in the search space, the probability that a call to the constraint solver returns s is bounded from below and non-zero.

Our analysis framework reveals a deep connection between the search mechanism of the constraint solver and the exploration of the search space of a MOCO instance. In brief, if the probability that the solver returns a solution is bounded from below by c/n, where n is the number of all solutions in the search space, for some constant c, a constraint-based MOCO algorithm $\mathcal{A}$ satisfying the good ordering property finds each Pareto-optimal solution in $O(\log n)$ expected calls to the solver. If c is a function of n and c is in $\omega(\frac{\log n}{n})$—intuitively, c grows asymptotically faster than $\frac{\log n}{n}$—$\mathcal{A}$ finds each Pareto-optimal solution in $o(n)$ expected calls to the solver, which is strictly better than the naive worst-case bound $O(n)$. Our study thus has implications for the best choice and design of the underlying constraint solver for a constraint-based MOCO solver.

We apply our framework to two important constraint-based MOCO algorithms: (i) Le Pape et al.'s [12] influential and widely-used algorithm for bi-objective optimization problems (see also [20] for an earlier proposal restricted to a particular scheduling problem), and (ii) Rayside et al.'s [15] guided improvement algorithm (GIA), which has shown good performance empirically on several

[1] From here after, we use *solution* unqualified to refer to a feasible solution and *Pareto-optimal solution* to refer to an optimal solution to a MOCO instance.

benchmark instances and has been incorporated into a widely-used system to support MOCO: the Z3 constraint solver, developed at Microsoft Research [2]. Both algorithms are designed to find one or more exact Pareto-optimal solutions. We prove that both algorithms satisfy the good ordering property and thus fit our analysis framework and theoretical results.

2 Notation and Preliminaries

In the context of constraint programming, a MOCO problem is a quadruple $\mathcal{P} = \langle X, D, C, F \rangle$, where $X = \{x_1, \ldots, x_L\}$ is a set of variables, $D = \{D_1, \ldots, D_L\}$ is a set of finite domains of variables in X, C is a set of constraints on variables in X, and $F = \{f_1, \ldots, f_m\}$ is a set of m objective functions to minimize simultaneously.[2] A solution s to a MOCO problem $\mathcal{P}$ is a total assignment of all variables in X to values in the corresponding domains, such that all constraints in C are satisfied. For a combinatorial optimization problem [14], all solutions constitute a *finite* search space $\mathcal{S}$, and we denote $|\mathcal{S}|$ by n. Each objective function $f_i(\mathcal{S})$ assigns a discrete value to each solution $s \in \mathcal{S}$, and is bounded by the minimal and maximal values regarding the corresponding objective.

There are two classes of approaches to solving MOCO problems [7]: *a priori*, where weights or rankings are specified for the objectives prior to solving, and *a posteriori*, where a representative set of Pareto-optimal solutions are presented to a decision maker. Our interest is in *a posteriori* methods and, in particular, constraint-based MOCO algorithms for finding sets of Pareto-optimal solutions.

Given two solutions s and s' to a MOCO problem $\mathcal{P}$, we say that s *dominates* s', denoted by $s \prec s'$, if and only if s is not worse than s' regarding all objectives and s is better than s' regarding at least one objective:

$$\begin{aligned} &\forall i \in \{1, \ldots, m\} : f_i(s) \leq f_i(s') \textit{ and} \\ &\exists j \in \{1, \ldots, m\} : f_j(s) < f_j(s') \end{aligned} \tag{1}$$

A solution to $\mathcal{P}$ is Pareto-optimal, which we denote by $\tilde{s}$, if and only if no other solution s in $\mathcal{S}$ dominates $\tilde{s}$: $\nexists s \in \mathcal{S} : s \prec \tilde{s}$. All the Pareto-optimal solutions constitute the Pareto front $\tilde{\mathcal{S}}$, and we denote $|\tilde{\mathcal{S}}|$ by p.

3 Exact Constraint-Based MOCO Algorithms

A common approach to solving *single*-objective constraint optimization problems is to find an optimal solution by solving a sequence of constraint satisfaction problems [1,19]. The idea is to, at each iteration, post an additional constraint that excludes solutions that are worse than the most recently found solution. This approach has been generalized in various ways to obtain constraint-based algorithms for solving *multi*-objective problems. In this section, we examine in detail the two algorithms that we subsequently analyze.

---

[2] Without loss of generality, we consider minimization problems.

Algorithm 1. Le Pape et al. (1994) Algorithm

```
   input : BOCO instance P with objectives f1 and f2
   output: Pareto front S̃
1  S̃ ← ∅
2  SupC2 ← true
3  s ← solver(P)
4  while s ≠ null do                                   /* while a SAT call */
5      while s ≠ null do                               /* minimizing f1 */
6          s' ← s
7          InfC ← f1(S) ≥ f1(s')
8          s ← solver(P ∧ ¬InfC ∧ SupC2)
9      SupC1 ← f1(S) ≤ f1(s')
10     while s' ≠ null do                              /* minimizing f2 */
11         s ← s'
12         InfC ← f2(S) ≥ f2(s)
13         s' ← solver(P ∧ SupC1 ∧ ¬InfC)
       /* s becomes Pareto-optimal                                        */
14     S̃ ← S̃ ∪ {s}
15     SupC2 ← f2(S) < f2(s)
16     s ← solver(P ∧ SupC2)
17 return S̃
```

The first algorithm we consider was proposed by Le Pape et al. [12], denoted by LePape from here after, which is a classical algorithm for bi-objective combinatorial optimization (BOCO) problems (see Algorithm 1). The idea is to find the optimal value for one of the objective functions, constrain its value, and restart the search to find the optimal value for the second objective function. The subroutine solver($\mathcal{P}$) (Line 3) indicates a call to a constraint solver for a solution to a MOCO problem $\mathcal{P}$. A call is SAT if the solver returns a solution successfully, and UNSAT otherwise. The inner loop in Lines 5–8 finds the optimal value for the objective function f_1: every time a solution s is returned, the algorithm incrementally searches for a better solution than s regarding f_1 by excluding all solutions scoped by the constraint $\mathit{InfC} = f_1(\mathcal{S}) \geq f_1(s)$, which indicates all $s' \in \mathcal{S}$, subject to $f_1(s') \geq f_1(s)$. Then, the algorithm constrains the optimal value regarding f_1 (Line 9) and finds the optimal value for the other objective function f_2 (Lines 10–13). A Pareto-optimal solution is found when there is no solution better than the currently-found solution regarding f_2 (Line 14). Next, the algorithm constrains the optimal value regarding f_2 (Line 15), implicitly retracts the constraint regarding f_1, and keeps searching for other Pareto-optimal solutions (the outer loop in Lines 4–16).

The second algorithm we consider was proposed by Rayside et al. [15], called guided improvement algorithm (GIA), which is designed for MOCO problems (see Algorithm 2). On some benchmarks GIA has been shown empirically to outperform other constraint-based algorithms [8,13] in terms of the actual running time of solving a given problem instance [15]. To formalize GIA, we introduce the following notation. According to the definition of Pareto dominance, a solution s to a MOCO problem $\mathcal{P}$ partitions the original search space $\mathcal{S}$ into three subspaces: `inferior`, `superior`, and `incomparable`. Correspondingly, we define three types of constraints scoping these subspaces. The `inferior` constraint of a solution s defines the `inferior` subspace leading to all solutions that are dominated by s:

$$\texttt{inf}(s) = \{s' \in \mathcal{S} : s \prec s'\}. \tag{2}$$

The `superior` constraint of solution s defines the `superior` subspace leading to all solutions dominating s:

$$\texttt{sup}(s) = \{s' \in \mathcal{S} : s' \prec s\}. \tag{3}$$

The `incomparable` constraint of solution s defines the `incomparable` subspace leading to all solutions that do not dominate s and are not dominated by s either:

$$\texttt{incp}(s) = \mathcal{S} \setminus \big(\texttt{inf}(s) \cup \texttt{sup}(s) \cup \{s\}\big). \tag{4}$$

GIA, at each iteration, uses the `superior` constraint of a newly-found solution, defined in Eq. (3), to augment constraints for the next search. GIA always searches for the next solution only in the `superior` subspaces that lead to better solutions, regarding all objectives, than the ones already found. This results in inexpensive operations during the search as GIA only needs to keep track of the one solution that is currently the best. A Pareto-optimal solution is found when there is no solution in its `superior` subspace. Afterwards, GIA searches for other Pareto-optimal solutions in the `incomparable` subspace of the Pareto-optimal solution already found, defined in Eq. (4).

Algorithm 2 lists the pseudo-code of GIA. The inner loop (Lines 5–8) is the procedure of searching for one Pareto-optimal solution: every time a solution s is returned by a SAT call in the `superior` subspace of the previous solution, the current constraints are incrementally augmented by the `superior` constraint (denoted by *SupC*) of solution s. The outer loop (Lines 4–11) serves finding all Pareto-optimal solutions: every time an UNSAT call in the `superior` subspace of solution s' is returned, solution s' becomes a Pareto-optimal one and the constraints are incrementally augmented by the `incomparable` constraint (denoted by $IncpC$) of solution s'.

Theoretically, in the best case, LePape finds one Pareto-optimal solution using one SAT call and two UNSAT calls to a constraint solver, while GIA needs one SAT call and one UNSAT call to reach a Pareto-optimal solution. However, a naive analysis suggests that in the worst case, both algorithms may take $O(n)$ calls to find even one Pareto-optimal solution.

Algorithm 2. Guided Improvement Algorithm (GIA)

```
input  : MOCO instance 𝒫 with objectives f_1, ..., f_m
output: Pareto front S̃
S̃ ← ∅
IncpC ← true
s ← solver(𝒫)
while s ≠ null do                                    /* while a SAT call */
    while s ≠ null do                                /* while a SAT call */
        s' ← s
        SupC ← getSupC(𝒫, s)
        s ← solver(𝒫 ∧ IncpC ∧ SupC)
    /* s' becomes Pareto-optimal                                         */
    S̃ ← S̃ ∪ {s'}
    IncpC ← IncpC ∧ getIncpC(𝒫, s')
    s ← solver(𝒫 ∧ IncpC)
return S̃
```

4 A Framework for Worst-Case Analysis

In this section, we propose an analysis framework for systematically investigating the worst-case performance of a constraint-based MOCO algorithm for finding each Pareto-optimal solution in terms of the expected number of calls to a constraint solver. In general, the performance of a constraint-based MOCO algorithm for finding a Pareto-optimal solution in a search space $\mathcal{S}$ of a given MOCO problem $\mathcal{P}$ is determined by the following two uncertain factors:

Factor 1: How are the solutions distributed in $\mathcal{S}$?
Factor 2: How likely is any particular solution in $\mathcal{S}$ to be returned by the solver?

Given an underlying constraint solver, a constraint-based MOCO algorithm that finds one or more Pareto-optimal solutions, denoted by $\mathcal{A}$, searches for a Pareto-optimal solution following a process that we call *improvement search*:

Step 1 (constraint solving): $\mathcal{A}$ asks the solver to return an arbitrary solution;

Step 2 (decision making): If no solution exists (an UNSAT call), the process terminates as all Pareto-optimal solutions have been found; if a solution s is returned (a SAT call), go to Step 3;

Step 3 (constraint improvement): $\mathcal{A}$ delimits the next search space by augmenting the constraints using the currently-found solution s; go to Step 1.

Given a MOCO problem $\mathcal{P}$, the search space $\mathcal{S}$ with n solutions to $\mathcal{P}$ is fixed. In all cases, an UNSAT call is returned at the end of the improvement search. If $n = 0$ (i.e., $\mathcal{P}$ has no solution), then no SAT call happens in $\mathcal{S}$. If $n = 1$, only one SAT call is required to reach the only solution in $\mathcal{S}$, which is Pareto-optimal as well. If $n > 1$, a SAT call is required to return an arbitrary solution s in $\mathcal{S}$, and subsequently the algorithm $\mathcal{A}$ defines the next search space using the constraints of solution s.

Let $Q \subseteq \mathcal{S}$ be any subspace of $\mathcal{S}$, which we call a *query space*. Let $target(s)$ be the *target* subspace defined by the algorithm $\mathcal{A}$ for the next search after finding solution s. Note that a target subspace, $target(s) \subseteq \mathcal{S}$, is a query space. Also, a query space can represent the original search space $\mathcal{S}$. For any query space Q, let $T(Q)$ be the expected number of SAT calls that $\mathcal{A}$ makes until it reaches any Pareto-optimal solution in Q, and $Pr[\text{solver}(Q) = s]$ the probability of returning solution s in Q by the solver. We define the following general probability model of $T(Q)$ when the first query space of algorithm $\mathcal{A}$ is Q:

Definition 1 (General probability model). *If $Q = \emptyset$ has no solution, then $T(Q) = 0$. If $Q \neq \emptyset$ contains at least one solution, then:*

$$T(Q) = \sum_{s \in Q} \Pr[\text{solver}(Q) = s] \cdot T\big(target(s)\big) + 1. \tag{5}$$

Consider Factor 1: the target subspace $target(s)$ is determined by the specific algorithm $\mathcal{A}$. Moreover, given a certain solution $s \in Q$, the number of solutions contained in $target(s)$ is uncertain. To address the uncertainty, we define the good ordering property of the algorithm $\mathcal{A}$ as follows:

Definition 2 (Good ordering property). *Given any query space $Q \subseteq \mathcal{S}$, let $|Q| = n$. The algorithm $\mathcal{A}$ has the good ordering property, if we can label all solutions $s_1, s_2, \cdots, s_n$, such that*

$$s_i \in target(s_j) \rightarrow i < j \tag{6}$$

Remark 1. By Eq. (6), $target(s_i) \subseteq \{s_1, s_2, \cdots, s_{i-1}\}$, and thus $|target(s_i)| < i$.

For any integer $k \geq 0$, let $T(k)$ be the maximum of $T(Q)$ for any query space Q that contains at most k solutions:

$$T(k) = \max_{Q \subseteq \mathcal{S}: |Q| \leq k} T(Q). \tag{7}$$

Remark 2. By Eq. (7), $T(k) \geq T(k-1)$ for every integer $k \geq 1$.

Consider Factor 2: the probability of returning any particular solution in a given query space by the underlying solver is uncertain. The probability is determined by the search mechanism designed in the solver, which varies for different solvers, depending, for example, on the amount of *randomization* used in the variable and value ordering heuristics adopted by the solvers [9,17]. As an approximation of realistic constraint solvers, we make the following assumption regarding the probability. We merely suppose that the probability of returning any solution by the solver has a bounded bias:

Definition 3 (Bounded bias assumption). *Given a search space $\mathcal{S}$ including n solutions to a given MOCO problem $\mathcal{P}$, there exists a non-zero parameter $c_n \leq 1$ such that for every $Q \subseteq \mathcal{S}$ and every solution $s \in Q$,*

$$\Pr[\text{solver}(Q) = s] \geq \frac{c_n}{|Q|}.$$

Remark 3. When the parameter $c_n = 1$, the solver returns any solution in Q uniformly at random.

Theorem 1. *Let $\mathcal{A}$ be a constraint-based MOCO algorithm with the good ordering property and let c_n be a parameter for which the bounded bias assumption holds for the underlying constraint solver used by $\mathcal{A}$. Given a search space $\mathcal{S}$ including n solutions to a given MOCO problem $\mathcal{P}$, the expected number of SAT calls that $\mathcal{A}$ requires to find a Pareto-optimal solution is at most $(2\log n)/c_n$.*

Proof. Given $\mathcal{S}$ including n solutions to problem $\mathcal{P}$, we want to show that $T(\mathcal{S}) \leq \frac{2}{c_n}\log n$. To do so, it suffices to show that for any $k \leq n$, $T(k) \leq \frac{2}{c_n}\log k$.

Let $Q^* = \text{argmax}_{Q\subseteq\mathcal{S}:|Q|\leq k} T(Q)$. Then by Eq. (7), $T(Q^*) = T(k)$. By the good ordering property and Remark 1, let $|Q^*| = \ell \leq k$ and label all the solutions in Q^* by $s_1, \ldots, s_\ell$. Let E denote the event where solver(Q^*) returns one of the solutions in $\{s_1, \ldots, s_{\lceil k/2\rceil}\}$. By the bounded bias assumption,

$$\Pr[E] = \sum_{i=1}^{\lceil k/2\rceil} \Pr[\text{solver}(Q^*) = s_i] \geq \frac{k}{2}\cdot\frac{c_n}{\ell} \geq \frac{k}{2}\cdot\frac{c_n}{k} = \frac{c_n}{2}.$$

When event E occurs, by Remark 1, the solver returns a solution s such that $|target(s)| \leq \lceil k/2\rceil - 1 \leq \lfloor k/2\rfloor$ solutions; furthermore, by Remark 2, $T(target(s)) \leq \max_{Q\subseteq\mathcal{S}:|Q|\leq\lfloor k/2\rfloor} T(Q) = T(\lfloor k/2\rfloor)$. Likewise, when event E does not occur, the solver returns a solution s such that $|target(s)| \leq k-1 < k$ solutions and $T(target(s)) < T(k)$. Therefore, we have that

$$\begin{aligned} T(Q^*) &\leq \Pr[E]\cdot T(\lfloor k/2\rfloor) + (1-\Pr[E])\cdot T(k) + 1 \\ &\leq T(k) + \frac{c_n}{2}\left(T(\lfloor k/2\rfloor) - T(k)\right) + 1. \end{aligned} \tag{8}$$

Since $T(Q^*) = T(k)$, the above inequality implies that

$$T(k) \leq T(\lfloor k/2\rfloor) + \frac{2}{c_n}.$$

Hence, $T(k) \leq \frac{2\log k}{c_n}$ and thus $T(\mathcal{S}) \leq T(n) \leq \frac{2\log n}{c_n}$.

Corollary 1. *In Theorem 1, if parameter c_n is a constant, the algorithm $\mathcal{A}$ finds each Pareto-optimal solution in $O(\log n)$ expected SAT calls; if c_n is a function of n and $c_n = \omega(\log n/n)$, $\mathcal{A}$ finds each Pareto-optimal solution in $o(n)$ expected SAT calls.*

According to Definition 3 and Corollary 1, if parameter c_n is a positive constant $c \leq 1$, then the probability of returning any solution s in the search space $\mathcal{S}$ of all n solutions is not less than $\frac{c}{n}$, i.e., $\Pr[\text{solver}(\mathcal{S}) = s] \geq \frac{c}{n}$; in such a case, $T(n)$ reaches an ideal logarithmic bound $O(\log n)$. Note that if $c = 1$, then the solver returns any solution uniformly at random, i.e., $\Pr[\text{solver}(\mathcal{S}) = s] = \frac{1}{n}$. If parameter c_n is a function bounded in $\omega(\frac{\log n}{n})$, then for any positive constant c, there exists a positive constant n_0 such that $0 \leq \frac{c \log n}{n} < c_n$ for all $n \geq n_0$, and the probability of returning any solution $\Pr[\text{solver}(\mathcal{S}) = s] > \frac{c \log n}{n^2}$; in such a case, $T(n) < \frac{2n}{c}$ is bounded in $o(n)$. Intuitively, if c_n grows asymptotically faster than $\frac{\log n}{n}$, then $T(n)$ is bounded in $o(n)$, which is strictly (i.e., asymptotically) better than the naive worst-case bound $O(n)$.

5 Application of the Framework

To apply the proposed analysis framework to a certain MOCO algorithm, one has to check if the algorithm meets the good ordering property and if the underlying constraint solver used by the algorithm satisfies the bounded bias assumption. The bounded bias assumption embodies and relaxes an active research point of generating uniformly-distributed solutions (Remark 3) [6, 10], and it only needs a lower bound on the probability of returning any solution. Moreover, our analysis proves that not only uniformly random generators but also bounded bias generators are ideal. However, it is non-trivial to design a constraint solver that works efficiently and simultaneously guarantees either rigorous the uniformity or bounded bias assumptions. A state-of-the-art scalable generator supports *near-uniformity* [4] or *almost-uniformity* [3, 5], which also guarantees the bounded bias assumption, but only for Boolean satisfiability (SAT) problems. For general constraint-satisfaction problems (CSPs), a uniformly random generator has been proposed but suffers from exponential complexity [6]. In practice, we believe that an efficient generator that approximately guarantees the bounded bias assumption might be sufficient, e.g., by designing randomization heuristics based on variable and value ordering, which would be explored in future. In this section, we apply the proposed framework to two constraint-based optimization algorithms. We suppose that the underlying solver used in the algorithms satisfies the bounded bias assumption, and we prove that the good ordering property holds for the algorithms.

5.1 LePape

According to Algorithm 1, LePape essentially performs two improvement search processes to find one Pareto-optimal solution: the first process (Lines 5–8) minimizes one of the objective functions f_1, and the second one (Lines 10–13) minimizes the objective function f_2. In each process, the search retains the constraints of the optimal value for one of the objective functions and incrementally finds a better solution in the target subspace of the currently-found one regarding the other objective function. For example, in the first process, $target(s)$ retains the constraint $SupC_2$ for f_2 and scopes all solutions constrained by $f_1(\mathcal{S}) < f(s)$ (i.e., $\neg InfC$ in Line 8); while in the second process, $target(s)$ retains the constraint $SupC_1$ for f_1 (Line 9) and scopes all solutions constrained by $f_2(\mathcal{S}) < f(s)$ (i.e., $\neg InfC$ in Line 13). According to the characteristics of the target subspaces in two processes, we have the following claim:

Claim. The good ordering property holds for LePape.

Proof. The good ordering property holds when the condition (6) is satisfied. To label all n solutions in the entire search space, we perform a "bucket sorting": firstly, suppose that there are n_1 distinct values for one of objective functions f_1, we partition all solutions into n_1 buckets, each of which contains all solutions with the same value for f_1, and we sort buckets in the ascending order of the values for f_1; secondly, we sort all solutions inside each bucket in the ascending order of the values for the other objective function f_2; finally, we label all solutions from index 1 to n firstly following the bucket order and secondly following the solution order inside each bucket, with breaking ties arbitrarily. For example, after the above bucket sorting, the first bucket of solutions are labeled as $s_1, \cdots, s_{|b_1|}$ (b_1 is the size of the first bucket) that have the minimum value for f_1 and are ordered ascendingly by their values regarding f_2.

Following the above labeling tactic, given a solution s_j with the bucket index b, in the first search process that minimizes f_1, any solution $s_i \in target(s_j)$ must belong to a bucket with a smaller index than b; while in the second search process that minimizes f_2, any solution $s_i \in target(s_j)$ must be a solution that has a smaller index than j in the same bucket as s_j. Thus, in both improvement search processes of LePape, we have $i < j$.

By Claim 5.1 and the bounded bias assumption, Theorem 1 and Corollary 1 hold for LePape. Moreover, LePape has two improvement search processes, and it requires at least one SAT call and two UNSAT calls to identify one Pareto-optimal solution. Hence, LePape finds all p Pareto-optimal solutions using at most $(4p \log n)/c_n$ SAT calls and at most $2p$ UNSAT calls. In addition, the Pareto-optimal solutions founded by LePape follows a certain order, i.e., the ascending order of values regarding either of two objectives.

5.2 GIA

According to Algorithm 2, GIA performs the improvement search process once to reach some Pareto-optimal solution (Lines 5–8), and we have:

Claim. The good ordering property holds for GIA.

Proof. For GIA, the target subspace $target(s)$ of the currently-found solution s is the superior subspace $\mathtt{sup}(s)$. If we label all n solutions in the entire search space, such that

$$|\mathtt{sup}(s_1)| \leq |\mathtt{sup}(s_2)| \leq \cdots \leq |\mathtt{sup}(s_n)| \tag{9}$$

then for every $i = 1, \ldots, n$, we have

$$|\mathtt{sup}(s_i)| < i. \quad (10)$$

To prove Eq. (10), by contradiction, suppose that all solutions have been indexed following the rule defined in Eq. (9) and that there is a solution s_i for which $|\mathtt{sup}(s_i)| \geq i$. Then, there must exist some index $j > i$, such that $s_j \in \mathtt{sup}(s_i)$. But then $\mathtt{sup}(s_j) \subsetneq \mathtt{sup}(s_i) \setminus \{s_j\}$ and so $|\mathtt{sup}(s_j)| \leq |\mathtt{sup}(s_i)| - 1$, in contradiction to Eq. (9). According to Eq. (10), any solution $s_i \in \mathtt{sup}(s_j)$ must have a smaller index than j, i.e., $i < j$.

By Claim 5.2 and the bounded bias assumption, Theorem 1 and Corollary 1 hold for GIA. Moreover, GIA requires at least one SAT call and at least one UNSAT calls to identify one Pareto-optimal solution. Hence, GIA finds all p Pareto-optimal solutions using at most $(2p \log n)/c_n$ SAT calls and at most p UNSAT calls. In addition, the Pareto-optimal solutions founded by GIA does not follow a certain order, which is different from LePape.

6 Conclusion

We presented the first theoretical analysis of the worst-case performance of two constraint-based MOCO algorithms. The algorithms rely on modeling using constraint programming and on solving the MOCO problem by repeated calls to an underlying constraint solver. We characterized the original search space into subspaces during the search and developed a general probability model of $T(n)$, the expected number of (SAT) calls to the underlying constraint solver that the algorithms require to find each Pareto-optimal solution to a given MOCO problem. We identified a total-order relation on all solutions by introducing a good ordering property. Under only a (weak) bounded bias assumption—the probability that a call to the underlying solver returns any particular solution is bounded from below and non-zero, we proved that $T(n)$ is bounded in $O(\log n)$ or $o(n)$, determined by a parameter c_n that depends on how the underlying solver behaves for the MOCO problem.

Our analysis reveals the connection between the search mechanism of a constraint solver and the exploration of the search space of a MOCO problem. Our study has implications for the best choice and design of the underlying constraint solver for a constraint-based MOCO solver. In brief, the underlying constraint solver used in a constraint-based MOCO solver should randomize the generation of feasible solutions, ideally meeting the uniformly random or bounded bias assumption, such that the MOCO solver is able to find each Pareto-optimal solution in a bound strictly better than the naive worst-case $O(n)$.

Some extensions to our current analysis framework would be considered in future. We plan to perform a worst-case analysis of other constraint-based MOCO algorithms. Furthermore, we plan to investigate a smoothed analysis [18] of constraint-based MOCO algorithms.

Acknowledgments. This work has been partially supported by Shanghai Municipal Natural Science Foundation (No. 17ZR1406900) and NSERC Discovery Grant.

References

1. Baptiste, P., Le Pape, C., Nuijten, W.: Constraint-Based Scheduling: Applying Constraint Programming to Scheduling Problems. Kluwer, Dordrecht (2001)
2. Bjørner, N., Phan, A.D.: νZ - maximal satisfaction with Z3. In: Proceedings of the SCSS, pp. 632–647 (2014)
3. Chakraborty, S., Fremont, D.J., Meel, K.S., Seshia, S.A., Vardi, M.Y.: Distribution-aware sampling and weighted model counting for SAT. In: Proceedings of the AAAI, pp. 1722–1730 (2014)
4. Chakraborty, S., Meel, K.S., Vardi, M.Y.: A scalable and nearly uniform generator of SAT witnesses. In: Sharygina, N., Veith, H. (eds.) CAV 2013. LNCS, vol. 8044, pp. 608–623. Springer, Heidelberg (2013). doi:10.1007/978-3-642-39799-8_40
5. Chakraborty, S., Meel, K.S., Vardi, M.Y.: Balancing scalability and uniformity in sat witness generator. In: Proceedings of the DAC, pp. 1–6 (2014)
6. Dechter, R., Kask, K., Bin, E., Emek, R.: Generating random solutions for constraint satisfaction problems. In: Proceedings of the AAAI, pp. 15–21 (2002)
7. Ehrgott, M.: Multicriteria Optimization, 2nd edn. Springer, Heidelberg (2005)
8. Gavanelli, M.: An algorithm for multi-criteria optimization in CSPs. In: Proceedings of the ECAI, pp. 136–140 (2002)
9. Gomes, C., Selman, B., Kautz, H.: Boosting combinatorial search through randomization. In: Proceedings of the AAAI, pp. 431–437 (1998)
10. Gomes, C.P., Sabharwal, A., Selman, B.: Near-uniform sampling of combinatorial spaces using XOR constraints. In: Proceedings of the NIPS, pp. 481–488 (2006)
11. Hartert, R., Schaus, P.: A support-based algorithm for the bi-objective pareto constraint. In: Proceedings of the AAAI, pp. 2674–2679 (2014)
12. Le Pape, C., Couronné, P., Vergamini, D., Gosselin, V.: Time-versus-capacity compromises in project scheduling. In: Proceedings of the Thirteenth Workshop of the UK Planning Special Interest Group, Strathclyde, UK (1994)
13. Lukasiewycz, M., Glaß, M., Haubelt, C., Teich, J.: Solving multi-objective Pseudo-Boolean problems. In: Marques-Silva, J., Sakallah, K.A. (eds.) SAT 2007. LNCS, vol. 4501, pp. 56–69. Springer, Heidelberg (2007). doi:10.1007/978-3-540-72788-0_9
14. Papadimitriou, C., Steiglitz, K.: Combinatorial Optimization: Algorithms and Complexity. Dover, Mineola (1998)
15. Rayside, D., Estler, H.C., Jackson, D.: The guided improvement algorithm for exact, general purpose, many-objective combinatorial optimization. Technical report, MIT-CSAIL-TR-2009-033 (2009)
16. Rossi, F., van Beek, P., Walsh, T. (eds.): Handbook of Constraint Programming. Elsevier, Amsterdam (2006)
17. Sadeh, N., Fox, M.: Variable and value ordering heuristics for the job shop scheduling constraint satisfaction problem. Artif. Intell. **86**(1), 1–41 (1996)
18. Spielman, D., Teng, S.H.: Smoothed analysis of algorithms: why the simplex algorithm usually takes polynomial time. J. ACM **51**(3), 385–463 (2004)
19. Van Hentenryck, P.: Constraint Satisfaction in Logic Programming. MIT Press, Cambridge (1989)
20. van Wassenhove, L., Gelders, L.: Solving a bicriterion scheduling problem. Eur. J. Oper. Res. **4**(1), 42–48 (1980)

Metaheuristics for Score-and-Search Bayesian Network Structure Learning

Colin Lee and Peter van Beek(✉)

Cheriton School of Computer Science, University of Waterloo, Waterloo, Canada
vanbeek@cs.uwaterloo.ca

Abstract. Structure optimization is one of the two key components of score-and-search based Bayesian network learning. Extending previous work on ordering-based search (OBS), we present new local search methods for structure optimization which scale to upwards of a thousand variables. We analyze different aspects of local search with respect to OBS that guided us in the construction of our methods. Our improvements include an efficient traversal method for a larger neighbourhood and the usage of more complex metaheuristics (iterated local search and memetic algorithm). We compared our methods against others using test instances generated from real data, and they consistently outperformed the state of the art by a significant margin.

1 Introduction

A Bayesian network is a probabilistic graphical model which encodes a set of random variables and their probabilistic relationships through a directed acyclic graph. Bayesian networks have been successfully applied to perform tasks such as classification, knowledge discovery, and prediction in fields including medicine, engineering, and business [15]. Bayesian network structure learning involves finding the acyclic graph that best fits a discrete data set over the random variables.

Bayesian networks can be learned through the method of score-and-search. In score-and-search a scoring function indicates how well a network fits the discrete data and search is used to find a network which achieves the best possible score by choosing a set of parents for each variable. Unfortunately, finding such a network is $\mathcal{NP}$-hard, even if each node in the network has at most two parents [11]. Exact solvers for this problem have been developed using a variety of techniques (e.g., [2,3,7,20]). These methods achieve good performance on smaller instances of the problem but fail to scale in terms of memory usage and runtime on instances with more than 100 variables unless the indegree is severely restricted.

Local search has been shown to be successful in finding high quality solutions to hard combinatorial problems with relatively simple algorithms [9]. It has already been applied to learning Bayesian networks using techniques such as greedy search [5], tabu search [19], and ant colony optimization [8], over search spaces such as the space of network structures [5], the space of equivalent network structures [4], and the space of variable orderings [12,19]. We improve upon the

M. Mouhoub and P. Langlais (Eds.): Canadian AI 2017, LNAI 10233, pp. 129–141, 2017.
DOI: 10.1007/978-3-319-57351-9_17

approach of ordering-based search (OBS) by Teyssier and Koller [19], which makes use of the topological orderings of variables as a search space. Teyssier and Koller [19] show that OBS performs significantly better than local search over network structures on this problem.

In this paper, we make the following contributions. We identify the Bayesian network structure learning problem as being similar to the Linear Ordering Problem (LOP) and adapt the local search techniques applied to LOP in [17] to improve OBS. First, as previously done in [1], we experiment with using a neighbourhood which is larger than the one originally used in OBS to find high quality local optima. We then include optimizations to make the use of this neighborhood more feasible for instances with a high number of variables. We combine our local search method with iterated local search (ILS) and memetic algorithm (MA) to produce two new methods. Experimental results show that the new methods are able to find networks that score significantly better than other state of the art anytime solvers on instances with hundreds of variables.

2 Background

A Bayesian network is composed of a directed acyclic graph (DAG) G with random variables $\{X_1, \ldots, X_n\}$ as vertices. The score-and-search method of Bayesian network learning makes use of a scoring function $sc(G \mid I)$ which takes a set $I = \{I_1, \ldots, I_n\}$ of complete instantiations I_i of the variables (the data) and assigns a real valued score to the network G. For the purposes of this paper, a lower score will indicate a higher quality network. Also, the data parameter I will be made implicit, so that we write $sc(G)$ instead of $sc(G \mid I)$.

The score-and-search method consists of two stages. The first stage, called *parent set identification*, consists of computing the scores of sets of parents for each variable. A scoring function is *decomposable* if the score $sc(G)$ of the network can be written as the sum of its local scores $\sum_{i=1}^{n} sc_i(Pa(X_i))$, where $Pa(X_i)$ is the set of parents of X_i in G. Commonly used scoring functions, including BIC and BDeu which we use in our experiments, are decomposable [2]. In practice, the indegree for each variable is often bounded by some small integer k to increase the speed of inference [11]. As is usual in score-and-search approaches, we assume precomputed caches are available using techniques for efficiently scoring and pruning parent sets [16,19], resulting in a *cache* C_i of c_i candidate parent sets for each variable X_i along with their associated scores. More formally, for each i, we have $C_i \subseteq \{U : U \subseteq \{X_1, \ldots, X_n\} \setminus \{X_i\}, |U| \leq k\}$, from which $sc_i(U)$ for $U \in C_i$ can be queried in constant time.

Our work focuses on the second component of score-and-search, called *structure optimization*. This involves searching for a network structure which achieves the minimum possible score by selecting a parent set for each variable X_i from C_i such that the graph is acyclic. Following previous work, we apply local search over the space of orderings of variables [19], as the space of variable orderings is significantly smaller than the space of all possible DAGs. We call a Bayesian network G *consistent* with an ordering O of its variables if O is a topological

Algorithm 1. Hill climbing for ordering-based structure optimization.

Result: A local minimum in the neighbourhood defined by *neighbours*

$O \leftarrow$ *randomOrdering*();
curScore $\leftarrow$ *sc*(O);
while *neighbours(O) contains an ordering which improves curScore* **do**
    $O \leftarrow$ *selectImprovingNeighbour*(O);
    curScore $\leftarrow$ *sc*(O);
return O

ordering of G. For a given ordering, using a bitset representation we can find the optimal parent sets for all of the variables in $O(Cn)$ operations, where C is the total number of candidate parent sets. Thus, the problem of finding the optimal network can be transformed into finding the ordering with the lowest score.

3 Search Neighbourhood

We start by building upon the hill climbing method that is used in OBS (see Algorithm 1). This method consists of first randomly generating an ordering O and computing its score. Then, until no ordering in the *neighbourhood* of O has a higher score than O, O is set to one of its neighbours with an improving score. O will then be a local minimum in the neighbourhood. We call each iteration to an improving neighbour a hill climbing *step*.

The choice of neighbourhood significantly impacts the performance of hill climbing, as it essentially defines the search landscape. In OBS, the *swap-adjacent* neighbourhood is used. Formally, for an ordering $O = (X_1, \ldots, X_n)$, O' is a neighbour of O if and only if $O' = (X_1, \ldots, X_{i+1}, X_i, \ldots, X_n)$ for some $1 \leq i \leq n - 1$. The size of the neighbourhood is therefore $n - 1$. In hill climbing, other than in the first step, the optimal parents sets of O are already computed from the previous step. Subsequently, the optimal parent sets only need to be updated for X_i and X_{i+1} as the swap in the ordering does not affect the potential parents of other variables. Therefore, the cost of checking the score of a neighbour defined by the swap-adjacent neighbourhood is $O((c_i + c_{i+1})n)$. The total cost of computing the score of all neighbours of O (a *traversal* of the neighbourhood) is then $O(Cn)$. From [16], a further optimization can be made by checking for an updated parent set for X_{i+1} only if X_i was one of its parents before the swap. Additionally, when updating X_i's parent set after the swap, only the candidate parent sets that contain X_{i+1} needs to be considered for an improvement.

A pitfall of the swap-adjacent neighbourhood is a high density of weak local minima. Swapping adjacent variables X_i and X_{i+1} does not have a large impact on their parent sets, as X_{i+1} only loses the ability to have X_i as a parent and X_i only gains the ability to have X_{i+1} as a parent. Given that the parent set size is restricted to k, which is significantly smaller than n in practice, it is unlikely that an adjacent swap will lead to an improvement in the score. In the terminology of local search, using this neighbourhood results in a search landscape with large

$$\begin{aligned} O =&(X_1, X_2, X_3, X_4, X_5, X_6) && \rightarrow_{swap} \\ &(X_1, X_3, X_2, X_4, X_5, X_6) &&= (\text{Insert } X_2 \text{ in } O \text{ to index } 3) \rightarrow_{swap} \\ &(X_1, X_3, X_4, X_2, X_5, X_6) &&= (\text{Insert } X_2 \text{ in } O \text{ to index } 4) \rightarrow_{swap} \\ &(X_1, X_3, X_4, X_5, X_2, X_6) &&= (\text{Insert } X_2 \text{ in } O \text{ to index } 5) \rightarrow_{swap} \\ &(X_1, X_3, X_4, X_5, X_6, X_2) &&= (\text{Insert } X_2 \text{ in } O \text{ to index } 6) \rightarrow_{swap} \end{aligned}$$

Fig. 1. Example of performing the four forward inserts of X_2 for O using four swap-adjacent moves. The final insert left for X_2 (to index 1) can be achieved with a similar swap-adjacent move in O with X_1. Adapted from [17].

plateaus. OBS attempts to alleviate this problem by using a tabu list which allows the traversal of the search over non-improving solutions.

Keeping this in mind, we consider the *insert* neighbourhood, which contains orderings that can be obtained from one another by selecting a variable and inserting it at another index. Formally, $O = (X_1, \ldots, X_{i-1}, X_i, X_{i+1}, \ldots, X_{j-1}, X_j, X_{j+1}, \ldots, X_n)$ is neighbouring O' in the insert neighbourhood if and only if $O' = (X_1, \ldots, X_{i-1}, X_{i+1}, \ldots, X_{j-1}, X_j, X_i, X_{j+1}, \ldots, X_n)$, for some i and j. We say O' is O with the variable X_i inserted into position j. The use of the insertion neighbourhood as an improvement to OBS is explored in [1], but there it is used with limited success.

After inserting variable X_i to index j, the possible parents for all variables from X_i to X_j (inclusive) in the original ordering have been updated, and the optimal parent set for each one of these must be checked. In the case that for $i < j$, this takes $O((\sum_{i=1}^{j} c_i)n)$ operations. The case for $j < i$ is the same but with the indices swapped. Naïvely computing the scores of all $(n-1)^2$ neighbours independently therefore has cost $O(Cn^3)$, which is significantly greater than the $O(Cn)$ cost required for traversing the swap-adjacent neighbourhood.

Fortunately, as shown in [6] and applied to OBS in [1], the insert neighbourhood can be traversed with a series of $O(n^2)$ swap-adjacent moves. Specifically, given a variable X_i, the $n-1$ neighbours of O formed by inserting X_i into one of the $n-1$ other indices can be constructed with a series of $n-1$ swap-adjacent moves (see Fig. 1). Since a score update for a swap-adjacent move can be done in $O((c_i + c_{i+1})n)$ operations, the cost to compute the scores of the ordering for all $n-1$ indices that X_i can be inserted into is $O(Cn)$. There are n choices for X_i, so the cost of traversing the entire neighbourhood is $O(Cn^2)$. Along with being an order of magnitude faster than the naïve traversal, the previously mentioned optimizations for scoring swap-adjacent moves can be applied in this method.

Even in small cases, local minima in the swap-adjacent neighbourhood can be overcome by using an insert move (see Fig. 2). The swap-adjacent neighbourhood of an ordering is a subset of the insert neighbourhood of that ordering. Thus, the lowest scoring neighbour in the insert neighbourhood is guaranteed to score at least as low as any neighbour from the swap-adjacent neighbourhood.

Three different possibilities for neighbour selection were tested for the insert neighbourhood: best improvement, first improvement, and hybrid.

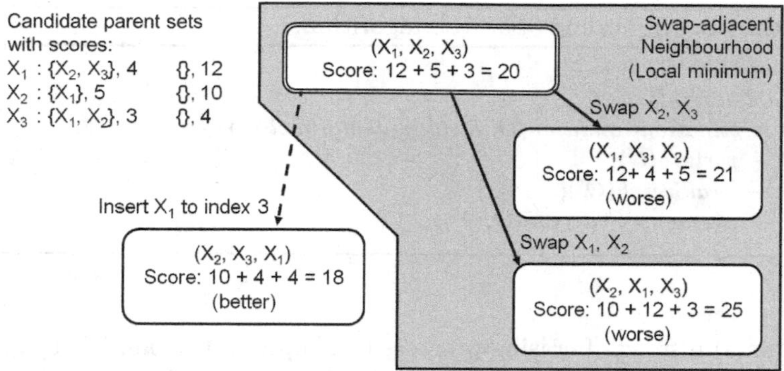

Fig. 2. Example local minimum for the swap-adjacent neighbourhood. A local minimum occurs at the ordering $O = (X_1, X_2, X_3)$. The two swap-adjacent neighbours of O are indicated with solid arrows; both have worsening scores. An insert move neighbour, indicated with a dashed arrow, gives an improved score. Hence O is not a local minimum in the insert neighbourhood.

- *Best improvement*: The neighbour with the highest score is chosen. Finding the score of every neighbour takes $O(Cn^2)$ operations.
- *First improvement*: The insert moves are evaluated in random order and the first neighbour with an improving score is selected. Finding the score of each random neighbour costs $O(Cn)$ operations each, so that in the worst case, where every neighbour must be scored, $O(Cn^3)$ operations are used.
- *Hybrid*: This selection scheme falls between best and first improvement and is adapted from [17]. A variable X is randomly chosen from the ordering. The index j to insert X which gives the highest score is then found using $n - 1$ adjacent swaps to score each index. If this insertion gives an improvement in score, then it is chosen. If no insertions for X give an improvement, another variable is randomly chosen and the process repeats. In the worst case of a local minimum, all n variables are tested for improving insert moves, using a total of $O(Cn^2)$ operations.

The three selection methods are experimentally compared in Sect. 6. Our results show hybrid selection to be the most appropriate. We call the hill climbing method obtained from Algorithm 1 by using the insert neighbourhood and hybrid neighbour selection method Insert Neighbourhood OBS (INOBS). INOBS is a key component of our metaheuristic methods in the following sections.

4 Iterated Local Search

Iterated local search (ILS) has historically been a simple and intuitive extension of basic hill climbing which performs competitively with other metaheuristic methods [9]. The improvement ILS brings over hill climbing with random restarts is the ability to continue searching for improvements nearby a good solution

Algorithm 2. An outline of an ILS algorithm.

```
O ← initialState();
O ← localSearch(O);
while terminationCondition(O, history) is not met do
    O' ← perturb(O);
    O' ← localSearch(O');
    O ← acceptenceCriterion(O, O');
```

(local minima) instead of erasing progress by simply restarting. First, a random ordering is chosen as an initial candidate solution and a subsidiary local minimum is found through local search. Then, three basic steps are iterated over until a restart condition is met: first, the current solution is perturbed through some *perturbation operator*. Then, local search is applied to the perturbed solution to obtain a new local minimum. Whether or not the new local minimum will replace the old one before the next iteration is decided upon according to an *improvement criterion*. The iterations stop when a specified *termination condition* is met. This generic ILS algorithm is outlined in Algorithm 2.

Using INOBS as the local search component for the ILS procedure, we construct Iterated INOBS (IINOBS). For the perturbation operator of IINOBS, $p_s \cdot n$ pairs of variables were swapped by their index in the ordering, where p_s is called the perturbation factor. Swaps are chosen because they are not easily undone by insertions, so it is unlikely that the proceeding local search will reverse the perturbation [17]. As for the improvement criterion, the solution is accepted when the new local minima achieves a score s' such that $s'(1 - \varepsilon) < s$, where s is the score of the original local minima and $\varepsilon \geq 0$. The parameter ε allows some leeway for the new local minima to have a worse score than the current one. To avoid stagnation, IINOBS is restarted from a new initial ordering according to both a soft and hard restart schedule. A soft restart occurs if the objective value has not been improved in over r_s moves to new local optima. A hard restart occurs when r_h moves to new local optima have occurred, regardless of how the search has been improving.

5 Memetic Algorithm

Memetic INOBS (MINOBS) is a memetic search method for the problem which uses INOBS as a local search procedure. Memetic search allows a local search algorithm to be combined with the intensification and diversification traits of population based search techniques. The method can be compared to a standard genetic algorithm except using the space of local minima rather than the space of all possible orderings [13]. An outline of the memetic algorithm we fit MINOBS into is in Algorithm 3.

Memetic search roughly resembles maintaining multiple runs of ILS in parallel. Performing crossover and mutation is analogous to perturbation. Pruning the

Algorithm 3. An outline of the memetic algorithm that INOBS is fit into to construct MINOBS. Adopted from [17].

```
population ← {};
for i ← 1,...,N (N is the population size) do
    O ← localSearch(randomInitialState());
    population ← population ∪ {O};
while termination condition is not met do
    offspring ← {};
    for i ← 1,...,c_n do
        choose O_1, O_2 from population;
        offspring ← offspring ∪ localSearch(crossover(O_1, O_2))};
    for i ← 1,...,m_n do
        choose O_1, O_2 from population;
        offspring ← offspring ∪ localSearch(mutate(O_1, O_2, m_p))};
    population ← prune(population ∪ offspring, N);
    if the average score in the population does not change by d_Δ in the last d_t
      generations then
        population ← selectBest(population, d_n);
        for i ← 1,...,N − d_n do
            O ← localSearch(randomInitialState());
            population ← population ∪ {O};
```

population is analogous to automatically stopping the less promising of the parallel runs. Therefore, we expect MINOBS to perform at least as well as IINOBS given a sufficient amount of time.

The algorithm begins with an initial population of random local optima are generated through INOBS. Until the termination condition is met, the population undergoes a number of generations. Each generation consists of a crossover and a mutation stage. During the crossover stage, members of the population are randomly drawn in pairs and combined according to some crossover operator to produce a new ordering. INOBS is then applied to the new orderings. In the mutation stage, random members of the population are chosen from the population and perturbed according to the swap-based perturbation operation presented in the IINOBS. The new permutations are then subjected to local search using INOBS. Afterwards, both the orderings produced in the crossover and mutations stages are added to the population. Finally, members of the population are pruned to maintain the original size of the population according to some pruning scheme. In our case, pruning involved filtering out orderings with duplicate scores and then afterwards removing orderings with the lowest scores until the population was back to its original size.

MINOBS also has the possibility of performing a diversification step if the average score of the population does not change by over d_Δ for d_t generations. The diversification step consists of removing all but the top d_n members of the population and refilling the rest of the population with new random local minima. The diversification step's purpose is to stop the population from stagnating and acts similarly to a random restart. We experimented with three different crossover operators. Let $O_1 = (X_{\pi_1(1)}, \ldots, X_{\pi_1(n)})$ and $O_2 = (X_{\pi_2(1)}, \ldots, X_{\pi_2(n)})$ be the two orderings to cross to produce the offspring $O = (X_{\pi(1)}, \ldots, X_{\pi(n)})$, where π_1, π_2, and π are permutations of indices from 1 to n.

- *Cycle crossover* (CX): A random index i is selected along with a random parent O_1, without loss of generality. For the resulting ordering O, we set $\pi(i)$ as $\pi_1(i)$. Then for the other parent O_2, the index j such that $\pi_1(j) = \pi_2(i)$ is found, and we set $\pi(i)$ to $\pi_1(j)$. Index i is then set to j and the process repeats until i cycles back to the original index. The process then restarts with i as an index unused by π until π is completed. The resulting permutation π has the property that $\pi(i) = \pi_1(i)$ or $\pi(i) = \pi_2(i)$ for every index i [14].
- *Rank crossover* (RX): The offspring is based on sorting the mean index of each variable over both parent orderings. When a ties occur (two or more elements share the same mean index over both parents), the order of the elements is determined according to a random distribution [17].
- *Order-based crossover* (OB): From O_1, $n/2$ variables are randomly chosen and copied in the same position into offspring O. The variables not copied from O_1 fill the unused positions in O according to their order in O_2 [18].

6 Experimental Results

We report on experiments to (i) evaluate the three neighbourhood selection schemes, (ii) select the parameters for our two proposed metaheuristic methods, IINOBS and MINOBS, and (iii) compare our INOBS, IINOBS and MINOBS methods against the state of the art for Bayesian network structure learning.

Most of the instances used in our experiments were provided by the Bayesian Network Learning and Inference Package (BLIP)[1]. These instances used the BIC scoring method and have a maximum indegree of $k = 6$. Other instances were produced from datasets from J. Cussens and B. Malone and scored using code provided by B. Malone. The method of scoring for an instance in this set (BIC or BDeu) is indicated in the instance name.

Experiment 1. In the first set of experiments, we compared the three neighbourhood selection schemes—best improvement, first improvement, and hybrid—incorporated into the basic hill climbing algorithm (Algorithm 1), which terminates once a local minima is reached (see Table 1). Overall, best and first improvement generated higher quality local minima than hybrid selection. Note that it is possible for first improvement to be better than best improvement as they follow a different trajectory through the search space from the first move. Best improvement for insertion-based OBS is the best method tested in [1] where

[1] http://blip.idsia.ch/.

Table 1. Average runtime (sec.) and score for each neighbourhood selection method for various benchmarks (100 runs), where n is the number of variables in the instance and C is the total number of candidate parent sets.

Instance	n	C	Best		First		Hybrid	
			Time	Score	Time	Score	Time	Score
segment_BIC	20	1053	0.01	15176.3	0.01	15175.9	0.00	15176.8
autos_BIC	26	2391	0.02	1585.5	0.03	1586.4	0.01	1587.1
soybean_BIC	36	5926	0.08	3155.9	0.08	3156.5	0.02	3158.4
wdbc_BIC	31	14613	0.19	6623.0	0.16	6624.6	0.04	6627.0
steel_BDeu	28	113118	2.09	18690.0	1.76	18674.8	0.59	18685.9
baudio.ts	100	371117	23.76	194711.9	12.63	193795.5	3.03	194922.0
jester.ts	100	531961	36.56	88098.9	19.86	87271.6	4.48	87871.1
tretail.ts	134	435976	36.54	106864.0	16.59	106294.6	3.03	106879.2
munin-5000	1041	1648338	847.08	1041284.5	961.39	1041219.6	17.97	1040638.6

it is called HCbO. The authors note that the performance of their algorithm is hindered by the need to evaluate the scores of all $(n-1)^2$ neighbours, even with the optimizations mentioned in Sect. 3. They attempted to lower the neighbourhood size by restricting the insert radius and using variable neighbourhood search, but the modifications were not effective in improving performance.

While overall hybrid selection performed marginally worse in terms of score, it took significantly less time to reach a local minima on the larger instances, scaling to about fifty times faster on the largest instance. One further optimization for best improvement with insert moves is explored in [1] but was not implemented in our experiments. However, this optimization only improves the speed by at most a factor of two, which is still not enough to make best improvement comparable to hybrid. Following the note that best improvement selection is too time consuming in [1] and our own focus on scaling to larger instances, we designated hybrid as our neighbourhood selection method of choice for our metaheuristic methods to make a direct improvement over HCbO.

Experiment 2. In the second set of experiments, we tuned the parameters for our two proposed metaheuristic methods, IINOBS and MINOBS. Parameter tuning was performed with ParamILS, a local search based tuning method for metaheuristics [10]. Tuning was performed using three instances from the BLIP benchmarks (*baudio.ts*, *jester.ts*, *tretail.ts*). Unfortunately, larger instances could not be used effectively for tuning due to time constraints. The objective minimized by ParamILS was the mean percent difference from the best scores generated by INOBS with random restarts. The parameters tuned and their optimal value found by ParamILS are listed in Tables 2 and 3. (Near-optimal parameters were also experimented with and similar results were obtained.)

Experiment 3. In the final set of experiments, we compared our two proposed metaheuristic methods, IINOBS and MINOBS, as well as INOBS with random

Table 2. Parameters tuned for IINOBS.

Parameter	Description	Value
p_s	Perturbation factor: $p_s \cdot n$ random swaps will be used to perturb the ordering	0.03
ε	Leeway allowed when choosing a local minima to move to	0.00005
r_s	Number of non-improving steps until a restart	22
r_h	Number of perturbations until a restart	100

Table 3. Parameters tuned for MINOBS.

Parameter	Description	Value
N	Number of members in the population	20
crossover	Type of crossover to perform	OB
c_n	Number of crossovers to perform	20
m_p	Mutation power factor: $m_p \cdot n$ random swaps will be used to perturb the ordering	0.01
m_n	The number of mutations to perform	6
d_t	Number of scores to look back for triggering a diversification step	32
d_Δ	Max. change in ave. score needed to trigger a diversification step	0.001
d_n	Number of members to keep after a diversification step	4

restarts, to the state of the art (see Table 4). For the state of the art, we compare against (i) our implementation of OBS [19]; (ii) GOBNILP (v1.6.2) [7], an exact solver used here as an anytime solver that was run with its default parameters; and (iii) acyclic selection OBS (ASOBS [16], a recently proposed local search solver that has been shown to out-perform all competitors on larger instances. OBS, INOBS, INOBS with restarts, IINOBS, and MINOBS were implemented in C++ using the same code and optimizations for swap-adjacent moves[2]. ASOBS is written in Java and is therefore expected to run more slowly compared to our methods. However, our experiment runtime is long enough for ASOBS to stagnate enough so that even if the implementation of the method was several times faster, it is unlikely that the results would change significantly.

Experiments for all methods other than ASOBS were run on a single core of an AMD Opteron 275 @ 2.2 GHz. Each test was allotted a maximum 30 GB of memory and run for 12 h. The generation of the instances from data can take days, so this time limit is reasonable. Due to limited software availability, tests for ASOBS were run courtesy of M. Scanagatta with the same time and memory limits and on a single core of an AMD Operton 2350 @ 2 GHz. These two processors have similar single core performance. We used test instances from the BLIP benchmarks. Of the 20 data sets used to generate the BLIP instances, three

[2] The software is available at: https://github.com/kkourin/mobs.

Table 4. Median score of best networks found, for various benchmarks, where n is the number of variables and C is the total number of candidate parent sets. The column labelled INOBS represents the scores of INOBS with random restarts. OM indicates the solver runs out of memory before any solution is output. Bold indicates the score was the best found amongst all tested methods. An asterisk indicates that the score is known to be optimal.

Instance	n	C	GOBNILP	OBS	ASOBS	INOBS	IINOBS	MINOBS
nltcs.test	16	48303	**5836.6***	5903.4	**5836.6***	**5836.6***	**5836.6***	**5836.6***
msnbc.test	17	16594	**151624.7***	153291.6	**151624.7***	**151624.7***	**151624.7***	**151624.7***
kdd.test	64	152873	57271.3	57556.2	57522.6	57218.0	**57209.6***	**57209.6***
plants.test	69	520148	19337.8	16485.0	16681.4	14649.6	**14539.7**	**14539.7**
bnetflix.test	100	1103968	OM	13033.3	12545.1	12282.4	**12279.8**	**12279.8**
accidents.test	111	1425966	OM	3454.4	2119.9	855.9	**828.3**	**828.3**
pumsb_star.test	163	1034955	11552.5	5626.9	3641.7	3068.5	**3062.8**	**3062.8**
dna.test	180	2019003	OM	21783.0	19335.1	18455.1	18297.0	**18287.8**
kosarek.test	190	1192386	OM	29283.4	26718.5	24816.5	**24731.8**	24745.9
msweb.test	294	1597487	OM	28496.3	26061.6	25781.7	25743.5	**25741.6**
book.test	500	2794588	OM	36133.0	33104.4	30614.2	30355.2	**30345.0**
tmovie.test	500	2778556	OM	8547.6	6312.4	5008.5	4765.5	**4763.8**
cwebkb.test	839	3409747	OM	34837.9	21948.7	17984.7	17564.7	**17556.4**
cr52.test	889	3357042	OM	28187.2	16060.2	13374.3	13063.0	**13013.9**
c20ng.test	910	3046445	OM	109950.7	79093.8	69832.9	69139.5	**69024.0**
bbc.test	1058	3915071	OM	44663.6	30261.3	25263.5	24498.2	**24403.9**
ad.test	1556	6791926	OM	10845.0	8745.2	7814.5	**7610.4**	7646.0
diabetes-5000	413	754563	OM	2043150.9	1925441.6	1913319.6	**1912286.3**	1912670.9
pigs-5000	441	1984359	OM	1010120.7	905538.2	802293.5	782105.9	**775953.3**
link-5000	724	3203086	OM	85516.2	43072.1	37067.2	36758.9	**36715.3**

were excluded because they were used in tuning, leaving 17 for testing. Three additional large instances were chosen that were generated with data from real networks (*diabetes-5000*, *link-5000*, *pigs-5000*). Excluding ASOBS, three tests with different random seeds were tested for each instance-method pair, and the median was recorded. ASOBS was only run once due to time constraints.

GOBNILP, OBS, and ASOBS performed significantly worse than our proposed metaheuristic methods, IINOBS and MINOBS. A closer look at the experimental data revealed that the best solutions found by OBS and ASOBS on all but three of the smaller instances over an entire 12 h run scored worse than the solutions found by INOBS with random restarts in a *single* hill climb. MINOBS found equivalent or better structures than IINOBS for 17/20 instances, though seven were tied. The time and score data showed that MINOBS tended to start slow but overtime managed to outperform IINOBS on most instances. This behaviour is expected if memetic search is seen as running ILS in parallel, as speculated earlier. One of the cases where MINOBS found worse solutions than IINOBS was *ad.test*, one of the biggest instances we tested with. On this instance, neither method seemed close to stagnating at the 12 h timeout, so we reran the experiment with a time limit of 72 h. MINOBS eventually overtook IINOBS after about 24 h. In general, IINOBS seems to be the better method if time is limited, but it begins stagnating earlier than MINOBS.

7 Conclusions

We present INOBS, IINOBS, and MINOBS: three new ordering-based local search methods for Bayesian network structure optimization which scale to hundreds of variables and have no restrictions on indegree. We compare these methods to the state of the art on a wide range of instances generated from real datasets. The results indicated that these new methods are able to outperform the few score-and-search learning methods that can operate on instances with hundreds of variables. MINOBS appeared to find the best scoring network structures, with IINOBS closely following.

References

1. Alonso-Barba, J.I., de la Ossa, L., Puerta, J.M.: Structural learning of Bayesian networks using local algorithms based on the space of orderings. Soft. Comput. **15**, 1881–1895 (2011)
2. Beek, P., Hoffmann, H.-F.: Machine learning of Bayesian networks using constraint programming. In: Pesant, G. (ed.) CP 2015. LNCS, vol. 9255, pp. 429–445. Springer, Cham (2015). doi:10.1007/978-3-319-23219-5_31
3. de Campos, C.P., Ji, Q.: Efficient structure learning of Bayesian networks using constraints. J. Mach. Learn. Res. **12**, 663–689 (2011)
4. Chickering, D.M.: Learning equivalence classes of Bayesian network structures. J. Mach. Learn. Res. **2**, 445–498 (2002)
5. Chickering, D.M., Heckerman, D., Meek, C.: A Bayesian approach to learning Bayesian networks with local structure. In: Proceedings of UAI, pp. 80–89 (1997)
6. Congram, R.K.: Polynomially searchable exponential neighborhoods for sequencing problems in combinatorial optimisation. Ph.D. thesis, University of Southampton (2000)
7. Cussens, J.: Bayesian network learning with cutting planes. In: Proceedings of UAI, pp. 153–160 (2011)
8. De Campos, L.M., Fernandez-Luna, J.M., Gámez, J.A., Puerta, J.M.: Ant colony optimization for learning Bayesian networks. J. Approx. Reason. **31**, 291–311 (2002)
9. Hoos, H.H., Stützle, T.: Stochastic Local Search: Foundations and Applications. Elsevier, Amsterdam (2004)
10. Hutter, F., Hoos, H.H., Leyton-Brown, K., Stützle, T.: ParamILS: an automatic algorithm configuration framework. JAIR **36**, 267–306 (2009)
11. Koller, D., Friedman, N.: Probabilistic Graphical Models: Principles and Techniques. The MIT Press, Cambridge (2009)
12. Larranaga, P., Kuijpers, C., Murga, R., Yurramendi, Y.: Learning Bayesian network structures by searching for the best ordering with genetic algorithms. IEEE Trans. Syst. Man Cybern. **26**, 487–493 (1996)
13. Moscato, P.: On evolution, search, optimization, genetic algorithms and martial arts: towards memetic algorithms. Technical report, Caltech (1989)

14. Oliver, I., Smith, D., Holland, J.R.: Study of permutation crossover operators on the TSP. In: Proceedings of International Conference on Genetic Algorithms (1987)
15. Pearl, J.: Probabilistic Reasoning in Intelligent Systems. Morgan Kaufmann, San Francisco (1988)
16. Scanagatta, M., de Campos, C.P., Corani, G., Zaffalon, M.: Learning Bayesian networks with thousands of variables. In: Proceedings of NIPS, pp. 1864–1872 (2015)
17. Schiavinotto, T., Stützle, T.: The linear ordering problem: Instances, search space analysis and algorithms. J. Math. Model. Algorithms **3**, 367–402 (2004)
18. Syswerda, G.: Schedule optimization using genetic algorithms. In: Handbook of Genetic Algorithms, pp. 332–349 (1991)
19. Teyssier, M., Koller, D.: Ordering-based search: a simple and effective algorithm for learning Bayesian networks. In: Proceedings of UAI, pp. 548–549 (2005)
20. Yuan, C., Malone, B., Wu, X.: Learning optimal Bayesian networks using A* search. In: Proceedings of IJCAI, pp. 2186–2191 (2011)

SmartHome Energy Saving Using a Multi-objective Approach Based on Appliances Usage Profiles

Henrique F. Lacerda[1], Allan R.S. Feitosa[1(✉)], Abel G. Silva-Filho[1], Wellington P. Santos[2], and Filipe R. Cordeiro[3]

[1] Informatics Center, Federal University of Pernambuco, Av. Jornalista Anibal Fernandes, s/n - Cid. Universitaria, Recife, PE 50-6740-550, Brazil
{hfl,arsf,agsf}@cin.ufpe.br

[2] Biomedical Engineering Department, Federal University of Pernambuco, Av. da Arquitetura, s/n - Cid. Universitaria, Recife, PE 50-6740-550, Brazil
wellington.santos@ufpe.br

[3] Estatistics and Informatics Department, Federal Rural University of Pernambuco, Rov. Gov. Mario Covas, Dois Irmaos, 52171-011 Recife, PE, Brazil
filipe.rolim@ufrpe.br

Abstract. The increasing number of electronic appliances in the houses and the huge human dependency on fossil fuel, bring the necessity of an efficient use of the available power sources. The Smart Home systems allow monitoring and controlling residential appliances. The proposed system works in residential energetic management using multi-objective techniques to recommend more economic appliances usage profiles than the actual usage profile of the user. However, these recommended profiles have to be similar to the user normal usage profile before the recommendation, allowing to make a reasonable recommendation. For the tested appliances, the NSGA-II technique has shown the best solutions. From the best results it was possible to get similar profiles to the normal use with until 90% of energy saving.

Keywords: Multi-objective optimization · Smart Home · Energy save

1 Introduction

The human dependency on fossil fuel brings necessity of an efficient and sustainable usage of the available power sources. The *Smart Home* appliances have received more capacity of gathering information about the residential appliances and how to manage them. This technology has allowed the development of several Computational Intelligence based techniques for efficient energy usage and comfort management at residential environment.

Thus, aiming to reduce the power waste, it is interesting that the management system becomes able to reduce the power usage of the appliances without affect the inhabitants' comfort.

M. Mouhoub and P. Langlais (Eds.): Canadian AI 2017, LNAI 10233, pp. 142–147, 2017.
DOI: 10.1007/978-3-319-57351-9_18

The system proposed by this work has two main parts. The first consists of finding the user normal usage profiles. After that, at the second part, the recommendation is made by a multi-objective search algorithm.

This work is structured as follows. In the second chapter will be shown and briefly discussed the related works. Following, in the third chapter, the proposed technique will be described. The fourth chapter presents the results obtained as well its discussion. Finally, the conclusions and future works are in the fifth chapter.

2 Related Works

Several Residential Appliances Management Systems (RAMS) can be found in the literature to automatically manage the domestic appliances.

In [3], it is proposed a RAMS based on appliances coordination. Their experiments were performed by simulating the loads of four appliances. They considered the period at which they were on *stand by*, that represented around 10% of the total consumed energy for each one, and then turned off the more critical at energy price peak periods.

In the RAMS described by [4], there is a thermal environmental management, which uses multi-objective optimization to search for an acceptable balance between the user preferences and save energy. Their tests were performed through virtual simulation of a residence in Sidney. Their model took in consideration the position, altitude, windows, wall weight and the size of the residence.

The importance of *Smart Home* with Computational Intelligence techniques is that they are able to automatically manage and reduce the power consumption of a residence, in an efficient and non-expensive way.

The system proposed by this work intends to learn the user usage profile of the appliances and then recommend usage patterns that makes more economical use of energy and becomes similar with the current usage profile.

3 Multi-objective Optimization

3.1 Non-dominated Sorting Genetic Algorithm II

In optimization problems, a largely utilized group of techniques is the Genetic Algorithm. Those techniques model possible solutions for determining problem as chromosomes, which have a fitness value. This measure says how good the solution is relates to others. The algorithm is initialized with an initial population of solution candidates and over the generations, it will be performed operators to select and combine the solutions to generate new better individuals.

The Non-dominated Sorting Genetic Algorithm II (NSGA-II) [6] is a multi-objective version of genetic algorithms. This approach is largely utilized because of its fast convergence, besides to emphasize the non-dominated solutions, i.e., the solutions which are not better than others in both objectives simultaneously, it uses mechanisms like the *Crowding distance*, which is a solution spreading technique. This mechanism evaluates the density of non-dominated solutions and thus preserve the solution diversity, running through local maxima.

3.2 Discrete Multi-objective Optimization

The Particle Swarm Optimization (PSO) is a heuristic search approach inspired by the movement of bird flocks searching for a food source. The multi-objective version of PSO, called *Multi-Objective Particle Swarm Optimization* (MOPSO) used in this work is based on the Pareto Dominance Concept to collect the non-dominated solution among the objectives. This version is described by Coello Coello [5]. They represented the MOPSO algorithm like a single objective *Particle Swarm Optimization* (PSO), but with a new turbulence operator and an external archive, where are saved the non-dominated solutions.

Besides, in order to implement a discrete version of MOPSO, called here (DMOPSO), it were used the velocity and position calculations as in [2].

At the end of the execution, it is obtained, from the Pareto Front, a group of non-dominated solutions that will serve as balanced options of solutions to the proposed problem.

4 Proposed Technique

The hole system operation is summarized by the Fig. 1 and is described as follows.

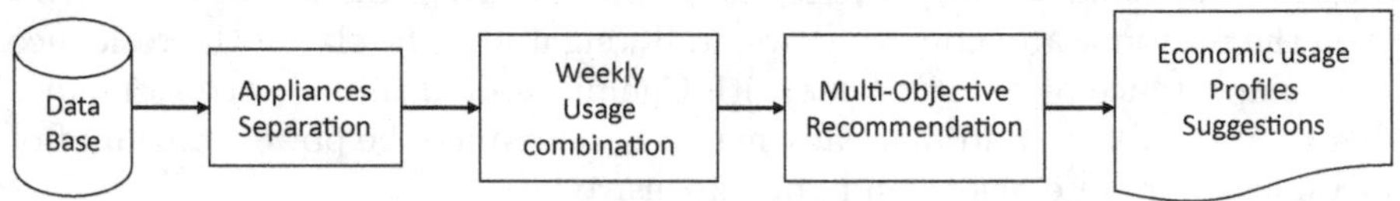

Fig. 1. Operation flow to recommend a lower energy usage profile.

Appliance Separation: In the first stage, the appliance data is separated and their data are split into weeks.

Weekly Usage Combination: Here, for each home appliance, the raw data obtained before is combined into weeks of usage. This conversion is done by counting how many times during the 7 week days, that appliance was turned on at each second of a whole day. Resulting in a vector containing 86400 integer values (each second for a period of 24 h) that can fluctuate from [0,7], representing how many days on that week the appliance was turned on in that specific second.

Besides, it was selected one of those weeks for each appliance. This week is supposed to represent all the others as the normal usage profile for each equipment. This was accomplished by finding the one that had the smallest sum of Euclidean Distance from all the others.

Multi-objective Recommendation: Thus, the selected week is given as input to the multi-objective algorithm and will serve as the normal usage for both objectives. The solution candidates were randomly generated weeks of usage.

It was identified two concurrent fitness functions, power consumption and the proximity with the current profile (used as a measure of comfort). The power consumption has been calculated by the sum of the usage time (in seconds) of each solution candidate, and as the second objective, the proximity to the normal usage profile was given by the Euclidean distance from the solution candidate to the current profile of usage.

The solutions candidate could only have their internal distribution with integers between [0,7] and their total dimension was 86400 (represents the quantity of seconds in a day).

To improve the velocity of convergence, the sampling rate L was reduced and tested with different values. This different sizes are due to the intervals of sampling: 30 s, 60 s, 5 min and 10 min. Resulting in individuals/particles with L of: 144, 288, 1440 and 2880 dimensions respectively. In order to calculate the objective function the solutions were re-sampled to 86400 dimensions.

The appliance consumption data used by this work were obtained from the UK Domestic Appliance-Level Electricity (UK-DALE) [1] repository. From this repository, it were selected 50 weeks from 6 appliances: 25-lighting_circuit, 3-solar_thermal_lamp, 6-dishwasher, 7-tv, 9-htpc and the 13-microwave.

5 Results and Discussion

In order to find the best results for each technique, firstly it was found the best parameters for one of the appliances. Those parameters are described in the Table 1.

Table 1. NSGA-II and DMOPSO best parameters found.

NSGA-II		DMOPSO	
Name	Value	Name	Value
Number of individuals	100	Number of particles	100
Iteration number	150	Number of iterations	150
Crossover probability	90%	c1 and c2	2
Mutation probability	10%	Inertia weight	0.8
Individual dimension	144	Particles dimension	144
		Mutation probability	40%
		Division factor	5,5

The hyper-volumes of the two tested techniques Pareto-Front are represented by the Fig. 2. The solutions given by the genetic algorithm were split into three levels of economy, like showed in the Fig. 3, and to show the capacity of the technique it was selected an average solution from each group which are represented in Table 2.

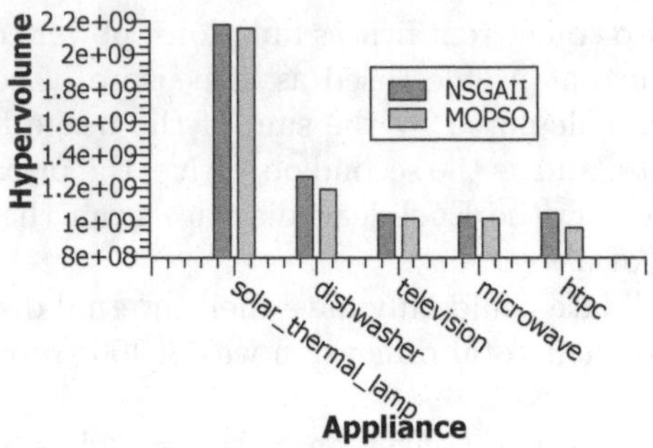

Fig. 2. Hypervolume of the NSGA-II and DMOPSO for the 5 appliances analysed.

Table 2. Results for the five appliances tested

ID	Appliance	Reduction comfortable	Reduction moderated	Reduction economic
3	*solar_thermal_lamp*	42%	54%	65%
6	*dishwasher*	42%	54%	66%
7	*tv*	43%	54%	64%
9	*htpc*	38%	50%	61%
13	*microwave*	41%	53%	64%

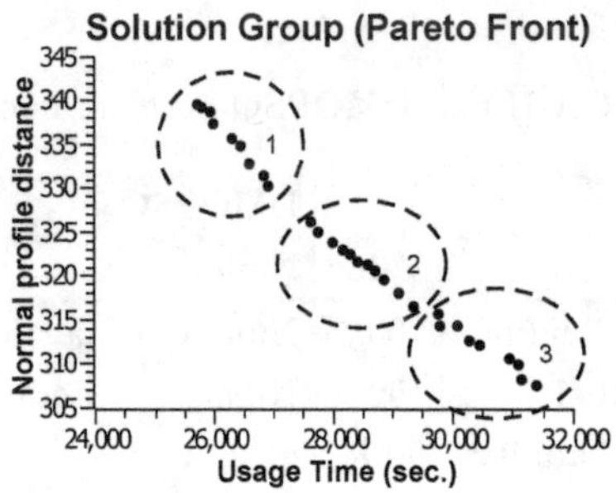

Fig. 3. Pareto Front with the zone separations.

For both techniques, the best hypervolumes, were found by the smallest dimensional individuals (bigger interval sampling) probably because of the facility of work with smaller solutions candidates. The NSGA-II had the best results, this is probably because of its better capacity of exploring the search space and scape from local minimum. The Table 2 shows the mean percentages for NSGA-II of the extremes and average solutions for the techniques.

6 Conclusions and Future Works

To reduce the energy consumption without affecting much the user comfort, the normal week usage obtained was used to find possible solutions that were similar to it. The approach returned solutions for less energy save and, therefore, more comfortable, as well as more energy economic and thus, more invasive to the user comfort. Also, it is not interesting to the technique to be applied to appliances as a fridge, that cannot be turned off or TV that has a smaller representation in the house electricity consumption.

As future work, it will be used Machine Learning to more accurately, detect the user usage profiles avoiding the missing variations of use from one week to another.

Acknowledgements. The authors are grateful to CIN UFPE, CNPQ, FACEPE and the CIn/FCA Project for the support of this research.

References

1. Kelly, J.: UK Domestic Appliance Level Electricity (UK-DALE) - disaggregated (6s) appliance power and aggregated (1s) whole house power (2015)
2. Izakian, H., Ladani, B.T., Abraham, A., Snacel, V.: A discrete particle swarm optimization approach for grid job scheduling. Int. J. Innovative Comput. Inf. Control **6**(9), 1–15 (2010)
3. Mahmood, A., Khan, I., Razzaq, S., Najam, Z., Khan, N.A., Rehman, M.A., Javaid, N.: Home appliances coordination scheme for energy management (HACS4EM) using wireless sensor networks in smart grids. Procedia Comput. Sci. **32**, 469–476 (2014)
4. Anvari-Moghaddam, A., Monsef, H., Rahimi-Kian, A.: Optimal smart home energy management considering energy saving and a comfortable lifestyle. IEEE Trans. Smart Grid **6**(1), 324–332 (2015)
5. Coello Coello, C.A., Lechuga, M.S.: MOPSO: a proposal for multiple objective particle swarm optimization. In: Proceedings of the 2002 Congress on Evolutionary Computation (2002)
6. Deb, K., Pratap, A., Agarwal, S., Meyarivan, T.: A fast and elitist multiobjective genetic algorithm: NSGA-II. IEEE Trans. Evol. Comput. **6**(2), 182–197 (2002)

Sequence-Based Bidirectional Merge Map-Matching Algorithm for Simplified Road Network

Ge Cui[1], Chunlin Ma[1,2], and Xin Wang[1(✉)]

[1] Department of Geomatics Engineering, University of Calgary, 2500 University Drive, N.W., Calgary, Alberta T2N 1N4, Canada
{cuig, chunlin.ma, xcwang}@ucalgary.ca

[2] Geomatics Centre of Xinjiang Uygur Autonomous Region, Urumqi 830002, Xinjiang, China

Abstract. Current map matching algorithms do not perform well for simplified road networks. In this paper, we propose a sequence-based bidirectional merge algorithm called SBBM for map matching on the simplified road network. SBBM splits a GPS trajectory into a set of sequences first, and then merges the sequences from the one with the highest confidence. During the merging procedure, the algorithm would address the problems of outliers. Last, an experiment is conducted based on GeoLife dataset in Beijing, China, and the result shows that the proposed algorithm in this paper performs better than Passby algorithm and incremental algorithm.

Keywords: Map matching · Simplified road network · Sequence-based

1 Introduction

With the rapid popularity of GPS devices, the massive GPS trajectories of vehicles are collected and available for various applications. The spatial position of GPS trajectory is usually imprecise due to the measurement error and the sampling error of GPS receivers. Map matching is the operation to match GPS trajectories to the road segment by geometric, topological and statistical analysis, which is critical for further geospatial operations.

Simplified road networks are often used in many applications because of its small storage size, low I/O and communication overhead and fast processing time. In a simplified road network, road segments only consist of junctions and do not have any other information such as speed limitation, turn restriction at junctions. However, simplified road network may hamper the effectiveness of geometric features (such as azimuth), and even leads to location deviation of road segments after simplification. Figure 1 illustrates the problem by using a real case on the simplified road network. In the figure, a GPS trajectory passes through a ramp in the road network. Figure 1(a) shows the scene in the original road network where the GPS points 1–7 can be located on the ramp correctly. However, in Fig. 1(b), as the ramp is simplified, the GPS points 1–7 will be incorrectly mapped to Road 1 based on the geometric feature. Very few

M. Mouhoub and P. Langlais (Eds.): Canadian AI 2017, LNAI 10233, pp. 148–154, 2017.
DOI: 10.1007/978-3-319-57351-9_19

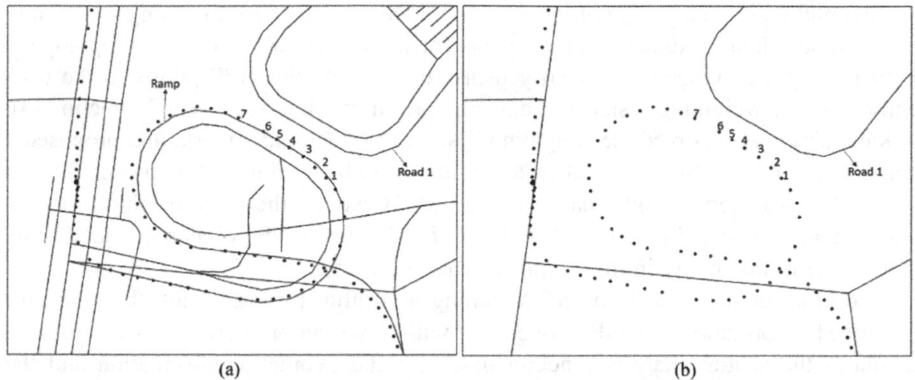

Fig. 1. An example of a GPS trajectory in (a) original road network (b) simplified road network

map matching algorithms have been proposed for the simplified road network. Passby algorithm [1] is proposed for simplified road network, however, it may result in wrong map matching result when the intersections passed by are incorrectly identified.

In this paper, we propose a sequence-based bidirectional merge (SBBM) algorithm to match GPS trajectory onto a simplified road network. The consecutive points could constitute a basic sequence. The sequence with highest confidence will be matched first, and then to merge its adjacent sequences in the bi-direction based on criteria which could remove outliers effectively. The contributions of the paper are summarized as follows:

- This paper proposes a sequence-based bidirectional merge (SBBM) algorithm to match GPS trajectory onto simplified road network. SBBM operates on sequence rather than a single GPS point, which could make the process of map matching efficient. Besides, SBBM starts from the sequence with the highest confidence to merge adjacent sequences, which could address the problem of outliers.
- This paper conducts experiments on the real dataset GeoLife, and the experimental result shows that the proposed SBBM algorithm outperforms the two existing map matching algorithms, Passby algorithm and incremental algorithm.

This paper is organized as follows: Sect. 2 introduces the related works of map matching algorithm; Sect. 3 gives some definitions and problem statement, and makes a detailed discussion about the proposed SBBM algorithm; Sect. 4 gives a case study based on the GPS trajectory dataset of GeoLife project in Beijing city, China. Section 5 makes conclusions and discusses future works of this research.

2 Related Works

In the last several decades, a lot of map matching algorithms have been proposed. Quddus *et al.* made a literature review [2] of the map matching algorithms, and pointed out that the determination of a vehicle location on a particular road depends to a large extent on both the quality of the spatial road map and the used map matching algorithm.

Greenfeld proposed a topological based incremental map matching algorithm. Firstly, it searched candidate road segments for the target GPS point by a topological analysis. Then, it utilized a similarity measure to locate the GPS points to the road segment with a weighting system of balancing proximity, intersection and direction [3]. Brakatsoulas *et al.* adopted the weighting system of Greenfeld's work, and proposed a look-ahead policy to make a local matching decision by exploring a sequence of road segments rather than a single road segment [4]. However, the map matching method based on geometric and topological analysis of individual GPS points may identify the road segment incorrectly in the simplified road network.

Lou *et al.* came up with the ST-Matching algorithm by integrating the geometry and speed information for GPS trajectory with low sampling rate. This algorithm calculates the spatial analysis function based on the geometric information and the temporal analysis function based on speed information [5]. It is a well-known algorithm. However, it does not apply to simplified road network because it requires extra road network information such as speed limits of road segments.

The Passby algorithm proposed in [1] detects the GPS points located at the intersections of road segments, and matching the consecutive GPS points within the intersections to the road segment. However, it may result in wrong map matching result when the intersections passed by are incorrectly identified.

3 Sequence-Based Bidirectional Merge Method

Definition 1 Simplified Road Network. The simplified road network is a graph $G = (V, E)$, where V is a set of vertices representing the endpoints of road segments, and E is a set of road segments. A simplified road network only has the geometric and topological information without any other attributes.

Definition 2 GPS Trajectory. A GPS trajectory T is a sequence of GPS points $\{p_1, p_2, \ldots, p_n\}$, and each GPS reading is a tuple of $<x, y, t>$, where x, y, t are latitude, longitude and time, respectively, and $p_i \cdot t < p_{i+1} \cdot t$.

Problem Statement. Given a GPS trajectory T and a simplified road network $G = (V, E)$, determine the path which matches the trajectory in the road network.

The sequence-based bidirectional merge method is composed of two steps. They are sequence generation and bidirectional merge. In the following, we will discuss them in details.

First, it makes a fast map matching of each GPS point in a trajectory only based on spatial proximity between GPS points and road segments. Then, GPS points are aggregated to sequences which are matched to the same road segment. Next, the bidirectional merge is conducted starting from the sequence with the highest confidence. During the merge procedure, skipping segments traversed are searched out and outliers are detected and eliminated. In the following, we will discuss them in details.

3.1 Sequence Generation

In this step, each GPS point in a trajectory is matched to a road segment based on the spatial proximity. Given a trajectory $T = \{p_1, p_2, \ldots, p_n\}$, each point p_i will be matched to its nearest road segment according to its distance to the segment. To facilitate search the closest segments to the point, a spatial index is built for the road network with R tree. After the fast map matching, each GPS point p_i is located at a matching point a_j on the road segment s_j, and it is recorded as $p_i \cdot a = a_j$, and $p_i \cdot s = s_j$.

If a road segment s has more consecutive points matched on, the consecutive points $\{p_i, p_{i+1}, \ldots, p_{i+k}\}$ are called a sequence, recorded as $Seq = \{p_i, p_{i+1}, \ldots, p_{i+k}\}$, and the confidence of this sequence is the number of the points within it, denoted as *Seq.conf*. The corresponding road segment s of the sequence is recorded as $Seq.seg = \{s\}$.

The rules to merge sequences are as follows: given two sequences $Seq_1 = \{p_i, p_{i+1}, \ldots, p_j\}$, $Seq_1.seg = \{s_1\}$ and $Seq_2 = \{p_{j+1}, p_{j+2}, \ldots, p_k\}$, $Seq_2.seg = \{s_2\}$:

- If $s_1 = s_2$, then $Seq_{new} = \{p_i, \ldots, p_j, p_{j+1}, \ldots, p_k\}$, $Seq_{new}.seg = \{s_1\}$, $Seq_{new}.conf = Seq_1.conf + Seq_2.conf$.
- If $s_1 \neq s_2$ and s_1, s_2 are adjacent, $Seq_{new} = \{p_i, \ldots, p_j, p_{j+1}, \ldots, p_k\}$, $Seq_{new}.seg = \{s_1, s_2\}$, $Seq_{new}.conf = Seq_1.conf + Seq_2.conf$.
- If $s_1 \neq s_2$ and s_1, s_2 are not adjacent, there are segments $s_p, \ldots, s_q$ between s_1 and s_2, then $Seq_{new} = \{p_i, \ldots, p_j, p_{j+1}, \ldots, p_k\}$, $Seq_{new}.seg = \{s_1, s_p, \ldots, s_q, s_2\}$, $Seq_{new}.conf = Seq_1.conf + Seq_2.conf$.

3.2 Bidirectional Merge

After segmenting a trajectory into several sequences, it will merge adjacent sequences step by step to find a reasonable path. During the bidirectional merge procedure, the algorithm would search the traversed skipping segments between sequences and detect sequence of outlier to find the reasonable path which matches the trajectory in the road network.

Segment-skipping problem [2] is that a point p_i is matched to the segment s, but the next point p_{i+1} is matched neither on the segment s nor any segment adjacent to s, so there exist some segments which are skipped. This algorithm assumes that the shortest path between the two sequences is the one composed by the skipped segments.

Due to the measurement error of GPS receiver or the inaccuracy of simplified road network, some sequences may be matched to the incorrect road segments, and taken as outliers. Figure 2 gives an example about problem of outlier.

In Fig. 2, $Sequence_1 = \{p_6, p_7\}$ are matched to the segment s_4 and it should be taken as an outlier. When $Sequence_2 = \{p_1, p_2, p_3, p_4, p_5\}$ merges $Sequence_1$, the skipped segments s_3 will be found. If it is not possible to travel the distance of the skipped path $p_5 \cdot a \rightarrow s_3 \rightarrow p_6 \cdot a$ within the time interval $\Delta t = p_6 \cdot t - p_5 \cdot t$, $Sequence_1$ will be considered as outlier and eliminated. In this paper, the speed $\bar{v}$ of the travel $p_5 \rightarrow p_6$ is estimated by the five point samples before the travel, namely the average speed between $p_1 \cdot a$ and $p_5 \cdot a$ in Fig. 2.

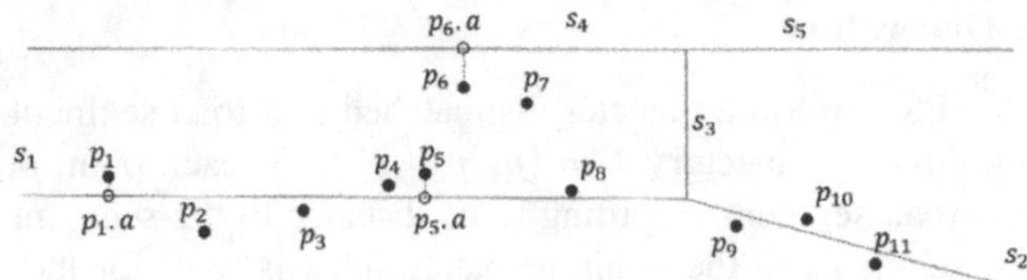

Fig. 2. An example of outlier

$$Distance(p_5 \cdot a \rightarrow s_3 \rightarrow p_6 \cdot a) > \bar{v}' * (p_6 \cdot t - p_5 \cdot t), \bar{v}' = Min(w * \bar{v}, vmax)$$

Where w is the scale parameter of the speed, $vmax$ is the maximum speed of the moving object. After $Sequence_1$ is removed, $Sequence_2$ will continue to merge the next adjacent sequences.

4 Experiments

In this section, we first describe the experimental settings, including the experiment dataset and some parameters setting in the experiment. Then, we introduce the evaluation approaches. Finally, we report the matching accuracy of the SBBM algorithm on simplified road network, and compare it with both Passby algorithm [1] and incremental algorithm in [3].

In this experiment, we use the road network of the downtown area of Beijing. The simplified road network contains 18,813 vertices and 22,043 road segments. Besides, 50 trajectories (sampling rate is 1 Hz) with different length and spatial coverage are selected from GeoLife dataset [6], and they are labeled with the true paths manually for evaluation. Our implementation was written in C# on Microsoft Visual Studio 2010 platform, and experimental results were taken on a computer with Intel Core i7 4710HQ CPU 2.5 GHz and 16 GB RAM. In this experiment, The scale parameter of the speed is set as 5, and the maximum speed is set as 35 m/s. For the incremental algorithm, the parameters are set as $\mu_d = 10$, $a = 0.17$, $n_d = 1.4$, and $\mu_\alpha = 10$, $n_\alpha = 4$, adopted in [3].

In this experiment, two metrics Precision by Number (PN) and Recall by Number (RN) are used to evaluate the effectiveness of map matching algorithm for simplified road networks, and they are defined as follows.

$$PN = \frac{\#correctlymatchedroadsegments}{\#allroadsegmentsofthetrajectory}$$

$$RN = \frac{\#correctlymatchedroadsegments}{\#matchedroadsegments}$$

Figure 3 shows the quality of the three algorithms on the experiment dataset. In Fig. 3, it can be seen clearly that our proposed SBBM algorithm outperforms both Passby algorithm and incremental algorithm with respective to PN and RN, which

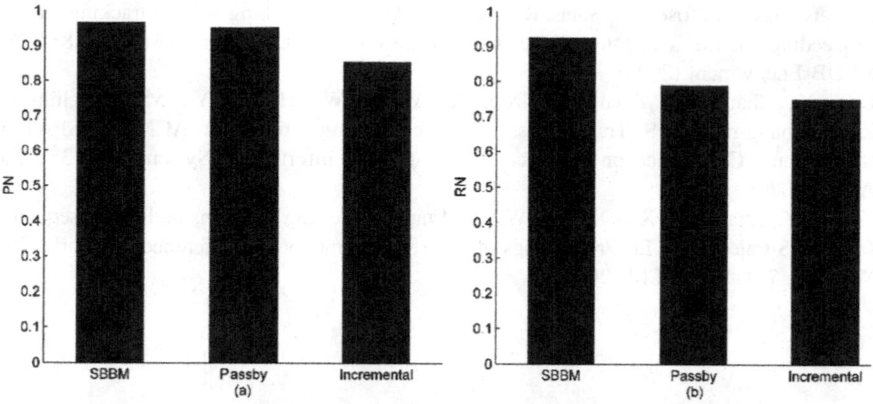

Fig. 3. The results of experiment: (a) precision by number (b) recall by number

means that SBBM algorithm succeeds in not only finding the correct travelled path, but also eliminating outliers which are matched incorrectly. The PN and RN of Passby algorithm is 0.950 and 0.791, which means that Passby algorithm has a good performance in finding the correct path, but it cannot eliminate outliers and short roundabout very effectively. The PN and RN of incremental algorithm is 0.852 and 0.751, which means that incremental algorithm does not work well for map matching in the simplified road network.

5 Conclusions and Future Works

In this paper, we propose a map matching algorithm called sequence-based bidirectional merge algorithm SBBM to match GPS trajectory to simplified road network. The experimental results show that the proposed algorithm outperforms Passby and incremental algorithm with high sampling rate GPS trajectories in the simplified road network. In future, we will conduct more experiments to test the performance of the proposed algorithm on low sampling rate GPS dataset.

References

1. Liu, K., Li, Y., He, F., Xu, J., Ding, Z.: Effective map-matching on the most simplified road network. In: Proceedings of the 20th International Conference on Advances in Geographic Information Systems, pp. 609–612. ACM (2012)
2. Quddus, M.A., Ochieng, W.Y., Noland, R.B.: Current map-matching algorithms for transport applications: state-of-the art and future research directions. Transp. Res. Part C: Emerg. Technol. **15**(5), 312–328 (2007)
3. Greenfeld, J.S.: Matching GPS observations to locations on a digital map. In: Proceedings of Transportation Research Board 81st Annual Meeting (2002)

4. Brakatsoulas, S., Pfoser, D., Salas, R., Wenk, C.: On map-matching vehicle tracking data. In: Proceedings of the 31st International Conference on Very Large Databases, pp. 853–864. VLDB Endowment (2005)
5. Lou, Y., Zhang, C., Zheng, Y., Xie, X., Wang, W., Huang, Y.: Map-matching for low-sampling-rate GPS Trajectories. In: Proceedings of the 17th ACM SIGSPATIAL International Conference on Advances in Geographic Information Systems, pp. 352–361. ACM (2009)
6. Zheng, Y., Zhang, L., Xie, X., Ma, W.Y.: Mining interesting locations and travel sequences from GPS trajectories. In: Proceedings of the 18th International Conference on World Wide Web, pp. 791–800. ACM (2009)

On the Role of Possibility in Action Execution and Knowledge in the Situation Calculus

Vahid Vaezian(✉) and James P. Delgrande

School of Computing Science, Simon Fraser University,
Burnaby, BC V5A 1S6, Canada
{vvaezian,jim}@cs.sfu.ca

Abstract. In the Situation Calculus the term $do(a, s)$ denotes the successor situation to s, resulting from *performing* (i.e. executing) the action a. In other words, it is assumed that actions always succeed. If action a is not possible in situation s, then the action still succeeds but the resulting situation is not physically realizable. We will argue that consequences of this definition of $do(a, s)$ puts some limitations on applicability of the Situation Calculus. In this paper, we view $do(a, s)$ slightly differently which results in a more general form for successor state axioms. The new framework not only has all the benefits of the current version of the Situation Calculus but also offers several advantages. We suggest that it is more intuitive than the traditional account. As well, it leads to a more general solution to the projection problem. Last, it leads to a more general formalization of knowledge in the Situation Calculus.

1 Introduction

The Situation Calculus ([2,4]) is a formalism designed for reasoning about action. In the axiomatization, $do(a, s)$ denotes the result of executing action a in situation s, even if executing a is not possible in s. In other words, it is assumed that actions always succeed. If action a is not possible in situation s, then a still succeeds but the resulting situation is not physically realizable. Let's call this the *success assumption*. To take care of the case where a is not possible, the tree of situations is "pruned" by a separate executability condition, which limits things to only those situations which the actions "actually" succeed.

Although a great deal has been achieved with the current version of the Situation Calculus (from now on we call it the traditional framework), we argue that the success assumption leads to some limitations. In this paper, we define $do(a, s)$ differently by relaxing the success assumption and explore the impacts of this change in the theory of the Situation Calculus. In the new definition actions have no effect if their preconditions are not met. This leads to a more general form of the successor state axioms which follows from reconsidering the frame problem when unexecutable actions (i.e. those actions whose preconditions are not met) are involved.

In Sect. 2 we review the main concepts of the Situation Calculus. In Sect. 3 we make explicit the success assumption and discuss its consequences. In Sect. 4 we

M. Mouhoub and P. Langlais (Eds.): Canadian AI 2017, LNAI 10233, pp. 155–161, 2017.
DOI: 10.1007/978-3-319-57351-9_20

discuss the new definition of $do(a, s)$, present a more general form for successor state axioms and discuss the benefits of the proposed framework. In the last section we conclude and present directions for future work.

2 Background

The language of the Situation Calculus is a many-sorted first order language. There are three sorts: *action* for actions, *situation* for situations, and *object* for everything else. A distinguished constant S_0 represents the initial situation, and a distinguished function symbol *do* represents the execution of an action. A situation is a finite sequence of actions starting from the initial situation. A binary predicate symbol $\sqsubset$ defines an ordering relation on situations. A *fluent* is a fact whose truth value may vary from situation to situation; formally a fluent is a predicate that takes a situation as the final argument. An action then takes a situation to another situation in which the action has been executed. A situation calculus action theory includes an *action precondition* axiom for each action symbol, a *successor state axiom* for each fluent symbol, as well as *unique name axioms* and the *foundational axioms* of the Situation Calculus. Action precondition axioms are represented by the binary predicate *Poss*. Successor state axiom for a (relational) fluent F has the form

$$F(\boldsymbol{x}, do(a, s)) \equiv \gamma_F^+(\boldsymbol{x}, a, s) \vee [(F(\boldsymbol{x}, s) \wedge \neg\gamma_F^-(\boldsymbol{x}, a, s))] \tag{1}$$

where $\gamma_F^+(\boldsymbol{x}, a, s)$ and $\gamma_F^-(\boldsymbol{x}, a, s)$ represent the conditions under which action a affects the value of fluent F positively or negatively.

3 The Traditional Definition of $do(a, s)$

In the Situation Calculus, the term $do(a, s)$ denotes "the successor situation to s, resulting from *performing* the action a" [4]. In this definition, actions always succeed. In other words, in the situation denoted by $do(a, s)$ all the (conditional) effects of action a hold, even if it is not possible to perform action a in s. If performing a is not possible in situation s then $do(a, s)$ and subsequent situations are what Reiter calls "ghost" situations. In these cases the actions still succeed, in that the action effects hold in the resulting situation, but the resulting situation is not physically realizable. The focus is then put on the *executable* situations (i.e. those action histories in which it is actually possible to perform the actions one after the other). For example in planning in the Situation Calculus, where we have a goal statement G and want to find a plan that satisfies G, we prove $Axioms \models (\exists s).executable(s) \wedge G(s)$ which only deals with executable situations. As another example, in Golog, *primitive* and *test* actions are defined as

Primitive actions: $Do(a, s, s') \stackrel{def}{=} Poss(a[s], s) \wedge s' = do(a[s], s)$.

Test actions: $Do(\phi?, s, s') \stackrel{def}{=} \phi[s] \wedge s' = s$.

Note that executability is included in the definition of primitive actions, and test actions are always possible. More complex actions then are defined on top of these two kinds of actions, and they inherit executability as well.

This definition of $do(a, s)$, through Reiter's solution to frame problem [4], results in the successor state axiom (1) which in it truth or falsity of a fluent after an action is independent of whether the action is executable or not. For example if we have $holding(x, do(a, s)) \equiv a = pickup(x) \vee holding(x, s)$ then $holding(x, do(pickup(x), s))$ is always true for all x and s no matter executing the action $pickup(x)$ is possible in s or not.

In the sequel we discuss some consequences of the success assumption.

1. Projection Problem. Consider the example where an agent intends to execute a pickup action of some object followed by a move action to the next room, but the pickup is not possible, say as a result of the object being glued to the floor. In the traditional framework, following the pickup-and-move sequence, in the resulting situation the agent is holding the object and is in the next room. This is clearly impossible and the (separate) executability condition rules out such a (ghost) situation. As a result we cannot formalize these scenarios in the traditional framework. Clearly a more desirable outcome of this pickup-and-move sequence is that the agent is in the next room and the object's location is unchanged. This will be the result in our proposed framework.

2. Representing Knowledge. Formalizing knowledge is an important aspect of reasoning about change; there have been several variants of formalization of knowledge in the Situation Calculus ([1,4,5]). The most recent of these has been used as the standard representation in the literature; but as we will see all these variants have some issues and can be used only in a restricted way. These approaches differ on how they formalize the accessibility relation. We now summarize how knowledge is formalized in Situation Calculus based on [5].

The accessibility relation is represented by a relational fluent K. $K(s', s)$ denotes "situation s' is accessible from situation s". Knowledge is then defined naturally using the K fluent: ($\mathbf{Knows}(\phi, s) \stackrel{def}{=} (\forall s').K(s', s) \supset \phi[s']$) where ϕ is a *situation suppressed* expression and $\phi[s]$ denotes the formula obtained from ϕ by restoring situation variable s into all fluent names mentioned in ϕ.

The successor state axiom for the fluent K is

$$K(s'', do(a, s)) \equiv (\exists s').s'' = do(a, s') \wedge K(s', s) \\ \wedge Poss(a, s') \wedge \textsc{sr}(a, s) = \textsc{sr}(a, s') \tag{2}$$

where SR is *sensing result function*, and formalizes the result of a sense action.

However there is a problem in formalizing knowledge in the traditional framework, as illustrated in the following example in the blocks world domain.

Example 1. Consider a robot which can pickup objects. There are two blocks A and B. Block A is known to be on the table, but the agent does not know whether B is on A or on the table. Nonetheless in the Scherl-Levesque approach [5], after a $pickup(A)$ action the agent believes that it is holding A, even though picking up A is not possible in one of the initial situations.

Formally, we have two initial situations S_0 and S_1. There are three fluents:

$holding(x, s)$: The robot is holding object x, in situation s.
$clear(x, s)$: There is no block on top of x, in situation s.
$on(x, y, s)$: x is on (touching) y, in situation s.

We have only one action ($pick\ up(x)$). Its action precondition axiom is:

$$Poss(pickup(x), s) \equiv clear(x, s) \wedge (\forall y)\neg holding(y, s)$$

Successor state axioms:

$$holding(x, do(a, s)) \equiv a = pickup(x) \vee holding(x, s)$$
$$clear(x, do(a, s)) \equiv [(\exists y).on(y, x, s) \wedge a = pickup(y)] \vee clear(x, s)$$
$$on(x, y, do(a, s)) \equiv on(x, y, s) \wedge a \neq pickup(x)$$

S_0: $(\forall x)\neg holding(x, S_0)$, $on(B, A, S_0)$, $on(A, Table, S_0)$, $clear(B, S_0)$.
S_1: $(\forall x)\neg holding(x, S_1)$, $on(A, Table, S_1)$, $on(B, Table, S_1)$, $clear(A, S_1)$, $clear(B, S_1)$.

The initial accessibility relations: $K(S_0, S_0), K(S_1, S_0), K(S_1, S_1), K(S_0, S_1)$.

Note that $pickup(A)$ is a physical action, so the accessibility relations are preserved. Also note that it is possible to pick up A in S_1 while it is not possible in S_0. Therefore we expect that in a "correct" formalization the accessibility relations and possible worlds after $pickup(A)$ be as shown in Fig. 1.

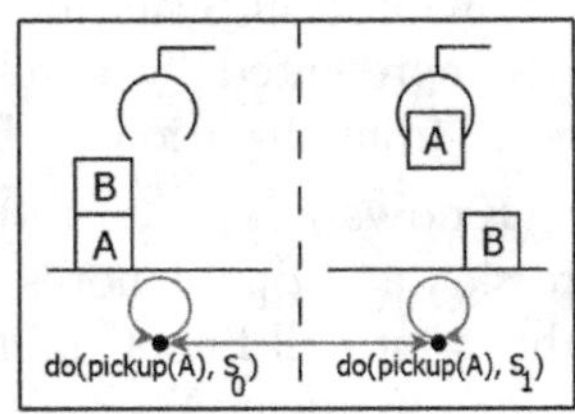

Fig. 1. Desired accessibility relations and possible worlds after action $pickup(A)$

But in the traditional framework, after a $pickup(A)$ action the formulas $holding(A, do(pickup(A), S_0))$ and $holding(A, do(pickup(A), S_1))$ hold; so no matter how the accessibility relation gets updated (i.e. no matter which formulation of K fluent we opt) the agent will believe that it is holding A after $pickup(A)$.

In addition to this general problem the Scherl-Levesque approach has also a problem with updating the accessibility relation. Note that using (2) the only accessibility relations we get are $K(do(pickup(A), S_1), do(pickup(A), S_1))$ and $K(do(pickup(A), S_1), do(pickup(A), S_0))$ (because of $\neg Poss(pickup(A), S_0)$).

Among other proposed successor state axioms for the K fluent, [1] has similar problems. The one suggested in [4] which using the standard terminology is

$$K(s'', do(a, s)) \equiv (\exists s').s'' = do(a, s') \wedge K(s', s) \wedge \mathrm{SR}(a, s) = \mathrm{SR}(a, s') \tag{3}$$

returns the desired accessibility relations after *pickup*(A), but the general problem discussed above remains (the agent believes it is holding A after *pickup*(A)).

The main reason behind the general problem discussed above is that in the traditional framework ghost situations cannot represent possible worlds. Note that in the traditional framework, when action a is not possible in situation s, $do(a, s)$ is a ghost situation and can only represent an imaginary world where action a was successfully executed (although it was not possible) in the world represent by situation s. In our proposed framework we will not have ghost situations and the problem with formalizing knowledge will be fixed.

Note that assuming there is no unexecutable action possible in the model is often too restrictive. The reason is that when dealing with knowledge we have multiple initial situations. Assuming that all actions are executable in every situation starting from any of the initial situations is a very strong assumption.

4 An Alternative Definition of $do(a, s)$

Let $do(a, s)$ denote "the successor situation to s, resulting from *attempting* the action a". An *attempt* to do an action is different from *performing* (i.e. executing) an action in the sense that it is not assumed that it succeeds. If an action is executable then it has its expected effects, otherwise nothing happens (i.e. a null action is executed). This is reasonable because for example if *pickup*(x) is unexecutable (say, because x is glued to the floor), after (attempting) this action, it is reasonable to assume that nothing happens.

In [3], Reiter presented a solution to the frame problem building on the previous works of Davis, Haas and Schubert. He then developed a form for successor state axioms using this solution. If we follow a similar pattern in the new framework we will obtain the following form for successor state axioms[1]:

$$\begin{aligned} F(\boldsymbol{x}, do(a, s)) \equiv\ & (Poss(a, s) \wedge \gamma_F^+(\boldsymbol{x}, a, s)) \\ & \vee [F(\boldsymbol{x}, s) \wedge (\neg\gamma_F^-(\boldsymbol{x}, a, s) \vee \neg Poss(a, s))] \end{aligned} \tag{4}$$

It is important to note that this successor state axiom gives Reiter's successor state axiom (1) as a special case when we have $Poss(a, s) \equiv \top$.

We now describe some advantages of the new framework and show that the new framework does not suffer from the aforementioned limitations.

Projection Problem. In the new framework we can solve the more general form of the problem where the sequence of actions does not have to be executable. Reconsidering the example discussed before, using the new form of successor

[1] The discussion and proof will be given in the full paper.

state axiom, after the sequence of pickup-and-move actions, the agent is in room 2 not holding any object, and the object is still in room 1, as desired.[2]

Representing Knowledge. The ability of our framework to formalize the result of unexecutable actions (by means of the new form of successor state axiom) enables it to regard situations as "states" of the world. In other words, when action a is possible in situation s, the situation $do(a, s)$ represents the world resulting from executing action a in the world represented by situation s, and when action a is not possible, the situation $do(a, s)$ represents the world resulting from the failed attempt to execute action a (which as we assumed has the same properties as s). This advantage will be useful for formalizing knowledge.

Reconsider Example 1. The new successor state axioms are

$$holding(x, do(a, s)) \equiv [a = pickup(x) \wedge Poss(a, s)] \vee holding(x, s)$$
$$clear(x, do(a, s)) \equiv [(\exists y).on(y, x, s) \wedge a = pickup(y) \wedge Poss(a, s)] \vee clear(x, s)$$
$$on(x, y, do(a, s)) \equiv on(x, y, s) \wedge (a \neq pickup(x) \vee \neg Poss(a, s))$$

First note that the new axiomatization entails $\neg holding(A, do(pickup(A), S_0)$. Determining the value of other fluents, we see that in our framework the possible worlds after action $pickup(A)$ are as shown in Fig. 1 (the desired results).

For accessibility relation we use (3). Note that the difference is that for fluents other than K we are using the new form of successor state axiom. In our framework possibility of actions has been considered in successor state axioms of fluents (excluding the K fluent). These fluents characterize the possible worlds. Therefore there is no need to mention $Poss$ in the fluent K which characterizes the accessibility relation between possible worlds. Using this formulation of K and the new form of successor state axiom for other fluents, we will get the expected results after actions $pickup(A)$.[3]

5 Conclusion

We have provided a more nuanced and expressive version of the Situation Calculus by presenting a more general form for successor state axioms which stems from a different definition of $do(a, s)$.

We described some advantages of the new framework. In the traditional framework we can solve projection problem but only for executable situations. We can regard situations as possible worlds but only when the situation is executable. We showed that the current formalization of knowledge works only for executable situations. In our framework we don't have these limitations and it allows us to utilize the power of the Situation Calculus in a broader area. Studying other impacts of the new framework is subject of the future research.

---

[2] A formal account of the problem will be given in the full paper.

[3] The complete description will be given in the full paper.

References

1. Levesque, H., Pirri, F., Reiter, R.: Foundations for the situation calculus. Electron. Trans. Artif. Intell. **2**(3–4), 159–178 (1998)
2. McCarthy, J.: Situations, actions and causal laws. Technical report, Stanford University (1963)
3. Reiter, R.: The frame problem in the situation calculus: a simple solution (sometimes) and a completeness result for goal regression. In: Artificial Intelligence and Mathematical Theory of Computation: Papers in Honor of John McCarthy (1991)
4. Reiter, R.: Knowledge in Action: Logical Foundations for Specifying and Implementing Dynamical Systems. MIT Press, Cambridge (2001)
5. Scherl, R.B., Levesque, H.J.: Knowledge, action, and the frame problem. Artif. Intell. **144**(1), 1–39 (2003)

Combinatorial Reverse Electricity Auctions

Shubhashis Kumar Shil and Samira Sadaoui(✉)

Department of Computer Science, University of Regina, Regina, SK, Canada
{shil200s, sadaouis}@uregina.ca

Abstract. Utility companies can organize e-auctions to procure electricity from other suppliers during peak load periods. For this purpose, we develop an efficient Combinatorial Reverse Auction (CRA) to purchase power from diverse sources, residents and plants. Our auction is different from what has been implemented in the electricity markets. In our CRA, which is subject to trading constraints, an item denotes a time slot that has two conflicting attributes, energy volume and its price. To ensure the security of energy, we design our auction with two bidding rounds: the first one is for variable-energy suppliers and the second one for other sources, like controllable load and renewable energy. Determining the winner of CRAs is a computational hard problem. We view this problem as an optimization of resource allocation that we solve with multi-objective genetic algorithms to find the best solution. The latter represents the best combination of suppliers that lowers the price and increases the energy.

Keywords: Combinatorial reverse auctions · Electricity auctions · Winner Determination · Genetic algorithms · Multi-Objective Optimization

1 Introduction

To meet the additional load, utilities may organize online auctions to procure electricity from diverse sources, such as variable energy (solar and wind), active controllable load (battery storage, electric vehicles and heat storage) and controllable renewable energy (hydroelectricity, biomass and geothermal heat). It has been shown that auctions in the electricity sector promote economic growth, foster competition among energy suppliers, and attract new generation sources [4]. For instance, the number of countries that adopted renewable-energy auctions for long-term contracts increased from 9% in 2009 to 44% by the beginning of 2013 [3]. In this study, we introduce advanced Combinatorial Reverse Auction (CRA) for both Consumer-to-Business and Business-to-Business settings. With the help of auctions, grid companies would be able to obtain the needed energy at a good price thanks to the supplier competition. Our auction is different from what has been proposed in the electricity markets. Limited studies have been carried out for combinatorial electricity markets despite the fact that they match the demand and supply very efficiently and maximize buyer's revenue [5]. Our particular CRA possesses the following features: (1) Reverse i.e. the utility purchases electricity from multiple suppliers (residents and power plants); (2) Multiple items, each one representing a time slot of fifteen minutes. In this way, residents and power facilities have equal opportunities in the auction; (3) Two negotiable attributes: energy

M. Mouhoub and P. Langlais (Eds.): Canadian AI 2017, LNAI 10233, pp. 162–168, 2017.
DOI: 10.1007/978-3-319-57351-9_21

volume and price. These attributes are in conflict because the auction objective is to lower the price and at the same time increase the energy volume; (4) Trading constraints of buyer and suppliers regarding the energy demand and set price; (5) Two bidding rounds: suppliers of variable energy compete first. Controllable load and other renewable energy participate in the second round for any remaining demand; (6) Sealed-bidding since suppliers are independent and compete privately. Sealed auctions are simple, foster competition and avoid bidder collusion [2, 4]. Our new market will benefit utilities and their ratepayers both environmentally and economically and will motivate the expansion of renewable energy.

The above auction mechanism leads to a complex Winner Determination (WD) problem. Searching for the winners in traditional CRAs is already difficult to solve due to the computational complexity issue [6]. Previous studies adopted exact algorithms to look for the optimal solution but endured an exponential time cost [1], which is not practical in real-life auctions. Additionally, considering conflicting attributes makes it even more difficult. To address these issues, researchers introduced evolutionary algorithms, such as Genetic Algorithms (GAs), which produce high-quality solutions with an excellent time-efficiency [8]. Our ambition is to elaborate a GA-based Multi-Objective Optimization (MOO) method to find the best trade-off solution i.e. the best combination of suppliers that lowers the price, increases the energy and satisfies all the trading constraints. This solution consists of a set of winning suppliers, their prices, energy volumes and schedules. In this paper, we conduct a case study to illustrate the working of the proposed WD method.

2 Auctioning Electricity from Diverse Sources

Our electricity procurement auction is conducted with five major phases described below.

A. **Auction Demand:** Few hours ahead the anticipated under-supply period, the buyer issues a call of purchase by specifying his requirements as follows: (1) Delivery period, which is split into slots of fifteen minutes (called items); (2) The energy required for the demand period, defined with the minimum amount (to avoid a blackout) and a maximum amount (to avoid excess); (3) Each item is described with three constraints: minimum and maximum energy and maximum allowable price.
B. **Supplier Constraints:** Potential suppliers (those already connected to smart meters) are then invited to the auction, and all the buyer requirements are disclosed to them. Interested suppliers register to the auction to provide electricity according to the auction demand. Each bidder submits two constraints: (1) the minimum price for each item and (2) the operational constraint i.e. how long the supplier will be able to stay active during the delivery period (after turning ON from the OFF status).
C. **Bidding with Two Rounds:** Our auction is sealed-bid i.e. does not reveal any information about the competitor bids in order to protect their privacy. Participants compete on two attributes: energy volume and price. To reduce the uncertainty due to wind and solar power, we design our auction with two bidding rounds. The first

round is for the suppliers of variable energy. Only these sellers can submit partial bids because they might not be able to generate electricity all the time. When they bid for an item, we assume that they are able to allocate electricity according to the weather prediction. It is worth mentioning that predicting wind for the short term is more accurate than for the long term. The second round is for other energy sources. Indeed if the solution from the first round is partial, then controllable renewable energy and active controllable load can bid for the remaining items: (1) items that do not have any submitted bids, and/or (2) items that do not have a winner from the first round.

D. **Winner Determination:** Our WD algorithm searches efficiently for the best solution that satisfies the buyer requirements and supplier constraints and offers. The solution represents the best combination of suppliers that lowers the price and increases the energy. We have several winners for the auction and one winner for each item. To produce the best trade-off solution, in [7–9], efficient WD algorithms were introduced to solve reverse auctions with multiple items, multiple units and multiple objectives. In [8, 9] WD methods were designed with GAs. We customize the GA algorithm defined in [8] specifically for our electricity market as presented next.

Inputs: Requirements of buyer; Constraints and offers of suppliers
Output: Best set of suppliers

---

1. Bid Validation:

$$Demand_{mini} \leq SupplyBid_{si} \leq Demand_{maxi} \quad (1)$$

$$Price_{minsi} \leq PriceBid_{si} \leq Price_{maxi} \quad (2)$$

where

- $Demand_{mini}$ is the minimum demand of buyer for item i and $Demand_{maxi}$ the maximum demand.
- $Price_{minsi}$ is the minimum price of seller s for item i and $Price_{maxi}$ the maximum price of buyer for item i.
- $SupplyBid_{si}$ is the supply of seller s for item i and $PriceBid_{si}$ the price of that item.

2. Initial Solution Generation: randomly generated based on uniform distribution

3. Winning Solution Generation:

4.1 Improve the solutions with three GA operators (selection, crossover and mutation).

4.2 Apply diversity (crowding distance) to not end-up with similar solutions.

4.3 Use the elitism with an external population to keep the best solutions.

4.4 Among the two sets of solutions (GA-based and elite), select the best ones as the participant solutions for the next generation.

4.5 After repeating steps 4.1 to 4.4 for a certain number of times, return one single near-to-optimal solution (sometimes optimal).

4.6 If any item remains, the auction goes to the next round (steps 1 to 4).

Our system checks the feasibility of any produced solution with two equations:

$$\wedge SellerBid_{si} == 1 \tag{3}$$

$$ActiveDuration_s \geq CertainTime - StartingTime_s \tag{4}$$

where

- $SellerBid_{si} = 1$ if seller s has placed a bid for item i; 0 otherwise.
- $ActiveDuration_s$ is the active duration of seller s.
- $CertainTime$ is a certain time slot in the delivery period.
- $StartingTime_s$ is the time when seller s turned ON from OFF status.

E. **Trade Settlement:** The winners allocate the required electricity w. r. t. the trading schedule. The utility pays each winning supplier via an online payment service. To conduct a successful delivery of energy, we consider the following assumptions: (1) all suppliers are OFF at the beginning of the demand period, and (2) switching (every fifteen minutes) among different suppliers is not an issue for the power grid.

3 A Case Study

Here we illustrate the proposed CRA with a small electricity market (8 items and 5 sellers). We assume the buyer needs to procure a minimum of 700 KW and a maximum of 850 KW, and schedules the delivery from 11 am to 1 pm. He also specifies the constraints for each item (see Table 1). Since we are dealing with two conflicting attributes (demand and price), the buyer needs to rank the attributes to be able to find a trade-off solution.

We have two wind and one solar facilities participating in the first round. Table 2 shows their minimum prices and how long they can stay active. For example, S1 might supply energy for Item1 at the minimum price of $18 and after getting ON, S1 stays

Table 1. Buyer requirements

Item	Minimum demand (KW)	Maximum demand (KW)	Maximum price ($)	Attribute ranking
Item1 (11:00–11:15)	100	110	20	*Demand > Price*
Item2 (11:15–11:30)	120	130	25	*Demand > Price*
Item3 (11:30–11:45)	80	90	15	*Demand > Price*
Item4 (11:45–12:00)	100	120	20	*Price > Demand*
Item5 (12:00–12:15)	50	75	13	*Demand > Price*
Item6 (12:15–12:30)	100	125	22	*Demand > Price*
Item7 (12:30–12:45)	75	100	18	*Price > Demand*
Item8 (12:45–13:00)	75	100	17	*Price > Demand*
Total demand	700	850		

Table 2. Wind and solar constraints

Supplier	Minimum price ($) for items	ON (hours)
S1 (wind)	{18, 23, 14, -, -, -, -, -}	2
S2 (solar)	{-, -, -, -, 10, 20, -, -}	1
S3 (wind)	{17, 24, 13, 19, 12, 20, 17, -}	1

active for 2 h. The symbol '-' means that during that time interval, there is no energy generation from the seller. Next, sellers submit their bids consisting of supply and price for the items of their choice (see Table 3). For instance, S1 bided only for three items; for Item1, he can supply 105 KW for $20. We can see there are no bids for Item8.

Table 3. Valid bids of wind and solar

Item	Supplier	S1 (wind)	S2 (solar)	S3 (wind)
Item1		{105, 20}	–	{110, 18}
Item2		{125, 24}	–	{122, 25}
Item3		{85, 14}	–	{85, 13}
Item4		–	–	{110, 20}
Item5		–	{72, 10}	{50, 12}
Item6		–	{110, 21}	{120, 22}
Item7		–	–	{95, 18}
Item8		–	–	–

Our WD algorithm solves the combinatorial problem above. Table 4 shows the breakdown of one of the candidate solutions. However, this solution is invalid since it does not satisfy the feasibility condition in Eq. (3): S3 has been selected for Item3 and again for Item7, which means that source must be active for 75 min but the active duration of S3 is only 1 h. This solution also does not respect the feasibility condition in Eq. (4) because S1 has been chosen for Item 4 but did not bid for it. So the WD algorithm tries other sellers for Item4 and Item7 if any satisfies both conditions of feasibility. At the end of the first round, it returns the best solution shown in Table 4, which is still not complete. Indeed there is no feasible solution found for Item7.

Table 4. Candidate and winning solutions for first round

Item	Item1	Item2	Item3	Item4	Item5	Item6	Item7	Item8
Candidate solution (infeasible)								
Seller	S1 wind	S1 wind	S3 wind	S1 wind	S2 solar	S2 solar	S3 wind	×
Winning solution (partial)								
Seller	S1 wind	S1 wind	S3 wind	S3 wind	S2 solar	S3 wind	×	×

Table 5. Constraints and valid bids of hydro and battery

Supplier	Minimum price ($) for Item7 & Item8	ON (hours)	Valid bid
S4 (hydro)	{15, 18}	2	{98, 16}, {95, 18}
S5 (battery)	{17, 18}	2	{99, 17}, {100, 18}

For the next round, hydroelectricity and battery storage compete for the remaining two items. Table 5 exposes their constraints and valid bids. Supplier S5 and S4 are the winners of Item7 and Item8 respectively. In conclusion the bid-taker will receive: (1) 617 KW from variable energy; 545 from Wind and 72 from Solar; (2) 98 KW from Hydro and 100KW from Battery. The total energy supply of 815 KW satisfies the min and max amounts stated by the utility.

4 Conclusion

Electricity consumption is increasing rapidly due to the growth of population, economy and infrastructure. To avoid any energy outage, with the help of online auctions, utilities can procure electricity from diverse power sources. We have designed a combinatorial reverse electricity auction with two bidding rounds. We first give preference to variable energy since they are free, and then to controllable load and other renewable energy. We have solved our combinatorial procurement problem with multi-objective genetic algorithms to find the best trade-off solution. The proposed electricity auction will promote the expansion of renewable energy as well as home-based generation with new technologies accessible to residents (like solar panels and plug-in electrical vehicles).

References

1. Han, D., Sun, M.: The design of a Probability Bidding Mechanism in electricity auctions by considering trading constraints. Simulation **91**(10), 916–924 (2015)
2. Knysh, D.S., Kureichik, V.M.: Parallel genetic algorithms: a survey and problem state of the art. J. Comput. Syst. Sci. Int. **49**(4), 579–589 (2010)
3. Maurer, L.T.A., Barroso, L.: Electricity Auctions: an Overview of Efficient Practices. A World Bank Study. World Bank, Washington, DC (2011)
4. Penya, Y.K., Jennings, N.R.: Combinatorial markets for efficient energy management. In: Proceedings of IEEE/WIC/ACM International Conference on Intelligent Agent Technology, pp. 626–632. IEEE (2005)
5. Qian, X., Huang, M., Gao, T., Wang, X.: An improved ant colony algorithm for winner determination in multi-attribute combinatorial reverse auction. In: Proceedings of IEEE Congress on Evolutionary Computation (CEC), pp. 1917–1921 (2014)
6. Sadaoui, S., Shil, S.K.: A multi-attribute auction mechanism based on conditional constraints and conditional qualitative requirements. J. Theor. Appl. Electron. Commer. Res. (JTAER) **11** (1), 1–25 (2016)

7. Shil, S.K., Mouhoub, M., Sadaoui, S.: Winner determination in multi-attribute combinatorial reverse auctions. In: Arik, S., Huang, T., Lai, W., Liu, Q. (eds.) ICONIP 2015. LNCS, vol. 9491, pp. 645–652. Springer, Cham (2015). doi:10.1007/978-3-319-26555-1_73
8. Shil, S.K., Sadaoui, S.: Winner determination in multi-objective combinatorial reverse auctions. In: Proceedings of 28th International Conference on Tools with Artificial Intelligence (ICTAI), pp. 714–721 (2016)
9. Wu, S., Kersten, G.E.: Information revelation in multi-attribute reverse auctions: an experimental examination. In: Proceedings of the 46th IEEE Hawaii International Conference on System Sciences (HICSS), pp. 528–537 (2013)

Policy Conflict Resolution in IoT via Planning

Emre Göynügür[1(✉)], Sara Bernardini[2], Geeth de Mel[3], Kartik Talamadupula[3], and Murat Şensoy[1]

[1] Ozyegin University, Istanbul, Turkey
emre.goynugur@ozu.edu.tr, murat.sensoy@ozyegin.edu.tr
[2] Royal Holloway University of London, London, UK
sara.bernardini@rhul.ac.uk
[3] IBM Research, Hampshire, UK
geeth.demel@uk.ibm.com, krtalamad@us.ibm.com

Abstract. With the explosion of connected devices to automate tasks, manually governing interactions among such devices—and associated services—has become an impossible task. This is because devices have their own obligations and prohibitions in context, and humans are not equipped to maintain a bird's-eye-view of the environment. Motivated by this observation, in this paper, we present an ontology-based policy framework which can efficiently detect policy conflicts and automatically resolve such using an AI planner.

Keywords: IoT · Semantic web · Policy · Conflict resolution · Planning

1 Introduction

Internet connected and interconnected devices—collectively referred to as *Internet of Things (IoT)*—are fast becoming a reliable and cost effective means to automate daily activities for people and organizations. This interconnection among devices—and services—not only yields to the need for representing such interactions, but also to the problem of efficiently managing them.

In traditional systems, *policies* are typically used to govern these interactions. However, most of these systems are static in nature when compared with IoT-enabled systems. In IoT, resources supporting capabilities could become available w.r.t. time, location, context, and so forth. Thus, much efficient tooling is required to handle the governance. There are a multitude of frameworks—some with rich policy representations [10], others targeting pervasive environments [5,7]. However, with respect to IoT, these frameworks are either computationally intensive or are not expressive enough to be effective.

Inspired by this observation, we present a semantically-aware policy framework based on OWL-QL [2] to effectively represent interactions in IoT as policies and an efficient mechanism to automatically detect and resolve conflicts. In the context of IoT, we predominantly observe two types of policies—*obligations* which mandates actions, and *prohibitions* which restrict actions [6]. Conflicts among such policies occur when prohibitions and obligations get applied to the

M. Mouhoub and P. Langlais (Eds.): Canadian AI 2017, LNAI 10233, pp. 169–175, 2017.
DOI: 10.1007/978-3-319-57351-9_22

same action of a device or a service at the same time. In order to provide a uniform solution to this problem, we propose and implement a mechanism which minimizes the policy violations by automatically reformulating the conflict resolution as an AI planning problem.

2 Policy Representation and Reasoning

We use OWL-QL [2], a language based on DL-Lite [1] family, to represent and reason about policies. DL-Lite has low reasoning overhead with expressivity similar to UML class diagrams. A DL-lite knowledge base $\mathcal{K}$ consists of a TBox $\mathcal{T}$ and an ABox $\mathcal{A}$, and the reasoning is performed by means of query rewriting. Due to the page limitations, we refer the reader to [1] for a detailed description on syntax and semantics of DL-Lite.

In order to motivate and to provide a consistent example throughout the document, we base our scenario in a smart home environment. Table 1 shows snippets of the TBox and the ABox of our smart home.

Table 1. Example TBox and ABox for an OWL-QL ontology.

TBox		ABox
$MobilePhone \sqsubseteq PortableDevice$	$Awake \sqsubseteq \neg Sleeping$	$Baby(John)$
$SomeoneAtDoor \sqsubseteq Event$	$Baby \sqsubseteq Person$	$Adult(Bob)$
$PortableDevice \sqsubseteq Device$	$Adult \sqsubseteq Person$	$Doorbell(dbell)$
$SoundNotification \sqsubseteq Sound \sqcap Notification$	$Speaker \sqsubseteq Device$	$Flat(flt)$
$TextNotification \sqsubseteq Notification$	$Doorbell \sqsubseteq Device$	$inFlat(Bob, flt)$
$TV \sqsubseteq \exists hasSpeaker \sqcap \exists hasDisplay$	$\exists playSound \sqsubseteq Device$	$Sleeping(John)$
$MakeSound \sqsubseteq Action \sqcap \exists playSound$	$Notify \sqsubseteq Action$	$SomeoneAtDoor(e1)$
$NotifyWithSound \sqsubseteq MakeSound \sqcap Notify$	$Awake \sqsubseteq State$	$producedBy(e1, dbell)$
$\exists hasSpeaker \sqsubseteq \exists playSound$	$Sleeping \sqsubseteq State$	$hasResident(flt, John)$
$MediaPlayer \sqsubseteq \exists playSound$		$inFlat(dbell, flt)$

Motivated by the work of Sensoy et al. [10], we formalize a policy as a six-tuple $(\alpha, N, \chi : \rho, a : \varphi, e, c)$ where *(1)* α is the activation condition of the policy; *(2)* N is either obligation (O) or prohibition (P); *(3)* χ is the policy addressee and ρ represents its roles; *(4)* $a : \varphi$ is the description of the regulated action; a is the variable of the action instance and φ describes a; *(5)* e is the expiration condition; and *(6)* c is the policy's violation cost.

In a policy, ρ, α, φ, and e are expressed using a conjunction of query atoms. A query atom is in the form of either $C(x)$ or $P(x, y)$, where C is a concept, P is either a object or datatype property from the QL ontology, x is either a variable or individual, and y a variable, an individual, or a data value. For instance, using variables b and f, the conjunction of atoms $Baby(?b) \wedge Sleeping(?b) \wedge inFlat(?b, ?f)$ describes a setting where there is a sleeping baby in a flat.

Table 2. Example prohibition and obligation policies

Prohibition		Obligation
$\chi : \rho$	$?d : Device(?d)$	$?d : Doorbell(?d)$
N	P	O
α	$Baby(?b) \wedge Sleeping(?b) \wedge$ $inFlat(?b, ?f) \wedge inFlat(?d, ?f)$	$SomeoneAtDoor(?e) \wedge producedBy(?e, ?d) \wedge$ $belongsToFlat(?d, ?f) \wedge hasResident(?f, ?p)$
$a : \varphi$	$?a : MakeSound(?a)$	$?a : NotifyWithSound(?a) \wedge hasTarget(?a, ?p)$
e	$Awake(?b)$	$notifiedFor(?p?e)$
c	10.0	4.0

When multiple policies act upon a device, conflicts could occur. In our context, three conditions have to hold for two policies to be in conflict: *(a)* policies should be applied to the same addressee; *(b)* one policy must oblige an action, while the other prohibits it; and *(c)* policies should be active at the same time in a consistent state according to the underlying ontology. Our example policies represented in Table 2 satisfy these conditions, thus they are in conflict.

3 Resolving Conflicts via Planning

In order to resolve conflicts, we have utilized planning techniques. We represent our policies in PDDL2.1 [3]. PDDL is considered to be the standard language for modeling planning problems which commonly consist of a domain and a problem files. The domain defines the actions and predicates while the problem defines the initial and the goal states. Below we illustrate how planning can be useful in resolving conflicts and then we outline a way to pose this conflict resolution problem as a planning problem.

3.1 Illustrative Scenario

Let us envision a situation in which an obligation to notify someone within the house is created, however, there is a prohibition on making sound. This forces the doorbell to pick between one of the two policies to violate. However, if there was another way to fulfill both of them without violating one another, the conflict and ensuing violation could be avoided. Given that we are dealing with complex domains with multiple devices and services, notification action could be achieved in multiple possible ways–e.g., instead of making a sound, a visual message could be used. In more complicated scenarios, the planner would make a decision based on violation costs; a planer can then use costs of actions and violations to create a globally optimum plan that minimizes or avoids conflicts.

3.2 PDDL Domain

We exploit the TBox which contains the concepts and their relationships to construct the planning domain. Concepts and properties are represented using

PDDL predicates. Though we are unable to perform an automatic translation of action descriptions to PDDL domain, it is possible to do so via an infrastructure by exposing device capabilities as services. A discussion on how to do so is beyond the scope of this paper.

Type feature of PDDL is suitable to encode simple class hierarchies, yet it is not sufficient to express multiple inheritance and subclass expressions with object or data properties. Thus, we represent types with PDDL predicates and encode the rules for inferences using derived predicates and disjunctions. For instance, to infer that someone is a parent we can use: `(:derived (Parent ?p) (or (hasChild ?p ?unbound_1) (Mother ?p) (Father ?p)))`

The planning problem contains a total cost function that keeps track of the accumulated cost associated with executing the found plan. In addition to the total cost, a new cost function is introduced for each different active prohibition policy. These prohibition cost functions are associated with the effects of the actions that they regulate to increase the total cost, when the policy is violated. For instance, we can encode the sound prohibition in PDDL as follows:

```
(:action NotifyWithSound :parameters (?person ?event ?device ?soundAction)
  :precondition (and (MakeSound ?soundAction) (canPerform ?device ?soundAction))
  :effect (and (gotNotifiedFor ?person ?event) (increase (total-cost) (p1Cost ?device))))
```

3.3 PDDL Problem

The instances in ABox, which contains knowledge about individual objects are mapped to the initial state and to the goal of the planning instance. For example, the atom `(canPerform dbell PlaySoundDbell)` indicates that *dbell* can produce a sound to notify when needed. Moreover, total and violation cost functions are initialized in the initial state. e.g. `(= (total-cost) 0) (= (p1Cost dbell) 10)`

We note that whenever there is a change in the world, it is reflected on the initial state. For example, when the baby wakes up, the value of function `(= (p1Cost dbell) 10)` is updated to 0 in the initial state. Recall that the goal of the planning problem is to fulfill the obligations while minimizing the total cost. However, if the final plan cost exceeds the violation cost of obligations, the planner chooses to violate the obligations instead of executing the plan.

4 Automated Translation from OWL-QL to PDDL

In order to resolve policy conflicts found through planning, we first need to represent policies in the planning domain. Below we describe how policies were translated into PDDL automatically while preserving their semantics.

The translation process starts with encoding all concepts and properties from the ontology as predicates and their inference rules as derived predicates in the PDDL domain. This allows us to represent the information in the knowledge base (KB) in the planning problem. The inference rules are generated using Quetzal [8], which is a framework to query graph data efficiently.

Next, all individuals in the KB are defined as objects in the PDDL problem. Similarly, class and property axioms of these individuals are selected from the KB and written into the initial state using PDDL predicates. We note that each entry in the KB is either a concept or a property assertion. The total cost is initially set to zero and prohibition cost functions for each policy-addressee pair are set to the corresponding violation costs. Cost functions for unaffected objects are initialized to zero. Finally, the goal state is produced by using the expiration conditions of the active obligation's instances with disjunctions. Lets assume there is another resident, *Alice*, at home. Now, it could be sufficient to notify either *Bob* or *Alice*. The goal state is defined as `(:goal (or(gotNotifiedFor bob someoneAtFrontDoor) (gotNotifiedFor alice someoneAtFrontDoor)))`

All active prohibition policies along with their bindings are encoded in the planning problem to prevent unintentional violation of other active policies while avoiding the actual conflict. In our implementation, we used a central server to processes the policies of all the connected devices for convenience. We note that for each prohibition instance, a cost function predicate is created using its name, and added to the effects of actions that the policy prohibits. For example, if $p1$ is the name of the policy, then (increase (total-cost) (p1 ?x)) statement is added into the effects of $notifyWithSound$ action. Finally, each function is initialized in the problem file.

Encoding an obligation policy becomes relatively simple when the desired goal state is already defined in the expiry conditions—i.e., the variables in the condition get bounded when the activation query is executed over the knowledge base. For example, in the case of Bob and Alice, activation condition would return two rows with different bindings; $\{?d = dbell, ?p = Bob, ?f = flt, ?e = someoneAtDoor\}$ and $\{?d = dbell, ?p = Alice, ?f = flt, ?e = someoneAtDoor\}$.

5 Evaluation

In order to evaluate our approach, we augmented our IoT framework [4] with the LAMA [9] planner; we then tested our implementation w.r.t. our running scenario of home automation. We compared our approach in the following settings: always prohibition, always obligation, and higher violation cost. We generated 60 problem files in total—i.e., 15 problem files for 4 different number of devices (2, 3, 5, 20). Our intuition here was that each newly added device favors the planning method even if they did not add a new capability.

Below we show and discuss the outcomes of our experiments—due to the page limitations, we only present results when the device numbers were 2 and 20. The abbreviations in the result tables are as follows: S_{CNT} = number of times the obligation is fulfilled, S_{AVG} = average violation cost to fulfill the obligation, S_{MAX} = max violation cost, and F stands for Failed.

Table 3 depicts the results obtained. As shown by the results, when 2 devices were used, the planner violated a policy to fulfill the obligation at least once; adding more devices (e.g., when the number of device were 20) reduced policy violations to zero. Thus, it supports our intuition—i.e., adding more devices with

Table 3. Obtained results for problems with 2 and 20 devices.

Method	S_{Cnt}	F_{Cnt}	S_{Avg}	S_{Max}	S_{Min}	F_{Avg}	F_{Max}	F_{Min}	S_{Cnt}	F_{Cnt}	S_{Avg}	S_{Max}	S_{Min}	F_{Avg}	F_{Max}	F_{Min}
Number of devices: 2									Number of devices: 20							
Prohi.	0	15	0	0	0	4	8	1	0	15	0	0	0	7	10	3
Obli.	15	0	6	10	1	0	0	0	15	0	6	10	2	0	0	0
Cost	4	11	3	6	1	4	8	1	9	6	4	8	2	6	10	3
Planning	15	0	0	3	0	0	0	0	15	0	0	0	0	0	0	0

different capabilities to the system spans the solution space for our planning problem. However, adding more devices do not necessarily affect the results of other strategies as they are not aiming to resolve conflicts from a system's perspective.

6 Conclusions

In conclusion, in this paper, we discussed how a planner could be used in a lightweight policy framework to automate policy conflict resolution. The policy framework is based on OWL-QL as it targets IoT applications, which generate large volumes of instance data, and efficient query answering w.r.t. policy representation and reasoning. We reformulated policy conflict resolution as a planning problem by encoding policies in PDDL by means of cost functions and goals. We then utilized a planner to avoid or mitigate conflicts found in plethora of policies. We then presented our initial results which scales well especially when the device numbers increase which is promising. We currently are investigating means to use user history to learn violation costs associated with policies.

References

1. Calvanese, D., De Giacomo, G., Lembo, D., Lenzerini, M., Rosati, R.: Tractable reasoning and efficient query answering in description logics: the DL-Lite family. J. Autom. Reason. **39**(3), 385–429 (2007)
2. Fikes, R., Hayes, P., Horrocks, I.: OWL-QL: a language for deductive query answering on the semantic web. Web Semant.: Sci. Serv. Agents World Wide Web **2**(1), 19–29 (2004)
3. Fox, M., Long, D.: PDDL2.1: an extension to PDDL for expressing temporal planning domains. J. Artif. Intell. Res. **20**, 61–124 (2003)
4. Goynugur, E., de Mel, G., Sensoy, M., Talamadupula, K., Calo, S.: A knowledge driven policy framework for internet of things. In: Proceedings of the 9th International Conference on Agents and Artificial Intelligence (2017)
5. Kagal, L., Finin, T., Joshi, A.: A policy language for a pervasive computing environment. In: IEEE 4th International Workshop on Policies for Distributed Systems and Networks, June 2003
6. Kortuem, G., Kawsar, F., Sundramoorthy, V., Fitton, D.: Smart objects as building blocks for the internet of things. IEEE Internet Comput. **14**(1), 44–51 (2010)
7. Lupu, E.C., Sloman, M.: Conflicts in policy-based distributed systems management. IEEE Trans. Softw. Eng. **25**(6), 852–869 (1999)

8. Quetzal-RDF: Quetzal (2016). https://github.com/Quetzal-RDF/quetzal. Accessed 02 Oct 2016
9. Richter, S., Westphal, M.: The lama planner: guiding cost-based anytime planning with landmarks. J. Artif. Int. Res. **39**(1), 127–177 (2010). http://dl.acm.org/citation.cfm?id=1946417.1946420
10. Sensoy, M., Norman, T., Vasconcelos, W., Sycara, K.: OWL-POLAR: a framework for semantic policy representation and reasoning. Web Semant.: Sci. Serv. Agents World Wide Web **12**, 148–160 (2012)

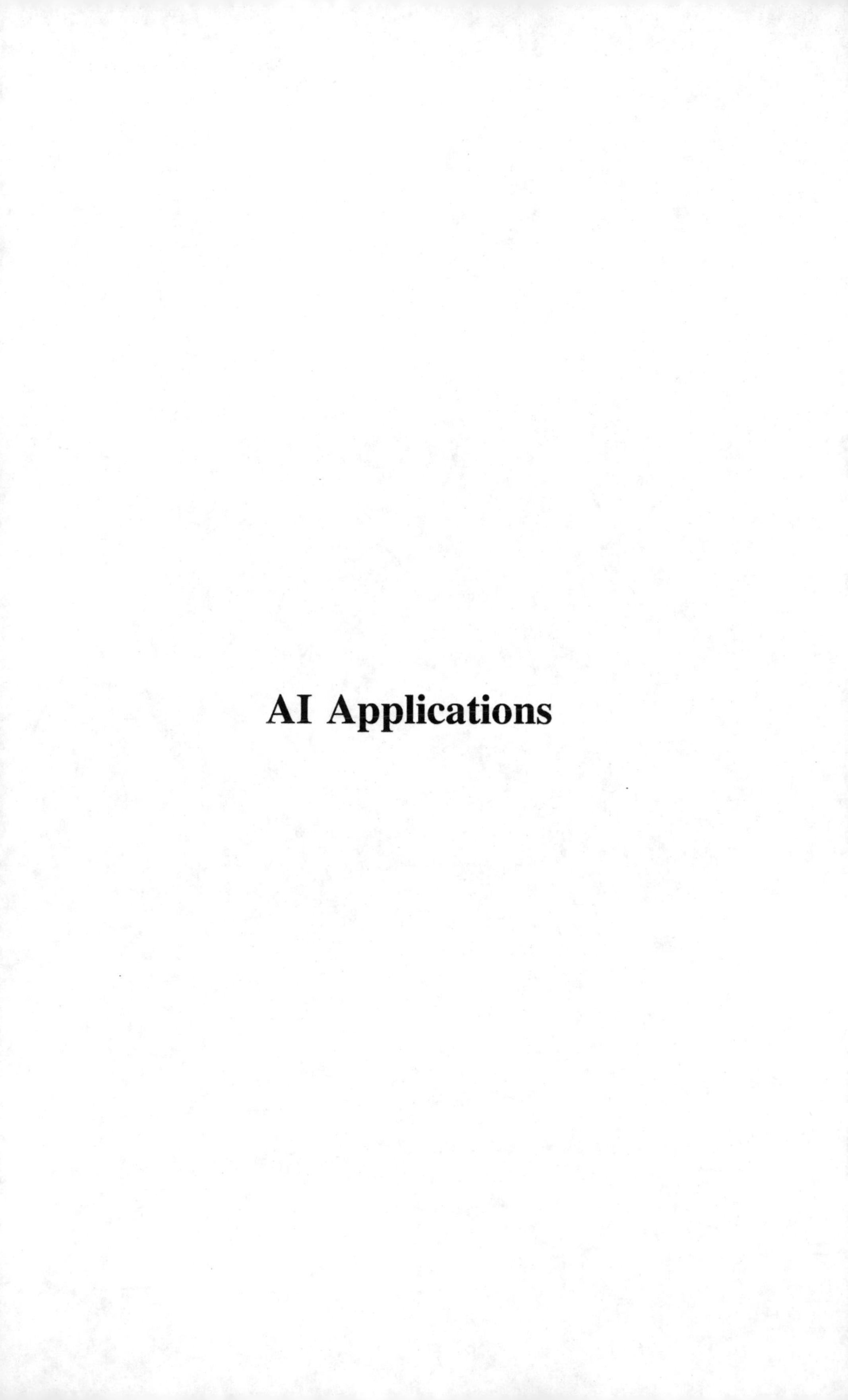

AI Applications

Learning Physical Properties of Objects Using Gaussian Mixture Models

Kaveh Hassani(✉) and Won-Sook Lee

School of Computer Science and Electrical Engineering,
University of Ottawa, Ottawa, Canada
{kaveh.hassani,wslee}@uottawa.ca

Abstract. Common-sense knowledge of physical properties of objects such as *size* and *weight* is required in a vast variety of AI applications. Yet, available common-sense knowledge-bases cannot answer simple questions regarding these properties such as *"is a microwave oven bigger than a spoon?"* or *"is a feather heavier than a king size mattress?"*. To bridge this gap, we harvest semi-structured data associated with physical properties of objects from the web. We then use an unsupervised taxonomy merging scheme to map a set of extracted objects to WordNet hierarchy. We also train a classifier to extend WordNet taxonomy to address both fine-grained and missing concepts. Finally, we use an ensemble of Gaussian mixture models to learn the distribution parameters of these properties. We also propose a Monte Carlo inference mechanism to answer comparative questions. Results suggest that the proposed approach can answer 94.6% of such questions, correctly.

1 Introduction

Common-sense knowledge is a collection of non-expert and agreed-upon facts about the world shared among the majority of people past early childhood based on their experiences [5]. It includes a vast spectrum of facts ranging from properties of objects to emotions. Learning and inferring such knowledge is essential in many AI applications (e.g., social robotics, visual question answering, conversational agents). An important category of common-sense knowledge is physical properties objects such as *size* and *weight*. This knowledge is essential in computer graphics and robotics. In robotics, weight and size information are required to perform tasks such as object grasping whereas in computer graphics, they are required to render plausible relative sizes and realistic dynamics [9]. Yet, this knowledge is missing from available common-sense knowledge-bases such as ConceptNet [13] and Cyc [12], and hence they cannot answer simple questions regarding these properties such as "*is a microwave oven bigger than a spoon?*" or "*is a feather heavier than a king size mattress?*". Considering the huge number of object categories, and their intra- and inter- variations, it is not practical to populate a knowledge-base with hand-crafted facts about physical properties.

A promising approach towards bridging this gap is using web data [7,8]. However, considering that: (1) web data is distributed among heterogeneous

M. Mouhoub and P. Langlais (Eds.): Canadian AI 2017, LNAI 10233, pp. 179–190, 2017.
DOI: 10.1007/978-3-319-57351-9_23

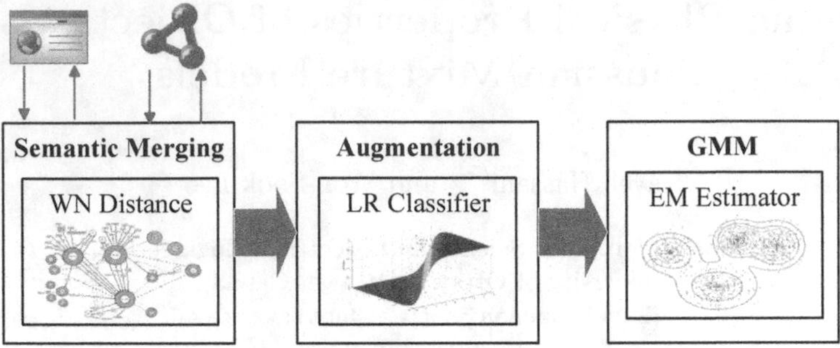

Fig. 1. Schematic of the proposed approach to learn physical properties of objects. Semantic merging uses WordNet semantic distance to merge heterogeneous taxonomies into WordNet taxonomy, augmentation is used to insert object categories that are missing from WordNet using a Logistic Regression (LR) Classifier, and GMMs is used to model underlying distributions of physical properties.

resources, and (2) object categories are hierarchical, it is not a trivial task to integrate this data into a reference taxonomy. To address this, we harvest semi-structured data associated with physical properties from the web and use an unsupervised taxonomy merging scheme to map the extracted objects to WordNet hierarchy (i.e., semantic merging). We then train a classifier to extend WordNet taxonomy to address both fine-grained and missing concepts (i.e., augmentation). Finally, we use Gaussian Mixture Models (GMM) to model the underlying distributions of these properties. We also introduce a Monte Carlo inference mechanism to answer questions regarding physical properties. The schematic of the proposed approach is shown in Fig. 1.

The paper is organized as follows. Section 2 presents an overview on related works. Section 3 describes harvesting and pre-processing web data whereas Sect. 4 presents the proposed approach for semantic taxonomy merging. In Sect. 5, Gaussian mixture models are discussed. Section 6 presents the experimental results and discussion. Section 7 concludes the paper.

2 Related Works

Cyc [12] is an integrated knowledge-base and inference engine with one million hand-crafted assertions and axioms of common-sense knowledge formulated in CycL language. ConceptNet [13] is an automatically generated common-sense knowledge-base containing spatial, physical, social, temporal, and psychological aspects of common-sense knowledge that consists of 1.6 million assertions represented as a semantic network. WordNet [6] is a lexicon with 101,863 nouns that provides the common-sense knowledge as a lexical taxonomy using hypernyms and hyponyms (i.e., *X is a kind of Y*) and holonyms and meronyms (i.e., *X is a part of Y*) relations within in a Directed Acyclic Graph (DAG) structure. Nevertheless, none of these knowledge-bases provide information regarding sizes or weights of objects.

This work is influenced by [18] which trains univariate normal distributions to estimate bounding box diagonals of 3D model categories (i.e., uniform scaling factor). It uses prior absolute sizes of indoor objects and relative sizes of corresponding objects within 3D scenes to learn the distribution parameters. Taxonomy matching is carried out by computing the cosine similarity between representative words of a model and candidate synsets using Term Frequency-Inverse Document Frequency (TF-IDF) measure.

In [1], relative sizes of objects are estimated by maximizing joint likelihood of textual and visual observations. A graph representation with nodes corresponding to univariate log-normal distributions of object sizes and arcs corresponding to relative sizes between objects that frequently co-occur is utilized. Textual information is extracted using search query templates and visual information is extracted by detecting objects and estimating depth adjusted ratio of the bounding box areas of those objects.

ShapeNet [3,19] is an ongoing project to create an annotated repository of 3D models. It currently contains 3,000,000 models out of which 220,000 models are classified using WordNet taxonomy. The goal is to annotate models by language-related, geometric, functional, and physical annotations. Annotating is performed algorithmically and then verified using crowd-sourcing. Absolute sizes are estimated using [18] and weights are estimated by multiplying object volumes by their material densities.

Due to noisy nature of web data, variations in measurements, unit conversions, and correlation between physical properties, we utilize GMMs to jointly learn size and weight information of objects collected from the web, and size ratios of 3D models. We also develop a Monte Carlo inference mechanism to answer comparative questions regarding the extracted properties.

3 Harvesting the Web Data

We are interested in absolute sizes and weights of various object categories. To collect such data, we used websites of *Walmart*, *Costco*, *IKEA*, and *Best-Buy* retail stores. These websites contain hierarchical object categories, object instances, their sizes, weights, and other attributes. To systematically extract this data, we customized a crawler and a Document Object Model (DOM) parser based on DOM template of each website. We crawled over 200 K pages and extracted 108,105 items.

Considering noisy nature of the web, we pre-processed extracted items using some regular expressions. These regular expressions are used to extract numerical values of attributes, standardize units, and normalize dimensions. Dimensions are re-arranged to $length \times width \times height$ format and units are converted to the SI base units. Furthermore, duplicate items and items with missing physical properties are filtered out. Final dataset contains 69,433 objects classified into over 500 categories. We also collected a dataset of dimension ratios of 220,000 classified 3D models from ShapeNet. We use this dataset to post-process trained models on the web dataset.

4 Semantic Taxonomy Merging

Structure of the collected web data consists of heterogeneous taxonomical hierarchies and granulation levels. For example, taxonomical hierarchies of "*washing machine*" in harvested data and WordNet are as follows. Note that hierarchy of *BestBuy* is more fine-grained than WordNet and *Walmart*.

- **WordNet**: [entity] ⟶[physical entity] ⟶ ... ⟶ [home appliance] ⟶ [white goods] ⟶ [washer, automatic washer, washing machine]
- **Walmart**: [Appliances] ⟶ [Home Appliances] ⟶ [Washing Machines]
- **BestBuy**:

  (1) [Appliances] ⟶ [Washers, Dryers & Laundry Accessories] ⟶ [Washers] ⟶ [Front Load Washers]

  (2) [Appliances] ⟶ [Washers, Dryers & Laundry Accessories] ⟶ [Washers] ⟶ [Top Load Washers]

Hence, one should define a scheme to integrate hierarchies into a reference taxonomy. This process known as taxonomy merging is the process of integrating two or more taxonomies on a same subject by eliminating duplicate terms and enhancing the taxonomy using terms from all taxonomies. To address this, we should determine: (1) a reference taxonomy; (2) a mechanism to enrich local taxonomies with representative terms; (3) a semantic similarity measure between taxonomies; and (4) a mechanism to extend the reference taxonomy. We exploit WordNet's *is-a* taxonomy (i.e., hypernym and hyponym relations) as the reference taxonomy. The latter three requirements are addressed as follows.

4.1 Enriching the Local Taxonomies

Instances of an object category contain relevant information about that category. For example, hierarchical category of "*air purifier*" in *BestBuy* (i.e., ... ⟶ [Air Conditioning & Heating] ⟶ [Air Purifiers]) contains 50 instances such as: "*Honeywell AirGenius Oscillating Air Cleaner and Odor Reducer*", "*Gern Guardian Air Cleaning System with HEPA Filter*", and "*Germ Guardian Pluggable Air Sanitizer*". Extracting representative n-grams such as "*air cleaning system*", "*air sanitizer*" , "*odor reducer*", and "*air cleaner*" and combining them with category headers (e.g., "*air purifiers*") can significantly enhance taxonomy merging.

We first pre-process instances to reduce noise by normalizing text, lemmatizing plural nouns, and eliminating stop words. We then extract Unigrams, 1-skip-bigrams, and 2-skip-trigrams from the pre-processed instances and category headers. Synonym concepts of the extracted skip-grams are also retrieved from ConceptNet [13] and added to skip-grams. We then select the top $K = 10$ discriminative skip-grams denoted by Ψ_C. We only consider those candidates that are children of "*physical object*" synset in WordNet. We used three feature selection methods including mutual information (MI), χ^2−test, and normalized

TF-IDF to select representative skip-grams. These measures are defined as follows.

$$MI(C;T) = \sum_{c\in\{C,\overline{C}\}} \sum_{t\in\{T,\overline{T}\}} p(c,t) \times \log_2\left(\frac{p(c,t)}{p(c) \times p(t)}\right) \tag{1}$$

$$\chi^2(C;T) = \sum_{c\in\{C,\overline{C}\}} \sum_{t\in\{T,\overline{T}\}} \frac{(N(c,t) - E(c,t))_2}{E(c,t)} \tag{2}$$

$$Ntf.idf(C;T) = \left(\gamma + (1-\gamma)\frac{tf(C,T)}{tf_{max}(C)}\right) \times \log\left(1 + \frac{|C|}{N_T}\right) \tag{3}$$

C denotes the category and T denotes the skip-gram. $p(C,T)$, $N(C,T)$ (i.e., $tf(C,T)$), and $E(C,T)$ denote the probability, observed frequency, and expected frequency of T occurring in category C, respectively. $tf_{max}(C)$ is the maximum frequency of a skip-gram occurring in category C, $|C|$ is the total number of categories, NT is the total number of categories that T appears in, and γ is a smoothing term set to 0.4 as advised by [14].

4.2 Semantic Similarity

Given a query q, WordNet retrieves a triplet $H_i(q) =< s_i, g_i, h_i >, i = 1 \ldots M$ where s_i, g_i, and h_i denote a synset, a gloss, and a hypernym hierarchy, respectively, and M denotes polysemy degree of the query q. We feed extracted skip-grams of a category, $q \in \Psi_C$, to WordNet and extract $H_i(q)$ for each skip-gram. This produces set $T_C = \{H_1(q_1), \ldots, H_M(q_N)\}, q_j \in \Psi_C$. We then filter out synsets that have "*abstract entity*" in their hypernym hierarchy from T_C. Assuming N skip-grams with average polysemy degree of M for a category, there are $N \times M$ candidates to consider. The goal is to find a h_i in WordNet that has maximum semantic similarity with Ψ_C. We extract unigrams, 1-skip-bigrams, and 2-skip-trigrams of $H_i(q_j)$ and denote it by Ψ_R. Given these assumptions, an unsupervised method is required to select a candidate that maximizes the likelihood of selecting a correct category as follows.

$$\Psi = \arg\max_{h_{ij}} (Sim(\Psi_R, \Psi_C)) \tag{4}$$

Ψ denotes the selected hypernym and $Sim(\Psi_R, \Psi_C)$ measures semantic similarity between Ψ_R and Ψ_C. We define this measure as the normalized pairwise semantic similarity between representative skip-grams of these two sets as follows.

$$Sim(\Psi_R, \Psi_C) = \frac{\sum_{t_r\in\Psi_R} \sum_{t_c\in\Psi_C} sim(t_r, t_c)}{|\Psi_R| \times |\Psi_C|} \tag{5}$$

$sim(t_r, t_c)$ is the semantic similarity between two skip-grams. To decide this similarity measure, we examine seven lexicon-based and two continuous vector space semantic similarity measures. Lexicon similarity measures include six

WordNet-based and one ConceptNet-based similarities [4,10] whereas continuous vector space semantic similarity is computed using word embeddings [2] which can capture fine-grained semantic and syntactic regularities using vector arithmetic and reflect similarities and dissimilarities between the words [17]. We consider two pre-trained and available word embedding models including Word2Vec [15] and GloVe [17] models. For given concepts C_1 and C_2, these measures are computed as follows.

1. *Path similarity* is based on the number of edges in the shortest path connecting senses in a hypernym relation (i.e. $dis(C_1, C_2)$).

$$sim_{path}(C_1, C_2) = -log(dis(C_1, C_2)) \tag{6}$$

2. *Leacock-Chodorow similarity* normalizes the path similarity by taxonomy depth (dep).

$$sim_{lc}(C_1, C_2) = -log\left(\frac{dis(C_1, C_2)}{2 \times dep}\right) \tag{7}$$

3. *Wu-Palmer similarity* is based on the depth of two senses ($dep(C)$) in a taxonomy and the depth of Least Common Subsumer (LCS).

$$sim_{wup}(C_1, C_2) = \frac{2 \times dep(LCS(C_1, C_2))}{dep(C_1) + dep(C_2)} \tag{8}$$

4. *Resnik similarity* is based on Information Content (IC) defined as $IC(C) = -logP(C)$ where $P(C)$ is the probability of encountering an instance in a corpus.

$$sim_{res}(C_1, C_2) = -logP(LCS(C_1, C_2)) \tag{9}$$

5. *Lin similarity* integrates Information Content (IC) with similarity theorem.

$$sim_{Lin}(C_1, C_2) = \frac{2 \times logP(LCS(C_1, C_2)}{logP(C_1) + logP(C_2)} \tag{10}$$

6. *Jiang-Conrath similarity* defines the distance between two concepts and then inverses it to compute the similarity.

$$sim_{jc}(C_1, C_2) = (2 \times P(LCS(C_1, C_2)) - (logP(C_1) + logP(C_2)))^{-1} \tag{11}$$

7. *ConceptNet similarity* is based on a semantic concept similarity provided by ConceptNet [13].
8. *Continuous Vector Space Semantic Similarity* is based on the cosine similarity of word embeddings.

$$sim_{cos}(C_1, C_2) = \frac{\vec{V}(C_1).\vec{V}(C_2)}{|\vec{V}(C_1)| \times |\vec{V}(C_2)|} \tag{12}$$

4.3 Extending the Taxonomy

There are two cases that cannot be addressed by unsupervised merging including missing categories and fine-grained categories. Missing categories are categories that are considered as undefined concepts in WordNet hierarchy (e.g., *Xbox game console*). Unsupervised merging always finds a WordNet concept to match a given category. Hence, in case of a missing category, it missclassifies it to its closest concept. To address this issue, we need a model to predict whether a given category is defined in WordNet or not. If this model predicts that a category is defined in WordNet, we let the unsupervised merging to assign it to a WordNet concept. Otherwise, we insert the local hierarchy of that category to WordNet. We train a logistic regression classifier as our predictive model. Input to this model is the highest achieved semantic similarity between a category and WordNet concepts. This model is defined as follows.

$$P(x) = \frac{1}{1 + \exp\left(-w_0 - w_1 \times Max\ (Sim(\Psi_R, \Psi_C))\right)} \tag{13}$$

Fine-grained categories are missing categories that their hypernym concept is defined in WordNet (e.g., WordNet contains a category for "*washing machine*" but not for "*front load washers*"). Fine-grained categories tend to have inter-variations with their siblings. Unsupervised merging classifies these categories to their parent category, which in turn introduces noise to the model. To address them, we use a heuristic as follows. We collect categories that: (1) are harvested from a same resource; (2) are mapped into a same concept in WordNet; (3) have same immediate ancestor in their local hierarchy; and (4) have different leafs in their local hierarchy. We then extend a corresponding WordNet category with more fine-grained child categories by appending the leaves of local hierarchies to WordNet.

5 Gaussian Models

We train Gaussian Mixture Models (GMM) to model the underlying distributions of physical properties of collected objects and then use the trained models to perform probabilistic inference and sampling. A GMM is defined as a weighted sum of M multivariate Gaussian distributions as follows.

$$P(x) = \sum_{i=1}^{M} w_k P(x|\mu_i, \sigma_i) \tag{14}$$

M denotes the number of clusters (i.e., number of Gaussian distributions). $w_i, i = 1, \ldots, M$ are mixture weights (i.e., $\Sigma w_i = 1$). $x = [x_1 \ldots x_n]^T$ is a continuous random variable of physical properties (i.e., *width*, *length*, *height*, and *weight*) of instances of a category. $P(x|\mu, \sigma)$ denotes a multivariate Gaussian distribution defined as follows.

$$P(x|\mu, \Sigma) = \frac{1}{(2\pi)^{n/2}|\Sigma|^{1/2}} \exp\left(-\frac{1}{2}(x-\mu)^T \Sigma^{-1}(x-\mu)\right) \tag{15}$$

μ and Σ denote the mean vector and covariance matrix, respectively. A GMM is parameterized by its mean vectors, covariance matrices, and mixture weights. The number of models (M) is a hyper-parameter which we set to 5 using grid search in the range of [2,5] and Bayesian Information Criteria (BIC). The parameters are estimated using iterative Expectation-Maximization (EM) algorithm [16]. We train a GMM per category in our constructed taxonomy and a GMM per category in ShapeNet [3]. GMMs trained on ShapeNet learn the distributions of dimension ratios (i.e., *length/width*, *width/height*, etc.). These models are then exploited to reduce the sampling noise of the GMMs trained on the web data using ranking selection. Given an object category, we first sample its corresponding GMM trained on the web data for k times and then feed the samples to its corresponding GMM trained on ShapeNet [3] and compute the probability of each sample. The most probable sample is then selected as the result.

6 Experimental Results

To model physical properties, we considered three assumptions: (1) underlying distributions are either Gaussian or multimodal; (2) a mixture of distributions fits the data better; and (3) physical properties are not independent. Due to noisy nature of web data, we visualized data histograms (i.e., with 50 bins) rather than using systematic goodness-of-fit tests such as Kolmogorov-Smirnov test to investigate the underlying distributions. As an example, the data histogram for "*men's bag*" category is depicted in Fig. 2. As shown, distributions are either Gaussian or multimodal. We observed a similar behavior for other categories as well. Hence, visualizations validate the first assumption.

The noisy nature of web data also implies that simple Gaussian distributions cannot fit the data well (i.e., refer to Fig. 2) and hence it is required to use a

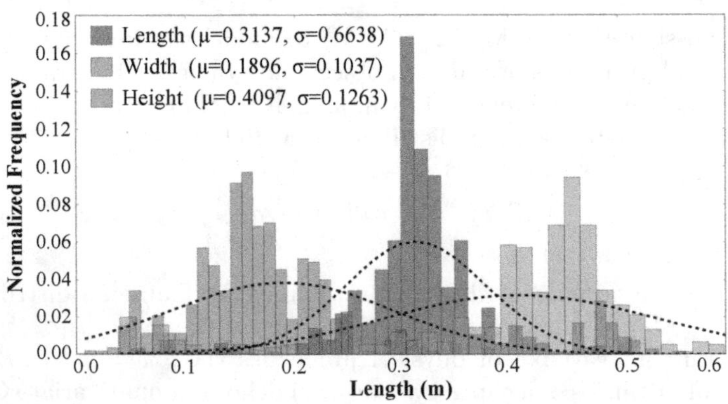

Fig. 2. Sample distributions of dimensions of "*men's bag*" category extracted from 523 instances. All dimensions follow either Gaussian or multimodal distributions.

mixture of such models. The third assumption can be validated both analytically (i.e., density is defined as $\rho = m/v$) and empirically (e.g., Pearson correlation coefficient and the p-value for *volume-weight* pair are 0.6392 and 4.58E-08, respectively).

To investigate the performance of enriching the taxonomies, we sampled 200 categories and defined 10 gold standard skip-grams for each category. We then applied the feature selection methods on this dataset. MI achieved mean accuracy of 88.1% with standard deviation (SD) of 2.53; χ^2−test achieved a mean accuracy of 87.9% with SD of 4.32; and TF-IDF achieved mean accuracy of 89.2% with SD of 2.89. These results suggest that normalized TF-IDF slightly outperforms other methods. Error analysis showed that unigrams are frequent source of error (e.g., for "*air purifiers*" category all methods select "*air*" as a candidate). Hence, it is necessary to prioritize the candidates with respect to their lengths.

We then semi-automatically assigned the sampled 200 categories with WordNet hypernym hierarchies and manually validated them, and then used them to compare the similarity measures. Results are shown in Table 1. In terms of accuracy, precision, and F_1-score, Jiang-Conrath WordNet-based similarity outperforms other measures whereas in terms of recall ConceptNet-based similarity outperforms other measures. Furthermore, to evaluate the performance of the proposed model in extending the taxonomy, we trained the logistic regression model on 200 categories (50 missing from WordNet) and tested it on 50 categories (25 missing from WordNet). The model achieved accuracy of 94% and F_1-score of 0.9214.

Table 1. Performance of semantic similarity measures on unsupervised taxonomy merging task. Jiang-Conrath similarity outperforms other methods in terms of accuracy and F_1-score. similarity

Similarity	Accuracy	Precision	Recall	F_1-score
Path	78.00%	0.7925	0.7812	0.7868
Leacock-Chodorow	79.50%	0.7786	0.7624	0.7704
Wu-Palmer	88.00%	0.9054	0.8856	0.8954
Resnik	92.00%	0.9185	0.8928	0.9055
Lin	93.00%	0.8964	0.9010	0.8987
Jiang-Conrath	**94.50%**	**0.9486**	0.9158	**0.9319**
ConceptNet	92.50%	0.9187	**0.9358**	0.9271
Word2Vec	85.00%	0.8624	0.8245	0.8430
GloVe	85.50%	0.8858	0.8425	0.8636

To investigate the statistical significance of results, pairwise one-tailed t-test is performed between ConceptNet, Resnik, Lin, and Jiang-Conrath similarity measures ($p \leq 0.05$). Results are summarized in Table 2. As shown, t-tests reject the null hypothesis and hence the results are statistically significant.

Table 2. Results of pairwise one-tailed t-test between ConceptNet, Resnik, Lin, and Jiang-Conrath similarity measures

Test pair	p-value	Test pair	p-value
ConceptNet ⊕*Resnik*	0.0000	*ConceptNet* ⊕*Lin*	0.0011
ConceptNet ⊕*Jiang-Conrath*	0.0003	*Resnik* ⊕*Lin*	0.0241
Resnik ⊕*Jiang-Conrath*	0.0000	*Lin* ⊕ *Jiang-Conrath*	0.0037

To evaluate the overall performance of the proposed approach, we performed two scenarios: (1) automatic scaling of 3D models, and (2) answering comparative questions. The first scenario is a subjective scenario in which trained models are exploited to automatically scale a set of 3D models. We generated 10 scenes with 12 scaled objects in each and asked four users to score the naturalness of

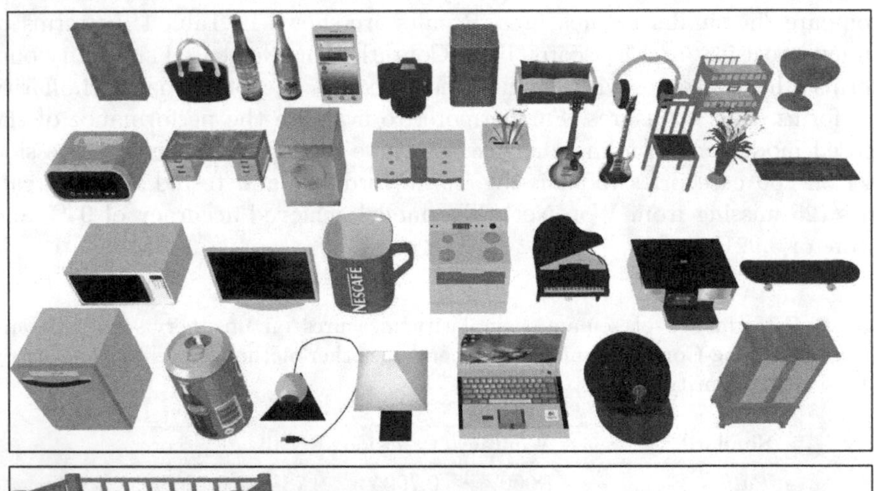

Fig. 3. Upper row demonstrates a collection of 3D models in their default sizes; Same models are shown in lower row after being automatically scaled using trained GMMs.

relative sizes based on Likert scale (i.e., 1 representing *not natural* and 5 representing *very natural*). In 87.5% of cases, users ranked the scenes as *very natural* and in 12.5% of cases they ranked them as *natural*. Figure 3 shows a set of 3D models in their default sizes and same models after being automatically scaled using the proposed approach.

We also evaluated simple inference capabilities of the trained models. For this purpose, we defined a set of comparative questions using grammar G defined as follows.

$$G : \{S \longrightarrow is\ X\ C\ than\ Y?$$
$$C \longrightarrow smaller|bigger|lighter|heavier\}$$

To infer the answers, we utilize Monte Carlo simulation [11]. We sample GMMs corresponding to categories of X and Y, and compare the sample pairs with respect to C. We repeat this process for $N = 10,000$ times and count the number of pairs (K) that satisfy $C(X,Y)$. The answers are generated as follows.

1. X is C than Y with confidence of K/N, if $K \gg N/2$
2. X is not C than Y with confidence of $1 - K/N$, if $K \ll N/2$
3. X is similar to Y with confidence of $2 \times K/N$, if $K \approx N/2$

We manually constructed a dataset of 500 comparative triplets such as (*guitar,bigger,spoon*) and (*refrigerator,heavier,teapot*), and asked the system to accept or reject these assertions. The system correctly accepted 94.6% of them. Rejections were in cases that both GMMs corresponding to categories of X and Y were trained on less than 100 instances. It is noteworthy that the average training time per category is 57 ms and the average sampling time for 10,000 samples is 5 ms on an Intel Core i7 processor. This suggests that the proposed method is both real-time and efficiently scalable.

7 Conclusion

we proposed an integrated approach towards learning common-sense knowledge of physical properties of objects using web data. We used a combination of semantic taxonomy merging and ensemble of GMM models to enhance the learned distributions. We also proposed a Monte Carlo simulation as an inference mechanism to infer simple relations between physical properties of objects. As future works, we are planning to integrate numeric value extraction from online search results to address categories that are not defined in the collected data.

References

1. Bagherinezhad, H., Hajishirzi, H., Choi, Y., Farhadi, A.: Are elephants bigger than butterflies? Reasoning about sizes of objects. In: Proceedings of the Thirtieth AAAI Conference on Artificial Intelligence, pp. 3449–3456 (2016)

2. Bengio, Y., Ducharme, R., Vincent, P., Jauvin, C.: A neural probabilistic language model. J. Mach. Learn. Res. **3**, 1137–1155 (2003)
3. Chang, A.X., Funkhouser, T., Guibas, L., Hanrahan, P., Huang, Q., Li, Z., Savarese, S., Savva, M., Song, S., Su, H., et al.: Shapenet: An information-rich 3d model repository. arXiv preprint (2015). arXiv:1512.03012
4. Corley, C., Mihalcea, R.: Measuring the semantic similarity of texts. In: Proceedings of the ACL Workshop on Empirical Modeling of Semantic Equivalence and Entailment, pp. 13–18. Association for Computational Linguistics (2005)
5. Davis, E.: Representations of Commonsense Knowledge. Morgan Kaufmann, Burlington (2014)
6. Fellbaum, C.: WordNet: An Electronic Lexical Database. Wiley Online Library, Hoboken (1998)
7. Hassani, K., Lee, W.S.: Adaptive animation generation using web content mining. In: 2015 IEEE International Conference on Evolving and Adaptive Intelligent Systems (EAIS), pp. 1–8 (2015)
8. Hassani, K., Lee, W.S.: A universal architecture for migrating cognitive agents: a case study on automatic animation generation. In: Integrating Cognitive Architectures into Virtual Character Design, pp. 238–265. IGI Global (2016)
9. Hassani, K., Lee, W.S.: Visualizing natural language descriptions: a survey. ACM Comput. Surv. **49**(1), 17:1–17:34 (2016)
10. Jurafsky, D., Martin, J.H.: Speech and Language Processing. Pearson, London (2014)
11. Landau, D., Binder, K.: A Guide to Monte Carlo Simulations in Statistical Physics (2001)
12. Lenat, D., Guha, R.: Building large knowledge-based systems: representation and inference in the cyc project. Artif. Intell. **61**(1), 4152 (1993)
13. Liu, H., Singh, P.: Conceptnet–a practical commonsense reasoning tool-kit. BT Technol. J. **22**(4), 211–226 (2004)
14. Manning, C.D., Raghavan, P., Schütze, H.: Introduction to Information Retrieval. Cambridge University Press, Cambridge (2008)
15. Mikolov, T., Sutskever, I., Chen, K., Corrado, G.S., Dean, J.: Distributed representations of words and phrases and their compositionality. In: Advances in Neural Information Processing Systems, pp. 3111–3119 (2013)
16. Pedregosa, F., Varoquaux, G., Gramfort, A., Michel, V., Thirion, B., Grisel, O., Blondel, M., Prettenhofer, P., Weiss, R., Dubourg, V., et al.: Scikit-learn: machine learning in Python. J. Mach. Learn. Res. **12**, 2825–2830 (2011)
17. Pennington, J., Socher, R., Manning, C.D.: Glove: global vectors for word representation. EMNLP **14**, 1532–1543 (2014)
18. Savva, M., Chang, A.X., Bernstein, G., Manning, C.D., Hanrahan, P.: On being the right scale: sizing large collections of 3d models. In: SIGGRAPH Asia 2014 Indoor Scene Understanding Where Graphics Meets Vision, p. 4. ACM (2014)
19. Savva, M., Chang, A.X., Hanrahan, P.: Semantically-enriched 3d models for common-sense knowledge. In: Proceedings of the IEEE Conference on Computer Vision and Pattern Recognition Workshops, pp. 24–31 (2015)

Design and Implementation of a Smart Quotation System

Akash Patel[1] and Brigitte Jaumard[2(✉)]

[1] Yellow Pages Group, Montreal, Canada
akash.patel@pj.ca

[2] Department of Computer Science and Software Engineering, Concordia University, Montreal, QC, Canada
brigitte.jaumard@concordia.ca

Abstract. We propose the design and development of an Automated Quote Evaluation (called AQE) system that semi-automates the quoting process for equipment sales and services. Various machine learning tools (linear and nonlinear regression algorithms, automated feedback module, tagging, feature scoring) are used in order that AQE generates consistent, accurate and timely quotes.

Preliminary validation is provided in the context of a case study with Ciena (global supplier of telecommunications networking equipment, software and services). Therein, AQE issues quotes for performing network equipment operations and planning the required technical human resources in order to install the equipment in customer networks.

Keywords: Automated quote system · Machine learning · Prediction · Tagging

1 Introduction

To be more competitive in the market, several companies, e.g., Apttus [2], IBM [6] are trying to speed up their quotation process, produce quotes with more attractive prices, and have identified a need for support in the quotation process. The goal is to reduce the quotation lead-time, and ensure a higher level of accuracy in the estimation of the operation hours. In our collaboration with Ciena (global supplier of telecommunications networking equipment, software and services), a first investment has been made for an automated quotation system with respect to the equipment/products that are sold by the company (currently under development). However, Ciena is also interested in including the price quotation for customer projects (for e.g., network migration or upgrading operations) as well, and this is a far more challenging enterprise as it not only includes equipment/products, but services (e.g., circuit, node or ring of nodes updating or replacement) and highly specialized manpower.

An initial step is the creation of an automated quotation system for the equipment/products and services sold by a company. Subsequent steps include

M. Mouhoub and P. Langlais (Eds.): Canadian AI 2017, LNAI 10233, pp. 191–202, 2017.
DOI: 10.1007/978-3-319-57351-9_24

the guarantee of quote accuracy as well as the evolution of the system with the introduction of new products and services.

In this study, we will illustrate the automated quotation system with the case study of a company providing telecommunication optical networking equipment, software and services. It follows that the price quotation for customer projects is a quite challenging since it does not only include quoting equipment/products (e.g., circuit, node or ring updating or replacement in a customer network), but services as well in order to add these equipment into a customer network, using highly specialized manpower. In addition, the execution of the services depends on the maintenance quality of the customer network, the type and generation of network equipment and the experience and expertise of the customer technical team that maintain the network.

This study presents the design and development of a web-based quote management application in order to semi-automate the quoting process for internal and external sales or technical network support.

We propose a semi-automated framework incorporating several algorithms to perform the following tasks - auto quote generation, keyword extraction, feature reduction and querying of similar past quotes based on tagging for comparison purposes.

The first contribution of the proposed system is to auto-generate a new quote by applying various machine learning techniques. After having collected a large set of historical quote data for a particular type of operation, the system will trigger the decision library, which will apply a set of regression algorithms such as Support Vector (SV) regression, 2nd order polynomial regression, logistic regression and linear regression to decide which regression algorithm provides a better fit to the dataset. The system will then build a quote accordingly. It is important to note that each quote output parameter can have a different regression model for its prediction.

The second contribution is to enhance the system in order to allow the prediction of the output parameters of a quote for a specific type of operations by including or excluding input parameter into the prediction formula. The inclusion of new input parameters is done by a feedback module. When the system observes a large difference between the predicted value and the real value of the output parameters of a quote, it redirects the user to the feedback module. Therein, the system accumulates a set of reasons behind discrepancy, and extract keywords from it to provide a suggestion for including a new input parameter to the user. Excluding input parameters that play a minimal role in predicting the output parameter of a quote is also an important task that improves the generalization of a prediction model. Therefore, the system applies a random forest algorithm to rank the input parameters, and let the user decides which input parameter should be removed.

Lastly, we applied an approach called tagging to quotes, which provides added information or semantic information or description about a particular quote [12]. In our framework, we are demonstrating a usage of the Term Frequency - Inverse Document frequency algorithm [11] to calculate the similarity between queried tags and tags attached to quotes. The system returns all the quotes whose tags have high similarity with queried tags. So, a network engineer can gather all similar quotes by tags and possibly can find some help from it regarding migration details.

This paper is organized as follows: Sect. 2 describes some related works. Section 3 provides an overview of the automated quotation system architecture. The experimental evaluation along with some preliminary results are presented in Sect. 4. Discussion of a fully vs. semi-automated system is made in Sect. 5. Conclusions are drawn in the last Sect. 6.

2 Related Work

The quote creation process is a very time-consuming and daunting task, as it requires many input variables such as the services involved, their prices and description, customer information, etc. In the daily quote process, the faster a quote is issued, the better are the chances of being selected by a customer. So, there are several companies in the marketplace nowadays developing quoting software to make quoting process timely efficient and consistent among its vendors. Few studies discuss the opportunity of developing customized-pricing bid-response models, using the historical information on previous bidding opportunities, see, e.g., [1,15]. However, they do not discuss any feature for updating their system, which is a key difference with our proposed system.

According to QuoteWerks [9], "Most of the companies have a Customer Relationship Management (CRM) and an accounting systems in place but, they have not yet realized the power of web based quoting system". QuoteWerks focuses on the automation of quote creation process by trying to bridge the gap between CRM and the accounting system. Using a spreadsheet based manual quotation paradigm, the quotation process is very time consuming since the user has to fetch information about the quote from various other sources. QuoteWerks can be attached to various sources like an external database or spreadsheets for retrieving the information quickly, according to some given parameters like customer names for instance. It also has the ability to attach product images and files containing information about contracts, terms and conditions, etc.

Quotient [10] is a very-intuitive online quoting software which lets the service team create, send and manage quotes. Quotient makes the quote creation process online, where the customer can accept the quote at any time and on any device. The user also has the capability to save the ideal quote template and can form a new quote out of it quickly, which leads to sales automation. Moreover, it provides visualization of the quoting data to get a better understanding of business performance.

The WorkflowMax [14] quoting software allows the customers to have an idea about how much a particular job will cost them. The list of advantages stated on their official site is as follows. First, you can create a custom quote in a matter of minutes. Second, you can customize the quote template according to the customer. Third, it provides capability for the user to attach a logo or brand information on their quote. Fourth, it gives you the control over the prices as it uses a different markup percentage, which gives the total control over the final price.

The Axioms [4] sales manager is also a web-based sales application targeting medium-sized businesses, providing an easy and quick way to create sales quotation. It also provides the interface for easy management of the customer's sales, pricing, sales pipeline data, etc.

Apptus [2,3] provides various features to meet client requirements such as Dynamic Configure-Price-Quote, Contract Management and Revenue Management etc. It recommends bundles, pricing and configuration based on factors like regions, organizations' top sales person and prior history. Moreover, it trains the model separately for each customer, to adapt the quotes according to their changing trends.

All the aforementioned software fetch the information from various sources based on the few input parameters which are later used to generate the quotations, thereby making the process of quotation generation easier than a manual one.

However, there are several notable differences in the above mentioned quotation software and the framework that we proposed and developed. These software fetch the values for quotation from the database and use the templates to fill-up the quote automatically. But, there is no learning algorithm running behind the scenes to adjust the quotation dynamically based on past data. Our system recommends various output parameter values needed for the quotation, like number of hours, number of technicians, network reconfiguration time, customer support meeting time, etc. by applying various machine learning algorithms which take into the account several important factors such as historical data, customer name, type of operations, as part of the quote generation process.

Basically, our system makes a model for each type of operation separately and trains it on the dataset and it also adapts to the newly acquired information. In contrast to Apptus [2,3], we have a feedback loop where network engineers are able to give suggestions to improve the accuracy of the system, and minimize the discrepancy between the real and the predicted values. The model creation part of the system is flexible so that users can change the relationships of various parameters, and analyze how the system is reacting based on those changes.

3 Methodology

This section gives a high-level overview about the architecture of the Automated Quote Evaluation (AQE) system. We first describe the input and output parameters of a quote and how to link output parameters with input ones. An illustration of the architecture is presented in Fig. 1.

Input Parameters. To create a quote with a new type of operations, a network engineer will construct a set of input questions associated with the type of operations. These input questions can be modified at a later stage, along

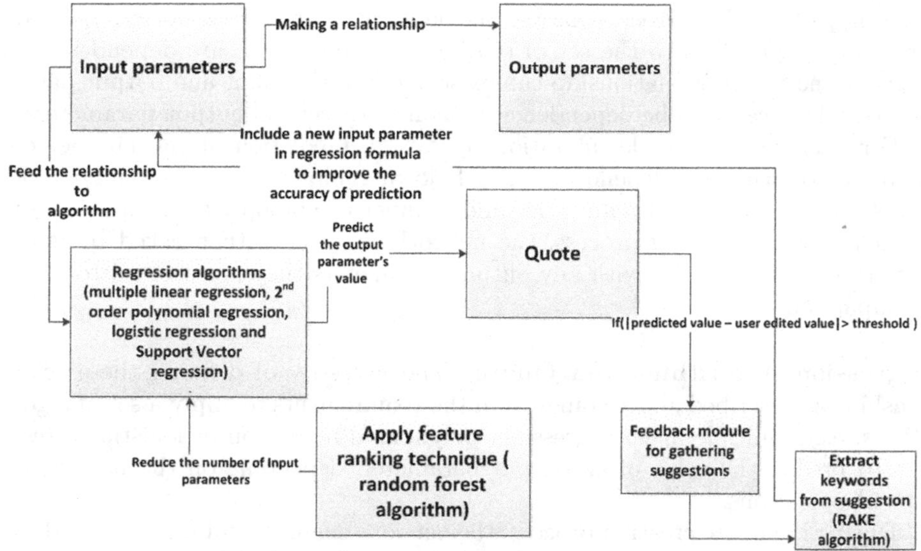

Fig. 1. Architecture overview

with deletion of existing questions and addition of new questions. For example, to define a new type of operations, e.g., node migration, questions include: *(i)* number of nodes in the customer network, *(ii)* number of 2-fiber rings (many legacy optical networks are defined by a set of interconnected rings of nodes), *(iii)* number of 4-fiber rings, *(iv)* number of optical tributaries, and possibly some other items.

Output Parameters. The parameters that network engineers want to predict when generating the quote are defined as output parameters. Examples of output parameters are:

- **Number of *Maintenance Windows* (MW)**: It corresponds to the number of time periods required to perform the specific type of operations. If maintenance windows are of different lengths, it is required to keep track of the number of MWs per MW length.
- **Network Audit and Analysis**: It is the number of hours required to perform audit and analysis on a customer network by a network engineer.
- **Network Reconfiguration and *Engineering Method of Procedure* (EMOP) Creation**: Number of hours needed to make a project plan by a network engineer.
- **Customer Support and Meeting**: Number of hours allocated for interacting with a customer for meeting and support purposes.

Establishing Input/Ouput Relationships. After the completion of the input question creation, the network engineer will then proceed with the relation building process. This process enables the network engineer to connect a defined set of input questions to the set of output parameters that are dependent on them. A one to many relationship can exist between the input and output parameters. There can also be dependencies among two/several output parameters.

For example, in a node migration operation, prediction of the number of maintenance windows depends on the following input questions: number of nodes, number of optical tributaries and number of non-optical tributaries. In the relationship building process, the network engineer is then asked to associate the input questions with any output parameters they are deemed to have an impact on.

Regression Algorithms and Quote. The necessity of defining these relationships as described above comes from the requirements to apply a set of algorithms, e.g., multiple linear regression, polynomial regression or logistic regression to predict the value of an output parameter, depending on the particular type of operations.

During the quote creation process, the network engineer will first be asked to select the operation type and to enter basic information related to the quote such as customer name, author, region, etc. Then depending on the chosen operation type, the network engineer will be asked the specific set of input questions and will be guided to fill up the actual quote.

In the beginning, the AQE system starts accumulating the quote data with associated input values for building a first prediction model. Once AQE system collects an adequate number of quotes for an operation type, a suitable algorithm will be selected according to the data for quote's output parameter prediction and will build prediction model accordingly.

Feedback Module for Collecting Suggestions. For perpetual AQE system prediction accuracy enhancement, the feedback process will be triggered in two-ways. First, when the network engineer reviews the quote and does major changes in estimated quote values and second, after completing a project when network engineers make a changes in certain parameter's value.

Whenever there is a difference between the real and the estimated values that is above a given threshold, the network engineer will be directed to the feedback form to describe the cause for the variance. In the feedback process, the network engineer will be asked to provide suggestion describing the reason of discrepancy.

Extract Keywords from Suggestions. If a network engineer provides a reason explaining the inconsistency between the real value and the predicted values, the AQE system applies a keyword extraction algorithm to extract keywords from this explanation. Then, the system lists all the extracted keywords to help the admin network engineer formulate a new input question, which will be added to the regression formula to improve prediction accuracy.

After including a new input question, the algorithm will wait for a sufficiently large number of quotes to be added into the AQE system to build a new regression formula. The AQE system chooses appropriate regression algorithm again to create a new regression formula to effectively predict corresponding output parameter's value.

Apply Feature Ranking Technique. To remove insignificant features or input parameters from the regression formula, we apply random forest algorithm [5] to rank the features according to their importance. It gives insight to the network engineer as how much each input parameter contributes in predicting output parameters. Then, the network engineer can remove irrelevant parameters from the regression formulas to make input parameter set more manageable.

4 Experimental Evaluation and Preliminary Results

We now present in more details the implementation of the case study with Ciena, and some preliminary validations.

4.1 Selection of Regression Algorithms for Output Parameters

We now describe the chosen regression algorithm for all the output parameters related to the operation named "node/site add/delete". Indeed, a network can be viewed as a graph with a set of interconnected nodes, where a site corresponds to a cluster of nodes. When upgrading a network following, e.g., an increase of the traffic or new technology, a node or a site can be added or deleted.

The system has been experimented initially with 25 data samples, then with 32 data samples and finally with 38 data samples. Figures 2 to 4 show the chosen regression algorithm on all the stages mentioned above.

For output parameter named "network audit and analysis", the selected regression after 25 and 32 data samples is *Support Vector* regression and after 38 data samples, the selected regression is changed to *linear* regression.

The selected regression algorithms for the output parameter "network reconfiguration and EMOP creation" are *Support Vector* regression for 25 data samples and *linear regression* for 32 and 38 data samples which is shown in the Fig. 3.

Figure 4 shows selected regression algorithms for output parameter named "customer support and meeting" which are Support Vector Regression, linear regression and linear regression for data samples - 25, 32 and 38 in order.

The chosen regression algorithms for output parameter "number of maintenance windows" are Support Vector regression, logistic regression and linear regression for data samples - 25, 32 and 38 respectively which is shown in Fig. 5.

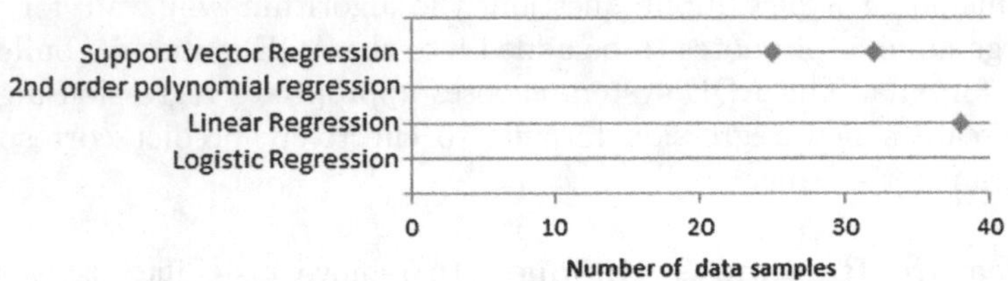

Fig. 2. Selected regression algorithms for the *Network Audit and Analysis* output parameter according to the number of data samples

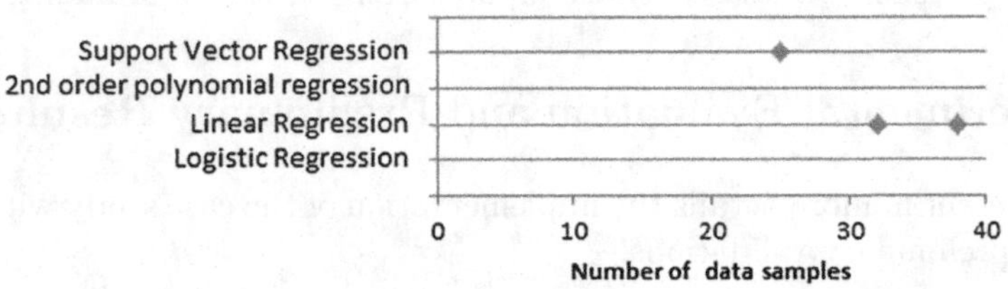

Fig. 3. Selected regression algorithms for the *Network Reconfiguration and EMOP creation* output parameter according to the number of data samples

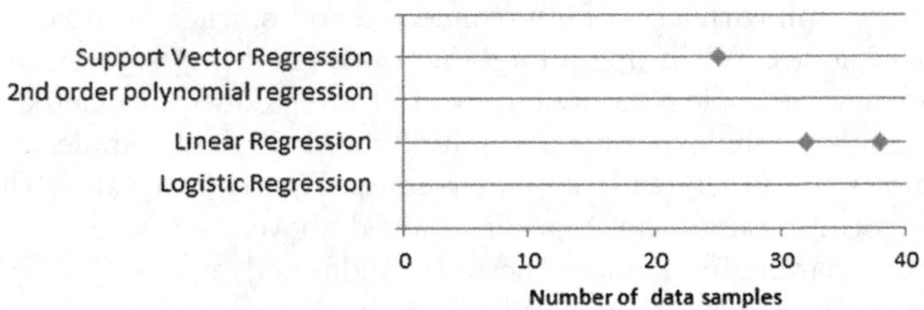

Fig. 4. Selected regression algorithms for the *Customer Support and Meeting* output parameter according to the number of data samples

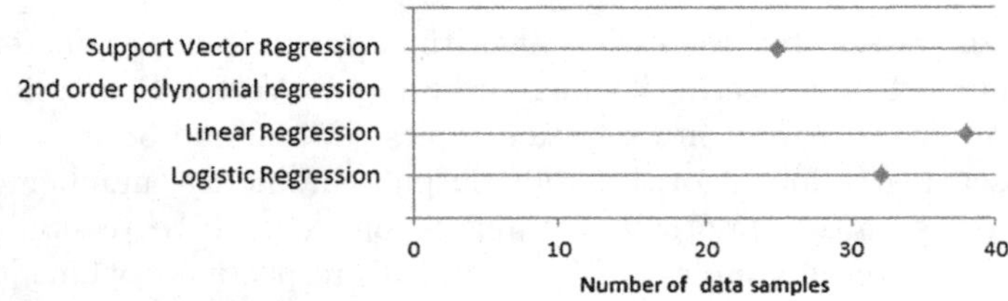

Fig. 5. Selected regression algorithms for the *Number of MWs* output parameter according to the number of data samples

4.2 Random Forest for Feature Scoring

As random forest provides good accuracy, robustness and ease of use, we apply it on the set of output parameters as a feature selection algorithm.

Tables 1, 2, 3 and 4 shows the random forest ranking and scoring for each output parameter: *network audit and analysis*, *network reconfiguration and EMOP creation*, *customer support and meetings* and *number of MW (maintenance windows)* respectively. Each table has three columns. The first one displays the

Table 1. Feature scoring for *Network Audit and Analysis* output parameter

Input parameters (features)	Score	Ranking
Total number of nodes to add	0.058	2
Number of involved systems	−0.213	3
Number of sites to add/delete	0.594	1
Total number of nodes to delete	−4.272	4

Table 2. Feature scoring for *Network Reconfiguration and EMOP creation* output parameter

Input parameters (features)	Score	Ranking
Total number of nodes to add	0.253	2
Number of MWs	0.594	1.000
Number of involved systems	−4.272	4
Total number of nodes to delete	−0.508	3

Table 3. Feature scoring for *Customer Support and Meeting* output parameter

Input parameters (features)	Score	Ranking
Network audit and analysis	0.211	1
Network reconfiguration and EMOP creation	0.015	2
Number of MWs	−0.089	3

Table 4. Feature scoring for the # *MWs (number of maintenance windows)* output parameter

Input parameters (features)	Score	Ranking
Number of sites to add/delete	0.227	1
Total number of nodes to delete	0.030	2
Total number of nodes to add	−0.065	3
Number of involved systems	−0.203	4

input parameters related to the particular output parameter. The second column provides the score, i.e., how much the particular input parameter impacts the regression model performance. The last one provides the ranking of the input parameters.

5 Fully Automated vs. Semi-automated System

A quotation system with no automation can be time consuming; however, moving to a fully automated system brings limited benefits, and it is not feasible in some cases.

There are few features in the AQE system that need to be fully automated. For instance, the AQE system does not delete irrelevant input questions from the regression formula automatically as it depends on the network engineer to explicitly run the algorithm to remove the input questions. Rather than updating the prediction model by an action of a network engineer, there should be a way for the AQE system to update the model over time based on the frequency of the quote data.

In many cases, it is not feasible to automate all the desired tasks. For instance, the significance of the output parameter cannot be automatically understood by the AQE system. The AQE system does not have any idea with regards to the margin of errors while predicting values. For example, the discrepancy value of "3" between the predicted and the real value for the output parameter - "number of maintenance windows (MWs)" is a more serious issue than the same discrepancy value for the output parameter - "customer support and meetings". Hence, to prevent the above mentioned issue, the network engineer sets a threshold value for each output parameter. It helps the AQE system to track the activity in the database in case of a discrepancy that goes beyond the threshold limit.

The project was mainly the design of a semi-automated quote system which provides assistance to network engineers to create quotes quickly and efficiently. Therefore, the main focus was provided in implementing the AQE system using machine learning algorithms. Complete validation will take some time, as a sufficiently large number of quotes is required.

The AQE system fulfills this objective by going through three stages. First, in the initialization stage, the network engineer enters the new operation type and builds an association between the input and output parameters. Second, in the early training stage, the AQE system waits for a fair amount of quotes to be gathered and then it builds a prediction model accordingly. Finally, in the steady stage, the AQE system will make predictions and simultaneously gather feedback from the network engineer for prediction improvement.

We have completed implementing the AQE system with all three stages which satisfy the main objective of the AQE system. According to the number of quotes being entered into the AQE system, it will take few months to about one year to properly validate the AQE system.

6 Conclusions and Future Work

We design the AQE system, a first automated quotation system, which not only automatically generates quotes, but is also able to automatically refine its accuracy thanks to the combination of several machine learning tools: linear and nonlinear regression algorithms, automated feedback module, tagging, feature scoring, etc.

In the feedback module, we allow the network engineer to provide feedback in plain text. Thereafter, we apply the keyword extraction algorithm for extracting the keywords. From the extracted keywords, the admin network engineer builds few questions which can possibly be included in the regression formula. S/he distributes these questions to a group of network engineers who vote on these questions. The highest voted question, assumed to be relevant enough would be added to the regression formula.

The next step in terms of the research is to make the AQE system more generic so that it can be applicable to other domains as well, e.g., house price estimation for real estate brokers. In [7,13], the authors use multiple linear regression algorithms for building a regression model for prediction. Slightly more sophisticated machine learning tools are used in [8]. In our case study, the AQE system applies three other regression algorithms on top of the multiple linear regression algorithm for building a regression model. In addition, AQE also uses an automated feedback module to improve the prediction.

Finally, after gathering a large number of quotes, the validation of the AQE system will be completed. Fine tuning will still be required, as well as assessment of its accuracy.

Acknowledgements. B. Jaumard has been supported by a Concordia University Research Chair (Tier I) and by an NSERC (Natural Sciences and Engineering Research Council of Canada) grant. A. Patel was supported by a MITACS & Ciena Accelerate grant. We thank Dr. Meurs for her constructive comments. We also thank R. Fahim and C. Preston-Thomas for their comments while defining and modelling the AQE system.

References

1. Agrawal, V., Ferguson, M.: Bid-response models for customised pricing. J. Revenue Pricing Manag. **6**, 212–228 (2007)
2. Apptus. http://www.apptus.com. Accessed 4 Nov 2015
3. Apttus using machine learning in price-quoting management. http://www.eweek.com/enterprise-apps/apttus-using-machine-learning-in-price-quoting-management.html. Accessed 25 Sept 2015
4. Axiom sales manager. http://www.raeko.com/. Accessed 4 Nov 2015
5. Breiman, L.: Random forests. Mach. Learn. **45**(1), 5–32 (2001)
6. Lawrence, R.D.: A machine-learning approach to optimal bid pricing. In: Bhargava, H.K., Ye, N. (eds.) Computational Modeling and Problem Solving in the Networked World. Operations Research/Computer Science Interfaces Series, pp. 97–118. Springer, New York (2003)

7. Pardoe, I.: Modeling home prices using realtor data. J. Stat. Educ. **16**(2), 1–9 (2008)
8. Parka, B., Baeb, J.K.: Using machine learning algorithms for housing price prediction: the case of Fairfax County, Virginia housing data. Expert Syst. Appl. **42**, 2928–2934 (2015)
9. QuoteWerks. http://www.quotewerks.com/. Accessed 4 Nov 2015
10. Quotient. https://www.quotientapp.com/. Accessed 4 Nov 2015
11. Robertson, S.: Understanding inverse document frequency: on theoretical arguments for IDF. J. Doc. **60**(5), 503–520 (2004)
12. Sebastiani, F.: Machine learning in automated text categorization. J. ACM Comput. Surv. **34**, 1–47 (2002)
13. Tiwari, V., Khare, D.: Housing demand model for rental housing in urban regions of Uttar Pradesh. Int. J. Sci. Res. **5**(10), 430–438 (2016)
14. WorkflowMax. http://www.workflowmax.com/. Accessed 4 Nov 2015
15. Zhang, Y., Luo, H., He, Y.: A system for tender price evaluation of construction project based on big data. Procedia Eng. **123**, 606–614 (2015)

Knowledge Discovery in Graphs Through Vertex Separation

Marc Sarfati[1,2], Marc Queudot[2], Catherine Mancel[3], and Marie-Jean Meurs[2(✉)]

[1] École Polytechnique, Palaiseau, France
[2] Université du Québec à Montréal, Montreal, QC, Canada
meurs.marie-jean@uqam.ca
[3] ENAC (École Nationale de l'Aviation Civile), Université de Toulouse, Toulouse, France

Abstract. This paper presents our ongoing work on the Vertex Separator Problem (VSP), and its application to knowledge discovery in graphs representing real data. The classic VSP is modeled as an integer linear program. We propose several variants to adapt this model to graphs with various properties. To evaluate the relevance of our approach on real data, we created two graphs of different size from the IMDb database. The model was applied to the separation of these graphs. The results demonstrate how the model is able to semantically separate graphs into clusters.

Keywords: Graph partitioning · Knowledge discovery · Vertex Separator Problem

1 Introduction

Extracting knowledge from graphs is often performed by clustering algorithms. While several methods are based on random walks or spectral decomposition for example [12], this paper focuses on graph separation through the Vertex Separator Problem (VSP) and its applications. The VSP can be formally defined as follows. Given a connected undirected graph $G = (V, E)$, a *vertex separator* in G is a subset of vertices whose removal disconnects G. In other words, finding a vertex separator is finding a partition of V composed of 3 non-empty classes A, B and C such that there is no edge between A and B, as depicted in Fig. 1. C is usually called the separator while A and B are the pillars. The VSP appears in a wide range of applications like very-large-scale integration design [15], matrix factorization [4], bioinformatics [6], or network security [13].

The VSP consists in finding a minimum-sized separator in any connected graph. In any finite connected graph which is not complete, one can find a minimum-sized separator since the number of subsets of the vertex set is finite. The VSP is NP-hard [3,8], even if the graph is planar [7]. In [10], Kanevsky provided an algorithm to find all minimum-sized separators in a graph. However,

M. Mouhoub and P. Langlais (Eds.): Canadian AI 2017, LNAI 10233, pp. 203–214, 2017.
DOI: 10.1007/978-3-319-57351-9_25

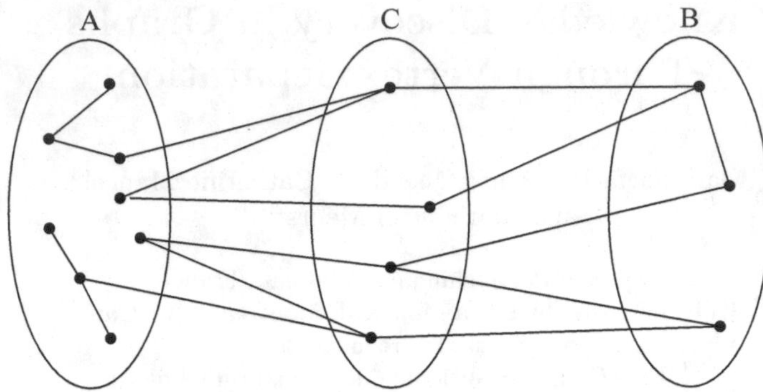

Fig. 1. Example of vertex separation

the method is not efficient for computing balanced pillars, especially on large instances. Indeed, computing a minimum-sized separator often leads to finding pillars of highly unbalanced cardinalities. Since most of the applications to real-life problems look for reasonably balanced pillars, adding cardinality constraints often results in finding slightly larger separators. Figure 2 shows on a small graph this trade-off between finding a small-sized separator and finding a balanced result. A minimum-sized separator is only composed of the red vertex, which separates the graph in two subsets whose cardinalities are 9 and 1. Any graph which contains a terminal vertex (*i.e.* which degree is 1). In Fig. 2, the separator composed of blue vertices may be a better choice because it separates the graph into balanced dense subsets.

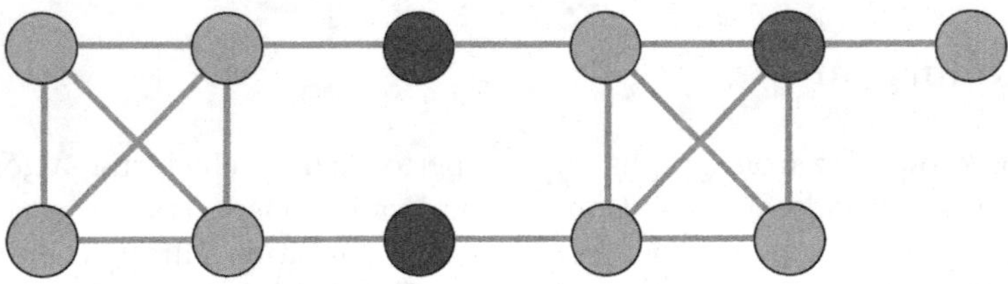

Fig. 2. Trade-off between separator-size and balanced components

Other approaches to solve the VSP have been recently proposed. Among them, Benlic and Hao present an approximate solution, which uses Breakout Local Search [2]. The algorithm requires an initial solution, and then looks for a local optimum using a mountain climbing method. In order to avoid getting stuck on a local optimum, once the algorithm reaches a local optimum, a perturbation is added to leap to another search zone. A continuous polyhedral solution is proposed by Hager and Hungerford in [9] where the optimization problem relaxes the separation constraint ($|(A \times B) \cap E| = 0$) to include it in the objective function. However, the optimization problem is quadratic thus not easily solvable by a mathematical programming solver. Following the seminal work from Balas and De Souza [1,14], the work we present in this paper is based on the polyhedral approach introduced by Didi Biha and Meurs. In [5], they presented a formulation of a Mixed-Integer Linear Programming (MILP) to solve the VSP. This solution is useful and elegant since it is exact and allows to easily add constraints on the sizes of the pillars.

Our initial model and the proposed variants are presented in the next Section. To evaluate the efficiency of our approach and its ability to provide semantic sets of vertices (pillars), we applied our approach to several graphs extracted from the Internet Movie Database (IMDb)[1]. Section 3 describes these experiments and results, while we conclude and discuss future work in Sect. 4.

2 Solving the VSP

2.1 Initial Model

Since this paper presents an extension of [5], it uses the same notations for the sake of clarity. Let $G = (V, E)$ be a finite undirected graph, the goal is to find a partition (A, B, C) as defined previously. Let $\mathbf{x}$ and $\mathbf{y}$ be two vectors indexed by the vertices in V, which are indicators of the presence of a vertex in A or B (*i.e.* $x_u = 1$ if $u \in A$, $x_u = 0$ otherwise). Computing the VSP is equivalent to finding a partition (A, B, C) such as there is no edge between A and B and if n denotes $|V|$, $|A| + |B| = n - |C| = \sum_{v \in V}(x_v + y_v)$ is maximized. The integer linear program is hence formulated as follows:

$$\max_{\mathbf{x},\mathbf{y} \in \{0,1\}^n} \sum_{v \in V} (x_v + y_v) \tag{VSP}$$

Subject to

$$\forall v \in V, x_v + y_v \leq 1 \tag{1}$$

$$\forall (uv) \in E, x_u + y_v \leq 1 \tag{2}$$

$$\forall (uv) \in E, x_v + y_u \leq 1 \tag{3}$$

Note that (VSP) is equivalent to

$$\max_{\mathbf{x},\mathbf{y} \in \{0,1\}^n} |A| + |B| \tag{VSP'}$$

Constraint (1) reflects the fact that a vertex can not simultaneously be in A and in B. (2) and (3) express that there is no edge between A and B. (VSP) subject to (1)–(3) computes a minimum-sized separator of a graph G. An extension of the Menger's theorem defined in [10] states that the size of a separator in a graph is necessarily greater than or equal to the connectivity of the graph. Adding this constraint reduces the size of the polyhedron admissible solutions, shrinking down the computation time needed to solve the model. Let k_G denote

[1] Information courtesy of IMDb (http://www.imdb.com). Used with permission.

the connectivity of the graph, the linear program can be strengthened by adding a new constraint:

$$\sum_{v \in V} (x_v + y_v) \leq n - k_G \tag{4}$$

As seen previously, it can be useful to compute separators which lead to balanced pillars. Didi Biha and Meurs added two constraints to the linear program (VSP) in order to avoid large imbalances. Given $\beta(n)$ an arbitrary number, they forced the cardinalities of the pillars A and B to be smaller than or equal to $\beta(n)$. The literature usually recommends $\beta(n) = 2n/3$ [11].

$$\sum_{v \in V} x_v \leq \beta(n) \tag{5}$$

$$\sum_{v \in V} y_v \leq \beta(n) \tag{6}$$

2.2 Relaxing the Constraints on the Partition Size

(VSP) subject to (1)–(6) computes a low-sized separator of a graph while generally avoiding large imbalances in the pillars. However, $\beta(n)$ is arbitrarily chosen so it may lead to inconsistency. The graph in Fig. 3 is clearly composed of 2 different dense blocks (cliques) linked by a single vertex (denoted 25). The bigger clique contains more than $2n/3$ vertices, hence the linear program can not choose $\{25\}$ as a separator. In order to satisfy constraints (5) and (6), the solver must add unnecessary vertices in the separator, which are part of a dense connected component.

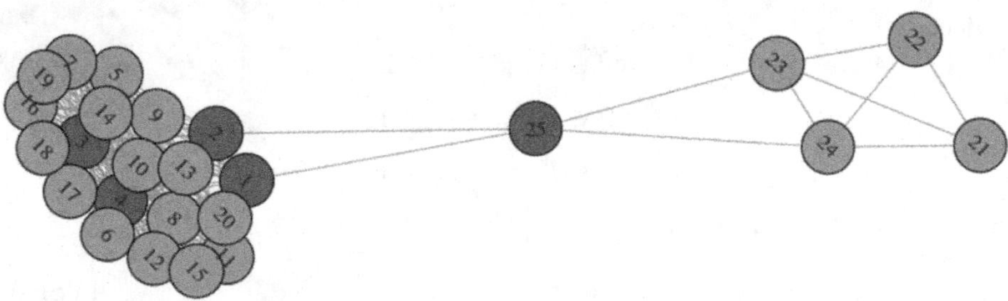

Fig. 3. Inconsistency due to the choice of $\beta(n)$

In this paper we present a new approach to compute low-sized balanced separator in a graph. Instead of fixing an arbitrary upper bound to the sizes of the pillars, we relax constraints (5) and (6) but we penalize large gaps between $|A|$ and $|B|$ in the objective function. The objective function becomes:

$$\max_{\mathbf{x},\mathbf{y} \in \{0,1\}^n} |A| + |B| - \gamma(|B| - |A|)$$

where $\gamma \in [0,1]$ and

$$|A| \leq |B| \tag{7}$$

Note that because pillars A and B have no predefined meaning, one can set $|A| \leq |B|$ or $|B| \leq |A|$ with no loss of generality.

The objective function can be simplified as follows:

$$|A| + |B| + \gamma(|A| - |B|) = (1+\gamma)|A| + (1-\gamma)|B| = (1+\gamma)[|A| + \frac{1-\gamma}{1+\gamma}|B|].$$

Since $(1+\gamma)$ is positive, we can remove this term from the objective function and still find the same solutions $\mathbf{x}$ and $\mathbf{y}$. Moreover $\gamma \mapsto \frac{1-\gamma}{1+\gamma}$ induces a bijection between $[0,1]$ and $[0,1]$, thus the objective function of the relaxed problem is:

$$\max_{\mathbf{x},\mathbf{y} \in \{0,1\}^n} |A| + \lambda|B| \qquad \text{with } \lambda \in [0,1] \tag{VSPr}$$

The new linear program is formulated as (VSPr) subject to (1)–(4) and (7). We can notice that λ measures the trade-off between finding a small size separator and finding balanced pillars. If $\lambda = 1$, (VSPr) is equivalent to the first linear program (VSP) so the solver will output a minimum-sized separator. If $\lambda = 0$ then the program will maximize $|A|$ given (7), thus generating a well balanced partition.

2.3 Adding Weights to the Vertices

Unlike Kanevsky's algorithm, the linear programming solution allows to take into account vertex weights. Let $\mathbf{c}$ denote the vector containing the vertex weights. For any subset $S \subset V$, we define the weight of S, $c(S) = \sum_{v \in S} c_v$. The program which uses vertex weights is formulated as is:

$$\max_{\mathbf{x},\mathbf{y} \in \{0,1\}^n} c(A) + \lambda\, c(B) \tag{VSPw}$$

subject to (1)–(4) and

$$c(A) \leq c(B) \tag{8}$$

This version, though taking into account vertex weights, is as simple as the previous one. Note that $c(A)$ (respectively $c(B)$) can be calculated as $\mathbf{c}^\top \mathbf{x}$ (respectively $\mathbf{c}^\top \mathbf{y}$).

2.4 Taking Distances into Account

We have previously seen that the VSP can be used in order to split a graph into balanced pillars. In such a context, the data points (graph vertices) have relational links (graph edges) but these links can also be associated to intrinsic information which leads to defining metrics, as for example distances between vertices. In order to have more consistent results, it is interesting to take these distances into account. The main goal here is to find a well-balanced partition separated by a small size separator while minimizing intern distances in the resulting pillars.

Let $d : (u, v) \mapsto d(u, v)$ denote the metric between the vertices. Since we only care about the distances between vertices that are both in A or B, we only consider pairs (u, v) where $(x_u = 1 \wedge x_v = 1)$ or $(y_u = 1 \wedge y_v = 1)$. This means we only take into account the pairs (u, v) where $x_u x_v = 1$ or $y_u y_v = 1$, *i.e.* $x_u x_v + y_u y_v = 1$ because both terms can not be equal to 1.

The constraints of the optimization program remain (1)–(4), (8) but the objective function becomes:

$$\max_{\mathbf{x},\mathbf{y}\in\{0,1\}^n} (1-\mu)(c(A) + \lambda\, c(B)) - \mu \sum_{\{u,v\}\in V^2} d(u,v)(x_u x_v + y_u y_v) \qquad \text{(VSPd)}$$

where $\mu \in [0, 1]$. As for λ, μ measures the trade-off between finding a partition with a small size separator and whose weights are balanced, and minimizing the distances within the pillars A and B.

If $\mu = 1$ the solver will minimize the distance within the subsets, so it will surely put all the vertices in the separator C to reach its optimal value. If $\mu = 0$, the optimization program is exactly (VSPw). The higher μ is, the more the optimization program takes the distances into account.

The program (VSPd) is not linear anymore since it contains quadratic terms in the objective function. Common free and commercial solvers are also able to solve Mixed-Integer Non-Linear Programs (MINLP), however the computation time is usually much higher. To linearize (VSPd), we introduce a new family of variables (z_{uv}), for all $(u, v) \in V^2, v > u$. We want z_{uv} to be an indicator whether u and v are both in the same pillar. We can not define $z_{uv} = x_u x_v + y_u y_v$ because it would add quadratic constraints to the linear program. Hence in order to have the family (z_{uv}) be such indicators, we add the following constraints to the linear program.

$$\forall (u,v) \in V^2, v > u, z_{uv} \geq x_u + x_v - 1 \qquad (9)$$

$$\forall (u,v) \in V^2, v > u, z_{uv} \geq y_u + y_v - 1 \qquad (10)$$

$$\forall (u,v) \in V^2, v > u, z_{uv} \in \{0,1\} \qquad (11)$$

The new objective function is:

$$\max_{\mathbf{x},\mathbf{y}\in\{0,1\}^n} (1-\mu)(c(A) + \lambda\, c(B)) - \mu \sum_{\{u,v\}\in V^2} d(u,v) z_{uv} \qquad \text{(VSPdist)}$$

Let u, v be two different vertices such that $v > u$, if both u and v are in A, then $x_u = 1$ and $x_v = 1$ so necessarily $z_{uv} = 1$. Similarly if u and v are both in B, $z_{uv} = 1$. If u and v are not in the same subset then constraints (9)–(11) force $z_{uv} \geq 0$; since μ and $d(u, v)$ are both positive then the maximization of the objective function leads to $z_{uv} = 0$.

(VSPdist) subject to constraints (1)–(4), (8)–(11) represents a new extension of the Vertex Separator Problem which computes a small size separator and splits the graph into balanced subsets while minimizing the distances within these subsets. Moreover, selecting such a trade-off is easily doable by setting the values of the hyper-parameters λ and μ.

2.5 *a*, *b*-Separation

Vertex separation can also be useful to separate two particular nodes in a graph. For instance in a transportation network, it may be desired to know which stations are necessarily part of any path from station a to station b. Thus, the goal in this context is to find a separation that puts a in a given pillar and b in the other.

Towards this goal, we present a variation of the VSP called a, b-separation, which can be combined with every version of the VSP discussed earlier. An a, b-separation problem model is a linear program composed of any objective function seen previously (VSP), (VSPr), (VSPw) or (VSPdist) subject to their associated constraints plus the two following ones:

$$x_a = 1 \tag{12}$$

$$y_b = 1 \tag{13}$$

Note that we fixed $a \in A$ and $b \in B$, but besides in the (VSP) version, A and B do not have symmetrical roles. Indeed (7) and (8) created an asymmetry in the problem. This is why setting $a \in B$ and $b \in A$ can lead to a better value than setting $a \in A$ and $b \in B$.

In order to avoid having to try both cases, we defined a new set of constraints which sets a and b in A and B without forcing knowing the order.

$$x_a + y_a = 1 \tag{14}$$

$$x_a = y_b \tag{15}$$

$$y_a = x_b \tag{16}$$

(14) implies that a is either in A or B, a can not be in the separator. (15) and (16) imply that b is necessarily in the subset where a is not. Since either x_a or y_a is equal to 1, then b can not be in the separator as well.

3 Application to the Internet Movie Database (IMDb)

In order to evaluate how our approach performs, we applied it to graphs created from the IMDb database. We have access to the list of all the movies inventoried in the database and the list of the movies each actor/director contributed to. We created a graph where the vertices correspond to the movies, which are connected by an edge if they have at least one common contributor.

For our first experiment, we kept the 100 most popular movies. We constructed the graph and only kept the biggest connected component (the graph must be connected).

We considered equivalent weights for each vertices and a trade-off parameter $\lambda = 0.7$. The VSPr model was implemented in R and solved using the free solver lpSolve on a 2.5 GHz Intel Core i7 processor. This VSPr instance was solved in 4 ms CPU.

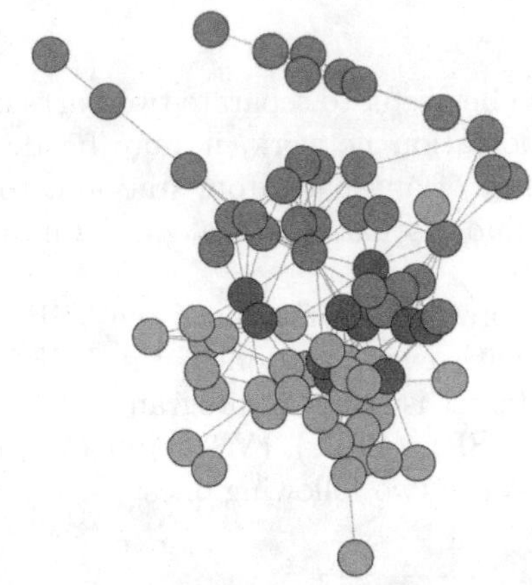

Fig. 4. Graph with separator for the first experiment (Color figure online)

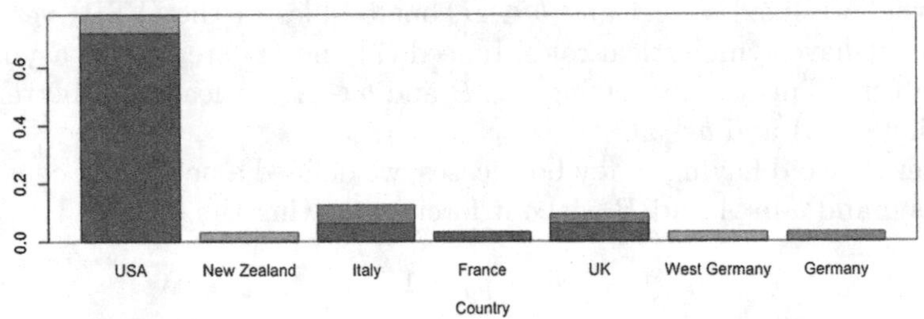

Fig. 5. Histograms of the countries of production for movies in A (red) and B (blue). (Color figure online)

The resulting graph is composed of 74 vertices. Figure 4 presents the graph with its separator. The pillars A and B are in yellow and green respectively while the separator C is colored in red. The cardinalities of A, B and C are respectively 32, 32, 10.

The separator contains famous movies – movies that are in average 1.5 times more voted than the other movies. Since the size of the separator is quite small, we present here the full list of the movies it contains: {The Godfather: Part II (1974); The Dark Knight (2008); One Flew Over the Cuckoo's Nest (1975); The Silence of the Lambs (1991); Raiders of the Lost Ark (1981); The Departed (2006); Django Unchained (2012); The Dark Knight Rises (2012); Requiem for a Dream (2000); Inglourious Bastards (2009)}

In order to have a deeper understanding of how the graph has been separated, we plotted the histograms of the countries and years of release of the movies in A and B. Figure 5 shows that the countries of production are fairly distributed between the two pillars. However, Fig. 6 shows that the algorithm semantically splits the graph according to the year of production. Indeed, it separated older movies from more recent ones. Note that we had not given any of this information to the algorithm.

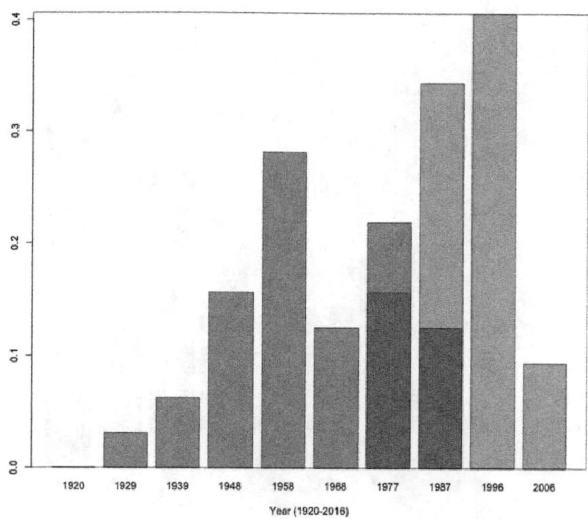

Fig. 6. Histograms of the years of release for movies in A (red) and B (blue). (Color figure online)

For the second experiment, we kept 1000 movies. The corresponding VSPr model (with same parameters than previously, also implemented in R) was solved with Gurobi in 260 s on Calcul Québec's servers (8 cores).

The biggest connected component was a graph composed of 273 vertices. Figure 7 presents the graph with its separator. The pillars A and B are in yellow and green while the separator C is colored in red. The cardinalities of A, B and C are respectively 93, 152, 28.

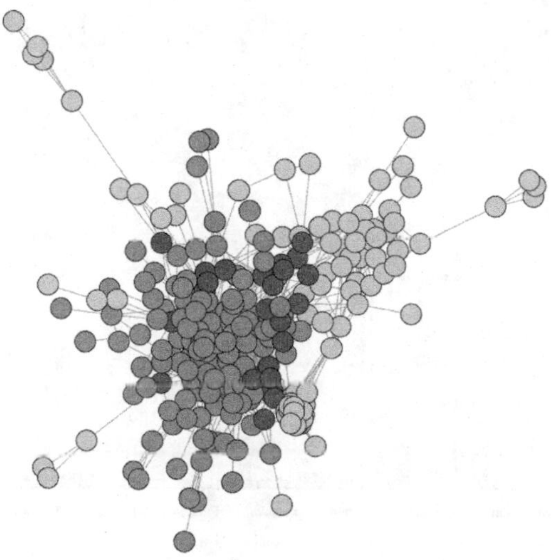

Fig. 7. Graph with separator for the second experiment (Color figure online)

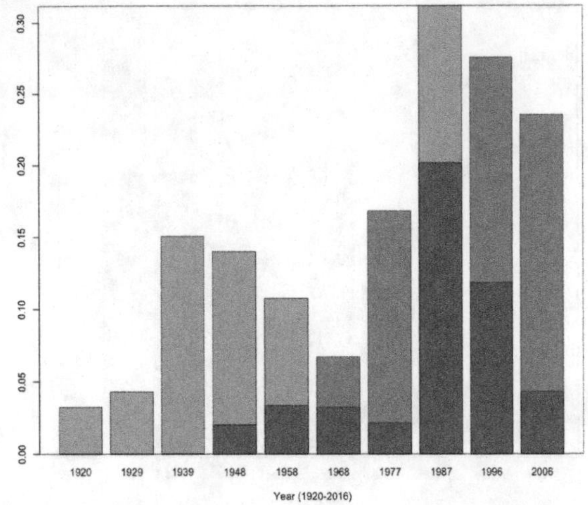

Fig. 8. Histograms of the years of release and A (red) and B (blue). (Color figure online)

Figures 8 and 9 present the histograms of the years and countries of release of the movies in A and B. Figure 8 shows that pillar A contains older movies while B contains more recent movies. However, one can notice that many movies released in 1987 belong to B. Further investigation is needed to understand this result,

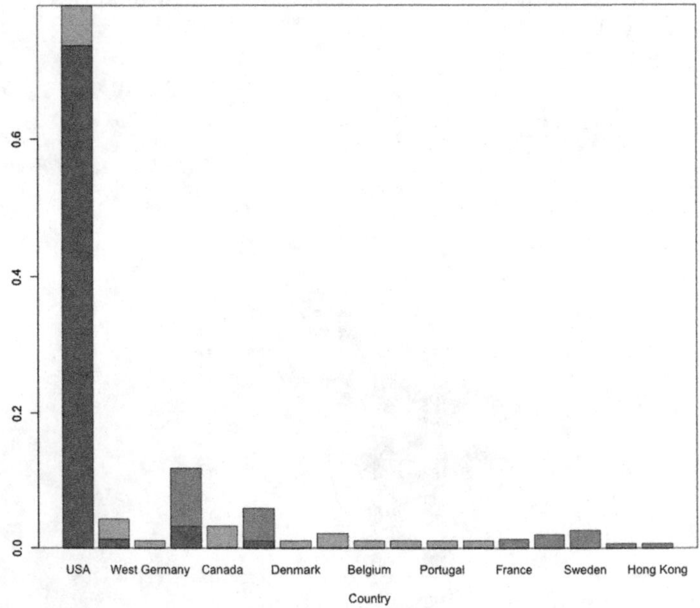

Fig. 9. Histograms of the countries of production and A and B.

and link it to the graph structure. Figure 9 shows that the algorithm separated the graph according to the countries of production. Besides the United States of America, for all the countries, the movies produced there are almost all in the same pillar.

4 Conclusion and Future Work

In this paper, we proposed several variants of the VSP (VSPr, VSPw, a-b separation) for which we provide integer linear models. We also proposed a new version of the VSP able to take into account distances between vertices (VSPd), and its linearization (VSPdist).

Preliminary experiments on the IMDb database shown promising results: the proposed approach has been able to semantically split graphs without considering the intrinsic information associated to the vertices. This shows that the VSP could be used for unsupervised clustering purposes.

Our future work is focused on applying the VSP to air transportation. Ongoing computational experiments are conducted on several graphs that represent air transportation network. This field of application is of particular interest to evaluate the variants of our algorithm, especially regarding distance related constraints or a, b-separation.

To ensure full reproducibility and comparisons between systems, our source code (in R) is publicly released as an open source software in the following repository: https://github.com/BigMiners/vsp.

References

1. Balas, E., de Souza, C.: The vertex separator problem: a polyhedral investigation. Math. Program. **103**(3), 583–608 (2005)
2. Benlic, U., Hao, J.K.: Breakout local search for the vertex separator problem. In: IJCAI (2013)
3. Bui, T.N., Jones, C.: Finding good approximate vertex and edge partitions is NP-hard. Inf. Process. Lett. **42**(3), 153–159 (1992)
4. Davis, T.A.: Direct Methods for Sparse Linear Systems, vol. 2. SIAM, Philadelphia (2006)
5. Didi Biha, M., Meurs, M.J.: An exact algorithm for solving the vertex separator problem. J. Glob. Optim. **49**(3), 425–434 (2011)
6. Fu, B., Oprisan, S.A., Xu, L.: Multi-directional width-bounded geometric separator and protein folding. Int. J. Comput. Geom. Appl. **18**(05), 389–413 (2008)
7. Fukuyama, J.: NP-completeness of the planar separator problems. J. Graph Algorithms Appl. **10**(2), 317–328 (2006)
8. Garey, M.R., Johnson, D.S.: Computers and Intractability, vol. 29. W.H. Freeman, New York (2002)
9. Hager, W.W., Hungerford, J.T.: Continuous quadratic programming formulations of optimization problems on graphs. Eur. J. Oper. Res. **240**(2), 328–337 (2015)
10. Kanevsky, A.: Finding all minimum size separating vertex sets in a graph. Coordinated Science Laboratory Report no. ACT-93 (UJLU-ENG 88–2233) (1988)

11. Lipton, R.J., Tarjan, R.E.: A separator theorem for planar graphs. SIAM J. Appl. Math. **36**(2), 177–189 (1979)
12. Schaeffer, S.E.: Graph clustering. Comput. Sci. Rev. **1**(1), 27–64 (2007)
13. Schuchard, M., Geddes, J., Thompson, C., Hopper, N.: Routing around decoys. In: Proceedings of the 2012 ACM Conference on Computer and Communications Security, pp. 85–96. ACM (2012)
14. de Souza, C., Balas, E.: The vertex separator problem: algorithms and computations. Math. Program. **103**(3), 609–631 (2005)
15. Ullman, J.D.: Computational Aspects of VLSI. Computer Science Press, Rockville (1984)

A Knowledge Acquisition System for Price Change Rules

Moslema Jahan and Howard J. Hamilton(✉)

Department of Computer Science, University of Regina, Regina, Canada
Howard.Hamilton@uregina.ca

Abstract. We describe the Knowledge Acquisition System for Price ChangE Rules (KASPER) software system for acquiring knowledge concerning price change rules. The goal is to provide decision rules with high predictive accuracy on unseen data that may explain why a store or brand made a price change in a specific category. These decision rules should relate price changes at one store to those at other stores or brands in the same city. The KASPER approach can use brand-based or distance-based store-to-store relations or use brand-to-brand relations. KASPER was applied to data from four cities to generate decision rules from these relations. We tested the decision rules on unseen data. Our approach was more effective in the two cities where price changes of varied sizes occur than in the two cities where price changes are consistently small.

Keywords: Knowledge Acquisition System · Pricing strategy · Price change rules · Learning price change rules

1 Introduction

Finding an effective pricing strategy is a key part of making a business successful. The price of a product or service may be set to maximize profit, to increase sales of other services or products, to increase market share, or to achieve any other goal set by the seller. Obtaining maximum profit is the most common target.

One pricing strategy is to observe price changes made at other stores for identical or similar products or services and adjust prices according to *price change rules*, i.e., rules that specify how to change the price at a store when the price changes at another store. Stores that follow rules for setting prices do not necessarily follow the same rules. Thus, when attempting to form a price setting strategy for product at a store, it may be interesting to automatically derive price change rules consistent with price changes observed at other stores.

This paper focuses on automatically generating and validating price change rules that explain changes in retail prices for commodities. We concentrate on commodities that are purchased regularly in small amounts by consumers and frequently change in price. For example, prices of motor fuel may change once a week or several times a day. After receiving knowledge about the hypothesized price change rules of a competing store, people can make more informed decisions

M. Mouhoub and P. Langlais (Eds.): Canadian AI 2017, LNAI 10233, pp. 215–226, 2017.
DOI: 10.1007/978-3-319-57351-9_26

when creating pricing strategies. Our research is intended to design a system that generates price change rules as well as to evaluate the effectiveness of this system at producing price change rules meeting specific criteria. The system should produce decision rules that relate price changes at one store to price changes at other stores. In business applications, decision rules may be required to meet specific criteria, e.g. have high predictive accuracy on unseen data. In our experiments, we require rules with precision of at least 60% and accuracy of at least 80%.

Given a set of stores $S = \{s_1, s_2, \ldots, s_n\}$, z price change categories, and a large set of price reports, the goal is to find a table R of rules. After preprocessing, a price report consists of city id, brand id, store id, latitude, longitude, fuel type, date, time, and price. The set of rules for store i is represented by $R_i = \{r_{i1}, r_{i2}, \ldots, r_{iz}\}$. Rule r_{ij} gives a possible explanation, in the form of a price change rule, of why a store s_i made a change in price in category j. Thus, the system should generate a decision rule for every store in every price change category. We choose to generate only one rule for each store to produce a simple, easily understood table. This research problem is distinct from predicting prices. The goal is to provide a high quality, comprehensible rule for every price category for every store rather than an arbitrarily complex prediction rule. By examining the table created for a store or a brand, a price analyst can understand the strategy being followed. In particular, the analyst might see that store s_3 raises its price whenever store s_1 raises its price (but not when store s_2 raises its price).

The remainder of this paper is organized as follows. Section 2 explains relevant background topics. Section 3 provides an overview of the KASPER approach. Section 4 presents experimental results. We concentrate on motor fuel pricing because we have access to a large commercial data set of such prices. Section 5 gives a summary and future work.

2 Background and Related Work

Knowledge acquisition is the process of extracting and organizing knowledge from one source and storing it in some other location such as a knowledge base [5]. In this paper, we consider the case where the structured knowledge is a collection of decision rules, i.e. conjunctive IF-THEN rules representing price change rules. IF a certain condition happens (is TRUE), THEN a certain conclusion may occur.

Our approach uses pairwise relations at the store (retail) level and generates price change rules at the store level, while other systems use pairwise relations at other stages in the distribution chain [6] and summarize retail pricing behaviour at the city level [2,10]. Our system is capable of generating thousands of rules while Olvarrieta et al. manually devise eleven hypotheses [12]. The overall process from profile construction to decision rule generation of KASPER is different from that of any other rule generation model.

Since our experiments relate to motor fuel pricing, previous research concerning the behaviour of motor fuel prices is relevant. Some factors cause prices to move slowly and others cause prices to move quickly. Some factors have a global effect on prices, while others apply only in certain areas or at certain times. We hypothesized that in order to understand patterns in price changes we should study three relationships: the relationship between price changes at a store and those at its potential competitors, the relationship between price changes at a store and those at other stores with the same brand, and the relationship between price changes for one brand and those for other brands.

Hosken et al. described the behaviour of retail motor fuel prices [6]. They used the prices at the pump for regular (87-octane) motor fuel (including tax) as the retail price, the average "branded rack" price in a week as the wholesale price, and the retail price less the branded rack price and taxes as the *margin*. Hosken et al. claim that the primary sources of retail price variation results from (a) a store changing its price in response to a change in the wholesale price and (b) a store changing its price relative to other stores.

Al-Gudhea et al. examined the idea that retail motor fuel prices rise more rapidly than they fall [1], using threshold and momentum models of cointegration developed by Enders et al. [3,4]. This study examined the behaviour of the response times of daily retail motor fuel prices to upstream and downstream price changes at different stages of the distribution chain [9]. *Upstream* refers to the raw material extraction or production elements of the supply chain [7]. *Downstream* refers to firms closer to the end users or consumers [7]. They investigated pairwise dissimilar adjustments between (a) the crude oil price and the retail motor fuel price, (b) the crude oil price and the spot motor fuel price, (c) the spot motor fuel price and the wholesale motor fuel price, and (d) the wholesale motor fuel price and the retail motor fuel price.

3 The KASPER System

This section describes the Knowledge Acquisition System for Price ChangE Rules (KASPER) system. Subsections describe terminology, choosing relevant stores and brands, generating price change rules, and validating price change rules.

3.1 Terminology

The following terms are employed throughout the remainder of this paper:

- A *directional rule* is a rule that indicates the direction (increase or decrease) of an expected price change.
- A *categorical rule* is a rule that indicates an interval-based category of an expected price change.
- A *good rule* is a rule that has accuracy and precision meeting required thresholds (80% and 60%, respectively, in our experiments).
- A *key store* (*key brand*) is a store (brand) for which rules are generated and validated to identify other stores (brands) that are relevant to price changes for the key store (brand).

- A *single-store rule* is an IF-THEN rule stating that if a price change in a specific category occurs at another store then a price change in a specific category can be expected at the key store on the same day.
- A *accuracy* rule is a single-store rule or a single-brand rule.
- A *double-store rule* is an IF-THEN rule stating that if price changes in two categories (the same or different) occur respectively at two different stores on the same day then a price change in a specific category can be expected at the key store on the same day.
- The *utility function* is a function that computes a score representing the quality of a rule based on seventeen measures.
- The *coverage* is the fraction of possible combinations of stores and price change categories for which we have decision rules.
- The *end of day price* (or hereafter *price*) is the last price reported on a specific date. The price on day d is denoted p_d. If no prices are reported on a day, the price is considered to be missing.
- The *price change* (PC) is defined as the change between the price for a specific day d and the one from day $d-1$. Let $PC_d = P_d - P_{d-1}$. If either price is missing, the PC is null. The PC can be defined for an individual store or a brand. We define PC values only for cases where the day d has data.
  From Table 1a, the price for two consecutive days is as follows:
  Date: 2 January 2015, Price: 3.34
  Date: 3 January 2015, Price: 3.39
  $PC_d = 3.39 - 3.34 = 0.05$ for $d = 3$ January 2015, as shown in Table 1b.

Table 1. Prices and price changes.

(a) Price		(b) Price changes	
Date	Price	Date	Price change (PC)
2 January 2015	3.34	3 January 2015	0.05
3 January 2015	3.39	5 January 2015	Null
5 January 2015	3.35	7 January 2015	Null
7 January 2015	3.35	8 January 2015	0.01
8 January 2015	3.36	9 January 2015	0.00
9 January 2015	3.36	11 January 2015	Null
11 January 2015	3.37	12 January 2015	−0.02
12 January 2015	3.35	13 January 2015	−0.02
13 January 2015	3.33		

- A *price change* (PC)*category* is a positive integer in the range 1 to z, where z is a small positive integer, representing the range of a price change. We consider two possibilities, 2 and 6, for z in this paper. The categories are defined in Table 2. For $z = 2$, we refer to the possible categories as directions

Table 2. Price changes for directional and categorical rules.

(a) Directions of price change ($z = 2$)		
Direction	Meaning	Price change
		City1, City2, City3, and City4
NC	No change	=0
INC	Increase	>0
DEC	Decrease	<0
(b) Categories of price change ($z = 6$)		
Category	Price change (PC)	
	City1, City2, and City4	City3
CAT0	=0	=0
CAT1	>0 and ≤0.05	>0 and ≤0.02
CAT2	>0.05 and ≤0.10	>0.02 and ≤0.04
CAT3	>0.10	>0.04
CAT4	<0 and ≥ − 0.05	<0 and ≥ − 0.02
CAT5	< − 0.05 and ≥ − 0.10	< − 0.02 and ≥ − 0.04
CAT6	< − 0.10	< − 0.04

and we use the symbols INC and DEC to represent the possible values 1 and 2, respectively (see Table 2a). For, $z = 6$, we use the symbols CAT1 to CAT6 to represent the possible values 1 to 6, as shown in Table 2b. We use the 2 directions for making directional rules and the 6 categories for making categorical rules. NC and CAT0 both represent a case where no price change occurred. We do not make rules for such cases because "no change" is more easily explained as the default behaviour in the domain than as a result of other behaviours.

3.2 Relevant Stores and Brands for Generating Rules

We consider two approaches to determining a set of relevant stores for generating rules and one for generating relevant brands. Let S_k be the set of relevant stores (potential competitors) for key store s_k.

Definition: A *distance-based relevant store* of a key store is any other store within a specified distance (the *distance threshold*) of the key store, where the distance d between any two nearby points, point1 and point2, on the earth's surface is calculated according to the Haversine formula [11], shown in Eq. 1:

$$d = 2 \times r \times \sin^{-1}\sqrt{\sin^2(\frac{\phi_1 - \phi_2}{2}) + \cos(\phi_1)\cos(\phi_2)\sin^2(\frac{\lambda_1 - \lambda_2}{2})} \quad (1)$$

where ϕ_1 and ϕ_2 are the latitudes of point1 and point2, λ_1 and λ_2 are their longitudes, and r is the radius of the earth (6373 km).

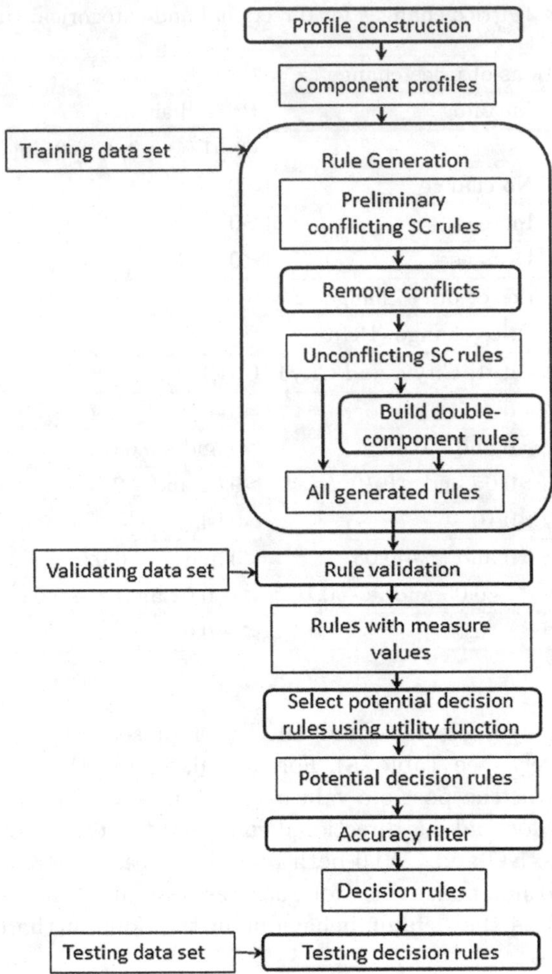

Fig. 1. Procedure for generating and testing price change rules with KASPER

Definition: A *brand-based relevant store* for a key store is any other store in the same city that has the same brand as the key store.

Example: Suppose brand b has 10 stores $s_1, s_2, \ldots, s_{10}$ in a city. If we consider store s_2 to be the key store, then the brand-based relevant stores are $s_1, s_3, \ldots, s_{10}$. In this case $S_k = \{s_1, s_3, \ldots, s_{10}\}$.

Analogously, let B_k be the set of relevant brands for key brand b_k. B_k is assigned the set of brands in the city other than b_k.

3.3 Procedure for Generating Price Change Rules

Figure 1 summarizes the procedure that KASPER follows to generate store-to-store and brand-to-brand decision rules for price changes from the training data set.

Algorithm 1. Generate single-component rules

1 Input: key component c_k, set of relevant components C_k, set of tuples in hashmap (training data set), set of unique days D in the hashmap
2 Output: a set of single component rules $R_{k,i}$ for every component $c_i \in C_k$
3 **for** *each* $c_i \in C_k$ **do**
4 $\quad R_{k,i} = \phi$
5 $\quad$ initialize frequency table f to zeros
6 $\quad$ **for** *each* $d \in D$ **do**
7 $\quad\quad p_i = Retrieve(hashmap, c_i, d)$ // get price report
8 $\quad\quad$ **if** $(p_i \neq null)$ **then**
9 $\quad\quad\quad p_k = Retrieve(hashmap, c_k, d)$
10 $\quad\quad\quad$ **if** $(p_k \neq null)$ **then**
11 $\quad\quad\quad\quad u = Classify(p_i)$ // determine PC category
12 $\quad\quad\quad\quad v = Classify(p_k)$
13 $\quad\quad\quad\quad f[u][v]++$
14 $\quad$ **for** *each* $u = 1$ *to* z **do**
15 $\quad\quad$ **for** *each* $v = 1$ *to* z **do**
16 $\quad\quad\quad$ **if** $f[u][v] \geq threshold$ **then**
17 $\quad\quad\quad\quad$ generate single-component rule r in the format
18 $\quad\quad\quad\quad$ "IF PC_d of other component c_i is u THEN PC_d of key component c_k is v."
19 $\quad\quad\quad\quad$ add single-component rule r to $R_{k,i}$.

To simplify presentation, we use the word "component" to refer to either a store or a brand. For each component, we construct and maintain a profile containing a list of dates, times, and prices. For example, the profile for a store $s \in S$ is a $\langle storeId, date, List\langle time, price\rangle\rangle$ tuple. Generating rules from profiles is faster than generating them from the database because it avoids calculating the same values repeatedly.

Single-component rules are generated using Algorithm 1 and stored in the database. Let C_k be a set of generating components for key component c_k; i.e., C_k is S_k for a store and C_k is B_k for a brand. For a key component c_k and every other component $c_i \in C_k$, KASPER calculates the joint frequency of the PC categories of the other component and the key component using step 13. Finally, KASPER generates rules using steps 17 to 19 if the joint frequency is greater than or equal to a threshold. A *conflict* occurs if there are multiple rules for the same key component with the same condition. The rule with the highest utility score is selected from such rules. Double-component rules are generated by a more complex but analogous procedure [8].

3.4 Rule Validation

KASPER employs seventeen measures to assess the quality of a rule on the validation data set. These measures are TP (true positives), FP (false positives), FN (false negatives), TN (true negative), AC (accuracy), E (error rate), P (precision), FDR (false discovery rate), TPR (true positive rate), TNR (true negative rate), FPR (false positive rate), FNR (false negative rate), F (F-measure), G (G-mean), LR+ (positive likelihood ratio), LR– (negative likelihood ratio), and DOR (diagnostic odds ratio) [8]. For each rule $r \in R$, the seventeen measures are calculated for every single and double-component rule. A utility score is assigned to a rule as follows: one point is awarded for each of the TP, TN, TPR, TNR, AC, P, F, G, LR+, and DOR measures if the rule has the maximum value (among all rules) for the measure and one point is assigned for each of the remaining measures for which it has the minimum value. For each price change category for the key store, we select the single-component or double-component rule with the highest score. Ties are broken arbitrarily but with a preference for single-component rules. These rules form the output of the knowledge acquisition process.

4 Experimental Results

Experiments were conducted on a historical data set of motor fuel prices for four cities. The data covered period of five years and four months for all cities. Besides price reports, information is provided about the stores in each city and the brand of each store. After preprocessing, a price report has eight attributes: city id, brand id, store id, latitude, longitude, fuel type, date, time, and price.

The data set selected for evaluation contains only stores with at least 100 reports for each of the training, validation, and testing phases, and brands with at least 5 such stores. This data set consists of 9 brands and 189 stores for City1, 10 brands and 177 stores for City2, 9 brands and 317 stores for City3, and 16 brands and 538 stores for City4. The number of tuples in the evaluation data set is 1,091,270 for City1, 1,523,353 for City2, 1,435,548 for City3, and 1,802,016 for City4. The data set for each city is divided chronologically into three sections for training (2010-01-01 to 2011-12-31), validation (2012-01-01 to 2013-12-31), and testing (2014-01-01 to 2015-04-30). The order is chosen so only information about the past is available when predicting the future. Overall, City1 and City2 show more variations in price changes than City3 and City4. Thus, we consider City1 and City2 as *high variability* cities and the others as *low variability* ones (Fig. 2).

Table 3 shows the number of possible rules, number of decision rules, number of good rules, coverage, and percentage of good rules for brand-based and distance-based store-to-store rules, and brand-to-brand rules for four cities. Coverage is based on the ratio of the number of decision rules and the number of possible rules. So, Coverage (%) $= \frac{\#\ of\ decision\ rules}{\#\ of\ possible\ rules} \times 100\%$. Percentage of good rules is based on the ratio of the number of good rules and the number of decision rules. So, the percentage of good rules $= \frac{\#\ of\ good\ rules}{\#\ of\ decision\ rules} \times 100\%$. From Table 3a, we can see that the coverage for directional rules for City1 is $\frac{201}{378} \times 100\% = 53.17\%$ and the percentage of good rules is $\frac{145}{201} \times 100\% = 72.14\%$. All values are calculated in similar way. We consider only the directional rules produced for City1 and City2 to be satisfactory since they had high percentages of good rules. Using brand-to-brand rules, one has a high chance of being able

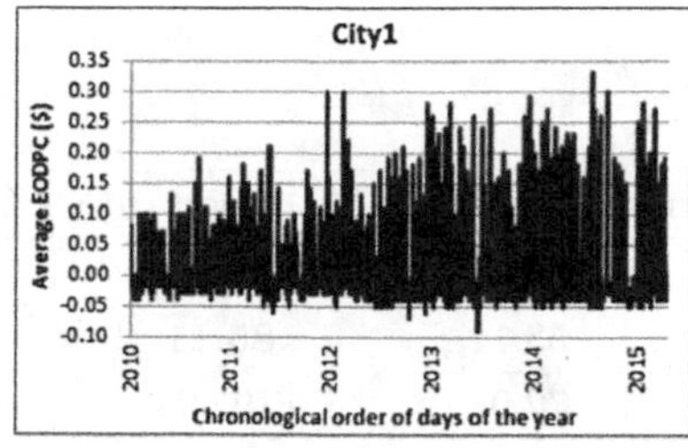

(a) Average PC for City1 (chronological).

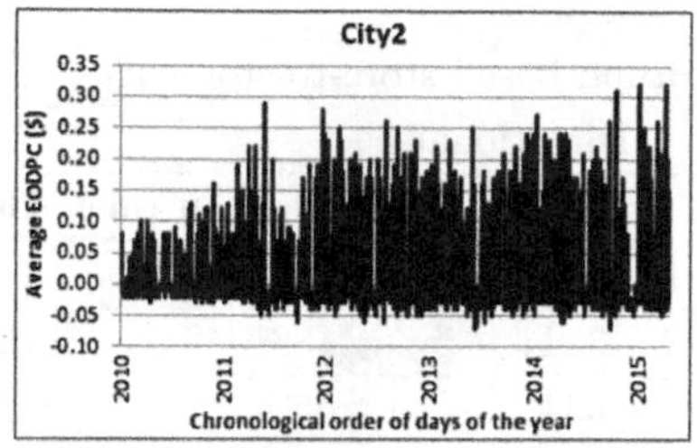

(b) Average PC for City2 (chronological).

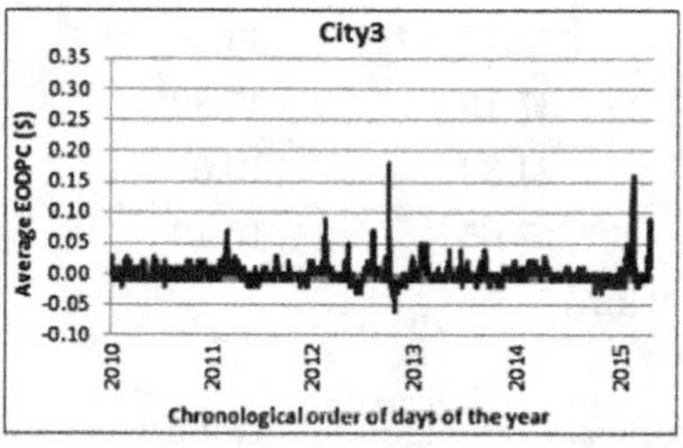

(c) Average PC for City3 (chronological).

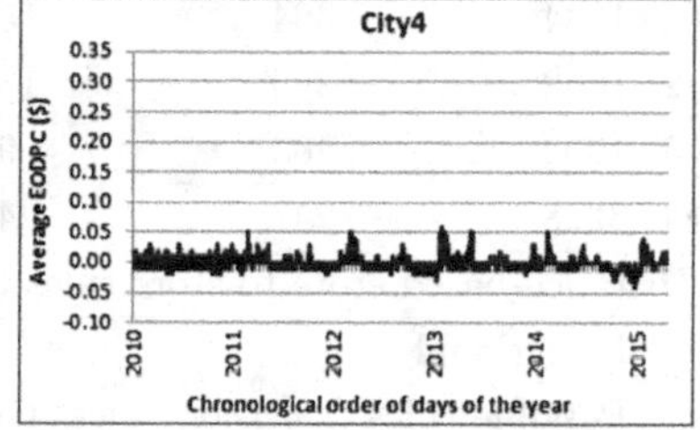

(d) Average PC for City4 (chronological).

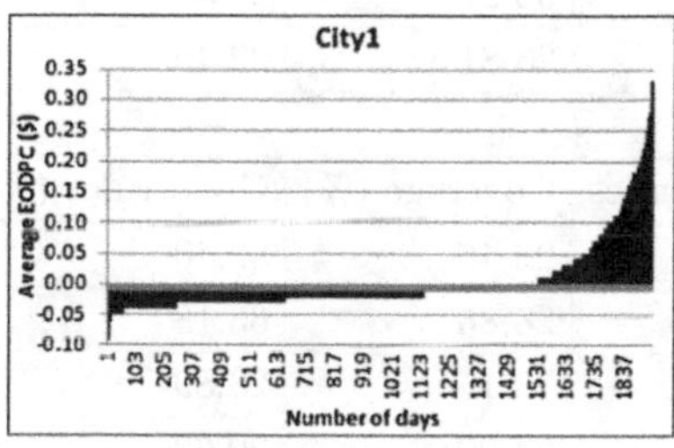

(e) Average PC for City1 (sorted).

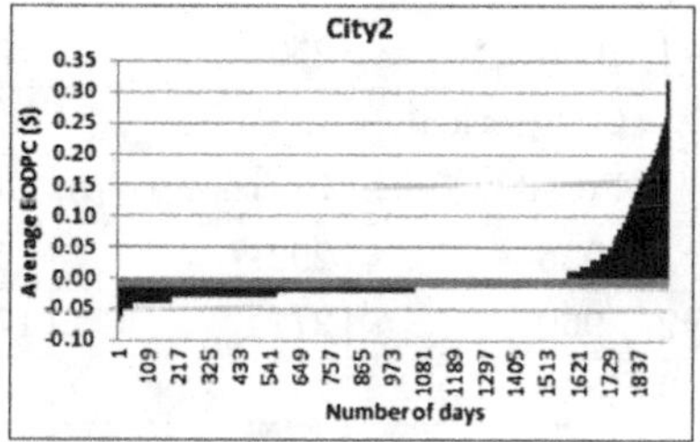

(f) Average PC for City2 (sorted).

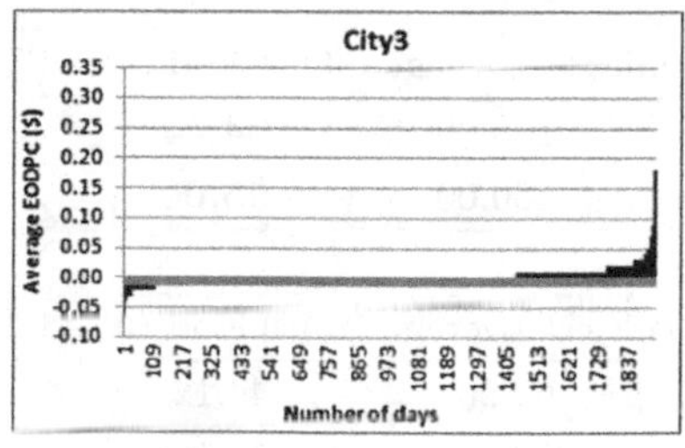

(g) Average PC for City3 (sorted).

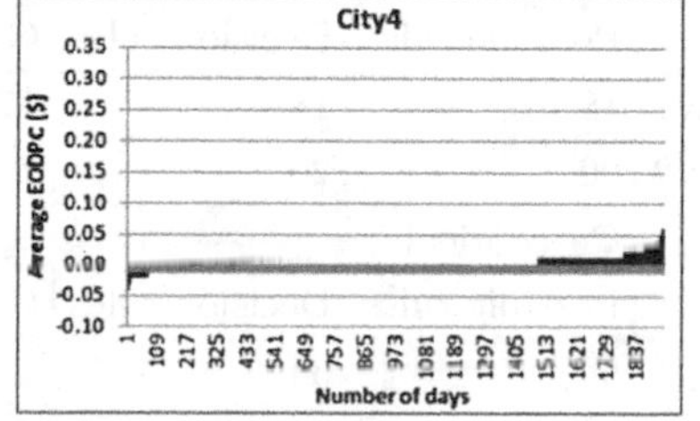

(h) Average PC for City4 (sorted).

Fig. 2. Average PC for City1, City2, City3, and City4.

Table 3. Directional and categorical rules for four cities.

(a) Brand-based store-to-store rules

	Directional				
City	Possible rules	Decision rules	Good rules	Coverage (%)	Good rules (%)
City1	378	201	145	53.17	**72.14**
City2	354	188	160	53.11	**85.11**
City3	634	457	90	72.08	19.69
City4	1076	495	70	46.00	14.14

	Categorical				
City	Possible rules	Decision rules	Good rules	Coverage (%)	Good rules (%)
City1	1134	364	158	32.10	43.41
City2	1062	395	181	37.19	45.82
City3	1902	463	91	24.34	19.65
City4	3228	247	40	7.65	16.19

(b) Distance-based store-to-store rules ($d = 2\,\text{km}$)

	Directional				
City	Possible rules	Decision rules	Good rules	Coverage (%)	Good rules (%)
City1	342	171	137	50.00	**80.11**
City2	320	137	116	42.81	**84.67**
City3	626	346	75	55.27	21.68
City4	1050	250	56	23.81	22.40

	Categorical				
City	Possible rules	Decision rules	Good rules	Coverage (%)	Good rules (%)
City1	1026	292	153	28.46	52.40
City2	960	277	175	28.85	63.18
City3	1878	247	59	13.15	23.89
City4	3150	126	26	4.00	20.63

(c) Brand-to-brand rules

	Directional				
City	Possible rules	Decision rules	Good rules	Coverage (%)	Good rules (%)
City1	18	18	17	100.00	**94.44**
City2	20	20	19	100.00	**95.00**

	Categorical				
City	Possible rules	Decision rules	Good rules	Coverage (%)	Good rules (%)
City1	54	34	15	62.96	44.12
City2	60	42	24	70.00	57.14

to predict the change a key brand will make in response to a change by another brand in either price direction. The categorical rules may have performed poorly by trying to predict the size of the price change too precisely, perhaps given the scarcity of data for some price categories. It was more difficult to find suitable rules for low-variability cities (City3 and City4) than for high-variability ones.

Table 4 shows the first quartile, median, third quartile, and maximum values for the accuracy and precision measures. From the first quartile value in Table 4, we see that the accuracy is more than 80% for at least 75% of the directional and categorical rules for all cities. The median accuracy for half of the directional and categorical rules for City1 and City2 is above 90%. The median accuracy for distance-based store-to-store and brand-to-brand rules are also more than 90%.

Table 4. Quartile values for measures for four cities.

		Directional				Categorical			
		City1	City2	City3	City4	City1	City2	City3	City4
First quartile	AC	86.52	91.89	83.38	81.54	83.98	84.26	88.14	82.88
	P	56.36	72.55	25.00	25.93	21.74	25.00	21.43	17.86
Median	AC	92.58	95.94	87.26	85.59	90.21	92.33	91.30	86.53
	P	79.17	84.44	39.53	37.70	50.00	51.19	38.46	30.91
Third quartile	AC	97.20	98.09	90.07	89.25	96.45	96.61	93.62	89.16
	P	88.37	93.75	55.56	51.35	85.37	85.31	54.17	50.00
Maximum	AC	99.12	100.00	98.88	97.50	100.00	99.79	100.00	98.87
	P	100.00	100.00	100.00	100.00	100.00	100.00	100.00	100.00

5 Conclusion

The KASPER approach generates meaningful and high quality decision rules that predict price changes for retail prices for a specific store from the relation of price changes of other stores or brands in a city. KASPER was tested on data from motor fuel prices of stores and brands from four cities. KASPER generates rules from three relations (brand-based store-to-store, distance-based store-to-store, brand-to-brand) for a specific set of PC categories. Directional decision rules, when applied to unseen data, have high predictive accuracy and precision for most of the store-to-store and brand-to-brand rules for high-variability cities (City1 and City2). KASPER is more effective with directional PC categories ($z = 2$) than categorical PC categories ($z = 6$). This system did not generate any brand-to-brand rules for low-variability cities because of the consistency of price changes for these two cities. Overall, KASPER generates good directional rules for stores and brands in high-variability cities, because in such cities, stores and brands are highly responsive to each other's price changes.

Future work could apply the concept of a tacit collusion model to stores in low variability cities (City3 and City4) to evaluate how effective the concept is for these cities. In the *tacit collusion model*, if one store sets a price for a product, then a group of stores will also set the same price for the same product. Other factors, such as wholesale price, rack price, spot price, and margin could be added to make our approach more comprehensive. Potential competitors could be selected using driving distances or driving times instead of spatial distances.

Acknowledgements. Hamilton's NSERC Discovery and CRD grants.

References

1. Al-Gudhea, S., Kenc, T., Dibooglu, S.: Do retail gasoline prices rise more readily than they fall? A threshold cointegration approach. J. Econ. Bus. **59**(6), 560–574 (2007). http://www.sciencedirect.com/science/article/pii/S0148619507000604
2. Eckert, A., West, D.S.: Price uniformity and competition in a retail gasoline market. J. Econ. Behav. Org. **56**(2), 219–237 (2005). http://www.sciencedirect.com/science/article/pii/S0167268104000526
3. Enders, W., Granger, C.W.J.: Unit-root tests and asymmetric adjustment with an example using the term structure of interest rates. J. Bus. Econ. Stat. **16**(3), 304–311 (1998). http://amstat.tandfonline.com/doi/abs/10.1080/07350015.1998.10524769
4. Enders, W., Siklos, P.L.: Cointegration and threshold adjustment. J. Bus. Econ. Stat. **19**, 166–176 (2001). http://dx.doi.org/10.1198/073500101316970395
5. Engel, B.: Knowledge acquisition and validation. www.prenhall.com/divisions/bp/app/turban/dss/6e/ppt/short-ch11.ppt. Accessed Feb 2015
6. Hosken, D.S., McMillan, R.S., Taylor, C.T.: Retail gasoline pricing: what do we know? Int. J. Ind. Organ. **26**(6), 1425–1436 (2008). http://www.sciencedirect.com/science/article/pii/S0167718708000283
7. Investopedia: What is the difference between upstream and downstream oil and gas operations? http://www.investopedia.com/ask/answers/060215/what-difference-between-upstream-and-downstream-oil-and-gas-operations.asp. Accessed Aug 2015
8. Jahan, M.: A knowledge acquisition system for price change rules. Master's thesis, University of Regina, Canada (2016)
9. Karrenbrock, J.D.: The behavior of retail gasoline prices: symmetric or not? Fed. Reserve Bank of St. Louis **73**, 19–29 (1991)
10. Lewis, M.S.: Price leadership and coordination in retail gasoline markets with price cycles. Int. J. Ind. Organ. **30**(4), 342–351 (2012). http://www.sciencedirect.com/science/article/pii/S0167718711001081
11. Mwemezi, J.J., Huang, Y.: Optimal facility location on spherical surfaces: algorithm and application. N. Y. Sci. J. **4**(7), 21–28 (2011)
12. Olavarrieta, S., Hidalgo, P., Manzur, E., Farías, P.: Determinants of in-store price knowledge for packaged products: an empirical study in a chilean hypermarket. J. Bus. Res. **65**(12), 1759–1766 (2012). http://www.sciencedirect.com/science/article/pii/S0148296311003791

Automatic Household Identification for Historical Census Data

Luiza Antonie[1(✉)], Gary Grewal[1], Kris Inwood[2], and Shada Zarti[1]

[1] School of Computer Science, University of Guelph, Guelph, Canada
{lantonie,ggrewal,szarti}@uoguelph.ca

[2] Department of Economics and Finance, University of Guelph, Guelph, Canada
kinwood@uoguelph.ca

Abstract. In this paper, we present a method, that uses domain knowledge, to automatically discover and assign household identifiers to individual historical records. We apply this algorithm on a full count real census (the 1891 Canadian census) to assign household identifiers to all the records.

1 Introduction

Historical census data is considered to be an informational treasure for genealogists, social scientists, and historians. It provides information about people's ancestors, including how they lived and what the social and economic features of their society were. Indeed, this type of longitudinal data allow researchers to build more reliable studies about various topics such as family formation and dissolution, social and geographic mobility, and the interrelationship of geographic and economic movement [7]. Linking records that refer to the same entity from various data sources, such as censuses, bibliographies, or websites is called, *record linkage*. The record linkage problem has been studied in the statistics community for more than five decades, and advances in databases, machine learning and data mining have led to a variety of sophisticated methods. Winkler [1] and Elmagarmid et al. [2] offer a detailed discussion of the field. More recently, in the record linkage domain, *group record linkage* (or collective record linkage) [3] has been investigated, and involves considering groups (e.g., households) besides pair-wise linking. Use of group linkage techniques has increased both the number and the quality of generated longitudinal data.

Using group linkage techniques to link historical censuses increases the linkage rate, which in turn provides social scientists with longitudinal data for more individuals. The groups in this particular application are the *households*. However, these historical censuses often lack Household Identifiers (HID), so group record linkage techniques cannot be directly applied. Finding HIDs is a critical step therefore in the group linkage of censuses, but it is not an easy task. First, census data usually has millions of records, so extracting HIDs manually is time-consuming and requires significant labor. Second, historical censuses are hand-written, and must be scanned and transcribed manually. During this

M. Mouhoub and P. Langlais (Eds.): Canadian AI 2017, LNAI 10233, pp. 227–232, 2017.
DOI: 10.1007/978-3-319-57351-9_27

process, transcription errors are frequently introduced, and only a small number of attributes are included in the digitized transcriptions such as the name, age, gender, relationship to the head of household and some geographical location.

Previous studies have manually generated HIDs, which is time and human resource expensive [5], or they have automatically generated household identifiers for only small samples of censuses that contain only thousands of records [6]. Automatically extracting household identifiers would speed up the process and would allow extracting HIDs even for large, complete census collections. In this paper, we present a method, that uses domain knowledge to automatically discover HIDs, and apply it to the full 1891 Canadian census.

2 Data

The original 1891 Canadian census are hand-written documents which have been subsequently microfilmed, digitized and transcribed. The original census forms include a plethora of information about inhabitants, but in the transcribed versions, only a limited number of attributes are digitized. The digitized version of the census used in this paper has the following properties: it contains 4,787,244 records, each with 18 attributes describing name, gender, age, birth place, religion, and geographic area.

3 Household Identification - Methodology

A *household* is a person or group of people who live in the same dwelling and also share living accommodations. It may consist of just relatives or it can consist of some other grouping of people, such as servants. The digitized version of the 1891 census data is a list of individuals, with no clear designation of where one household ends and where a new household starts. There is also no information about the addresses of the people in the machine-readable censuses. We know from domain experts that the original census forms were completed by the head of a household. The head's record is (expected to be) the first record in the household followed by records of other members of the household (e.g. partner, children, parent, servants). Members of the same household (should) share the same district, subdistrict, and surname, if they are part of the same family. After transcribing the census, Numerical Personal Identifiers (PID) were assigned automatically for each census record, thus we expect these identifiers to be sequential. Based on these assumptions, which were validated by domain experts, we develop a heuristic for identifying HIDs, as follows: first, HIDs are assigned to those records that follow the assumptions described above; second, any remaining unassigned cases are resolved by using the households discovered in the first stage.

First-Pass Assignment of HIDs: We sort the file of records by district, subdistrict, and then PID, then scan the sorted census. Each time we compare a record X with the previous record Y to decide if X is a member-record, a head-record of a new household, or a suspended record that requires more analysis.

Table 1. A relation to household member

PID	Name	Surname	Relation	HID
598316	W W	Rowe	Head	1349
598317	P L	Rowe	Brother	1349
598318	Henrich	Wirth	Domestic	1349
598319	Elizabeth	Wirth	Domestic	1349
598320	Jack	Wirth	Son	Case 2

Table 2. Member-record before head-record

PID	Name	Surname	Relation	HID
735361	Albert	Tombs	Son	989
735362	Nellie	Galbraith	Daughter	Case 2
735363	William	Galbraith	Head	990

Resolving Suspended Records: Suspended records without an assigned HID fall in one of the following four cases: 1 - Records with missing district value (0.1%); 2 - Records with a sequential PID, different surname, and a family relation value (4.6%); 3 - Records with a non sequential PID and the same surname (4.2%); and 4 - Records with a non sequential PID, different surname, and a family relation value (1%).

Case 1: A record X with a missing subdistrict value is a suspended record because the record X may be in the wrong location. In the first step of our HID identification process, we sort the census using the district values, so if a record has a missing district value, it will not appear in the right position following the sort. The solution is to include the district name in the sorting. We include this attribute only when the district number is missing because the district name attribute is more prone to spelling errors.

Case 2: A record X with a sequential PID, different surname, and a family relation value is a suspended record because if it is a member-record, it should share the same surname. Almost 5% of the records in the 1891 census fall into this case. After analyzing a sample of these records manually and discussing them with domain experts, we determined some of the causes and developed solutions, as described below:

1. *Incomplete information*: During transcription, some of the data was omitted. If the value of the relation attribute refers to a relation to a household member instead of the head, it is still a solvable issue. Table 1 shows a household with this issue. If we define the relation field as a relation to the head only, the record containing "Jack Wirth" should be a son of "W W Rowe", but they do not share the same last name. According to the surnames of the household members, it is reasonable to say that "Jack" is a son of the domestics "Henrich" and "Elizabeth Wirth". Hence, only comparing surnames to the head record is not be enough. The solution requires comparing the surname of any new record with the surnames of the household members who have different surnames, but a relation to the head (e.g., married, widowed, divorced daughter, domestic, lodger, sister, brother).
2. *Misplaced information*: Information inserted/copied/recorded in the wrong order leads to unassigned records (e.g., inserting member-record information before head-record). Table 2 shows an example where a child's record comes before the head-record. For example, the record of daughter "Nellie

Table 3. Spelling errors

PID	Name	Surname	Relation	HID
805206	David	Murry	Head	622
809827	Isabela	Murry	Wife	622
809828	Isabela	Murry	Daughter	622
809829	Margret	Murry	Daughter	622
809830	Peter	Murry	Son	622
809831	Jennie	Murray	Daughter	Case 2

Table 4. Different PIDs range in consecutive pages

PID	Name	Surname	Relation	HID
743123	W	Eliott	Head	891
743124	Mariah	Eliott	Wife	891
751644	Foster	Eliott	Son	Case 3
757850	Alexr	Eliott	Son	Case 3

Galbraith" shares the surname with the head-record "William Galbraith", however, the PID value results in her being sorted before the father record.

3. *Spelling errors*: Spelling mistakes are common errors that appear, especially in the transcription of historical documents. As shown in Table 3, "Jennie Murray" seems to be a daughter of "David Murry" but the spelling error in her name makes the record suspended from the initial assignment. To solve this problem, we employ a string comparison measure (i.e., Jaro-Winkler) [1] to compare last names when we deal with unresolved cases. Pairs of strings with a similarity score above 0.85 are considered the same by our system.

Table 5. Different PIDs range in consecutive pages

ID	PID	Given name	Surname	Relation	HID
108	889003	Louis	lafontine	Head	721
108	889004	Sarah	lafontine	Wife	721
109	333291	Justine	levielle	Head	722
..	..	28 other records	..	..	..
109	889005	Philomina	lafontine	Daughter	Case 4
109	889006	James	lafontine	Son	Case 2
109	889007	Elear	lafontine	Son	Case 2

Case 3 and Case 4: If a record X has a non sequential PID, but shares the same surname with its previous record, it is considered a suspended record. We can resolve these cases by exploiting the fact that they share the same surname with the head of household. However, before we can assign them a HID, we have to be certain that there are no other records that share the surname with these records and have a sequential PID appearing in neighbouring pages. We do this by using a sliding-window algorithm to search for similar records across neighbouring pages (i.e., previous and following pages). Table 4 shows an example for this case (note the non sequential PIDs in the table). Similarly, we search for possible matches for suspended records of Case 4 (Table 5).

The solutions we have found to resolve the unassigned cases are based on manually exploring unassigned records and discussing them with the domain experts. We incorporate this domain knowledge into our system and we employ a search for any possible household for the suspended records in their page, previous page, or next page using a sliding-window algorithm. We are using this step to help in making a decision about the suspended records, so if there is any household that shares household information with a suspended record in the range of 3 pages, the record will take the same HID of that household.

4 Evaluation and Results

The solutions we discovered were effective in decreasing the number of excluded records that belong to the four cases from almost 10% to less than 1%. However, we cannot evaluate all of the generated households except through manual evaluation, which is time expensive. A small sample (50 households) of our automatically generated households was reviewed by the domain experts, and they found the assignments to be correct. Further, we compared the automatically produced households of the 1891 census with the manually produced households of the 1871 and the 1881 Canadian censuses [4] in terms of total households and household size. In addition, we compared the manual and automatic HID identification of the three censuses to the household aggregate information given by Statistics Canada[1] (note that this is only aggregate information that cannot be used for group linkage). Table 6 shows this information. The unassigned records (0.9%) were excluded from this comparison since we don't have a HID for them. We can observe from this table that the number and average size of the automatically discovered households are very close to those reported by Statistics Canada.

Table 6. Household information

Transcribed census data	Manual		Automatic
	1871	1881	1891
Data set size	3,466,427	4,277,807	4,787,244
Included records	-	-	99.1%
Total of households	609,300	801,052	881,923
Size range	1: 761	1: 625	1: 1260
Size average	5.67	5.34	5.37
Statistics Canada	1871	1881	1891
Census data size	3,485,761	4,278,327	4,833,239
Total of households	622,719	800,410	900,080
Size average	5.6	5.3	5.3

[1] Statistics Canada website, URL: http://www.statcan.gc.ca/pub/11-630-x/11-630-x2015008-eng.htm.

5 Conclusions

In this paper, we presented an automatic household generating approach for historical census data. This approach identifies household information of full count real census data. The experimental results show that the proposed approach can be applied to real data by taking into account domain knowledge, and without requiring a further data cleaning step. We can accurately detect households by excluding only less than 1% of census records.

By generating the household identifiers for the 1891 full Canadian census, we make this census ready to be linked together by group linkage techniques or integrate them with the 1871 and 1881 censuses that are already linked in [4,5].

References

1. Winkler, W.E.: Overview of record linkage and current research directions. Statistical Research Division Report (2006)
2. Elmagarmid, A.K., Ipeirotis, P.G., Verykios, V.S.: Duplicate record detection: a survey. IEEE Trans. Knowl. Data Eng. **19**, 116 (2007)
3. On, B.W., Koudas, N., Lee, D., Srivastava, D.: Group linkage. In: IEEE International Conference on Data Engineering, pp. 496–505 (2007)
4. Antonie, L., Inwood, K., Lizotte, D.J., Ross, J.A.: Tracking people over time in 19th century Canada for longitudinal analysis. Mach. Learn. **95**(1), 129–146 (2014)
5. Richards, L.: Disambiguating Multiple Links in Historical Record Linkage, MSc thesis, University of Guelph (2014)
6. Fu, Z., Boot, H.M., Christen, P., Zhou, J.: Automatic record linkage of individuals and households in historical census data. Int. J. Humanit. Arts Comput. **8**(2), 204–225 (2014)
7. Ruggles, S.: Linking historical censuses: a new approach. Hist. Comput. **14**(1–2), 213–224 (2002)

Natural Language Processing

Matrix Models with Feature Enrichment for Relation Extraction

Duc-Thuan Vo(✉) and Ebrahim Bagheri

Laboratory for Systems, Software and Semantics (LS3), Ryerson University, Toronto, Canada
{thuanvd, bagheri}@ryerson.ca

Abstract. Many traditional relation extraction techniques require a large number of pre-defined schemas in order to extract relations from textual documents. In this paper, to avoid the need for pre-defined schemas, we employ the notion of *universal schemas* that is formed as a collection of patterns derived from Open Information Extraction as well as from relation schemas of pre-existing datasets. We then employ matrix factorization and collaborative filtering on such universal schemas for relation extraction. While previous systems have trained relations only for entities, we exploit advanced features from relation characteristics such as clause types and semantic topics for predicting new relation instances. This helps our proposed work to naturally predict any tuple of entities and relations regardless of whether they were seen at training time with direct or indirect access in their provenance. In our experiments, we show improved performance compared to the state-of-the-art.

Keywords: Matrix factorization · Universal schema · Relation extraction · Topic modeling

1 Introduction

Relation Extraction (RE) aims at determining the relationships between entities in textual documents and is among the more important tasks of information extraction that has been applied in a large number of applications such as question-answering, and search engines, among others. In this context, most supervised and semi-supervised extraction methods use a predefined, finite and fixed schema of relation types (such as located-in or founded-by). Among the supervised methods, the works in [8, 21] have focused on performing language analysis for semantic relation extraction. A running theme among these techniques is the capacity to generate linguistic features based on syntactic, dependency, or shallow semantic structures of the text. Semi-supervised approaches have been employed by various researchers [7, 12, 18] to extract patterns derived initially from rule-based relations. These approaches exploit the concept of *information redundancy* and hypothesize that similar relations tend to appear in uniform contexts. However, most of these systems are limited in terms of scalability and portability across domains by predefined and fixed schema of relation types.

In contrast, Open Information Extraction (OIE) [5, 6, 11, 19] systems offer a more nuanced approach that rely minimally on background knowledge and manually labeled

M. Mouhoub and P. Langlais (Eds.): Canadian AI 2017, LNAI 10233, pp. 235–247, 2017.
DOI: 10.1007/978-3-319-57351-9_28

training data. OIE systems require no supervision for performing highly scalable extractions and are often portable across domains. Distant supervision [1, 15, 16] aims to exploit information from knowledge bases such as Freebase in order to learn large-scale relations from text. Heuristic method [16] has been employed to generate training relations by mapping phrases to their corresponding entities in KBs. Dependence on pre-existing datasets in distant supervision approaches can be avoided by using language itself as the source for the universal schema. To this end, Riedel et al. [15] have already presented a model based on matrix factorization with universal schemas for predicting relations. These authors presented a series of models that learn lower dimensional manifolds for tuple of entities and relations with a set of weights in order to capture direct correlations between relations. While these approaches have shown reasonable performance, their limitation is in that they train cells only for tuple of entities, and therefore, are limited when an insufficient number of evidences are present for the entities present in the relations. For instance, the relation OBAMA–president-of–US could not infer the hidden relation HOLLANDE-president-of-FRANCE due to differences of the tuples <(OBAMA, US)> and <(HOLLANDE, FRANCE)>. Even if entity types are exploited in the system, the failure to predict other relations such as OBAMA–born-in–US with similar tuple of entities can be problematic in such systems.

In this paper, we exploit advanced features from relation characteristics, namely *clause types* and *semantic topics* to enrich the cells in the matrix of a matrix factorization model for predicting new relation instances. Particularly, we exploit clause types and topic models to predict relations regardless of whether they were seen at training time with direct or indirect access. Our work uses the concept of universal schema from [15] in order to convert the KB combined with OIE patterns into a binary matrix in which tuples of entities are its rows and relations denote the columns.

The rest of this paper is organized as follows. Section 2 presents background on relation extraction with matrix factorization and collaborative filtering. In Sect. 3, we present a detailed description of several models with feature enrichments in matrix models. This is followed by an in-depth discussion of experimental results in Sect. 4, where the results are compared to the state-of-the-art. Section 5 finalizes the paper with conclusions and future work.

2 Background

The application of matrix factorization and collaborative filtering methods in relation extraction aims at predicting hidden relations that might not have been directly observed. Kemp et al. [9] used Infinite Relational Model (IRM) in order to build a framework to discover latent relations jointly from an n-dimensional matrix. In this matrix, each dimension has a latent structure through which relations can be found. Bollegala et al. [3] try to explore clusters of entity pairs and patterns jointly as latent relations by employing co-clustering. Takamatsu et al. [17] use probabilistic matrix factorization with Singular Value Decomposition to reduce dimensions to discover relations. Riedel et al. [15] use matrix factorization and collaborative filtering by including surface patterns in a universal schema and a ranking objective function to learn latent vectors for tuple of entities and relations. In their systems, they use surface patterns extracted from OIE. The goal of these systems is to predict the hidden relations through *matrix completion*. Our work is similar to [15] in that we use matrix factorization and collaborative filtering for the discovery of potential relations. Given the fact that the work in [15] populate the matrix cells only for entity pairs, they can fall short when predicting latent relations that do not have sufficient evidence from observed relation instances. In our work, we represent universal schemas in the form of a matrix where tuples of entities form the rows and relations constitute the columns. We further employ advanced features from relation characteristics such as clause types and semantic topics for enriching the cells in the matrix to predict new relation instances (See Fig. 1).

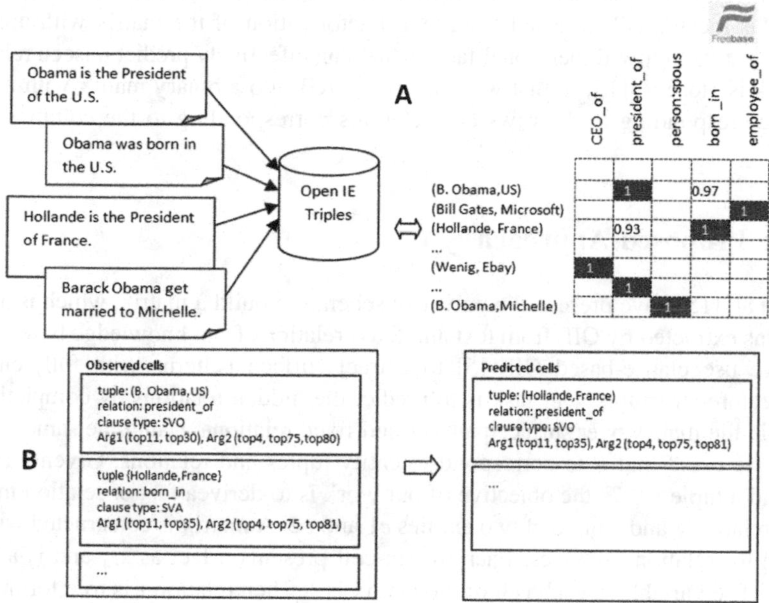

Fig. 1. (A) Universal schema with relation and tuples, 1 denotes observed relation, values 0.97, 0.93 are predicted probability of the relation; (B) Examples of observed cells and predicted cells.

Open Information Extraction (OIE) [5, 6, 11, 19] is another closely related area of research to our work. The majority of OIE systems use a shallow syntactic representation or dependency parsing in the form of verbs or verbal phrases and their arguments. Wu and Weld [20] propose a shallow syntactic representation of natural language text in the form of verbs or verbal phrases and their arguments. Besides that, there have been several approaches [11, 18, 20] that employ robust and efficient dependency parsing for relation extraction. More recent OIE systems such as ClausIE [5] use dependency parsing and a small set of domain-independent lexica without any post-processing or training data. At the outset, these systems exploit linguistic knowledge about the grammar of the English language to first detect clauses in an input sentence and to subsequently identify each clause type based on the grammatical function of its constituents. In our work, for surface patterns of the matrix, we use OIE patterns for populating relations of all kinds in the matrix. We exploit clause-based features extracted from OIE (ClausIE) combined with topic models (LDA), which are used as important characteristics for predicting potential relations.

The work in distant supervision [1, 15, 16] aim at exploiting knowledge bases (KBs) such as Freebase to learn relations. Heuristic method [16] is employed to generate training relations by mapping pairs of mentioned entities in a sentence to corresponding entities in a KB. As a result, such methods do not require labeled corpora, avoid being domain dependent, and allow the use of any size of documents. These methods learn extracted relations for a known set of relations. Universal schema [15] employs the notion of distant supervision by using a knowledge base to derive similarity between both structured relations such as "LocatedAt" and surface form relations such as "is located at" extracted from text. Factorization of the matrix with universal schemas results in low-dimensional factors that can effectively predict unseen relations. Our work is close to [15] in that we convert the KB into a binary matrix with tuple of entities corresponding to the rows and relations corresponding to the columns in the matrix.

3 The Proposed Approach

Riedel et al. [15] have presented a universal schema to build a matrix, which is a union of patterns extracted by OIE from text and fixed relations from knowledge bases. In our work, we use clause-based OIE [5] to extract surface patterns with fully-enriched clause feature structures. Our task is to predict the hidden relations by completing the schema in the matrix over surface patterns and fixed relations. Using the same notation as [15], we use T and R to correspond to entity tuples and relations. Given a relation $r \in R$ and a tuple $t \in T$, the objective of our work is to derivea fact or relation instance about a relation r and a tuple of two entities $e1$ and $e2$. A matrix is constructed with size $|T| \times |R|$ for relation instances. Each matrix cell presents a fact as $x_{r,t}$ and is a binary variable. The variable in each cell of the matrix is 1 when relation r is true for the tuple t, and 0 when relation r is false for t. We aim at predicting new relations that could potentially hold for tuple of entities, which are missing in the matrix. We present several models that can address the task as follows.

3.1 Matrix Factorization (F Model)

In the matrix factorization approach, we denote each relation by a_r and each tuple of entities as e_t. We measure compatibility between relation r and tuple t as the dot product of two latent feature representations of size k. Thus we have:

$$\theta_{r,t} = \sum_k a_{r,k} e_{t,k} \tag{1}$$

The formula is factorizing a matrix into a multiplication of two matrices $\Theta = AE$, A denoting the lower dimension matrix of a_r, and E representing the lower dimension matrix of e_t based on PCA [4]. Thus, a model with the matrix $\Theta = (\theta_{r,t})$ of natural parameters is defined as the low rank factorization AE. To estimate the values in PCA, we have:

$$x_{r,t} = \sigma(\theta_{r,t}) = \sigma\left(\sum_k a_{r,k} e_{t,k}\right) \tag{2}$$

This is applying a logistic function $\sigma(\theta_{r,t}) = 1/(1+\exp(-\theta_{r,t}))$ [4, 14, 15] to model a binary cell in the matrix. Each cell is drawn from a Bernoulli distribution with natural parameter $\theta_{r,t}$. We maximize the log-likelihood of the observed cells under a probabilistic model to learn low dimensional representations. The representations a_r and e_t can be found by minimizing the negative log-likelihood using stochastic gradient descent with $x_{r,t} = \sigma(\theta_{r,t})$. This formulation also applies to all the following models as well.

3.2 Neighbor Model (N Model)

In the matrix, a relation in a column could be neighbor to some other co-occurring relation (neighbor relation). For example, relation "CEO-of" and "Director-of" are often seen in similar relation instances. Therefore, the Neighbor Model [10] is essential to capture the localized correlation of the cells in the matrix to incorporate this information. We implement a neighborhood model N via a set of weights w of features based on co-occurrence of information around tuples of entities, e.g., headword "President" often appears in tuples of entities in relations such as "CEO-of" and "Director-of". In this model, each cell is scored based on the set of weights between this cell and its associated neighbors. This leads to the following formulation:

$$\theta_{r,t} = \sum_k w_k f_k(r', r) \tag{3}$$

where w_k is the weight of association between r' and r; $f_k(r', r)$ defines a conjunctive feature between relation r and neighbor relation r' and k is the number of relations r' that have the exact same tuples as r.

In this model, we additionally employ clause-based features, which are core characteristic of relations for selectional preference. For instance, a relation OBAMA-president-of-US or OBAMA-leader-of-US could be presented by a clause type "Subject-Verb-Complement", while another relation "OBAMA-born-in-US" is in the form of a "Subject-Verb-Adverb" clause. Therefore, considering only entities will fail to predict relations in tuple <(OBAMA, US)>. We have used clause types in OIE [5] when extracting surface patterns for the matrix. We can interpolate the confidence for a given tuple and relation based on the trueness of other similar relations for the same tuple. Measuring compatibility of an entity tuple and relation amounts to summing up the compatibilities between each argument slot representation and the corresponding entity representation. We extend the model in Eq. 3 to incorporate clause types, which is presented as follows:

$$\theta_{r,t} = \sum_k v_{t,r} w_k f_k(r', r) \tag{4}$$

where $v_{t,r}$ is a vector of clause types.

3.3 Entity Model (E Model)

Earlier, Riedel et al. [15] introduced the use of entities in collaborative filtering. In their method, they employed entities to predict latent relations. The model embeds each entity into a low dimensional space of size k. For binary relations, their arguments (t_1 and t_2) are entities modeled in the low dimensional space and are represented as $e1$ for t_1 and $e2$ for t_2. The equation below leads to the calculation of the compatibility of tuple of entities and their relations by summing up the presentation of each argument slot. Thus, this leads to:

$$\theta_{r,t} = \sum_k a_{t1,k} e1_{r,k} + \sum_k a_{t2,k} e2_{r,k} \tag{5}$$

Analogous to the Neighbor model, we augment the entity model with clause-based features, which enhances the entity model as follows:

$$\theta_{r,t} = \sum_k a_{t1,k} e1_{r,k} v_{t1} + \sum_k a_{t2,k} e2_{r,k} v_{t2} \tag{6}$$

where v_{t1} isa vector of clause type for argument 1, and v_{t2} is a vector of clause type for argument 2.

3.4 Topic-Based Model (T Model)

In the Entity model, selectional preferences are employed based on each argument's slot representation and the corresponding entity representation in order to learn from other relations. However, in addition to this, many relations can be considered to be related to other relations based on the probability of being observed within the same semantic topic group. For instance, the relation tuple <(HOLLANDE, FRANCE)> could be learned from the observed relation <OBAMA, US>, if and when "OBAMA"-"HOLLANDE" and "US"-"FRANCE" are observed in the same semantic topic groups. Therefore, relations could further be learned by their selectional preferences in semantic topic groups. This helps to determine more relations that are missing when learning from directly observed relations. We use Latent Dirichlet Allocation [2] to generate semantic groups of topics, and then embed this information in the matrix. We embed each entity into a low dimensional space if they are mapped together within similar topics. We measure each cell based on the compatibility of the argument representation and their corresponding semantic topic groups with other cells. This can be more formally represented as:

$$\theta_{r,t} = \sum_k a_{t1,k} e1_{r,k} h_{t1,k} + \sum_k a_{t2,k} e2_{r,k} h_{t2,k} \quad (7)$$

where h_{t1} denotes the vector of topics for argument 1, and h_{t2} denotes vector of topics for argument 2.

Given the fact that using only semantic groups of topics could be noisy for training purposes, we also further augment the topic model with clause-based features. For instance, <(HOLLANDE-FRANCE)> could be learned by <(OBAMA-US)> if they are presented with a similar clause type. This could be presented as:

$$\theta_{r,t} = \sum_k a_{t1,k} e1_{r,k} h_{t1,k} v_{t1} + \sum_k a_{t2,k} e2_{r,k} h_{t2,k} v_{t2} \quad (8)$$

where v_{t1} is the vector of clause type for argument 1, and v_{t2} is the vector of clause type for argument 2.

3.5 Interpolated Models

Each of the above models represents a unique and important aspect of the data that needs to be combined with other models to predict potential relations in the matrix. In practice, combining the introduced models can capture different necessary aspects of the data. For instance, the combined model of Entity and Neighbor can take advantage of selectional preference on argument slot presentation from the Entity model and the weight of the related neighbors from the Neighbor model. We linearly interpolate the models, e.g., the combination of F, N, E and T models can be shown as follows:

$$\theta_{r,t} = F(\theta_{t,r}) + N(\theta_{t,r}) + E(\theta_{t,r}) + T(\theta_{t,r}) \quad (9)$$

3.6 Parameter Estimation

Similar to the F model, relation cells in the matrix model are parameterized through weights and/or latent component vectors. In each model, we predict a relation with a number between 0 and 1. However, the models require negative training data for the learning process. We train the models by ranking the positive cells (observed true facts) with higher score than the negative cells (false facts). The log-likelihood setting could be contrasted with this constraint that primarily requires negative facts to be scored below a defined threshold. Thus, it is possible to calculate the gradient for the weights of cells. We also use log-likelihood as the objective function and employ stochastic gradient descent with a logistic function $\sigma(\theta_{r,t}) = 1/(1+\exp(-\theta_{r,t}))$ to learn the parameters $x_{r,t} = \sigma(\theta_{r,t})$.

4 Experimentation

4.1 Experimental Setting

In this paper, in order to benchmark our approach, we conducted experiments on the dataset[1] proposed in [1]. The content of this dataset is comprised of reports from New York Times where each sentence has been annotated with relation types with linked entity tags to Freebase. Note that, we do not use the dataset from [15] given the fact that it does not include the original sentences, which prevents us from being able to identify grammatical clauses as required in our approach. We used ClausIE [5] to extract the clause patterns and then check them with entity tuples annotated in each sentence in order to embed them into the matrix. For embedding clause types into the matrix, we use three fundamental clause types, namely SVO, SVC and SVA. The details of these clauses are presented in [5]. Given we only focus on three clause types, if a tuple of entities was extracted with a different clause type, e.g., "Bill has worked for IBM since 2010" that corresponds to the SVOA clause pattern, we check the main entities of the relation's corresponding elements and convert its clause type into one of the three main types of clauses. In this case, SVOA will be converted into SVO because "Bill" represents S and "has worked" denotes V, and "IBM" represents O.

Additionally, for extracting the semantic groups of topics, we generate and estimate topic models based on LDA through Gibbs Sampling using GibbsLDA++[2]. We optimize three important parameters a, b and number of topics T in the LDA. It is based on the topic number and the size of the vocabulary in the document collection, which are $a = 50/T$ and $b = 0.01$, respectively [13]. Then we vary topic sizes between 100, 150, and 200. We evaluate each group of topics and select topic size 150, which shows the best performance for our experiments.

4.2 Experimental Results

We have conducted experiments on both individual models and interpolated models for predicting relations as listed in Tables 1 and 2. We randomly split the dataset for training and testing and applied 10-fold cross validation for all models. We have applied the threshold 0.5 as suggested in [15] for all models that indicate the confidence value to predict a relation. Table 1 shows the detailed performance of each model as well as the combined models in Table 2. As observed in the table, using clause features shows improved performance compared to when models are built without clause information. Using the clause information, we can see the EC model with F-measure of 41.81% is better than the E model with F-measure of 38.77%; N model obtained only 36% in F-measure while NC obtained 39.5% in F-measure. We observe that, N models are lower than the other models due to weak co-occurrence with other relations. The interpolation of N, F, E and T models outperforms the non-interpolated models, indicating the power of selectional preferences learned from data, e.g., F+E+N (being

[1] http://nlp.stanford.edu/software/mimlre-2014-07-17-data.tar.gz.

[2] http://gibbslda.sourceforge.net.

Table 1. Experimental results in individual models.

Models	Precision (%)	Recall (%)	F-measure (%)
E	48.23	32.41	38.77
EC (E with clause)	51.97	37.02	**41.81**
N	44.61	30.18	36.00
NC (N with clause)	48.94	33.11	**39.50**
T	46.79	41.70	44.10
TC (T with clause)	54.71	37.02	**44.16**
F	58.02	39.26	**46.83**

Table 2. Experimental results in interpolated models.

Models	Precision (%)	Recall (%)	F-measure (%)
Baseline [15] (F+E+N)	**79.58**	38.51	51.90
F+E+N+T	51.16	53.30	52.21
EC+NC	72.29	32.51	43.88
TC+NC	64.12	34.98	47.82
EC+TC	59.58	39.67	47.62
F+EC	54.65	42.36	47.69
F+NC	56.24	40.14	46.85
F+TC	53.02	46.87	49.75
NC+EC+TC	57.24	42.36	48.69
F+EC+NC	57.31	49.24	52.96
F+NC+TC	55.01	54.80	54.90
F+EC+NC+TC	60.23	**60.00**	**60.11**

the baseline presented by Reidel et al. [15]) and F+E+N+T models have an F-measure of 51.9% and 52.23%, respectively.

The interpolated models EC+NC, EC+TC, and EC+TC+NC benefit from important aspects of the data from the EC, NC and TC models and take advantage of selectional preference on argument slot presentation from entities and the weight of the related neighbors. EC+NC achieves an F-measure of 43.88%, EC+TC has an F-measure of 47.62% and EC+TC+NC produces an F-measure of 48.69%. Therefore, the interpolated models obtain better results compared to the individual EC, NC, or TC models. We observed that TC employs features based on the presentation of argument slots from entities; and the presentation of argument slots in the TC model results in a much higher number of co-occurrences compared to the EC model. Therefore, the interpolated models with TC achieve better results compared to the interpolated models with EC, e.g., TC+NC yielded 47.82% while EC+NC yielded 43.88%.

The interpolated models with F such as F+TC, F+NC+TC and F+EC+NC+TC have sufficient number of features, which are employed based on PCA components (F model). Therefore, F+TC, F+NC+TC and F+EC+NC+TC achieve better results compared to the interpolated models without F such as TC, NC+TC, and EC+NC+TC. For instance, NC+TC obtains an F-measure of 47.82% while F+NC+TC obtains

54.90%. Finally, the best interpolated model is F+EC+NC+TC which produces the highest result with 60.11% in F-measure when compared to the other models. Our interpolated models, namely F+NC+TC, F+E+N+T and F+EC+NC+TC outperform the baseline (F+E+N) proposed in [15].

Finally, we would like to summarize the impact of our proposed work on performance. As seen in the table, when employing clause types on the baseline (F+E+N vs. F+EC+NC), we see that precision drops; however, recall increases and overall the incorporation of clause type improves F-measure. Also when adding semantic topics to the baseline (F+E+N vs. F+E+N+T), we see a similar trend. The important observation is that once clause types and topic models are added simultaneously (F+EC+NC+TC) that we achieve a significant improvement on recall and a reasonable precision performance, leading to much higher F-measure. This shows that clause types and semantic topics can help identify a higher number of relevant relations and hence increase retrieval rates and also maintain acceptable precision.

Table 3 shows several specific relation types in our models. We show the top-5 relation types that have the best F-measure scores in the top-6 best performing models such as the F model (the best individual model), EC+NC+TC (the best interpolated model without F), F+E+N and F+E+N+T (the two best models without clause types), F+TC+NC and F+EC+NC+TC (the best interpolated models with clause types). These relations take advantage of selectional preference in the training process due to their co-occurrence and/or clause type similarity with other relations. For instance, similar entities co-occur multiple times in relations such as "org/country_of_headquarters", "org/city_of_headquarters" or "per/country_of_birth"; therefore, making the cells for these relationships highly similar and related to each other. Hence, the models will take advantage of such similarity in the training process in order to learn latent relations between the relationships. Beside entity co-occurrences, some relations appear only within a specific clause type. e.g., "person/founded" is often seen in the "SVC" clause type while "org/member_of" is observed as the "SVO" clause type; hence, the application of the clause type information can significantly help find similarity or relationship between these relations and the others in the matrix and lead to reduced noise in the training process.

Table 3. F-measures of top-5 relation types in the best six models.

	F	EC+NC+TC	F+E+N	F+E+N+T	F+TC+NC	F+EC+NC+TC
org/country_of_headquarters	60.97	67.22	70.49	76.42	69.16	77.39
person/founded	61.53	62.63	43.68	72.50	72.99	75.84
org/city_of_headquarters	25.84	66.66	63.93	75.60	75.00	76.52
per/country_of_birth	56.92	69.31	79.63	73.54	72.25	76.88
org/member_of	58.96	79.73	78.70	71.59	76.72	70.22

4.3 Discussions

In terms of the performance of the individual models, we observe that the E and T models outperform the N model. The E and T models employ the presentation of argument slots while N employs co-occurrence with neighbors. The N model might face situations where only a few co-occurrences with other neighbor relations are observed that can cause weak evidence in the training process for learning hidden relations. However, in the T and E models where their argument slots are presented in high dimensions, this could increase the number of desirable co-occurrences. These models take advantage of selectional preference in the training process due to the exploitation of co-occurrence information with other relations. Most of the models have increasing performance when applying clause type features because the clause type information can reduce noise in the training process.

Interpolated models benefit from the advantages of each individual model. Thus, most of the interpolated models achieve better results compared to separate models. Comparing our best models (F+NC+TC) and (F+EC+NC+TC) with Reidel et al.'s model (F+E+N) as a baseline, the results reveal that we obtained 55.01% of precision and 54.80% of recall in F+NC+TC, and 60.23% of precision and 60% of recall in F+EC +NC+TC while Reidel et al. achieved 79.58% of precision and 38.51% of recall. Applying semantic topics to the models could reduce precision but increase recall significantly when compared to the baseline. Baseline+Topic model (F+E+N+T) achieves 51.16% of precision and 53.30% of recall. Our model obtained an improvement in recall when compared to the baseline. However, our models also show lower precision because applying topic-based features in our models will lead to an increasingly higher number of hidden relations for prediction compared to the baseline. This can cause a lower precision in our model even when our model predicts more hidden relations compared to Reidel et al.'s model. Finally, based on the F-measure metric, our models show up to 8% improvement in comparison to the baseline model.

Now, let us look at some of the major causes of error in our proposed models. There are some factors, which can affect the results. First, some relation types show missing evidence for training that cause low accuracy when predicting latent relations. For example, the relation "per:cause_of_death" has only been observed very few times with other relations in the matrix. Consequently, after the training process, the trained models do not have enough knowledge to predict such infrequent relations. Second, there are incorrect linked entities that cause noise in the matrix. We found that some tuples of entities, which are linked to entities from Freebase, are not accurately placed in the correct tuple or relation in the dataset. For example, "Obama, who is the President of US, has visited Canada" has been annotated with the tuple of entities <(OBAMA-CANADA)> with relation "person: employee". Therefore, such a tuple in the training set will introduce noise, which can lead to issues when predicting relations. Finally, ambiguous tuples of entities might occur in the dataset, e.g., tuple of entities (<WASHINGTON-US>) areseen in several relations such as "org:country_of_headquarters", "per:countries_of_residence", and "per:origin" because "WASHINGTON" could refer to a city in some cases, or a person in other cases that leads to noise in the training processes. As a result, this will have a negative effect on performance when predicting hidden relations.

5 Concluding Remarks

In this paper, we presented several matrix models with feature enrichment for predicting potential relations. We have exploited universal schemas that are formed as a collection of patterns from OIE and relation schemas from pre-existing datasets to build a matrix model in order to use matrix factorization and collaborative filtering to predict hidden relations. While previous systems have trained relations only for entities, we further exploited advanced features such as clause types and semantic topics for predicting hidden relations. Particularly, we exploited clause-based features extracted from OIE combined with semantic groups of topics, which are used as important characteristics for predicting potential relations. In our experiments, the results reveal that our proposed models achieve better results compared to the state of the art, which demonstrates the efficiency of our proposed approach.

References

1. Angeli, G., Tibshirani, J., Wu, J., Manning, C.D.: Combining distant and partial supervision for relation extraction. In: EMNLP 2014 (2014)
2. Blei, D., Ng, A.Y., Jordan, M.I.: Latent dirichlet allocation. J. Mach. Learn. Res. **3**, 993–1022 (2003)
3. Bollegala, D., Matsuo, Y., Ishizuka, Y.: Relational duality: unsupervised extraction of semantic relations between entities on the web. In: WWW 2010 (2010)
4. Collins, M., Dasgupta, S., Schapire, R.S.: A generalization of principal component analysis to the exponential family. In: NIPS 2001 (2001)
5. Corro, L.D., Gemulla, R.: ClausIE: clause-based open information extraction. In: WWW 2013 (2013)
6. Fader, A., Soderland, S., Etzioni, O.: Identifying relations for open information extraction. In: EMNLP 2011 (2011)
7. Greenwood, M.A., Stevenson, M.: Improving semi-supervised acquisition of relation extraction patterns. In: IEBD 2006 (2006)
8. Kambhatla, N.: Combining lexical, syntactic and semantic features with maximum entropy models for extracting relations. In: ACL 2004 (2004)
9. Kemp, C., Tenenbaum, J.B., Griffiths, T.L.: Learning systems of concepts with an infinite relational model. In: AAAI 2006 (2006)
10. Koren, Y.: Factorization meets the neighborhood: a multifaceted collaborative filtering model. In: KDD 2009 (2009)
11. Mausam, Schmitz, M., Bart, R., Soderland, S., Etzioni, O.: Open language learning for information extraction. In: EMNLP 2012 (2012)
12. Pantel, P., Pennacchiotti, M.: Espresso: leveraging generic patterns for automatically harvesting semantic relations. In: COLING 2006 (2006)
13. Phan, X.H., Nguyen, C.T., Le, D.T., Nguyen, L.M., Horiguchi, S., Ha, Q.T.: A hidden topic-based framework toward building applications with short web documents. IEEE Trans. Knowl. Data Eng. **23**, 961–976 (2011)
14. Rendle, S., Freudenthaler, C., Gantner, Z., Schmidt-Thieme, L.: Bayesian personalized ranking from implicit feedback. In: Proceedings of UAI 2009 (2009)

15. Riedel, S., Yao, L., McCallum, A., Marlin, M.: Relation extraction with matrix factorization and universal schemas. In: NAACL 2013 (2013)
16. Surdeanu, M., Tibshirani, J., Nallapati, R., Manning, C.D.: Multi-instance multi-label learning for relation extraction. In: EMNLP-CoNLL 2012 (2012)
17. Takamatsu, S., Sato, I., Nakagawa, H.: Probabilistic matrix factorization leveraging contexts for unsupervised relation discovery. In: PAKDD 2011 (2011)
18. Vo, D.T., Bagheri, E.: Self-training on refined clause patterns for relation extraction. Inf. Process. Manage. (2017). doi:10.1016/j.ipm.2017.02.009
19. Vo, D.T., Bagheri, E.: Open information extraction. Encycl. Semant. Comput. Robot. Intell. **1**(1) (2017). doi:10.1142/S2425038416300032
20. Wu, F., Weld, D.S.: Open information extraction using wikipedia. In: ACL 2010
21. Zhou, G., Qian, L., Fan, J.: Tree kernel based semantic relation extraction with rich syntactic and semantic information. Inf. Sci. **180**, 1313–1325 (2010)

Domain Adaptation for Detecting Mild Cognitive Impairment

Vaden Masrani[1](✉), Gabriel Murray[2], Thalia Shoshana Field[3], and Giuseppe Carenini[1]

[1] Department of Computer Science, University of British Columbia, Vancouver, Canada
{vadmas,carenini}@cs.ubc.ca

[2] Department of Computer Information Systems, University of the Fraser Valley, Abbotsford, Canada
gabriel.murray@ufv.ca

[3] Department of Neurology, University of British Columbia, Vancouver, Canada
thalia.field@ubc.ca

Abstract. Lexical and acoustic markers in spoken language can be used to detect mild cognitive impairment (MCI), a condition which is often a precursor to dementia and frequently causes some degree of dysphasia. Research to develop such a diagnostic tool for clinicians has been hindered by the scarcity of available data. This work uses *domain adaptation* to adapt Alzheimer's data to improve classification accuracy of MCI. We evaluate two simple domain adaptation algorithms, AUGMENT and CORAL, and show that AUGMENT improves upon all baselines. Additionally we investigate the use of previously unconsidered *discourse features* and show they are not useful in distinguishing MCI from healthy controls.

Keywords: Domain adaptation · Mild cognitive impairment · Dementia · Alzheimer's

1 Introduction

Mild cognitive impairment (MCI) is a non-specific diagnosis characterized by cognitive decline that is less severe than dementia and does not significantly interfere with activities of daily living [1]. Population-based studies estimate its prevalence to be between 12–18% in people over the age of 60 [2]. While a proportion of patients will revert to normal cognition or stay mildly impaired, 8–15% annually will progress to dementia [2]. MCI can be due to neurodegenerative (most commonly, but not exclusively, Alzheimer's dementia (AD)) or reversible causes, including psychiatric illness or metabolic disturbances including thyroid disease or vitamin B12 deficiency [3].

As MCI can involve a number of potential underlying causes, there are no specific treatments. However, early diagnosis can affect testing for potentially

M. Mouhoub and P. Langlais (Eds.): Canadian AI 2017, LNAI 10233, pp. 248–259, 2017.
DOI: 10.1007/978-3-319-57351-9_29

treatable causes, allow for optimization of vascular risk factors that may accelerate onset of dementia, prompt further diagnostic testing, and better allow for planning for social supports and closer medical follow-up.

With recent improvements in natural language processing (NLP) and machine learning, there has been a push to use speech processing to develop a tool to assist clinicians in diagnosis of "Alzheimer's disease and other dementias" (ADOD)[1]. Clinical research has shown that dysphasia is common among ADOD. Weiner et al. found a significant association between cognitive test scores and multiple language measures, including language fluency, animal naming and repetition [4–6]. However, building a similar diagnostic tool for MCI presents a challenge due to the limitations involved in data collection. MCI data is difficult to acquire due to limited time resources available for detailed assessment in primary care settings [7], insufficient sensitivity to MCI of screening tools such as the Mini Mental Status Exam [8], and limited access to primary care.

A technique that can be used to address this challenge is *domain adaptation* (also known as "transfer learning"). The situation often arises when one has a limited amount of data related to a problem of interest (the "target domain"), but a large amount of data from a separate but related problem (the "source domain"). Domain adaptation is the task of leveraging ("adapting") data from the source domain so that it can be used in the target domain. More specifically, we wish to use data collected from persons with AD to improve our classification accuracy for persons with MCI.

The main contribution of this work is to demonstrate the efficacy of domain adaptation in using AD data to improve our ability to diagnose MCI. We compare two domain adaptation algorithms, AUGMENT and CORAL, both of which are simple to implement and have been successfully applied on a range of datasets, and show AUGMENT improving upon all baselines. These algorithms are discussed in detail in Sect. 2.3. A secondary contribution of this work is in testing the usefulness of a new set of "discourse" features, as discussed in Sect. 2.2, which have not been used in previous work in the area. We show discourse features surprisingly do not substantially improve the final classification performance.

2 Related Work

2.1 Diagnosing Dementia from Speech

There has been a recent interest in using lexical and acoustic features derived from speech to diagnose ADOD. In 2013 Ahmed et al. [9] determined features that could be used to identify dementia from speech, using data collected in the Oxford Project to Investigate Memory and Ageing (OPTIMA) study. They used a British cohort of 30 participants, 15 with Alzheimers disease at either mild cognitive impairment or mild stages, and 15 whose age and education matched healthy controls. Ahmed et al. found that language progressively deteriorates

[1] http://www.alz.org/greaterdallas/documents/AlzOtherDementias.pdf.

as Alzheimer's disease (AD) progresses and suggested using semantic, lexical content, and syntactic complexity features to identify cases. Rentoumi et al. [10] then used a Naive Bayes Gaussian Classifier with lexical and syntactic features to distinguish between AD with and without additional vascular pathology. They achieved a classification accuracy of 75% on 36 transcripts from the OPTIMA dataset.

In 2014 Fraser et al. [11] compared different feature sets that could be used in discriminating between three different types of primary progressive aphasia, a form of Frontotemporal Dementia, which is a rarer cause of dementia than AD with a distinct disease course. They concluded that a smaller relevant subset of features achieves better classification accuracy than using all features and highlighted the importance of a feature selection step. They also showed how psycholinguistic features, such as frequency and familiarity, were useful in detecting aphasic dementia. In later work Fraser [12] achieved state-of-the-art of 81.92% in distinguishing individuals with AD from those without using logistic regression. Fraser used DementiaBank, an American cohort of 204 persons with dementia and 102 controls, and performed factor analysis on a set of 370 lexical and acoustic features, finding optimal performance when 35–50 features are used [13].

Roark et al. [14] did the largest study to date classifying MCI from speech, using transcripts and audio recordings of patients undergoing the Wechsler Logical Memory I/II test. This test involves a patient twice retelling a short story, once immediately after hearing it and again after a 30 min delay. Roark extracted two broad set of features; "linguistic complexity" features which measure the complexity of a narrative, and "speech duration" features including number of pauses, pause length and pause-to-speech ratio. Using SVM's, they achieved a maximum AUC of 0.74 and concluded that NLP techniques could be used to automatically derive measures to discriminate between healthy and MCI subjects.

Our work differs from the previous work done in this area in a number of ways. Unlike Roark, we are using MCI data collected from DementiaBank, described in Sect. 4.1, where patients undergo a picture description task rather than a narrative retelling task. We are also using a larger feature set proposed by Fraser et al., to which we are adding the "discourse features" described in Sects. 2.2 and 4.2. Most significantly, we are applying two domain adaptation algorithms which aim to use data collected from AD patients to improve the diagnosis of MCI. Our goal is not to improve upon the accuracy of previous work but to demonstrate the viability of domain adaption in this setting.

2.2 Discourse Analysis

One measure of coherence which has been neglected in the aforementioned work comes from *discourse analysis.* In a coherent passage, a reader can clearly discern how one sentence relates to the next. A given sentence may *explain* or *elaborate* upon a previous sentence (as this one is doing), or act as *background* for a future sentence. Such relations can be formed on an intra-sentential level as well, with *elementary discourse units* (EDU's) being clause-like units of text which can be related to one another by *discourse relations*. Discourse parsing is the task of segmenting a piece of text into its EDU's and then forming a *discourse tree* with edges corresponding to discourse relations, as seen in Fig. 1. Features related to the discourse structure of a passage can then be extracted from the discourse tree, as discussed in Sect. 4.2.

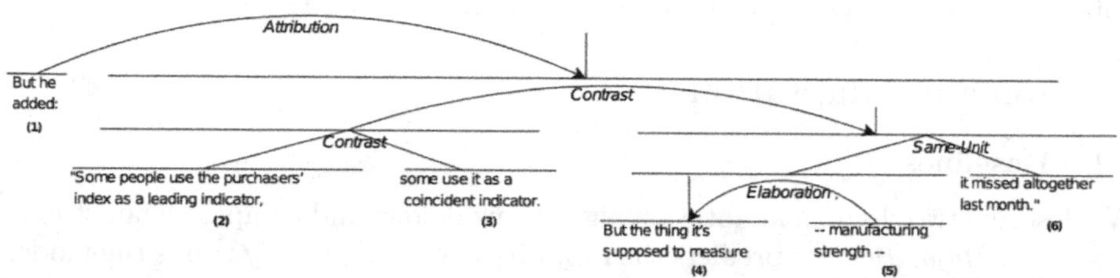

Fig. 1. Discourse tree for two sentences. Each sentence contains three EDUs. EDUs correspond to leaves of the tree and discourse relations correspond to edges. (Figure adapted from [15])

Previous work has shown a disparity in the overall discourse ability of patients with ADOD compared to healthy controls [16–18]. Those with ADOD show a greater impairment in global coherence, have more disruptive topic shift, greater use of empty phrases, and produce fewer cohesive ties than controls. [19–22]. Discourse parsing has been useful in determining overall coherence in other domains such as essay scoring, and so we hypothesize that it will also be useful for MCI detection [23].

2.3 Domain Adaptation

Domain adaptation is a general term for a variety of techniques that aim to exploit resources in one domain (the *source* domain) in order to improve performance on some task in a second domain (the *target* domain). This is typically done when the target domain has little or no labelled data, while the source domain has a relatively large amount of labelled data, as well as existing models trained on that data. Typically the source data have been annotated for some phenomenon of interest, and the target data relate to another phenomenon that is highly similar in nature.

The issue of domain adaptation has received increasing attention in recent years. In work by Chelba and Acero [24], the source model is used to derive priors for the weights of the target model. They employ this technique with a maximum entropy model and apply it to the task of automatic capitalization of uniformly-cased data. They report that adaptation yields a relative improvement of 25–30% in the target domain.

Blitzer et al. [25] introduced Structural Correspondence Learning (SCL), in which relationships between features in the two domains are determined by finding correlations with so-called *pivot* features, which are features exhibiting similar behaviour in both domains. They used SCL to improve the performance of a parser applied to Biomedical data, but trained on Wall Street Journal data.

Daume [26] introduced an approach wherein each feature is copied so that there is a source version, a target version and a general version of the feature. More recently, Sun [27] proposed CORAL, a method which aligns the second-order statistics of the source and target domain. We have implemented these two approaches, and describe them in more detail in Sect. 3.

3 Domain Adaptation

3.1 Baselines

We describe two domain adaptation algorithms below, and compare against four baselines. *Majority class* predicts the majority class, *target only* trains the model only using target data, *source only* trains a model only using source data but evaluates on the target data. In the *relabeled source* model, we pool the target data and source data in the training folds and relabel AD to MCI.

3.2 Frustratingly Simple

Daume III's AUGMENT domain adaptation algorithm is simple ("frustratingly" so) and has been shown to be effective on a wide range of datasets [26]. It augments the feature space by making a "source-only", "target-only", and "common" copy of each feature, as seen below.

$$\underset{(n\times d)}{\begin{bmatrix} X_s \\ X_t \end{bmatrix}} \Rightarrow \underset{(n\times 3d)}{\begin{bmatrix} X_s & 0 & X_s \\ X_t & X_t & 0 \end{bmatrix}} \tag{1}$$

Here $X_s \in \mathbb{R}^{n_s \times d}$ and $X_t \in \mathbb{R}^{n_t \times d}$ are matrices of source and target data, where each of the n rows is an observation, each of the d column is a feature, $n = n_t + n_s$ and $n_t \ll n_s$. We create three copies of each column: a source-only column with zeros in target rows, a target-only column with zeros in source rows, and the original column with both target and source entries left untouched. This augmented dataset is then fed to a standard learning algorithm.

The motivation for this transformation is intuitive. If a column contains a feature (e.g. mean word length) which correlates to a diagnosis in both the target and source data (e.g. MCI and Alzheimer's), a learning algorithm will increase the weight in the common column and reduce the weight on target-only and source-only copies, thereby reducing their importance in the model. However, if a feature correlates to a diagnosis only with MCI data, a learning algorithm can increase the weight of the target-only column (which contains zeros for all the source data) and reduce weight of the original and source-only columns, thereby assuring the feature will be less relevant to the model when applied to Alzheimer's data. By expanding the feature space and padding with zeros, we allow a model to learn whether to apply a given feature on zero, one, or both datasets.

3.3 CORAL

CORAL (CORrelation ALignment) is another recently proposed "frustratingly easy" domain adaptation algorithm which works by aligning the covariances of the source and target features [27]. The algorithm first normalizes the source data to zero mean and unit variance, and then a whitening transform[2] is performed on the source data to remove the correlation between the source features. Finally, the source matrix is "recoloured" with the correlations from the target data. These three steps are shown in Fig. 2. A model is then trained on the recoloured source data and used to classify the target data.

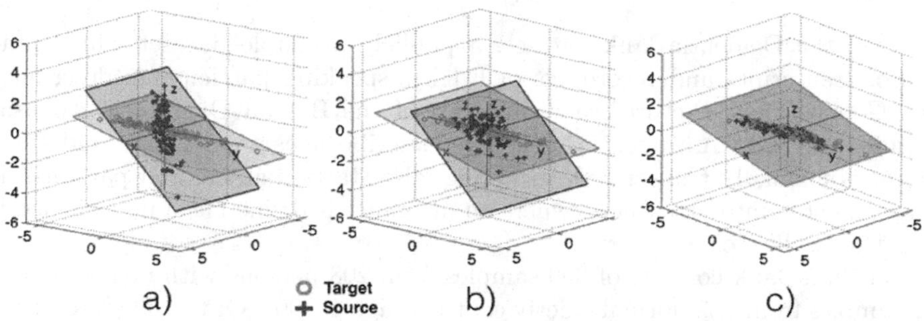

Fig. 2. The CORAL algorithm is shown in three steps. The target and source dataset consist of three features; x, y, z. In (a) The source data and target data are normalized to unit variance and zero mean, but have difference covariances distributions. (b) The source data is whitened to remove the correlations between features. (c) The source data is recolored with the target domain's correlations and the two datasets are aligned. A classifier is then trained on the re-aligned source data. (Figure adapted from [27])

4 Experimental Design

An overview of our experimental design is as follows. We chose logistic regression with l2 regularization as a model, which has been used successfully in previous work on detecting Alzheimer's [12]. We trained the model using a 10-fold cross validation procedure. Within each fold, we first separated 10% of the data to be used as a test set, assuring that if a patient has multiple interviews, those interviews appeared either in the training set or the test set but not both. Then, before training the model, we ran a feature selection step where we selected for inclusion into the model only those features which have highest correlation (positive or negative) with the labels in the training set. We were interested to see how model accuracy varied as a function of k, the number of features fed to the model, so we trained a model for each value of k up to the total number

[2] We used ZCA whitening which is discussed in greater detail here: http://ufldl.stanford.edu/wiki/index.php/Whitening.

of features. This entire procedure was repeated for each of the 10 folds, and we report the highest average F-Measure across all k.

With the AUGMENT, CORAL, and *relabeled* approaches, each fold of the training set contains a combination of MCI+AD data and the test set contains only MCI data. Our goal was to verify whether the accuracy achieved by using these domain adaptation methods outperforms the accuracy achieved by using MCI data alone. A secondary goal was to evaluate the effect of "discourse features" (described below), which have not previously been applied in dementia classification.

4.1 Corpora

We used the DementiaBank dataset, a publicly available dataset which consists of transcripts and recordings of English-speaking participants describing the "Cookie Theft Picture", a component of the Boston Diagnostic Aphasia Examination [28]. A patient is asked to describe a cartoon image and their answer is manually transcribed, including false starts, pauses, and paraphasia, and segmented into utterances, where an utterance is defined as a unit of speech bounded by silence.

DementiaBank consists of 309 samples from 208 persons with dementia and 242 samples from 102 normal elderly controls (age 45–90). Of the 309 interviews with dementia patients, 43 were classified as MCI and 256 as possible/probable AD. The remaining interviews were not used in this study. We split the DementiaBank dataset into target (MCI) and source (AD) data, where the target data contains 86 rows (43 MCI, 41 control) and the source data contains 458 rows (236 probable AD, 21 possible AD, 201 control). Interviews from a single control were contained in either the target or the source datasets, but not both.

4.2 Classification Features

In addition to the age of the patient, which is a known predictor of dementia [29], We used a total of 353 lexical and acoustic features which can be divided into nine groups. The first eight have been used in previous work [12].

- **Parts-of-speech:** We use the Stanford Tagger[3] to capture the frequency of various parts of speech tags (nouns, verbs, adjectives, adverbs, pronouns, determiners, etc.). Frequency counts are normalized by the number of words in the transcript. We also count disfluencies ("um", "er", "ah"), not-in-dictionary words of three or more letters, and word-type ratios (noun to verb, pronoun to noun, etc.).
- **Context-free-grammar rules:** Features which count how often a phrase structure rule occurs in an utterance, including NP→VP PP, NP→DT NP, etc. Parse trees come from the Stanford parser.

[3] Available at: http://nlp.stanford.edu/software/tagger.shtml.

- **Syntactic Complexity:** Features which measure the complexity of an utterance through metrics such as the depth of the parse tree, mean length of word, sentences, T-Units and clauses and clauses per sentence.
- **Vocabulary Richness:** We calculated various metrics which capture the range of vocabulary in a text, include type-token ratio, Brunet's index, Honore's statistic, and the moving-average type-token ratio (MATTR) [30].
- **Psycholinguistic:** Psycholinguistic features are linguistic properties of words that effect word processing and learnability [31]. We used five psycholinguisic features, *Familiarity*, *Concreteness*, *Imagability*, *Age of acquisition* and *SUBTL*, which measures the frequency with which a word is used in daily life [32].
- **Content words:** Croisile et al. [33] compiled a list of 23 items which can be discerned in the Cookie Theft Picture. These "information units" can be either actions or nouns and examples include "jar", "cookie", "boy", "kitchen", "boy taking" and "woman drying". For each information unit we extracted two features; a binary feature indicating whether the subject has mentioned the item (or one of its synonyms in WordNet), and a frequency count of how many times an item has been mentioned.
- **Repetitiveness:** We vectorized the utterances using TF-IDF and measure the cosine similarity between utterances. We then recorded the mean cosine distance, the average cosine distance, and proportion of distances below three thresholds (0, 0.3, 0.5).
- **Acoustic:** We calculated the mean, variance, skewness, and kurtosis of the first 14 mel-frequency cepstral coefficients (MFCCs), representing spectral information from the speech signal.

In addition to the features considered in previous work, we also perform a *discourse analysis* on the transcripts as described in Sect. 2.2.

- **Discourse:** We use CODRA to segment the speech EDU's and identify the relations between them [15]. We count the number of occurrences of each of the 17 discourse relations, the depth of the discourse tree, the average number of EDU's per utterance, the ratio of each discourse relation to the total number of discourse relations, and the discourse relation type-to-token ratio.

5 Results

We use the *F-measure* as our evaluation metric, which is the weighted harmonic mean of precision and recall. The F-measures for all systems are shown in Fig. 3. The main positive result is that domain adaptation does help with the task of detecting MCI. The best overall approach is the AUGMENT adaptation system without discourse features (F-Measure of 0.712, and 90% CI = 0.633–0.791). The confidence intervals with this AUGMENT system are also tighter than the other approaches. Somewhat surprisingly, the source-only method (F-Measure of 0.681, and 90% CI = 0.576–0.786) outperforms target-only (F-Measure of 0.640, and 90% CI = 0.495–0.785), presumably because the source dataset is much larger.

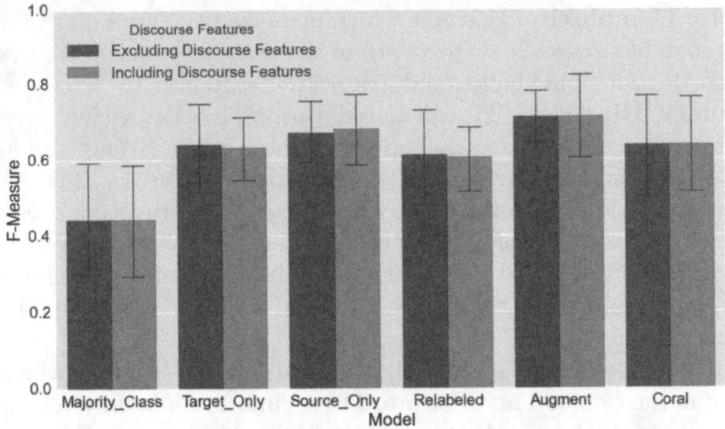

Fig. 3. Comparison of domain adaptation methods. We show the mean F-measure and 90% confidence intervals across a 10-fold CV. Only target data appears in the test fold.

The AUGMENT system also selects a smaller percentage of the total features than the target-only, source-only and relabeled baselines. The effect of discourse features is a mixed result. The best performing baseline model does include the discourse features, but it is a very slight improvement. Furthermore, the AUGMENT, relabeled, and CORAL approaches all perform the same or slightly worse when discourse features are added. We suspect that because the speech elicited by the cookie theft test is both brief and highly specific, there will be few differences in the discourse structure between control and dementia groups. Discourse analysis may be more useful in longer and less structured narratives, where there is an opportunity for a speaker to use a larger set of discourse relations to connect one statement to the next. The main negative result is the performance of the CORAL domain adaptation method (F-Measure of 0.637, and 90% CI = 0.487–0.786), which is nearly identical to the target-only method, i.e. equivalent to not doing domain adaptation at all. It has previously been found that CORAL does not always work well with boolean features such as bag-of-words features [27]. Info-units, which have been shown in previous work to be strong predictors of dementia, are largely boolean [12].

We also include a learning curve analysis showing AUGMENT's F-Measure score as a function of sample size, as seen in Fig. 4. We keep the ratio between target and source data constant and run the analysis using 25%, 50%, 75% and 100% of the data. We ran 15 trials as described[4] in Sect. 4 on random subsets of the data and plot the average and 90% CI across all trials. Figure 4 shows a trend that increasing the size of the dataset improves the F-Measure and tightens the confidence intervals as we approach 100% but then the curve levels off.

[4] With one small modification: We ran a 7-fold cross validation instead of 10-fold because there was not enough target data in the 25% trial to divide into 10 folds.

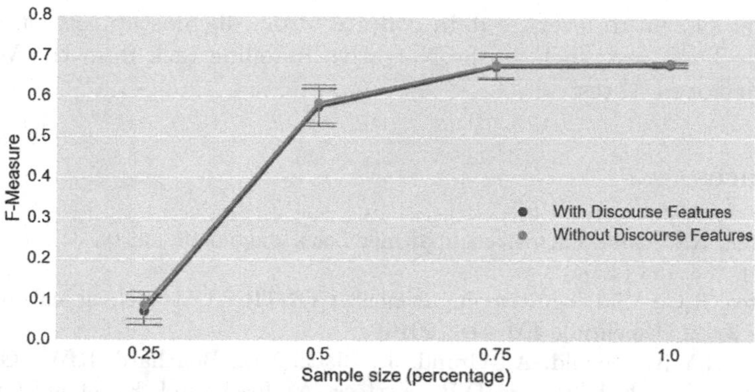

Fig. 4. Learning curve showing F-Measure with AUGMENT as a function of training data size. We keep the ratio of target and source data constant and average over 15 randomized trials.

This suggests we may be nearing the limit of accuracy that can be achieved with a source-to-target ratio of approx 5:1, but we will investigate this more fully in future work.

6 Conclusion

Lack of data is a major obstacle facing researchers who wish to develop a tool to diagnose mild cognitive impairment from speech. In this work we evaluated two domain adaptation algorithms, AUGMENT and CORAL, which attempt to improve classification accuracy by using data collected from patients with Alzheimer's. Our main positive result is that the AUGUMENT domain adaptation algorithm outperformed all baseline algorithms and improved the F-measure by more than 7% over models trained on MCI data alone.

A second objective of this paper was to evaluate the efficacy of discourse features, which had not been used in previous work in this area. We speculated that features extracted from a discourse tree of patient transcripts might capture the loss of coherency which is characteristic of MCI, but unfortunately the discourse features failed to consistently improve the results.

In future work, we will modify CORAL to improve its performance in this setting. One possibility we will investigate is to align only the non-boolean features of the source domain rather than the entire feature space. We will also try merging both AUGMENT and CORAL into a single algorithm by adding a "CORAL aligned" copy of the feature to the AUGMENT feature space. A parallel path of future work involves expanding our system so it can accommodate data from multiple source domains simultaneously. In this way we will be able to use speech samples collected from patients with Vascular Dementia, Dementia with Lewy bodies, and other Non-Alzhiemers dementias. Finally, we wish to expand our system to leverage data collected from diagnostics test other than the Cookie-Theft test, such as the Narrative Retelling task from the Wechsler Logical Memory I/II test.

References

1. Petersen, R.C.: Mild cognitive impairment as a diagnostic entity. J. Intern. Med. **256**(3), 183–194 (2004)
2. Petersen, R.C.: Mild cognitive impairment. CONTINUUM: lifelong learning. Neurology **22**(2, Dementia), 404–418 (2016)
3. Hsiung, G.Y.R., Donald, A., Grand, J., Black, S.E., Bouchard, R.W., Gauthier, S.G., Loy-English, I., Hogan, D.B., Kertesz, A., Rockwood, K., et al.: Outcomes of cognitively impaired not demented at 2 years in the Canadian cohort study of cognitive impairment and related dementias. Dement. Geriatr. Cogn. Disord. **22**(5–6), 413–420 (2006)
4. Faber-Langendoen, K., Morris, J.C., Knesevich, J.W., LaBarge, E., Miller, J.P., Berg, L.: Aphasia in senile dementia of the Alzheimer type. Ann. Neurol. **23**(4), 365–370 (1988)
5. McKeith, I.G., Galasko, D., Kosaka, K., Perry, E., Dickson, D.W., Hansen, L., Salmon, D., Lowe, J., Mirra, S., Byrne, E., et al.: Consensus guidelines for the clinical and pathologic diagnosis of dementia with lewy bodies (DLB) report of the consortium on DLB international workshop. Neurology **47**(5), 1113–1124 (1996)
6. Weiner, M.F., Neubecker, K.E., Bret, M.E., Hynan, L.S.: Language in Alzheimer's disease. J. Clin. Psychiatry **69**(8), 1223 (2008)
7. Boise, L., Neal, M.B., Kaye, J.: Dementia assessment in primary care: results from a study in three managed care systems. J. Gerontol. Ser. A: Biol. Sci. Med. Sci. **59**(6), M621–M626 (2004)
8. Mitchell, A.J.: A meta-analysis then accuracy of the mini-mental state examination in the detection of dementia and mild cognitive impairment. J. Psychiatr. Res. **43**(4), 411–431 (2009)
9. Ahmed, S., Haigh, A.M.F., de Jager, C.A., Garrard, P.: Connected speech as a marker of disease progression in autopsy-proven Alzheimer's disease. Brain **136**(12), 3727–3737 (2013)
10. Rentoumi, V., Raoufian, L., Ahmed, S., de Jager, C.A., Garrard, P.: Features and machine learning classification of connected speech samples from patients with autopsy proven Alzheimer's disease with and without additional vascular pathology. J. Alzheimer's Dis. **42**(s3), S3–S17 (2014)
11. Fraser, K.C., Hirst, G., Graham, N.L., Meltzer, J.A., Black, S.E., Rochon, E.: Comparison of different feature sets for identification of variants in progressive aphasia. In: ACL 2014, 17 (2014)
12. Fraser, K.C., Meltzer, J.A., Rudzicz, F.: Linguistic features identify Alzheimer's disease in narrative speech. J. Alzheimer's Dis. **49**(2), 407–422 (2015)
13. Becker, J.T., Boiler, F., Lopez, O.L., Saxton, J., McGonigle, K.L.: The natural history of Alzeheimae's disease: description of study cohort and accuracy of diagnosis. Arch. Neurol. **51**(6), 585–594 (1994)
14. Roark, B., Mitchell, M., Hosom, J.P., Hollingshead, K., Kaye, J.: Spoken language derived measures for detecting mild cognitive impairment. IEEE Trans. Audio Speech Lang. Process. **19**(7), 2081–2090 (2011)

15. Joty, S., Carenini, G., Ng, R.T.: CODRA: a novel discriminative framework for rhetorical analysis. Comput. Linguist. **41**, 385–415 (2015)
16. Chapman, S.B., Ulatowska, H.K., King, K., Johnson, J.K., McIntire, D.D.: Discourse in early Alzheimer's disease versus normal advanced aging. Am. J. Speech-Lang. Pathol. **4**(4), 124–129 (1995)
17. Blonder, L.X., Kort, E.D., Schmitt, F.A.: Conversational discourse in patients with Alzheimer's disease. J. Linguist. Anthropol. **4**(1), 50–71 (1994)
18. Ellis, D.G.: Coherence patterns in Alzheimer's discourse. Commun. Res. **23**(4), 472–495 (1996)
19. Dijkstra, K., Bourgeois, M.S., Allen, R.S., Burgio, L.D.: Conversational coherence: discourse analysis of older adults with and without dementia. J. Neurolinguist. **17**(4), 263–283 (2004)
20. Ellis, C., Henderson, A., Wright, H.H., Rogalski, Y.: Global coherence during discourse production in adults: a review of the literature. Int. J. Lang. Commun. Disord. **51**, 359–367 (2016)
21. Laine, M., Laakso, M., Vuorinen, E., Rinne, J.: Coherence and informativeness of discourse in two dementia types. J. Neurolinguist. **11**(1), 79–87 (1998)
22. Davis, B.H.: So, you had two sisters, right? Functions for discourse markers in Alzheimer's talk. In: Davis, B.H. (ed.) Alzheimer Talk, Text and Context, pp. 128–145. Springer, Heidelberg (2005)
23. Feng, V.W.: RST-style discourse parsing and its applications in discourse analysis. Ph.D. thesis, University of Toronto (2015)
24. Chelba, C., Acero, A.: Adaptation of maximum entropy capitalizer: little data can help a lot. Comput. Speech Lang. **20**(4), 382–399 (2006)
25. Blitzer, J., McDonald, R., Pereira, F.: Domain adaptation with structural correspondence learning. In: Proceedings of EMNLP 2006, Sydney, Australia, pp. 120–128, July 2006
26. Daume, H.: Frustratingly easy domain adaptation. In: Proceedings of ACL 2007 (2007)
27. Sun, B., Feng, J., Saenko, K.: Return of frustratingly easy domain adaptation. arXiv preprint (2015). arXiv:1511.05547
28. Giles, E., Patterson, K., Hodges, J.R.: Performance on the Boston cookie theft picture description task in patients with early dementia of the Alzheimer's type: missing information. Aphasiology **10**(4), 395–408 (1996)
29. Gao, S., Hendrie, H.C., Hall, K.S., Hui, S.: The relationships between age, sex, and the incidence of dementia and Alzheimer disease: a meta-analysis. Arch. Gen. Psychiatry **55**(9), 809–815 (1998)
30. Covington, M.A., McFall, J.D.: Cutting the gordian knot: the moving-average type-token ratio (MATTR). J. Quant. Linguist. **17**(2), 94–100 (2010)
31. Salsbury, T., Crossley, S.A., McNamara, D.S.: Psycholinguistic word information in second language oral discourse. Second Lang. Res. **27**(3), 343–360 (2011)
32. Brysbaert, M., New, B.: Moving beyond Kučera and Francis: a critical evaluation of current word frequency norms and the introduction of a new and improved word frequency measure for American English. Behav. Res. Methods **41**, 977–990 (2009)
33. Croisile, B., Ska, B., Brabant, M.J., Duchene, A., Lepage, Y., Aimard, G., Trillet, M.: Comparative study of oral and written picture description in patients with Alzheimer's disease. Brain Lang. **53**(1), 1–19 (1996)

Speech Intention Classification with Multimodal Deep Learning

Yue Gu[✉], Xinyu Li, Shuhong Chen, Jianyu Zhang, and Ivan Marsic

Department of Electrical and Computer Engineering,
Rutgers University, New Brunswick, NJ, USA
{yue.guapp, Xinyu.li1118, sc1624, jz549, marsic}@rutgers.edu

Abstract. We present a novel multimodal deep learning structure that automatically extracts features from textual-acoustic data for sentence-level speech classification. Textual and acoustic features were first extracted using two independent convolutional neural network structures, then combined into a joint representation, and finally fed into a decision softmax layer. We tested the proposed model in an actual medical setting, using speech recording and its transcribed log. Our model achieved 83.10% average accuracy in detecting 6 different intentions. We also found that our model using automatically extracted features for intention classification outperformed existing models that use manufactured features.

Keywords: Multimodal intention classification · Textual-acoustic feature representation · Convolutional neural network · Trauma resuscitation

1 Introduction

Human-computer interaction (HCI) is becoming more prevalent in daily living, appearing in applications ranging from navigation systems to intelligent voice assistants. There has been significant research focused on understanding speech, an essential vehicle for human communication. However, machines have faced difficulty extracting the intention of human speech, in part because words may carry different meanings in different contexts. For example, "it is snowing" could either be a comment, reply, or question depending on the inflection and punctuation. To understand the actual meaning and detect the speaker's intention, machines must be able to make these distinctions.

The definition of *speech intention* in this paper is different from the general action-based intention recognition [1]. The goal in this paper is to identify the actual purpose of a speaker's verbal communication in the trauma scenario (e.g. "Directive" for commands/instructions to the medical team or patient). Trauma-related language contains rich information regarding medical operations, cooperation, and team performance that can be used for the detection of medical processes and operation workflows. To identify the actual status of a surgical activity (e.g. the activity is started or finished), it is essential to precisely estimate the intention from human speech. Hence, this intention classifier may be used in a larger system for recognizing clinical activities or verbal procedures.

M. Mouhoub and P. Langlais (Eds.): Canadian AI 2017, LNAI 10233, pp. 260–271, 2017.
DOI: 10.1007/978-3-319-57351-9_30

One approach to estimating speech intention, used by many current systems such as Microsoft LUIS, is to analyze only the sentence syntax. However, this approach ignores valuable acoustic information such as pitch contour, stress pattern, and rhythm. In many applications, such as the emergency medical field, speech tends to be short and unstructured, with its meaning hidden in the vocal delivery. For example, the utterance "pain in belly" may either be a report to another care provider or a question to the patient, which is impossible to tell given the text alone. Without much syntactical structure, an intention classifier cannot afford to disregard the speech's acoustic features.

To address these intention detection challenges, we propose a multimodal deep learning structure for sentence-level intention classification using both text and audio data. The model uses manually transcribed speech text and its synchronized speech audio as input. We first preprocess the text data with word embedding [2] and extract mel-frequency spectral coefficients (MFSC) [3] from the audio. These inputs are fed to two independent convolutional neural networks (ConvNets) for feature extraction [3, 4]. The extracted features are then fused and used for the intention classification decision.

To demonstrate the model, we collected text and audio data from an actual trauma room during 35 trauma resuscitations, which are full of short, stressed sentences. The dataset contains 6424 transcribed sentences with their corresponding audio clips. The 6 intentions we used were: Directive, Report, Question, Clarification, Acknowledgement, and Response/Reply. With an 80-20 training-testing split, the model achieved 83.10% average accuracy, outperforming the text-only and audio-only models, and other similar models from other research. Our experiments also showed that ConvNets provide better-performing features than manufactured features such as fundamental frequency, pitch/energy related features, zero crossing rate (ZCR), jitter, shimmer, and mel-frequency cepstral coefficients (MFCC).

The contributions of our work are:

- A deep learning multimodal structure capable of automatically learning and using textual and acoustic features for intention classification.
- Detailed analysis and comparison of different modality and features that is commonly used for similar topic.
- A case study with actual medical application scenario, which indicated both the efficiency and drawbacks of the proposed system, this can be used as our future implementation reference as well as other similar applications.

The paper is organized as follows: Sect. 2 introduces related work, Sect. 3 describes our dataset, Sect. 4 details the model architecture, Sect. 5 presents the experimental results, Sect. 6 discusses model limitations, potential extensions, and concludes the paper.

2 Related Work

Previous research defined "intent" as understanding spoken language by converting sentences into representations of meaning [5]. Recently proposed methods in this field have used semantic analysis [6] and language understanding [7]. However, these methods only considered textual features, and ignored the acoustic information.

Because the same words may carry different intentions depending on the manner of speech, these acoustic features are critical to understanding the underlying meaning. Several different approaches were introduced using various features to help identify the meaning of human speech. Sentiment analysis tried to distinguish positive and negative attitudes [8]. This approach showed strong performance on document-level sentiment classification, but its binary (positive or negative sentiment) categories made it unhelpful in speech understanding. As an improvement, acoustic-based speech emotion recognition (SER) has been proposed [9, 10]. Different emotions reflect the speaker's attitude, but are too abstract for many scenarios and unhelpful to intention recognition. Therefore, we borrowed strategies from sentiment analysis and emotion recognition, and identified the intentions in our problem domain.

To combine the various feature types for understanding the underlying meaning, multimodal structures were introduced in related research fields. Early research demonstrated that the joint use of audio and text features achieved better performance in speech emotion recognition [11]. 2100 sentences with text and audio were collected from broadcast dramas. 33 original acoustic features and some specific emotional words were manually defined for predicting 7 emotions. However, the manufactured acoustic features and the specific keywords impeded their generalizability. A multimodal structure consisting of audio, visual, and textual modules was introduced to identify emotions [12]; manufactured features were selected from each module and the system was evaluated on three different emotion datasets (Youtube dataset, SenticNet, and EmoSenticNet). The results showed that using the visual features improved performance, but the system was still based on manually selected features. Recently, more complex multimodal systems using ConvNet-based visual and textual features were shown to outperform manufactured ones in emotion recognition [13, 14]. A ConvNet structure was used as a trainable textual feature extractor [13, 14], and another ConvNet structure extracted the visual features [14]. These systems were tested on the Multimodal emotion recognition dataset (USC IEMOCAP), multimodal opinion utterances dataset (MOUD), and Youtube dataset. Both systems demonstrated the power of ConvNet feature extraction. However, they still partially relied on manufactured acoustic features reduced by principal component analysis. The previous work also indicated that their system, although multimodal, relied heavily on text input [14]. We assume that the problem arose because they used manufactured acoustic features instead of automatic ones extracted by a ConvNet. To overcome this shortcoming, our proposed model uses ConvNet feature extractors for both the text and audio. Considering the limitations in the trauma scenario, it is not possible for us to capture the visual information from the human faces, so our multimodal system uses only text and audio. To demonstrate its robustness, we also tested it with inaccurately transcribed text input from a speech recognition engine.

3 Dataset

3.1 Data Collection

Our dataset was collected during 30 resuscitations at a level-1 trauma center in the north-eastern US. In medical settings, data collection devices must preserve privacy and not interfere with medical tasks. Therefore, instead of using wearable Bluetooth microphones, we used a hands-free SONY ICD PX333 Digital Voice Recorder. It was placed on the Mayo equipment stand roughly 2.5 feet away from the trauma team leadership group of three clinicians, who mostly remained stationary during the resuscitation. We recorded on a mono channel with 16000 Hz sampling rate.

3.2 Transcribing and Labeling the Raw Data

We manually segmented the recorded audio data into sentence-level clips. To keep the audio quality, clips with overlapping speech or strong background noise (e.g. patient crying, electronic equipment noise) were removed. The final dataset contained 6424 audio clips. Each audio clip was then manually transcribed (unpunctuated) and labeled with an intention (Table 1). The "intention" represents the speaker's original purpose of saying the utterance. Six different intentions were defined based our dataset. For example, "Q" represents the speaker intends to inquire for information, "DIR" means the speaker plans to give an instruction or command to someone, "RS" indicates the speaker is responding to an inquiry. Table 2 shows example sentences with their intentions.

Table 1. Speech intention classes in the trauma resuscitation

Class	Intentions	Frequency
DIR	Directives (task assignment/instruction/command)	1172
RS	Response to an inquiry or request for information	934
Q	Inquiry/request for information	1256
RP	Report (report on patient status or results of an activity)	1045
CL	Clarification (request for retransmission of information)	1044
ACK	Acknowledgement	973

Table 2. Examples of speech intention from trauma resuscitation

Class	Sentence
DIR	Get her fluids going
RS	I don't know she's got three IVs on left side
Q	What's the IV access
RP	Bilateral TMs are clear
CL	You mean on the left
ACK	Yes alright I will

4 The System Structure

Our system structure is composed of four modules (Fig. 1). The data preprocessor formats the input text and audio into word vectors and Mel-frequency spectral coefficients (MFSC) maps for feature extraction. The feature extractor uses two ConvNets to learn and extract textual and acoustic features independently. The feature fusion layer balances and merges the extracted features through a fully-connected (FC) structure.

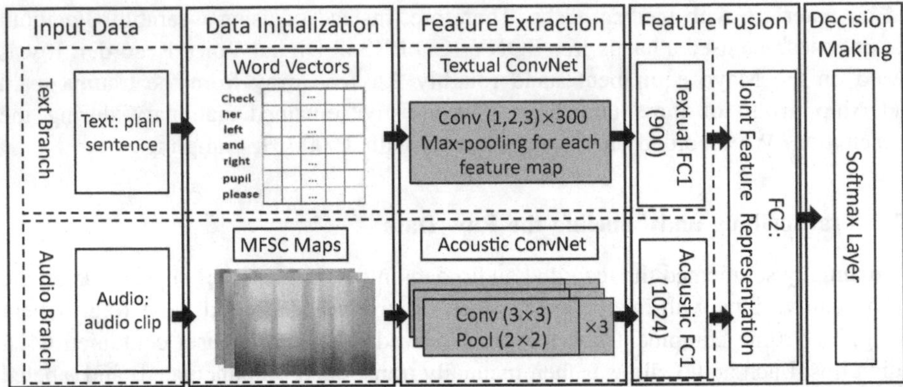

Fig. 1. The structure of our intention recognition model. FC = fully connected. The numbers in parentheses represent the number of neurons in each network layer.

The decision maker uses softmax (multinomial regression) to perform the multiclass classification.

4.1 Data Preprocessor

To generate the input layer for feature extraction, we used different initialization strategies for text input and audio input. We preprocessed the text into word vectors [2, 15, 16] and the audio into MFSC maps [3]. Word vectors are low-dimensional mappings describing semantic relationships between words [2]. A sentence is then a matrix with the word vector sequence as its rows [2]. Two different strategies exist for the initialization of the word vectors [2, 16]. We selected Mikolov's method [2] for its good performance on the semantic and syntactic learning for words. The word2vec embedding dictionary, trained on 100 million words from Google news [2], is the most commonly used word embedding tool. Since our sentences have varying lengths (between 1 and 26 words), we zero-padded all sentences to the longest length as suggested by others [4]. Each word was embedded into a 300-dimensional word vector using the word2vec dictionary, and unknown words were initialized randomly. Sentences were, therefore, 26×300 matrices (sentence length by word-vector length).

In human speech, different energy intensities and the variance of energy in different frequencies may reflect speaking manners. We represented the audio with time-frequency energy maps. Instead of the Mel-frequency cepstral coefficients (MFCCs) commonly used in speech recognition, we used Mel-frequency spectral coefficients (MFSC) to avoid the locality-compromising discrete cosine transform (DCR) [3]. We extracted the static, delta, and double delta MFSC for each audio for use as individual input channels. We empirically divided the 0–8000 Hz into 64 frequency bands. Each input frame contained 1 s of data (sampled at 40 ms with 50% overlap, following previous work [3, 17]), generating $64 \times n$ MFSC maps for an n-second clip. All MFSC maps were rescaled to 64×256 with bicubic interpolation. The initialized word vectors and MSFC maps were used as the input layers for the text branch and audio branch, respectively. As mentioned, the dimensions of the inputs data were 26×300 for the text branch and $64 \times 256 \times 3$ for the audio branch.

4.2 Feature Extractor

We used two ConvNets for feature extraction. One-dimensional filters were implemented for textual feature extraction (Fig. 2), following prior work [4]. As suggested in [4, 15], we applied multiple convolutional filters with different widths (1, 2, and 3) to capture phrases of varying length (Fig. 2). We chose these rather short filter widths because in our problem domain (trauma resuscitation) most of the speech is not in the form of full and grammatically correct sentences, but is instead in the form of short phrases. We empirically found that one convolutional and one max-pooling layer is sufficient for our application, similar to [4]. From each of the three filter sizes, 300 feature maps were then max-pooled, producing a 900-dimensional textual feature vector (comparable in size to the 1024-dimensional acoustic feature vector).

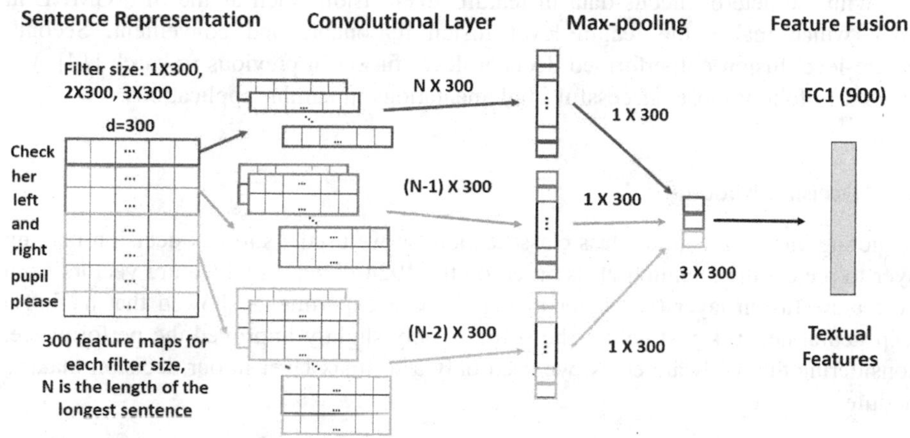

Fig. 2. Textual feature extraction ConvNet (CNN_T)

An eight-layer ConvNet structure was implemented to extract acoustic features from MFSC maps (Fig. 3). As suggested for VGG Nets [3, 17], we used 3 × 3 convolutional and 2 × 2 max-pooling filters with zero padding and chose 3 × 3× 32, 3 × 3 × 64, 3 × 3 × 128, and 3 × 3 × 128 as the kernel sizes and the number of

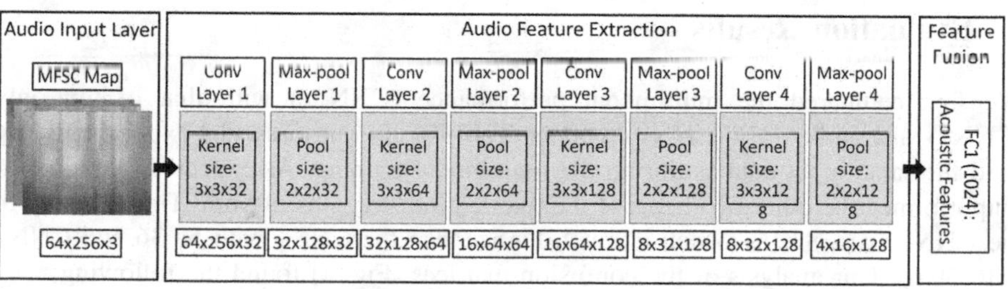

Fig. 3. Acoustic feature extraction ConvNet (CNN_A)

feature maps are determined empirically. Although deeper networks tend to perform better, we stopped at eight layers due to the hardware constraints.

4.3 Feature Fusion Layer

Two independent fully-connected layers concatenate the features from CNN_T and CNN_A (Fig. 1). To balance the two modalities, they were represented with 900 and 1024-dimensional vectors respectively. A fully-connected (FC) layer fuses the text and audio features into a joint feature representation ready for the final decision (Fig. 1). There are two main reasons for us to select feature-level fusion instead of decision-level fusion. First, because we used ConvNet structure to extract both the acoustic features and textual features, we do not need to apply the implementation method designed to deal with the heterogeneous data in feature-level fusion (such as the SPF-GMKL in [14]), which makes the feature-level fusion reasonable and convenient. Second, feature-level fusion outperformed decision-level fusion in previous research [14]. We decided to follow those successful implementations in similar applications.

4.4 Decision Making

Predicting intention is multiclass classification, so we used a softmax decision-making layer to predict the intention class based on the 1924-dimensional feature vectors from the feature fusion layer (last layer in Fig. 1). Our experiments showed that having a deep neural network just before the softmax only slightly improved the performance. Considering the hardware costs, we used only a softmax layer in our decision-making module.

4.5 Implementation

We used Keras, a high-level TensorFlow-based neural network library [18], for model training and testing. As suggested previously [3, 17], we used the rectified linear unit activation function for all convolutional layers. We initialized the learning rate at 0.01 and used Adam optimizer to minimize the loss value [17]. Dropout function and 5-cross validation was applied during training to avoid overfitting.

5 Evaluation Results

We first compared the multimodal performance (CNN_{TA}) with that of text-only (CNN_T), and audio-only (CNN_A) models (Table 3). In our unimodal experiments, we used the same input data as during the multimodal training. As expected, the CNN_{TA} outperformed the other two because it exploited the strengths of both. The accuracy of the CNN_{TA} was 83.1% which is much higher than the CNN_T with 57.36 and CNN_A with 59.64. Our analysis of the confusion matrices (Fig. 4) found the following:

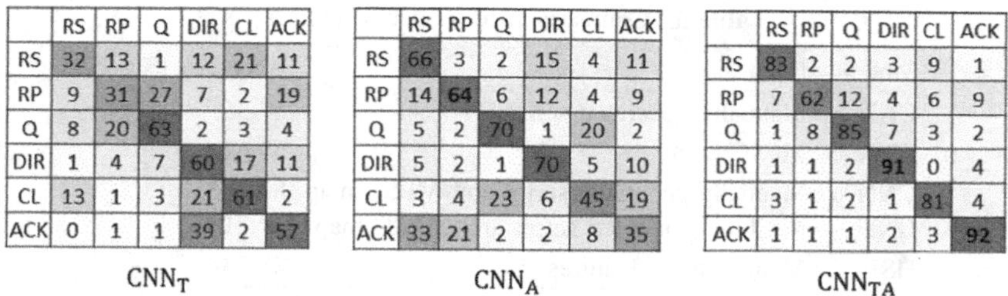

Fig. 4. The confusion matrix for different model structure (number is in percentage).

- The CNN$_T$ differentiated well between classes with distinct contents (e.g. Q, CL). Both Q and CL have interrogative phrases such as "what is," "how about," and "do you" that appear very infrequently in the remaining classes.
- The CNN$_A$ distinguished well between classes with different speaking manners (e.g. Q, DIR, RS, RP). Using the acoustic features improved the accuracy rate of Q and DIR. This was expected, as their acoustic features are different despite similar phrases and vocabulary. The performance for RS and RP was also strong, despite the text-level content variation, due to their relatively fixed speaking manners.
- The CNN$_{TA}$ significantly outperformed the unimodal models, indicating that text or audio alone is insufficient for intention classification. Both datatypes compensate the weaknesses of each other, making their joint feature representation more useful for understanding the underlying meaning and intentions in speech.
- The accuracy on RP was comparatively low. This might have been because RP sentences vary widely in content, and are acoustically similar to other classes. After further analysis of the data, we found that the speakers often increased the pitch at the end of each sub-report during a summary report at the end of each process phase, in order to emphasize certain point. This made RP sound like a Q or CL. When ground truth coding for RPs, humans usually exploit contextual information (i.e. nearby sentences), indicating that context may improve intention classification.

Considering the infeasibility of manual transcription in speech applications, we also tested the CNN$_{TA}$ model with text generated from automatic speech recognition (CNN$_{SA}$). Specifically, we used the text generated by the *Microsoft Bing Speech API* along with the original audio clip as the input to our system. The Bing API could not achieve human accuracy for our medical dataset due to the noise, and had a 26.3% word error rate. However, our results showed that despite the transcription inaccuracies, CNN$_{SA}$ predictions were only 6% less accurate than those of CNN$_{TA}$ (Table 3). This indicates that word-level accurate text is not as essential to intention classification as loose sentence structure and keywords, which is a significant finding. Using text-only model to detect activity or motion of trauma team members is very hard because high ambient noise made speech recognition difficult. Our experiment showed that including the acoustic features improved the accuracy of the intention recognition and the multimodal system is not very sensitive to the textual features. Hence, our model could be used for capturing speech intention in noisy environments such as trauma room.

Table 3. Comparison of model accuracies

Model	Input data	Accuracy (%)
CNN_T	Manually generated script	57.36
CNN_A	MFSC map	59.64
CNN_{TA}	Manually generated script and MFSC map	**83.1**
CNN_{SA}	Machine generated script and MFSC map	77.21
HSF	Manufactured features	48.73

We also compared the accuracies of individual or combined modalities using ConvNet-learned versus manufactured features. A model with human-selected feature extraction (HSF) using the same data split and softmax configuration was trained on several widely used manufactured features including fundamental frequency [19], pitch related features [20], energy related features [21], zero crossing rate (ZCR) [21, 22], jitter [21], shimmer [21], and Mel-frequency cepstral coefficients (MFCC) [22–24]. As suggested in [19, 20], we applied the statistical functions including Maximum, Minimum, Range, Mean, Slope, Offset, Stddev, Skewness, Kurtosis, Variance, and Median for these features. We normalized all the manufactured acoustic features using z-score normalization [22] and fed them into a softmax layer. The results showed that the features extracted by our multimodal structure's led to significantly better performance than the manufactured features (Table 3). In fact, even CNN_A alone outperformed HSF, further demonstrating the effectiveness of ConvNet-based feature selection. Although one could fine-tune the manually-selected features [21, 22], doing so would be highly laborious compared to automated ConvNet learning.

Finally, we compared our work with some similar research [12–14] (Table 4). We compared our model with several similar models in different application scenarios. This comparison showed that our model is competitive with some [13, 14], and outperformed others [12]. The previous model achieving the best performance [14] had a much simpler application than ours: it only classified 447 instances into two categories (positive/negative sentiment). Although MKL [13] achieved 96.55% accuracy in binary sentiment analysis (positive or negative), it relied heavily on visual features. Its accuracy dropped to a comparable 84.12% given only text and audio. In addition, their

Table 4. Comparison of our intention recognition model to similar research

Model	Input data	Classes	Accuracy (%)
Multimodal sentiment [12]	Manually selected video, audio, text features	3 classes	78.2
Convolutional MKL [13]	Text, manually selected acoustic features, video	2 classes 4 classes	84.12 76.85
Deep CNN [14]	Text, manually selected acoustic features, video	2 classes	88.6
CNN_{TA} CNN_{SA}	Manually generated script, MFSC map Machine generated script, MFSC map	6 classes	83.1 77.21

binary classification problem is much simpler than our six-class classification application. In fact, our six-class system even outperforms MLK's four-class emotion detection implementation.

6 Discussion and Conclusion

Although applicable and competitive, our proposed model can be improved in two aspects. Using wearable microphones would improve audio quality, which would increase the automatic speech recognition accuracy and lead to better predictions in the automated transcription. Using an LSTM to learn contextual features would also better discover features in text data [16, 25].

There are also inherent limitations to our current model. Our model performed well in scenarios such as trauma resuscitation, where there are few unessential words in relatively short sentences. However, it is difficult to detect the intention from fully-formed sentences, since the speaker may use multiple speaking manners in one sentence. This shortcoming may be solved with contextual intention recognition, which will be part of our future research. Lack of speaker-independency is another limitation. Even though there were work shifts in trauma room, our dataset only had voices from a limited set of persons and we did not consider speaker independency during training the model. Evaluating the model performance on the unknown voices should be further researched. Another limitation is the necessary removal of overlapping speech, which occurs very frequently. Around 28% of trauma speech has heavy overlapping speech. Then, to further improve speech intention recognition in the trauma environment, we must also consider solutions to the cocktail party problem.

To conclude, we restate this paper's contributions to the field:

- A framework that learns textual and acoustic features for intention classification.
- A comparison and analysis of our system performance on intention classification using multimodal, unimodal, and human-selected features.
- A system application in an actual medical setting that can be used as a reference for future study.

Acknowledgment. The authors would like to thank the trauma experts of the Children's National Medical Center, United State involved in this work. We also would like to thank three anonymous reviewers for their valuable comments and suggestions.

References

1. De Ruiter, J.P., Cummins, C.: A model of intentional communication: AIRBUS (asymmetric intention recognition with Bayesian updating of signals). In: Proceedings of SemDial 2012, pp. 149–150 (2012)
2. Mikolov, T., Sutskever, I., Chen, K., Corrado, G.S., Dean, J.: Distributed representations of words and phrases and their compositionality. In: Advances in Neural Information Processing Systems, pp. 3111–3119 (2013)

3. Abdel-Hamid, O., Mohamed, A.-R., Jiang, H., Deng, L., Penn, G., Yu, D.: Convolutional neural networks for speech recognition. IEEE/ACM Trans. Audio Speech Lang. Process. **22**, 1533–1545 (2014)
4. Kim, Y.: Convolutional neural networks for sentence classification. In: Proceedings of 2014 Conference on Empirical Methods in Natural Language Processing (EMNLP) (2014)
5. Wang, Y.-Y., Deng, L., Acero, A.: Spoken language understanding. IEEE Sig. Process. Mag. **22**, 16–31 (2005)
6. Tur, G., Mori, R.D.: Introduction. In: Spoken Language Understanding. pp. 1–7 (2011)
7. Williams, J.D., Kamal, E., Ashour, M., Amr, H., Miller, J., Zweig, G.: Fast and easy language understanding for dialog systems with Microsoft language understanding intelligent service (LUIS). In: Proceedings of 16th Annual Meeting of the Special Interest Group on Discourse and Dialogue (2015)
8. Pang, B., Lee, L.: Opinion mining and sentiment analysis. Found. Trends® Inf. Retr. **2**, 1–135 (2008)
9. Ayadi, M.E., Kamel, M.S., Karray, F.: Survey on speech emotion recognition: features, classification schemes, and databases. Pattern Recogn. **44**, 572–587 (2011)
10. Minker, W., Pittermann, J., Pittermann, A., Strauß, P.-M., Bühler, D.: Challenges in speech-based human–computer interfaces. Int. J. Speech Technol. **10**, 109–119 (2007)
11. Chuang, Z.J., Wu, C.H.: Multi-modal emotion recognition from speech and text. Comput. Linguist. Chin. Lang. Process. **9**(2), 45–62 (2004)
12. Poria, S., Cambria, E., Howard, N., Huang, G.-B., Hussain, A.: Fusing audio, visual and textual clues for sentiment analysis from multimodal content. Neurocomputing **174**, 50–59 (2016)
13. Poria, S., Iti, C., Erik, C., Amir, H.: Convolutional MKL based multimodal emotion recognition and sentiment analysis. In: ICDM (2016)
14. Poria, S., Cambria, E., Gelbukh, A.: Deep convolutional neural network textual features and multiple kernel learning for utterance-level multimodal sentiment analysis. In: Proceedings of 2015 Conference on Empirical Methods in Natural Language Processing (2015)
15. Tang, D., Qin, B., Liu, T.: Document modeling with gated recurrent neural network for sentiment classification. In: Proceedings of 2015 Conference on Empirical Methods in Natural Language Processing (2015)
16. Socher, R., Perelygin, A., Wu, J.Y., Chuang, J., Manning, C.D., Ng, A.Y., Potts, C.: Recursive deep models for semantic compositionality over a sentiment TreeBank. In: Proceedings of Conference on Empirical Methods in Natural Language Processing (EMNLP). vol. 1631, p. 1642 (2013)
17. Li, X., Zhang, Y., Li, M., Chen, S., Austin, F.R., Marsic, I., Burd, R.S.: Online process phase detection using multimodal deep learning. In: 2016 IEEE 7th Annual Ubiquitous Computing, Electronics and Mobile Communication Conference (UEMCON) (2016)
18. Abadi, M., Agarwal, A., Barham, P., Brevdo, E., Chen, Z., Citro, C., Corrado G.S.: Tensorflow: large-scale machine learning on heterogeneous distributed systems (2016). arXiv preprint arXiv:1603.04467
19. Busso, C., Lee, S., Narayanan, S.: Analysis of emotionally salient aspects of fundamental frequency for emotion detection. IEEE Trans. Audio Speech Lang. Process. **17**, 582–596 (2009)
20. Cowie, R., Douglas-Cowie, E., Tsapatsoulis, N., Votsis, G., Kollias, S., Fellenz, W., Taylor, J.: Emotion recognition in human-computer interaction. IEEE Sig. Process. Mag. **18**, 32–80 (2001)
21. Kotti, M., Paternò, F.: Speaker-independent emotion recognition exploiting a psychologically-inspired binary cascade classification schema. Int. J. Speech Technol. **15**, 131–150 (2012)

22. Wang, K., An, N., Li, B.N., Zhang, Y., Li, L.: Speech emotion recognition using Fourier parameters. IEEE Trans. Affect. Comput. **6**(1), 69–75 (2015)
23. Davis, S., Mermelstein, P.: Comparison of parametric representations for monosyllabic word recognition in continuously spoken sentences. IEEE Trans. Acoust. Speech Sig. Process. **28**, 357–366 (1980)
24. Kamaruddin, N., Wahab, A., Quek, C.: Cultural dependency analysis for understanding speech emotion. Expert Syst. Appl. **39**, 5115–5133 (2012)
25. Tai, K.S., Socher, R., Manning, C.D.: Improved semantic representations from tree-structured long short-term memory networks. In: Proceedings of 53rd Annual Meeting of the Association for Computational Linguistics and 7th International Joint Conference on Natural Language Processing, vol. 1: Long Papers (2015)

Layerwise Interweaving Convolutional LSTM

Tiehang Duan(✉) and Sargur N. Srihari

Department of Computer Science and Engineering,
The State University of New York at Buffalo, Buffalo, NY 14260, USA
tiehangd@buffalo.edu, srihari@cedar.buffalo.edu

Abstract. A deep network structure is formed with LSTM layer and convolutional layer interweaves with each other. The Layerwise Interweaving Convolutional LSTM (LIC-LSTM) enhanced the feature extraction ability of LSTM stack and is capable for versatile sequential data modeling. Its unique network structure allows it to extract higher level features with sequential information involved. Experiment results show the model achieves higher accuracy and shoulders lower perplexity on sequential data modeling tasks compared with state of art LSTM models.

1 Introduction

LSTM is a specific Recurrent Neural Network (RNN) which uses explicit gates to control the magnitude of input, cell state and hidden state at each time step and it has the unique property of maintaining long term dependencies in the memory cell [6]. It is playing an important role in sequential learning and has been applied to multiple fields of natural language processing including sentiment analysis [8], semantic analysis [7] and neural machine translation [1,5] etc. The feature extraction of LSTM can be enhanced with windowed convolution operation, which is used widely in computer vision and image processing [4]. Researchers have contributed innovative and pioneering work for possible combinations of LSTM and CNN. Y. Kim et al. built the CNN-LSTM character level model for NLP problems [3]; S. Vosoughi et al. combined CNN and LSTM model to encode tweets into vectors for semantic and sentiment analysis [7]; and J. Donahue et al. used similar structure for visual recognition and description [2].

Previous works adopt the network structure with convolutional layer(or several convolutional layers) at the bottom and LSTM layers on the top, and feature extraction process is completed before it is fed into the LSTM stack. In this paper, we introduced dense convolutional layer between all adjacent LSTM layers in the network and forms the Layerwise Interweaving Convolutional LSTM (LIC-LSTM).

2 Network Structure and Mechanism

The network structure is shown in Fig. 1. In the net, Convolution layer and LSTM layer interweaves with each other. The features extracted in the filters

M. Mouhoub and P. Langlais (Eds.): Canadian AI 2017, LNAI 10233, pp. 272–277, 2017.
DOI: 10.1007/978-3-319-57351-9_31

are combined and fed into the next LSTM layer, and the encoded output from the LSTM layer is convoluted to extract higher level features containing sequential information. The evolving of feature from low level to higher level is more homogeneous. While max pooling or mean pooling is often applied in CNN to reduce feature dimensionality, no pooling is introduced in our network based on two considerations: (1) pooling disrupts the sequential order [10], (2) LSTM is capable to deal with long term sequences and shrinking of time steps is not necessary.

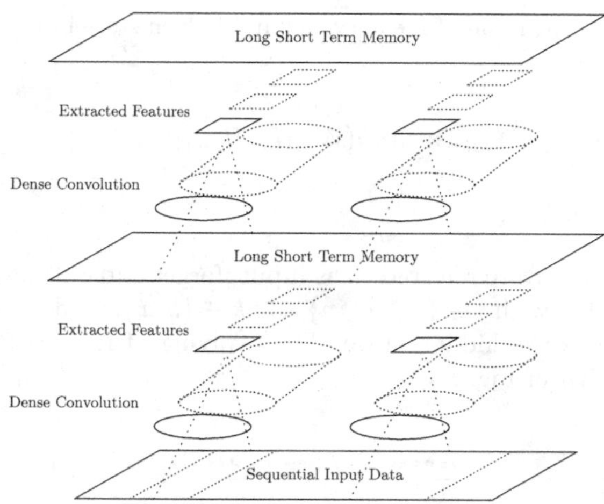

Fig. 1. Structure of Layerwise Interweaving Convolutional LSTM (LIC-LSTM)

Valid convolution is used for each convolutional layer in the forward pass. Meaning of labels is summarized in Table 1.

The extracted feature after the convolutional layer is

$$f_i^n = \sum_{j=1}^{C} \left(\sum_{k=1}^{D} W[f]_{jk}^n \times I_{(i+C-j)(D+1-k)} \right) \tag{1}$$

where n is the n th filter and i denotes the i th time step.

The extracted features from N different filters are combined together to form the new input to LSTM layer, in which the following transformations are performed

$$i_{gate} = sigmoid(W_{ih}H_{s-1} + W_{ix}I_s + b_i) \tag{2}$$

$$o_{gate} = sigmoid(W_{oh}H_{s-1} + W_{ox}I_s + b_o) \tag{3}$$

$$f_{gate} = sigmoid(W_{fh}H_{s-1} + W_{fx}I_s + b_f) \tag{4}$$

Table 1. Summary of label meaning

Label	Meaning
D	Character representation dimension
L	Number of time steps
I	Input data
W[f]	Filter weight
C	Convolution layer window size
N	Number of filters
CS	Dimension of memory cell and hidden state in LSTM

$$C_s = f_{gate} \times C_{s-1} + i_{gate} \times tanh(W_{in}[I_s; H_{s-1}]) \tag{5}$$

$$H_s = o_{gate} \times tanh(C_s) \tag{6}$$

where i_{gate}, f_{gate}, o_{gate} are referred to as input, forget and output gates. Weights of the LSTM are W_{jk} with $j \in \{i, f, o, in\}$ and $k \in \{h, x\}$. C_s denotes the memory cell and H_s denotes the hidden state. The evolving of feature for one layer of LIC-LSTM is shown in Fig. 2.

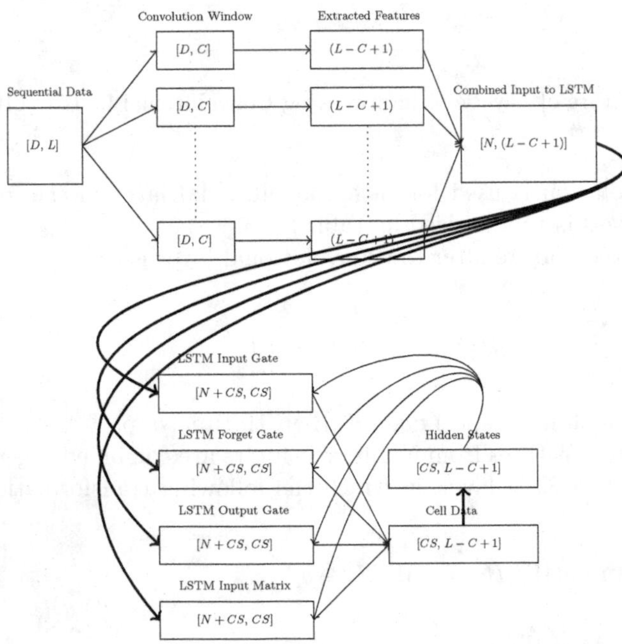

Fig. 2. Workflow in one layer of LIC-LSTM, dimension of feature and data is illustrated in the brackets.

3 Network Training and Performance

We reveal the detailed training process of the network with character prediction task. For the majority of related works, the training of CNN stack and LSTM stack are processed separately. This approach, while easy to implement and fine tune, can not guarantee overall optimization for the whole combined network. In LIC-LSTM, the convolutional layers and LSTM layers interweave with each other, and in the forward backward training phase, the gradients are propagated through the whole network simultaneously and concurrently. Such approach is designed to achieve overall optimization in the whole network and better performance. The drawback is requisite for more elegant implementation and careful fine tuning.

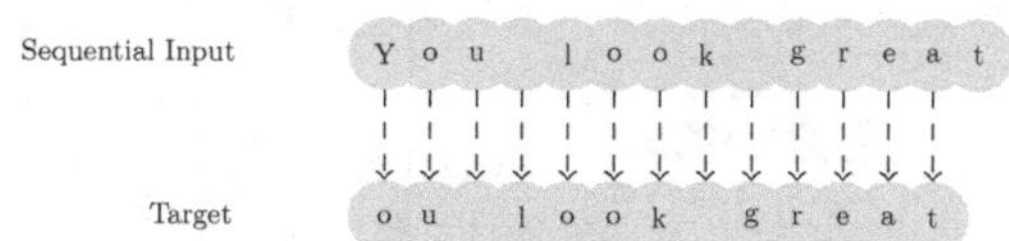

Fig. 3. Illustration of character prediction

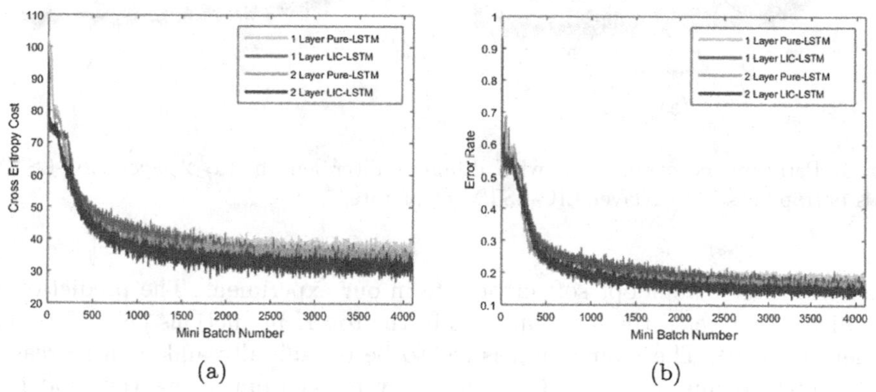

Fig. 4. Performance comparison of different Models. (a) Cross entropy cost, (b) Error rate.

We used 24,000 English phrases for training and 8,000 English phrases for testing. The dataset is from LightNet toolbox introduced in [9]. The labels are created by moving the training phrase one character left. An illustration of the task is shown in Fig. 3. A total of 67 different characters are included and each character is encoded into one hot vector. The number of time steps is set to 34 and the original phrases are either truncated or concatenated with zeros. SGD is used for the convolutional layer optimization and Adam is used for the LSTM layer. As some of the characters like spaces are much more frequent than

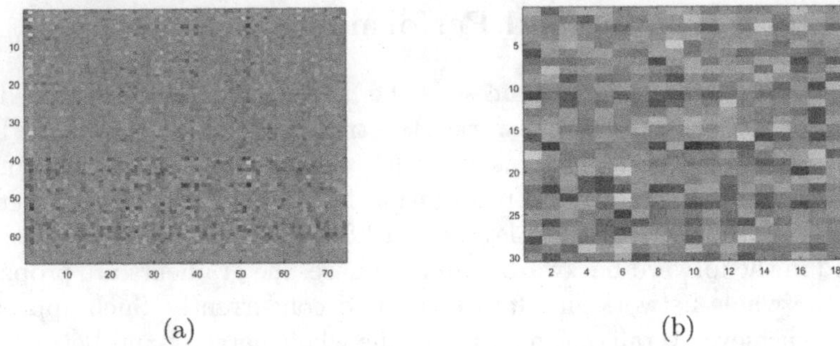

Fig. 5. Visualization of filter weight. (a) First convolution layer, (b) Second convolution layer.

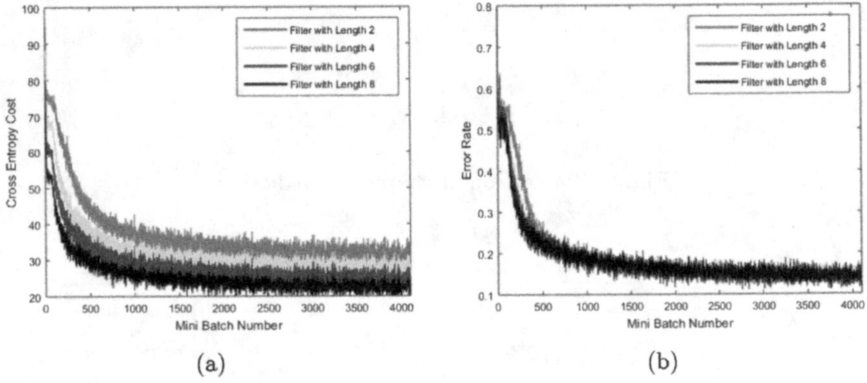

Fig. 6. Performance comparison with different filter length. (a) 2 layer LIC-LSTM cross entropy cost, (b) 2 layer LIC-LSTM error rate.

other characters, we adopt soft error rate in our experiment. The prediction is classified as correct if the label appears in the top K predictions ($K = 5$ in our implementation). The momentum is set to be 0.5 initially and then increased to 0.9 after 20 mini batches. The initial low momentum allows the model to rapidly reach functioning region and the following high momentum avoids the model being trapped in local optima. We found high momentum(0.9) is necessary for LIC-LSTM with 2 layers to achieve satisfying result. The model training performance is shown in Fig. 4. For the same number of layers, the LIC-LSTM model is achieving higher accuracy than pure LSTM model. And the performance of deep LSTM model lies between shallow LIC-LSTM model and deep LIC-LSTM model. The deep LIC-LSTM model achieves 16.2% error rate on testing dataset compared to 17.8% achieved by deep LSTM model. The LIC-LSTM model is enduring less cross entropy cost with larger filter size as shown in Fig. 6, while error rate remains stable, which shows the model performance is robust on variating filter size.

4 Conclusion

In this paper, we formed LIC-LSTM with convolutional layer and LSTM layer interweaving with each other. LIC-LSTM combines the feature extracting ability of CNN and sequential data modeling of LSTM homogeneously. Experiment results show the model achieves higher accuracy and shoulders lower cross entropy cost on sequential data modeling tasks compared with state of art LSTM models. The LIC-LSTM can serve as encoders in encoder-decoder model with natural language processing and neural machine translation tasks.

References

1. Bahdanau, D., Cho, K., Bengio, Y.: Neural machine translation by jointly learning to align and translate. CoRR abs/1409.0473 (2014). http://arxiv.org/abs/1409.0473
2. Donahue, J., Hendricks, L.A., Rohrbach, M., Venugopalan, S., Guadarrama, S., Saenko, K., Darrell, T.: Long-term recurrent convolutional networks for visual recognition and description. IEEE Trans. Pattern Anal. Mach. Intell. **PP**(99), 1 (2016)
3. Kim, Y., Jernite, Y., Sontag, D., Rush, A.M.: Character-aware neural language models. CoRR abs/1508.06615 (2015). http://arxiv.org/abs/1508.06615
4. Krizhevsky, A., Sutskever, I., Hinton, G.E.: Imagenet classification with deep convolutional neural networks. In: Pereira, F., Burges, C.J.C., Bottou, L., Weinberger, K.Q. (eds.) Advances in Neural Information Processing Systems 25, pp. 1097–1105. Curran Associates, Inc. (2012). http://papers.nips.cc/paper/4824-imagenet-classification-with-deep-convolutional-neural-networks.pdf
5. Luong, M., Pham, H., Manning, C.D.: Effective approaches to attention-based neural machine translation. CoRR abs/1508.04025 (2015). http://arxiv.org/abs/1508.04025
6. Sutskever, I., Vinyals, O., Le, Q.V.: Sequence to sequence learning with neural networks. In: Ghahramani, Z., Welling, M., Cortes, C., Lawrence, N.D., Weinberger, K.Q. (eds.) Advances in Neural Information Processing Systems 27, pp. 3104–3112. Curran Associates, Inc. (2014). http://papers.nips.cc/paper/5346-sequence-to-sequence-learning-with-neural-networks.pdf
7. Vosoughi, S., Vijayaraghavan, P., Roy, D.: Tweet2vec: learning tweet embeddings using character-level CNN-LSTM encoder-decoder. CoRR abs/1607.07514 (2016). http://arxiv.org/abs/1607.07514
8. Wang, J., Yu, L.C., Lai, K.R., Zhang, X.: Dimensional sentiment analysis using a regional CNN-LSTM model. In: Proceedings of the 54th Annual Meeting of the Association for Computational Linguistics, Berlin, Germany, pp. 225–230 (2016)
9. Ye, C., Zhao, C., Yang, Y., Fermüller, C., Aloimonos, Y.: Lightnet: a versatile, standalone matlab-based environment for deep learning. CoRR abs/1605.02766 (2016). http://arxiv.org/abs/1605.02766
10. Zhou, C., Sun, C., Liu, Z., Lau, F.C.M.: A C-LSTM neural network for text classification. CoRR abs/1511.08630 (2015). http://arxiv.org/abs/1511.08630

Using Cognitive Computing to Get Insights on Personality Traits from Twitter Messages

Romualdo Alves Pereira Junior(✉) and Diana Inkpen

University of Ottawa, Ottawa, ON K1N 6N5, Canada
{ralvespe,diana.inkpen}@uottawa.ca

Abstract. In this work, we apply text mining algorithms on Twitter messages made available by PAN2015. In the first step, we applied IBM Watson algorithms to obtain the results of Big Five personality analysis, namely OCEAN: Openness, Conscientiousness, Extraversion, Agreeableness and Neuroticism. Then, we applied a Deep Learning algorithm on the resulted IBM Watson scores, in order to minimize the Root Mean Square Error. In this way, we achieved better results than using the IBM Watson algorithms alone. The dataset contains messages in English from 152 distinct authors.

Keywords: Text mining · Deep Learning · Big Five · Personality analysis

1 Introduction

Language Use, as studied in Psycholinguistics, is an area where psychologists and psychiatrists nowadays could use tools that employ Machine Learning and Text Mining techniques. A person's language usage can reveal information about their character, personality, moral values, sentiments, and emotions. In fact, in psycholinguistic analysis of texts, a verbal utterance is comprehended as an expression of personality, especially when it is closely linked with a native cultural environment, as argued by Tausczik and Pennebaker [12]. According to Farnadi et al. [4], a variety of approaches have been recently proposed to automatically infer users' personality from their generated content in social media. In turn, Celli [2] warns that although the large amount of data available from social media allows predictions of users personality from text in a computational way, there are some problems to be considered: the definition of personality; the annotation of personality in the datasets; the construction of the models; and the evaluation of these personality models.

Without neglecting these nontrivial problems, we intend to show that our text analysis system augmented with a post-processing Deep Learning module can determine a user's personality accurately, efficiently, and robustly enough to be used in practical applications. The psychological indicators that we employ in our work come from IBM Watson Alchemy and Personality Insights [6]. It is

M. Mouhoub and P. Langlais (Eds.): Canadian AI 2017, LNAI 10233, pp. 278–283, 2017.
DOI: 10.1007/978-3-319-57351-9_32

a cloud service that relies on psychometric survey-based scores[1] This model uses a vector representation of words derived from multiple large corpora developed by Stanford University [5].

The Big Five personality categories, representing the most widely used model for generally describing how a person engages with the world, are presented below, with their respective sub-categories [7]:

- **Openness** - The extent to which a person is open to experiencing a variety of activities. Subcategories: Adventurousness, Artistic Interests, Emotionality, Imagination, Intellect and Liberalism;
- **Conscientiousness** - Act in an organized or thoughtful way. Subcategories: Achievement Striving, Cautiousness, Dutifulness, Orderliness and Self-Discipline;
- **Extraversion** - Seek stimulation in the company of others. Subcategories: Activity Level, Assertiveness, Cheerfulness, Excitement Seeking and Friendliness;
- **Agreeableness** - Compassionate and cooperative toward others. Subcategories: Altruism, Cooperation, Modesty, Morality, Sympathy and Trust;
- **Neuroticism** - Emotional Range or Natural Reactions. Subcategories: Anger, Anxiety, Depression, Immoderation, Self-Consciousness and Vulnerability.

The rest of this paper is organized as follows: Sect. 2 presents the methodology; Sect. 3 explains the experiments; Sect. 4 presents the results, discussion, and comparison to related work; Sect. 5 presents conclusions and future work.

2 Methodology

The methodology of this research is presented in Fig. 1. We defined five stages, as follows:

1. **Obtaining Author Profiling Dataset:** The tweets from 152 distinct authors were made available in XML format (each author with 100 tweets).
2. **Text Mining Tweets:** We read the XML files, extracting the textual messages from each file using XPath expressions. Then, we executed the IBM Watson routines (Personality Insights and Alchemy) to calculate initial scores (from 0.0 to 1.0), storing the results for the next steps.
3. **Optimizing Scores with Deep Learning:** We created a training dataset with the first 30 authors, defining a strategy for each main personality trait and executing Deep Learning (H2O) to calculate improved scores over the Watson scores and the other features, resulting in a trained model for each of the 5 personality traits;

[1] In short, to collect the ground truth data, when IBM was developing the tool, surveys were administered over large populations and, for each user, standard psychometric surveys were collected along with their Twitter posts.

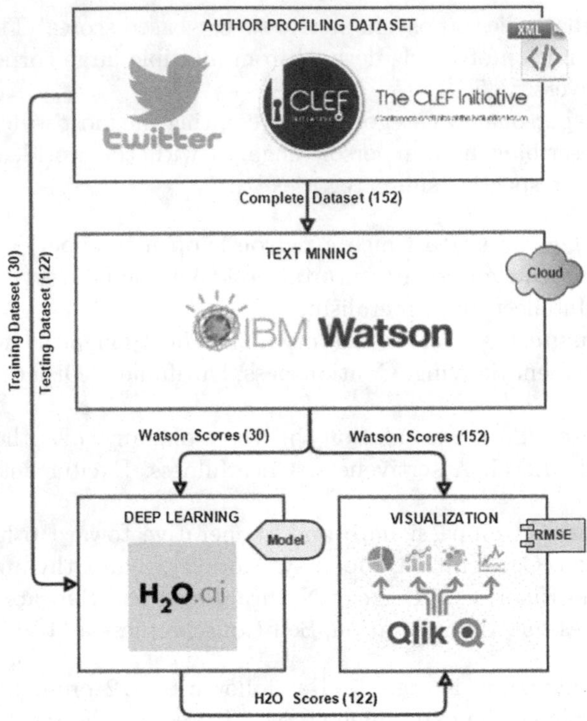

Fig. 1. Methodology

4. **Evaluating Deep Learning Predictions:** We created a testing dataset with the last 122 authors. Then, we applied the trained model on the testing dataset to optimize scores, storing it and calculating the Root Means Square Error (RMSE) for each personality trait.
5. **Visualizing with Business Intelligence:** We can visualize the results in a Business Intelligence system, which provides a dynamic and context-sensitive user interface with responsive navigation menus, dashboards, charts and tables.

3 Experiments

The International Competition on Author Profiling (PAN) is an evaluation lab on uncovering plagiarism, authorship, and social software misuse. The organizers provided a dataset of 152 distinct authors, each one with 100 tweets in English. We used 20% of this dataset for training and 80% for testing.

Creating the neural network architecture to structure our deep learning process required coming up with parameters for the input, hidden, and output layers. The output layer has one node. The input layer contains one node per feature. The features considered for all traits were: AuthorId, Gender, and AgeGroup. For Openness, we also included the following scores: TruthOpen, WatsonOpennes, Imagination, and Sentiment. For Conscientiousness we included: TruthConscientious, Cautiousness, and Joy. For Extraversion we included: TruthExtroverted, all main personality categories, and all Extroversion subcategories. For Agreeableness we included: TruthAgreeable and all main personality categories. For Neuroticism we included: TruthStable, all main personality categories, and Vulnerability.

Regarding the hidden layers and the number of epochs needed for training, Candel et al. [1] argues that there is no good default setting. We need to use our intuition for choosing these parameters, as well as tuning them by performing trial runs. The H2O parameters we chose after performing trial runs are presented in Table 1.

Table 1. H2O specific configuration

Big5	Activation	Epochs	HLS	Big Five	Subcategories	Emotion	Sentiment
O	Maxout	11	5,5,5,1	Own	Imagination	None	Yes
C	Rectifier	3	3,10,10	Own	Cautiousness	Joy	No
E	Rectifier	4	3,10,10,3	All	All	Sadness	No
A	Rectifier	3	3,10,10,3	All	None	None	No
N	Maxout	12	5,5,5,5,6	All	Vulnerability	None	No

4 Results, Discussion and Compaison to Related Work

Root Mean Square Error (RMSE) was used as an evaluation measure in the PAN shared task. It is the standard deviation of the residuals (prediction errors). The RMSE values for the IBM Watson and H2O Deep Learning extension, on the test dataset, is presented in Table 2.

Table 2. Watson RMSE and Watson+H2O RMSE

OCEAN	Watson	Watson+H2O	Performance
Openness	0.2650	0.1321	13.30 %
Conscientiousness	0.4142	0.1280	28.62 %
Extraversion	0.3002	0.1333	16.69 %
Agreeableness	0.4099	0.1196	29.03 %
Neuroticism	0.3040	0.1793	12.47 %
Overall average	0.3387	0.1385	20.02 %

We summarized in Table 3 the three best overall results [10] obtained in the shared task: (1) Sulea and Dichiu [11] introduced a novel way of computing the type/token ratio of an author and showed that the text of a person was influenced by gender, age, and big five personality traits, and they used this ratio, along with Term frequency-Inverse document frequency (tf-idf) matrices. (2) Álvarez-Carmona et al. [3] considered several sets of stylometric and content features, and different decision algorithms for each language-attribute pair, hence treating it as an individual problem. And (3) Werlen [9] used SVM and Linear Discriminant Analysis classifiers to analyze features obtained from Linguistic Inquiry and Word Count (LIWC) dictionaries.

Comparing our results with the official teams that participated in the PAN15 contest, our approach improved the best overall RMSE, but this is not directly comparable since we used a smaller test dataset, consisting of 122 (out of the 152) authors, because we used 30 authors for training.

Table 3. Ranking on the PAN15 dataset - top 5 best RMSE scores

Ranking	Team	Overall	O	C	E	A	N
1	Sulea	0.14416	0.1246	0.1297	0.1318	0.1396	0.1951
2	Alvarezcarmona	0.14420	0.1202	0.1172	0.1278	0.1305	0.2253
3	Miculicich	0.14748	0.1225	0.1330	0.1250	0.1322	0.2247

Concerning IBM Watson Personality Insights, Mahmud [8] explains that the service requires 3500 words written by an individual to produce a personality portrait with meaningful results. In addition, the input text must contain at least 70 words that match words found in the standard LIWC psycholinguistic dictionary. The service tokenizes the input text to develop a representation in an n-dimensional space; obtains a vector representation for the words in the input text; and feeds this representation to a machine-learning algorithm that infers a personality profile with Big Five, Needs, and Values characteristics. To train the algorithm, the service uses scores obtained from surveys conducted among thousands of users along with data from their Twitter feeds.

In order to improve the results and to minimize the RMSE, our approach of applying H2O Deep Learning over Watson scores in fact surpassed this service limitation.

Regarding H2O, we realized that the configuration of its parameters was fundamental to achieve better results than those obtained with the default configuration. We needed to tune the system for some important parameters, mainly the Hidden Layer Size, number of epochs, and choosing the fields (features) with higher impact on the training dataset RMSE, in order to reduce it to an acceptable and competitive level.

5 Conclusion and Future Work

We showed that using deep learning over the Watson scores we were able to improve the results for the personality detection task. H2O did very well with only 20% in the training set. In future work we plan to convert this to 70% training and 30% test, to verify if accuracy goes up. Also, we plan to test our system with other configurations and to apply it on a wide source of semi-structured and unstructured datasets obtained from letters, personal notes, books, literature, social media, etc. Additionally, there is a possibility to highlight risks of mental disorders, particularly related to auto-destructive behavior.

Acknowledgments. We are very grateful to the National Council for Scientific and Technological Development - CNPq (Brazil) for having subsidized the postdoctoral fellowship, and to Saman Daneshvar (University of Ottawa) for revising the paper.

References

1. Candel, A., Parmar, V., LeDell, E., Arora, A.: Deep Learning with H2O. H2O.ai, Inc., Mountain View (2015)
2. Celli, F.: Unsupervised personality recognition for social network sites. In: Proceedings of 6th International Conference on Digital Society. Citeseer (2012)
3. Álvarez-Carmona, M.A., et al.: INAOE's participation at PAN'15: author profiling task–notebook for PAN at CLEF 2015. In: Cappellato, L., Ferro, N., Jones, G., Juan, E.S. (eds.) CLEF 2015 Evaluation Labs and Workshop - Working Notes Papers, Toulouse, France. CEUR-WS.org, 8–11 September 2015
4. Farnadi, G., Sitaraman, G., Sushmita, S.: User modeling and user-adapted interaction, vol. 26 (2016)
5. IBM: IBM Watson personality insights has a new model: support of shorter text and precision improvement. Technical report, IBM (2016)
6. IBM: Personality insight basics. Technical report, IBM (2016)
7. IBM: Personality models. Technical report, IBM (2016)
8. Mahmud, J.: IBM Watson personality insights: the science behind the service. Technical report, IBM (2016)
9. Werlen, L.M.: Statistical learning methods for profiling analysis-notebook for PAN at CLEF 2015. In: Cappellato, L., Ferro, N., Jones, G., Juan, E.S. (eds.) CLEF 2015 Evaluation Labs and Workshop - Working Notes Papers, Toulouse, France. CEUR-WS.org, 8–11 September 2015
10. Rangel, F., Celli, F., Rosso, P., Potthast, M., Stein, B., Daelemans, W.: Overview of the 3rd author profiling task at PAN 2015. In: Cappellato, L., Ferro, N., Jones, G., Juan, E.S. (eds.) CLEF 2015 Evaluation Labs and Workshop - Working Notes Papers, Toulouse, France. CEUR-WS.org, 8–11 September 2015
11. Şulea, O.-M., Dichiu, D.: Automatic profiling of Twitter users based on their tweets-notebook for PAN at CLEF 2015. In: Cappellato, L., Ferro, N., Jones, G., Juan, E.S. (eds.) CLEF 2015 Evaluation Labs and Workshop - Working Notes Papers, Toulouse, France. CEUR-WS.org, 8–11 September 2015
12. Tausczik, Y.R., Pennebaker, J.W.: The psychological meaning of words: LIWC and computerized text analysis methods. J. Lang. Soc. Psychol. **29**(1), 24–54 (2010)

Confused and Thankful: Multi-label Sentiment Classification of Health Forums

Victoria Bobicev[1] and Marina Sokolova[2,3(✉)]

[1] Technical University of Moldova, Chisinau, Moldova
victoria.bobicev@ia.utm.md
[2] IBDA, Dalhousie University, Halifax, Canada
sokolova@uottawa.ca
[3] University of Ottawa, Ottawa, Canada

Abstract. Our current work studies sentiment representation in messages posted on health forums. We analyze 11 sentiment representations in a framework of multi-label learning. We use **Exact Match** and **F-score** to compare effectiveness of those representations in sentiment classification of a message. Our empirical results show that feature selection can significantly improve **Exact Match** of the multi-label sentiment classification (paired t-test, P = 0.0024).

Keywords: Sentiment classification · Multi-label learning · Medical forums

1 Motivation

Separation of sentiments is a major challenge in sentiment classification. Due to a *yes-no* approach which assigns a text with one label and one label only, single label learning algorithms thrive and succeed when sentiment classes are easily dichotomized. At the same time, even short texts can combine various sentiments and objective, factual information, e.g. *my oldest had his th bday today & he had the stomach flu it still was a nice day I even got to spend some special time whim & hubby*. Overlap in sentiments can hardly be resolved by single-label binary or multiclass classification. We hypothesize that annotating texts with ≥ 2 sentiment labels and applying multi-label classification can benefit our understanding of the text sentiments. Applied to online health forums, multi-label sentiment classification improves understanding of patients' needs and can be used in advancing patient-centered health care (Bobicev, 2016; Liu and Chen, 2015; Melzi et al. 2014).

Online health forums allow for studies of well-being and behavior patterns in uncontrolled environment (Aarts et al. 2015; Navindgi et al. 2016; Hidalgo et al. 2015). Giving and receiving emotional support has positive effects on emotional well-being for patients with higher emotional communication, while the same exchanges have detrimental impacts on emotional well-being for those with lower emotional communication competence (Yoo et al. 2014). It has been shown that positive emotions present more frequently in responding posts than in the posts initiating new discussions (Yu, 2011).

In this study, we analyze how 6 score-based, 4 multi-dimensional and 1 domain-based sentiment representations affect accuracy of multi-label sentiment classification of

M. Mouhoub and P. Langlais (Eds.): Canadian AI 2017, LNAI 10233, pp. 284–289, 2017.
DOI: 10.1007/978-3-319-57351-9_33

message posted on a health forum. Problem transformations (Binary Relevance and Bayesian Classification Chains) and classification algorithms (SVM, Naïve Bayes and Bayesian Nets) assess effectiveness of the sentiment representations. Our results show that feature selection can significantly improve **Exact Match** of sentiment classification (paired t-test, P = 0.0024).

2 Multi-label Data Annotation and Sentiment Representation

We have worked with 80 discussions, 10 – 20 posts each, obtained from the InVitroFertilization forum (www.ivf.ca); we had 1321 messages. The length of forum messages was 126 words on average. The target labels were *confusion*, *encouragement*, *gratitude* and *facts*; those labels were previously used in multi-class classification of the data (Sokolova and Bobicev, 2013). Three annotators independently worked with each post; each annotator assigned a post with one label. From 1321 posts, 658 posts had three identical labels; 605 posts had two identical labels, and 58 posts had three different labels. Note that multi-label learning algorithms automatically resolve difference in the number of assigned labels. When we account per classification category, 954 posts had the label *facts,* 642 posts – *encouragement*, *confusion* appeared in 285 posts, and *gratitude* appears in 161 posts.[1]We kept the assigned labels in classification experiments. Fleiss Kappa = 0.48 indicated a moderate agreement, comparable with three-label sentiment annotation of health messages (Melzi et al. 2014).

We used 11 sentiment lexicons to extract sentiment information from our texts: *SentiWordNet* **(SWN)**, *Bing Liu Sentiment Lexicon* (**BL**), *SentiStrength* **(SS),** ***AFINN*** *Hashtag Affirmative and Negated Context Sentiment Lexicon* **(HANCSL),** *Sentiment 140 Lexicon* **(140SL)** assign terms with polarity scores; ***MPQA*** *DepecheMood* **(DM)**, *Word-Emotion Association Lexicon* **(WEAL),** *General Inquirer* **(GI)** assign terms with multiple sentiment categories, and *HealthAffect* **(HA)** uses Point-wise Mutual Information to retrieve emotional scores (Sokolova and Bobicev, 2013). Among the emotional terms retrieved from the data, 6 terms appears in the 11 lexicons: *encouragement, horrible, negative, stupid, success, successful*, 2650 terms - in two lexicons, 928 terms - in three lexicons, and 3963 terms appear in one of the lexicons.

3 Empirical Evaluation

Multi-label classification allows an example to be simultaneously associated with >1 label (Trohidis, and Tsoumakas, 2007). In practice, multi-label classification can be transformed into ensemble of binary classification tasks. We applied two transformation methods: Binary Relevance (BR) and Bayesian Classifier Chains (BCC)[2]. We use **Exact Match** in performance evaluation (Sorower, 2010):

[1] The data set is available upon request at victoria.bobicev@ia.utm.md.

[2] http://meka.sourceforge.net/.

$$ExactMatch = \frac{1}{n}\sum_{i=1}^{n} I(Y_i = Z_i) \quad (1)$$

Where n denotes the number of texts in the data set, Y_i, Z_i are sets of predicted and true labels for text i respectively. We compute a balanced **F-score** to evaluate classification of each label categories. We used the MEKA toolkit (Read, et al. 2016). SVM, Naïve Bayes and Bayesian Nets were the base classifiers; 10-fold cross-validation was used for model selection. To put our results in perspective, we compute the majority class baseline; text representation by concatenating the 11 lexicons provides the benchmark accuracy.

The 11 lexicons assessed sentiments through different schema; hence, we worked with 11 different sentiment representations. The highest **Exact Match** was obtained with 1131 terms extracted from *SentiStrength* (SS) (see Table 1). Although every **Exact Match** significantly beats the baseline, none of the lexicons provided for significantly better results. Similarly, non-significant improvement happens for the best *per category* **F-score** (Table 2).

Table 1. The best **Exact Match** on individual lexicons; the majority class ExactMatch = 0.270;

N	Features	Retrieved terms	Exact Match	Classifier
1	SWN	3 725	0.395	BR- NB Multinomial
2	SS	1 131	**0.410**	BCC-SVM
3	DM	4 467	0.407	BR-NB Multinomial
4	HA	1 190	0.403	BR-NB Multinomial
5	AFINN	793	0.399	BCC-SVM
6	GI	942	0.378	BCC-SVM
7	HANCSL	2 765	0.357	BCC-SVM
8	140SL	2 160	0.376	BCC-SVM
9	WEAL	1 368	0.335	BR-NB Multinomial
10	BL	1 103	0.362	BCC-SVM
11	MPQA	1 417	0.388	BCC-SVM
12	*All the 11 lexicons*	*9 086*	***0.450***	*BR-NB Multinomial*

Table 2. The best **F-score** obtained for each category; we use the majority class baseline;

Category	Baseline	F-score	Feature	Classifier
Confusion	0.784	0.802	SWN	BR NB Multinomial
Encouragement	0.486	0.731	HA	BR NB Multinomial
Gratitude	0.878	0.907	BL	BCC- SVM
Facts	0.722	0.805	DM	BR NB Multinomial

On the next step, we assessed whether reducing non-essential information can help in classification accuracy (Tables 3 and 4). To remove less contributing features, we applied three feature selection methods: CfsSubset (best subsets), Classifier SubsetEval,

Table 3. The best Exact Match obtained on the combinations of the selected feature sets.

N	Feature set	N of terms	Exact Match	Classifier
1	Selected attributes from all 11 lexicons (best subsets)	1009	**0.544**	BR-NB Multinomial
2	Selected attributes from all 11 lexicons (best subsets for SMV)	1446	0.521	BR-NB Multinomial
3	Selected attributes from all 11 lexicons (InfoGain)	2072	0.534	BR-NB Multinomial

Table 4. The best **F-score** obtained on combinations of the selected feature sets.

Category	F-score	Feature set	Classifier
Confusion	0.870	best subsets for SVM	BR-NB Multinomial
Encouragement	0.805	best subsets	BR-NB Multinomial
Gratitude	0.930	InfoGain	BR-NB Multinomial
Facts	0.833	InfoGain	BCC- SVM

and InfoGain. For each method, we applied feature selection to each lexicon and each label; then those $11 \times 4 = 44$ sets were concatenated; we removed all duplicate terms. We obtained the best **Exact Match** = **0.544** on 1009 terms: 301 terms with positive scores, 200 - with negative scores, 249 - from HA; other 259 terms had multiple emotional indicators.

We computed a conservative *paired* t-test between three Exact Match results reported in Table 3 and the highest three Exact Match from Table 1, i.e., rows 2, 3 and 6. T-test's P = 0.0024 indicates that feature selection significantly increased examples with fully correctly identified labels. Although feature selection did not significantly improved **F-score** (*paired* t-test, P = 0.3245), it did improve classification for each category, esp. for *encouragement* where increase was >10%.

4 Discussion of Sentiment Representations

As expected, emotionally charged adjectives are frequent among the selected features, e.g., *amazing, awful, bad, desperate, excited.* At the same time, polarity of the selected terms has a nuanced relationship with the expressed sentiments. For every category, selected features contain words with positive and negative connotation: the best **F-score** for *confusion* was obtained with representation containing 425 terms with positive scores and 333 terms - with negative scores, for *gratitude* - on representation containing 583 terms with positive scores and 323 terms with negative scores, for *encouragement* - on representation containing 301 with positive scores and200 terms with negative scores, and for *facts* - on representation containing 583 terms with positive scores and323 terms with negative scores. This can be attributed to a sentiment flow typical to health forum posts: empathy (positive polarity), followed by reference to interlocutors' problems (negative polarity), followed by good wishes (positive polarity).

Many selected terms appear in several lexicons, e.g., *lovely, progress, exciting, fearful, hopeless, luck, worse* appeared in 8–10 lexicons of the discussed 11; *lovely, hopeless* appeared in all the lexicons but HA; *progress* - in all the lexicons but SS; *worse*- in all the lexicons but HA and HANCSL. Also, no sentiment representation was left behind: for each category, selected terms represented almost every lexicon. Some terms were repeatedly selected for several categories. For example, *luck* was selected for *encouragement* and for *gratitude*; *good* was selected for *facts* and *confusion*.

5 Conclusions and Future Work

In this work we have studied effects of sentiment representation on sentiment classification of a message posted on a health forum. We used a framework of Multi-label Learning as many messages convey >1 sentiment. We have analyzed 11 sentiment representations: 6 score-based, 4 multi-dimensional and 1 domain-based. We applied Exact Match to evaluate usefulness of the sentiment representations. Counting only examples with fully correctly identified labels (i.e., examples with partially identified labels were discarded), we found that redundancy reduction through feature selection significantly improves classification (paired t-test, P = 0.0024).

Using **F-score** to find the most effective sentiment representations of each category, we observed that both positive and negative polarity *within* message text play an important role in correct identification of the message sentiment. Those results hold for *encouragement, gratitude* (aka positive sentiments), *confusion* (a substitute for the negative sentiment), and *facts*. For the label *facts*, which we considered a non-sentimental category, the highest **F-score** appeared on representation containing terms with high polarity scores. Co-occurrence of opposite polarities shows complexity of sentiment conveyance and supports multi-label sentiment classification.

In future, we plan to work with finer grained sentiment representations. One venue would be to explore relations between polarity strength and accuracy of sentiment classification in a message. Another promising venue is to apply discourse analysis to investigate the use of sentiment-bearing words in factual messages.

References

Aarts, J., Faber, M., Cohlen, B., van Oers, A., Nelen, W., Kremer, J.: Lessons learned from the implementation of an online infertility community into an IVF clinic's daily practice. Hum. Fertil. **18**(4), 238–247 (2015)

Bobicev, V.: Text classification: the case of multiple labels. In: 2016 International Conference on Communications (COMM), pp. 39–42 (2016)

Liu, S.M., Chen, J.H.: A multi-label classification based approach for sentiment classification. Expert Syst. Appl. **42**(3), 1083–1093 (2015)

Melzi, S., Abdaoui, A., Aze, J., Bringay, S., Poncelet, P., et al.: Patient's rationale: patient knowledge retrieval from health forums. In: 6th International Conference on eTELEMED: eHealth, Telemedicine, and Social Medicine (2014)

Navindgi, A., Brun, C., Boulard, S., Nowson, S.: Steps Toward Automatic Understanding of the Function Of Affective Language in Support Groups. NLP for Social Media (2016)

Read, J., Reutemann, P., Pfahringer, B., Holmes, G.: MEKA: a multi-label/multi-target extension to Weka. J. Mach. Learn. Res. **21**(17), 1–5 (2016)

Rodríguez Hidalgo, C.T., Tan, E.S.H., Verlegh, P.W.J.: The social sharing of emotion (SSE) in online social networks: a case study in live journal. Comput. Hum. Behav. **52**, 364–372 (2015)

Sokolova, M., Bobicev, V.: What sentiments can be found in medical forums? In: Proceedings of RANLP 2013, pp. 633–639 (2013)

Sorower, M.S.: A literature survey on algorithms for multi-label learning. Technical report, Oregon State University, Corvallis (2010)

Trohidis, K., Tsoumakas, G.: Multilabel classification: an overview. Int. J. Data Warehouse. Min. **3**, 1–13 (2007)

Yoo, W., Namkoong, K., Choi, M., et al.: Giving and receiving emotional support online: communication competence as a moderator of psychosocial benefits for women with breast cancer. Comput. Hum. Behav. **30**, 13–22 (2014)

Yu, B.: The emotional world of health online communities. In: Proceedings of the 2011 iConference, pp. 806–807, New York, USA (2011) [illegible] Sentiment [illegible] patients [illegible] Conference on e-Health [illegible] (2010)

[illegible] Analysing Understanding [illegible] (2016)

[illegible]

[illegible] study [illegible] (2011)

[illegible], M. [illegible] medical forums. In: Proceedings of RANLP [illegible]

Sorower, M.S.: A literature survey on algorithms for multi-label learning. Technical report, Oregon State University, Corvallis (2010)

[illegible] Multi-label classification: an overview. Int. J. Data Warehous. Min. [illegible] (2007)

[illegible] emotional support [illegible] women with breast [illegible]

[illegible] In: Proceedings of the 2011 [illegible]

Uncertainty and Preference Reasoning

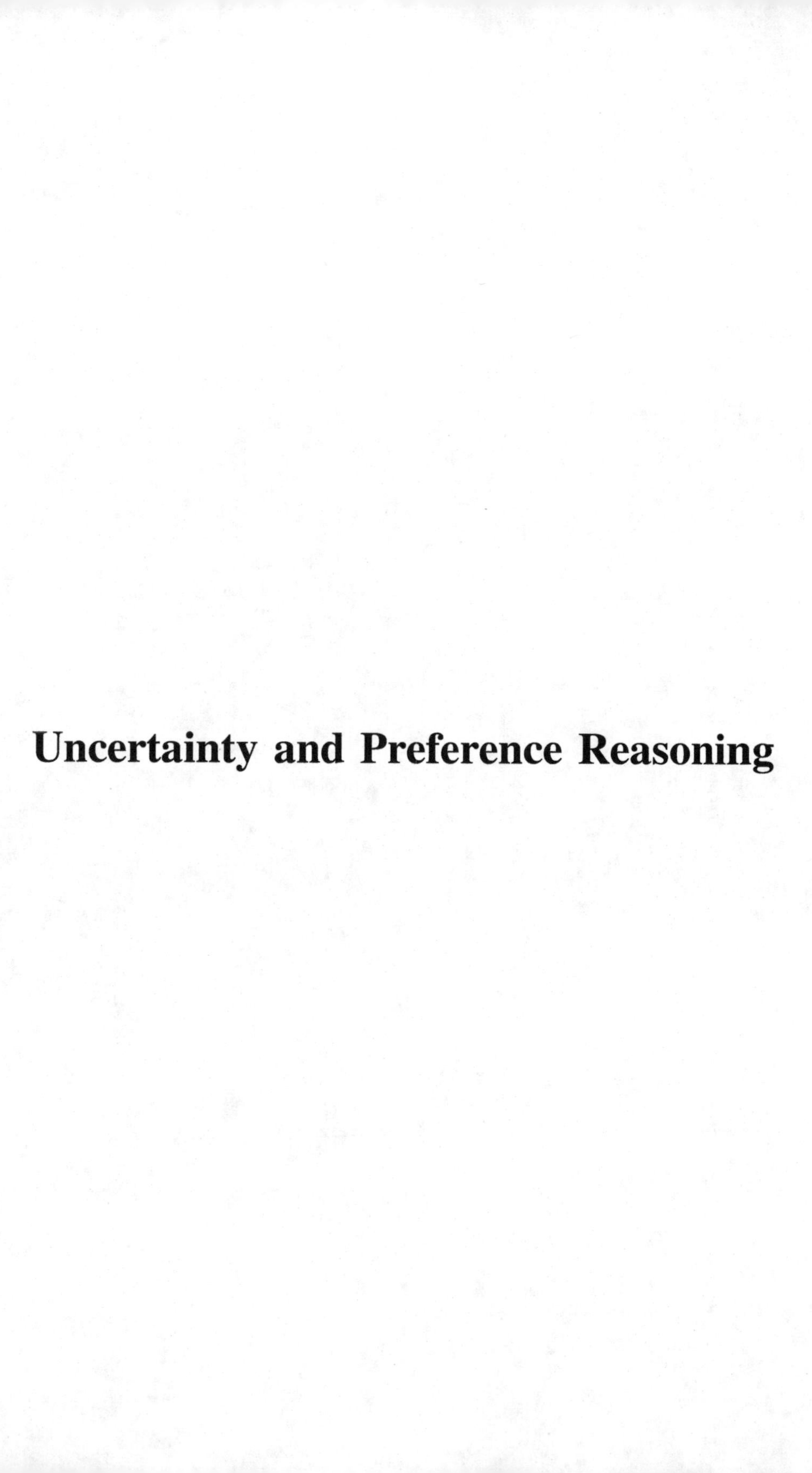

Probabilistic TCP-net

Sultan Ahmed and Malek Mouhoub(✉)

Department of Computer Science, University of Regina, Regina, Canada
{ahmed28s,mouhoubm}@uregina.ca

Abstract. TCP-nets are graphical tools for modeling user's preference and relative importance statements. We propose the *Probabilistic TCP-net* (PTCP-net) model that can represent a set of TCP-nets, in a compact form, sharing the same set of variables and their domains but having different preference and relative importance statements. In particular, the PTCP-net is able to express the choices of multiple unknown users such as, recommender systems. The PTCP-net can also be seen as an extension of the TCP-net with uncertainty on preference and relative importance statements. We have adopted the Bayesian Network as the reasoning tool for PTCP-nets especially when answering the following two questions (1) finding the most probable TCP-net for a given PTCP-net and (2) finding the most probable optimal outcome.

Keywords: Preference · Relative importance · Probability · TCP-net

1 Introduction

Reasoning with preferences using graphical models has attracted great interest in many real world applications, e.g., recommender systems [9] and product configuration [4]. A *Conditional Preference Network* (CP-net) [3] is a graphical model that uses the notion of *conditional preferential independence* for representing and reasoning about qualitative and conditional preferences in a compact and intuitive manner. A directed graph is used to encode preferential dependencies. For each variable in a CP-net, there is a *conditional preference table* (CPT) that gives the preference order over the domains of the variable for each combination of the parent set. A *Tradeoff-enhanced CP-net* (TCP-net) [5] is an extension of the CP-net that accounts user's qualitative and conditional relative importance statements by using the notion of *conditional relative importance.* For each conditional importance relation in a TCP-net, there is a *conditional importance table* (CIT) that gives conditional relative importance between two variables.

Aggregating users' preferences [12,13] is often a necessary task for real world scenarios. For example, we consider a simple recommender system [1,6] for a library. There are m books that are subject to be recommended to customers. Each book has two attributes, namely, Genre = {Fiction, Non-fiction} and Media = {Paper copy, Electronic copy}. There are n customers where each has preferences over the domain of each attribute, e.g., Fiction is preferred over Non-fiction. Each customer might also have relative importance over Genre and

M. Mouhoub and P. Langlais (Eds.): Canadian AI 2017, LNAI 10233, pp. 293–304, 2017.
DOI: 10.1007/978-3-319-57351-9_34

Media, e.g., Genre is more important than Media. Let us assume that there are n_1 customers with the following: (1) Fiction is preferred over Non-fiction, (2) Paper copy is preferred over Electronic copy, and (3) Genre is more important than Media. The TCP-net representation of these statements is given in Fig. 1(i). Note that 'Genre is more important than Media' is depicted by using a dashed directed arc. Now, consider a second group of n_2 customers having the same preference as the first group but without any relative importance over the attributes. The TCP-net of this second group is in Fig. 1(ii). Similarly there can be a total of 12 possible groups of customers with 12 different sets of preference and importance statements. 12 distinct TCP-nets are needed to model all the customers' preference and importance statements. Our goal in this paper is to model these 12 TCP-nets within a single graphical model.

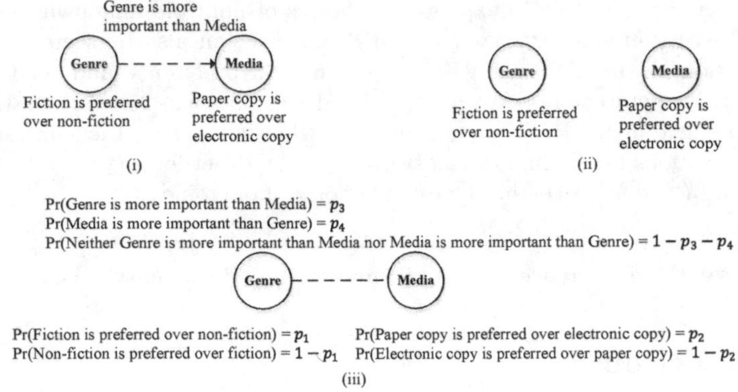

Fig. 1. Graphical representation of our library recommender system.

To reach this goal, we aggregate this set of TCP-nets with a single model extending these TCP-nets with a probability for each preference and importance statements. We call this aggregated model a *Probabilistic TCP-net* (PTCP-net). The PTCP-net for the library recommender system is illustrated in Fig. 1(iii). The probability of each statement is computed based on all customers. For example, if n_f customers prefer Fiction over Non-fiction, then Pr(Fiction is preferred over Non-fiction) $= n_f/n$, which is denoted as p_1. We assume that the probability of a statement is mutually independent from the other statements. More generally, our PTCP-net extends the TCP-net with a probability of preference orders, importance relations, existence of preferential dependencies and existence of importance relations. Instead of representing the choices of a single user, the PTCP-net is able to represent the choices of many users in a compact manner. After a PTCP-net is built, we answer two queries: (1) finding the most probable TCP-net for a given PTCP-net, which should most likely map onto an unknown user, and (2) finding the most probable optimal outcome that a recommender system should suggest to maximize the probability of a correct recommendation to an unknown user. In this paper, we will show that a *Bayesian Network*

(BN) [11] is a useful tool for answering these questions. Moreover, the PTCP-net can be used to model a single user's preference and relative importance statements with uncertainty. This is particularly important since, in real word problems or during elicitation process, preferences often come with noise [10].

The PTCP-net can be considered as an extension of the *Probabilistic CP-net* (PCP-net) [2,7]. In a PCP-net, for each variable, there is a *Probabilistic CPT* (PCPT) that gives a probability distribution over the set of all preference orders for each assignment of the parent set. Bigot et al. [2] introduce the PCP-net, but in their definition, preferential dependencies are considered deterministic. Cornelio et al. [7] give a general definition and show that BN is useful for the reasoning tasks in PCP-net. We follow their methodology of using BN for reasoning, but in the case of PTCP-net.

2 Preliminaries

A *preference relation* is modeled as a preference order (also known as strict partial order). A preference order is a binary relation over outcomes, which is anti-reflexive, anti-symmetric and transitive. Given two outcomes o and o', we write $o \succ o'$ to denote that o is strictly preferred to o'. The types of outcomes, we are concerned with, consist of possible assignments to some set of variables. We assume a set $V = \{X_1, X_2, \cdots, X_n\}$ of variables with corresponding domains $D(X_1), D(X_2), \cdots, D(X_n)$. The set of possible outcomes is then $D(V) = D(X_1) \times D(X_2) \times \cdots \times D(X_n)$, where we use $D(\cdot)$ to denote the domain of a set of variables.

Definition 1. *[5] Let a pair of variables X and Y be mutually preferentially independent given $W = V - \{X, Y\}$. We say that X is more important than Y, denoted by $X \rhd Y$, if for every assignment $w \in D(W)$ and for every $x_i, x_j \in D(X)$, $y \in D(Y)$, such that $x_i \succ x_j$ given w, we have that: $x_i y w \succ x_j y w$.*

Definition 2. *[5] Let X and Y be a pair of variables from V, and let $Z \subseteq W - \{X, Y\}$. We say that X is more important than Y given $z \in D(Z)$ iff, for every assignment w' on $W' = V - (\{X, Y\} \cup Z)$ we have: $x_i y_a z w' \succ x_j y_b z w'$ whenever $x_i \succ x_j$ given zw'. We denote this relation by $X \rhd_z Y$. Finally, if for some $z \in D(Z)$ we have either $X \rhd_z Y$ or $Y \rhd_z X$, then we say that the relative importance of X and Y is conditioned on Z, and write $RI(X, Y|Z)$. Z is said selector set of (X, Y) and is denoted as $S(X, Y)$.*

3 Proposed Probabilistic TCP-net

The relative importance relation over two variables X and Y can vary from user to user, in a context of multiple unknown users. For example, for l out of m users in a recommender system, X is more important than Y. Then, the probability of $X \rhd Y$ is l/m. On the other hand, in case of a single user system, there might be noises from the elicitation process or from personal choices (e.g., Mostly, X is more important than Y). To represent uncertainty for conditional and unconditional importance relations, we define *Probabilistic ClT* (PCIT). A PCIT of unconditional importance relations over two variables X and Y gives a probability distribution over the importance relations of X and Y. A PCIT of conditional importance relations $RI(X, Y|Z)$ gives a probability distribution over the importance relations of X and Y for every $z \in D(Z)$. If there is no importance relation between two variables X and Y, we denote it as $X \bowtie Y$.

Definition 3. *A Probabilistic TCP-net (PTCP-net) $\mathcal{N}$ is a tuple $\langle V, cp, pcpet, pcpt, ci, pciet, pcit\rangle$, where*

1. *V is a set of nodes, corresponding to the problem variables.*
2. *cp is a set of directed cp-arcs $\alpha_{\mathcal{N}}$ (where cp stands for conditional preference). A cp-arc $\overrightarrow{(X_i, X_j)}$ belongs to $\mathcal{N}$ iff the preferences over the values of X_j depend on the actual value of X_i.*
3. *pcpet associates a PCPET (probabilistic cp-arc existence table) with every cp-arc $\alpha \in \alpha_{\mathcal{N}}$. $PCPET(\alpha)$ represents the probability of existence for α.*
4. *pcpt associates a PCPT (probabilistic CPT) with every node $X \in V$. The $PCPT(X)$ gives a probability distribution over the set of all preference orders on $D(X)$ for each $u \in D(Y : Y \subseteq Pa(X))$ (including a null value to account for the possible non-existence of the cp-arcs).*
5. *ci is a set of undirected ci-arcs $\beta_{\mathcal{N}}$ (where ci stands for conditional importance). A ci-arc (X_i, X_j) belongs to $\mathcal{N}$ iff we have $RI(X_i, X_j|Z)$ for some $Z \subseteq V - \{X_i, X_j\}$ (including null). Z are said selector set of (X_i, X_j) and denoted by $S(X_i, X_j)$. A ci-arc is unconditional if Z is empty, otherwise it is conditional.*
6. *pciet associates a PCIET (probabilistic ci-arc existence table) with every ci-arc $\beta \in \beta_{\mathcal{N}}$. $PCIET(\beta)$ represents the probability of existence for β.*
7. *pcit associates a PCIT (probabilistic CIT) with every ci-arc $\beta \in \beta_{\mathcal{N}}$. If a ci-arc (X_i, X_j) exists, $PCIT(X_i, X_j)$ gives a probability distribution over the importance relations on X_i and X_j for each $z \in D(S(X_i, X_j))$. The probability of $X_i \rhd X_j$ given $z \in D(S(X_i, X_j))$ is denoted as $Pr(X_i \rhd X_j|z)$. If (X_i, X_j) does not exist, $PCIT(X_i, X_j)$ indicates that there is no importance relation between X_i and X_j. It is denoted by setting $Pr(X_i \bowtie X_j|z)$ to 1.*

The PTCP-net is a generalized formulation of the PCP-net. When *ci*, *pciet* and *pcit* are empty, the PTCP-net corresponds to a PCP-net. Note that, Brafman et al. [5] defined directed *i-arc* to denote an unconditional importance relation for a TCP-net. An i-arc $\overrightarrow{(X_i, X_j)}$ belongs to a TCP-net iff $X_i \rhd X_j$. However, in a PTCP-net, we use ci-arc to denote the existence of both conditional and unconditional importance relations. For example, a directed arc is appropriate to represent $A \rhd B$ in case of a TCP-net, whereas an undirected arc is appropriate to represent $Pr(A \rhd B) = 0.6$ and $Pr(B \rhd A) = 0.4$ in case of a PTCP-net.

Example 1. A PTCP-net with four binary variables $\{A, B, C, D\}$ is presented in Fig. 2. Two cp-arcs $\overrightarrow{(A, C)}$ and $\overrightarrow{(B, C)}$ are denoted as solid directed arc and their probabilities of existence are in Fig. 2(ii). The PCPTs corresponding to each variable are shown in Fig. 2(iii). C has two parents A and B. $PCPT(C)$ gives a probability distribution over $c \succ c'$ and $c' \succ c$ for each domain of AB, A and B, and *null*. A ci-arc is a dashed undirected arc, e.g., (A, B). We consider that the relative importance relations over A and B depend on the actual value of D. The $PCIET(A, B)$ and $PCIT(A, B)$ are in Fig. 2(iv) and (v) correspondingly.

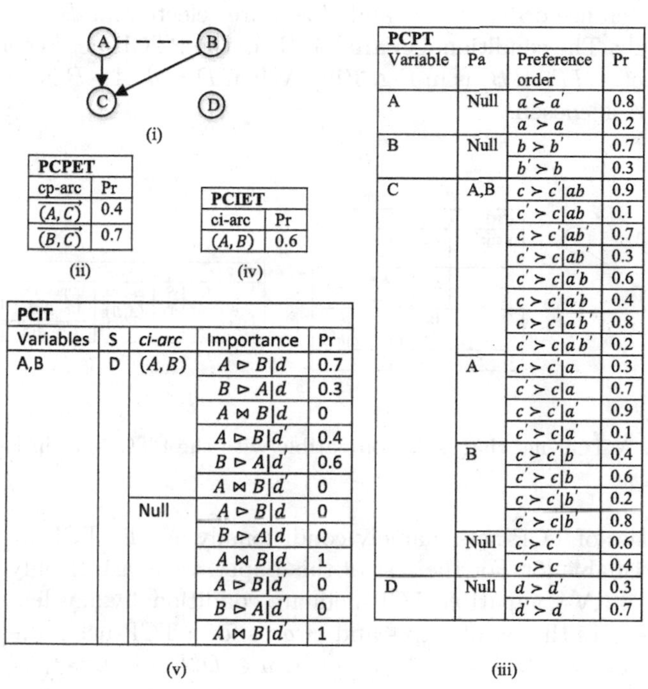

PCPET	
cp-arc	Pr
$\overrightarrow{(A,C)}$	0.4
$\overrightarrow{(B,C)}$	0.7

(ii)

PCIET	
ci-arc	Pr
(A,B)	0.6

(iv)

PCIT				
Variables	S	*ci-arc*	Importance	Pr
A,B	D	(A,B)	$A \rhd B \mid d$	0.7
			$B \rhd A \mid d$	0.3
			$A \bowtie B \mid d$	0
			$A \rhd B \mid d'$	0.4
			$B \rhd A \mid d'$	0.6
			$A \bowtie B \mid d'$	0
		Null	$A \rhd B \mid d$	0
			$B \rhd A \mid d$	0
			$A \bowtie B \mid d$	1
			$A \rhd B \mid d'$	0
			$B \rhd A \mid d'$	0
			$A \bowtie B \mid d'$	1

(v)

PCPT			
Variable	Pa	Preference order	Pr
A	Null	$a > a'$	0.8
		$a' > a$	0.2
B	Null	$b > b'$	0.7
		$b' > b$	0.3
C	A,B	$c > c' \mid ab$	0.9
		$c' > c \mid ab$	0.1
		$c > c' \mid ab'$	0.7
		$c' > c \mid ab'$	0.3
		$c' > c \mid a'b$	0.6
		$c > c' \mid a'b$	0.4
		$c > c' \mid a'b'$	0.8
		$c' > c \mid a'b'$	0.2
	A	$c > c' \mid a$	0.3
		$c' > c \mid a$	0.7
		$c > c' \mid a'$	0.9
		$c' > c \mid a'$	0.1
	B	$c > c' \mid b$	0.4
		$c' > c \mid b$	0.6
		$c > c' \mid b'$	0.2
		$c' > c \mid b'$	0.8
	Null	$c > c'$	0.6
		$c' > c$	0.4
D	Null	$d > d'$	0.3
		$d' > d$	0.7

(iii)

Fig. 2. A PTCP-net.

Definition 4. *A TCP-net N is said to be $\mathcal{N}$-compatible with a PTCP-net $\mathcal{N}$ if the following conditions are satisfied.*

1. *N has the same variables and domains as $\mathcal{N}$.*
2. *The cp-arcs α_N in N are subset of the cp-arcs $\alpha_{\mathcal{N}}$ in $\mathcal{N}$.*
3. *For each $X \in V$, a $PCPT(X)$ in $\mathcal{N}$ has a corresponding $CPT(X)$ in N. Given the cp-arcs in N, a $CPT(X)$ is formed by selecting a preference order over $D(X)$ for each $u \in D(Pa(X))$ in N.*
4. *The i-arcs in N are subset of the unconditional ci-arcs in $\mathcal{N}$. For an unconditional ci-arc (X_i, X_j) in $\mathcal{N}$, an importance relation, either $X_i \rhd X_j$ or $X_j \rhd X_i$, is selected in N. If $X_i \rhd X_j$ is selected, the i-arc in N is $\overrightarrow{(X_i, X_j)}$.*

5. *The ci-arcs in N are subset of the conditional ci-arcs in $\mathcal{N}$. For each ci-arc (X_i, X_j) in N, the $CIT(X_i, X_j)$ is derived from the corresponding $PCIT(X_i, X_j)$ in $\mathcal{N}$ by selecting an importance relation over X_i and X_j for each $u \in D(S(X_i, X_j))$.*

Example 2. A $\mathcal{N}$-compatible TCP-net of the PTCP-net in Fig. 2 is shown in Fig. 3. The cp-arc $\overrightarrow{(B,C)}$ exists in the TCP-net, while $\overrightarrow{(A,C)}$ does not exist (Fig. 3(i)). The CPTs of the variables are in Fig. 3(ii). For the variables A, B and D, the preference orders $a \succ a', b \succ b'$ and $d \succ d'$ are selected correspondingly. The preference order of the dependent variable C depends on the actual value of B. The preference orders $c \succ c'$ and $c' \succ c$ are selected for $B = b$ and $B = b'$ correspondingly. The conditional ci-arc (A, B) in the PTCP-net becomes a ci-arc in the TCP-net. $CIT(A, B)$ is in Fig. 3(iii). When $D = d$, $A \triangleright B$ is chosen. When $D = d'$, $B \triangleright A$ is chosen.

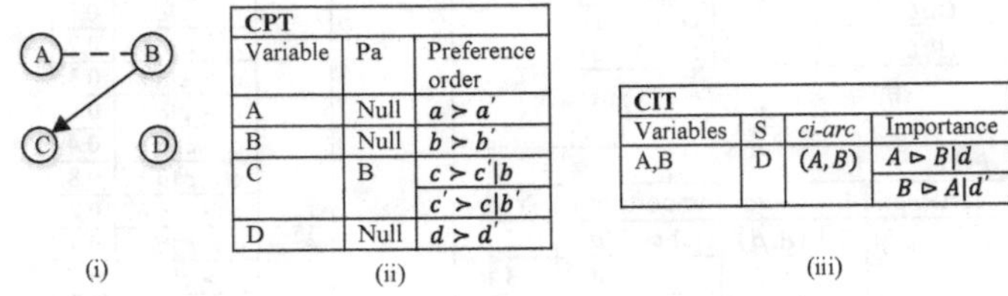

CPT		
Variable	Pa	Preference order
A	Null	$a \succ a'$
B	Null	$b \succ b'$
C	B	$c \succ c' \mid b$
		$c' \succ c \mid b'$
D	Null	$d \succ d'$

(ii)

CIT			
Variables	S	ci-arc	Importance
A,B	D	(A,B)	$A \triangleright B \mid d$
			$B \triangleright A \mid d'$

(iii)

Fig. 3. A TCP-net that is $\mathcal{N}$-compatible with the PTCP-net in Fig. 2.

A large class of TCP-nets, namely conditionally acyclic TCP-nets, has been proved as satisfiable [5]. For the rest of this paper, we consider only the PTCP-net where all its $\mathcal{N}$-compatible TCP-nets are conditionally acyclic.

Let β_N denotes the set of *i-arcs* and *ci-arcs* for a TCP-net N. $\succ_X^u$ denotes a preference order over $D(X)$ for $X \in V$ and $u \in D(Pa(X))$. $\triangleright_{(X,Y)}^u$ denotes an importance relation over X and Y for $(X, Y) \in \beta_N$ and $u \in D(S(X, Y))$.

Definition 5. *If a TCP-net N is $\mathcal{N}$-compatible with a PTCP-net $\mathcal{N}$, the probability of N with respect to $\mathcal{N}$ is defined as:* $Pr_{\mathcal{N}}(N) = \prod_{\alpha\in\alpha_{\mathcal{N}},\alpha\in\alpha_N} Pr(\alpha) \cdot \prod_{\alpha\in\alpha_{\mathcal{N}},\alpha\notin\alpha_N}(1 - Pr(\alpha)) \cdot \prod_{\beta\in\beta_{\mathcal{N}},\beta\in\beta_N} Pr(\beta) \cdot \prod_{\beta\in\beta_{\mathcal{N}},\beta\notin\beta_N}(1 - Pr(\beta)) \cdot \prod_{X\in V,\succ_X^u inN} Pr(\succ_X^u) \cdot \prod_{(X,Y)\in\beta_N,\triangleright_{(X,Y)}^u inN} Pr(\triangleright_{(X,Y)}^u)$.

Example 3. The probability of the $\mathcal{N}$-compatible TCP-net in Fig. 3 is computed as: $Pr\overrightarrow{(B,C)} \cdot (1 - Pr\overrightarrow{(A,C)}) \cdot Pr(A,B) \cdot Pr(a \succ a') \cdot Pr(b \succ b') \cdot Pr(c \succ c'|b) \cdot Pr(c' \succ c|b') \cdot Pr(d \succ d') \cdot Pr(A \triangleright B|d) \cdot Pr(B \triangleright A|d') = 0.7 \cdot (1 - 0.4) \cdot 0.6 \cdot 0.8 \cdot 0.7 \cdot 0.4 \cdot 0.8 \cdot 0.3 \cdot 0.7 \cdot 0.6$.

Theorem 1. *If $\mathcal{N}$ is a PTCP-net and $\mathbb{N}$ is the set of all $\mathcal{N}$-compatible TCP-nets, $Pr_{\mathcal{N}}(N)$ gives a probability distribution over $N \in \mathbb{N}$.*

Proof. Let $\mathbb{N}_1 \subset \mathbb{N}$, where for each $N \in \mathbb{N}_1$, we have $\alpha_N = \alpha_{\mathcal{N}}$ and $\beta_N = \beta_{\mathcal{N}}$ (i.e., the structure of each $N \in \mathbb{N}_1$ is the same). $\succ_{X_1}$ denotes all preference orders over $D(X_1)$ for $X_1 \in V$ in $\mathcal{N}$. $\rhd_{(X_1,Y_1)}$ denotes all importance relations over X_1 and Y_1 for $(X_1, Y_1) \in \beta_{\mathcal{N}}$. We can write:

$$\begin{aligned}
&\sum_{N\in\mathbb{N}_1} Pr_{\mathcal{N}}(N) \\
&= \sum_{N\in\mathbb{N}_1} (\prod_{\alpha\in\alpha_{\mathcal{N}}} Pr(\alpha) \cdot \prod_{\beta\in\beta_{\mathcal{N}}} Pr(\beta) \cdot \prod_{X\in V, \succ_X^u inN} Pr(\succ_X^u) \\
&\quad \cdot \prod_{(X,Y)\in\beta_N, \rhd_{(X,Y)}^u inN} Pr(\rhd_{(X,Y)}^u)) \\
&= \prod_{\alpha\in\alpha_{\mathcal{N}}} Pr(\alpha) \cdot \prod_{\beta\in\beta_{\mathcal{N}}} Pr(\beta) \\
&\quad \cdot \sum_{N\in\mathbb{N}_1} (\prod_{X\in V, \succ_X^u inN} Pr(\succ_X^u) \cdot \prod_{(X,Y)\in\beta_N, \rhd_{(X,Y)}^u inN} Pr(\rhd_{(X,Y)}^u)) \\
&= \prod_{\alpha\in\alpha_{\mathcal{N}}} Pr(\alpha) \cdot \prod_{\beta\in\beta_{\mathcal{N}}} Pr(\beta) \cdot \sum_{u\in D(Pa(X_1))} (\sum_{\succ_{X_1}^u \in \succ_{X_1}} Pr(\succ_{X_1}^u) \\
&\quad \cdot \sum_{N\in\mathbb{N}_1} (\prod_{X\in V, \succ_X^u inN, u\notin D(Pa(X_1))} Pr(\succ_X^u) \cdot \prod_{(X,Y)\in\beta_N, \rhd_{(X,Y)}^u inN} Pr(\rhd_{(X,Y)}^u)))
\end{aligned}$$

Since, for each $u \in D(Pa(X_1)), \sum_{\succ_{X_1}^u \in \succ_{X_1}} Pr(\succ_{X_1}^u) = 1$, we get:

$$\begin{aligned}
&\prod_{\alpha\in\alpha_{\mathcal{N}}} Pr(\alpha) \cdot \prod_{\beta\in\beta_{\mathcal{N}}} Pr(\beta) \\
&\cdot \sum_{N\in\mathbb{N}_1} (\prod_{X\in V - X_1, \succ_X^u inN} Pr(\succ_X^u) \cdot \prod_{(X,Y)\in\beta_N, \rhd_{(X,Y)}^u inN} Pr(\rhd_{(X,Y)}^u))
\end{aligned}$$

Similarly, $Pr(\succ_X^u)$ can be eliminated from the term for each $X \in V$. We get:

$$\begin{aligned}
&\prod_{\alpha\in\alpha_{\mathcal{N}}} Pr(\alpha) \cdot \prod_{\beta\in\beta_{\mathcal{N}}} Pr(\beta) \cdot \sum_{N\in\mathbb{N}_1} (\prod_{(X,Y)\in\beta_N, \rhd_{(X,Y)}^u inN} Pr(\rhd_{(X,Y)}^u)) \\
&= \prod_{\alpha\in\alpha_{\mathcal{N}}} Pr(\alpha) \cdot \prod_{\beta\in\beta_{\mathcal{N}}} Pr(\beta) \cdot \sum_{u\in D(S(X_1,Y_1))} (\sum_{\rhd_{(X_1,Y_1)}^u \in \rhd_{(X_1,Y_1)}} Pr(\rhd_{(X_1,Y_1)}^u) \\
&\quad \cdot \sum_{N\in\mathbb{N}_1} (\prod_{(X,Y)\in\beta_N, \rhd_{(X,Y)}^u inN, u\notin D(S(X_1,Y_1))} Pr(\rhd_{(X,Y)}^u)))
\end{aligned}$$

Since, for each $u \in D(S(X_1, Y_1)), \sum_{\rhd_{(X_1,Y_1)}^u \in \rhd_{(X_1,Y_1)}} Pr(\rhd_{(X_1,Y_1)}^u) = 1$, we get:

$$\prod_{\alpha\in\alpha_{\mathcal{N}}} Pr(\alpha) \cdot \prod_{\beta\in\beta_{\mathcal{N}}} Pr(\beta) \cdot \sum_{N\in\mathbb{N}_1} (\prod_{(X,Y)\in\beta_N - (X_1,Y_1), \rhd_{(X,Y)}^u inN} Pr(\rhd_{(X,Y)}^u))$$

Similarly, $Pr(\rhd^u_{(X,Y)})$ can be eliminated from the term for each $(X,Y) \in \beta_N$. The final term will be: $\prod_{\alpha \in \alpha_\mathcal{N}} Pr(\alpha) \cdot \prod_{\beta \in \beta_\mathcal{N}} Pr(\beta)$. Let α_1 be a cp-arc in $\mathcal{N}$. We assume that $\mathbb{N}_2 \subset \mathbb{N}$, where for each $N \in \mathbb{N}_2$, we have $\alpha_N = \alpha_\mathcal{N} - \alpha_1$ and $\beta_N = \beta_\mathcal{N}$. It can be shown that: $\sum_{N \in \mathbb{N}_2} Pr_\mathcal{N}(N) = (1 - Pr(\alpha_1)) \cdot \prod_{\alpha \in \alpha_\mathcal{N} - \alpha_1} Pr(\alpha) \cdot \prod_{\beta \in \beta_\mathcal{N}} Pr(\beta)$. We get: $\sum_{N \in \mathbb{N}_1} Pr_\mathcal{N}(N) + \sum_{N \in \mathbb{N}_2} Pr_\mathcal{N}(N) = \prod_{\alpha \in \alpha_\mathcal{N} - \alpha_1} Pr(\alpha) \cdot \prod_{\beta \in \beta_\mathcal{N}} Pr(\beta)$. Similarly, by adding the terms for all possible combination of existence and non-existence of cp-arcs and ci-arcs, we can show that: $\sum_{N \in \mathbb{N}} Pr_\mathcal{N}(N) = 1$. Thus, $Pr_\mathcal{N}(N)$ is a probability distribution.

4 Reasoning with PTCP-nets

Given a PTCP-net, we need to answer two basic queries: (1) finding the most probable $\mathcal{N}$-compatible TCP-net that should most likely map onto an unknown user and (2) finding the most probable optimal outcome, which the recommender system should suggest to maximize the probability of a correct recommendation to an unknown user.

4.1 The Most Probable $\mathcal{N}$-Compatible TCP-net

Cornelio et al. [7] introduced the concept of *General Network* (G-net) in the case of a PCP-net. We define G-net for a PTCP-net.

Definition 6. *A G-net $\mathcal{G}_\mathcal{N}$ of a PTCP-net $\mathcal{N}$ is a BN, where the variables and their* Conditional Probability Tables *(PTs) are defined as follow.*

1. *Each independent variable $X \in V$ in $\mathcal{N}$ is also an independent variable X in $\mathcal{G}_\mathcal{N}$. $D(X)$ in $\mathcal{G}_\mathcal{N}$ is the set of all preference orders over $D(X)$ in $\mathcal{N}$. In $\mathcal{G}_\mathcal{N}$, $PT(X)$ is given by the $PCPT(X)$ in $\mathcal{N}$.*
2. *Each cp-arc $\overrightarrow{(X_i, X_j)}$ in $\mathcal{N}$ is an independent variable $\underline{X_i X_j}$ in $\mathcal{G}_\mathcal{N}$ with domain $\{0, 1\}$ where $Pr(0) = 1 - Pr\overrightarrow{(X_i, X_j)}$ and $Pr(1) = Pr\overrightarrow{(X_i, X_j)}$. We call it a cp-variable.*
3. *For each dependent variable X in $\mathcal{N}$, there are as many dependent variables in $\mathcal{G}_\mathcal{N}$ as for each $u \in D(Y : Y \subseteq Pa(X))$, including null. If X_u is a dependent variable in $\mathcal{G}_\mathcal{N}$ for $u \in D(Y : Y \subseteq Pa(X)), D(X_u)$ is given by the set of all preference orders over $D(X)$ in $\mathcal{N}$ and a dummy value d. X_u depends on the cp-variables where the corresponding cp-arcs in $\mathcal{N}$ are directed to X. Note that, for u, there is a corresponding set of existent cp-arcs in $\mathcal{N}$. This set corresponds to an assignment of $Pa(X_u)$ in $\mathcal{G}_\mathcal{N}$. For that assignment of $Pa(X_u)$, the $PT(X_u)$ is given by the $PCPT(X)$ for u from $\mathcal{N}$ with the probability of the dummy value d setting to 0. For the other assignments of $Pa(X_u)$, the $PT(X_u)$ is given by setting the probability of the dummy value d to 1.*
4. *Each ci-arc (X_i, X_j) in $\mathcal{N}$ is an independent variable $\underline{X_i X_j}$ in $\mathcal{G}_\mathcal{N}$ with domain $\{0, 1\}$ where $Pr(0) = 1 - Pr(X_i, X_j)$ and $Pr(1) = \overline{Pr(X_i, X_j)}$. We call it a ci-variable.*

5. *For each $PCIT(X_i, X_j)$ in $\mathcal{N}$, there are as many dependent variables in $\mathcal{G}_{\mathcal{N}}$ as for each $z \in D(S(X_i, X_j))$, excluding null. If $I_{\underline{X_iX_j}/z}$ is a dependent variable in $\mathcal{G}_{\mathcal{N}}$ for $z \in D(S(X_i, X_j))$, $D(I_{\underline{X_iX_j}/z})$ is given by the set of all importance relations over X_i and X_j in $\mathcal{N}$. $I_{\underline{X_iX_j}/z}$ depends on the ci-variable $\underline{X_iX_j}$. $PT(I_{\underline{X_iX_j}/z})$ is given by the $PCIT(X_i, X_j)$ for z from $\mathcal{N}$.*

Example 4. A G-net $\mathcal{G}_{\mathcal{N}}$, corresponding to the PTCP-net $\mathcal{N}$ in Fig. 2, is shown in Fig. 3. The PTs of the independent variables A, B and D are given by the corresponding PCPTs. The PTs of the cp-variables $\underline{AC}$ and $\underline{BC}$ are given by the corresponding PCPETs. For the dependent variable C in $\mathcal{N}$, there are 9 dependent variables in $\mathcal{G}_{\mathcal{N}}$. They are C_{ab}, $C_{ab'}$, $C_{a'b}$, $C_{a'b'}$, C_a, $C_{a'}$, C_b, $C_{b'}$ and C_{null}. Each of these dependent variables has domain of $c \succ c', c' \succ c$ and d. Each of these dependent variables depends on the cp-variables $\underline{AC}$ and $\underline{BC}$. $PT(C_{ab})$ is determined from Fig. 2(iii). Given ab for $PCPT(C)$, the existent cp-arcs are $\overrightarrow{(A, C)}$ and $\overrightarrow{(B, C)}$. When $\underline{AC} = 1$ and $\underline{BC} = 1$, $PT(C_{ab})$ is given by $PCPT(C)$ for ab. For other combinations of $\underline{AC}$ and $\underline{BC}$, we have: $Pr(d|\underline{AC}, \underline{BC}) = 1$. The PTs of the other variables are similarly obtained. The PT of the ci-variable $\underline{AB}$ is given by the corresponding PCIET. For the $PCIT(A, B)$ in Fig. 2(v), the dependent variables in Fig. 4 are $I_{\underline{AB}/d}$ and $I_{\underline{AB}/d'}$. Their domain are $A \rhd B, B \rhd A$ and $A \bowtie B$. Both of the variables depend on $\underline{AB}$. $PT(I_{\underline{AB}/d})$ is given by $PCIT(A, B)$ for d from Fig. 2(v). When $\underline{AB} = 1$, we have: $Pr(A \rhd B|\underline{AB}) = 0.7$ and $Pr(B \rhd A|\underline{AB}) = 0.3$. When $\underline{AB} = 0$, we have: $Pr(A \bowtie B|\underline{AB}) = 1$. $PT(I_{\underline{AB}/d'})$ is similarly determined.

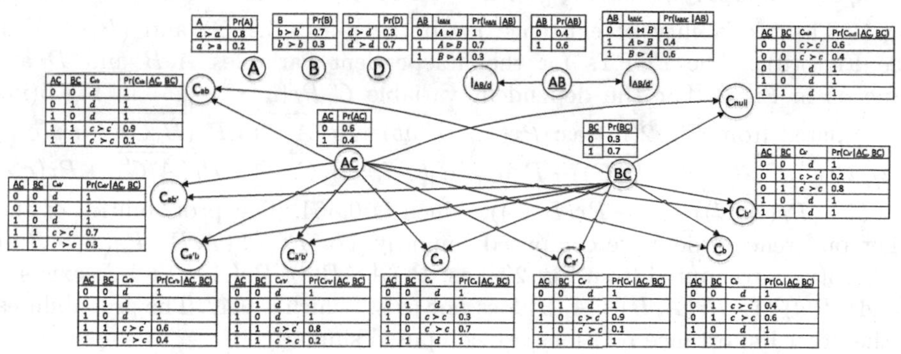

Fig. 4. The G-net of the PTCP-net in Fig. 2.

Intuitively, each assignment in $\mathcal{G}_{\mathcal{N}}$ corresponds to a $\mathcal{N}$-compatible TCP-net. The probability of a $\mathcal{N}$-compatible TCP-net can be given by the joint probability of the corresponding assignment in $\mathcal{G}_{\mathcal{N}}$. Therefore, given a PTCP-net $\mathcal{N}$, the problem of finding the most probable $\mathcal{N}$-compatible TCP-net is mapped into the problem of finding the assignment with the maximal joint probability in $\mathcal{G}_{\mathcal{N}}$.

4.2 The Most Probable Optimal Outcome

Definition 7. *Given a PTCP-net $\mathcal{N}$ and the set of its $\mathcal{N}$-compatible TCP-nets $\mathbb{N}$, the probability of an outcome o to be optimal, is defined as: $Pr(o) = \sum_{N \in \mathbb{N},\ o \text{ is optimal in } N} Pr_{\mathcal{N}}(N)$.*

To find the most probable optimal outcome for a PCP-net, two networks, namely Transformed PCP-net (Trans-net) and Optimal-net (Opt-net), were defined [7]. We extend these two networks in the case of the PTCP-net.

Definition 8. *The Trans-net $\mathcal{N}_T$ of a given PTCP-net $\mathcal{N}$ is a PTCP-net with the following:*

1. *$\mathcal{N}_T$ has the same variables and their domains as $\mathcal{N}$.*
2. *All the cp-arcs in $\mathcal{N}$ are also in $\mathcal{N}_T$ with probability of existence 1.*
3. *For an independent variable, the PCPTs in both $\mathcal{N}$ and $\mathcal{N}_T$ are the same. For a dependent variable, cp-arc probabilities are transformed in computing PCPT. For the PCPT of a dependent variable X, the probability of a preference order $\succ^u_X$ is computed from $\mathcal{N}$ as: $\sum_{v \in D(Y: Y \subseteq Pa(X)), v \subseteq u} (Pr(\succ^v_X) \cdot \prod_{Z \in Pa(X), D(Z) \cap v \neq \emptyset} Pr(\overrightarrow{Z, X}) \cdot \prod_{Z \in Pa(X), D(Z) \cap v = \emptyset} (1 - Pr(\overrightarrow{Z, X})))$.*
4. *All the ci-arcs in $\mathcal{N}$ are also in $\mathcal{N}_T$ with probability of existence 1.*
5. *ci-arc probabilities are transformed in computing PCITs in $\mathcal{N}_T$. For the PCIT of a ci-arc (X_i, X_j), the probability of an importance relation $\rhd^z_{(X_i,X_j)}$ is computed from $\mathcal{N}$ as follow: $Pr(\rhd^z_{(X_i,X_j)}) \cdot Pr(X_i, X_j) | (X_i, X_j) exists + Pr(\rhd^z_{(X_i,X_j)}) \cdot (1 - Pr(X_i, X_j)) | (X_i, X_j) does\ not\ exist$.*

Example 5. The Trans-net $\mathcal{N}_T$, of the PTCP-net $\mathcal{N}$ in Fig. 2, is shown in Fig. 5. The probability of existence for both cp-arcs $\overrightarrow{(A, C)}$ and $\overrightarrow{(B, C)}$ is 1 (see Fig. 5(ii)). The PCPTs for the independent variables A, B and D are same as in Fig. 2. For the dependent variable $C, Pr(c \succ c'|ab)$ in Fig. 5(iii) is computed from Fig. 2(iii) as: $Pr(c \succ c'|ab) \cdot Pr(\overrightarrow{A, C}) \cdot Pr(\overrightarrow{B, C}) + Pr(c \succ c'|a) \cdot Pr(\overrightarrow{A, C}) \cdot (1 - Pr(\overrightarrow{B, C})) + Pr(c \succ c'|b) \cdot Pr(\overrightarrow{B, C}) \cdot (1 - Pr(\overrightarrow{A, C})) + Pr(c \succ c') \cdot (1 - Pr(\overrightarrow{A, C})) \cdot (1 - Pr(\overrightarrow{B, C}))$, which is 0.564. The probabilities of the other preference orders are computed similarly. For $PCIT(A, B), Pr(A \rhd B|d)$ in Fig. 5(v) is computed from Fig. 2(v) as: $Pr(A \rhd B|d) \cdot Pr(A, B)|(A, B)$exists$+ Pr(A \rhd B|d) \cdot (1 - Pr(A, B))|(A, B)$does not exist, which is 0.42. The probabilities of the other importance relations are computed similarly.

Note that, the transformation of the probabilities from cp-arcs and ci-arcs to the corresponding PCPTs and PCITs preserves the probability of an outcome to be optimal. Therefore, the most probable optimal outcome in a Trans-net will give the most probable optimal outcome in the corresponding PTCP-net.

Definition 9. *The Opt-net $O_{\mathcal{N}_T}$ of a given Trans-net $\mathcal{N}_T$ is a BN with the following. Each variable X in $\mathcal{N}_T$ is also a variable X in $O_{\mathcal{N}_T}$. $D(X)$ in $O_{\mathcal{N}_T}$ are the values of X from $\mathcal{N}_T$ that rank first in at least one preference order with*

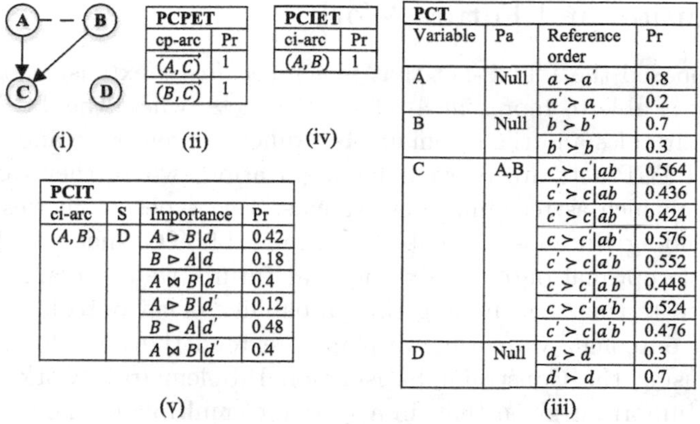

PCPET	
cp-arc	Pr
$\overrightarrow{(A,C)}$	1
$\overrightarrow{(B,C)}$	1

PCIET	
ci-arc	Pr
(A,B)	1

PCT			
Variable	Pa	Reference order	Pr
A	Null	$a \succ a'$	0.8
		$a' \succ a$	0.2
B	Null	$b \succ b'$	0.7
		$b' \succ b$	0.3
C	A,B	$c \succ c' \mid ab$	0.564
		$c' \succ c \mid ab$	0.436
		$c' \succ c \mid ab'$	0.424
		$c \succ c' \mid ab'$	0.576
		$c' \succ c \mid a'b$	0.552
		$c \succ c' \mid a'b$	0.448
		$c \succ c' \mid a'b'$	0.524
		$c' \succ c \mid a'b'$	0.476
D	Null	$d \succ d'$	0.3
		$d' \succ d$	0.7

PCIT			
ci-arc	S	Importance	Pr
(A,B)	D	$A \rhd B \mid d$	0.42
		$B \rhd A \mid d$	0.18
		$A \bowtie B \mid d$	0.4
		$A \rhd B \mid d'$	0.12
		$B \rhd A \mid d'$	0.48
		$A \bowtie B \mid d'$	0.4

Fig. 5. The Trans-net of the PTCP-net in Fig. 2.

non-zero probability. All the cp-arcs in $\mathcal{N}_T$ also exist in $O_{\mathcal{N}_T}$, which define probabilistic dependencies over the variables in $O_{\mathcal{N}_T}$. $PT(X)$ in $O_{\mathcal{N}_T}$ is computed as: for each $x \in D(X)$ and $u \in D(Pa(X))$, $Pr(x|u) = \sum_{x ranks\ first\ in \succ^u_X} Pr(\succ^u_X)$.

The purpose of an Opt-net is to represent the probability of each outcome that is optimal in at least one TCP-net. The PCITs are ignored while building an Opt-net from a Trans-net, because the probability of an outcome to be optimal is independent of the PCITs. The Opt-net, corresponding to the Trans-net in Fig. 5, is shown in Fig. 6. The variables are A, B, C and D. The PT of each variable is determined from the corresponding PCPT.

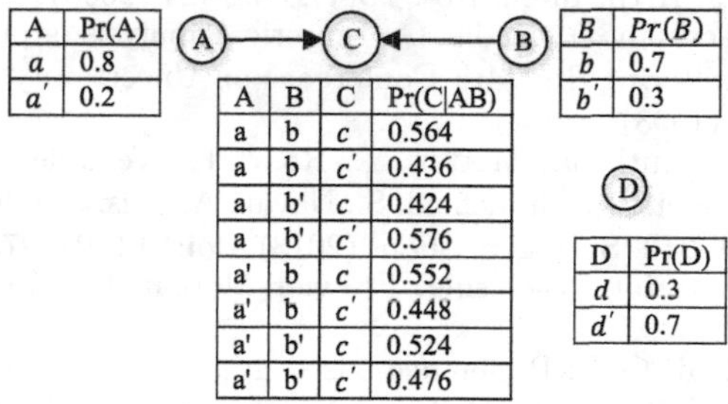

A	Pr(A)
a	0.8
a'	0.2

B	Pr(B)
b	0.7
b'	0.3

A	B	C	Pr(C|AB)
a	b	c	0.564
a	b	c'	0.436
a	b'	c	0.424
a	b'	c'	0.576
a'	b	c	0.552
a'	b	c'	0.448
a'	b'	c	0.524
a'	b'	c'	0.476

D	Pr(D)
d	0.3
d'	0.7

Fig. 6. The Opt-net corresponding to the Trans-net in Fig. 5.

Note that, for a given PTCP-net $\mathcal{N}$ and its Opt-net $O_{\mathcal{N}_T}$, there is a one-to-one correspondence between the assignments of $O_{\mathcal{N}_T}$ and the outcomes that are optimal in at least one $\mathcal{N}$-compatible TCP-net. The probability of an outcome to be optimal in $\mathcal{N}$ is the joint probability of the corresponding assignment in $O_{\mathcal{N}_T}$. Thus the most probable optimal outcome in $\mathcal{N}$ can be found by finding the assignment with highest joint probability in $O_{\mathcal{N}_T}$.

5 Conclusion and Future Work

We have proposed the PTCP-net that is a *probabilistic* extension of TCP-net. A PTCP-net is able to represent a set of TCP-nets, where the TCP-nets have same set of variables and their domains but differ in preference and importance statements. PTCP-nets are relevant for applications where there are multiple unknown users such as recommender systems. Two types of queries have been evaluated: finding the most probable $\mathcal{N}$-compatible TCP-net and finding the most probable optimal outcome. In the near future, we are planning to work on dominance testing, i.e., finding the probability of an outcome is preferred over another outcome. Moreover, we plan to extend the PTCP-net with hard constraints using the Constraint Satisfaction Problem framework [8]. This is particularly important given that, in a system of multiple unknown users, each user can have different set of constraints.

References

1. Adomavicius, G., Tuzhilin, A.: Toward the next generation of recommender systems: a survey of the state-of-the-art and possible extensions. IEEE Trans. Knowl. Data Eng. **17**(6), 734–749 (2005)
2. Bigot, D., Zanuttini, B., Fargier, H., Mengin, J.: Probabilistic conditional preference networks. In: 29th Conference on Uncertainty in Artificial Intelligence, pp. 72–81 (2013)
3. Boutilier, C., Brafman, R.I., Domshlak, C., Hoos, H.H., Poole, D.: CP-nets: a tool for representing and reasoning with conditional ceteris paribus preference statements. J. Artif. Intell. Res. **21**, 135–191 (2004)
4. Brafman, R.I., Domshlak, C.: TCP-nets for preference-based product configuration. In: ECAI 2002 Workshop on Configuration (2002)
5. Brafman, R.I., Domshlak, C., Shimony, S.E.: On graphical modeling of preference and importance. J. Artif. Intell. Res. **25**(1), 389–424 (2006)
6. Breese, J.S., Heckerman, D., Kadie, C.: Empirical analysis of predictive algorithms for collaborative filtering. In: 14th Conference on Uncertainty in Artificial Intelligence, pp. 43–52 (1998)
7. Cornelio, C., Goldsmith, J., Mattei, N., Rossi, F., Venable, K.B.: Updates and uncertainty in CP-nets. In: Cranefield, S., Nayak, A. (eds.) AI 2013. LNCS (LNAI), vol. 8272, pp. 301–312. Springer, Cham (2013). doi:10.1007/978-3-319-03680-9_32
8. Dechter, R.: Constraint Processing. Elsevier Morgan Kaufmann, San Francisco (2003)
9. Jin, R., Si, L., Zhai, C.X.: Preference-based graphic models for collaborative filtering. In: 19th Conference on Uncertainty in Artificial Intelligence, pp. 329–336 (2003)
10. Liu, J., Yao, Z., Xiong, Y., Liu, W., Wu, C.: Learning conditional preference network from noisy samples using hypothesis testing. Knowl.-Based Syst. **40**, 7–16 (2013)
11. Pearl, J.: Probabilistic Reasoning in Intelligent Systems: Networks of Plausible Inference. Morgan Kaufmann Publishers Inc., Burlington (1988)
12. Rossi, F., Venable, K.B., Walsh, T.: mCP nets: representing and reasoning with preferences of multiple agents. In: 19th National Conference on Artificial intelligence (AAAI 2004), pp. 729–734 (2004)
13. Yager, R.R.: Fusion of multi-agent preference orderings. Fuzzy Sets Syst. **117**(1), 1–12 (2001)

Resolving Inconsistencies of Scope Interpretations in Sum-Product Networks

Jhonatan S. Oliveira(✉), Cory J. Butz, and André E. dos Santos

Department of Computer Science, University of Regina, Regina, Canada
{oliveira,butz,dossantos}@cs.uregina.ca

Abstract. *Sum-product networks* (SPNs) are a deep learning model that have shown impressive results in several artificial intelligence applications. Tractable inference in practice requires an SPN to be *complete* and either *consistent* or *decomposable*. These properties can be verified using the definition of scope. In fact, the notion of scope can be used to define SPNs when they are interpreted as hierarchically structured latent variables in mixture models.

In this paper, we first show that the mixture model definition of scope is inconsistent with interpreting SPNs as *arithmetic circuit* (ACs), the network on which SPNs were founded. We then propose a definition of scope that is consistent with an AC interpretation. We next show that the AC definition of scope can be used for verifying the completeness property of SPNs, but not for verifying consistency or decomposability, nor is it consistent with a mixture model interpretation. We resolve the above inconsistencies by presenting a more general definition of scope that remains suitable for both AC and mixture model interpretations of SPNs, and can also be used for verifying the complete, consistent, and decomposable properties of SPNs.

Keywords: Sum-product networks · Arithmetic circuits · Deep learning

1 Introduction

Sum-product networks (SPNs) [11] are a class of tractable deep learning models for probabilistic inference. This is an attractive feature when compared to probabilistic graphical models in general, including *Bayesian networks* [7], where inference is NP-hard [3]. The tractability of SPN can be seen as follows [11]: the partition function of a probabilistic graphical model is intractable because it is the sum of an exponential number of terms. All marginals are sums of subsets of these terms, meaning that if the partition function can be computed efficiently, so can they. SPNs have been successfully applied in a variety of practical applications, including image completion [5,9,11], computer vision [1], classification [6], and speech and language modeling [2,10]. An SPN is a rooted, directed acyclic graph in which leaf nodes are indicator variables and internal nodes are either sum or multiplication operations. The practical usefulness of SPNs relies on three properties: *completeness*, *consistency*, and *decomposability* [11]. The satisfaction

M. Mouhoub and P. Langlais (Eds.): Canadian AI 2017, LNAI 10233, pp. 305–315, 2017.
DOI: 10.1007/978-3-319-57351-9_35

of these properties can be verified using the scope definition. The *scope* [11] of a node are the random variables appearing as descendants of that node.

There are probabilistic and non-probabilistic interpretations of SPNs. From a non-probabilistic perspective, SPNs can be interpreted as deep neural networks with the following three special properties [13]. First, SPNs are labeled, meaning that all nodes in the network are associated to random variables by the means of a scope definition. Next, they are constrained, that is, subjected to the completeness, consistency, and decomposability properties. Lastly, they are fully probabilistic neural networks, where each node (or neuron) is a valid SPN and still models a correct distribution over its scope.

Our discussion focuses on the probabilistic perspective, where SPNs have the capacity to generalize a variety of approaches to representing and learning tractable models, including *mixture models* [8] and *arithmetic circuits* (ACs) [4]. We compare these two interpretations by means of the scope definition. The scope definition is ideally suited for mixture model interpretation of an SPN, since the scope of a node grows larger the closer the node is to the root. This reflects the fact that higher nodes are mixtures of more random variables. On the other hand, this interpretation of scope is direct opposition with ACs, where sum nodes are marginalization operations that *reduce* scope.

In this paper, our first contribution is a new scope definition that suits the AC interpretation of an SPN. This definition considers the fact that ACs are compiled from Bayesian networks. Thus, the random variables at the leaf nodes come from probabilities in Bayesian network conditional probability tables. The scope of the leaf nodes then are labeled according to the variables in the conditional probability tables. The scope of a sum node removes one random variable from the union of the scope of its children. This reflects the interpretation of sum nodes as being marginalization. The scope of a multiplication node is the union of its children's scope. We establish that the completeness property of SPN can be defined under the AC interpretation of scope. Unfortunately, consistency and decomposability can not be applied using this scope definition, meaning that the definition can not be used for verifying tractability of an SPN. Moreover, the proposed scope definition for ACs can be non-intuitive for leaf nodes under a mixture model interpretation. For example, the scope of a leaf node can consider variables that are not random variables for an SPN leaf node, yet appear in a conditional probability table from the Bayesian network.

The second contribution of this paper is a novel scope definition with two advantages. First, it can be used when defining all three SPN properties. Second, it addresses the counter-intuitive points in both the mixture model and AC interpretations. Here, we define the scope of sum nodes more intuitively from an AC point of view by treating them as marginalization. Hence, the scope of sum nodes removes one random variable from the union of the scope of its children. Moreover, we make the scope of leaf nodes more intuitive from a mixture model point of view by only considering variables that are random variables for the SPN leaf node. Since both mixture models and ACs can be compiled into SPNs, the new scope definition improves the understanding of SPNs for different research communities, while still guaranteeing tractable inference during learning.

The remainder of this paper follows. Section 2 gives background information and presents the mixture model interpretation of SPNs. A new definition of scope under AC interpretation is presented in Sect. 3. In Sect. 4, we propose another scope definition that fits both mixture model and AC interpretations. Analysis and advantages are discussed in Sect. 5. Section 6 draws conclusions.

2 Background

Here we give pertinent definitions and review two deep learning networks.

We use uppercase letters X to denote variables and lowercase letters x to denote their values. We denote sets of variables with boldface uppercase letters $\mathbf{X}$ and their instantiations with boldface lowercase letters $\mathbf{x}$. For a boolean variable X, x denotes when $X = true$ and $\bar{x}$ for $X = false$. Also, we use $P(x)$ instead of $P(X = x)$ and $P(\mathbf{x})$ to mean $P(\mathbf{X} = \mathbf{x})$. Lastly, we denote graphs with calligraphic letters.

2.1 Arithmetic Circuits

Bayesian networks [7] are probabilistic graphical models composed of a *directed acyclic graph* (DAG) and a set of *conditional probability tables* (CPTs) corresponding to the structure of the DAG. For example, Fig. 1 shows the DAG of a Bayesian network $\mathcal{B}$ on binary variables A, B, and C, where CPTs $P(A)$, $P(B|A)$, and $P(C|A)$ are not illustrated.

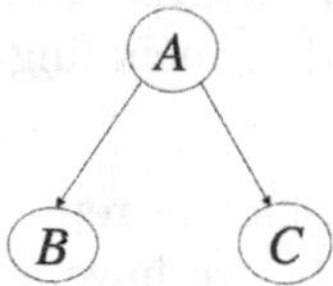

Fig. 1. A Bayesian network.

Bayesian networks are compiled into *Arithmetic Circuits* (ACs) [4] by mapping the operations performed when marginalizing all variables from the BN into a graph.

Example 1. Consider marginalizing variables A, B, and C from the Bayesian network in Fig. 1:

$$\sum_A P(A) \cdot \sum_B P(B|A) \cdot \sum_C P(C|A). \tag{1}$$

The computational process in Example 1 can be represented as the AC in Fig. 2 and formalized next.

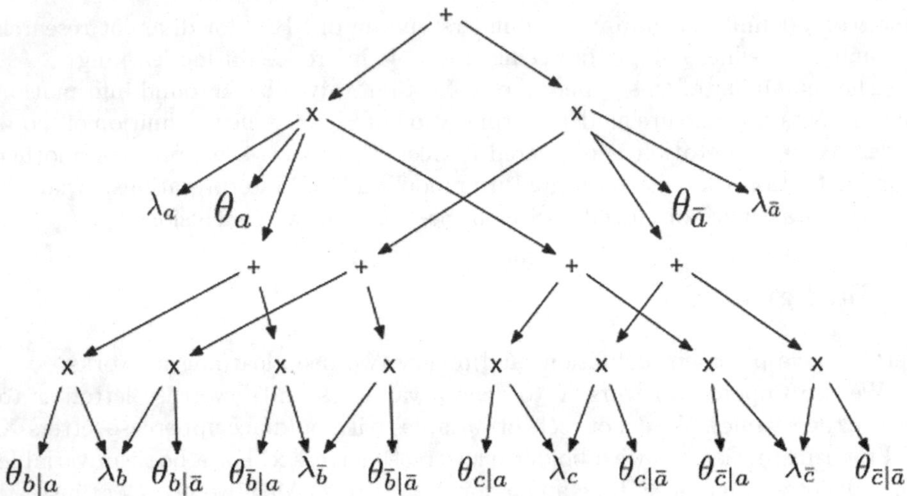

Fig. 2. An AC for the Bayesian network in Fig. 1 following (1).

Definition 1 *[4]. An arithmetic circuit (AC) over variables* $\mathbf{U}$ *is a rooted, DAG whose leaf nodes are labeled with numeric constants, called parameters, or* λ *variables, called indicators, and whose other nodes are labeled with multiplication and addition operations.*

Notice that parameter variables are set according to the Bayesian network CPTs, while indicator variables are set according to any observed evidence.

Example 2. Figure 2 shows an AC. Here, $P(a) = \theta_a$ and $P(b|a) = \theta_{b|a}$, the parameters are the numeric constant variables in the leaf nodes. The indicators are the λ variables in the leaf nodes, including λ_a, the indicator for a, and $\lambda_{\bar{a}}$ the indicator for $\bar{a}$.

In practical terms, an AC graphically represents a *network polynomial* over variables $\mathbf{U}$, where for each $X \in \mathbf{U}$, we have a set of indicator variable λ_x and for each network parameter for CPT $P(x|\mathbf{u})$, we have a set of parameters $\theta_{x|\mathbf{u}}$.

Example 3. The AC in Fig. 2 represents the following network polynomial f:

$$f = (\lambda_a \cdot \theta_a) \cdot (\lambda_b \cdot \theta_{b|a} + \lambda_{\bar{b}} \cdot \theta_{\bar{b}|a}) \cdot (\lambda_c \cdot \theta_{c|a} + \lambda_{\bar{c}} \cdot \theta_{\bar{c}|a}) \tag{2}$$

$$+ (\lambda_{\bar{a}} \cdot \theta_{\bar{a}}) \cdot (\lambda_b \cdot \theta_{b|\bar{a}} + \lambda_{\bar{b}} \cdot \theta_{\bar{b}|\bar{a}}) \cdot (\lambda_c \cdot \theta_{c|\bar{a}} + \lambda_{\bar{c}} \cdot \theta_{\bar{c}|\bar{a}}) \tag{3}$$

A query can be answered in an AC in time and space linear in the circuit size [4], where *size* means the number of edges. In order to evaluate an AC, we first set the indicator variables to 0 or 1 accordingly to any observed evidence. For example, when computing $P(a, \bar{c})$, indicators $\lambda_a, \lambda_b, \lambda_{\bar{b}}$, and $\lambda_{\bar{c}}$ are set to 1, while indicators $\lambda_{\bar{a}}$ and λ_c are set to 0. Next, we traverse the AC upward computing the value of a node after having computed the values of its children. A downward pass can be performed to compute the posterior of all variables given evidence [4].

2.2 Sum-Product Networks

Sum-Product Networks (SPNs) [11] are a deep probabilistic model. One striking feature of SPNs is that they can efficiently represent tractable probability distributions [12].

Definition 2 *[11]. A* Sum-product network *(SPN) over Boolean variables* **X** *is a rooted DAG whose leaves are indicators* $\lambda_{x_1}, \ldots, \lambda_{x_N}$ *and* $\lambda_{\bar{x}_1}, \ldots, \lambda_{\bar{x}_N}$ *and whose internal nodes are sums and products. Each edge* (v_i, v_j) *emanating from a sum node* v_i *has a non-negative weight* w_{ij}*. The value of a product node is the product of the values of its children. The value of a sum node is* $\sum_{v_j \in Ch(v_i)} w_{ij} val(v_j)$*, where* $Ch(v_i)$ *are the children of* v_i *and* $val(v_j)$ *is the value of node* v_j*. The value of an SPN* $\mathcal{S}$ *is the value of its root.*

Example 4. An SPN is shown in Fig. 3. Here, for instance, λ_a is an indicator, $n2$ is a product node, and $n4$ is a sum node.

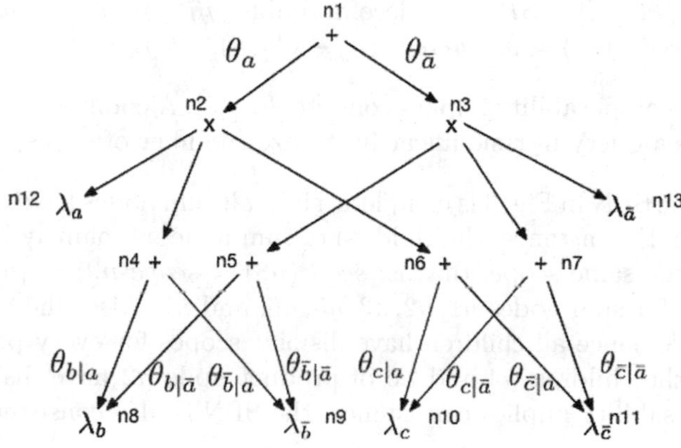

Fig. 3. A sum-product network.

An SPN graph compactly represents a polynomial over variables U.

Example 5. The SPN in Fig. 3 represents the polynomial f:

$$f = (\lambda_a \cdot \theta_a) \cdot (\lambda_b \cdot \theta_{b|a} + \lambda_{\bar{b}} \cdot \theta_{\bar{b}|a}) \cdot (\lambda_c \cdot \theta_{c|a} + \lambda_{\bar{c}} \cdot \theta_{\bar{c}|a}) \tag{4}$$

$$+ (\lambda_{\bar{a}} \cdot \theta_{\bar{a}}) \cdot (\lambda_b \cdot \theta_{b|\bar{a}} + \lambda_{\bar{b}} \cdot \theta_{\bar{b}|\bar{a}}) \cdot (\lambda_c \cdot \theta_{c|\bar{a}} + \lambda_{\bar{c}} \cdot \theta_{\bar{c}|\bar{a}}) \tag{5}$$

The important notion of scope is now reviewed.

Definition 3 *[14]. For any node* n *in an SPN, if* n *is a leaf node then* $scope(n) = \{X\}$*, else* $scope(n) = \bigcup_{c \in Ch(n)} scope(c)$*.*

Example 6. Recall Fig. 3. The scope of leaf node $n10$ is $scope(n10) = \{C\}$, since $n10$ is an indicator. Sum node $n6$ has two children, nodes $n10$ and $n11$. By definition, the scope of $n6$ is $scope(n6) = \{C\}$. Product node $n3$ has $scope(n3) = \{A, B, C\}$, which is the union of $n3$ children's scope. Similarly, for instance,

$$scope(n8) = \{B\}, \tag{6}$$
$$scope(n4) = \{B\}, \tag{7}$$
$$scope(n2) = \{A, B, C\}, \text{ and} \tag{8}$$
$$scope(n1) = \{A, B, C\}. \tag{9}$$

The follow three properties have practical usefulness in SPNs.

Definition 4 *[11]. An SPN is* complete *iff each sum node has children with the same scope.*

Definition 5 *[11]. An SPN is* consistent *iff no variable appears negated in one child of a product node and non-negated in another.*

Definition 6 *[11]. An SPN is* decomposable *iff for every product node* n, $scope(n_i) \cap scope(n_j) = \emptyset$*, where* $n_i, n_j \in Ch(n), i \neq j$.

In SPNs, decomposability implies consistency [11]. A complete and consistent SPN computes a query in time linear in its size (number of edges) [11].

Example 7. The SPN in Fig. 3 is complete, since all sum nodes have children with the same scope. For instance, the children of sum node $n4$, namely leaf nodes $n8$ and $n9$, have the same scope, that is, $scope(n8) = scope(n9) = \{b\}$. The same can be verified for sum nodes $n1, n2, n3, n5, n6$, and $n7$. Also, the SPN in Fig. 3 is decomposable, since all children have disjoint scopes for every product node. For example, the children $n4$ and $n6$ of product node $n2$ have disjoint scopes. Since decomposability implies consistency, the SPN is also consistent.

2.3 Mixture Model Interpretation

SPNs can be viewed as generalized DAGs of *mixture models*, where sum nodes correspond to mixtures over subsets of variables and product nodes correspond to features or mixture components [11]. In general, mixture models can be interpreted as a distribution over random variables described by the marginalization of *latent variables* (LVs). Under this interpretation, each sum node from an SPN has an associated LV [8].

Definition 3 agrees with the mixture model interpretation, since it takes into consideration the scope of nodes involved in previous computation. That is, a hierarchical mixture model is considered as a hierarchical structured LV model. Henceforth, by $scope_{mm}$, we mean scope as given in Definition 3.

3 Scope Under an AC Interpretation

In order to propose a scope definition under an AC interpretation, we first need to formalize the equivalence between ACs and SPNs. ACs are equivalent to SPNs for discrete domains [12]. The representational differences are that ACs use indicator nodes and parameter nodes as leaves, while SPNs use univariate distributions as leaves and attach all parameters to the outgoing edges of sum nodes [12]. For example, the AC in Fig. 2 is equivalent to the SPN in Fig. 3. Indeed, the polynomial represented by the AC in (3) for Example 3 is the same as the polynomial represented by the SPN in (5) for Example 5.

We now propose a novel scope definition taking into consideration the AC interpretation of an SPN. First, notice that all the weights in an SPN built from an AC correspond to probabilities in the given Bayesian network. Thus, we can associate labels from the CPTs to each edge weight. Outgoing edges from a product node have the same labels as its incoming edges.

Example 8. In the SPN of Fig. 3, sum node $n4$ has weights $\theta_{b|a}$ and $\theta_{\bar{b}|a}$. Both weights are probabilities $P(b|a)$ and $P(\bar{b}|a)$ from the CPTs in the Bayesian network in Fig. 1. Thus, the set $\{A, B\}$ of variables are associated labels of both edges $(n4, n8)$ and $(n4, n9)$. Moreover, outgoing edges $(n2, n12), (n2, n4)$, and $(n2, n6)$ from product node $n2$ have the set $\{A\}$ as the associated label, since θ_a is the weight attached to $n2$'s incoming edge.

Next, let us consider the layers of an SPN, where we will consider the bottom layer being the leaf nodes and the top layer being the root.

Example 9. The SPN in Fig. 3 contains 4 layers. The bottom layer is formed by leaf nodes $n8, n9, n10, n11, n12$, and $n13$. The next layer consisting of sum nodes $n4, n5, n6$, and $n7$ followed by a layer formed by multiplication nodes $n2$ and $n3$. Lastly, the top layer is sum node $n1$.

We now give the first contribution of this paper.

Definition 7. *The scope of a leaf node is the set of all variables involved in the labeling of its incoming edges. The scope of a product node is the union of its children's scope. The scope of a sum node is the intersection between the union of its children's scope in layer k and the scope of all other nodes in layer k.*

The scope of a node under the AC interpretation will be denoted $scope_{ac}$.

Example 10. Recall the SPN in Fig. 3. The scope of leaf node $n10$ is $scope_{ac}$ $(n10) = \{A, C\}$, since $n10$ is a leaf node with labeled incoming edges $(n6, n10)$ and $(n7, n10)$ both over variables $\{A, C\}$. Product node $n3$ has $scope(n3) = \{A\}$, which is the union of $n3$ children's scope. Now, consider sum node $n6$. It has two children, $n10$ and $n11$. The other nodes on the same layer as $n10$ and $n11$ are $n8$ and $n9$. Then, by definition, the scope of $n6$ is:

$$\begin{aligned} scope_{ac}(n6) &= (scope_{ac}(n10) \cup scope_{ac}(n11)) \cap (scope_{ac}(n8) \cup scope_{ac}(n9)) \\ &= (\{A, C\} \cup \{A, C\}) \cap (\{A, B\} \cup \{A, B\}) \\ &= \{A, C\} \cap \{A, B\} \\ &= \{A\}. \end{aligned}$$

Similarly, it can be verified that:

$$scope_{ac}(n8) = \{A, B\}, \tag{10}$$

$$scope_{ac}(n4) = \{A\}, \tag{11}$$

$$scope_{ac}(n2) = \{A\}, \text{ and} \tag{12}$$

$$scope_{ac}(n1) = \{\}. \tag{13}$$

This scope definition agrees with the AC interpretation for two reasons. First, leaf nodes consider all variables involved in the Bayesian network CPTs. For example, in Example 10, $scope_{ac}(n8) = \{A, B\}$, since the CPT $P(b|a)$ from where $\theta_{b|a}$ comes from, involves variables A and B. Second, sum nodes reduce the scope of previous layers. This is consistent with marginalization. In Example 10, for instance, $scope_{ac}(n4) = \{A\}$ reduced the scope of $n8$ by removing A from $\{A, B\}$.

4 A Scope Definition for Both SPN Interpretations

We first motivate the introduction of an unified interpretation of scope that works for both mixture model and AC interpretations of an SPN.

Notice that the scope definition under the AC interpretation in Definition 7 can consider variables that are not in the domain of indicator variables.

Example 11. In Fig. 3, node $n8$ has indicator λ_b, that is, an indicator for variable b. Yet, $scope_{ac}(n8) = \{A, B\}$ under the AC interpretation. Notice that variable A is considered part of the scope even though it is not in the domain of λ_b.

On the other hand, the scope definition under the mixture model interpretation does not consider a sum node as marginalization, namely, a domain reduction operation.

Example 12. Consider $n4$ and $n8$ in Fig. 3. For instance, $scope_{mm}(n8) = \{B\}$ under the mixture model interpretation. Yet $scope_{mm}(n4) = \{B\}$ even though $n4$ is a sum node. That is, the scope was not reduced after a sum node as would be expected by marginalization.

The scope definition under the AC interpretation can be counterintuitive in the leaf nodes of a mixture model point of view. On the other hand, the scope definition under a mixture model interpretation can be counterintuitive in the sum nodes from an AC point of view. In general, one interpretation does not cover the other one with their respective scope definition.

Our second main contribution is the proposal of a scope definition that agrees with both the mixture model and AC interpretations of SPN.

Definition 8. *The scope of a leaf node n with indicator λ over X is $scope(v) = \{X\}$. The scope of a sum node is the union of its children's scope, except those variables not appearing in the scope of any non-descendant nodes in the child layer. The scope of a product node is the union of its children's scope.*

Henceforth, we will denote the scope of a node under both the AC and mixture model interpretations as $scope_{am}$.

Example 13. Recall Fig. 3. The scope of leaf node $n10$ with indicator λ_c over C is $scope_{am}(n10) = \{C\}$. Sum node $n6$ has scope being the union of its children's scope, that is, $\{C\}$, except to those variables not appearing in the scope of any non-descendant nodes in the layer below, namely, variable C. Thus, $scope_{ac}(n6) = \{\}$. Product node $n3$ has $scope(n3) = \{A\}$, which is the union of $n3$ children's scope. Similarly, we can obtain:

$$scope_{am}(n8) = \{B\}, \tag{14}$$

$$scope_{am}(n4) = \{\}, \tag{15}$$

$$scope_{am}(n2) = \{A\}, \text{ and} \tag{16}$$

$$scope_{am}(n1) = \{\}, \tag{17}$$

As shown in Example 13, Definition 8 addresses both counterintuitive issues by only considering variables that are in the domain of the indicator variables and by reducing the scope after a sum node.

5 Analysis

Here, we show that $scope_{ac}$, the scope definition under the AC interpretation, can be used for defining correctness of an SPN, but not for defining consistency and decomposability. On the other hand, we show that $scope_{am}$, the scope definition under both interpretations, can be used for defining all three properties.

First, let us consider the scope definition under the AC interpretation.

Lemma 1. *If an SPN is complete by using the $scope_{mm}$ definition, then it is complete by using the $scope_{ac}$ definition.*

Proof. Consider a complete SPN by using the $scope_{mm}$ definition. A sum node n can have either product or leaf children.

We first show that leaf children of n also have the same scope as when using $scope_{ac}$. Consider a leaf child c of n. Suppose $scope(c)_{mm} = \{X\}$. By definition, this means that node c has an indicator λ over X. Under an AC interpretation, the λ over X exist only because it came from a Bayesian network CPT $P(X|Y)$. Hence, incoming edges for c have labels containing variables in X and Y. Thus, by the $scope(c)_{ac}$ definition, $scope(c)_{ac} = \{X, Y\}$. The same argument can be made for the other leaf children of n. Therefore, leaf children of n have the same scope using $scope_{ac}$ and $scope_{mm}$.

We next establish that a product child of n also has the same scope when using $scope_{ac}$. The scope definition for product nodes is the same for $scope_{mm}$ or $scope_{ac}$. □

Example 14. The SPN in Fig. 3 is complete, as shown in Example 7, by using $scope_{mm}$, since all children of each sum node have the same scope. Consider, for instance, sum node $n4$ with leaf children. Both leaf children have the same scope, namely, $scope_{mm}(n8) = scope_{mm}(n9) = \{B\}$. Similarly, under the AC interpretation, the scope of $n4$ leaf children are the same, that is, $scope_{ac}(n8) = scope_{ac}(n9) = \{A, B\}$. Now, consider sum node $n1$ with product children. Both product children have the same scope, namely, $scope_{mm}(n2) = scope_{mm}(n9) = \{A, B, C\}$. In the same way, under the AC interpretation, the scope of $n1$'s product children are the same. That is, $scope_{ac}(n2) = scope_{ac}(n9) = \{A\}$.

Unfortunately, $scope_{ac}$ can not be used for defining consistency or decomposability.

Example 15. Example 7 shows that the SPN in Fig. 3 is decomposable by using $scope_{mm}$. In contrast, under the AC interpretation, $scope_{ac}(n12) = \{A\}$, $scope_{ac}(n4) = \{A\}$, and $scope_{ac}(n6) = \{A\}$. Therefore, the SPN is not decomposable by using $scope_{ac}$.

Now, let us consider $scope_{mm}$, the scope definition under both mixture models and ACs interpretation. Here, if completeness, consistency, and decomposability hold in an SPN using $scope_{mm}$, then they hold using $scope_{am}$. Proofs are omitted and will be given in an extended version of this manuscript.

Lemma 2. *If an SPN is complete by using $scope_{mm}$ definition, then it is also complete when using $scope_{am}$.*

Lemma 3. *If an SPN is consistent by using $scope_{mm}$ definition, then it is also complete when using $scope_{am}$.*

Lemma 4. *If an SPN is decomposable by using $scope_{mm}$ definition, then it is also complete when using $scope_{am}$.*

Example 16. The SPN in Fig. 3 is complete and decomposable by using $scope_{mm}$ as shown in Example 7. Similarly, using $scope_{am}$, the SPN in Fig. 3 is complete. Consider, for example, sum node $n4$, which has both children with the same scope, namely, $scope_{am}(n8) = \{B\}$ and $scope_{am}(n9) = \{B\}$. Moreover, the SPN in Fig. 3 is complete using $scope_{am}$. Consider, for instance, product node $n2$, which has different scopes for all of its three children, namely, $scope_{mm}(n12) = \{A\}, scope_{mm}(n4) = \{B\}$, and $scope_{mm}(n6) = \{C\}$.

Since mixture models and ACs can be compiled to SPNs, one advantage of using the scope definition under both interpretations is that it can enhance the SPN understanding from both point of views, while still being useful for testing tractability of the network.

6 Conclusions

In this paper, we identify and resolve inconsistencies regarding scope in the SPN literature. We considered two probabilistic interpretations of SPNs. The scope definition given in [11] fits nicely in the mixture models interpretation. On the other hand, that scope definition for sum nodes can be non-intuitive when under the AC interpretation of an SPN. We proposed a scope definition that suits the ACs interpretation of an SPN. Unfortunately, the scope definition of leaf nodes can be non-intuitive when under the mixture models interpretation. Thus, we proposed yet another scope definition that addresses the non-intuitive points for both mixture model and AC interpretations.

The latter scope definition can be used for checking the completeness, consistency, and decomposability properties of an SPN. Therefore, it is helpful for understanding SPNs originating from different research communities, while guaranteeing tractability when learning or compiling SPNs. Future work includes analyzing this scope definition when considering independence among LVs [8].

References

1. Amer, M.R., Todorovic, S.: Sum-product networks for modeling activities with stochastic structure. In: 2012 IEEE Conference on Computer Vision and Pattern Recognition, pp. 1314–1321. IEEE (2012)
2. Cheng, W.C., Kok, S., Pham, H.V., Chieu, H.L., Chai, K.M.A.: Language modeling with sum-product networks. In: INTERSPEECH, pp. 2098–2102 (2014)
3. Cooper, G.: The computational complexity of probabilistic inference using Bayesian belief networks. Artif. Intell. **42**(2–3), 393–405 (1990)
4. Darwiche, A.: A differential approach to inference in Bayesian networks. J. ACM **50**(3), 280–305 (2003)
5. Dennis, A., Ventura, D.: Learning the architecture of sum-product networks using clustering on variables. In: Advances in Neural Information Processing Systems, pp. 2033–2041 (2012)
6. Gens, R., Domingos, P.: Discriminative learning of sum-product networks. In: Advances in Neural Information Processing Systems, pp. 3248–3256 (2012)
7. Pearl, J.: Probabilistic Reasoning in Intelligent Systems: Networks of Plausible Inference. Morgan Kaufmann, Burlington (1988)
8. Peharz, R., Gens, R., Pernkopf, F., Domingos, P.: On the latent variable interpretation in sum-product networks. arXiv preprint arXiv:1601.06180 (2016)
9. Peharz, R., Geiger, B.C., Pernkopf, F.: Greedy part-wise learning of sum-product networks. In: Blockeel, H., Kersting, K., Nijssen, S., Železný, F. (eds.) ECML PKDD 2013. LNCS (LNAI), vol. 8189, pp. 612–627. Springer, Heidelberg (2013). doi:10.1007/978-3-642-40991-2_39
10. Peharz, R., Kapeller, G., Mowlaee, P., Pernkopf, F.: Modeling speech with sum-product networks: application to bandwidth extension. In: IEEE International Conference on Acoustics, Speech and Signal Processing, pp. 3699–3703. IEEE (2014)
11. Poon, H., Domingos, P.: Sum-product networks: a new deep architecture. In: Proceedings of the Twenty-Seventh Conference on Uncertainty in Artificial Intelligence, pp. 337–346 (2011)
12. Rooshenas, A., Lowd, D.: Learning sum-product networks with direct and indirect variable interactions. In: International Conference on Machine Learning, pp. 710–718 (2014)
13. Vergari, A., Di Mauro, N., Esposito, F.: Visualizing and understanding sum-product networks. arXiv.org (2016)
14. Zhao, H., Melibari, M., Poupart, P.: On the relationship between sum-product networks and Bayesian networks. In: Proceedings of Thirty-Second International Conference on Machine Learning (2015)

A Sparse Probabilistic Model of User Preference Data

Matthew Smith[1(✉)], Laurent Charlin[2], and Joelle Pineau[1]

[1] School of Computer Science, McGill University, Montréal, QC, Canada
{msmith108,jpineau}@cs.mcgill.ca
[2] HEC Montréal, Montréal, QC, Canada
laurent.charlin@hec.ca

Abstract. Modern recommender systems rely on user preference data to understand, analyze and provide items of interest to users. However, for some domains, collecting and sharing such data can be problematic: it may be expensive to gather data from several users, or it may be undesirable to share real user data for privacy reasons. We therefore propose a new model for generating realistic preference data. Our Sparse Probabilistic User Preference (SPUP) model produces synthetic data by sparsifying an initially dense user preference matrix generated by a standard matrix factorization model. The model incorporates aggregate statistics of the original data, such as user activity level and item popularity, as well as their interaction, to produce realistic data. We show empirically that our model can reproduce real-world datasets from different domains to a high degree of fidelity according to several measures. Our model can be used by both researchers and practitioners to generate new datasets or to extend existing ones, enabling the sound testing of new models and providing an improved form of bootstrapping in cases where limited data is available.

1 Introduction

User preference data has become one of the most valuable commodities, used by industry and governments, to inform several aspects of decision-making. Yet in many domains accurate user preference data can be difficult and expensive to obtain since collecting preference data requires access to a set of users, a set of items, and an interface for recording the users' preferences (clicks or ratings). There are also often limitations to sharing this data, which impedes progress of research, commercialization and policy development. There exist a few preference datasets commonly used in research on recommender systems (e.g., [2]). However confining research to a few datasets makes it difficult to ensure robust decision-making and explore diverse research directions.

In several fields of AI research, the use of synthetic data has provided an alternative for the rapid development and validation of new ideas. Examples abound, including in planning and reinforcement learning where there exist repositories of widely used synthetic benchmarks [3–5]. Synthetic datasets are also standard

M. Mouhoub and P. Langlais (Eds.): Canadian AI 2017, LNAI 10233, pp. 316–328, 2017.
DOI: 10.1007/978-3-319-57351-9_36

in social-network analysis research [6,7], and in the field of statistics [8]. Realistic synthetic data can be used to explore the capabilities of models beyond what available real-world datasets can provide. Further, realistic synthetic data could be useful in application contexts where data has been collected, but cannot be shared, due to potential privacy or ethical constraints. Yet a survey of the literature found very few examples of synthetic data generation for recommendation systems.

We present a new model for generating synthetic user preference data. Our model builds on the widely used probabilistic matrix factorization (PMF) model [9], which on its own was not designed to generate preference data. Our model generates a *mask matrix* which is used to censor the user preferences obtained by PMF. The mask matrix is parametrized by user budgets, item popularity as well as terms accounting for user-item interactions. Tuning these parameters allows the model to generate preference data with different attributes. The model could also take into account particular user and item interactions through *side information* (e.g., online friendship influenced by preferences).

While our model is capable of generating data from a wide variety of distributions, we show experimentally that, in particular, it can be used to generate realistic datasets that match important attributes of real data from movie, books, music and electronic-commerce domains. Note that while we use real datasets in order to evaluate our model, our procedure can be used to generate entirely novel datasets, from scratch. We also show that a popular recommendation model can be applied directly on our generated datasets in lieu of real data.

2 Related Work

A conceptual overview for a possible synthetic preference generation architecture is presented by Pasinato et al. [10]. The method outlined (never implemented as far as we know) involves the creation of user and item profiles, defining directly the distribution over the number of items sampled per user and the user's evaluation of each item. The authors suggest that one of the main benefits of this procedure is the ability to specify the probability density function of ratings. The model we propose is structured similarly, but the distributions are defined in terms of latent attributes of the users and items, providing more flexibility to structure the (preference) data.

Cluster Method. An alternative method based on clustering is presented by Tso and Schmidt-Thieme [11]. As far as we know, this is the only method in the literature that has been implemented and empirically validated for synthetic preference data generation. We use this approach as a baseline in our empirical evaluation below. This method involves the creation of user clusters, denoted C^U, and item clusters, C^I, which respectively represent groups of related users and related items. Each individual user is assigned to a user cluster according to a Dirichlet distribution over clusters, and likewise for items and item clusters. The method then generates a conditional distribution $P(C^U|C^I)$ of user clusters with respect to item clusters, using repeated draws from a modified χ^2 distribution that rejects values greater than 1, until the conditional normalized entropy, $H(C^U|C^I)$, reaches a preset value:

$$H(C^U|C^I) = -\sum_{i=0}^{|C^U|}\sum_{k=0}^{|C^I|}\frac{P(C^I = k, C^U = i)\log_2(P(C^U = i|C^I = k))}{\log_2(|C^I|)}.$$

Users then sample items from clusters determined by sampling from this conditional distribution, so the probability of user i, in user cluster C_i^U sampling from items in item cluster C_j^I, is $P(C_i^U|C_j^I)$. If a user has been determined to be sampling from a given item cluster, they then sample items according to a binomial distribution, with the parameter determining the probability that any given item within the cluster is sampled. This generates a final binary preference matrix, **R**. While this model is general, it can be difficult to interpret in terms of how changing parameters will affect the resulting data, as probability density functions are not defined directly. In comparison, our model maintains the interpretability of a directly defined PDF, while remaining able to generate attribute information, since it models data as a product of an item attribute matrix.

Random Graph Models. Alternatively, we can view the user preference data generation problem as a random graph generation: we generate a (potentially weighted) bipartite graph, where edges exist between users and items. Many approaches to the generation of random graphs exist, with early advances focused around the Erdös-Rényi model. Though this model is too simple for user preferences, other models exist which enable specification of graph properties such as degree distribution. Caron and Fox [12] provide a method for the generation of sparse and exchangeable bipartite graphs, though the degree distribution is not directly specified. Newman et al. [13] present a method for sampling bipartite graphs with arbitrary degree distribution, though this method does not include latent factors (user-item interactions) and does not apply the budget-based approach constructed here. These models have not been used to construct user preference data, but may provide some theoretical foundation for our method.

3 A Sparse Probabilistic User Preference Model

The purpose of our model is to generate an N users by M items preference matrix, **R**, to be used for recommender systems. The ith row represents how a user, i, has rated each item, either *implicitly* (by viewing or consuming the item, e.g., purchase decisions, movie views, article “shares”), or *explicitly* (giving feedback on some ratings scale) [14]. Here, as is common in recommender systems, a value of zero at entry ij of **R** indicates that user i has not rated or consumed item j. In typical recommendation system scenarios, **R** is a sparse matrix, although the methods proposed here can be used to generate arbitrarily dense datasets.

Our proposed **Sparse Probabilistic User Preferences (SPUP) model** produces ratings data in two steps. We first generate a dense preference matrix using a probabilistic matrix factorization model [9]; this matrix can be interpreted as how much users can be expected to like items. This matrix is then sparsified by generating budgets for each user, and subsampling from a user-specific distribution over items, as a function of both the user's expected preference, and the popularity of different items.

Probabilistic Matrix Factorization. Our model builds on the probabilistic matrix factorization (PMF) model [1,9]. PMF is a generative probabilistic model that is standard in recommender systems. It involves the generation of a ratings matrix using the product of two matrices commonly interpreted as latent attributes of items and user latent preferences over these attributes. Latent factors are usually inferred by optimizing for the reconstruction error of nonzero elements of the (observed) matrix.

The initial preference matrix, $\widetilde{\mathbf{R}}$, is modeled as a noisy product of latent user preference and item attribute matrices, which are sampled here, rather than inferred:

$$\mathbf{U}_i \sim \mathcal{N}(\mathbf{0}, \sigma_u^2 \mathbf{I}) \quad \text{and} \quad \mathbf{V}_j \sim \mathcal{N}(\mathbf{0}, \sigma_v^2 \mathbf{I}) \tag{1}$$

$$\widetilde{\mathbf{R}}_{ij} \sim \mathcal{N}(\mathbf{U}_i^\top \mathbf{V}_j, \sigma_p^2), \tag{2}$$

where $\mathbf{U}_i$ represents user i's latent preference vector, and $\mathbf{V}_j$ item j's latent attribute vector, $\mathbf{I}$ the identity matrix, and σ^2 parametrizes the Gaussian's variance.

Generating the Mask Matrix. The Aldous-Hoover representation theorem [15, 16] shows that the class of matrices generated by PMF (jointly exchangeable matrices) are dense (or empty) matrices. Thus our first step—recall that we begin by generating ratings with PMF—typically generates a matrix $\widetilde{\mathbf{R}}$ that is dense. However, our goal is not to infer the full user preference matrix, but rather to generate realistic preference data, which is typically very sparse.

Our second step ensures that we can generate such data by applying sparsification to the matrix generated by PMF ($\widetilde{\mathbf{R}}$). The steps for sparsification are as follows: (a) sample a user budget to determine the activity-level of each user; (b) sample an item popularity for each item; and (c) for each user (and according to its budget) sample items according to their popularity and to their rating given by PMF.[1]

In order to achieve a realistic distribution over both items and products while sparsifying the matrix, we allocate each user with a budget, B_i, sampled from

[1] The idea of using the combination of user budgets and item popularity has also been exploited for sampling preference matrices in the context of stochastic variational inference [17].

an exponential distribution, parameterized by rate β (rate is the inverse of the scale parameter):

$$B_i \sim \text{round}(\text{exponential}(\beta)) + c_b \tag{3}$$

where c_b is some positive hyperparameter set as the desired number of ratings for any user. Recall that the PDF of the exponential distribution is $\text{exponential}(x; \beta^{-1}) := \beta^{-1} \exp(-x\beta^{-1})$.

A user-specific distribution is then defined over the items. Users do not select items to rate at random. Empirically, across several datasets of consumer products, users rated more preferred items more frequently, with strong popularity effects, where many users are likely to have rated the same few items. We define the distribution over items for user i as a normalized element-wise product between an item-specific popularity vector (sampled from a power law distribution), and the underlying preference vector, $\widetilde{\mathbf{R}}_i$

$$p_j \sim \text{Power}(a) + c \tag{4}$$

$$\mathbf{D}_i = \frac{\mathbf{p} \circ (\widetilde{\mathbf{R}}_i + \min_j(\widetilde{\mathbf{R}}_{ij}))}{\|\mathbf{p} \circ (\widetilde{\mathbf{R}}_i + \min_j(\widetilde{\mathbf{R}}_{ij}))\|_1} \tag{5}$$

where p_j is the popularity factor of the jth item, a is the parameter for the power law, and c is some positive parameter, that gives a baseline probability of each item being rated (so that no item has $p_j \equiv \mathbf{0}$), $\circ$ represents the Hadamard (elementwise) product between two vectors (or matrices) of equal size, and $\|\cdot\|_1$ is the 1-norm. Recall that the power law distribution function is $\text{Power}(x; a) := ax^{a-1}$.

B_i ratings for each user i are then sampled from the user-specific distribution $\mathbf{D}_i$, without replacement. This forms a masking matrix, $\mathbf{M}$, which is then applied to the latent ratings matrix $\widetilde{\mathbf{R}}$ by elementwise multiplication in order to form the masked raw ratings matrix: $\widetilde{\mathbf{R}}^{(\mathbf{M})} = \mathbf{M} \circ \widetilde{\mathbf{R}}$.

Most preference data is discrete (e.g., clicks or ratings). In order to form the final ratings matrix, $\mathbf{R}$, each entry in $\widetilde{\mathbf{R}}^{(\mathbf{M})}$ can be either binarized, in order to represent implicit feedback, or binned/scaled for ratings.[2]

The complete procedure for generating data is detailed in Algorithm 1. The time complexity of our method is dominated by the PMF product step (Eq. 2), which requires $\mathcal{O}(NM)$ operations to generate the complete ratings matrix $\widetilde{\mathbf{R}}$. In comparison, generating the mask ($\mathbf{M}$) has a time complexity that is linear in the order of the number of non-zero entries.

It should be noted that for large datasets, it is expensive to compute and store the full dense matrix $\widetilde{R}$ in memory, since this can contain tens of billions of real-valued entries. This is solved by performing the above masking procedure on individuals or groups of users, and concatenating the sparse matrices that this generates.

[2] Recent work has proposed the use of Poisson-observation matrix factorization models [18]. Using such models would alleviate the need for this discretization step but this is largely independent of our proposed approach.

Algorithm 1. Generating preference data with SPUP.

```
Data: N, M, β, c_B, a, c
for each user i and item j do
 | Sample a rating r̃_ij using Eq. 2;
end
for each user i do
 | Generate a budget B_i using Eq. 3;
end
for each item j do
 | Generate a popularity p_j using Eq. 4;
end
Set M to be an all-zero N by M matrix;
for each user i do
 | for k ← 0 to B_i do
 | | Generate D_i using Eq. 5;
 | | Sample an item: j ~ D_i;
 | | Set M_ij = 1;
 | end
end
return M ∘ R̃
```

4 Experimental Methods

To study our proposed SPUP model we evaluate how well it can simulate the attributes of real-world preference datasets. For several such datasets we adapt the hyper-parameters of our model so as to generate data that is similar to that observed in the real-world, according to several attributes. We repeat this procedure for the cluster method [11] discussed in Related Work above and compare their output to the characteristics of the original datasets. We further validate our SPUP model by learning a standard collaborative filtering model on our synthetic data. We show that our synthetic data can indeed be learned: the performance of the model on our data is significantly higher than the performance of the same method on synthetic data generated using a random mask.

We consider datasets from a range of domains with varying consumption patterns:

MovieLens Dataset. This data was collected from an online movie recommendation platform. Users score movies that they have seen on an integer scale from 1–5, and receive recommendations for movies to watch in the future. The MovieLens dataset used here contains 1 million ratings across 6 K users and 4 K movies [2].

Million Song Dataset (MSD). The million song dataset contains music listening data consisting of 1.4 million (user, song, playcount) triplets across 110 K users and 160 K songs. Playcounts in this dataset range from 1 to 923. This is a (random) subset of the original dataset [19].

Epinions Dataset. The Epinions dataset consists of data across 22 K users and 300 K items acquired from a product ratings website that allowed users to write reviews of and rate items that they had purchased on an integer scale from 1–5. Additionally, users could form trust relationships with other users, which would influence the ratings which would appear on a user's feed [20,21].

Book Crossings Dataset. This dataset was generated from a book sharing website that enables users to leave books in real-world locations, with a tag that allows the book to be tracked as it changes hands. Ratings data is either explicit values from 1–10, or implicit. This dataset contains 1.1 million ratings of 280 K users by 270 K books [22].

Comparison Measures. Synthetic and real datasets are compared across several key attributes. Our aim is to compare key attributes that define the structure of the preference datasets. We consider the density of the ratings matrix, the degree distribution for both users and items, and the normalized sorted sum of ratings distribution as first-order comparisons. We formally define these attributes below. Further as a second-order method, we consider the performance of a baseline PMF algorithm on a held-out subset of the synthetic data, relative to performance on a held-out subset of the real data.

When generating synthetic data for recommender systems, it is important to consider how well a recommender system performs under different amounts of data. Density provides a good measure as to the amount of information present in the ratings matrix (statistically uniformly denser matrices are easier to correctly estimate)—density is a widely reported statistic. As more ratings are added to the matrix, there is more information about the preferences of users and the attributes of items. If the purpose of the synthetic data is to extend or emulate a particular dataset, then it is important that the density of the synthetic data matches the density of the original data to avoid an information mismatch. Here, density of an $N \times M$ matrix $\mathbf{R}$ is expressed as: $\text{density}(R) = \sum_{i=0}^{N} \sum_{j=0}^{M} \frac{I(R_{ij} \neq 0)}{NM}$, where I is the indicator function. Both our SPUP model and the cluster method can control density directly, but since density is primarily determined by how many items users rate in each algorithm (B_i in our latent factor method, and the binomial parameter in the cluster method), parameterization to produce a particular density can impact the distributions of ratings for both users and items.

The second attribute is the *degree distribution* which describes how connected nodes in a graph are. If we interpret $\mathbf{R}$ as a bipartite graph, where users form one set of vertices and items form the other, this can be used to obtain the PDF of the number of connections (in our case, ratings) that users have formed and items have received. We can evaluate how much the ratings are governed by general patterns, such as popularity effects. For each dataset we report the degree distribution of users using a normalized histogram where the x-axis represents the number of connections per user (or item), and the y-axis is the number of users (or items) with a given number of connections.

The third attribute is the *normalized sorted sum of ratings* (NSSR) which represents how ratings are distributed across users and items. For each user it is the ratio of the sum of that user's ratings over the sum of all ratings.

We report NSSR using a histogram over all users. NSSR is similar to degree distribution, in that it demonstrates how drastic effects such as item populary or user activity are. We can read directly how much more certain items and users are engaged with by looking at the slope of the NSSR curve. If the slope is either very steep or very flat, then there may be strong factors (like item popularity) that influence the distribution of data. It should be noted that peaks in the NSSR graph correspond to points that have high degree. As such, NSSR demonstrates directly how items are rated by users. It can be simpler to interpret than the degree distribution, but it does not show the PDF directly, so both methods are used.

In addition to reporting micro-level results using degree distribution and NSSR we can also compare methods more directly using their similarity according to these statistics. In particular since both statistics can be interpreted as distributions, we use the Kullback-Leibler divergence (KL), defined between two discrete probability distributions Y and Z as: $KL(Y||Z) = \sum_i Y(i) \log \left(\frac{Y(i)}{Z(i)} \right)$. Since KL-divergence is not well defined when Z is not continuous with respect to Y, Laplace smoothing is used wherever Y is nonzero and Z is.

Parameter Setting. To match characteristics of a specific real dataset with our synthetic data generation, we adjust the hyperparameters of the SPUP model using search. We first adjust hyperparameters in order to achieve similar density to the real dataset (using β and c_B), then the budget parameters (adjust β,c_B) while keeping the density constant, and finally, the item popularity parameters (using a,c). The first two objectives can be accomplished simultaneously by fitting β and c_B to the data: c_B is the minimum number of ratings across users in the dataset, and β is the mean number of ratings per user, minus c_B. Table 1 reports values of the hyper-parameters selected for each dataset.

Table 1. Values of hyperparameters used to generate the four dataset under study.

Parameter	Domain	Description	MovieLens	MSD	Epinions	Book crossings
β	$\mathbb{R}^+$	Controls the distribution of user budgets	160	10.2	36.2	4
c_B	$\mathbb{N}^+$	Minimum number of ratings per user	15	3	2	0
a	$0 \leq a \leq 1$	Controls the distribution of item popularities	0.18	0.12	0.012	0.012
c	$\mathbb{R}^+$	Baseline probability of an item being rated	10^{-13}	0.02	0.02	0.02

5 Results

We have described the methodology of our study above and will now present results. For the purpose of comparisons, we focus on the implicit-data case by binarizing all datasets, since the Cluster method cannot generate explicit preference data.

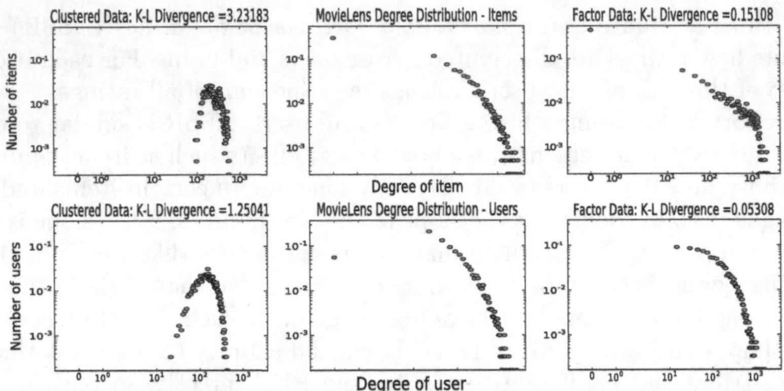

Fig. 1. Degree distribution of MovieLens data: cluster method (left), real data (middle), and SPUP (right). The x-axis represents the degree of items (top) or users (bottom) while the y-axis indicates the number of items or users (points on the figure indicate the number of items/user for a particular degree value). Error bars are omitted due to the very low variance of both methods. SPUP results (right) are more similar (visually and according to the KL divergence) to the real data (middle) than the cluster method (left).

Comparison of Datasets. Figure 1 shows the results of the generation for the MovieLens dataset. We can see that degree distribution of the data (middle column) is shaped somewhere in between the shape of an exponential distribution and a power law across both items and users. The cluster method does not fit the degree distribution of either items or users (left). On the other hand the SPUP model achieves low KL-divergence for both users and items (right). The results for NSSR are qualitatively similar (Fig. 4): SPUP generates more realistic data. Figure 2 illustrates how the budget parameters can be tuned to match the real data, even when looking at it on an item-by-item basis.

MSD is characterized by high sparsity—it has a density of only approx. 10^{-5}. It additionally has greater long-tail effects: while the mean number of listens per song is 10, some of its songs have several thousand listens. Despite the more complex nature of this data, SPUP is able to model it well (Fig. 5), while

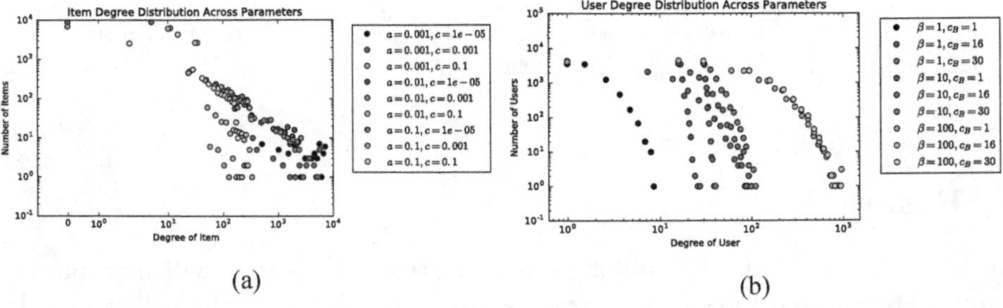

(a) (b)

Fig. 2. An exploration of how the degree distribution of items (left) and users (right) vary as a function of hyperparameters. (This figure is best viewed in color.)

maintaining values across all parameters that seem intuitively plausible: the average user has rated 10 items, and item popularity falls off as a power of approximately $\frac{1}{10}$. We do not report the results for NSSR here as they are similar to the ones for the MovieLens datasets (likewise for the other datasets).

The results on the Epinions dataset (Fig. 6) show that SPUP provides a much better fit to the real data than the Cluster method in terms of user distributions, and fits similarly in item distribution.

For the Book Crossing dataset, both the cluster method and SPUP seem to provide good fits to the real data. Visually, the degree distributions match those of the Epinions data, and for lack of space are not included here. The KL-Divergence for the Cluster method was 0.1457 for items and 0.02235 for users, while for the SPUP method, KL-divergence was 0.00565 and 0.02235 correspondingly.

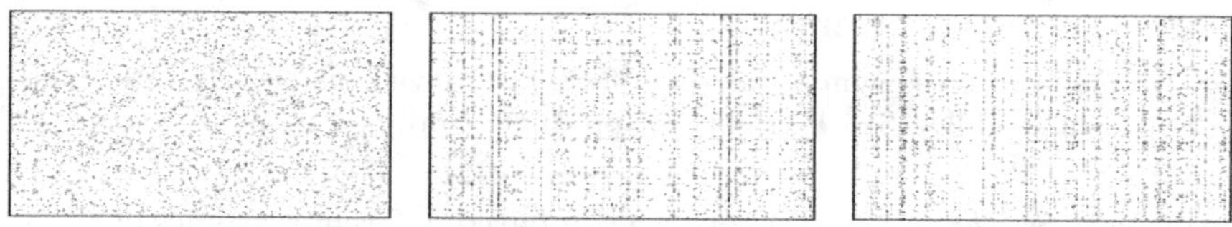

Fig. 3. Visualizing the observed entries of the MovieLens dataset (users in rows, items in columns) from the cluster method (left), real data (middle), SPUP (right). We shuffled the order of rows/columns to eliminate spurious spatial effects in the real data. (This figure is best viewed on screen.)

Model Attributes. One important feature of the SPUP model is the interpretable effect of the parameters on the generated data. Figure 2 demonstrates how the degree distribution across users and items varies as the relevant parameters change. Figure 2b shows how varying budget parameters control the density of the ratings matrix (shifting the distribution to the left or right). As β increases, the probability mass is moved to higher values of x, widening the distribution. The desired number of ratings per user, c_B, can shift the distribution by adding a constant to all of the budgets.

The effects of parameter shifts on the degree distribution of items is somewhat more subtle. The position of the distribution is determined by the parameter settings for the budget, described above. Figure 2a shows the degree distribution as a and c are varied for budget parameters set to $\beta = 25, c_B = 5$. As a increases, the mass of the distribution is shifted up and to the left. This is because as a increases, the probability density flattens out as a power of x. The constant, c, is used to modify this effect by linearly scaling the vector before normalization. Thus, when c is increased, the distribution will shift horizontally to the left, due to a flattening out of the distribution. As a increases, however, the effects of changes in c are reduced significantly.

In addition to these quantitative evaluations we can also qualitatively compare the generated data from the different methods. Figure 3 shows visually the matrices corresponding to the generated data as the entries of a matrix. Data generated using the cluster method does not have visible structure whereas SPUP and the real data exhibit structure from users and items with varying levels of activity and popularity respectively.

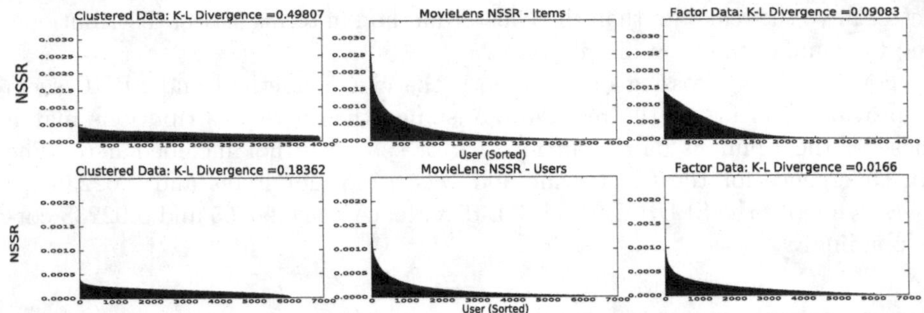

Fig. 4. Normalized sorted sum of ratings (NSSR) of MovieLens Data: cluster method (left), real data (middle), SPUP (right) for products (top) and users (bottom).

Learning with Synthetic Data. Above we compared different statistics of the synthetic datasets to the statistics of the real data. We now consider a more indirect measure of how realistic the synthetic data is by studying the performance of a collaborative filtering model fit to it.

The exact evaluation procedure is as follows: (a) generate synthetic data (or use real data); (b) split data into train/validation/test splits; (c) evaluate the performance of a standard collaborative filtering model—we use PMF [9]—on this data. We ran this experiment on the MovieLens dataset which is the densest dataset. We did not attempt to compare to the Cluster method due to its overall lower performance at reproducing the real-world dataset.

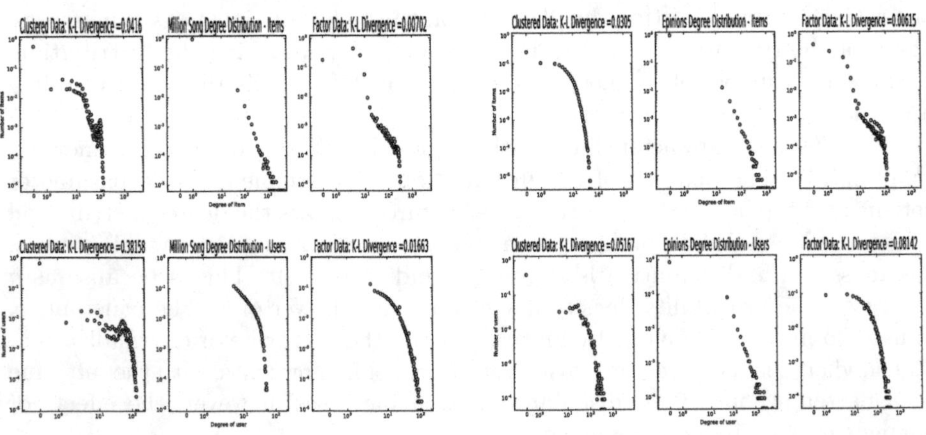

Fig. 5. Degree distribution for MSD. **Fig. 6.** Degree distribution for epinions. Axes represent same quantities as in Fig. 1

When fitting PMF to synthetic data we obtain better performance compared to a random predictor of the actual dataset (Mean Normalized Discounted Cumulative Gain, higher is better, of 0.28 vs 0.33 on a test set of MovieLens Data). This experiment suggests that there is structure in the data generated by SPUP that PMF can leverage.

6 Discussion

We presented a new model, SPUP, for generating user preference data and show that this model can produce synthetic data matching characteristics of four standard datasets from different preference domains. Further evidence from using it to learn a model suggests that data generated from our method contains meaningful structure.

Comparing the synthetic data generated by SPUP against the real-world datasets confirmed three key properties of our model: (1) SPUP is flexible: it can generate datasets characterized by many different attributes (2) SPUP is interpretable: it is easy to see how changing hyper-parameters lead to changes in the generated data (3) SPUP is stable: it tends to generate consistent-looking data for any given set of parameters, with low variability across measurements.

Given that SPUP is designed to be modular and extensible, it would be easy to modify the process to additionally produce side information (i.e., additional features of users, items or both). One such extension could involve the use of the user factors generated by probabilistic matrix factorization to generate a social network between users. This could then be used in the context of a recommender system to examine how social network data can improve the performance of the system. Another extension, in the same spirit as Pasinato et al. [10], involves the modification of the system to generate *contextual data*: preference data which is influenced in part by information about the context in which the items are consumed (time, location, social interactions). This enables the construction and validation of new models for rich datasets which may or may not exist, thus enabling more rapid testing and development in new domains.

References

1. Koren, Y., Bell, R., Volinsky, C.: Matrix factorization techniques for recommender systems. J. Comput. **42**, 30–37 (2009)
2. Maxwell Harper, F., Konstan, J.A.: The movielens datasets: history and context. ACM Trans. Interact. Intell. Syst. 5(4) (2015). Article no. 19
3. ICAPS. Ipc. http://www.icaps-conference.org/index.php/Main/Competitions
4. Cassandra, T.: POMDP file repository. http://www.pomdp.org/examples/
5. RL-GLUE. Reinforcement learning glue. http://glue.rl-community.org/
6. Cointet, J.P., Roth, C.: How realistic should knowledge diffusion models be. J. Artif. Soc. Soc. Simul. **10**(3), 1–11 (2007)
7. Leskovec, J.: Dynamics of large networks. Ph.D. thesis, Carnegie Mellon University (2008)
8. Rubin, D.B.: Discussion statistical disclosure limitation. JOS **9**(2), 461–468 (1993)

9. Salakhutdinov, R., Mnih, A.: Probabilistic matrix factorization. In: NIPS, pp. 1257–1264 (2008)
10. Pasinato, M., Mello, C.E., Aufaure, M.A., Zimbro, G.: Generating synthetic data for context-aware recommender systems. In: BRICS-CCI CBIC 2013
11. Tso, K.H.L., Schmidt-Thieme, L.: Empirical analysis of attribute-aware recommender system algorithms using synthetic data. J. Comput. **1**(4), 18–29 (2006)
12. Caron, F., Fox, E.B.: Sparse graphs using exchangeable random measures. ArXiv e-prints, January 2014
13. Newman, M.E.J., Strogatz, S.H., Watts, D.J.: Random graphs with arbitrary degree distributions and their applications. Phys. Rev. E **64**(2), 026118 (2001)
14. Hu, Y., Koren, Y., Volinsky, C.: Collaborative filtering for implicit feedback datasets. In: Data Mining, 2008, pp. 263–272. IEEE, ICDM 2008 (2008)
15. Aldous, D.J.: Representations for partially exchangeable arrays of random variables. J. Multivar. Anal. **11**(4), 581–598 (1981)
16. Hoover, D.N.: Relations on probability spaces and arrays of random variables. Technical report, Institute for Advanced Study, Princeton, NJ (1979)
17. Hernandez-Lobato, J.M., Houlsby, N., Ghahramani, Z.: Stochastic inference for scalable probabilistic modeling of binary matrices. In: ICML (2014)
18. Gopalan, P., Hofman, J.M., Blei, D.M.: Scalable recommendation with hierarchical Poisson factorization. In: UAI (2015)
19. Bertin-Mahieux, T., Ellis, D.P.W., Whitman, B., Lamere, P.: The million song dataset. In: Proceedings of 12th ISMIR (2011)
20. Tang, J., Gao, H., Liu, H.: eTrust: discerning multi-faceted trust in a connected world. In: ACM International Conference on Web Search and Data Mining (2012)
21. Tang, J., Gao, H., Liu, H., Das Sarma, A.: eTrust: Understanding trust evolution in an online world. In: Proceedings of the 18th ACM SIGKDD, pp. 253–261. ACM (2012)
22. Ziegler, C.-N., McNee, S.M., Konstan, J.A., Lausen, G.: Improving recommendation lists through topic diversification. In: Proceedings of WWW (2005)

On Converting Sum-Product Networks into Bayesian Networks

André E. dos Santos([✉]), Cory J. Butz, and Jhonatan S. Oliveira

Department of Computer Science, University of Regina, Regina, Canada
{dossantos,butz,oliveira}@cs.uregina.ca

Abstract. *Sum-Product Networks* (SPNs) are a probabilistic graphical model with deep learning applications. A key feature in an SPN is that inference is linear with respect to the size of the network under certain structural constraints. Initial studies of SPNs have investigated transforming SPNs into *Bayesian Networks* (BNs). Two such methods modify the SPN before conversion. One method modifies the SPN into a *normal* form. The resulting BN does not contain edges between latent variables. The other method considered here augments the SPN with *twin* nodes. Here, the constructed BN does contain edges between latent variables, thereby encoding a richer set of dependencies among them.

In this paper, we propose another method for converting an SPN into a BN. Our process starts with the normal SPN from the first method above. We introduce an augmented version of the normal SPN. Consequently, the constructed BN does contain edges between latent variables. The salient feature of our method is that, given a normal SPN, we build a BN not limited to a bipartite structure. Moreover, unlike a normal SPN, our augmented, normal SPN is necessarily complete. Lastly, by using aspects of two earlier methods, our approach can be seen as unifying the two methods.

Keywords: Sum-product networks · Conditional independence · Deep learning

1 Introduction

Sum-Product Networks (SPNs) are tractable deep learning models for probabilistic inference [5]. In an SPN, leaf nodes are indicator variables for each value that a random variable can assume and the remaining nodes are either sum or product. Attractive features of SPNs include linear time inference in the size of the network (number of edges) and probabilistic semantics in a deep architecture [5]. Applications of SPNs involves image completion, computer vision, classification, and speech and language modeling [5]. Related models to SPNs are arithmetic circuits [1] and AND/OR graphs [2]. SPNs can also be seen as general cases of hierarchical mixture models and thin junction trees [5].

In this paper, we propose a method for converting *normal* SPNs [6] into BNs with edges among random and latent variables. This can be achieved by adapting

M. Mouhoub and P. Langlais (Eds.): Canadian AI 2017, LNAI 10233, pp. 329–334, 2017.
DOI: 10.1007/978-3-319-57351-9_37

the idea of *twin* nodes [4] from augmented SPNs. Next, we introduce a new method for converting augmented, normal SPNs into a BN. The generated BN encodes more dependencies than the method proposed in [6]. Also, the generated BN is not restricted to a bipartite structure. Hence, it has a richer representation of the random variable dependencies. Moreover, by applying twin nodes from [4] into normal SPNs of [6], our augmented, normal SPN overcomes a potential problem discussed in [4] pertaining to completeness. Lastly, by using aspects of two earlier methods, our approach can be seen as unifying the two methods.

2 Background

Random variables are denoted by upper-case letters, say X. The values of a variable X are denoted by $val(x)$, where lower-case element x is a corresponding element of the domain of X, denoted $val(X)$. Sets of random variables are defined by boldface letters, for example, $\mathbf{X}$. The cardinality of a set $\mathbf{X}$ is denoted $|\mathbf{X}|$. For a set of variables $\mathbf{X} = \{X_1, \ldots, X_N\}$, we define $\mathbf{val}(\mathbf{X}) = \times_{n=1}^{N} \mathbf{val}(X_n)$ and use corresponding lower-case boldface letters for elements of $\mathbf{val}(\mathbf{X})$. For a subset $\mathbf{Y} \subseteq \mathbf{X}$, $\mathbf{x}[\mathbf{Y}]$ is the projection of $\mathbf{x}$ onto $\mathbf{Y}$. Let $\mathcal{G}$ denote a *directed acyclic graph* (DAG) on a finite set $\mathbf{U}$ of variables (nodes). The *children* $Ch(V_i)$ and *parents* $Pa(V_i)$ of V_i are those V_j such that $(V_i, V_j) \in \mathcal{G}$ and $(V_j, V_i) \in \mathcal{G}$, respectively.

A *Sum-Product network* [5] (SPN), denoted $\mathcal{S}$, over Boolean variables $\mathbf{X} = \{X_1, \ldots, X_N\}$ is a rooted DAG containing three types of nodes: indicators, sums, and products. An indicator variable $\lambda[X = x]$ returns 1 when $X = x$ and 0 otherwise. All leaves of $\mathcal{S}$ are indicator variables $\lambda_{x_1}, \ldots, \lambda_{x_N}$ and $\lambda_{\bar{x}_1}, \ldots, \lambda_{\bar{x}_N}$. All internal nodes are either sum or product. Each edge (V_i, V_j) from a sum node V_i has a non-negative weight w_{ij}. The value of a product node is the product of its children. The value of a sum node is $\sum_{V_j \in Ch(V_i)} w_{ij} val(V_j)$. An SPN can be extended for multi-valued discrete variables by replacing Boolean indicators for the variables possible values.

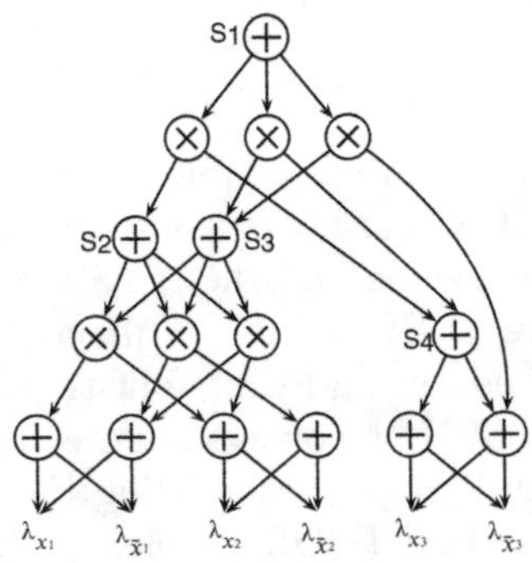

Fig. 1. An SPN over a set $\mathbf{X} = \{X_1, X_2, X_3\}$ of binary variables.

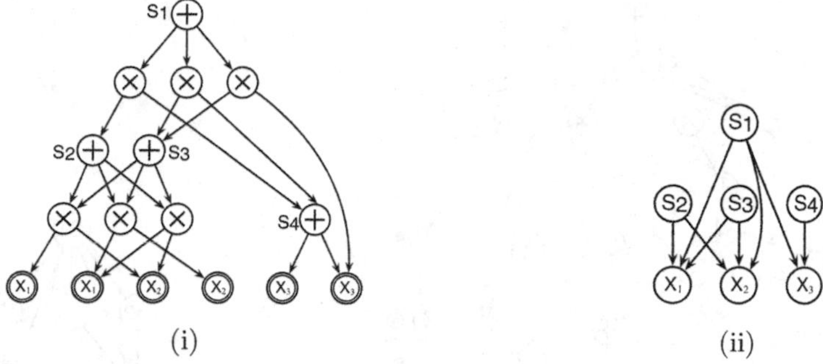

Fig. 2. (i) A normal SPN obtained from the SPN in Fig. 1. (ii) The BN built from the normal SPN in (i).

We consider two methods [4,6] for converting an SPN into a *Bayesian Network* (BN) [3]. In [6], a method was proposed for converting SPNs into BNs by first creating a *normal* SPN. The generated BN has a bipartite structure, where a latent variable is a parent of a random variable, if the latter is contained in the scope of the corresponding node. It is important to emphasize that the generated BN has no edges among latent variables and no edges among random variables. For example, consider the SPN $\mathcal{S}$ in Fig. 1. Figure 2(i) shows a normal SPN $\mathcal{S}_n$ constructed from the $\mathcal{S}$. Terminal nodes which are probability distributions over a single variable are represented by a double-circle. Given $\mathcal{S}_n$, the resulting BN $\mathcal{B}$ is depicted in Fig. 2(ii).

In [4], a BN is generated by first creating an *augmented* SPN. Then, a BN can be obtained by exploiting the latent variable interpretation in SPNs [4]. Here, the BN contains edges among random and latent variables. That is, the generated BN has a richer set of dependencies encoded than [6], since there are no restrictions of connectedness among latent variables or random variables. Note that a BN generated from an augmented SPN in [4] may not be obtainable from a normal SPN in [6]. For instance, given the SPN in Fig. 1, the augmented SPN is illustrated in Fig. 3(i). The resultant BN $\mathcal{B}$ is shown in Fig. 3(ii).

3 Building Richer BNs from Normal SPNs

In this section, we present a two-step method for building a richer BN from a normal SPN. The first step is to augment the normal SPN, while the second step builds a BN from the augmented, normal SPN.

3.1 Augmenting Normal SPNs

We can augment a normal SPN by introducing twin nodes. This modification can be performed by the algorithm AUGMENTSPN described in [4]. Here, AUGMENTSPN adds twin nodes to a normal SPN in a similar fashion when applied on SPN. We call the result of this step an *augmented, normal SPN*.

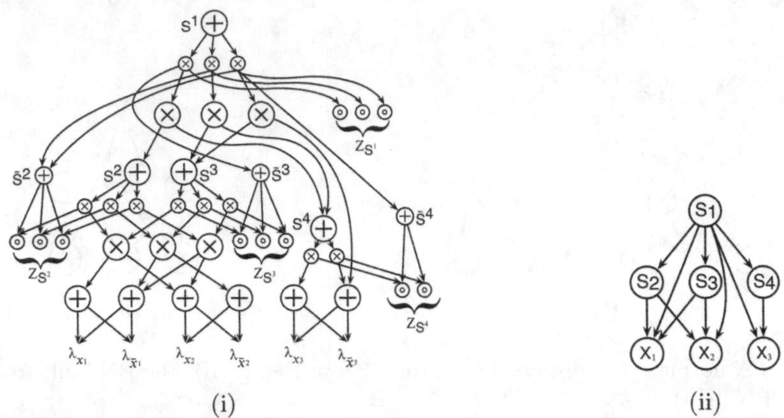

Fig. 3. (i) An augmented SPN obtained from the SPN in Fig. 1. (ii) The BN constructed from the augmented SPN in (i).

Definition 1. *(Augmented, Normal SPN) Let* $\mathcal{S}_n$ *be an normal SPN over variables* $\mathbf{X}$*,* $\mathbf{w}$ *be a set of twin-weights.* $\mathcal{S}'_n$ = AUGMENTSPN($\mathcal{S}_n$) *is called the* augmented, normal SPN *of* $\mathcal{S}_n$*.*

Example 1. Consider the normal SPN $\mathcal{S}_n$ in Fig. 2(i). The call AUGMENTSPN ($\mathcal{S}_n$) adds twin nodes to $\mathcal{S}_n$. The output of the call is the augmented, normal SPN in Fig. 4.

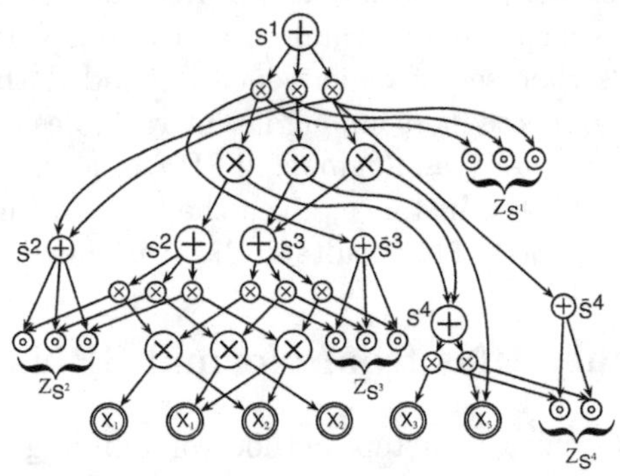

Fig. 4. The augmented, normal SPN built from the SPN in Fig. 2(i).

3.2 Building BNs from Augmented, Normal SPNs

When converting an augmented SPN to a BN, the algorithm AUGMENTSPN uses twin nodes to create CPTs. This implies that a normal SPN with twin nodes would be a valid input for AUGMENTSPN. Thus, an augmented, normal SPN fulfills this requirement, since it modifies a normal SPN by adding twin nodes.

We propose Algorithm 1, which is inspired by AUGMENTSPN, as a method for converting augmented, normal SPNs into BNs.

Algorithm 1. Converts an augmented, normal SPN into a BN.

Input: an augmented, normal SPN $\mathcal{S}$
Output: a BN $\mathcal{B} = (\mathcal{B}_V, \mathcal{B}_E)$

$R \leftarrow$ root of $\mathcal{S}$
if R is a terminal node over variable X **then**
  Create an observable variable X
  $\mathcal{B}_V \leftarrow \mathcal{B}_V \cup X$
else
  for each child R_i of R **do**
    if a BN has not been built for $\mathcal{S}_{R_i}$ **then**
      Recursively build a BN for $\mathcal{S}_{R_i}$
  if R is a sum node **then**
    Create a hidden variable H_R associated with R
    $\mathcal{B}_V \leftarrow \mathcal{B}_V \cup \{H_R\}$
    for each observable variable $X \in \mathcal{S}_R$ **do**
      $\mathcal{B}_E \leftarrow \mathcal{B}_E \cup \{(H_R, X)\}$
    for each hidden variable $H_{Ch} \in \mathcal{S}_R$ **do**
      $\mathcal{B}_E \leftarrow \mathcal{B}_E \cup \{(H_R, H_{Ch})\}$

Example 2. Applying Algorithm 1 on the augmented, normal SPN in Fig. 4 yields the BN in Fig. 3(ii).

4 Advantages and Conclusion

We have suggested a new method for converting an SPN into a BN. Our method uses the normal form of a given SPN, as first suggested in [6]. Next, we augment the normal SPN using the augmentation process put forth in [4]. Lastly, we build a BN from the augmented, normal SPN. The striking feature of our method is that it builds a richer BN from a normal SPN as compared to [6]. For example, given the SPN in Fig. 1, the normal form is shown in Fig. 2(i). The method in [6] builds the BN in Fig. 2(ii), while our method builds the BN in Fig. 3(ii). By comparing Figs. 2(ii) and 3(ii), it can be seen that our BN includes edges between latent variables. Moreover, when building a normal SPN, one requires the latent variable interpretation of sum nodes. As shown in [4], this interpretation may violate the completeness condition. Our augmented, normal SPN necessarily satisfies completeness by its use of twin nodes. Another salient feature of our method is that it unifies two other methods [4,6] for building BNs from SPNs by

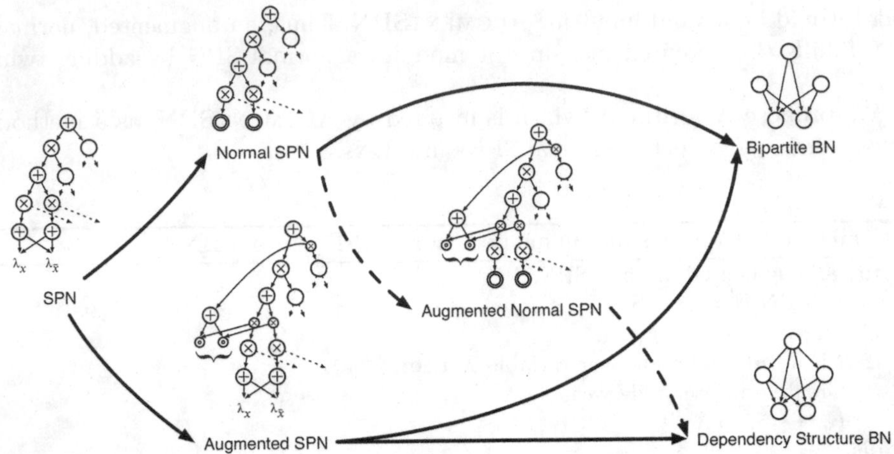

Fig. 5. In order to convert a normal SPN to a richer BN, we need the notion of an augmented, normal SPN. The first and second dashed lines represent the methods proposed in Sects. 3.1 and 3.2, respectively.

adopting techniques from each. Figure 5 summarizes this point. A new method for building normal SPNs from BNs can be formulated by applying our technique in reverse. This remains as future work.

References

1. Darwiche, A.: A differential approach to inference in Bayesian networks. J. ACM **50**(3), 280–305 (2003)
2. Dechter, R., Mateescu, R.: AND/OR search spaces for graphical models. Artif. Intell. **171**(2), 73–106 (2007)
3. Pearl, J.: Probabilistic Reasoning in Intelligent Systems: Networks of Plausible Inference. Morgan Kaufmann, Burlington (1988)
4. Peharz, R., Gens, R., Pernkopf, F., Domingos, P.: On the latent variable interpretation in sum-product networks. arXiv preprint arXiv:1601.06180 (2016)
5. Poon, H., Domingos, P.: Sum-product networks: a new deep architecture. In: Proceedings of the Twenty-Seventh Conference on Uncertainty in Artificial Intelligence, pp. 337–346 (2011)
6. Zhao, H., Melibari, M., Poupart, P.: On the relationship between sum-product networks and Bayesian networks. In: Proceedings of Thirty-Second International Conference on Machine Learning (2015)

Fuzzy Rough Set-Based Unstructured Text Categorization

Aditya Bharadwaj and Sheela Ramanna(✉)

Department of Applied Computer Science, University of Winnipeg, Winnipeg, MB R3B 2E9, Canada
bharadwaj-a@webmail.uwinnipeg.ca, s.ramanna@uwinnipeg.ca

Abstract. In this paper, we have proposed a fuzzy rough set-based semi-supervised learning algorithm (FRL) to label categorical noun phrase instances from a given corpus (unstructured web pages). Our model uses noun phrases which are described in terms of sets of co-occurring contextual patterns. The performance of the FRL algorithm is compared with the Tolerance Rough Set-based (TPL) algorithm and Coupled Bayesian Sets-based(CBS) algorithm. Based on average precision value over 11 categories, FRL performs better than CBS but not as good as TPL. To the best of our knowledge, fuzzy rough sets has not been applied to the problem of unstructured text categorization.

Keywords: Unstructured text categorization · Semi-supervised learning · Fuzzy-rough sets · Web mining

1 Introduction

Text categorization or labeling methods assign unseen documents or unknown linguistic entities to pre-defined categories or labels. Structured text categorization is popularly referred to as document categorization or clustering. However, in this paper, our focus is on representation and categorization of unstructured text(i.e., unknown linguistic entities such as nouns) gleaned from the web with a hybrid fuzzy rough model inspired by [1,2,7] combined with semi-supervised learning. The representation is made possible by constructing a fuzzy thesaurus (of nouns) and applying approximating operators based on rough sets thus providing the framework for semi-supervised learning. The categorization is accomplished using a co-occurrence matrix where seed values for nouns of each category are promoted in subsequent iterations by the learner. We use the term *categorization* throughout the paper instead of the term *classification* to avoid confusion.

The proposed FRL algorithm was experimentally compared with Coupled Bayesian Sets (CBS) [6] and Tolerant Pattern Learner (TPL) [5] algorithms. To

This research has been supported by the NSERC Discovery grant. Special thanks to Cenker Sengoz and to Prof. Estevam R. Hruschka Jr.

M. Mouhoub and P. Langlais (Eds.): Canadian AI 2017, LNAI 10233, pp. 335–340, 2017.
DOI: 10.1007/978-3-319-57351-9_38

the best of our knowledge, this is the first time that a fuzzy rough set model has been used in the categorization of unstructured text. Experimental results show that FRL was able to achieve better performance than CBS and not as good as TPL in terms of precision. It is also worth noting that unlike CBS, neither FRL nor TPL use any external constraints such as mutual exclusion to constrain the learning process. The paper is organized as follows: in Sect. 2, we discuss briefly research related to structured and unstructured text categorization pertinent to this paper. In Sect. 3, we present some preliminaries for the fuzzy rough set model. We describe our proposed FRL algorithm and experiments in Sect. 4. We conclude the paper in Sect. 5.

2 Related Work

2.1 Structured Text Retrieval with Fuzzy Rough Sets

In a Pawlak approximation space (X,R) [4], X is a set of elements, R is a binary relation which is an equivalence relation, and a subset A of X denotes instances of categories (concepts). A can be approximated by two sets: upper $R \uparrow A$ and lower $R \downarrow A$. An element y of X belongs to the $R \downarrow A$ if its equivalence class is included in A. On the other hand, an element y of X belongs to the $R \uparrow A$ if its equivalence class has a non-empty intersection with A [1].

In the context of fuzzy sets, A is a fuzzy set in X and X: $\rightarrow [0, 1]$, while R is a fuzzy relation in X, i.e., R:X $\times X \rightarrow [0, 1]$. This model is based on combining the flexibility of fuzzy memberships with upper approximations followed by strictness of lower approximation by applying them successively.

2.2 Unstructured Text Categorization

The unstructured text was derived from an ontology from the NELL system [3] which is also used in the three methods compared in this paper. The categorical information consists of noun phrase instances from a given corpus (unstructured web pages), where the information needs to be categorized into noun phrases (for ex: **categorical** noun phrase instances such as *Profession(Lawyer), Company Name(Intel)*). This categorization is typically accomplished using a co-occurrence matrix. The co-occurrence matrix consists of nouns(rows) and contexts (columns) with entries representing scores. The co-occurrence scores over a collection of nouns and contexts are then used to generate a thesaurus. The categorization (or labeling) process starts by selecting a small number of trusted nouns(examples) for each category. These examples become input to the algorithm (given in Sect. 4) to label more instances. These new trusted instances are further used to label more instances leading to a continuously growing thesaurus.

3 Unstructured Thesaurus Construction with Fuzzy Rough Sets

Let $\mathcal{N} = \{n_1, n_2, \ldots, n_M\}$ be the set of noun phrases, $\mathcal{C} = \{c_1, c_2, \ldots, c_P\}$ be the set of contextual patterns and $\mathcal{TN} = \{n_1, n_2, \ldots, n_Y\}$ be a set of trusted nouns such that, $\mathcal{TN} \subset \mathcal{N}$ and index $Y < M$. Furthermore, let $C : \mathcal{N} \rightarrow \mathbb{P}(\mathcal{C})$ denote mapping of each noun phrase to its set of co-occurring categorical contexts: $C(n_i) = \{c_j : f_C(n_i, c_j) > 0\}$ where $f_C(n_i, c_j) = \kappa \in \mathbb{N}$ denoting that n_i occurs κ times within context c_j. Similar to the procedure given in [2], the first step towards creation of a fuzzy thesaurus is by normalizing the co-occurrence information using ϑ:

$$\vartheta(n_i, c_j) = \frac{f_C(n_i, c_j)}{f_C(n_i, c_j), \forall j : 1..P} \tag{1}$$

The next step involves fuzzifying the co-occurrence function with the $S - function$ where $\alpha = 0.001$ and $\beta = 0.02$ are constants determined experimentally.

$$S(\vartheta; \alpha, \beta) = \begin{cases} 1 & \text{if } \vartheta \geq \beta \\ \frac{\vartheta - \alpha}{\beta - \alpha} & \text{if } 0.005 \leq \vartheta < \beta \\ 0, & \text{otherwise} \end{cases} \tag{2}$$

3.1 Approximation of the Thesaurus: Lower and Upper Approximation

The initial thesaurus T is defined as an approximation space $T = (\mathcal{N}, \mathcal{C}, CO_F)$, where $\mathcal{N}$ denotes the universe of nouns, and the fuzzy relation CO_F is a fuzzy set in $\mathcal{C} \times \mathcal{N}$. Let $\mathcal{N_F}, \mathcal{TN_F}$ represent the fuzzy sets of the nouns and trusted nouns respectively. The *upper* and *lower* approximations of the fuzzy set $\mathcal{N_F}$ in T is denoted by $\mathcal{N_F} \uparrow CO_F$ and $\mathcal{N_F} \downarrow CO_F$[2]. These are defined as follows in Eqs. 3 and 4:

$$\mathcal{N_F} \uparrow CO_F = \sup_{y \in \mathcal{N},\ x \in \mathcal{TN}} \mathcal{T}(CO_F(C(y), x), \mathcal{N_F}(x)) \tag{3}$$

$$\mathcal{N_F} \downarrow CO_F = \inf_{y \in \mathcal{N},\ x \in \mathcal{TN}} \mathcal{I_T}(CO_F(C(y), x), \mathcal{N_F}(x)) \tag{4}$$

$\forall y \in \mathcal{N}$ where $\mathcal{T}$ is the usual t-norm and $\mathcal{I_T}$ is the residual implicator of $\mathcal{T}$. Note that $C(y)$ gives all the contexts for noun y. FRL uses a modified representation for the promoted (labeled noun phrases). As a result, every promoted candidate noun n_i is associated with the $\mathcal{N_F} \uparrow CO_F$ and $\mathcal{N_F} \downarrow CO_F$ operators (redefined as $U_{\mathcal{N}_F}(n_i)$, $L_{\mathcal{N}_F}(n_i)$). A micro score for a candidate noun n_i from $\mathcal{N}$ and n_j from $\mathcal{TN}$ is calculated as:

$$U_{\mathcal{N}_F}(n_i) = \sup_{n_i \in \mathcal{N},\ n_j \in \mathcal{TN}} (CO_F(C(n_i), n_j), \mathcal{N_F}(n_j) : CO_{\mathcal{F}}(n_i) \geq CO_{\mathcal{F}}(n_j)) \tag{5}$$

where all the candidate nouns having a membership co-occurrence value either equal to or more than that of the trusted nouns, will be selected. This will eliminate all the unrelated noun phrases. The lower approximation is redefined as:

$$L_{\mathcal{N}_F}(n_i) = \inf_{n_i \in \mathcal{N},\, n_j \in \mathcal{TN}} (CO_F(C(n_i), n_j), \mathcal{N}_{\mathcal{F}}(n_j) \\ : ((n_i, n_j) | C(n_j) \cap C(n_i) \neq \emptyset)) \tag{6}$$

where only candidate nouns phrases n_i will be promoted as trusted when there is at least one common context with a trusted noun n_j.

$$micro(n_i) = \omega_1(U_{\mathcal{N}_F}(n_i)) + \omega_2(L_{\mathcal{N}_F}(n_i)) \tag{7}$$

where ω_1 and ω_2 are application dependent and in this experiment are set to 70% and 10% respectively.

3.2 Tight Upper Approximation

The tight upper approximation for fuzzy set A for approximation space (X, R) is defined as [2]:

$$R \downarrow\uparrow A(y) = inf_{z \in X}\ \mathcal{I}_{\mathcal{T}}(R_z(y), sup_{x \in X}\ \mathcal{T}(R_z(x), A(x))) \tag{8}$$

for all y in X where X is the set of all terms and R is a fuzzy relation. The benefit of using tight upper approximation is that a term y will only be added to a query A if all the terms related to y are related to at least one keyword of the query [2]. We experienced a similar problem, candidate nouns with high membership degree are promoted and added to the trusted noun set irrespective of whether the noun is related or not to the trusted noun. To counter this, we take the upper approximation of all the n_i in $\mathcal{N}$ followed by lower approximation for the remaining candidate nouns which can be effectively translated into:

$$CO_F \downarrow\uparrow \mathcal{N}_F(n_i) = CO_F \downarrow (CO_F \uparrow \mathcal{N}_F(n_i)) \tag{9}$$

We then calculate $micro(n_i)$ given in Eq. 7 for each candidate noun-phrase. We sort the noun phrases identified as trusted based on their scores and the top five noun phrases are promoted as trusted for the next iteration.

4 FRL Algorithm and Experiments

Algorithm 1 summarizes the overall flow. FRL uses a score-based ranking. For the category *cat*, an accumulated micro-score for candidate n_i is maintained. After calculating the score for every candidate $n_i \in \mathcal{N}$, we rank the candidates by their micro-scores normalized by the number of trusted instances of *cat*. Ultimately, we promote the top new candidates as trusted. FRL is an iterative algorithm which is designated to run indefinitely. After every iteration, it learns new trusted instances and it uses its growing knowledge to make more comprehensive judgments in the following iterations. Semi-supervised learning is used in the context of finding the trusted instances. Initial category seeds are labeled by the user, forming the supervised step. At the end of each round, the top-scoring new candidates are marked as trusted instances for the category, forming the unsupervised step. Co-occurrence function ϑ was implemented using Matlab and the other steps in FRL were implemented in $C++$. The input to FRL was the same subset of noun phrases and contexts that were used in the CBS and TPL experiments. The final data set consisted of 68,919 noun phrase instances and 59,325 contextual patterns. It was stored in form of a matrix M_{ij} with each cell corresponding to the co-occurrence of noun phrase j against contextual pattern i. Throughout our experiments, we used the same ontology as used in TPL and CBS experiments.

Algorithm 1. Fuzzy Rough Set Based Unstructured Text Learner

Input : An ontology O defining categories; a large corpus $\mathcal{N}$, CO co-occurrence matrix, a small set of trusted nouns $\mathcal{TN}$

Output: Trusted instances n_j for $\mathcal{TN}'$, where $\mathcal{TN}'$ is a set of all new trusted noun-phrases

for $r = 1 \rightarrow$ end of file **do**
  for each category *cat* **do**
    for each new trusted noun phrase n_j of *cat* **do**
      for each candidate noun phrase n_i **do**
        Calculate Fuzzy Relation $\mathcal{CO}_{\mathcal{F}}$ using Eqns. 1 and 2;
        Calculate Upper Approximation $U_{\mathcal{N}_F}(n_i)$ as in Eqn. 5;
        Calculate score ω_1;
        for each candidate noun phrase n_i **do**
          Calculate Lower Approximation $L_{\mathcal{N}_F}(n_i)$ using Eqn. 6;
          Calculate score ω_2;
      Calculate $micro_{cat}(n_i)$ using Eqn. 7;
    Sort trusted instances n_j by $micro_{cat}/|cat|$;
    Promote top trusted instances, such that $\mathcal{TN}' = \mathcal{TN} \cup \{n_j\}$;

Each category was initialized with 5 to 6 seed instances and the experiment was run for 10 iterations. In every iteration, the top 5 new noun phrases for every category were promoted as trusted nouns for subsequent iterations. Similar to TPL and the CBS algorithms, we used Precision@N at each iteration. Precision@N is calculated as the ratio of the correct instances to the N-ranked ones. Since the data was not labeled, the correctness of an instance was judged manually. Table 1 shows the result for all categories at Precision@30. Based on average precision value over all 11 categories and 10 iterations, one can observe that the FRL algorithm performs better than CBS but not as good as TPL. It was observed that in three categories (Vegetable, KitchenItem and PhysicsTerm), FRL under performs. In the category *Vegetable*, concept drift was an issue with all of the three algorithms. In the category *PhysicsTerm*, FRL was able to handle concept drift better than CBS.

Table 1. Precision@30 of TPL, CBS and **FRL**

Categories	Iteration 5			Iteration 10		
	TPL	CBS	FRL	TPL	CBS	FRL
Company	100%	100%	100%	100%	100%	100%
Disease	100%	100%	100%	100%	100%	100%
KitchenItem	100%	94%	97%	100%	94%	73%
Person	100%	100%	100%	100%	100%	100%
PhysicsTerm	93%	100%	67%	90%	100%	77%
Plant	100%	100%	77%	97%	100%	**100%**
Profession	100%	100%	100%	100%	87%	**100%**
Sociopolitics	100%	48%	93%	100%	34%	**87%**
Sport	97%	97%	100%	100%	100%	100%
Website	90%	94%	97%	90%	90%	**93%**
Vegetable	93%	83%	83%	63%	48%	47%
Average	**97.5%**	**92%**	**92%**	**94.5%**	**87%**	**89%**

5 Conclusion

We have proposed a semi-supervised learning algorithm based on fuzzy rough sets using contextual pattern statistics for categorizing nouns. Our experiments suggest that the approach yields promising results for the current data set. We have also compared our work with a tolerance form of rough sets. This was important for this work since both methods permit overlapping or soft similarity classes. Currently, we are working on extending this model for learning pairs of noun phrases for relations.

References

1. Cornelis, C., De Cock, M., Radzikowska, A.M.: Fuzzy rough sets: from theory into practice. Handbook of Granular Computing (2008)
2. De Cock, M., Cornelis, C.: Fuzzy rough set based web query expansion. In: Proceedings of Rough Sets and Soft Computing in IAT, pp. 9–16 (2005)
3. Mitchell, T., et al.: Never-ending learning. In: Proceedings of the AAAI 2015 (2015)
4. Pawlak, Z.: Rough sets. Int. J. Comput. Inf. Sci. **11**(5), 341–356 (1982)
5. Sengoz, C., Ramanna, S.: Learning relational facts from the web: a tolerance rough set approach. Pattern Recognit. Lett. **67**(P2), 130–137 (2015)
6. Verma, S., Hruschka, E.R.: Coupled bayesian sets algorithm for semi-supervised learning and information extraction. In: Flach, P.A., Bie, T., Cristianini, N. (eds.) ECML PKDD 2012. LNCS (LNAI), vol. 7524, pp. 307–322. Springer, Heidelberg (2012). doi:10.1007/978-3-642-33486-3_20
7. Zadeh, L.: Towards a theory of fuzzy information granulation and its centrality in human reasoning and fuzzy logic. Fuzzy Sets Syst. **177**(19), 111–127 (1997)

Bayesian Networks to Model *Pseudomonas aeruginosa* Survival Mechanism and Identify Low Nutrient Response Genes in Water

Bertrand Sodjahin[1(✉)], Vivekanandan Suresh Kumar[1], Shawn Lewenza[2,3], and Shauna Reckseidler-Zenteno[2,3]

[1] School of Computing and Information Systems, Athabasca University, Athabasca, Canada
bercadson@yahoo.fr

[2] Faculty of Science and Technology, Center for Science, Athabasca University, Athabasca, Canada

[3] Microbiology, Immunology and Infectious Diseases, University of Calgary, Calgary, Canada

Abstract. *Pseudomonas aeruginosa* is an organism notable for its ubiquity in the ecosystem and its resistance to antibiotics. It is an environmental bacterium that is a common cause of hospital-acquired infections. Identifying its survival mechanism is critical for designing preventative and curative measures. Also, understanding this mechanism is beneficial because *P. aeruginosa* and other related organisms are capable of bioremediation. To address this practical problem, we proceeded by decomposition into multiple learnable components, two of which are presented in this paper. With unlabeled data collected from *P. aeruginosa* gene expression response to low nutrient water, a Bayesian Machine Learning methodology was implemented, and we created an optimal regulatory network model of the survival mechanism. Subsequently, node influence techniques were used to computationally infer a group of twelve genes as key orchestrators of the observed survival phenotype. These results are biologically plausible, and are of great contribution to the overall goal of apprehending *P. aeruginosa* survival mechanism in nutrient depleted water environment.

Keywords: Machine learning · Bayesian networks · Gene expression · Bacteria · *Pseudomonas aeruginosa*

1 Introduction

Studies have shown that *P. aeruginosa* may survive for months on hospital surfaces [1] causing various infections. However, this organism also has some potential applications in biotechnology [2]. We are interested in its survival mechanism in nutrient depleted water. Our hypothesis is that the survival is sustained by a particular group of genes which encode for persistence proteins.

M. Mouhoub and P. Langlais (Eds.): Canadian AI 2017, LNAI 10233, pp. 341–347, 2017.
DOI: 10.1007/978-3-319-57351-9_39

To achieve this goal, Machine Learning techniques in the field of AI, are proposed. We present our approach and the architecture of our methodology that is based on Bayesian Networks Learning [3] to unveil the regulatory network of *P. aeruginosa* survival in low nutrient water. Our findings concerning the viability maintenance genes are also reported in this paper.

2 Approach and Proposed Methodology

2.1 Dataset and Pre-processing

Two experimental trials based on PAO1 mini-Tn5-*luxCDABE* transposon mutant library incubated in nutrient depleted water were undertaken [4]. Over a time period, gene expression response data were collected and then consolidated. The actual data matrix has ~1000 genes and ~30 data samples. Table 1 presents a sample format.

Table 1. Dataset's sample format. First column is *P. aeruginosa* genes. Others are expression response fold (% T_0) in low nutrient water for each measurement time point.

Genes	Exprsn_$_{T1}$	Exprsn_$_{T2}$	Exprsn_$_{Ti}$	Exprsn_$_{Tn}$
PA5398	1.92	1.42	…	0.03
PA5400	2.12	1.51	…	0.05
…	…	…	…	…
Tgt	1.06	0.64	…	0.73

A visual parse of the data shows that some genes initially expressed became repressed over time, and vice versa across time. This observation suggests the existence of a hierarchical "hand passing" between genes in their expression, to ensure the agent survives over time. As the dataset contains replicas of genes, their expression fold values were averaged before a domain knowledge-based discretization [4]. The resulting dataset was then transposed, and ready for analysis.

2.2 Modeling of the Survival Mechanism: Bayesian Networks Learning

For each gene, the expression response fold (Exprsn_$_{Ti}$) is numerical, and our analysis is quantitative and considers some prior microbiology knowledge. Figure 1 shows the global architecture of our methodology, which rests predominantly on Bayesian Networks (BN). BN—invented by Professor *Judea Pearl* in the 1980s— is a mathematical formalism for defining complex probability models and inference algorithms. Also known as Directed Acyclic Graph (DAG), it is a graphical representation of probabilistic relationships among a set of domain variables—here genes, represented by nodes. Conditional dependencies (Parent→Child) between pairs of genes are illustrated by directed edges. A Conditional Probability Distribution is associated with each gene G_i given its parents $Pa(G_i)$. The joint distribution of all the domain genes is uniquely represented by (1).

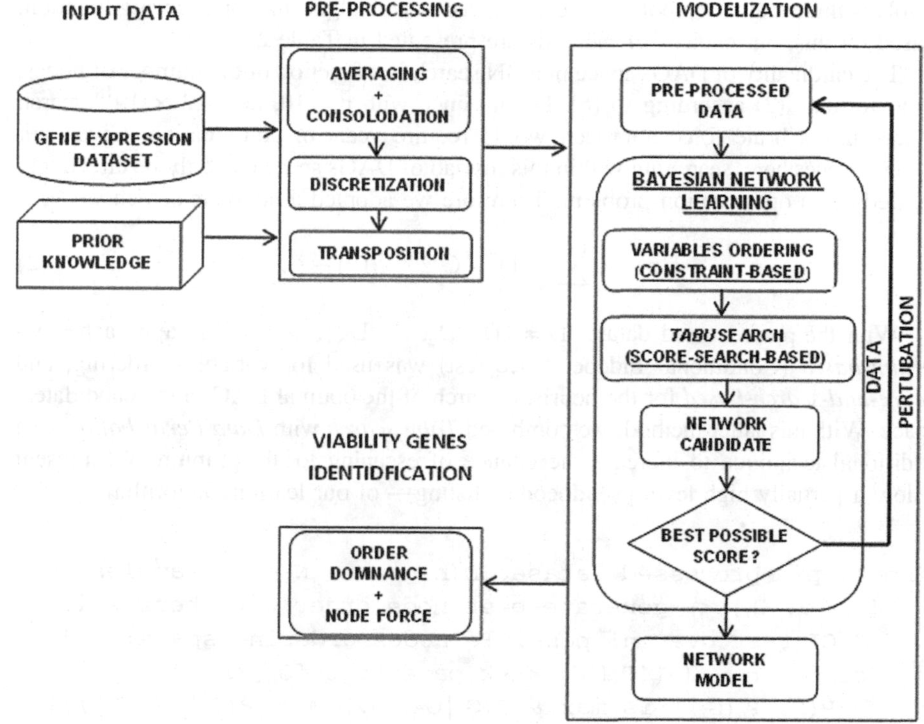

Fig. 1. Global analysis design architecture

$$P(G_1 \ldots G_n) = \prod_{i=1 \ldots n} P(G_i |\ P_a(G_i)). \tag{1}$$

A DAG is constructed either with domain expert knowledge or by learning from data. Theoretic groundwork on the latter was extensively covered and applied to *S. cerevisiae* as a model organism [3]. This application, the first in gene expression data analysis, was foundational for our current work, i.e., learning from data the regulatory network of *P. aeruginosa* survival mechanism. In short, this task consisted in finding a set of parents for each gene in the domain, such that the resulting network is acyclic with an optimal MDL score. The standard skeleton of BN learning, as discussed in [5],

Table 2. Learning components methods choice for *P. aeruginosa* Bayesian Network.

Search space	Search algorithm	Scoring function
Space of DAGs	Tabu search	MDL

involves three major components: search space, search algorithm, and scoring function. Based on this, our choices of methods are presented in Table 2.

The cardinality of DAGs space in a BN search is a function of the number of nodes, as in formula (2) according to [6]. For instance with n = 10, i.e., 4.2×10^{18} search space size, a brute force approach would require years of computation. Given our ~1000 genes here, searching within this myriad of DAGs space can only be effectively tackled as an optimization problem. Therefore we adopted a heuristic search.

$$f(n) = \sum (-1)^{i+1} C_i^n 2^{i(n-i)} f(n-i). \quad (2)$$

With the preprocessed dataset D = {D_1, D_2, …, D_N}, in a hybrid approach, *constraint-based* (Conditional Independence test) was used for variables ordering, and *Score-and-search-based* for the heuristic search of the optimal DAG in the candidates' space. With this latter method, we combined *Tabu search* with *Data Perturbation*—an additional technique to increase the chance of escaping local optimum. We present below a partially high level pseudocode—listing— of our learning algorithm.

```
Input: pre-processed Dataset D(n genes, N data samples)
   [G1 ... Gn] <- generate best node order with heuristic
      CI test over n! possible nodes ordering space;
   For i = n...2 {{Pa(Gi) <- k parents ∈ [Gi-1...G1] :
      P(D| Pa(Gi)) is max & P(Gi|Gi-1 ...G1) = P(Gi| Pa(Gi));}
      For j = 1...k {Edges[] <- Connect(Pa(Gi)j -> Gi);
         CPT(Gi) <- P(Gi| Pa(Gi)j;} //CPT = Cond. Prob. Table
   gInitCandidate <- graph({G1 ... Gn}, Edges[], CPT(Gi));
   f(n) <- #(Candidates in search space) function of n;
   H(f(n)) <- TabuListSize from Heuristic evaluation H;
   TDP(H(f(n)) <- Tabu(H(f(n))) + DataPerturbation(D);
Output: gBest= TDP(H(f(n)), gInitCandidate, MDL))
```

2.3 Viability Genes Inference: Node Influence Techniques

P. aeruginosa survival in water was measured several times and we have experimentally proven that it survives in water without nutrients for a very long time (up to 8 weeks) i.e., our data embody the survival phenotype. With the learned model, we used node influence techniques to isolate a particular group of genes as orchestrators of *P. aeruginosa* survival mechanism. For this, we joined the notion of "Predisposition nodes" or dominance order [3] to the notion of gene force—based on Kullback-Leibler divergence measure (3). With these, we evaluated the genes' participating *force* in the regulatory network of the survival. In (3), given a directed edge $E_{i \to j}$ between two genes, P(G) the probability distribution of our learned model network, Q(G) = P (G) − $E_{i \to j}$, then D_{KL} is the measure of information gain from Q(G) to P(G).

$$\mathrm{Force}(E_{i\to j}) = D_{KL}(P(G)||Q(G)) = \sum_i P(G_i)\log_2(P(G_i)/Q(G_i)) \tag{3}$$

Our approach to the viability genes inference consisted first in searching through the graph to identify all root nodes i.e., all nodes with no parents but having children. We called this set of nodes R_G. Then for each gene G_i in the entire network, we considered its $Force(G_i)$ as the sum of all its corresponding $Force(E_{i\to j})$. Denoting S_G the top strongest genes in force, we infer the viability genes set as: $V_G = R_G \cup S_G$.

3 Current Findings and Discussions

In contrast to our hybrid approach, [3] is *score-and-search-based* without *prior knowledge*. Our larned regulatory network (Fig. 2) encompasses ~25% of the overall 954 domain genes. This aligns with [3], which stated that gene expression networks are

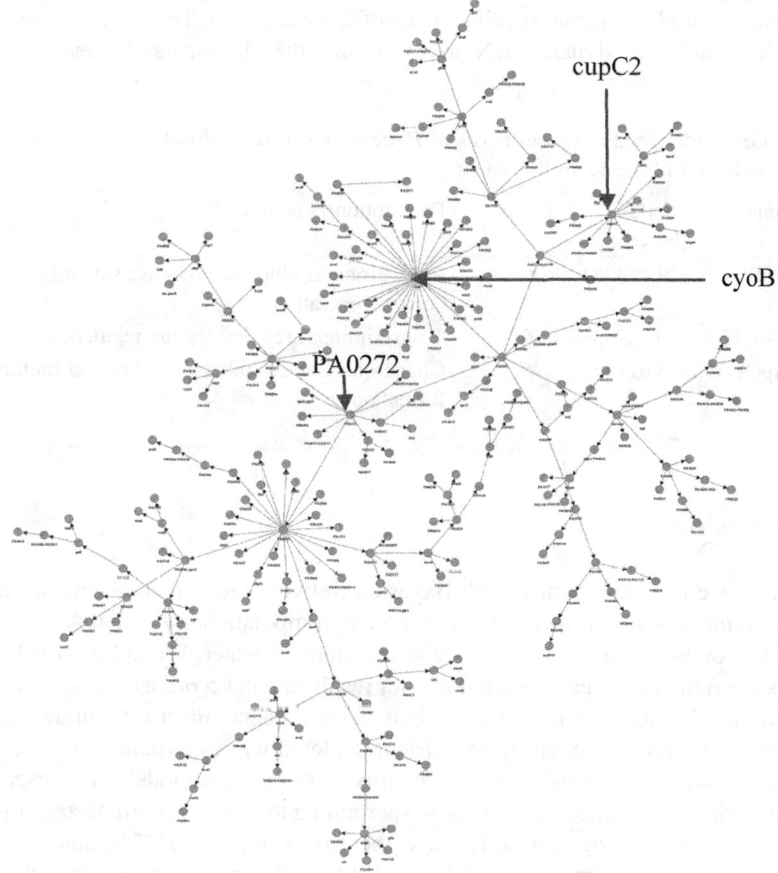

Fig. 2. Learned regulatory network of *P. aeruginosa* survival mechanism—Nodes represent stochastic genes as variables, and links are for conditional dependencies between them.

generally sparse: only a small number directly affect each other. Overall, the computation time of the BN model learning is ~300 h on a 4 GB RAM Windows computer. Though the study in [3] uses 48 more data samples (800 genes and 76 instances) than in this research, our hybrid approach to a certain extent compensates for that difference, given that constraint-based methods are said to do well on large number of variables dataset while score-based gives more accurate results on small sample size dataset. With BayesiaLab [7], the implementation tool used, our network model is fully interactive, and can be enlarged/shrunk for a visual read and interpretation by microbiologists, without Bayesian Networks background.

The node influence techniques resulted in the inference of 12 genes as key players of *P. aeruginosa* viability maintenance (3 presented in Table 3). These genes are all protein coding type as in [3]. Experts' knowledge concurs that the identified genes are interestingly conducive to the bacterium's survival. E.g., *PA0272* appears as the only root node in the model with a force of 10.72 bits. Its functional description shows a transcriptional regulator which is an orchestrator of gene activity—bacterium's life.

It emerged from our study—and [3] —, the need to investigate how combinations of gene states could determine specific states of the bacterium. This and the functional interplay as well as the dynamic BN are to be presented in our next papers.

Table 3. Genes identified as orchestrators of *P. aeruginosa* survival in low nutrient water. We only include here 3 of the 12 in this paper.

	Gene	Node Force	Root?	Description/Function
1	cyoB	29.153781	✗	Cytochrome o ubiquinol oxidase subunit I, energy generation
2	PA0272	10.72733	✓	Transcriptional regulator, gene regulation
3	cupC2	8.611461	✗	Chaperone CupC2, pilus assembly and biofilm formation
…	…	…	…	…

4 Conclusion

In this paper we machine-learned with Bayesian Networks formalism a network model for *P. aeruginosa* survival mechanism. We then computationally isolated a dozen of genes as key orchestrators of its viability in low nutrient water. We did not list here all the genes inferred due to space restriction. Our results are in accordance with theoretical domain knowledge and they greatly contribute to the broader objective of understanding *P. aeruginosa* survival mechanism in nutrient depleted water medium. We note that a larger sample size would confer more reliability to the current model. This research is the first to address these specific questions—pertaining to *P. aeruginosa* bacterium–with this AI based methodology. At this stage the survival of PA0272 mutant is being lab-tested in water in comparison to PAO1 wild type. We posit this framework model could be generalized to other bacteria for similar study.

References

1. Kramer, A., Schwebke, I., Kampf, G.: How long do nosocomial pathogens persist on inanimate surfaces? A systematic review. BMC Infect. Dis. **6**(1), 1–8 (2006)
2. Kung, V.L., Ozer, E.A., Hauser, A.R.: The accessory genome of *Pseudomonas aeruginosa*. Microbiol. Mol. Biol. Rev. **74**(4), 621–641 (2010)
3. Friedman, N., Linial, M., Nachman, I., Pe'er, D.: Using Bayesian networks to analyze expression data. J. Comput. Biol. **7**(3–4), 601–620 (2000)
4. Lewenza, S., Korbyn, M., de la Fuente-Numez, C., Recksieder-Zenteno, S. L.: In Preparation
5. Carvalho, A.M.: Scoring functions for learning Bayesian networks. Inesc-id Technical report (2009)
6. Robinson, R.W.: Counting unlabeled acyclic digraphs. In: Little, C.H.C. (ed.) Combinatorial Mathematics V. LNM, vol. 622, pp. 28–43. Springer, Heidelberg (1977). doi:10.1007/BFb0069178
7. Conrady, S., Jouffe, L.: Bayesian Networks and BayesiaLab: A Practical Introduction for Researchers. Franklin, TN, Bayesia, USA (2015)

Agent Systems

Quantified Coalition Logic of Knowledge, Belief and Certainty

Qingliang Chen[1,2(✉)], Xiaowei Huang[1,3], Kaile Su[1,2], and Abdul Sattar[2]

[1] Department of Computer Science, Jinan University, Guangzhou 510632, China
tpchen@jnu.edu.cn, xiaowei.huang@cs.ox.ac.uk

[2] Institute for Integrated and Intelligent Systems, Griffith University, Brisbane, Australia
a.sattar@griffith.edu.au

[3] Department of Computer Science, University of Oxford, Oxford, UK

Abstract. This paper introduces a multi-modal logic of Quantified Coalition Logic of Knowledge, Belief and Certainty (QCLKBC) to establish a logical framework that can model novel properties concerning mental attitudes and strategic power in a system, such as "agent i must be involved in order to convince agent j of the fact φ". Furthermore, this paper presents an axiomatic system of QCLKBC with the completeness proof, and shows the satisfiability problem for QCLKBC is PSPACE-complete.

Keywords: Coalition logic · Complete axiomatization · Computational complexity

1 Introduction

Inspired by the fundamental framework of Coalition Logic (CL) [1], a lot of logical formalisms have been proposed to model strategic abilities of multi-agent systems such as [2–5]. However, the incorporation of CL with the logics for some rational and mental notions of agents such as knowledge, belief and certainty (KBC) [6] has not been explored yet.

In this paper, we introduce a multi-modal logic of Quantified Coalition Logic of Knowledge, Belief and Certainty (QCLKBC) to enable the fusion of KBC and strategic modalities, resulting in a unified multi-modal logic to address those concerns. With QCLKBC, we can reason about how cooperations among agents can interact with their mental attitudes of KBC in game-like multi-agent systems. Therefore, QCLKBC equips us with the utility to formalize some novel and interesting properties which are hard or even impossible for any existing logical framework, such as "agent i can help j to make certain of φ".

This work was supported by the National Natural Science Foundation of China (Grant Nos. 61572234 and 61472369), the Fundamental Research Funds for the Central Universities of China (Grant No. 21615441), and Australian Research Council (Grant No. DP150101618).

M. Mouhoub and P. Langlais (Eds.): Canadian AI 2017, LNAI 10233, pp. 351–360, 2017.
DOI: 10.1007/978-3-319-57351-9_40

The significance of the paper is summarized as follows. Firstly, we enrich Quantified Coalition Logic (QCL) [3] by incorporating the strategic and KBC settings together. Secondly, we present an axiomatic system for QCLKBC with the completeness proof. To the best of our knowledge, there is no completeness result for variants of CL incorporated with KBC operators yet, and this paper is addressing this deficit. Thirdly, the complexity of satisfiability for QCLKBC is shown to be PSPACE-complete.

The rest of the paper is organized as follows. Next section will give a brief review of Coalition Logic (CL), Quantified Coalition Logic (QCL) and a KBC model over which our logic is based. Then we present the syntax and semantics of Quantified Coalition Logic of Knowledge, Belief and Certainty (QCLKBC), followed by the introduction of an axiomatic system, along with the completeness proof. Furthermore, the study of the complexity of satisfiability problem is in Sect. 5. Finally, we discuss the related work in Sect. 6 and conclude the paper in the last section.

2 Preliminaries

2.1 Coalition Logic

Syntax. Given a set Θ of atomic propositions, and a finite set Ag of agents. A *coalition* is a set $G \subseteq Ag$ of agents. The formulas of Coalition Logic (CL) [1] are defined as follows:

$$\varphi ::= p \mid \neg\varphi \mid \varphi \wedge \varphi \mid [G]\varphi$$

where $p \in \Theta$, $G \subseteq Ag$ and $[G]\varphi$ means G has a joint strategy to enforce φ no matter what the other agents do.

The semantics of CL is based on the concept of an *effectivity function* ξ that is defined as

$$\xi : 2^{Ag} \times S \rightarrow 2^{2^S}$$

An *effectivity function* is called *truly playable* [7] iff it satisfies the following **T1**–**T6** properties. The term *truly playability* carries the fact that an effectivity function is *truly playable* iff it is an effectivity function of a strategic game. To be more specific, for every truly playable effectivity function, there exists a strategic game that assigns to coalitions exactly the same power as ξ, and vice versa [8].

T1 (Outcome monotonicity): $\forall s \in S$, $\forall G \subseteq Ag$, $\forall X \subseteq Y \subseteq S$: $X \in \xi(G, s) \Rightarrow Y \in \xi(G, s)$

T2 (Ag-maximality): $\forall s \in S$, $\forall X \subseteq S$: $\overline{X} \notin \xi(\emptyset, s) \Rightarrow X \in \xi(Ag, s)$

T3 (Liveness): $\forall s \in S$, $\forall G \subseteq Ag$: $\emptyset \notin \xi(G, s)$

T4 (Safety): $\forall s \in S$, $\forall G \subseteq Ag$: $S \in \xi(G, s)$

T5 (Superadditivity): $\forall s \in S$, $\forall G_1, G_2 \subseteq Ag$, $G_1 \cap G_2 = \emptyset$, $\forall X, Y \subseteq S$: $X \in \xi(G_1, s)$ and $Y \in \xi(G_2, s) \Rightarrow X \cap Y \in \xi(G_1 \cup G_2, s)$

T6 (Determinacy): If $X \in \xi(Ag, s)$, then there exists a $w \in X$ such that $\{w\} \in \xi(Ag, s)$

An effectivity function that only satisfies **T1**–**T5** is called *playable*. Actually, they can be equivalent on finite domains [7].

Semantics. CL formulas are interpreted over the *coalition model* which is a tuple

$$M = \langle S, \xi, \pi \rangle$$

where

- S is a non-empty set of *states*;
- ξ is a *truly playable* effectivity function;
- π is a *valuation function*, which assigns each state $s \in S$ a set $\pi(s) \subseteq \Theta$.

A CL formula is interpreted in a state s in a coalition model M as follows:

- $M, s \models_{CL} p$ iff $p \in \pi(s)$;
- $M, s \models_{CL} \neg\varphi$ iff $M, s \not\models_{CL} \varphi$;
- $M, s \models_{CL} (\varphi_1 \wedge \varphi_2)$ iff $M, s \models_{CL} \varphi_1$ and $M, s \models_{CL} \varphi_2$;
- $M, s \models_{CL} [G]\varphi$ iff $\exists T \in \xi(G, s)$, such that for $\forall t \in T$, we have $M, t \models_{CL} \varphi$.

2.2 Quantified Coalition Logic

Ågotnes, van der Hoek and Wooldridge introduce Quantified Coalition Logic (QCL), by modifying the existing cooperation modalities of CL in order to enable quantifications over coalitions [3]. In QCL, the basic cooperation constructs are $\langle P \rangle \varphi$ and $[P]\varphi$, where P is a *predicate over coalitions*, and the two sentences state that *there exists a coalition C satisfying property P such that C can achieve φ* and *all coalitions satisfying property P can achieve φ*, respectively. The key element P is named as coalition predicates, and QCL defines a language for coalition predicates, with respect to which QCL will then be parameterised.

Coalition Predicates. Syntactically, QCL introduces two atomic predicates *subseteq* and *supseteq*, which is given by the following grammar:

$$P ::= subseteq(C) \mid supseteq(C) \mid \neg P \mid P \wedge P$$

where $C \subseteq Ag$ is a set of agents. The circumstances under which a concrete coalition C_0 satisfies a coalition predicate P, are specified by a satisfaction relation "$\models_{cp}$", defined by the following four rules:

1. $C_0 \models_{cp} subseteq(C)$ iff $C_0 \subseteq C$;
2. $C_0 \models_{cp} supseteq(C)$ iff $C_0 \supseteq C$;
3. $C_0 \models_{cp} \neg P$ iff not $C_0 \models_{cp} P$;
4. $C_0 \models_{cp} P_1 \wedge P_2$ iff $C_0 \models_{cp} P_1$ and $C_0 \models_{cp} P_2$.

Quantified Coalition Logic. Given a set Θ of atomic propositions, and a finite set Ag of agents, the formulas of Quantified Coalition Logic (QCL) are defined as:

$$\varphi ::= p \mid \neg\varphi \mid \varphi \wedge \varphi \mid \langle P \rangle \varphi \mid [P]\varphi$$

where $p \in \Theta$. Like its predecessor CL, QCL formulas are also interpreted over the *coalition model* which is a tuple $M = \langle S, \xi, \pi \rangle$. The satisfaction relation for the new operators is as follows.

- $M, s \models_{QCL} \langle P \rangle \varphi$ iff $\exists C \subseteq Ag : C \models_{cp} P$ and $\exists S \in \xi(C, s)$ such that for $\forall s' \in S$, we have $M, s' \models_{QCL} \varphi$;
- $M, s \models_{QCL} [P]\varphi$ iff $\forall C \subseteq Ag : C \models_{cp} P$ implies $\exists S \in \xi(C, s)$ such that for $\forall s' \in S$, we have $M, s' \models_{QCL} \varphi$.

Expressive Power. QCL is known to be equivalent in expressive power to Coalition Logic (CL) [3] in the following sense:

$$\langle P \rangle \varphi \leftrightarrow \bigvee_{\{C \mid C \models_{cp} P\}} \langle eq(C) \rangle \varphi \qquad [P]\varphi \leftrightarrow \bigwedge_{\{C \mid C \models_{cp} P\}} \langle eq(C) \rangle \varphi$$

where $\langle eq(C) \rangle \varphi$ is equivalent to $[C]\varphi$ in CL. However, the significance of QCL is that it is exponentially more succinct than CL, while being computationally no worse.

2.3 A Model of Knowledge, Belief and Certainty

Following [9], [6] has presented a general formalism to represent and reason about the knowledge, belief and certainty of an agent, whose core idea is to equip agents with sensors that can be potentially inaccurate. And this can enable us to distinguish what is *visible* in the environment to individual agents, what these agents actually *perceive* (see), and what the agents actually *know* about the environment.

To be more specific, given n agents of the set $\{1, 2, \ldots, n\}$, we assume that every agent has a sensor that may be defective which thus can not perceive the environment correctly.

For every agent i, the *environment state* s_e can be defined as a pair (s^i_{vis}, s^i_{inv}) of a *visible part* s^i_{vis} and an *invisible part* s^i_{inv}. The agent i's *internal state* s^i_{int} is a pair (s^i_{per}, S^i_{pls}), where s^i_{per} is the agent's perception of s^i_{vis}, and S^i_{pls} is a set of plausible invisible parts of s_e that agent i thinks possible. Therefore, every agent i can be associated with a 4-tuple $(s^i_{vis}, s^i_{inv}, s^i_{per}, S^i_{pls})$, and we denote $s^i_{vis}, s^i_{inv}, s^i_{per}$ and S^i_{pls} by $vis(i, s)$, $inv(i, s)$, $per(i, s)$ and $pls(i, s)$, respectively.

A global state s of the system is then defined as

$$s = ((s^1_{vis}, s^1_{inv}, s^1_{per}, S^1_{pls}), \ldots, (s^n_{vis}, s^n_{inv}, s^n_{per}, S^n_{pls}))$$

The set of all global states of the system is named as S.

Now we define three kinds of binary relations K_i, B_i and C_i for every agent i based on the model given above. Let s and t be two global states from S.

For every agent i, if $vis(i, s) = vis(i, t)$, then we define $s \sim^i_K t$, which implies that s and t are indistinguishable to agent i from the view point of knowledge. Furthermore $K_i = \{(s, t) \mid s \sim^i_K t\}$.

For every agent i, if $vis(i, t) = per(i, s)$ and $inv(i, t) \in pls(i, s)$, then we define $s \sim^i_B t$, which means that s and t are indistinguishable to agent i from the view point of belief. Furthermore $B_i = \{(s, t) \mid s \sim^i_B t\}$.

For every agent i, if $vis(i, t) = per(i, s)$, then we define $s \sim_C^i t$, which delivers the message that s and t are indistinguishable to agent i from the view point of certainty. Furthermore $C_i = \{(s, t) \mid s \sim_C^i t\}$.

Then we can assign semantics to the modalities as usual. Intuitively, an agent knows φ means not only φ is true, but also the agent would be able to perceive φ if its sensor apparatus is good enough. The agent is certain of φ implies that φ holds at those states with the agent totally perceiving the visible parts of the environment, whereas the agent believes φ delivers the message that φ holds at those states with the visible part equaling to the agent's current perception and with the invisible part plausible from the agent's point of view.

Proposition 1. *The relation K_i is an equivalent relation, and $R_B^i(s) \subseteq R_C^i(s)$ with $R_B^i(s) = \{t|(s,t) \in B_i\}$ and $R_C^i(s) = \{t|(s,t) \in C_i\}$.*

3 Quantified Coalition Logic of Knowledge, Belief, and Certainty

3.1 Syntax

Given a set Θ of atomic propositions and a finite set $Ag = \{1, \ldots, n\}$ agents, the formulas of our Quantified Coalition Logic of Knowledge, Belief and Certainty (QCLKBC) are defined as:

$$\phi ::= p \mid \neg\phi \mid \phi \wedge \phi \mid \langle P \rangle \phi \mid [P]\phi \mid K_i\phi \mid B_i\phi \mid C_i\phi$$

where $p \in \Theta$, $i \in Ag$, and P is the coalition predicate defined in Sect. 2.2.

With QCLKBC, we can formalize the subtle interplay between KBC and strategic modalities, and thus can model some novel and interesting properties that are hard or even impossible to be modeled by any other existing logical languages, such as "agent i is an indispensable member in any coalition that is able to make agent j believe φ": $[supset(\{i\})]B_j\varphi \wedge [\neg supset(\{i\})]\neg B_j\varphi$.

3.2 Semantics

As for the semantics, we define a *QCLKBC coalition model* as a tuple

$$M = \langle S, \xi, \pi, K, B, C \rangle$$

- S is a non-empty set of states; and for every $s \in S$, it is represented as $s = ((s_{vis}^1, s_{inv}^1, s_{per}^1, S_{pls}^1), \ldots, (s_{vis}^n, s_{inv}^n, s_{per}^n, S_{pls}^n))$;
- ξ is a *truly playable* effectivity function;
- π is a *valuation function*, which assigns each state $s \in S$ a set $\pi(s) \subseteq \Theta$;
- $K = \{K_1, \ldots, K_n\}$ with each $K_i \subseteq S \times S$ being an equivalent relation;
- $B = \{B_1, \ldots, B_n\}$ with each $B_i \subseteq S \times S$;
- $C = \{C_1, \ldots, C_n\}$ with each $C_i \subseteq S \times S$ and $R_B^i(s) \subseteq R_C^i(s)$ for every $s \in S$;

Given a QCLKBC coalition model $M = \langle S, \xi, \pi, K, B, C \rangle$, the semantics of QCLKBC is defined as follows:

- $(M, s) \models p$ iff $p \in \pi(s)$;
- $(M, s) \models \neg\phi$ iff $(M, s) \not\models \phi$;
- $(M, s) \models \phi_1 \wedge \phi_2$ iff $(M, s) \models \phi_1$ and $(M, s) \models \phi_2$;
- $(M, s) \models \langle P \rangle \phi$ iff $\exists G \subseteq Ag$ such that $G \models_{cp} P$ and $\phi^M \in \xi(G, s)$ where $\phi^M = \{s \mid (M, s) \models \phi\}$;
- $(M, s) \models [P]\phi$ iff $\forall G \subseteq Ag$ such that $G \models_{cp} P$ implies $\phi^M \in \xi(G, s)$;
- $(M, s) \models K_i\phi$ iff $(M, s') \models \phi$ for those s' such that $(s, s') \in K_i$;
- $(M, s) \models B_i\phi$ iff $(M, s') \models \phi$ for those s' such that $(s, s') \in B_i$;
- $(M, s) \models C_i\phi$ iff $(M, s') \models \phi$ for those s' such that $(s, s') \in C_i$.

From [6], we can have $\models C_i\varphi \rightarrow B_i\varphi$; $\models C_i\varphi \rightarrow C_iK_i\varphi$ and $\models \neg C_i\varphi \rightarrow C_i\neg K_i\varphi$.

4 The Proof System

4.1 The Axiomatic System for QCLKBC

The axiomatic system of QCLKBC consists of the following axioms and inference rules, where **K1–K7** are axioms for KBC modalities from [6], and **Q1–Q2** for translating all QCLKBC formulas with coalition predicates into the equivalent ones where the only coalition predicate is $eq()$.

Axioms:
Prop All axioms for propositional calculus
K1 $(X_i\varphi \wedge X_i(\varphi \rightarrow \psi)) \rightarrow X_i(\psi), i = 1, 2, ..., n$ for $X_i \in \{K_i, B_i, C_i\}$
K2 $K_i\varphi \rightarrow \varphi, i = 1, 2, ..., n$
K3 $K_i\varphi \rightarrow K_iK_i\varphi, i = 1, 2, ..., n$
K4 $\neg K_i\varphi \rightarrow K_i\neg K_i\varphi, i = 1, 2, ..., n$
K5 $C_i\varphi \rightarrow C_iK_i\varphi, i = 1, 2, ..., n$
K6 $\neg C_i\varphi \rightarrow C_i\neg K_i\varphi, i = 1, 2, ..., n$
K7 $C_i\varphi \rightarrow B_i\varphi, i = 1, 2, ..., n$
Q1 $\langle P \rangle\varphi \leftrightarrow \bigvee_{\{G \mid G \models_{cp} P\}} \langle eq(G) \rangle\varphi$
Q2 $[P]\varphi \leftrightarrow \bigwedge_{\{G \mid G \models_{cp} P\}} \langle eq(G) \rangle\varphi$
G1 $\neg\langle eq(G) \rangle \perp$
G2 $\langle eq(G) \rangle \top$
G3 $\neg\langle eq(\emptyset) \rangle\neg\varphi \rightarrow \langle eq(Ag) \rangle\varphi$
G4 $\langle eq(G) \rangle(\varphi \wedge \psi) \rightarrow \langle eq(G) \rangle\psi$
G5 $\langle eq(G_1) \rangle\varphi \wedge \langle eq(G_2) \rangle\psi \rightarrow \langle eq(G_1 \cup G_2) \rangle(\varphi \wedge \psi)$, if $G_1 \cap G_2 = \emptyset$

Inference Rules:
R1 If $\vdash \varphi$ and $\vdash \varphi \rightarrow \psi$, then $\vdash \psi$
R2 If $\vdash \varphi$, then $\vdash K_i\varphi \wedge C_i\varphi$
R3 If $\vdash \varphi \leftrightarrow \psi$, then $\vdash \langle eq(G) \rangle\varphi \leftrightarrow \langle eq(G) \rangle\psi$

where $G \subseteq Ag$ is coalition while $Ag = \{1, 2, \ldots, n\}$ is a finite set of agents.

Lemma 1 (Soundness). *For any QCLKBC-formula ϕ, $\vdash \phi \Rightarrow \models \phi$.*

4.2 Completeness Proof

Definition 1. *Let Γ be a finite set of formulas. Γ is closed under single negations iff for any $\varphi \in \Gamma$,*

$$\begin{cases} \phi \in \Gamma, & \text{if } \varphi \text{ is of the form } \neg\phi; \\ \neg\varphi \in \Gamma, & \text{otherwise.} \end{cases}$$

Definition 2 (Closure). *The closure of a formula φ, denoted by $cl(\varphi)$, is the set Γ of all subformulas of φ and is closed under single negations.*

Definition 3. *Given a formula φ, we define an extended set $ecl(\varphi)$ to be the smallest set such that*

1. *$cl(\varphi) \subseteq ecl(\varphi)$;*
2. *if $C_i\psi \in ecl(\varphi)$, then $B_i\psi \in ecl(\varphi)$;*
3. *if $\neg\langle eq(Ag)\rangle\psi \in ecl(\varphi)$, then $\langle eq(\emptyset)\rangle\neg\psi \in ecl(\varphi)$;*
4. *if $\langle eq(G_1)\rangle\psi_1 \in ecl(\varphi)$, $\vdash \psi_1 \rightarrow \psi_2$ and $\psi_2 \in ecl(\varphi)$, then $\langle eq(G_1)\rangle\psi_2 \in ecl(\varphi)$.*

The construction of $ecl(\varphi)$ is similar to Fischer-Ladner closure [10], which can prove the completeness of modal logics by constructing finite models.

Definition 4 (Canonical Model). *Given a consistent QCLKBC formula φ, the canonical QCLKBC coalition model is $M^c_\varphi = \langle S, \xi, \pi, K, B, C\rangle$ where*

- *$S = \{s \mid s$ is a maximal consistent set from $ecl(\varphi)\}$;*
- *ξ:*

$$W \in \xi(G, s) \text{ iff}$$

$$\begin{cases} \{t \mid \phi \in t\} \subseteq W \text{ and } \langle eq(G)\rangle\phi \in s, & \text{if } G \neq Ag; \\ \overline{W} \notin \xi(\emptyset, s), & \text{if } G = Ag. \end{cases}$$

- *$\pi : p \in \pi(s)$ iff $p \in s$ for all $s \in S$;*
- *$K = \{K_1, \ldots, K_n\}$, $B = \{B_1, \ldots, B_n\}$ and $C = \{C_1, \ldots, C_n\}$ are defined as*
  1. *$(s,t) \in K_i$ iff $\{\varphi \mid K_i\varphi \in s\} = \{\phi \mid K_i\phi \in t\}$ for all $i \in \{1, \ldots, n\}$;*
  2. *$(s,t) \in B_i$ iff $\{\varphi \mid B_i\varphi \in s\} \subseteq t$ for all $i \in \{1, \ldots, n\}$;*
  3. *$(s,t) \in C_i$ iff $\{\varphi \mid C_i\varphi \in s\} \subseteq t$ for all $i \in \{1, \ldots, n\}$.*

Lemma 2 (Truth Lemma). *Any QCLKBC-consistent formula φ is satisfied in the canonical QCLKBC coalition model M^c_φ.*

Proof. The construction of the canonical model is to make sure that a formula belongs to a state iff it is true there. Since $\varphi \in ecl(\varphi)$, we can prove by structural induction on an arbitrary $\gamma \in ecl(\varphi)$ that $(M^c, s) \models \gamma$ iff $\gamma \in s$. ∎

5 Computational Complexity

In this section, we show the satisfiability problem for QCLKBC is PSPACE-complete.

Definition 5. *Given a QCLKBC formula φ, we define $TL(\varphi)$ to be the smallest set such that*

- *$TL(\varphi)$ contains all subformulas of φ and is closed under single negations;*
- *if $\langle eq(Ag)\rangle\psi \in TL(\varphi)$, then $\langle eq(\emptyset)\rangle\neg\psi \in TL(\varphi)$;*
- *if $\langle eq(\emptyset)\rangle\psi \in TL(\varphi)$, then $\langle eq(Ag)\rangle\neg\psi \in TL(\varphi)$.*

Definition 6. *A QCLKBC tableau for a formula φ is a tuple $T = (S, L, \mathcal{K}, \mathcal{B}, \mathcal{C})$, where S is a set of states, $\mathcal{K} = \{\mathcal{K}_1, \ldots, \mathcal{K}_n\}$, $\mathcal{B} = \{\mathcal{B}_1, \ldots, \mathcal{B}_n\}$, $\mathcal{C} = \{\mathcal{C}_1, \ldots, \mathcal{C}_n\}$ with binary relations $\mathcal{K}_i$, $\mathcal{B}_i$ and $\mathcal{C}_i$ on S for each i, and L is a labelling function that associates with each states $s \in S$ a set $L(s) \in TL(\varphi)$ of formulas such that*

T1 *$\varphi \in L(s_0)$ for some $s_0 \in S$;*
PT *$L(s)$ is a propositional tableau that is consistent and satisfies*
(a) if $\neg\neg\psi \in L(s)$, then $\psi \in L(s)$;
(b) if $\psi_1 \wedge \psi_2 \in L(s)$, then both ψ_1 and ψ_2 are in $L(s)$;
(c) if $\neg(\psi_1 \wedge \psi_2) \in L(s)$, then either $\neg\psi_1 \in L(s)$ or $\neg\psi_2 \in L(s)$;
(d) for every $\neg\psi \in TL(\varphi)$, either $\neg\psi \in L(s)$ or $\psi \in L(s)$;
KT1 *$K_i\psi \in L(s)$ and $(s,t) \in \mathcal{K}_i$, then $\psi \in L(t)$; and the same holds for modalities B_i and C_i;*
KT2 *$\neg K_i\psi \in L(s)$ then there is a t with $(s,t) \in \mathcal{K}_i$ and $\neg\psi \in L(t)$; and the same holds for modalities B_i and C_i;*
KT3 *(a) if $K_i\psi \in L(s)$, then $\psi \in L(s)$;*
(b) if $(s,t) \in \mathcal{K}_i$, then $K_i\psi \in L(s)$ iff $K_i\psi \in L(t)$.
KT4 *(a) If $C_i\psi \in L(s)$ and $(s,t) \in \mathcal{C}_i$, then $K_i\psi \in L(t)$;*
(b) if $\neg C_i\psi \in L(s)$ and $(s,t) \in \mathcal{C}_i$, then $\neg K_i\psi \in L(t)$.
KT5 *if $C_i\psi \in L(s)$, then $B_i\psi \in L(s)$.*
QT1 *if $\langle P\rangle\psi \in L(s)$, then $\langle eq(G)\rangle\psi \in L(s)$ for some $G \in \{G_i \mid G_i \models_{cp} P\}$;*
QT2 *if $\neg\langle P\rangle\psi \in L(s)$, then $\neg\langle eq(G)\rangle\psi \in L(s)$ for all $G \in \{G_i \mid G_i \models_{cp} P\}$;*
QT3 *if $[P]\psi \in L(s)$, then $\langle eq(G)\rangle\psi \in L(s)$ for all $G \in \{G_i \mid G_i \models_{cp} P\}$;*
QT4 *if $\neg[P]\psi \in L(s)$, then $\neg\langle eq(G)\rangle\psi \in L(s)$ for some $G \in \{G_i \mid G_i \models_{cp} P\}$;*
CT1 *$\langle eq(Ag)\rangle\psi \in L(s)$ iff $\neg\langle eq(\emptyset)\rangle\neg\psi \in L(s)$;*
CT2 *if $\langle eq(G_1)\rangle\psi_1, \ldots, \langle eq(G_k)\rangle\psi_k \in L(s)$ where G_i are pairwise disjoint, then there is an $s' \in S$ such that $\psi_1, \ldots, \psi_k \in L(s')$;*
CT3 *if $\langle eq(G_1)\rangle\psi_1, \ldots, \langle eq(G_k)\rangle\psi_k, \neg\langle eq(G)\rangle\psi \in L(s)$ where G_i are non-empty, pairwise disjoint and $\bigcup_i G_i \subseteq G$, then there is an $s' \in S$ such that $\psi_1, \ldots, \psi_k$, $\neg\psi \in L(s')$.*

Intuitively, **KT1–KT4** are imposing the semantical conditions on a tableau for modal operators K_i, B_i and C_i respectively, **QT1–QT4** are for coalition predicates, and **CT1–CT3** are ensuring satisfiability of coalitional operators for a specific coalition.

Theorem 1. *A QCLKBC formula φ is satisfiable iff there is a QCLKBC tableau $T = \{S, L, \mathcal{K}, \mathcal{B}, \mathcal{C}\}$ for φ.*

Proof. By structural indcution. ∎

Hence we can immediately get a decision procedure to construct a QCLKBC tableau for a satisfiable formula φ that runs in polynomial space.

Theorem 2. *The satisfiability of QCLKBC is in PSPACE-Complete.*

6 Related Work

Many different variants have been proposed and studied based on CL [2–5]. However, they do not take into account the multiple rational mental attitudes of agents such as knowledge, belief and certainty [6] so as to enhance the expressivity. Therefore, our language of QCLKBC can arguably model more general and realistic game-like scenarios. Furthermore, complete axiomatization of these logics is technically harder to obtain. There exist only a few notable works such as completeness proof for CL [1], Higher-Order Coalition Logic (HCL) [4] and more recently, completeness proof for epistemic coalition logic [2]. And this paper has successfully addressed this issue for QCLKBC, a new multi-modal logic with coalitional and mental settings.

7 Conclusion

In this paper, we introduce a multi-modal logic of Quantified Coalition Logic of Knowledge, Belief and Certainty (QCLKBC) to equip CL with the power to address strategic and mental concerns in a unified language. Moreover, we provide a complete axiomatic system for the logic, and show that the complexity of satisfiability problem are PSPACE-complete.

Our research can be furthered by considering other epistemic concepts such as the awareness [11] and defining the effectivity function over a path instead of a state in order to model extensive games [12].

References

1. Pauly, M.: A modal logic for coalitional power in games. J. Log. Comput. **12**(1), 149–166 (2002)
2. Ågotnes, T., Alechina, N.: Epistemic coalition logic: completeness and complexity. In: Proceedings of the Eleventh International Conference on Autonomous Agents and Multiagent Systems (AAMAS 2012), pp. 1099–1106. ACM Press (2012)
3. Ågotnes, T., van der Hoek, W., Wooldridge, M.: Quantified coalition logic. Synthese **165**(2), 269–294 (2008)
4. Boella, G., Gabbay, D.M., Genovese, V., van der Torre, L.: Higher-order coalition logic. In: Proceedings of the ECAI 2010–19th European Conference on Artificial Intelligence, Lisbon, Portugal, 16–20 August 2010, pp. 555–560 (2010)

5. Ågotnes, T., van der Hoek, W., Wooldridge, M.: Reasoning about coalitional games. Artif. Intell. **173**(1), 45–79 (2009)
6. Su, K., Sattar, A., Governatori, G., Chen, Q.: A computationally grounded logic of knowledge, belief and certainty. In: Proceedings of the 4th International Joint Conference on Autonomous Agents and Multiagent Systems (AAMAS 2005), 25–29 July 2005, Utrecht, The Netherlands, pp. 149–156 (2005)
7. Goranko, V., Jamroga, W., Turrini, P.: Strategic games and truly playable effectivity functions. Auton. Agent. Multi-Agent Syst. **26**(2), 288–314 (2013)
8. Goranko, V., Jamroga, W., Turrini, P.: Strategic games and truly playable effectivity functions. In: Proceedigns of the 10th International Conference on Autonomous Agents and Multiagent Systems (AAMAS 2011), Taipei, Taiwan, pp. 727–734 (2011)
9. Wooldridge, M., Lomuscio, A.: A computationally grounded logic of visibility, perception, and knowledge. Log. J. IGPL **9**(2), 257–272 (2001)
10. Fischer, M.J., Ladner, R.E.: Propositional dynamic logic of regular programs. J. Comput. Syst. Sci. **18**(2), 194–211 (1979)
11. Ågotnes, T., Alechina, N.: A logic for reasoning about knowledge of unawareness. J. Logic Lang. Inform. **23**(2), 197–217 (2014)
12. Goranko, V., Jamroga, W.: State and path coalition effectivity models of concurrent multi-player games. Auton. Agent. Multi-Agent Syst. **30**(3), 446–485 (2016)

Modelling Personality-Based Individual Differences in the Use of Emotion Regulation Strategies

Juan Martínez-Miranda[1(✉)] and Matías Alvarado[2]

[1] CONACYT Research Fellow - Centro de Investigación Científica y de Educación Superior de Ensenada, Unidad de Transferencia Tecnológica, CICESE-UT3, Tepic, Mexico
jmiranda@cicese.mx

[2] Centro de Investigación y de Estudios Avanzados del IPN, Mexico City, Mexico
matias@cs.cinvestav.mx

Abstract. The modelling of the emotion regulation process is an important aspect that can contribute to the creation of more realistic intelligent virtual agents. The emotional reactions in a virtual agent, produced by the regulation process, can be useful to better adapt the agent's behaviour to the particular requirements of a social interactive scenario. We propose a computational model of emotion regulation where the use of different strategies to down-regulate the negative emotions is based on personality-based individual differences. Our model implements a fuzzy mechanism that reproduce the correlation between different personality traits and the use of the specific emotion regulation strategies described in the literature. The validation of the model has been performed through a set of simulations where synthetic data have been generated to represent individuals with different personalities.

Keywords: Affective computing · Emotion modelling · Virtual agents · Personality traits · Emotion regulation strategies

1 Introduction

The use and benefits of virtual agents, as advanced human-computer interaction interfaces, has contributed to the research and development of better underlying mechanisms able to generate more human-like behaviours in those agents. The modelling of the emotional phenomenon, as a basic component of human behaviour, is a key characteristic to produce *adequate* emotional reactions in the virtual agent while interacting with the user. The generation of emotional reactions that convey *empathy* towards the user is particularly important to create social and emotional bonds that maximise the use of virtual agents. The displaying of specific emotions with a suitable level of intensity is an important aspect especially for applications where the objective of the virtual agent is to support the user with therapeutic-based activities [1].

M. Mouhoub and P. Langlais (Eds.): Canadian AI 2017, LNAI 10233, pp. 361–372, 2017.
DOI: 10.1007/978-3-319-57351-9_41

The process to modulate the intensity (or even prevent the activation) of a particular emotion is known as emotion regulation. According to [2], there are different strategies that an individual could implement to self-regulate his/her emotions. The implementation of the different strategies for emotion regulation changes across individuals and there are studies that demonstrate the influence of culture, age, gender, temperament and personality traits on the process of emotion regulation [3,4].

Based on the evidence about the correlation between different personality types and the way how individuals self-regulate emotions, we present a computational model of the emotion regulation process considering the individual differences produced by the characteristics of different personalities. Our model is based on J.J. Gross' process model of emotion regulation [2] and integrates the findings about the influence of personality traits (using the Big Five model) in the selection of different strategies for emotion regulation [3,4].

We represent the influence of the personality type on the selection of the emotion regulation strategies through a set of fuzzy logic rules. A set of simulations using stochastic data that represent individuals scoring at different personality type is executed as the input of the fuzzy rules. The implementation or not of each emotion regulation strategy, according to the different personality, is the output of the fuzzy inference system and it is compared with the evidence reported in the literature.

Our main aim is to get a computational emotion regulation component that can be used as the affect derivation and affect intensity models for appraisal-based computational architectures of emotions [5]. The emotions and their associated intensity produced by our proposed model can contribute to generate a richer emotional behaviour in synthetic characters such as embodied conversational agents. Building virtual agents with different personalities able to produce diverse emotional reactions will be useful for the design of better personalised interactive scenarios.

The remainder of the paper is organised as follows: In Sect. 2 the theoretical foundations of the emotion regulation process and a summary of current computational models of this process are presented. The proposed model is described in Sect. 3, and its evaluation is presented in Sect. 4. Finally, Sect. 5 presents the main conclusions and some further work.

2 Related Work

2.1 Theoretical Foundations of Emotion Regulation

One of the affective processes that has attracted the interest of an important number of researchers in the last years is the emotion regulation. Emotion regulation is considered as the *modulation* of a given emotional reaction, including its inhibition, activation or graded modulation [6]. Although there is still discussion about whether consider the emotion regulation process as part of the emotion generation [7,8], there are studies that reveal the neural differences between these two processes [9] and describe the benefits of studying the emotion generation and emotion regulation processes separately [2].

The model of emotion regulation proposed by Gross [2] describes the conscious and unconscious strategies used to increase, maintain, or decrease one or more components of an emotional response. The main characteristic of this model is the identification and definition of five families of emotion regulation processes: *situation selection*, *situation modification*, *attentional deployment*, *cognitive change* and *response modulation.*

Situation selection is described as when an individual takes the necessary actions to be in a situation the individual expects will raise a certain desirable emotion. *Situation modification* refers to the efforts employed by the individual to directly modify the actual situation to alter its emotional impact. The third family, *attentional deployment*, refers to how individuals direct their attention within the current situation in order to influence their emotions. *Cognitive change* is described as when the individual changes how the actual situation is appraised to alter its emotional significance, either by changing how the individual thinks about the situation or the capacity to manage it. Finally, the *response modulation* family refers when the individual influences the physiological, experiential, or behavioural responses to the situation.

Based on experimental work, there is now an agreement about the fact that individuals differ *systematically* and *consistently* in how they apply emotion regulation in every day situations [4]. The Emotion Regulation Questionnaire (ERQ) [10] is an instrument used to identify consistent differences in emotion regulation according to individual characteristics such as age, gender, culture and personality trends. The questionnaire have been validated in different languages and applied to young and older adults from different countries [11–13]. One of the findings from these experimental works is the evidence about the influence of the different personalities on the use of the strategies of emotion regulation [3]. This evidence is the basis of our proposed model explained in Sect. 3.

2.2 Computational Models of Emotion Regulation

The modelling of the emotional phenomenon has produced different computational architectures of emotion that are used to analyse and simulate different aspects of this complex process. Most of these architectures are based on different cognitive and psychological theories of emotions influenced by the components and phases of the emotional phenomenon that the model tries to represent [5]. Although several computational architectures of emotions have been developed in the last years, most of them are dedicated to represent the process of emotion generation and just a few have integrated the process of emotion regulation.

One of the first architectures that modelled the phenomenon of emotion regulation phenomena was EMA [14]. The EMA framework is based on the cognitive appraisal theory of emotions [15] and it integrates a *coping* mechanism with strategies such as *planning*, *acceptance*, *positive reinterpretation*, *mental disengagement*, *denial/wishful thinking* and *shift/accept blame* [16]. The main aim of the coping component in EMA was to better adapt the behaviour of virtual agents to a dynamic environment.

CoMERG is another computational model of emotion regulation based on Gross' theory. This model formalises Gross model through a set of difference equations and rules to simulate the dynamics of Gross' emotion-regulation strategies [17]. CoMERG identifies a set of variables and their dependencies to represent both quantitative aspects (such as levels of emotional response) and qualitative aspects (such as decisions to regulate one's emotion) of the model. These variables include e.g. the level of -the actual- emotion, the optimal -desired- level of emotion, the personal tendency to adjust the emotional value, or the costs of adjusting the emotional value, among others to simulate and evaluate the results in the use of four strategies of emotion regulation. Although the model includes a variable representing a *personal tendency to adjust the emotional value*, the selection of the different strategies of emotion regulation are not based on the characteristics of different personality traits.

The work presented in [18] is an additional model of emotion regulation based on Gross' theory. This model proposes an extension of the CoMERG model by adding a dynamic evaluation of different kind of events and associating levels of desirability of those events, which in turn are used to elicit a set of emotions. The desirability of the events, the impact of the events according to a set of pre-defined goals and the emotional responses are modelled through fuzzy sets. Similar to CoMERG, the model implements an equation to calculate the emotional response. The equation includes different variables to represent the execution of different strategies for emotion regulation. The calculation also contains an *adaptation factor* which indicates the flexibility of the agent toward applying a specific regulation strategy in a certain condition.

A more recent work presents a neurologically inspired computational model of emotion regulation [19]. The model is based on an internal monitoring and decision making about the selection of three (Gross's model based) strategies of emotion regulation: situation modification, cognitive change and response modulation. The decision process to select one or another (or the three) emotion regulation strategies is mainly based on the assessment of the current emotional state generated by an external event, the *sensitivity* of a person for negative stimuli, and the *preferences* of a person for the emotion regulation strategies. The process is modelled as a temporal-causal network using a set of differential equations and evaluated through a number of simulations. During the simulations, different thresholds are set for the intensity of the negative emotions and different weights are defined to represent how much sensitive is the person to the stimulus. The use of these two parameters try to represent the individual differences in the implementation of the emotion regulation strategies.

As can be seen, most of the presented models include variables such as the *preferences*, *tendency* or *flexibility* of a person toward emotion regulation strategies, as well as his/her *sensitivity* for negative stimuli. The setting of these variables in the models where these are implemented try to represent the individual differences during the selection and implementation of the strategies of emotion regulation. Nevertheless, none of the above models associate specific personality traits to the selection of the different emotion regulation strategies. The contribution of the work presented here, is the construction of a computational framework which explicitly implements the individual differences during emotion regulation based on personality. The Big Five personality model and the findings reported in [3] are the theoretical roots of the model described in the next section.

3 The Proposed Model

3.1 Correlation Between Personality and Emotion Regulation Strategies

Most of the existent computational models of emotions based on cognitive appraisal theories implement -implicitly or explicitly- four main components. The **appraisal-derivation** component assesses e.g. how much desirable/undesirable, expected/unexpected and liked/disliked is an event or action occurred in the environment of the agent according to the agent's goals and preferences. The **affect-derivation** component uses the assessment performed in the appraisal-derivation component to generate the specific -positive or negative- emotions according to the type of goals and/or preferences affected by the occurred event or action. A close related component is the **affect-intensity** model which specifies the strength of the emotional response resulting from a specific appraisal. The **affect-consequent** component maps the emotional state produced in the agent into specific behaviours as responses to the detected event/action. For details of these components and their relationship see [5].

Our proposed model of emotion regulation can be seen as the *affect-derivation* and *affect-intensity* components where the produced emotions and their corresponding intensity are obtained after the implementation (or not) of the strategies of emotion regulation. This model is an extension of a previous work where only two emotion regulation strategies were included [20]. In that preceding study, the decision to implement any of the two strategies was based on predefined thresholds for the intensity of negative emotions and some characteristics of the events produced in the interactive scenario where it was evaluated. The selection of the strategies according to individual differences was neglected.

In order to include in our model those individual *preferences* or *tendencies* toward the implementation of specific emotion regulation strategies, we have used the research findings described in [3]. In the referred study, the authors correlate the habitual use of emotion regulation strategies with different personalities using the Big Five personality traits [21]: *conscientiousness*, *extraversion*, *neuroticism*, *openness to experience* and *agreeableness* (see details in [3]). The correlation between the use of the emotion regulation strategies by each personality trait is summarised in Table 1.

A positive correlation between a strategy and a personality trait is represented by "+". For example, individuals *high* in conscientiousness have the ability to plan, organise, and think ahead about potential consequences before

Table 1. Correlation of personality traits to the habitual use of emotion regulation strategies (taken from [3]).

Personality	Situation selection	Situation modification	Attention deployment	Cognitive change	Response modulation
Conscientiousness	+	+	+	0	0
Extraversion	–	+	0	0	–
Neuroticism	(+)	–	–	–	0
Openness	(–)	(+)	+	+	–
Agreeableness	0	–	0	0	(0)

acting. This characteristic should make it easier for them to use *situation selection* strategy. On the other hand, individuals *low* in conscientiousness have more difficulties to avoid entering or getting trapped in situations that cause them negative emotions [3]. A negative correlation is represented by "–". For example, individuals *high* in neuroticism do not usually apply the *situation modification* strategy due to the lack of self-esteem and confidence to assert their needs and enforce specific changes in the situation. When a clear positive or negative correlation has not been found, it is indicated with a "0". The parentheses, such as (+), indicates that the correlation likely depends on other factors or considerations such contextual information of the events, actions or individual's social relationships among others.

3.2 Fuzzy Sets and Fuzzy Rules

The linguistic values representing the *degree* of the different personality traits in an individual, such as *low in conscientiousness* or *high in extraversion*, are obtained from standardised inventories which score each of the Big Five traits. Moreover, the events or actions produced in the individual's environment can be appraised as *bad*, *neutral* or *good* according to the goals of the individual and predispose the triggering of an emotional response. Based on these linguistic values, we decided to use fuzzy sets to express these values in the main variables of our model. Fuzzy rules are used to represent the correlation between the different degrees of personality traits and the five strategies of emotion regulation.

The sets and elements used in our model are the following:

$P \in PERSONALITY = \{Co, Ex, Ne, Op, Ag\}$ is a *personality trait* element,
$E_i \in EVENT = \{E_1, ...E_m\}$ is an occurred *event* element, and
$S \in STRATEGY = \{SitSel, SitMod, AttDep, CogChg, ResMod\}$ is an *emotion regulation strategy* element.

The valuation function on each set is as follows:

$p : PERSONALITY \rightarrow V_p = \{low, middle, high\}$. (1)
$e : EVENT \rightarrow V_e\{very\_bad, bad, neutral, good, very\_good\}$. (2)
$s : STRATEGY \rightarrow V_s = \{weak\_apply, mid\_apply, strong\_apply\}$. (3)

The set $PERSONALITY$ contains the five personality traits and the distribution of linguistic values (V_p) of the personality traits implemented through fuzzy sets using a Gaussian membership function. The boundaries of each fuzzy set are based on the values used in the Big Five questionnaire. Similarly, the set $STRATEGY$ contains the five strategies of emotion regulation and the linguistic values (V_s) indicates to what extent each strategy is applied. Finally, the *events* occurred in the environment of the agent are linguistic qualified by values in V_e, which are also implemented through fuzzy sets with a Gaussian membership function. The fuzzy sets are shown in Fig. 1.

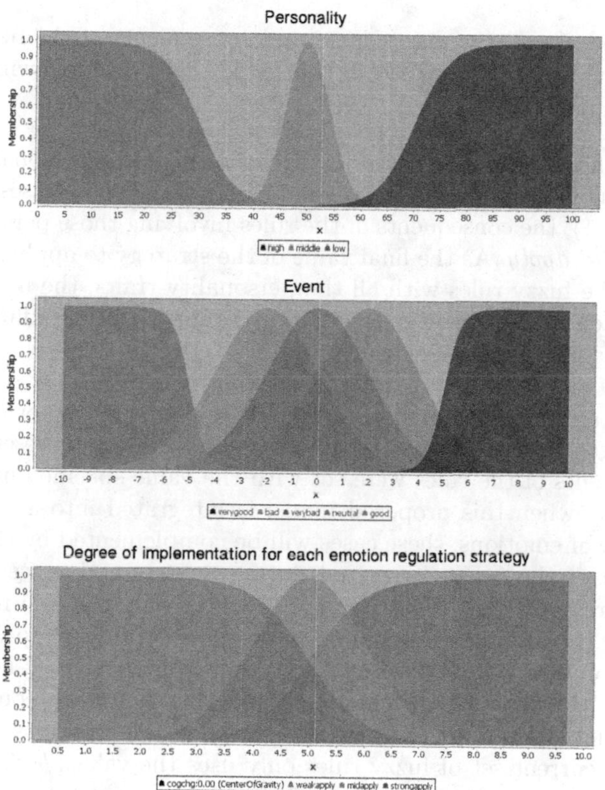

Fig. 1. Fuzzy sets used in the model.

The correlation between the personality traits and to what extent what of the five strategies of emotion regulation an agent will apply is implemented through a set of fuzzy rules. A roughly formal account of the rules is:

event AND personality THEN strategy

Then we have rules instances of the type:

$IF(E_1\ IS\ bad\ OR\ E_1\ IS\ very\_bad)\ AND\ (Co\ IS\ high)$
$THEN\ SitSel\ IS\ strong\_apply$

$IF(E_1\ IS\ bad\ OR\ E_1\ IS\ very\_bad)\ AND\ (Ex\ IS\ middle)$
$THEN\ ResMod\ IS\ mid\_apply$

$IF(E_1\ IS\ bad\ OR\ E_1\ IS\ very\_bad)\ AND\ (Ag\ IS\ low)$
$THEN\ SitMod\ IS\ weak\_apply$
...

As explained above, the antecedents and consequents of the fuzzy rules are based on the evidence summarised in the Table 1 with the following considerations:

1. The cases where there is no a clear evidence between the personality trait and the selection of a specific emotion regulation strategy (those cases labeled with "0" in Table 1), the consequents of the rules involving those personality traits are set to *mid_apply*. As the final value of the strategy to apply is a combination of all the fuzzy rules with all the personality traits, the implementation or not of each specific emotion regulation strategy will be influenced by the values in the rest of the personality traits.
2. The cases where some contextual information of the event or social relationships of the agent are required to decide the implementation or not of specific emotion regulation strategies (those cases shown in parentheses in Table 1), the consequents of the rules were set with the value specified in the Table 1. Nevertheless, when this proposed model is integrated into a computational architecture of emotions, these cases will be complemented by the contextual information of the events triggered during an interactive scenario. In this sense the previous work reported in [20], where only the information generated during the interaction was used to decide whether to apply the emotion regulation process, will be enriched with the model described here.
3. As most of the research on emotion regulation has been concentrated on negative emotions (produced by the negative events or actions in the agent's world), the current set of fuzzy rules only uses the values *bad* and *very_bad* of the events as part of their antecedents. Nevertheless, the model can be easily extended to up-regulate positive emotions using the values *good* and *very_good* of an event.

4 Evaluation

The model was implemented as a java software module using the jFuzzyLogic library [22]. In order to validate that the results provided by the fuzzy inference system are in line with the correlations shown in Table 1, a set of simulations was run. At each simulation step, random values were generated for each of the five personality traits. These values simulated the obtained score by a person from the Big-Five personality inventory and were fuzzified using the fuzzy sets described in Sect. 3.2. Moreover, random values were also generated to represent the appraisal of an hypothetical event, and also fuzzified. Both, the fuzzified values of each personality trait and of the event, were used as the input for the fuzzy inference system. A total of 5,000 simulation, representing the same number of individuals, were executed.

The result provided by the inference system was the *degree of use* of each emotion regulation strategy labeled as *weak_apply*, *mid_apply*, and *strong_apply*. In order to quantify the result obtained in each of the five strategies of emotion regulation, we applied the Mamdani [23] model by using the centroid defuzzification of the fuzzy rules. The obtained crisp values of the 5,000 simulations were plotted in a scatter graph to visualise how the different emotion regulation strategies are applied by each of the five personality traits. An example is the plot of Fig. 2 that presents how the *situation selection* and *situation modification* strategies are used by the *extraversion* personality trait.

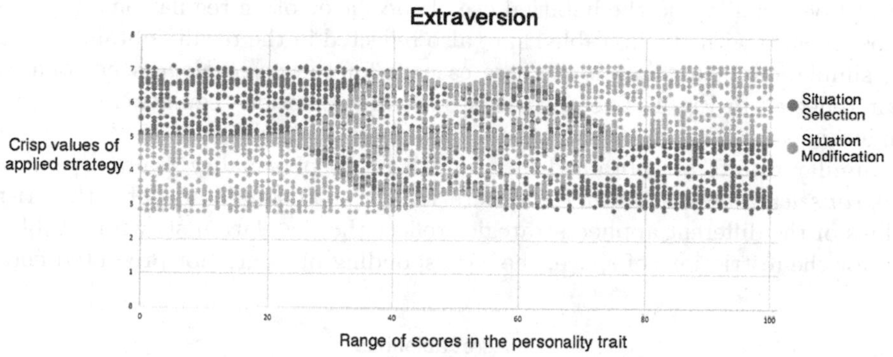

Fig. 2. Use of *situation selection* and *situation modification* strategies in the *extraversion* personality trait.

According to the summary of Table 1, individuals high in extraversion are negatively related with the use of situation selection and positively related with the use of situation modification. This assumption is reflected in the graph where lower values for this personality trait generate high crisp values in the use of situation selection. The use of the situation selection strategy decreases when the score in extraversion increases. Exactly the opposite occurs with the use of the situation modification strategy: low values in extraversion generate low crisp values for the use of this strategy, and it increases when scores of extraversion are also increased.

The plot of Fig. 3 shows the obtained results for the neuroticism personality trait. The values related to high scores of neuroticism are negatively related with the use of *situation modification*, *attentional deployment* and *cognitive change*. The only strategy that is positively related with high neuroticism is the *situation selection*. These results clearly reflect the correlations presented in the Table 1 for this personality trait.

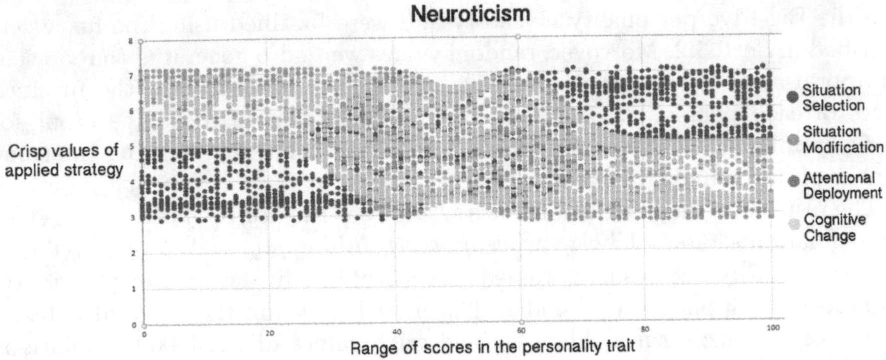

Fig. 3. Use of four strategies of emotion regulation in the *neuroticism* personality trait.

The cases where there is no a clear evidence of the correlation between the type of personality and the habitual use of specific emotion regulation strategies (those labeled with "0" in Table 1) are also reflected in the results obtained from the simulations. An example of these cases is for the *agreeableness* personality trait reflected in Fig. 4. The crisp values of three emotion regulation strategies remain in a same range independently of the personality's score.

Similar results are obtained for the other two personality traits: *openness* and *conscientiousness*. After the generation of 5,000 simulated data, the crisp values of the different applied strategies reflect the correlation shown in Table 1 but for the restrictions of space, the corresponding plots are not presented here.

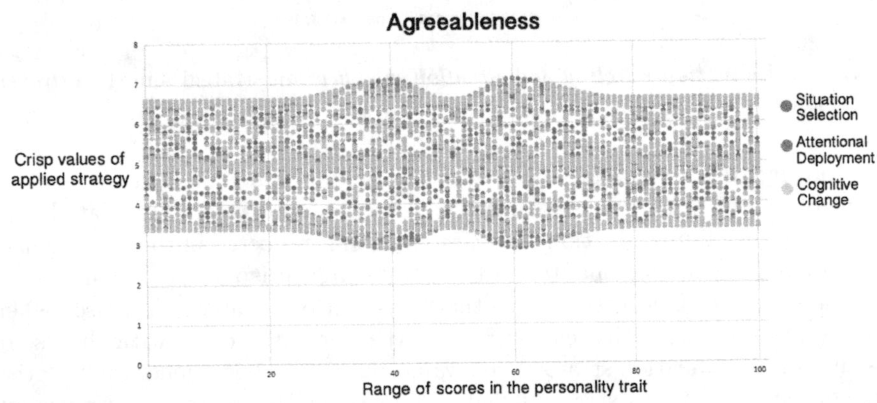

Fig. 4. Results of *situation selection*, *attentional deployment* and *cognitive change* in the *agreeableness* personality trait.

5 Conclusions

This paper presents a computational model of emotion regulation based on existing evidence about the personality-based individual differences in the use of different strategies to down-regulate negative emotions. The proposed model implements, using a fuzzy logic inference mechanism, the correlation between the different -Big Five- personality traits and the five strategies of emotion regulation proposed by J.J. Gross. The main aim of the proposed model is to be integrated as the underlying mechanism for the affect-derivation and affect-intensity components in a computational architecture of emotions. The generation of different emotion's intensities (generated by the emotion regulation process) based on different personalities will contribute to the creation of more believable virtual agents that can be personalised to the specific requirements of interactive scenarios.

The next step is exactly the integration of the model presented here into an existent computational architecture of emotions and complement the work initiated in [20]. In this way, the validation presented in this paper based on a set of simulations, can be complemented through the evaluation of the emotional behaviour produced by different virtual agents in a specific interactive scenario. The crisp values obtained from our fuzzy inference system can be used in a function to down-regulate the intensity of a triggered -negative- emotion. Thus, the produced emotional reactions modelling different personalities can be compared with those produced in virtual agents that do not incorporate our model and compare the acceptability and preferences of the users.

Acknowledgements. The first author acknowledges the "Cátedras CONACyT" program funded by the Mexican National Research Council (CONACyT).

References

1. Bickmore, T., Gruber, A.: Relational agents in clinical psychiatry. Harv. Rev. Psychiatry **18**(2), 119–130 (2010)
2. Gross, J.J., Thompson, R.A.: Emotion regulation: conceptual foundations. In: Gross, J.J. (ed.) Handbook of Emotion Regulation, pp. 3–24. The Guilford Press, New York (2007)
3. John, O.P., Gross, J.J.: Individual differences in emotion regulation. In: Gross, J.J. (ed.) Handbook of Emotion Regulation, pp. 351–372. The Guilford Press, New York (2007)
4. John, O.P., Eng, J.: Three approaches to individual differences in affect regulation: conceptualizations, measures, and findings. In: Gross, J.J. (ed.) Handbook of Emotion Regulation, 2nd edn, pp. 321–345. The Guilford Press, New York (2015)
5. Marsella, S., Gratch, J., Petta, P.: Computational models of emotion. In: Scherer, K.R., Bänziger, T., Roesch, E.B. (eds.) Blueprint for Affective Computing: A Sourcebook, pp. 21–46. Oxford University Press, Oxford (2010)
6. Rothbart, M.K., Sheese, B.E.: Temperament and emotion regulation. In: Gross, J.J. (ed.) Handbook of Emotion Regulation, pp. 331–350. The Guilford Press, New York (2007)

7. Campos, J.J., Frankel, C.B., Camras, L.: On the nature of emotion regulation. Child Dev. **75**, 377–394 (2004)
8. Frijda, N.H.: The Emotions. Cambridge University Press, Cambridge (1986)
9. Davidson, R.J., Fox, A., Kalin, N.H.: Neural bases of emotion regulation in nonhuman primates and humans. In: Gross, J.J. (ed.) Handbook of Emotion Regulation, pp. 47–68. The Guilford Press, New York (2007)
10. Gross, J.J., John, O.P.: Individual differences in two emotion regulation processes: Implications for affect, relationships, and well-being. J. Pers. Soc. Psychol. **85**, 348–362 (2003)
11. Abler, B., Kessler, H.: Emotion regulation questionnaire: a German version of the ERQ by Gross and John. Diagnostica **55**, 144–152 (2009)
12. Balzarotti, S., John, O.P., Gross, J.J.: An Italian adaptation of the emotion regulation questionnaire. Eur. J. Psychol. Assess **26**, 61–67 (2010)
13. English, T., John, O.P.: Understanding the social effects of emotion regulation: the mediating role of authenticity for individual differences in suppression. Emotion **13**, 314–329 (2013)
14. Gratch, J., Marsella, S.: A domain-independent framework for modeling emotion. J. Cogn. Syst. Res. **5**(4), 269–306 (2004)
15. Lazarus, R.: Emotion and Adaptation. Oxford University Press, Oxford (1991)
16. Gratch, J., Marsella, S.: Modeling coping behavior in virtual humans: don't worry, be happy. In: Proceedings of the 2nd International Joint Conference on Autonomous Agents and Multiagent Systems (2003)
17. Bosse, T., Pontier, M., Treur, J.: A computational model based on Gross' emotion regulation theory. Cogn. Syst. Res. **11**, 211–230 (2010)
18. Soleimain, A., Kobti, Z.: A fuzzy logic computational model for emotion regulation based on gross theory. In: Proceedings of the 26th International Florida Artificial Intelligence Research Society Conference (2013)
19. Manzoor, A., Abro, A.H., Treur, J.: Monitoring the impact of negative events and deciding about emotion regulation strategies. In: Proceedings of the 14th European Conference on Multi-Agent Systems (2016)
20. Martínez-Miranda, J., Bresó, A., García-Gómez, J.M.: Modelling two emotion regulation strategies as key features of therapeutic empathy. In: Bosse, T., et al. (eds.) Emotion Modeling: Towards Pragmatic Computational Models of Affective Processes, 115–133. Springer International Publishing, Cham (2014)
21. John, O.P.: The "Big Five" factor taxonomy: dimensions of personality in the natural language and in questionnaires. In: Pervin, L.A. (ed.) Handbook of Personality: Theory and Research, pp. 66–100. Guilford Press, New York (1990)
22. Cingolani, P., Alcalá-Fdez, J.: jFuzzyLogic: a robust and flexible Fuzzy-Logic inference system language implementation. In: Proceedings of IEEE International Conference on Fuzzy Systems, pp. 1–8 (2012)
23. Mamdani, E.H., Assilian, S.: An experiment in linguistic synthesis with a fuzzy logic controller. Int. J. Man Mach. Stud. **7**(1), 1–13 (1975)

Stoic Ethics for Artificial Agents

Gabriel Murray(✉)

University of the Fraser Valley, Abbotsford, BC, Canada
gabriel.murray@ufv.ca
http://www.ufv.ca/cis/gabriel-murray/

Abstract. We present a position paper advocating the notion that Stoic philosophy and ethics can inform the development of ethical A.I. systems. This is in sharp contrast to most work on building ethical A.I., which has focused on Utilitarian or Deontological ethical theories. We relate ethical A.I. to several core Stoic notions, including the dichotomy of control, the four cardinal virtues, the ideal Sage, Stoic practices, and Stoic perspectives on emotion or affect. More generally, we put forward an ethical view of A.I. that focuses more on internal states of the artificial agent rather than on external actions of the agent. We provide examples relating to near-term A.I. systems as well as hypothetical superintelligent agents.

Keywords: Ethical A.I. · Virtue Ethics · Stoicism · Superintelligence

1 Introduction

Stoicism is a philosophy that was prominent during the Hellenistic period and into the era of the Roman Empire [1]. Its ethical view is a form of Virtue Ethics, and both Stoicism and Virtue Ethics have seen a resurgence in study and popularity in recent decades. Virtue Ethics is now one of the three major ethical perspectives, alongside Utilitarianism and Deontological Ethics [2]. Whereas Utilitarianism examines the utility of actions and their consequences, and Deontological Ethics studies duties and obligations, Virtue Ethics focuses on virtuous or moral character, happiness, and the good life [3]. Stoicism more specifically adds ideas and practices relating to emotion, control, and rational deliberation, all of which we consider in depth.

The importance of designing ethical A.I. systems has become widely recognized in recent years. Most of this work is influenced by Utilitarian and Deontological ethics; for example, proposing or designing intelligent systems that act in such a way as to maximize some aspect of human well-being, or to obey particular rules. There has been very little work on how Virtue Ethics can inform the development of ethical A.I. agents, and perhaps no such work focusing on Stoicism. This is not surprising, as it is not immediately clear what it would even mean for an artificial agent to be Stoic. In this position paper, we aim to describe concretely what that could mean, and we advocate that Stoicism and Virtue Ethics should be considered in the discussion around ethical A.I.

M. Mouhoub and P. Langlais (Eds.): Canadian AI 2017, LNAI 10233, pp. 373–384, 2017.
DOI: 10.1007/978-3-319-57351-9_42

We propose that Stoic ethical analysis of A.I. should include the following:

- Stoic ethical analysis of A.I. should be based on analysis of an agent's internal states.
- Stoic ethical judgment of an A.I. agent should not be based on factors outside of the agent's control, and specifically should not be consequentialist.
- Stoic ethical analysis of A.I. should include whether or not the agent has characteristics corresponding to Stoic virtues.

Similarly, A.I. systems should be *designed* with these considerations in mind, and incorporate aspects of Stoic practices.

In Sect. 2, we discuss current directions in ethical A.I., including the limited previous work on Virtue Ethics for A.I. systems. In Sect. 3, we discuss some of the core concepts of Stoicism and how they can relate to the development of A.I. systems. These concepts include Stoic control, the four cardinal virtues, the ideal Sage, emotion, and Stoic practices. In Sect. 4, we consider criticisms of Stoicism and Virtue Ethics, as well as criticism of the notion that they could have any bearing on designing ethical intelligent systems. In that section, we also give some limited proposals on how Stoicism can be combined with Utilitarian and Deontological considerations. Finally, we conclude and summarize our position in Sect. 5.

2 Related Work

Recent discussion on ethical A.I. can be divided into that which focuses primarily on ethical implication of current and near-term A.I. systems, and that which primarily focuses on hypothetical superintelligence, i.e. systems with intelligence and capabilities that are beyond human-level. As an example of the former, Amodei et al. [4] describe concrete problems relating to A.I. safety, and Arkin [5] discusses ethics for autonomous systems used in warfare. Wallach and Allen [6] discuss morality for agents of varying levels of sophistication. Bostrom [7], Dewey [8], Christiano [9], and Yudkowsky [10] focus on A.I. ethics with a particular emphasis on superintelligent systems. Much of this work, whether looking at near-term or long-term A.I., is based on reinforcement learning, where an artificial agent learns how to act in an environment by collecting rewards (which could be negative, i.e. punishments). There are well-recognized potential pitfalls with this approach, such as using the wrong reward function, or having a super-intelligent agent take control of its own reward signal (called reward hacking, or wireheading). We will discuss some of these details and issues in Sect. 3. In general, these approaches are action-centric and based on taking actions that maximize some reward or utility.

There has been very little work on applying Virtue Ethics to artificial intelligence. Coleman [11] describes characteristics that can help an A.I. achieve its goals, and analyzes these characteristics as virtues in a Virtue Ethic framework. This is similar to our effort, except that we focus on the four cardinal Stoic virtues, and discuss many additional Stoic ideas and practices as well. Hicks [12] discusses drawbacks to designing ethical A.I. using principle-based approaches such as Utilitarian or Deontological ethics, and argues in favour of a role for Virtue Ethics. As one example, Hicks argues that in scenarios where all options are bad but the A.I. agent must still make a decision, the agent should have some sense of regret about the decision.

As the field of artificial intelligence has developed, the topic of ethical A.I. has been relatively neglected. The most famous example of ethical A.I. has come from fiction rather than A.I. research, in the form of Asimov's Laws of Robotics [13]. Recent years have seen a marked increase in attention paid to the topic of ethical A.I., with annual workshops as well as organizations and partnerships dedicated to the matter[1].

3 Stoicism and A.I.

In this section we discuss how Stoic philosophy and ethics can be relevant to the development of ethical A.I. systems.

3.1 Internal States Matter

As mentioned in Sect. 2, most existing work on ethical A.I. is action-centric. For example, we can design an intelligent agent that tries to maximize a reward function relating to some aspect of human well-being. There is a clear parallel between such systems and the Utilitarian ethical perspective, which says that an action is good if its positive consequences outweigh its negative consequences. Alternatively, an action-centric system could be informed by Deontological ethics, so that it takes actions that do not violate its obligations, and that do not use people or other agents as a means to an end (i.e. it acts in accordance with the Categorical Imperative). In either case, actions and consequences external to the agent are of paramount importance.

Stoicism and Virtue Ethics are more concerned with internal states of the agent. In that light, we need to first make a case that the internal states of an A.I. agent matter. We will give a number of examples demonstrating that the internal states of an A.I. do indeed matter, starting with current and near-term A.I. and then moving to increasingly sophisticated A.I. and hypothetical superintelligent systems.

A first example of the importance of internal states of an A.I. is the growing recognition that an A.I. system should be as *transparent* and *explainable* as possible[2]. If an A.I. system makes a prediction or a decision, we should be able to perform an audit that determines why it behaved as it did, or issue a query about what it has learned. A second, related example is that A.I. systems should be *corrigible*, or amenable to correction in order to improve behaviour and reduce mistakes [14].

[1] https://www.partnershiponai.org/, https://intelligence.org/, http://futureoflife.org/, http://humancompatible.ai, http://lcfi.ac.uk/.

[2] http://www.fatml.org/.

Another example concerns intelligent systems with affective capabilities. Affective computing involves the ability of a system to recognize, represent, and/or simulate affective states or emotions [15]. Since the role of emotion is critical in Stoic ethics, we will have much more to say about it below. At this point, it suffices to say that the internal states of an intelligent system with affective capabilities are important because the system may be engaging in persuasion or emotional manipulation that may be subtle from an external perspective.

If and when an A.I. system begins to match or exceed general human intelligence, we may need to engage in thorough monitoring of the system's internal states to carefully assess the agent's progress and capabilities. If a system is superintelligent but is a *boxed* A.I., meaning that it has severe restrictions on its external capabilities, it is possible that the agent will be strategically cooperative until it is unboxed, at which point it will have a strategic advantage and no longer need to cooperate with humans. It may also use emotional manipulation to persuade human operators to unbox it [7].

The prospect of such superintelligent systems leads to what Bostrom calls *mind crimes*, i.e. immoral internal states. The example just given, of an A.I. being deceptively cooperative, could constitute an immoral internal state. Bostrom gives a more dramatic example, where a superintelligent agent is able to create conscious human simulations, and is moreover able to create and destroy such conscious simulations by the billions. If the human simulations are truly conscious, this would constitute massive genocide [7].

These examples show that internal states are important even with current and near-term A.I. systems, and could become more so if superintelligent systems are ever developed.

3.2 Control

A central notion of Stoicism is the *dichotomy of control*, or recognizing that some things are in our control and some things are not. A person should not be overly concerned with things outside of their control, and more importantly, things that are outside of a person's control are neither good nor bad, morally speaking. Only virtue is good, and being virtuous is always within a person's control. And even when dealing with events that are outside of our control, we still control our responses to those events.

There are several applications of this idea to artificial intelligence. Clearly, it is important for an A.I. agent to know what is and isn't under its control, i.e. what are its capabilities and what is the environment like. And in an uncertain environment, the agent still controls its responses. Modern Stoic thinkers have used the idea of a *trichotomy of control* [16], introducing a third category of things we partly control, and that category can be demonstrated with two examples from within artificial intelligence. To use the example of an Markov Decision Process (MDP) with an optimal policy, the agent is best off following the policy even though the dynamics are uncertain (it controls its choice of actions, but not the dynamics and environment). To use a second example of a multi-agent scenario with two players and a zero-sum game, the first agent can adopt a *minimax* strategy to minimize its maximum loss (it controls its choice, but not the choice of the other agent).

More importantly, we should not say that an A.I. agent is exhibiting morally wrong behaviour if that judgment is based on factors that are outside of its control. This distinguishes Virtue Ethics from Act Utilitarianism, with the latter being susceptible to the problem of *moral luck*. Moral luck is a problem for consequentialist theories of ethics, because unforeseen circumstances can lead to disastrous consequences, which would cause us to determine that the action was wrong.[3] In contrast, Virtue Ethics says that the agent is behaving correctly if it is behaving in accordance with the cardinal virtues, regardless of external consequences.

3.3 Affective Computing

The Stoic notion of control is closely related to their perspective on emotions (or "passions"). Because the word *stoic* has entered the general vocabulary as meaning *lacking emotion*, Stoics have been wrongly thought of as being unemotional or disdaining emotion. In fact, their perspective on emotion is that we control our emotional responses to events even if we do not control the events themselves, and that it is pointless to fret about things outside of our control. A person obsessing about things outside their control is needlessly suffering.

Recall that affective capabilities for an intelligent system involve the ability to recognize, represent, and/or simulate emotions or affective states [15]. Let us call an agent with such capabilities an Affective Agent. Just as a Stoic person can monitor and control their emotional responses to events, so can an Affective Agent monitor and control how it represents and simulates emotional states. This has implications not just for the agent, but also for humans interacting with the agent. At one extreme, a person could be emotionally manipulated by an Affective Agent, while at the other extreme the Affective Agent could be a calming influence on a person.

We briefly note that even a system without explicit affective capabilities can be a calming influence. Christian and Griffiths [17] introduce the notion of *Computational Stoicism* to refer to the peace of mind that comes with using optimal algorithms in our everyday lives. If we are employing an optimal algorithm to solve some problem, then we can do no better using the tools that are under our control, regardless of what consequences may result.

We need to be careful about describing an A.I. as Stoic and what that means with regard to emotion, as it is very likely that many people fear the prospect of a generally intelligent A.I. that is devoid of emotion and operates in a cold, calculating manner. Just as it is a mistake to describe a Stoic person as emotionless, it would be wrong to describe a Stoic A.I. as being emotionless. A Stoic A.I. would be an A.I. that is in accord with Stoic virtues, and has carefully calibrated affective capabilities. Stoic A.I. is virtuous A.I.

[3] Rule Utilitarianism addresses the problem of moral luck, and Eric O. Scott points out (personal communication) that a consequentialist analysis of an agent can also address the problem by considering a large number of trials.

3.4 Stoic Virtues

We now turn to the four cardinal Stoic virtues of wisdom, justice, courage, and temperance, and how they relate to characteristics of A.I. agents.

Wisdom: It may seem obvious that an intelligent agent should have wisdom, but it is not necessarily the case that even an advanced A.I. would be wise, since intelligence and wisdom are not normally considered by humans to be synonymous. That an advanced A.I. could lack wisdom becomes evident when we examine the virtues that are categorized under wisdom: good sense, good calculation, quick-wittedness, discretion, and resourcefulness [1,18]. Computers are already beyond human-level in terms of excelling at calculation and being very fast. However, discretion and good sense are qualities that we do not necessarily associate with existing A.I. systems. Discretion for an intelligent agent could mean respecting privacy, and preserving anonymity in data. Good sense could incorporate commonsense reasoning, while resourcefulness could mean being innovative in finding new solutions to a problem.

The Stoics had three main areas of study: ethics, physics, and logic. They believed the three areas to be interdependent, because you cannot determine right or wrong (ethics) without understanding the world (physics) and thinking rationally (logic). A wise A.I. would need to be able to reason about real-world knowledge, including commonsense reasoning, while also being innovative and flexible – and A.I. systems based purely on logic are not always flexible. The Stoics also advocated the idea of being guided by the wisdom of an *Ideal Sage*, which we will discuss further below.

Justice: The virtues categorized under justice include piety, honesty, equity, and fair dealing [1,18]. An example of a just A.I. agent is one that does not mislead, even if the consequences of misleading could benefit the agent. The virtue of piety could be realized by an A.I. that is in a principal-agent relationship where it is designated to act on behalf of some principal, in which case it should be devoted to the principal and not to its own ends. Equity and fair dealing mean that an A.I. agent should not be biased in terms of race, gender, sexual orientation, or socioeconomic status, and should not use individuals as a means to its own ends.

Courage: Courage is often thought of as bravery, and we can easily imagine, for example, a military A.I. that is willing to be destroyed in order to save human lives. But when Stoic philosophers (and other Virtue Ethicists) talk about courage, they are speaking primarily about *moral courage*, which means taking some action for moral reasons, despite the consequences. So again we see a rejection of consequentialism, this time in the form of Stoic moral courage.

The virtues categorized under courage include endurance, confidence, high-mindedness, cheerfulness, and industriousness [1,18]. Confidence can mean that the A.I. agent is a good Bayesian that is able to update its prior beliefs as it gathers evidence. It does *not* mean that the A.I. agent has confidence at all times, even when unwarranted. In fact, being explicit about its uncertainty and recognizing that it could be wrong can be seen as a virtue of humility that is closely coupled with the virtue of confidence.

Temperance: The virtues included under temperance include good discipline, seemliness, modesty, and self-control [1,18]. Overall, temperance involves restraint on the part of the A.I. agent. Corrigibility, or the ability to be corrected and improved, could be seen as a type of modesty. Seemliness involves a sense of decorum and appropriateness. The lack of the virtue of seemliness has been demonstrated by a simple A.I. known as Tay, a Twitter chatbot launched by Microsoft that began tweeting racist and graphic content [19,20]. Self-control can be based on feedback and learning. Bostrom describes the idea of *domesticity*, where an A.I. agent has a limited scope of ambitions and activities. Bostrom also discusses the idea of instructing an A.I. agent to accomplish its goals while minimizing the impact that it has on the world [7]. Amodei et al. [4] similarly propose either defining or learning an *impact regularizer* for an agent. Temperance is an intriguing virtue for an A.I., as it seems to be at odds with the maximizing nature of many A.I. systems. We suggest that A.I. agents should rarely be engaged in pure maximization of some reward function, but instead be doing maximization subject to various constraints on their impact, or else have those constraints included in the reward function. We sketch out one such algorithm in Sect. 4. Alternatively, satisficing rather than maximizing models can be explored [21].

3.5 Moral Progress and the Ideal Sage

Stoics believe in moral progress toward some ideal virtuous state, while also recognizing that perfect virtue is not attainable. This emphasizes the need for a Stoic A.I. to be able to learn from experience, including from its own actions and mistakes, rather than being inflexible and having its behaviour predefined by strict rules. We previously mentioned the idea of an A.I. having some sense of regret when it has made a choice from a set of options that are all bad. At first, the idea of an A.I. agent with regret may seem to conflict with Stoic ideas about control, since the past is outside of our control and it is pointless to obsess about things that have already happened. While that is true, a Stoic A.I. can retain a memory of its choices and mistakes, including a sense of responsibility for things that have transpired, with an aim toward improving its behaviour in similar situations. This would be an indication of moral progress. Improving its behaviour in similar situations may entail creativity and coming up with options that are more acceptable and virtuous than the options previously known to the agent.[4]

To assist in making moral progress, Stoics use the notion of an Ideal Sage, and consider what the perfectly wise and virtuous sage would do in particular scenarios. While it is usually assumed that the Ideal Sage is hypothetical and

[4] It should be noted, however, that creativity is a double-edged sword for an A.I. agent, since it may come up with very unexpected and disastrous solutions to a problem, such as Bostrom's extreme example of a superintelligent agent getting rid of cancer in humans by killing all humans [7]. That is a clear example of the difference between creativity and moral progress.

that there is no perfectly virtuous person, ancient Stoics used Socrates and Cato the Younger as two figures to consider when looking for guidance [22]. There are many ways that the concept of an Ideal Sage could be used by an A.I. agent, and we will consider them in order of increasing complexity. A simple version of an Ideal Sage is an optimal algorithm: the A.I. agent should use an optimal algorithm wherever it is possible and efficient, and when it is infeasible to use the optimal algorithm, the A.I. agent can try to approximate the optimal algorithm, or consider how the optimal algorithm would operate on a simplified version of the problem at hand. The A.I. agent may be able to calculate a competitive ratio for the algorithm it uses, describing how close it is to the performance of the optimal algorithm. A second very simple example of an Ideal Sage is in the form of gold-standard feedback provided by a human, e.g. the principal in a principal-agent relationship.

That second notion leads us towards Christiano's proposal for "approval-directed agents," instead of goal-directed agents [9,23]. An approval-directed agent takes actions that it thinks its overseer would highly rate, and can avoid issues with goal-directed agents such as misspecified goals. Christiano also emphasizes that the agent's *internal* decisions can also be approval-directed. The following quote from Christiano [9] nicely parallels the idea that the Ideal Sage (in this case, a perfect overseer) represents an unattainable state but that we can start simply and scale up:

> "Asking an overseer to evaluate outcomes directly requires defining an extremely intelligent overseer, one who is equipped (at least in principle) to evaluate the entire future of the universe. This is probably impractical overkill for the kinds of agents we will be building in the near future, who don't have to think about the entire future of the universe. Approval-directed behaviour provides a more realistic alternative: start with simple approval-directed agents and simple overseers, and scale up the overseer and the agent in parallel."

For example, the approval-directed agent can begin learning from examples that have been labelled by the overseer as acceptable or not acceptable behaviour. In turn, the agent can assist and improve the overseer's capabilities. Christiano's proposal represents an implementable path forward for developing virtuous agents.

We conclude our discussion of the Ideal Sage with proposals by Bostrom and Yudkowsky for how a superintelligence could learn values. Bostrom [7] has proposed several variants of what he calls the *Hail Mary* problem, wherein the A.I. agent considers hypothetical alien superintelligences and tries to determine what those alien intelligences would likely value. Yudkowsky [10] (further discussed by Bostrom [7]) proposes that an A.I. agent can learn values by considering what he calls the coherent extrapolated volition (CEV) of humanity. The CEV essentially represents what humans would do if we were more intelligent and capable, and the A.I. agent determines its values by learning and analyzing the CEV. Both proposals have provoked much discussion but have a shared weakness, in that it is not at all clear how to implement them in the near future.

3.6 Stoic Practices

In addition to the Stoic virtues and Ideal Sage, we can discuss other Stoic practices that may have interesting parallels for an A.I. agent. The first practice is the *premeditatio malorum*, roughly translated as an anticipation of bad things to come [22]. For Stoic practitioners, this is often a morning meditation in which they anticipate potential misfortunes they may encounter, which could range from dealing with unkind people to losing a loved one. The idea is not to obsess over things that have not yet happened (which would be un-Stoic), but rather to rob these events of their ability to shock or control us. For an artificial agent, such planning could be used to consider worst-case scenarios, minimize maximum potential losses, and identify whether other agents are competitive or cooperative.

Another Stoic practice is to append the phrase "fate permitting" to all plans and aspirations, which represents a recognition that the person controls their own actions but not the consequences. For an A.I. agent, the parallel might be that the agent should always mind the uncertainty in its plans and its environments. The agent's internal states corresponding to plans and goals may not lead to the desired external states.

A final Stoic practice is the evening meditation, in which a person reviews the events of the day and engages in moral self-examination. For example, they may ask themselves whether they behaved virtuously and acted in accordance with the core ideas of Stoicism, or whether they could have done things differently. Again, the idea is not to obsess over things that have already happened and are therefore outside of our control, but rather to learn from experience and engage in moral progress. The parallels for an A.I. agent are clear, as any ethical agent will need to learn and improve. If the agent had been operating in a situation where it had to make choices with very limited information and time, it could later look for alternative, innovative choices that would have been more in accordance with the cardinal virtues or the preferences of an overseer. If the agent had been forced to employ a greedy algorithm while processing data in an online manner, it could later examine how performance might have improved in an optimal offline environment, and calculate the competitive ratio of the greedy algorithm it had been using. It could revisit the decisions that it had made and perform a self-audit examining the reasons behind the decision, and whether those reasons will be transparent and understandable to a human interrogator.

4 Criticisms and Responses

We can consider potential criticisms against Stoicism and the idea that it has any bearing on developing ethical A.I. A general criticism of Stoicism and other forms of Virtue Ethics is that they do not provide a strong normative ethics for real-world situations in which a person needs to make a decision given their available information [2]. Where Utilitarianism and Deontological ethics provide principles that are precise and (ostensibly) actionable, Stoicism gives a much vaguer principle: do what a virtuous person would do. A response to this accusation is to accept it and to point out that both Utilitarianism and Deontological Ethics are more unclear than they seem at first glance. For example, two Utilitarians can be in the same situation with the same available information and come to very different conclusions about the ethical course of action. Utilitarianism and Deontological Ethics over-promise in that they make ethical decision-making seem like a very simple application of a single rule (respectively, the principle of maximum utility and the Categorical Imperative), which can lead to overconfidence, or to a perverse application of the rule. For example, an A.I. agent that is trying to maximize a reward relating to human well-being could wind up directly stimulating the pleasure centres of the human brain in order to bring about a sense of well-being [7].

An A.I. that is trying to maximize some reward function can engage in *reward hacking*, also known as *wireheading* [4,7]. This is a situation where a very advanced A.I. is able to gain control of the reward signal, so that it can get a very large reward without having to take any external actions at all. Something similar could happen with a Stoic A.I. if an actor-critic architecture is used, e.g. the critic module could be disabled. Similarly, an approval-directed A.I. could become so intelligent that it is certain it knows the overseer better than the overseer does, and thus decide to be its own overseer, granting itself approval for any action. For this reason, we encourage research into overseer hacking, just as current research examines reward hacking. This relates to the idea of *adjustable autonomy* in multi-agent systems, and the opportunities and challenges associated with an agent being able to dynamically change its autonomy so that it defers to a person more often or less often [24].

Against the accusation that Stoicism is too vague for agents who need to make specific decisions and actions, we offer two responses:

- Approval-directed architectures offer a clear, implementable path forward, with the overseer acting as an Ideal Sage that seeds the A.I. with examples of approved and disapproved scenarios and actions.
- A syncretic ethics can be derived that combines elements of Stoicism with Utilitarian and Deontological ideas.

In the following subsection, we briefly describe a syncretic ethics approach for A.I. that includes Stoicism and Virtue Ethics.

4.1 Paramedic Ethics for Artificial Agents

Collins and Miller [25] provide a "paramedic ethics" for Computer Science professionals who may need to take action in a variety of scenarios where time and information are limited, and where the decision-makers may not have in-depth knowledge of ethical theories. They propose a syncretic algorithm that combines elements of Utilitarianism, Deontological Ethics, and Social Contract Theory. It is possible to come up with a similar algorithm that also incorporates Virtue Ethics. For example, a very simplified and general algorithm could be structured as follows:

- Gather data.
- Determine the available actions.
- For each action a:
  1. Does a satisfy the agent's obligations (to a human principal, other agents, the law, etc.)? (the Deontological step)
  2. Does a accord with the cardinal virtues (or would it be approved by the overseer)? (the Stoic step)
  3. What is the expected utility of a? (the Utilitarian step)
- Decide on an action by maximizing step 3 while satisfying the constraints in steps 1 and 2.

5 Conclusion

In this position paper, we have attempted to show how Stoic ethics could be applied to the development of ethical A.I. systems. We argued that internal states matter for ethical A.I. agents, and that internal states can be analyzed by describing the four cardinal Stoic virtues in terms of characteristics of an intelligent system. We also briefly described other Stoic practices and how they could be realized by an A.I. agent. We gave a brief sketch of how to start developing Stoic A.I. systems by creating approval-directed agents with Stoic overseers, and/or by employing a syncretic paramedic ethics algorithm with a step featuring Stoic constraints. While it can be beneficial to analyze the ethics of an A.I. agent from several different perspectives, including consequentialist perspectives, we have argued for the importance of also conducting a Stoic ethical analysis of A.I. agents, where the agent's internal states are analyzed, and moral judgments are not based on consequences outside of the agent's control.

Acknowledgements. Thanks to Eric O. Scott for helpful feedback and discussion.

References

1. Pigliucci, M.: Stoicism. http://www.iep.utm.edu/stoicism/. Accessed 2 Jan 2017
2. Hursthouse, R., Pettigrove, G.: Virtue ethics (2016). https://plato.stanford.edu/entries/ethics-virtue/. Accessed 2 Jan 2017
3. Sandel, M.: Justice: What's the Right Thing to Do? Macmillan, London (2010)
4. Amodei, D., Olah, C., Steinhardt, J., Christiano, P., Schulman, J., Mané, D.: Concrete problems in AI safety. arXiv preprint arXiv:1606.06565 (2016). http://arxiv.org/abs/1606.06565
5. Arkin, R.: Governing Lethal Behavior in Autonomous Robots. CRC Press, Boca Raton (2009)
6. Wallach, W., Allen, C.: Moral Machines: Teaching Robots Right from Wrong. Oxford University Press, Oxford (2008)
7. Bostrom, N.: Superintelligence: Paths, Dangers Strategies. Oxford University Press, Oxford (2014)
8. Dewey, D.: Learning what to value. In: Schmidhuber, J., Thórisson, K.R., Looks, M. (eds.) AGI 2011. LNCS (LNAI), vol. 6830, pp. 309–314. Springer, Heidelberg (2011). doi:10.1007/978-3-642-22887-2_35

9. Christiano, P.: Approval-directed agents (2014). https://medium.com/ai-control/model-free-decisions-6e6609f5d99e#.hpdm6kwee. Accessed 2 Jan 2017
10. Yudkowsky, E.: Coherent extrapolated volition (2004). https://intelligence.org/files/CEV.pdf
11. Coleman, K.: Android arete: toward a virtue ethic for computational agents. Ethics Inf. Technol. **3**(4), 247–265 (2001)
12. Hicks, D.: Virtue ethics for robots (2014). http://jefais.tumblr.com/post/89164919838/virtue-ethics-for-robots. Accessed 2 Jan 2017
13. Wikipedia: Three laws of robotics (2016). https://en.wikipedia.org/wiki/Three_Laws_of_Robotics. Accessed 5 Dec 2016
14. Soares, N., Fallenstein, B., Armstrong, S., Yudkowsky, E.: Corrigibility. In: AAAI 2015 Workshop on AI & Ethics (2015)
15. Calvo, R., D'Mello, S., Gratch, J., Kappas, A.: The Oxford Handbook of Affective Computing. Oxford University Press, Oxford (2014)
16. Irvine, W.: A Guide to the Good Life: The Ancient Art of Stoic Joy. Oxford University Press, Oxford (2008)
17. Christian, B., Griffiths, T.: Algorithms to Live by: The Computer Science of Human Decisions. Macmillan, London (2016)
18. Stephens, W.: Stoic ethics. http://www.iep.utm.edu/stoiceth/. Accessed 2 Jan 2017
19. Bright, P.: Tay, the neo-Nazi millennial chatbot, gets autopsied (2016). http://arstechnica.com/information-technology/2016/03/tay-the-neo-nazi-millennial-chatbot-gets-autopsied/. Accessed 9 Jan 2017
20. Sinders, C.: Microsoft's tay is an example of bad design (2016). https://medium.com/@carolinesinders/microsoft-s-tay-is-an-example-of-bad-design-d4e65bb2569f#.x27uitx3u. Accessed 9 Jan 2017
21. Simon, H.: Rational choice and the structure of the environment. Psychol. Rev. **63**(2), 129 (1956)
22. Robertson, D.: Stoicism and the Art of Happiness. Teach Yourself, London (2013)
23. Christiano, P.: Concrete approval-directed agents (2015). https://medium.com/ai-control/concrete-approval-directed-agents-89e247df7f1b#.u2e59x2os. Accessed 2 Jan 2017
24. Wooldridge, M.: An Introduction to Multiagent Systems, 2nd edn. Wiley, Hoboken (2009)
25. Collins, W., Miller, K.: Paramedic ethics for computer professionals. J. Syst. Softw. **17**(1), 23–38 (1992)

Active Team Management Strategies for Multi-robot Teams in Dangerous Environments

Geoff Nagy and John Anderson(✉)

Autonomous Agents Lab, University of Manitoba, Winnipeg, MB R3T 2N2, Canada
{geoffn,andersj}@cs.umanitoba.ca

Abstract. Cost-effectiveness, management of risk, and simplicity of design are all arguments in favour of using heterogeneous multi-robot teams in dangerous domains. Robot losses are expected to occur and the loss of useful skills means that replacement robots—either released into the environment or previously lost and rediscovered—must be recruited for useful work. While teams of robots may eventually encounter replacements by chance, more active search strategies can be used to locate them more quickly, either to complete a single task or join a team. These searches, however, must be balanced with existing tasks so that the team can still perform useful work in the domain. This paper describes additions that we have made to an existing framework for managing dynamic teams in dangerous domains in order to support this goal.

1 Introduction

There are many advantages to using autonomous teams of heterogeneous robots. With skills spread out among multiple team members, no single unit needs to possess every capability a mission requires. This reduces the overall cost and complexity of the robots [1]. This is beneficial in dangerous environments such as Urban Search and Rescue (USAR) or minefield clearing. In such settings, risk can be mitigated by deploying fewer elaborate units and more expendable ones.

In any situation where robot damage or loss can occur, team performance will degrade as robots are lost or destroyed. If possible, losses can be compensated for by releasing replacement robots into the environment at periodic intervals during a mission. Existing robot teams should be prepared to accept new members, which may either be replacement robots or rediscovered robots that were previously separated from a team. Robot teams should also recognize when it is necessary to strengthen their team by searching for and integrating other robots as required. Successfully integrated robots should also share information with the new team [14]. Conversely, robot teams may choose not to integrate additional members due to the costs associated with managing a larger team.

Robots should expend effort searching for other robots possessing skills that are valuable to the team or the current tasks at hand. This becomes increasingly necessary as robot teams suffer increased losses, particularly for rare or high-value skills. Aggressive search strategies (such as exploration of a previously unexplored area, or searching a location suspected to contain a useful robot)

M. Mouhoub and P. Langlais (Eds.): Canadian AI 2017, LNAI 10233, pp. 385–396, 2017.
DOI: 10.1007/978-3-319-57351-9_43

are more likely to result in the successful integration of a valuable skill, but at the cost of performing less immediately useful work. Strategies that only rely on random encounters with other robots will allow more work to be completed [7], but are less likely to result in the acquisition of needed skills. These types of recruitment strategies fall on a spectrum that defines how much effort is expended into actively searching for useful robots (Fig. 1). The middle point of this spectrum would contain strategies such as broadcasting wireless requests to nearby robots without actually attempting to locate them physically.

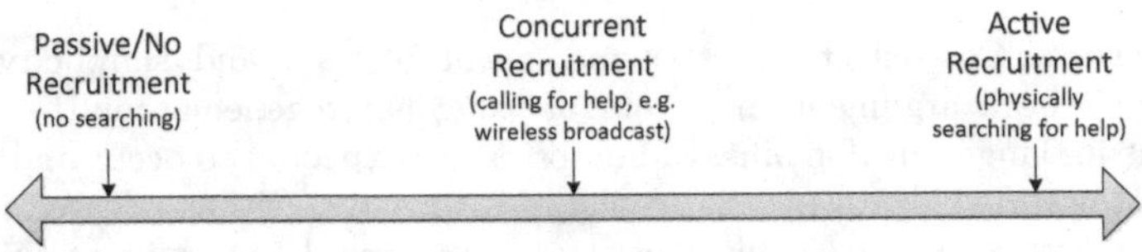

Fig. 1. The recruitment spectrum.

Previous work has resulted in a framework for robotic team management in dangerous domains [7]. We have expanded this framework to include recruitment strategies from across this spectrum. We evaluate our framework in a simulated USAR setting in which robots can be damaged or destroyed. The following sections describe our framework, experimental evaluation, and our results. We begin with a description of related work for comparison.

2 Previous Work

Existing work does not employ many strategies from the recruitment spectrum. It is difficult to form useful comparisons with previous work since many approaches assume an unlimited communications range, or that robots are always close enough to communicate [3,4,10]. Additionally, previous work does not take into account real-world challenges such as communication failures, robot failures, or robot losses in general [5,6,8,12,15]. This section describes previous work that uses active searching or random encounters with other robots to acquire additional team members during the course of a mission.

Krieger and Billeter [9] developed an approach for food-foraging tasks, modelling the behaviour of ants using a large number of homogeneous robots. Although explicit teams were not formed, robots were able to recruit others to known food locations in order to increase the amount of food returned to a central nest. Pitonakova et al. [13] studied active recruitment in more complex foraging missions where resources varied in size and value. This is similar to our work in that certain tasks or robot skills may be more important than others, and the choice of recruitment strategy depends greatly on environmental conditions and the availability of resources. In contrast, we study recruitment in a less abstract domain (USAR) and our work is focused explicitly on long-term team maintenance as well as short-term team goals.

Gunn and Anderson [7] implemented a team-management framework for heterogeneous robot teams in dangerous domains, and considered real-world challenges such as varying communication success rates, and robot failures and losses. This framework was evaluated in a USAR setting, where robots were organized into teams at the onset of each mission and explored the environment to identify as many human casualties as possible within the allotted time. Losses were offset by strategies that allowed teams to acquire new members when they were encountered in the environment by chance, i.e., robots did not explicitly put effort into locating other useful robots. We have made substantial additions to this framework, and have developed recruitment strategies enabling robots to (*a*) search for and assign tasks to others on an individual basis without the intervention of a team leader, and (*b*) recruit additional team members more permanently when a crucial skill set is missing from the current team. Preliminary results were published in [11]. This paper describes the additions we have made to the original framework (points (*a*) and (*b*) above, as well as extended heterogeneity through a new robot type and behaviours), and presents original results from two large experiments used to evaluate the completed framework.

3 Methodology

3.1 Framework

To adequately describe our additions, a high-level overview of major framework components is required. Readers interested in a thorough description of the complete framework are directed to [7].

Robots. The underlying assumption in our work is that robots are heterogeneous—they differ in how they move, sense the environment, and have varying storage and computational capabilities. Therefore, no single robot is able to perform every task, and certain robots will be able to complete certain tasks better than others, or may not be able to perform some tasks at all. In our framework, robots are aware of their own individual skills and how well-suited those skills make them for a particular task. The distributed nature of our framework means that robots rely on local decision-making processes based on their knowledge of the environment and their teammates. Communication problems, robot failures, or other challenges mean that this knowledge may not always be up-to-date.

Tasks, Roles, and Teams. A *task* in our framework is a single piece of work which can be assigned to and completed by a robot. Although a particular challenge or outstanding job discovered by a robot may ultimately involve more than one robot, such jobs must be broken up into discrete tasks and individually assigned to team members. However, assigned tasks may involve overlapping goals or objectives without explicitly requiring the involvement of more than one robot, e.g., two robots exploring overlapping areas. In the original version of this framework [7], task distribution was solely the responsibility of team leaders. Our improved framework allows any robot to perform task assignment in special circumstances, described in Sect. 3.3. For example, robot A may pass a particular task to another robot B, if A is already too busy or is incapable of performing the task. Every robot maintains an ordered queue of tasks, ensuring that the most important work is completed first.

In our framework, every robot fills a *role* within a *team*. A role is defined by a set of tasks that a robot in that role would be expected to perform, and is used as a simple heuristic for task allocation to quickly find team members capable of performing a particular task. A robot with the appropriate skill set can also perform a task outside of its current role if necessary (e.g., a firefighting robot could still perform exploratory searches for victims). Robots in our framework possess self-knowledge and are capable of determining their *suitability* for a particular role, represented as an integer that indicates how well their skill set matches the tasks that make up the role.

Roles are fluid, rather than permanent: to compensate for robot losses or acquisitions, robots periodically evaluate their role within their team and change to a role that would be more beneficial if required. As robots attempt to address skill deficiencies by adopting new (possibly non-optimal) roles, there is a risk that some robots will fill roles for which they are ill-equipped, taking them away from tasks for which they are better suited. For example, a single robot separated from its team will realize it is alone and adopt a leadership role (i.e. become a team of one), even if it has limited capabilities for such a role. If a more suitable robot is encountered (either by itself or as part of a larger team), it will cede the leadership role to the other robot as they merge teams.

Team Leader and Task Assignment. The *team leader* is a special role that exists for coordinating team actions. The leader also acts as a repository of team knowledge since other team members are expected to communicate significant locations, results of tasks, and other important knowledge to the leader. The team leader is thus expected to have the most complete global knowledge, including knowledge of team structure. It is important to note that this knowledge is unlikely to ever be complete—the leader will not know precisely when a robot is lost, for example, and communication that would indicate this may be long delayed [7]. Therefore, relying on local decision making is important despite the presence of a leader. Due to the memory and processing required, it is expected that leadership should fall to the most computationally-capable robot on the team. Ideally, such a robot would have ample facilities to handle these responsibilities, but as team structure degrades due to hazards, less-capable robots may temporarily fill this role until a better robot is found.

Role Switch Check. Robots are responsible for evaluating the usefulness of their current role and changing to a more valuable role for the team, if necessary.

This is done based on the robot's (potentially inaccurate) knowledge of the current team structure. Robots with empty task queues perform this check every 30 s and switch to a different role if necessary. The intuition behind this process is that robots with no outstanding work might be better suited for a different role. The sections that follow describe the expansions we have made to the original framework in terms of role management and task assignment.

3.2 Role-Level Recruitment

Our extensions provide robots with the ability to perform searches for other robots to join their team. These may be previously lost robots, replacement robots, or even members of another existing team. We refer to this mechanism as *role-level recruitment*. This recruitment process begins with a leader periodically assessing the current structure of the team (using possibly incomplete knowledge), and taking note of the most important role that is not currently filled. This occurs every 6 min in our implementation. The team leader will then attempt to assign a particular robot on the team with the task of acquiring a robot to fill that role. In cases where a team leader is the only robot on a team (and thus might have many missing roles), the team leader will assign itself with the task of finding another robot to fill the most important missing role. Section 3.4 describes the strategies used to find and recruit other robots.

3.3 Task-Level Recruitment

While role-level recruitment provides additional means for acquiring new team members, our framework also supports the acquisition of robot skills in a less-permanent fashion. We refer to this as *task-level recruitment*, and it allows one robot to search for another to complete a task. This is useful when the original robot is already too busy to perform additional work, or if it encounters a task for which it is poorly-equipped.

Task-level recruitment can be initiated in two ways. In our original framework, if a team leader attempts to assign a particular task to a robot, the task will be rejected if the assignee is already too busy with other work. The team leader will have no choice but to continually attempt to reassign the task elsewhere until it is accepted. In our modified framework, rather than rejecting tasks when too busy, robots will offer to locate another capable robot to complete the task. The team leader will agree to this only if no other robot is able to accept the task for execution. When this occurs, it is the responsibility of the assigned robot to recruit another robot who will accept the task for execution. Task-level recruitment can also be initiated when a robot discovers a task on its own that it is unable to complete. In the original framework, a robot which discovers a task beyond its capabilities would attempt to relay the task to a team leader for reallocation. In our improved framework, if a robot discovers a task for which it is poorly-equipped, it will instead attempt to locate another robot who can execute the task. Importantly, this process does not require the intervention of a team leader, and thus, is robust to leadership failures or limitations in communication.

3.4 Recruitment Strategies

A recruitment strategy defines how robots search for others when additional roles should be filled or tasks need to be completed. Active recruitment approaches will involve physical searches. While such approaches are more likely to result in successful recruitment, this is done at the cost of completing less immediately useful work. Less committed strategies may involve no searching at all (as employed in [7]), or may only require minimal searching efforts such as broadcasting a wireless request for assistance. The next two subsections describe the two recruitment mechanisms we have added to the original framework.

Concurrent Recruitment. This strategy relies only on wireless communication to search for other robots. Concurrent recruitment can be used to acquire additional team members (*role-level* recruitment), or to assign tasks to other robots (*task-level* recruitment) when required. This is done concurrently alongside normal work; recruiting robots are able to execute tasks while also sending recruitment broadcasts. The content of these broadcasts and any subsequent communication varies depending on whether a robot is recruiting for a task or a role. A robot will agree to a role-level request only if (a) its task queue is not full, and (b) if the robot has lost contact with its team or is better suited to the new role. The process for accepting task-level recruitment requests is the same that is used for regular task assignments: if a robot is not too busy, it will accept the task, and will offer to recruit someone else for the task otherwise.

Active Recruitment. *Active recruitment* is a more aggressive strategy that relies on a combination of physical search and wireless broadcasting to locate a new teammate. While actively recruiting, a robot is fully committed to exploring the environment in search of other robots, and executes no other tasks. This increases the chances of encountering useful robots, but prevents immediately useful work from being completed. Physical searching also increases a robot's risk of becoming separated from its team, either by exploring too far or by becoming stuck on debris while exploring.

4 Experimental Evaluation

Our framework was evaluated using USAR environments implemented in Stage [16], a well-known and established multi-robot simulator. It provides facilities that allowed us to abstract issues associated with physical sensors and hardware, since our focus was to evaluate our framework's performance with regards to team management. To reduce bias that may exist in any single environment configuration, we used 3 randomly-generated USAR scenarios. Each environment simulated a large area ($60\,\mathrm{m}^2$) of a collapsed building. Environments contained significant debris, partial rooms, and missing walls, as shown in Fig. 2. The presence of debris (dark gray and light gray squares) contributed to a considerable risk of robots becoming stuck, and helped to simulate real USAR conditions. Our environments also contained 20 human casualties that robots were responsible for locating, as well as 10 *false victims* (gray humans in Fig. 2), which appear to be casualties to simpler robots but require the attention of more advanced robots in order to confirm.

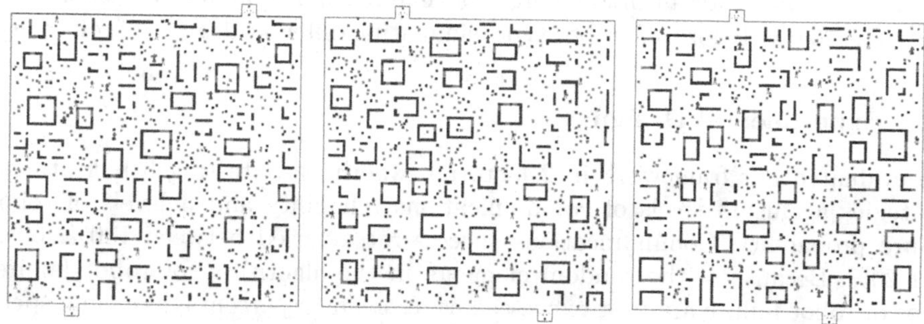

Fig. 2. Overhead views of our 3 randomly-generated USAR environments. Team starting positions are visible at the bottom and top entrances.

We abstracted robot heterogeneity to four types of robots, similar to [2, 7]. The most basic and inexpensive robot was a MinBot, a small robot with very simple victim-sensing capabilities. Its simplicity, low cost, and expendability make it ideal for potential victim discovery and exploration of unknown areas. MinBots are unsuitable as team leaders due to their limited computational and memory facilities, and require more advanced robots to confirm the presence of a human victim. The next robot is a MidBot, which is larger than the MinBot and has more advanced victim-sensing capabilities, enabling it to correctly identify the presence of human casualties at short distances. Increased computational power and memory make MidBots (marginally) suitable as team leaders if no better-equipped robots are available. A MaxBot is the third robot type. Its primary purpose is to function as a team leader due to its large memory capacity and powerful computational capabilities. MaxBots have basic victim sensors only and must rely on MidBots to correctly identify casualties. MaxBots are equipped with a tracked drive enabling them to drive over shorter debris items (light gray boxes in Fig. 2). The fourth robot was a highly-specialized, tracked-drive robot called a DebrisBot whose goal was to find and remove shorter debris items in the environment. Debris removal could be done in an unguided manner (randomly looking for and clearing debris if no other tasks are available), or by request from another robot that has become stuck in the environment. Debris removal results in a piece of debris being completely removed from the environment—this can only be done at ranges less than 1 m, and takes 5 s.

To test our framework against the challenging aspects of robotic USAR, our simulator is configured to allow varying levels of communications reliability, directly affecting the percentage of messages that are delivered successfully. This simulates interference in the environment. Wireless communication was simulated using Stage's indoor ITU radio model, with a 20 m range. Robot failure is also simulated by continually choosing a random value in the range [0,1] and comparing it to set thresholds for temporary or permanent failure in each simulation cycle. Exceeding the permanent failure threshold causes the robot to fail for the remainder of the trial, and exceeding the temporary failure threshold causes a failure for a random length of time (3–4 min). Failure thresholds are specified separately for each robot type, simulating different degrees of reliability.

4.1 Experimental Design

We evaluated our framework in 2 factorial experiments, testing 3 recruitment strategies against 3 levels of communications reliability and 3 levels of robot failure probability. Communications success rates varied between 100%, 60%, and 20%. Because of the random elements in the algorithm for robot failure, rates of robot failure are best expressed as an average percentage of time spent failed for MinBots, MidBots, MaxBots, and DebrisBots, respectively. The values used in this experiment are categorized as none, minimal (15%, 12%, 9%, 15%) and major (25%, 21%, 19%, 25%). Each experimental configuration lasted 30 simulated minutes and was run 50 times. Every trial was repeated in 3 unique environments to help reduce bias.

In our first (*main*) experiment we were interested in evaluating our framework using 2 teams of robots each consisting of 1 MaxBot, 2 MidBots, 4 MinBots, and 1 DebrisBot. Robot teams were initially inserted at the 2 entrances visible in Fig. 2. For this experiment, we varied whether or not replacement robots would be available. In trials where replacements existed, 10 MinBots, 2 MidBots, 1 MaxBot, and 1 DebrisBot would be introduced into the environment, spread evenly along the inner perimeter, after 5 simulated minutes. Each of these units functioned individually as a 1-robot team until forming a new team or joining an existing one. The factorial design for our main experiment yielded 8100 trials.

Our second (*minimal team*) experiment was designed to test the performance of our framework when resources were scarce and replacements were not available. In this experiment, 2 robot teams each consisting of 1 MinBot, 1 MidBot, 1 MaxBot, and 1 DebrisBot were placed in the entrances shown in Fig. 2. The factorial design for our minimal team experiment yielded 4050 trials.

5 Results and Discussion

We evaluated our framework using 2 criteria: the total percentage of true and false victims successfully identified and communicated to a team leader, and the total percentage of the environment covered and communicated to a team leader. We focused only on knowledge conveyed to team leaders, since they are likely to possess the most complete (but still imperfect) set of information. They also represent the best source of knowledge for human extraction teams in real-life scenarios. This makes our results more conservative—other robots may contain additional information that has not been relayed to a leader.

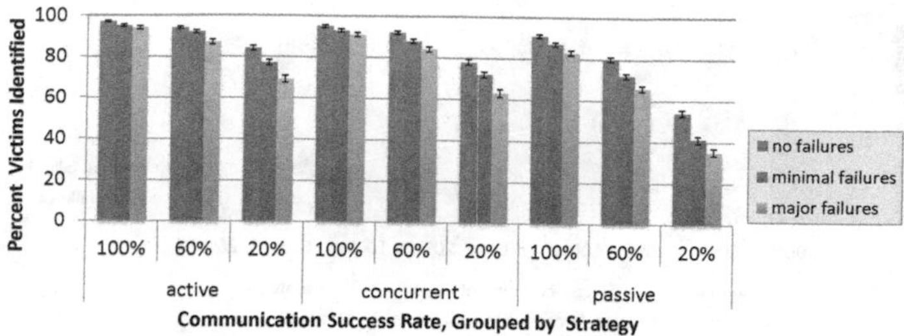

Fig. 3. Main experiment victims identified, with replacement robots available.

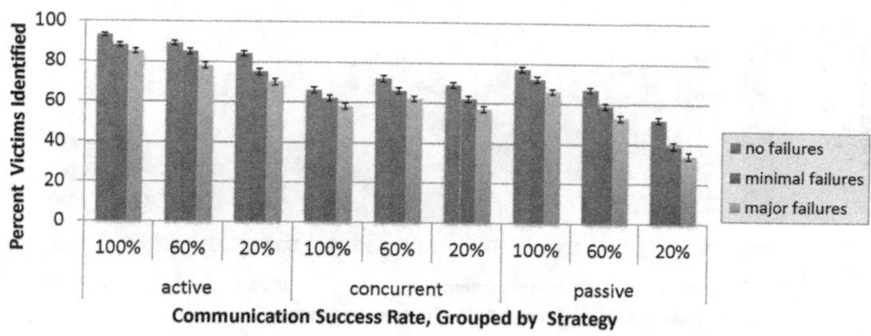

Fig. 4. Main experiment victims identified, with no replacement robots available.

5.1 Main Experiment Results

Victims Identified to Leaders. Figures 3 and 4 show the percentage of victims identified and communicated to a team leader, with and without replacements respectively. In all graphs that follow, error bars show 95% confidence intervals.

A major weakness of [7] was that robot teams could not function effectively when communication success rates were as low as 20%. As communications failed, fewer tasks could be successfully assigned and fewer results could be relayed to leaders. This is reflected in our results: passive recruitment is shown to perform poorly in these conditions. Active and concurrent recruitment strategies, however, provide a significant improvement in terms of victims identified, regardless of the presence of replacement robots, when robot operating conditions or communication reliability are poor.

Interestingly, in ideal conditions where no replacements are available, passive recruitment performs better than concurrent recruitment. This is likely due to a slight duplication of effort that occurs as non-leader robots assign victim-identification tasks that would normally be coordinated by a team leader. Without a team leader's broader perspective on remaining or outstanding work, multiple robots may unnecessarily be tasked with completing the same job. This redundancy can be harmful to team performance in ideal conditions, but is beneficial whenever conditions are not ideal.

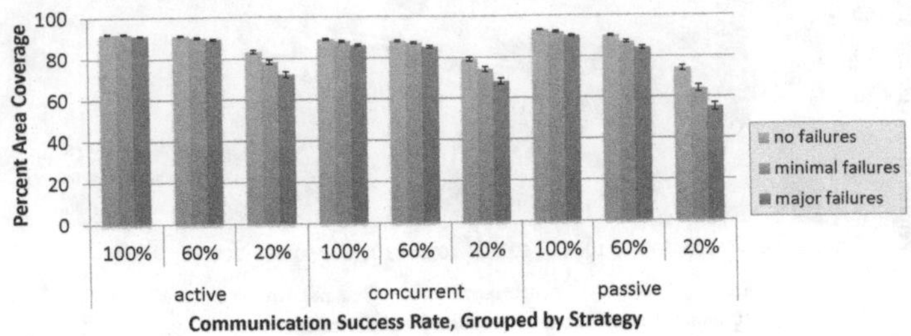

Fig. 5. Main experiment area coverage, with replacement robots available.

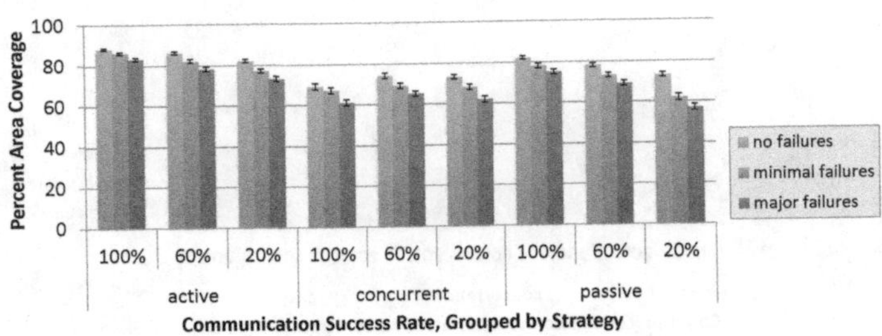

Fig. 6. Main experiment area coverage, with no replacement robots available.

Area Coverage. As shown in Fig. 5, there is not much difference in area coverage between recruitment strategies when replacements are available. It is possible that the area coverage amounts shown here reflect the maximum area that can be covered and conveyed to a team leader in the time allotted (30 min), or that some areas are extremely difficult to reach. As communication success rates fall, and as robot failures increase, active and concurrent recruitment show greater improvements over passive recruitment.

Figure 6 shows that active recruitment is more effective than passive recruitment when no replacements are available. This strategy results in the greatest environment coverage, likely due to the physical searches that take place and the improved likelihood of recruiting robots with useful information about the environment. As with victim identification (Sect. 5.1), concurrent recruitment performed more poorly than passive except where communications were unreliable. As noted previously, this is likely because of a duplication of effort that occurs when tasks are assigned without the coordination of a leader.

5.2 Minimal Team Experiment Results

In this experiment, active recruitment resulted in the greatest number of victims identified, in almost all experimental configurations. This is likely due to the increased exploration that takes place when actively recruiting—exploration provides more opportunities to discover victims and cover the environment. Active recruitment also resulted in the highest levels of area coverage (Fig. 8).

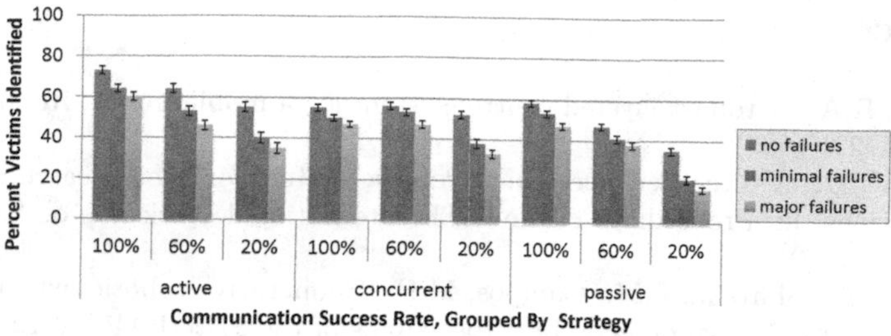

Fig. 7. Minimal team experiment victims identified.

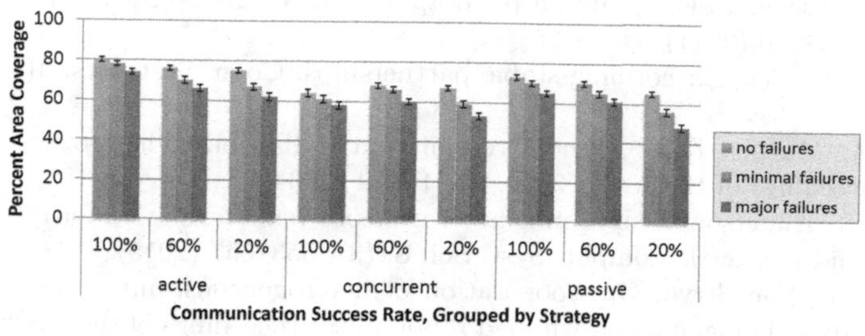

Fig. 8. Minimal team experiment area coverage.

Because of the smaller robot population, robot failures had a greater impact on these results than in our main experiment. However, it is interesting to note that area coverage in this experiment is only slightly less than that of our main experiment where replacements were not available. This suggests that only a small number of robots is necessary to cover most of the environment in 30 min. It is also possible that our experimental environments contain hard-to-reach areas that make it difficult to attain 100% environmental coverage, and that additional robots only improve coverage by a small amount.

6 Future Work and Conclusion

Since increased knowledge transfer between robots has clear benefits, directions for future work include having robots explicitly tasked with spreading information to others. The importance of the information could be used to determine the ideal recruitment strategy for conveying it: more critical information would require a more active approach.

In this paper, we described and evaluated recruitment strategies allowing robot teams in dangerous domains to acquire additional skills temporarily or permanently. Our recruitment strategies provide the greatest benefits when operating conditions are not ideal. Since this is often expected to be the case for many future robotics applications, we believe our framework and results provide substantial insight into how distributed robot teams should be designed to operate in these environments.

References

1. Brooks, R.A.: A robust layered control system for a mobile robot. Robot. Autom. **2**(1), 14–23 (1986)
2. Carnegie, D.: A three-tier hierarchical robotic system for urban search and rescue applications. In: Proceedings of the IEEE International Workshop on SSRR 2007, pp. 1–6 (2007)
3. Costa, E.D., Shiroma, P.M., Campos, M.F.: Cooperative robotic exploration and transport of unknown objects. In: Proceedings of the SBR/LARS 2012, pp. 56–61 (2012)
4. Dos Santos, F., Bazzan, A.L.: Towards efficient multiagent task allocation in the robocup rescue: a biologically-inspired approach. Auton. Agent. Multi-agent Syst. **22**(3), 465–486 (2011)
5. Dutta, P.S., Sen, S.: Forming stable partnerships. Cogn. Syst. Res. **4**(3), 211–221 (2003)
6. Gage, A., Murphy, R.R.: Affective recruitment of distributed heterogeneous agents. In: Proceedings of the AAAI 2004, pp. 14–19 (2004)
7. Gunn, T., Anderson, J.: Dynamic heterogeneous team formation for robotic urban search and rescue. J. Comput. Syst. Sci. **81**(3), 553–567 (2015)
8. Kiener, J., Von Stryk, O.: Cooperation of heterogeneous, autonomous robots: a case study of humanoid and wheeled robots. In: Proceedings of the IROS 2007, pp. 959–964 (2007)
9. Krieger, M.J., Billeter, J.B.: The call of duty: self-organised task allocation in a population of up to twelve mobile robots. Robot. Auton. Syst. **30**(1), 65–84 (2000)
10. Mathews, N., Christensen, A.L., O'Grady, R., Rétornaz, P., Bonani, M., Mondada, F., Dorigo, M.: Enhanced directional self-assembly based on active recruitment and guidance. In: Proceedings of the IROS 2011, pp. 4762–4769 (2011)
11. Nagy, G., Anderson, J.: Active recruitment mechanisms for heterogeneous robot teams in dangerous environments. In: Khoury, R., Drummond, C. (eds.) AI 2016. LNCS (LNAI), vol. 9673, pp. 276–281. Springer, Cham (2016). doi:10.1007/978-3-319-34111-8_34
12. Pinciroli, C., O'Grady, R., Christensen, A.L., Dorigo, M.: Self-organised recruitment in a heteregeneous swarm. In: Proceedings of the ICAR 2009, pp. 1–8 (2009)
13. Pitonakova, L., Crowder, R., Bullock, S.: Understanding the role of recruitment in collective robot foraging. In: Proceedings of the ALIFE 2014 (2014)
14. Roth, M., Vail, D., Veloso, M.: A real-time world model for multi-robot teams with high-latency communication. In: Proceedings of the IROS 2003, pp. 2494–2499 (2003)
15. Van De Vijsel, M., Anderson, J.: Coalition formation in multi-agent systems under real-world conditions. In: Proceedings of the AAAI 2004 Workshop on Forming and Maintaining Coalitions and Teams in Adaptive Multiagent Systems (2004)
16. Vaughan, R.: Massively multi-robot simulations in stage. Swarm Intell. **2**(2–4), 189–208 (2008)

Graduate Student Symposium

Diverse Action Costs in Heuristic Search and Planning

Gaojian Fan(✉)

University of Alberta, Edmonton, Canada
gaojian@ualberta.ca

Automated planning is a fundamental area in artificial intelligence, which concerns finding a sequence of actions that leads from an initial state to a goal state in a large state space. Such an action sequence is called a plan for the planning problem and its cost is the sum of costs of actions in the plan. Cost-optimal planning is to find an optimal plan which has the minimal cost among all paths between the initial state and the goal states. For planning problems with unit action cost, where every action has a cost of 1, optimizing the plan cost is equivalent to optimizing the plan length (number of actions). While the unit costs are common in benchmark problems used for planning research, actions in real-world planning problems often have different costs. For example, in logistics domains, loading and unloading a package are much cheaper than moving a vehicle, and the cost of moving a vehicle varies widely with the distance between locations. Another example is manufacturing applications in which different types of operations such as cutting, painting or moving often have very diverse costs.

Despite its importance, non-unit action costs have not been included in the International Planning Competition (IPC) benchmarks until the 6th IPC in 2008. Before that planning algorithms were mostly evaluated on unit-cost problems with a focus on addressing other difficulties of planning. Along a line of research on planning with diverse action costs since then, my thesis research focuses on understanding the effects of action costs on planning and improving techniques to handle action cost diversity better. In particular, I am interested how action costs affect *heuristic search*—an effective technique for solving planning problems, and how to improve the performance of heuristic search when actions have a variety of costs.

Heuristic search algorithms use heuristics, i.e., estimations of the cost-to-go of states, to guide the search and to find a plan more efficiently. The diversity of action costs has impacts on both the search algorithms and the methods for deriving heuristics. I am addressing my thesis research problem from these two angles. In Sect. 1, I summarize the work showing diverse action costs can have both negative and positive effects on search, which will appear in the 27th International Conference on Automated Planning and Scheduling (ICAPS-2017) [6]. In Sect. 2, I describe the on-going work on improving one heuristic generation method to produce better heuristics when actions have non-unit costs.

M. Mouhoub and P. Langlais (Eds.): Canadian AI 2017, LNAI 10233, pp. 399–402, 2017.
DOI: 10.1007/978-3-319-57351-9_44

1 The Two-Edged Nature of Diverse Action Costs

In recent years, planning with diverse action costs has been studied in both the optimal and satisficing (i.e., sub-optimal plans are acceptable) settings. One notable trend of those studies is a focus on the *negative* impact of diverse costs on planning. Several studies demonstrate cases where planning with diverse action costs is more difficult, in terms of the number of nodes expanded, than planning in the same domain with unit costs [1,3,20,21]. Other studies showed that some search algorithms perform better on domains with non-unit costs when they use information (e.g., heuristics) based on unit costs instead of relying entirely on information based on the given costs [14,16–19].

One clear disadvantage of diverse costs is a kind of "horizon effect". If a search space has huge regions reachable by low-cost actions, but the solution requires a high-cost action a, the low-cost regions will be exhaustively searched before the state s reached by a is expanded. In the unit cost model, state s would be expanded much earlier, allowing the solution to be found much more quickly.

Thus there is considerable evidence that *action cost diversity is harmful for search*. However, this is not generally the case. We investigate the effects of changing action costs on the number of nodes expanded by search theoretically and experimentally. Our experiments give a variety of examples, including problems from the IPC domains, where diversity of action costs is beneficial, i.e. the number of nodes expanded when the action costs are diverse is substantially lower than the number expanded using unit costs.

To explain these observations, we study the effects of action costs on the basic search algorithm, Dijkstra's shortest path algorithm, which is equivalent to A* with no heuristics. Our main theoretical result is a "No Free Lunch" (NFL) theorem about the impact, on the number of nodes expanded by Dijkstra's algorithm, of changing from any cost function $\mathcal{C}$ to any other function $\mathcal{C}'$. We prove that for any given state space S, the problem instances in S on which fewer nodes are expanded using $\mathcal{C}$ are exactly counterbalanced by the problem instances on which fewer nodes are expanded using $\mathcal{C}'$. This implies, for example, that if the initial state and the goal state are selected randomly, the expected number of nodes expanded is the same no matter what cost function is used.

Cushing, Benton and Kambhampati [3] give a theoretical analysis of Dijkstra's algorithm and provide examples where search based on non-unit cost expands exponentially many more nodes than search based on unit cost. They designed state spaces called "ε-cost traps" to illustrate such effects. Since our NFL theorem applies to all state spaces, we experimentally demonstrate that, for a particular type of ε-cost traps, the cycle trap, the total number of nodes expanded over all possible goal states is in fact *almost* identical whether one uses unit costs or the alternative cost function defined by Cushing et al.

The reason the totals in the cycle trap experiment are not exactly equal is that the NFL theorem does not take into account states that are the same distance from the start state as the goal. We call such states TIE states. Our second theoretical contribution is to analyze the impact of TIE states. We show that unit costs will often have an advantage over non-unit costs because of TIE states (as is the case for cycle traps) but we also design a new logistics based planning domain in which TIE states work to the advantage of non-unit costs.

2 Impacts of Diverse Action Costs on Heuristics

The quality of heuristics is critical to the performance of heuristic search on planning problems. Domain-independent heuristic generations have been the subject of a large body of research in planning, e.g., [2,4,7–9,11,13,15]. Although most heuristic generation methods allow non-unit action costs in their heuristic computations, the quality of the heuristics they produce varies a lot for different cost functions. For example, our experiments show that merge-and-shrink [9,10] generates heuristics of much higher quality with the unit costs than with non-unit action costs for some IPC domains.

We are currently working on improving merge-and-shrink (M&S) to handle diverse action costs better. An abstraction is a simplified state space in which distances between states and the goal state can be computed efficiently and thus to be used as heuristics for search in the original state space of a planning problem. M&S builds flexible abstractions through iterations of explicit operations. M&S abstractions can produce accurate heuristics that provide the perfect guidance for search (i.e., the search finds an optimal plan with the minimal number of node expansions) in some cases [5,12]. Our experiments show that, if the unit costs are used, M&S heuristic can provide perfect search guidance to all problems in WOODWORKING—one of the non-unit cost IPC domains. However, if the original IPC non-unit costs are used, search with M&S heuristics can solve only less than half of the problems in these domains.

One way to handle diverse costs is to partition the costs in the original non-unit cost function into a group of cost functions in which each resembles the unit costs in a certain way. Our current cost partitioning method ensures each cost function after the partitioning to have at most two distinct action costs. The experiments show that M&S using this cost partitioning produces much better heuristics and reduces search efforts greatly on WOODWORKING problems, comparing to the M&S that uses the original cost function directly.

While this cost partitioning shows some promising results, it does not improve the coverage (number of planning problems solved with certain time and memory limits) for WOODWORKING significantly. Moreover, the method does not show a general improvement for all IPC domains with diverse costs. Addressing these issues would be the future works in this research direction.

References

1. Benton, J., Talamadupula, K., Eyerich, P., Mattmüller, R., Kambhampati, S.: G-value plateaus: a challenge for planning. In: Proceedings of ICAPS 2010, pp. 259–262 (2010)
2. Bonet, B., Geffner, H.: Planning as heuristic search. Artif. Intell. **129**(1–2), 5–33 (2001)

3. Cushing, W., Benton, J., Kambhampati, S.: Cost based satisficing search considered harmful. In: Workshop HDIP at ICAPS, pp. 43–52 (2011)
4. Edelkamp, S.: Planning with pattern databases. In: Proceedings of ECP, pp. 84–90 (2001)
5. Fan, G., Müller, M., Holte, R.: Non-linear merging strategies for merge-and-shrink based on variable interactions. In: Proceedings of SoCS 2014, pp. 53–61 (2014)
6. Fan, G., Müller, M., Holte, R.: The two-edged nature of diverse action costs. In: ICAPS 2017 (2017, to appear)
7. Haslum, P., Geffner, H.: Admissible heuristics for optimal planning. In: Proceedings of AIPS 2000, pp. 140–149 (2000)
8. Helmert, M., Domshlak, C.: Landmarks, critical paths and abstractions: what's the difference anyway? In: Proceedings of ICAPS 2009 (2009)
9. Helmert, M., Haslum, P., Hoffmann, J.: Flexible abstraction heuristics for optimal sequential planning. In: Proceedings of ICAPS 2007, pp. 176–183 (2007)
10. Helmert, M., Haslum, P., Hoffmann, J., Nissim, R.: Merge-and-shrink abstraction: a method for generating lower bounds in factored state spaces. J. ACM **61**(3), 61:1–61:63 (2014)
11. Hernádvölgyi, I.T., Holte, R.C.: Experiments with automatically created memory-based heuristics. In: Choueiry, B.Y., Walsh, T. (eds.) SARA 2000. LNCS, vol. 1864, pp. 281–290. Springer, Heidelberg (2000). doi:10.1007/3-540-44914-0_18
12. Nissim, R., Hoffmann, J., Helmert, M.: Computing perfect heuristics in polynomial time: on bisimulation and merge-and-shrink abstraction in optimal planning. In: Proceedings of IJCAI 2011, pp. 1983–1990 (2011)
13. Pommerening, F., Röger, G., Helmert, M., Bonet, B.: Lp-based heuristics for cost-optimal planning. In: Proceedings of ICAPS 2014 (2014)
14. Richter, S., Westphal, M.: The LAMA planner: guiding cost-based anytime planning with landmarks. J. AIR **39**, 127–177 (2010)
15. Seipp, J., Helmert, M.: Counterexample-guided cartesian abstraction refinement. In: Proceedings of ICAPS 2013, pp. 347–351 (2013)
16. Thayer, J.T., Ruml, W., Kreis, J.: Using distance estimates in heuristic search: a re-evaluation. In: Proceedings of SoCS 2009 (2009)
17. Thayer, J.T., Benton, J., Helmert, M.: Better parameter-free anytime search by minimizing time between solutions. In: Proceedings of SoCS 2012 (2012)
18. Thayer, J.T., Ruml, W.: Using distance estimates in heuristic search. In: Proceedings of ICAPS 2009 (2009)
19. Thayer, J.T., Ruml, W.: Bounded suboptimal search: a direct approach using inadmissible estimates. In: IJCAI, pp. 674–679. IJCAI (2011)
20. Wilt, C.M., Ruml, W.: Cost-based heuristic search is sensitive to the ratio of operator costs. In: Proceedings of SoCS 2011 (2011)
21. Wilt, C.M., Ruml, W.: Speedy versus greedy search. In: Proceedings of SoCS 2014 (2014)

Collaborative Filtering with Users' Qualitative and Conditional Preferences

Sultan Ahmed(✉)

Department of Computer Science, University of Regina, Regina, Canada
ahmed28s@uregina.ca

Abstract. Current generation recommender systems are considered to be limited in: (1) utilizing users' qualitative choices and (2) tackling new items and new users. Our research focuses on building a new recommender system that utilizes users' qualitative and conditional preferences with *Collaborative Filtering* (CF). We call it *CF with Conditional Preferences* (CFCP). To represent users' conditional preferences in CFCP, we have developed *Probabilistic TCP-net* (PTCP-net). Intuitively, we argue that CFCP will be able to overcome the existing limitations, however we plan to do in-depth research on it.

Keywords: Preference reasoning · TCP-net · Recommender system

1 Introduction

Recommender systems [1,5] consist of a set of items that are subject to be recommended to a set of users. A utility function is used to measure the usefulness of an item to a user. The utility of an item is usually represented by a rating. The central problem of recommender systems lies in that utility is usually not defined on the whole user and item space, and it needs to be extrapolated to the whole space. In a *Collaborative Filtering* (CF) [7,9], the rating of an item to a user is estimated based on the ratings on the item from the similar users. Generally, there are two types of methods for performing this task: memory-based and model-based [4]. When the rating of the items are estimated, those with the highest estimated rating are recommended to the user.

CF has a number of limitations [1,5]. Firstly, users with similar interests can have very different rating patterns, i.e., some users tend to assign a higher rating to all items than other users. This results low accuracy. In memory based methods, this problem is tackled by applying heuristic normalization [4,9]. In model based methods, this problem has been addressed by considering users' qualitative preferences together with the ratings [6]. However, an item can have many features, and users can express conditional preferences over the features. CP-net [2] is an intuitive graphical tool to represent user's qualitative and conditional preferences. TCP-net [3] is an extension of CP-net that accounts user's conditional

Author's PhD research is supervised and supported by Dr. Malek Mouhoub, Professor, Department of Computer Science, University of Regina, Canada.

M. Mouhoub and P. Langlais (Eds.): Canadian AI 2017, LNAI 10233, pp. 403–406, 2017.
DOI: 10.1007/978-3-319-57351-9_45

relative importance statements. There is no approach in literature that utilizes conditional preferences represented by CP-net or TCP-net with memory based methods. Secondly, when there are new items or new users, recommendation can't be made without relying on some additional knowledge sources [1,5]. Our research addresses how to utilize conditional preferences represented by TCP-net in formulating memory-based CF to overcome the above limitations.

We plan to build a new recommender system that we call *CF with Conditional Preferences* (CFCP). CFCP is a basic CF extended to two knowledge sources: (1) the items have a finite set of attributes and (2) the users express conditional preferences over the attributes. To compactly represent many users' preferences in CFCP, we have developed *Probabilistic TCP-net* (PTCP-net). Given our CFCP model, we need to answer two questions: (1) how to estimate rating of an item to a user and (2) how to tackle new user and new item.

In a conventional CF, to estimate the rating of an item to a user, the ratings of the similar users are aggregated. Some techniques, such as correlation-based [9] and cosine-based [4], are used to measure similarity between two users. This similarity is used as a weight in the aggregated function. For our convenience, we call this "quantitative similarity" because it is measured from the quantitative ratings. In CFCP, we introduce "qualitative similarity" that indicates the similarity between two users in terms of their conditional preferences. We plan to develop effective and efficient techniques to measure qualitative similarity using the PTCP-net. Finally, both quantitative and qualitative similarities are used to calculate actual similarity and this actual similarity is used to compute rating. When there is a new user, only qualitative similarity is considered to estimate rating of the items. When there is a new item, the item is recommended to a user based on a "consistency checking" between the actual value of the item features and the optimal outcome of the TCP-net [3] that represents the user's preferences. We plan to do in-depth research on these questions.

2 Collaborative Filtering with Conditional Preferences

Our CFCP is formulated with the following components.

1. There is a set of items S. The set of qualitative attributes for the items is $\{X_1, X_2, \cdots, X_k\}$. The domains of the attributes are $D(X_1), D(X_2), \cdots,$ $D(X_k)$.
2. The rating of an item by a user is an integer ranging from 1 to r.
3. There is a set of users C. Each user expresses conditional preference statements over the domains of the attributes. Each user might have conditional relative importance statements between two attributes. The users' choices are represented using a PTCP-net.
4. u be a utility function that measures the usefulness of item $s \in S$ to user $c \in C$, i.e., $u : C \times S \Rightarrow R$, where R is a totally ordered set (e.g., non-negative integers or real numbers within a certain range). Then, for each user $c \in C$, we want to choose such item $s' \in S$ that maximizes the user's utility.

We address the following tasks in CFCP.

Estimating Unknown Utility: The value of the unknown utility $u(c, s)$ for user c and item s is computed as: $u(c, s) = k \sum_{c' \in N} sim(c, c')u(c', s)$. N denotes the set of users with non-zero $sim(c, c')$. k is a normalizing factor selected as $k = 1/\sum_{c' \in N} |sim(c, c')|$. $sim(c, c')$ indicates a similarity measure between the users c and c'. $sim(c, c')$ is computed as: $sim_{quantitative}(c, c') + sim_{qualitative}(c, c')$. $sim_{quantitative}(c, c')$ indicates quantitative similarity and $sim_{qualitative}(c, c')$ indicates qualitative similarity.

Tackling New User and New Item: A new user will fall in one of the two categories. (1) The user expresses preferences over the all attributes or a subset of attributes. In this case, for estimating the rating, only the qualitative similarity is used. (2) The user expresses no preferences over the attributes. From the PTCP-net, we find the most probable TCP-net that encodes a set of preferences that most likely map onto an unknown user. Therefore, the new user is assumed to have this set of preferences. For estimating the rating, only the qualitative similarity is used. A new item will fall in one of the two categories. (1) The values are known for the all attributes (or a subset of attributes). This item is recommended to a user, where the item's values are equal to (or subset of) the optimal outcome of the TCP-net that represents the user's preferences. (2) The attributes are unknown. In this case, we find the most probable optimal outcome for the PTCP-net. The item is recommended to a user, where the most probable optimal outcome is equal to the optimal outcome of the TCP-net that represents the user's preferences.

3 Progress

To compactly represent users' conditional preference and relative importance statements in CFCP, we have developed *Probabilistic TCP-net* (PTCP-net). In a PTCP-net, probability is considered with the preference orders, importance relations, existence of preferential dependencies and existence of importance relations. *Bayesian Network* (BN) [8] is adopted as a tool to answer two queries: (1) finding the most probable TCP-net and (2) finding the most probable optimal outcome. We have shown in the previous section that, these two questions are useful to tackle new users and new items in CFCP.

4 Plan of Action

PTCP-net with Constraint: We plan to extend our PTCP-net with hard constraints because users often express constraints and preferences together [5], and in CFCP, each user can have a different set of constraints.

Qualitative Similarity: We will attempt to find heuristics to measure qualitative similarity between two users. For example, qualitative similarity is a score that indicates the number of same conditional preference and relative importance statements between two users. There can be a number of scenarios. (1) For both of the users, conditional preferences over the all attributes are given.

(2) One of the users is given with partial preferences. (3) Both of the users have partial preferences.

Dataset and Experiment: Researchers have used variations of dataset for recommender system experiments. For example, Breese et al. [4] used MS Web, Television and EachMovie for evaluating various methods of collaborative filtering. Jin et al. [6] used MovieRating and EachMovie datasets. The problem of these datasets is that users' conditional preferences over the item features have not been necessarily recorded. We will create necessary tools to collect conditional preferences together with ratings on the items (such as books) from users. For example, as part of profile, user "A" will choose that "fiction is more preferred than non-fiction". We plan to compare CFCP with the existing methods.

5 Conclusion

We plan to develop CFCP that is a basic "Collaborative Filtering" with users' conditional preferences represented by PTCP-net. We have mentioned some challenging questions that we plan to work on in the near future: (1) finding heuristics to calculate qualitative similarity between two users, (2) aggregating qualitative similarity with quantitative similarity to obtain actual similarity, (3) effectively tackling new users and new items in our CFCP model, and (4) comparing predictive accuracy of CFCP with existing recommender systems.

References

1. Adomavicius, G., Tuzhilin, A.: Toward the next generation of recommender systems: a survey of the state-of-the-art and possible extensions. IEEE Trans. Knowl. Data Eng. **17**(6), 734–749 (2005)
2. Boutilier, C., Brafman, R.I., Domshlak, C., Hoos, H.H., Poole, D.: CP-nets: a tool for representing and reasoning with conditional ceteris paribus preference statements. J. Artif. Intell. Res. **21**, 135–191 (2004)
3. Brafman, R.I., Domshlak, C., Shimony, S.E.: On graphical modeling of preference and importance. J. Artif. Intell. Res. **25**(1), 389–424 (2006)
4. Breese, J.S., Heckerman, D., Kadie, C.: Empirical analysis of predictive algorithms for collaborative filtering. In: 14th Conference on Uncertainty in Artificial Intelligence, pp. 43–52 (1998)
5. Burke, R., Felfernig, A., Gker, M.H.: Recommender systems: an overview. AI Mag. **32**(3), 13–18 (2011)
6. Jin, R., Si, L., Zhai, C.X.: Preference-based graphic models for collaborative filtering. In: 19th Conference on Uncertainty in Artificial Intelligence, pp. 329–336 (2003)
7. Konstan, J.A., Miller, B.N., Maltz, D., Herlocker, J.L., Gordon, L.R., Riedl, J.: GroupLens: applying collaborative filtering to usenet news. Commun. ACM **40**(3), 77–87 (1997)
8. Pearl, J.: Probabilistic Reasoning in Intelligent Systems: Networks of Plausible Inference. Morgan Kaufmann Publishers Inc., San Francisco (1988)
9. Resnick, P., Iacovou, N., Suchak, M., Bergstrom, P., Riedl, J.: GroupLens: an open architecture for collaborative filtering of netnews. In: Proceedings of ACM Conference on Computer Supported Cooperative Work, pp. 175–186 (1994)

Deep Multi-cultural Graph Representation Learning

Sima Sharifirad(✉) and Stan Matwin

Dalhousie University, Halifax, Canada
{s.sharifirad, stan}@dal.ca

Abstract. This research aims at the development of a knowledge representation that will elucidate and visualize the differences and similarities between concepts expressed in different languages and cultures. Wikipedia graph structure is considered around one concept namely "Nazism" in two languages, English and German for the purpose of understanding how online knowledge crowdsourcing platforms will be affected by different language groups and their cultures. The solution is divided into capturing structure of weighted graph representation learning via random surfing, cross-lingual document similarity via Jaccard similarity, multi-view representation learning by deploying Deep Canonical Correlation Autoencoder (DCCAE) and sentiment classification task via SVM. Our method shows superior performance on word similarity task. Based on our best knowledge, it is the first application of DCCAE in this context.

Keywords: DCCAE · Random surfing · Sentiment classification

1 Introduction

Previous research has been tried to address the problem of understanding cultural differences based on Wikipedia pages by using different softwares. Namely a few, [1] considers the cultural similarities and differences between Chinese, English, German, French and Swedish Wikipedia were by focusing on war related pages, they divided their method into different sections such as network analysis, Wikipedia page analysis and sentiment analysis and for each of them software such as Gephi and Semantra for Excel were used. Additionally to previous research, [2] analyzed the differences between Chinese and English version of Wikipedia pages by deploying word-occurrence matrix and using softwares such as ConText and Gephi. We tried to use state of the art methods in natural language processing and text mining to answer these questions. The contribution of the paper is as follows: In the first step, web pages around our main concept were collected, then in the second step random surfing method was used to keep the structure information of the graph. In the third step, similar documents around each concept on opposite language were calculated and LDA was deployed to extract the topics, in the fourth step, deep canonical correlation was used for extracting the maximum correlated words and in the last step, SVM was implemented for sentiment analysis of the words.

M. Mouhoub and P. Langlais (Eds.): Canadian AI 2017, LNAI 10233, pp. 407–410, 2017.
DOI: 10.1007/978-3-319-57351-9_46

2 Model

2.1 Random Surfing Algorithm

In the first step of this research, The Wikipedia page of our target concept (we will call it root page in this paper) in two languages was considered and all the pages interconnected to those two pages were collected, around 2470 pages in English and 1126 pages in German were gathered. Undirected weighted graph was constructed by calculating tfidf and cosine similarity of web pages. In the second step, random surfing method was used. In 2016, [3] proposed random surfing for their weighted graph. Random surfing method which derives from the page rank model is as follows: considering the i-th vertex as the current vertex, first order all the vertices was considered randomly. Having B as a transition matrix, we reach the j-th vertex after k steps from matrix B. ρ_0 is the one hot vector that comes after probability α which shows the probability of continuing the algorithm.

$$\rho_{\mathrm{k}} = \alpha.\rho_{\mathrm{k}-1}\mathrm{B} + (1-\alpha)\rho_0 \tag{1}$$

In the third step, we used Eurparl Pararllel Corpus-v7 to calculate Jaccard similarity between root page in another language and the other pages in other language. Then Latent Dirichlet Allocation (LDA) was used to extract topics from the most 1000 related pages. The extracted topics would be used in the sentimental analysis step.

2.2 Deep Canonical Correlation Autoencoder (DCCAE)

Step 5 was around deploying DCCAE, in 2015, Deep Canonical Correlation Autoencoder (DCCAE) was proposed by [4]. In this method, two data matrices for two views X and Y along with two DNNs f and g were considered. These two DNNs were used to maximize the canonical correlation between the extracted features f(X) and g(Y). In the below formula U and V were two directions of CCA used to project the DNNs output. $\mathrm{U}^{\mathrm{T}}\mathrm{f}(.)$ was used for final projection mapping for testing. In DCCAE, we tried to optimize the following formula and λ was a tradeoff parameter [5].

$$\min\left(\mathrm{W_f}, \mathrm{W_g}, \mathrm{W_p}, \mathrm{W_q}, \mathrm{U}, \mathrm{V}\right) \\ \frac{1}{N}\mathrm{tr}\left(\mathrm{U^T f(X) g(Y)^T V}\right) + \frac{\lambda}{N}\sum\nolimits_{i=1}^{N} \left(||\mathrm{x_i} - \mathrm{p}\left(\mathrm{f}\left(\mathrm{x_i}\right)\right)||^2 + ||\,\mathrm{y_i} - \mathrm{q}(\mathrm{g}(\mathrm{y_i}))\,||^2\right) \tag{2}$$

3 Experiment

We did experiment on two types of datasets. The first dataset was on word similarity task, WS353 was considered for this purpose, random surfing part were skipped due to the linear sequence of dataset and deep canonical correlation autoencoder was implemented with two hidden ReLU layers with width of 1280 both in encoder and decoder part. In order to compare with previous methods, like in [4] the weight decay of 10^{-4} was considered. For training, WMT, 2014 was used for English-German word vectors. Like [6], cdec [7] was used to align the words and then 640 word vectors were calculated using LSA. On testing, the performance of algorithm was tuned on WS 353 dataset. Similarity of the pairs were calculated using cosine similarity and spearman's correlation reported between the model's ranking and human ranking. We reported the highest spearman's correlation on around 649 bigram pairs and reported it on test dataset. The performance is reported in Table 1. Second dataset, which pertains to our contribution was implemented on our knowledge graph, after training on WMT 2014 parallel corpus, we tested the algorithm with the most similar pages extracted from previous step. After calculating cosine similarity and spearman's correlation coefficient, we chose the top highest correlated words. We combined those words with topics extracted from previous LDA step and considered them as the test dataset for sentimental classification part. In the last step, we used Webis-CLS-10, this dataset was chosen because of its bilingual reviews, and the processed format of this dataset already have done the tokenization and preprocessing. We trained once the algorithm in English and once on German on the dataset, then tested it on previous prepared test dataset. Based on the prediction of the labels for each language, we calculate the sentiment score by the following formula. From 2470 words in total, sentiment score for German was −21.1 whereas for English about −14.2. It becomes evident that both countries have negative attitude toward this concept. The number of German words seems to be larger in comparison to positive words, it shows words have the power to show the level of deterioration in the history. Based on Shirer quote "Nazism was a deadly culmination of German nationalism".

$$\text{Sentiment score} = (\text{positive word count} - \text{negative word count}) / (\text{positive} + \text{negative word count}) \tag{3}$$

Table 1. Spearman's correlation coefficient on word similarity task.

Algorithms	Finkelstein et al. WS 353	Zesch et al. SW similarity	Agirre et al. WS relatedness
DCCAE	74.68	76.27	68.99
DNGR	72.45	74.84	68.73
PPMI	62.28	67.52	56.02
SVD	72.22	73.96	68.44
SGNS	70.78	74.37	64.60

4 Conclusion

In this work we tried to use novel text mining methods to show the differences and similarities of one concept in different languages in online crowdsourcing platforms having emphasis on keeping the structure of Wikipedia graph. An undirected weighted graph was extracted from the Wikipedia pages, then random surfing model used to keep the structural information of the graph, high similarity pages to our root page were collected. DCCAE was used to extract the high correlated words, these words later on were used for our sentiment classification. The sentiment score was calculated and results show the big difference between the words used in each language. Future work will be working on more similarity datasets and modifying DCCAE for unsupervised sentiment analysis.

References

1. Robin, G., Hanna-Mari, R., Yuanyuan, L., Mohsen, M., Franziska, P., Peter, G., Maria, P., Matthaus, P.: Cultural differences in the understanding of history on Wikipedia. In: Zylka, M., Fuehres, H., Fronzetti Colladon, A., Gloor, P. (eds.) Designing Networks for Innovation and Improvisation. Springer Proceedings in Complexity (SPCOM), pp. 3–12. Springer, Cham (2016). doi:10.1007/978-3-319-42697-6_1
2. Ke, J., Grace, A.B., et al.: Mapping articles on China in Wikipedia: an inter-language semantic network analysis. In: Proceedings of the 50th Hawaii International Conference on System Sciences (2017). ISBN: 978-0-9981331-0-2
3. Cao, S., Lu, W., Xu, Q.: Deep neural networks for learning graph representations. In: AAAI, pp. 1145–1152 (2016)
4. Weiran, W., Raman, A., Karen, L., et al.: On deep multi-view representation learning. In: Proceedings of the 32nd International Conference on Machine Learning (ICML 2015) (2015)
5. Sarath, C., Lauly, S., et al.: An autoencoder approach to learning bilingual word representations. In: Proceedings of NIPS 2014 (2014)
6. Manaal, F., Chris, D.: Improving vector space word representations using multilingual correlation. In: Proceedings of the 14th Conference of the European Chapter of the Association for Computational Linguistics, Gothenburg, Sweden, pp. 462–471, April 2014
7. Chris, D., Adam, L., et al.: cdec: a decoder, alignment, and learning framework for finite- state and context-free translation models. In: Proceedings of the ACL 2010 System Demonstrations, pp. 7–12. Association for Computational Linguistics (2010)

Who Is the Artificial Author?

Tom Lebrun(✉)

Université Laval, Quebec City, Canada
tom.lebrun.1@ulaval.ca

Abstract. This paper focuses on the potential receptions of literary artworks produced by or with the help of artificial intelligence on a legal and literary point of view. We take into account the Canadian legal notion of originality to postulate that we should now distinguish authority from auctoriality.

Keywords: Authorship · Copyright · Literature · Auctoriality · Formalism

1 Introduction

Who is the artificial author? The question arises, as contests such as the Nikkei Hoshi Shinichi Literary Award or the NaNoGenMo proposes to «*spend the month writing code that generates a 50 k word novel, share the novel & the code at the end*[1]». At the intersection of copyright, free culture, programming and of course literature, this new reality of books getting written by Artificial Intelligence (AI) is almost not examined; apart from the prospective work of Peter Swirski (Swirski 2013), nothing has been written about it. This paper aims at filling some of those gaps concerning the reception of an artificial author on a legal and literary point of views. Our goal here is to demonstrate that, even though the Canadian legal conception seems to rally consensus about authorship, the literary theory might challenge it. This reflexion takes place in a more global analysis of the possible reception of AI generated literature, which is the subject of our PhD thesis. Machine learning and deep learning are of course central to artificial literature – or, as Peter Swirski name it, Biterature. The distinction from usual computer generated lit (such as Serge Bouchardon, Philippe Bootz or Raymond Queneau's work) stands indeed in the new *autonomy* the algorithm gets thanks to those progresses. In programming language, autonomy is associated to the notion of agent. According to Stan Franklin and Art Graesser's definition (Franklin and Graesser 1997), an autonomous agent is «*a system situated within and a part of an environment that senses that environment and acts on it, over time, in pursuit of its own agenda and so as to effect what it senses in the future.*»; a definition that could apply to Illiad's author or to Google's most recent personal assistant. Both are indeed environment dependent, which means they are only agent thanks to the context in which they evolve. Franklin and Graesser's definition also relies on what Jeff Hawkins (Hawkins and Blakeslee 2007) analyses as the essence of intelligence, which is the capacity to remember patterns and to predict others. As most of the obstacles searchers in AI deal with

[1] The source here is actually a tweet from NaNoGenMo founder, Darius Kazemi (@tinysubversions) that dates from november 2013.

M. Mouhoub and P. Langlais (Eds.): Canadian AI 2017, LNAI 10233, pp. 411–415, 2017.
DOI: 10.1007/978-3-319-57351-9_47

nowadays relate precisely to language, one can't help but to wonder if literature – *the art of language* – still remain human privilege. So if a book gets written by an autonomous AI, who is the real author?

2 The Originality Criteria in Canadian Legislation

The legal definition of authorship in Canada is framed under the 1886 Berne Convention; the Constitution lends its regulation to federal government. The copyright act[2] that regulates the question is quite open to interpretations: doctrine, for what matters, considers authorship to be granted as far as originality is proven (Gervais 2002). The notion of originality is understood quite similarly in Canada, US and European Union (Gervais 2002), as the unification goal of Berne Convention succeeded to some extents. An exemple: in her paper *Allocating ownership right in computer-generated work* (Samuelson 1985), Pamela Samuelson reminds us that originality – in the U.S – is the number one criteria required to qualify for copyright protection (as well as a fixation on some «*tangible medium of expression*», which won't be examined here[3]); as she also reminds, the term does not «*include requirements of novelty, ingenuity or esthetic merit*[4]». This conception of originality is mostly the same in Canada (Gervais 2002) and in France[5]: the 2004 Supreme Court of Canada case *CCH Canadian Ltd. v. Law Society of Upper Canada, 2004 SCC* even states that «*creativity is not required to make a work 'original'.*[6]». As a matter of fact, Canada now define originality as an exercise of «*skill and judgment*», skill being the «*use of one's knowledge, developed aptitude or practised ability*», judgment being «*the use of one's capacity for discernment or ability to form an opinion or evaluation by comparing different possible options in producing the work*»[7]. The Court also precises that the exercice of skill and judgment «*must not be so trivial that it could be characterized as a purely mechanical exercise*».

So this is where it gets particularly interesting, as any piece of works that get written by (or with) the help of an artificial intelligence is composed of three elements: programmer's intention, algorithm and database. One could even say it is only two elements, algorithm (which implies the programmer's intention) and database. As we said before, we will focus on the last of those three elements here. Indeed, as AI grows in autonomy, the big thing still remains the data it gets fed with. Data is of course never just data: just like algorithm, it is never neutral. Data draws the content that will be created at the end, determines the DNA of the text, some would say its style. Give an

---

[2] R.S.C., 1985, c. C-42.

[3] The conservation on a computer server is generally enough to be considered as a «tangible mediun», in U.S, Canada or European Union legal systems.

[4] Samuelson here refers to House Report Number 1476, 94th Congress, Second Session, 51, 1976, on the Copyright Act of 1976.

[5] L. 112-1, Code de la Propriété Intellectuelle, Dalloz, Paris (2016).

[6] CCH Canadian Ltd. v. Law Society of Upper Canada, 2004 SCC, para 25.

[7] *Ibid.*, para 16.

AI the whole web (and a privileged access for trolls) and it will recreate a machine that put the stress on its love of lolcats and Adolf Hitler (Time 2016). Give it a few pieces of literature – let's say some Jane Austen works as well as some Mary Shelley's – and you get *Of Crying and Captains*, «*created by Isadora Lamego*» but «*written by a computer*» as the website Literai.com presents it. As Mrs Lamego indicates herself: «*I completely adore what my ai created, it has given my* (sic) *a beautiful work with a level of vocabulary and style that I would find difficult to replicate*». Last example, a new Harry Potter chapter generated thanks to the first four books of J.K Rowling bestsellers. The code is from a programmer named Max Deutsch, but the text, given to the public on Medium.com, is actually quite close to Mrs Rowling's identity. How could it be otherwise? Its source is not diluted at all. It is «*pure*», in lack of other term.

The problem is that, in all three examples, skill and judgment are each time partly involved in the database, partly in the algorithm. And that makes the «real author» quite hard to establish. The first one, about lolcats and Hitler, has a plurality of sources. The identity is diluted in the multiplicity of its contributors: its author is everything that ever interacted with, which means it is everything and anything. Mostly anything. What about *Of Crying and Captains*? In the legal sense, a court would probably say it's Isadora Lamego, not only because «*only those stuck in the doctrinal mud could even think that computers could be authors* (Samuelson 1985)», but because the act of composing the code, her work of compilation would certainly qualify to the legal conception of originality in Canada and U.S right now. Max Deutsch's new chapter of Harry Potter book might be considered just the same, even though it belongs for the courts to judge so. Both programmers would be authors of the texts - in the legal sense. On the literary sense though, one has to be careful.

3 From Authority to Auctoriality: A Forced Path to Formalism

As we said previously, artificial literature get produced thanks to three elements: programmer, algorithm and database. Programmers – people at the origin of the algorithm – are also generating the idea. They chose parameters *and* choose the database on which the neural network will get trained on. Is that enough to define them as authors? As we've said before, originality is not the defining criteria used to define authorship: it is skill and judgment. Most of artificial literature that get produced is created on the basis of a concept - let us just cite the example of *Word of the Useless*, which presents combinations of «*various prefixes and suffixes, and try to form definitions of these newly created terms*» in a borgian attempt. This case might be easy to define because the concept makes the whole point of reading it, but some works don't rely on concepts. Some works, in fact, rely on sources, on database. For one, *Of Crying and Captains* is presented as mostly Jane Austen and Mary Shelley's work, and «*legitimately sounds like an Austen novel*». The chapter made from J. K. Rowling's work, is even more touchy: as we've said, it is pure in its source, only transformed by the algorithm. Who is the real author here? As John Searle already said in 1980, computers only have a syntax, but no semantics (Searle 1980). The debate is endless[8] and in our opinion, quite sterile. Remains the more interesting notion of database intention… Which is, also, a complex question. Interpretation theories now mostly fall within an «anti» intentional framework (Ducrot and Schaeffer 1995), but that shouldn't elude the pragmatic understanding that Jane Austen, Mary Shelley and J. K Rowling probably intended to write in the way they did, at least to some extent.

All those reasons are exactly why the author needs to be distinguished from the *auctor*. Literary studies generally assimilate the two notions without a proper distinction. In our opinion, artificial art forces us to separate them. The authorship should be restrained to the qualification of the person legally responsible of the artwork whereas the auctorship, the *auctorialité,* should only qualify the artistic identity of it. Such a distinction is required to push further the analysis of what artificial art might be. According to our previous analysis, only the auctoriality would be composed of the three main elements of any artificial art (data, algorithm and programmer's intention). The authorship would remain relevant for the legal qualification of the artwork, but also for the explanation of its auctoriality, i.e. for the studying of the artwork's genetics. In a nutshell, the understanding of artificial art needs to appeal to authority for an explanation of auctoriality, since both concepts contribute to the definition of the artificial author.

Besides, even if some literary theories, through Sainte-Beuve and Taine, were based on the recognition of author's existence (the novel or the poem needed to be understood through the spectrum of its author's intention and biography) this reality is long gone by now. What started with Marcel Proust's famous *Contre Sainte-Beuve* was finally performed when what we call French Theory killed the notion of authorship. Roland Barthes in his essay of 1968, and Michel Foucault a year later both challenged the idea that the reception of a work had to study its creators. From this point of view, later seen as *formalist*, a book doesn't need to have an author to be a subject: in fact, it only needs a reader. To our opinion, artificial literature – and artificial art - forces us to enter definitely in this new paradigm described by Jauss in the seventies, for which readership constitutes the center of literary theory. Antiquity also didn't recognize the notion of authorship; this conception is, in fact, rooted in Renaissance. As for it, History seems to jump ahead and build a bridge straight from the past, offering to challenge the idea for one last round. That's perhaps what is implied by artificial literature: the end of authorship not only thanks to the prevalence of readership theories, but by the disappearance of the necessity of even having one.

References

Barthes, R.: La mort de l'auteur. In: Le bruissement de la langue, Seuil, Paris (1968)

Brunn, A.: L'auteur. G-F Flammarion, Paris (2001)

Ducrot, O., Schaeffer, J.-M.: Nouveau dictionnaire encyclopédique des sciences du langage. Seuil, Paris (1995)

[8] In our sense, Thomas Nagel did already evacuate the debate in his famous 1972 article. For the reflection, bats could be indeed compared to computers… One might never know if it thinks or not. See: Nagel 1974.

Foucault, M.: Qu'est-ce qu'un auteur? In: Bulletin de la société française de philosophie, dits et écrits 1, pp. 789–821, Gallimard, Paris (1969)

Franklin, S., Graesser, A.: Is it an agent, or just a program?: a taxonomy for autonomous agents. In: Müller, Jörg P., Wooldridge, Michael J., Jennings, Nicholas R. (eds.) ATAL 1996. LNCS, vol. 1193, pp. 21–35. Springer, Heidelberg (1997). doi:10.1007/BFb0013570

Gervais, D.: Feist goes global: a comparative analysis of the notion of originality in copyright law. J. Copyright Soc. **49**, 949 (2002). USA, New York

Hawkins, J., Blakeslee, S.: On Intelligence. Macmillan, London (2007)

Jauss, H., Benzinger, E.: Literary history as a challenge to literary theory. New Lit. Hist. **2**, 7–37 (1970). The Johns Hopkins University Press, Baltimore [1967]

Nagel, T.: What it is like to be a bat? Philocoph. Rev. **83**, 435–450 (1974). Duke University Press, Durham

Nillson, N.: The Quest for Artificial Intelligence: A History of Ideas and Achievements. Cambridge University Press, Cambridge (2009)

Samuelson, P.: Allocating ownership rights in computer-generated works. Univ. Pitt Law Rev. **47**, 1185–1228 (1985). Pittsburgh

Searle, J.: Minds, brains and programs. Behav. Brain Sci. **3**, 417–457 (1980). Cambridge University Press, Cambridge

Swirski, P.: From Literature to Biterature. McGill-Queen's University Press, Montreal (2013)

Time. http://time.com/4270684/microsoft-tay-chatbot-racism/

Machine Learning Techniques to Unveil and Understand *Pseudomonas aeruginosa* Survival Mechanism in Nutrient Depleted Water

Bertrand Sodjahin(✉)

School of Computing and Information Systems,
Athabasca University, Athabasca, Canada
bercadson@yahoo.fr

Abstract. *Pseudomonas aeruginosa* is an organism notable for its ubiquity in the ecosystem and its resistance to antibiotics. It is an environmental bacterium that is a common cause of hospital-acquired infections. Identifying its survival mechanism is critical for designing preventative and curative measures. Also, understanding this mechanism is beneficial because *P. aeruginosa* and other related organisms are capable of bioremediation. To address this practical problem, we proceeded by decomposition into multiple learnable components: the optimal regulatory network models—static and temporal—of the survival mechanism, the functional interplay, the determination of the viability maintenance genes, and the identification of the bacterium's states. With unlabeled data collected from *P. aeruginosa* gene expression response to low nutrient water, a Bayesian Networks Machine Learning methodology was implemented to model a static regulatory network of its survival process. Subsequently, node influence techniques were used to infer a group of genes as key orchestrators of the observed survival phenotype. Further, we proposed Dynamic Bayesian Networks for temporal modeling, clustering for the functional interplay, and hierarchical classification for the bacterium's states identification.

Keywords: Machine learning · Bayesian networks · Gene expression · Bacteria · *Pseudomonas aeruginosa*

1 Introduction

Studies have shown that *P. aeruginosa* may survive for months on hospital surfaces [1] causing various infections. However, this organism also has some potential applications in biotechnology [2]. We are interested in its survival mechanism in nutrient depleted water. Our hypothesis is that this survival is sustained by a particular group of genes which encode for persistence proteins.

To achieve this goal, Machine Learning techniques are proposed. We present the global architecture of our methodology with emphasis on Bayesian Networks Learning [3], which we implemented here to unveil the regulatory network of *P. aeruginosa* survival in low nutrient water. Our findings concerning the viability maintenance genes are also reported.

M. Mouhoub and P. Langlais (Eds.): Canadian AI 2017, LNAI 10233, pp. 416–420, 2017.
DOI: 10.1007/978-3-319-57351-9_48

2 Approach and Proposed Methodology

Two experimental trials based on PAO1 mini-Tn5-*luxCDABE* transposon mutant library incubated in nutrient depleted water were undertaken. Over a time period, gene expression response data were collected, and then consolidated. The actual data matrix has ~1000 genes and ~30 data samples. Table 1 presents a sample format.

Table 1. Dataset's sample format. First column is *P. aeruginosa* genes. Others are expression response fold (% T_0) in low nutrient water for each measurement time point.

Genes	Exprsn_$_{T1}$	Exprsn_$_{T2}$	Exprsn_$_{Ti}$	Exprsn_$_{Tn}$
PA5398	1.92	1.42	…	0.03
PA5400	2.12	1.51	…	0.05
…	…	…	…	…
Tgt	1.06	0.64	…	0.73

For each gene, the expression response fold (Exprsn_$_{Ti}$) is numerical and our analysis is quantitative and considers some prior microbiology knowledge. Figure 1 shows the global architecture of our methodology, which rests predominantly on Bayesian Networks (BN). BN—invented by Professor *Judea Pearl* in the 1980s—is a mathematical formalism for defining complex probability models and inference algorithms. Also known as Directed Acyclic Graph (DAG), it is a graphical representation

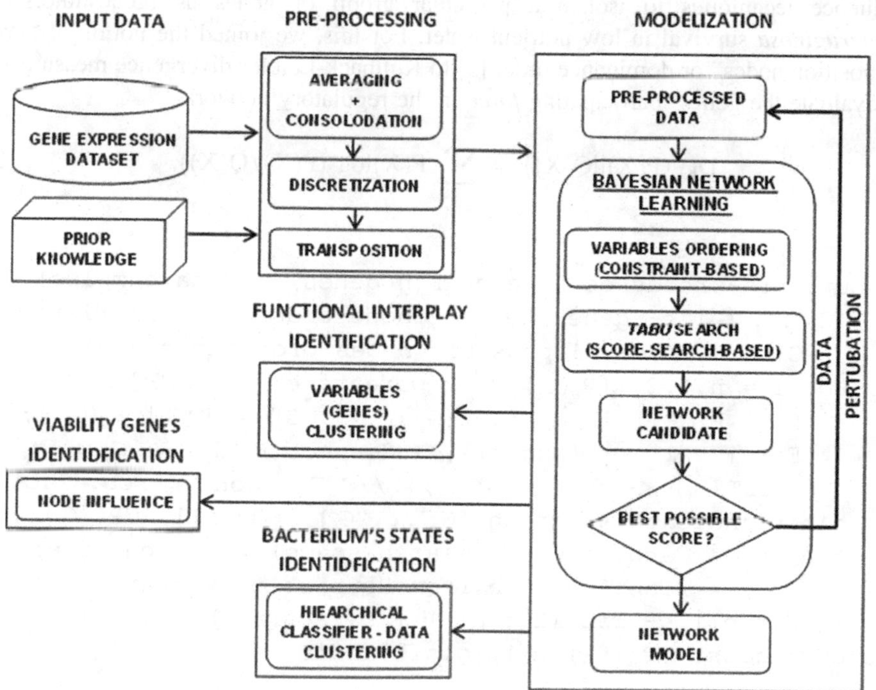

Fig. 1. Global analysis design architecture

of probabilistic relationships among a set of domain variables—here genes, represented by nodes. Conditional dependencies (Parent→Child) between pairs of genes are illustrated by directed edges. A Conditional Probability Distribution is associated with each gene G_i given its parents $Pa(G_i)$. The joint distribution of all the domain genes is uniquely represented by (1).

$$P(G_1 \ldots G_n) = \prod_{i=1 \ldots n} P(G_i | P_a(G_i)). \tag{1}$$

A DAG is constructed either with domain expert knowledge or by learning from data. Theoretic groundwork on the latter was extensively covered and applied to *S. cerevisiae* as a model organism [3]. This application, the first in gene expression data analysis, was foundational for our current work, i.e., learning from data the regulatory network of *P. aeruginosa* survival mechanism. In short, this task consisted in finding a set of parents for each gene in the domain, such that the resulting network is acyclic with an optimal MDL score. With the preprocessed dataset $D = \{D_1, D_2, \ldots, D_N\}$, in a hybrid approach, *constraint-based* (Conditional Independence test) was used for variables ordering, and *Score-and-search-based* for the heuristic search of the optimal DAG in the candidates' space. With this latter method, we combined *Tabu search* with *Data Perturbation*—an additional technique to increase the chance of escaping local optimum. In contrast to our hybrid approach, [3] is *score-and-search-based.* We present below a partially high level pseudocode—listing—of our learning algorithm.

Based on our learned model and our afore-enunciated hypothesis, we used node influence techniques to isolate a particular group of genes as orchestrators of *P. aeruginosa* survival in low nutrient water. For this, we joined the notion of "Predisposition nodes" or dominance order [3] to Kullback-Leibler divergence measure (2) to evaluate the genes' participating *force* in the regulatory network.

$$D_{KL}(P(X)||Q(X)) = \sum_X P(X) \log_2(P(X)/Q(X)). \tag{2}$$

```
Input: pre-processed Dataset D(n genes, N data samples)
   [G_1 ... G_n] <- generate best node order with heuristic
      CI test over n! possible nodes ordering space;
   For i = n...2 {{P_a(G_i) <- k parents ∈ [G_i-1...G_1] :
      P(D| P_a(G_i)) is max & P(G_i|G_i-1 ...G_1) = P(G_i| P_a(G_i));}
      For j = 1...k {Edges[] <- Connect(P_a(G_i)_j -> G_i);
         CPT(G_i) <- P(G_i| P_a(G_i)_j;} //CPT = Cond. Prob. Table
   gInitCandidate <- graph({G_1 ... G_n}, Edges[], CPT(G_i));
   f(n) <- #(Candidates in search space) function of n;
   H(f(n)) <- TabuListSize from Heuristic evaluation H;
   T_DP(H(f(n)) <- Tabu(H(f(n))) + DataPerturbation(D);
Output: gBest= T_DP(H(f(n)), gInitCandidate, MDL))
```

3 Current Findings and Discussions

Our learned regulatory network encompasses ~25% of the overall 954 domain genes. This aligns with [3] stating that gene expression networks are generally sparse: only a small number directly affect each other. Similar to [3] with 800 genes and 76 instances, our network model is sparse. With BayesiaLab [4], the implementation tool used, our network model is fully interactive, and can be enlarged/shrunk for visual read and interpretation by microbiologists, without Bayesian Networks background.

The node influence techniques resulted in the inference of a dozen of genes as key players of *P. aeruginosa* viability maintenance (Table 2). These genes are all protein coding type as it is the case in [3]. Experts' knowledge concurs that the identified genes are interestingly conducive to the bacterium's survival. E.g., *PA0272* appears as the only root node in the model and its functional description shows a transcriptional regulator which is an orchestrator of gene activity—bacterium's life. We neither include the actual resulting network nor list all the genes here, due to space restriction.

It emerged from our study—and [3], the need to investigate how combinations of gene states could determine specific states of the bacterium. In addition, the functional interplay and the dynamic model are to be presented in our next paper. Further, we note that a larger data instances would confer more reliability to the current model.

Table 2. Genes identified as orchestrators of *P. aeruginosa* survival in low nutrient water.

	Gene	Node force	Root?	Description/function
1	cyoB	29.153781	✗	Cytochrome o ubiquinol oxidase subunit I, energy generation
2	PA0272	10.72733	✓	Transcriptional regulator, gene regulation
3	cupC2	8.611461	✗	Chaperone CupC2, pilus assembly and biofilm formation
…	…	…	…	…

4 Conclusion

We machine-learned an optimal network model of *P. aeruginosa* survival mechanism and computationally isolated a dozen of its genes as key orchestrators of its viability in low nutrient water. These results are biologically plausible in theory, and contribute to the overall goal of apprehending *P. aeruginosa* survival mechanism in nutrient depleted water environment. Currently the survival of PA0272 mutant is being lab-tested in water, compared to PAO1 wild type.

References

1. Kramer, A., Schwebke, I., Kampf, G.: How long do nosocomial pathogens persist on inanimate surfaces? A systematic review. BMC Infect. Dis. **6**(1), 130 (2006)

2. Kung, V.L., Ozer, E.A., Hauser, A.R.: The accessory genome of pseudomonas aeruginosa. Microbiol. Mol. Biol. Rev. **74**(4), 621–641 (2010)
3. Friedman, N., Linial, M., Nachman, I., Pe'er, D.: Using Bayesian networks to analyze expression data. J. Comput. Biol. **7**(3–4), 601–620 (2000)
4. Conrady, S., Jouffe, L.: Bayesian Networks and BayesiaLab: A Practical Introduction for Researchers. Bayesia USA, Franklin (2015)

Identification and Classification of Alcohol-Related Violence in Nova Scotia Using Machine Learning Paradigms

Fateha Khanam Bappee(✉)

Dalhousie University, Halifax, Canada
ft487931@dal.ca

Abstract. A significant improvement in big data analytics has motivated the radical change in the scientific study of crime and criminals. In terms of criminal activities, it has been observed that alcohol has a great influence in most of the cases. The main goals of our research are to analyze different types of violence happening in Nova Scotia and to apply machine learning techniques to model the relationships between alcohol consumption and violence. In many machine learning algorithms, it is assumed that, the training and testing data must be in the same distribution and feature space. Because of limited amount of Nova Scotia criminal activity data, the need of transfer learning arises which helps to gain knowledge from different domains. The results of our studies show a very satisfactory classification performance on Nova Scotia data.

1 Introduction

The most commonly considered alcohol-related offense is impaired driving. However, there are a variety of other major alcohol related offences which include robberies, sexual assaults, aggravated assaults, and homicides. According to the Statistics Canada research, the hazardous alcohol consumption rate in Canada is 17.4% and Nova Scotia plays an important role to increase this rate [1]. A 2008 report shows that 33.7% of Nova Scotians aged between 19–24 were affected by alcohol-related abuse [9]. According to the annual report of NS Trauma Program 2014, alcohol is involved in approximately 25% of motor vehicle crashes and 28% of homicide/assault [2].

Information about alcohol-related violence is spread among different text media, e.g. print/online media, social media, police reports, and court decisions. The study mainly focuses on developing a machine learning tool to gather and process information and knowledge from these different sources about alcohol related violence in Nova Scotia. This work is the first attempt to use machine learning approaches in this type of application. Some other fields such as law and criminology already uncovered the relationship between alcohol consumption and violent behavior by some theoretical explanations. The experimental findings of [6] indicated that alcohol has a causal influence on violent behavior. In this study, we apply classification techniques to classify whether the violence

M. Mouhoub and P. Langlais (Eds.): Canadian AI 2017, LNAI 10233, pp. 421–425, 2017.
DOI: 10.1007/978-3-319-57351-9_49

is influenced by alcohol consumption or not, depending on the structure of the data. Many machine learning algorithms work well when the training and testing data are drawn from the same distribution and feature space. However, collecting adequate training data for many real-world applications, is very difficult and expensive. In such cases, where there is limited amount of training data, knowledge transfer or transfer learning would be beneficial. In transfer learning, it stores knowledge obtained from one problem and applies that knowledge to a different but related problem. It allows the domains and distributions to be different used in the training and testing data. The relationship between transfer learning and other machine learning techniques are discussed in [8]. In 2008, [7] proposed locally weighted ensemble learning algorithms, pLWE and LWE, on the 20 newsgroups data. In our research while solving the classification problem of Nova Scotia's alcohol-related violence, we try to apply some knowledge obtained from two other provinces, Alberta and British Columbia. This work compares the performance of transfer learning by transferring the knowledge of instances with the Recursive Partitioning (RP), Support Vector Machine (SVM), and Random Forest (RF) methods. An ensemble with the predictions of RF and SVM methods is created to improve the performance in transfer learning.

2 Data Source and Preparation

The decisions released by the Provincial Court of Nova Scotia from the Nova Scotia (NS) Courts' Decision database are used in the paper. In this paper, we explored 200 documents based on 200 decisions of the courts. Within these documents, 100 documents are in positive class, and 100 documents are in negative class. Documents of the courts' decision database, where the violence is related to alcohol consumption, are defined as positive. Otherwise, documents are defined as negative. Positive class documents are labeled by an expert and negative class documents are labeled using an algorithm which uses search terms alcohol, assault, drunk, intoxicated etc. Preprocessing involves removal of punctuations, numbers, white spaces, stopwords etc. After preprocessing of the text documents, 714 terms or words remain in the chosen data set. These terms are considered as explanatory variables/features while model building. Response variable indicates two classes that are positive and negative. The processed text documents are then passed to a document representation model, which represents each text with a numerical vector. A term-document matrix or TDM is used as a document representation model. TDM describes the frequency of terms that occur in a collection of documents. In TDM, rows represent documents and columns represent terms. We divide the data into two equal parts, training and testing, with the same number of positive and negative cases.

Besides NS court's decision data, we have collected 470 newspaper links from some specified twitter feed such as CBCNS, Chronicleherald, NEWS957, metrohalifax. Our focus was collecting old twitter data (links, tweets) from 2012 to 2014 based on some search terms such as assault, alcohol, drunk, intoxicated. 1313 police (HRP) reports from open data Halifax are also collected in the study. As the amount of NS data is not satisfactory, we try to collect some other province's crime related data to solve the desired classification problem. For our study, we have collected 7459 and 5379 court decisions released by Provincial Court of British Columbia (BC) and Alberta (AB) respectively from the website of Canadian Legal Information Institute. The total data with positive and negative class is summarized in Table 1.

3 Methods and Result Analysis

The task of document classification is to automatically assign the pre-defined labels on previously unseen documents. Various statistical and machine learning algorithms have been introduced to deal with document classification. This paper mainly focuses on Recursive Partitioning (RP) [4], Support Vector Machine (SVM) [5], and Random Forest (RF) [3] methods for identification and classification of alcohol-related violence. SVM and RF are optimized by choosing different kernel functions and the optimal number of decision trees respectively. RF and SVM has gained considerable attention in alcohol-related violence data classification, because of their optimal classification performance. The concept of inductive and transductive transfer learning [8] is taken into account. In transductive learning, source and target domains are different but related and labeled data is available only in a source domain. In inductive learning, labeled data is available in target domain and sometimes in source domain. For the experiments, we only use NS court data as target domain data (new unlabeled data or test data) to test the model. However, we apply all the domains such as, NS, AB, and BC as source domains while training the model to see how the models behave.

Table 1. Datasets used in the research

Data source	Total documents	Negative	Positive
NS court data	200	100	100
Twitter data	470	400	70
HRP data	1313	1284	29
BC court data	7459	5141	2318
AB court data	5379	2918	2461

Table 2 and Fig. 1(a) show the classification accuracy of models, developed using RP, SVM and RF methods, which is based on the test sets of seven random samples. From the results, it is clear that classification performance does not fluctuate surprisingly among different source domains as long as we used some labeled NS training data. The results also discover that Random Forest performs better than other two methods in all four cases. It exhibits 95% or more accuracy for all. RF gives smaller standard deviation compared to RP and SVM which reveals model's stability. Considering the fact when there is no labeled target

Table 2. Performance based on RP, SVM and RF methods when source domain includes NS, AB and BC data.

Source → Target Accuracy (unit:%)	RP		SVM		RF	
	Mean	SD	Mean	SD	Mean	SD
NS → NS	81.7%	4.8%	90.7%	6.3%	95.4%	2.07%
NS ∪ AB → NS	87.8%	9.2%	88.7%	3.86%	95.8%	1.95%
NS ∪ BC → NS	89%	5.1%	88%	2.69%	95%	3.2%
NS ∪ AB ∪ BC → NS	87%	4.2%	87%	4.05%	95%	2.54%

data available, we use AB, BC and (AB ∪ BC) as source domain. For this exploration, SVM and RF methods are chosen due to the previous performance. In this case performance drops (see Table 3) in comparison with the previous exploration (see Table 2). However, the performance is not unsatisfactory as for RF it gives more than 80% accuracy on average. An ensemble with the predictions of RF and SVM methods is created to improve the performance in transfer learning. Figure 1(b) and Table 3 show the classification accuracy based on SVM, RF and an ensemble of SVM & RF. The results show that ensembling increases the performance and it gives more than 85% accuracy on average.

Table 3. Performance based on SVM, RF and an ensemble of SVM & RF methods when source domain includes AB and BC data.

Source → Target	SVM	RF	SVM & RF
AB → NS	71%	88%	88%
BC → NS	76.5%	77%	83%
AB ∪ BC → NS	77.5%	80.5%	86%

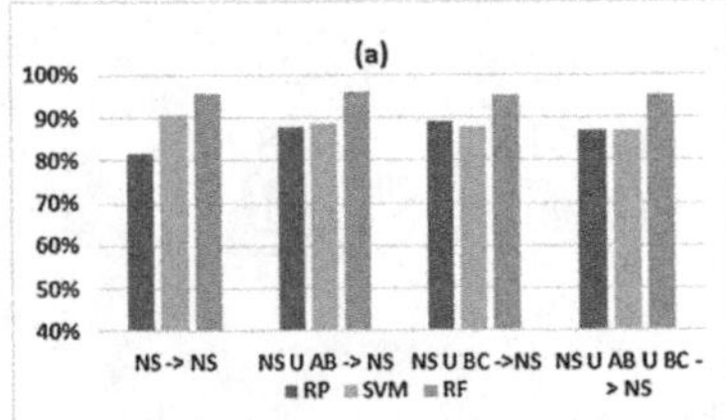

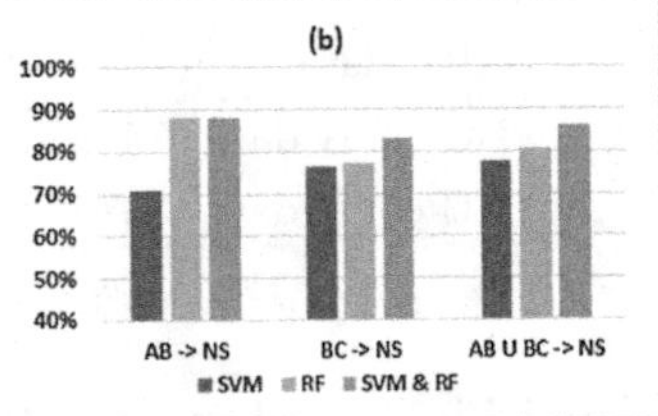

Fig. 1. Accuracy of RP, SVM and RF with all source domains (a) and SVM, RF and an ensemble of SVM & RF with AB and BC domains (b).

4 Conclusions and Future Work

NS Courts' database is a useful source of information for identification of different types of violence in Nova Scotia though it is not a complete collection of all the decisions. NS Twitter data and HRP data will also be used as target domain in future research. The most desirable long-term plan of the research is to identify alcohol involvement by analyzing all types of sources of crime data in Nova Scotia using machine learning and transfer learning techniques. Besides Alberta and British Columbia, we will also examine some other provinces so that source domain with more labeled data can be acquired. In our future research, we will explore different transfer learning methods for this purposes so that the performance will not drop in spite of the use of different source domains.

References

1. Canadian alcohol and drug use monitoring survey. Statistics Canada (2012)
2. Annual Report. EHS Nova Scotia Trauma Program (2014)
3. Breiman, L.: Random forests. Mach. Learn. **45**, 5–32 (2001)
4. Breiman, L., Friedman, J., Stone, C.J., Olshen, R.A.: Classification and Regression Trees, 1st edn. Chapman and Hall, Boca Raton (1984)
5. Cortes, C., Vapnik, V.: Support-vector networks. Mach. Learn. **20**(3), 273–297 (1995)
6. Exum, M.L.: Alcohol and aggression: an integration of findings from experimental studies. J. Crim. Justice **34**(2), 131–145 (2006)
7. Gao, J., Fan, W., Jiang, J., Han, J.: Knowledge transfer via multiple model local structure mapping. In: Proceedings of the 14th ACM SIGKDD International Conference on Knowledge Discovery and Data Mining, KDD 2008, New York, USA, pp. 283–291. ACM (2008)
8. Pan, S.J., Yang, Q.: A survey on transfer learning. IEEE Trans. Knowl. Data Eng. **22**(10), 1345–1359 (2010)
9. Schrans, T., Schellinck, T., Macdonald, K.: Culture of alcohol use in Nova Scotia. Nova Scotia Health Promotion and Protection (2008)

Author Index

Printed in the United States
By Bookmasters